BLACK AMERICAN WRITERS PAST AND PRESENT:

A Biographical and Bibliographical Dictionary

by
Theressa Gunnels Rush
Carol Fairbanks Myers
Esther Spring Arata

Volume I: A-I

The Scarecrow Press, Inc.
Metuchen, N. J.   1975

Library of Congress Cataloging in Publication Data

Rush, Theressa Gunnels, 1945-
    Black American writers past and present.

    Bibliography: v. 2, p.
    1. American literature--Negro authors--Bio-biblio-
graphy. I. Myers, Carol Fairbanks, joint author.
II. Arata, Esther Spring, joint author. III. Title.
Z1229.N39R87   016.8108'08'96073   74-28400
ISBN 0-8108-0785-8

DEDICATIONS

To Dwayne whose patience and understanding have been remarkable.

To my parents, Mr. and Mrs. Fred Gunnels, whose love, parental devotion, and hard work enabled all of their ten children to attend college.

T G R

To John, my husband, whose loyalty and well-timed sense of humor saw it through--

To my Mother, Father, brothers and sisters who always champion my cause--

To Mr. Earl C. Gleason, the grade school teacher I remember the most, and whose efforts of instruction I now gratefully acknowledge.

E S A

To Art and Clara Fairbanks who started me on my way;

To Paul who has shared the passage;

To my sons, Ted, Lee and Timothy.

C F M

Eau Claire, Wisconsin
May 30, 1974

TABLE OF CONTENTS

Volume 1

Volume 2

ACKNOWLEDGMENTS

During the 1960's when the tremendous surge towards Black culture quickened, publishers, librarians, and program directors were deluged with requests for available materials and resources needed to initiate and organize Black Studies courses. Marguerite Fox Randall, Mott Adult Education Program, Flint, Michigan, was one director who took action and arranged for me to research and publish a source book, <u>Black Power in the Arts</u>, Flint, Michigan: The Mott Foundation, 1970. Had it not been for Mrs. Randall's direction and encouragement, so generously offered when <u>Black Power in the Arts</u> was put together, this particular <u>Dictionary</u> would not have been compiled.

The research on Black artists had revealed the need for a reference book designed to introduce the reader to the wealth of written works done by Black men and women in America, from the time of slavery until the present. Encouraged by Mrs. Randall to compile this much needed reference book, in 1970 I began filing facts relevant to each Black author, living and deceased.

Three years later, in January 1973, Theressa Rush and Esther Arata agreed to co-edit and compile this reference with me.

While in essence we three have worked together, researching, writing and editing collected data for inclusion in the <u>Dictionary</u>, there were occasions when individual initiative contributed greatly towards the preparation of this reference. In the fall of 1973, Esther Arata assumed the responsibility to write grant proposals seeking financial assistance to allow for travel and further research in other city and university libraries. The University of Wisconsin-Eau Claire responded, and the grant funds provided monies and the incentive to pursue the information needed to complete the compilations.

vii

In the summer of 1973, with the aid of this grant, Ms. Rush met with Black writers in Chicago, New York, Los Angeles, and San Francisco to discuss the project, and to gather current information about Black authors. Ms. Rush also edited the material in this Dictionary making certain that the references included not only reflected the mood of Black writers, but that they also met the needs of Black readers.

Compiling such a reference work is a cooperative undertaking and we wish to acknowledge our indebtedness to the following:

The University of Wisconsin-Eau Claire for the University Grant;

Dr. John Ridge and Mr. Edmund Ellworthy, Institutional Studies.

Dr. Kenneth A. Spaulding, Chairman, English Department.

Mr. Robert Fetvedt, Director of the Wm. D. McIntyre Library and his staff, in particular Mary Alexander, Richard Bell, Eileen Diambra, Eugene Engeldinger, Jane Marshall and Evelyn Rounds.

Student assistants: Linda Glenn, Susan Johnson, Glenda McGee, Mary Oliver, Maureen Slawson.

Mrs. Caryl Laubach, Mrs. Glenn Derouin, typists.

Susan Taylor, assistant.

Mrs. Hilda Carter, publicity.

The Director and staff of the Rare Books Collection, University of Wisconsin-Madison.

Mrs. Lorraine Kearney, Eau Claire Technical Institute Library

Ms. Lillian L. Hubbel, Librarian, St. Louis Missouri, Public Library.

Eugene B. Redmond, author of the Introduction.

Leolin Azelma Craigg and Timya Moyo who invited Theressa to stay in their homes during her visits to New York and Chicago.

Mwalimu Haki R. Maghabuti (Don L. Lee), Safisha Maghabuti, Johnie Scott, Buriel Clay, Mr. and Mrs. Wayne Santinac, Nola Richardson, Birdell Chow Moore, St. Claire Bourne, Larry Melford, Akinyele Bolade, Cliff Frazier, Burgess "Snooks" Howard, Ohene Myanian, Yau Nyanian, Tony Eaton, G. Fitz Bartley, Kofi Moyo, Makini Obadina, Adesina Obaiye who invited Theressa to their homes out to dinner, to workshops and other gatherings in order to compile information for the Dictionary.

James Kilgore, Eugene Redmond, Sarah Wright, Charles Lynch, Melvin Lapley, Dudley Randall, and Nick Aaron Ford, who offered their expertise in locating materials and identifying writers.

DeLeon Harrison, Sue Irons, Julia Lewis, Wali Karim, Ojenke, John Otterbridge, Jim Potts, Francis Ward, Al Young, Bruce Mc-Marion Wright, Wesley Brown, Eric Priestley, Ed Spriggs, Carroll Clarke, Edafe Oddo, Louise Meriwether, Ineb Ellessac, Stephany Fuller, Mrs. Brown, Mrs. Micheaux (at the National Memorial Bookstore), and Harry Dolan whose contributions of valuable information for the Dictionary made Theressa's research tour profitable.

Claude D. Grant, Anna Land Butler, Fannie Ellison, George Barlow, Herbert Woodard Martin, Alvin Aubert, Mary E. Mebane, Russell Atkins, Ron Welburn, Gayl Jones, Saundra Sharp, Percy Johnston, Dan Simmons, Lloyd Richards, Bette Howard, Florene Wiley, Novella Nelson, Vinnette Carroll and Israel Hicks, who provided many valuable addresses.

Publishers and their staffs who also helped us locate writers: Len Fulton, Dustbooks; Karen M. Fraser, Pyramid Publications; Florence Schwartz, Crown Publishers; A. George, Carlton Press; T. Reed, William-Frederick Press; Shiela Nieves, Vantage Press; Dudley Randall, Broadside Press; Farrar, Straus & Giroux; Appleton-Century-Crofts; World; Karol White, Naylor; Loa Snyder, Warner Press; Popular Library; Alonzo Smith, Exposition Press; Follette Publishing Company; Dietz Press; Charles Scribner's; Michelle Lawrence, Dorrance; Review & Herald Publishing Association; Golden Quill Press; Franklin Watts, Inc.; Pageant-Poseidon Ltd. (formerly Pageant Press International); Associated Publishers; Warner Paperback Library; Julian Richardson, Publisher.

Alumni Offices all over the nation who helped us get in touch with their graduates.

Carol Fairbanks Myers

NOTE TO READERS

This Dictionary, which includes over 2000 Black American writers, living and deceased, was designed as a single source to provide information about both these writers' lives and their works in the various literary genres, from the early 18th century to the present. It is to aid librarians, teachers, students, and writers interested in the literary contributions made by Black American writers. At the time of this writing, May 1974, it is recognized that the Dictionary is neither complete nor perfect.

It has been the intent of the compilers to emphasize Black writers of novels, dramas, poetry, short stories, literature for children and young adults, and literary criticism. The principles determining the selection of writers have been modified to include (1) those writers of non-fiction whose works are studied in Black Literature courses, and whose works frequently appear in Black Literature anthologies, and (2) those writers from Africa and the West Indies who live and/or publish in the United States, and who also identify with Black American writers.

BIOGRAPHICAL INFORMATION

Only that biographical information provided for this Dictionary by the writers themselves has been included. However, to enable the reader to locate biographical material about other living writers listed in this book, a reference to biographical essays and other sources has been noted. Many anthologies, newspapers, and periodicals cited in this reference also provide brief biographies on the writers.

An attempt has been made to provide as much biographical information about deceased writers as possible. This area, in

particular, demonstrates the great need for further exploration and
research to determine whether or not such information does exist,
or had ever been published.

BIBLIOGRAPHICAL INFORMATION

The bibliography attached to each writer's entry includes all
known published books by that person.   Non-fiction works are included because they may be relevant to literary research.   The hardbound books listed in the 1973 edition of Books in Print are desig-
nated (*); soft cover books (†).

For work published in anthologies and periodicals, the Dictionary provides only partial information.   While it may be useful to
know, for example, that William Melvin Kelley's short story, "The
Dentist's Wife, " appears in Black Writers in America, and that it
had appeared originally in Playboy magazine, such detailed bibliographical notation lies outside the province of this study, which lim-
its itself to guiding researchers to additional information.   Each list
of anthologies, on the other hand, provides a source for those teachers and students desirous for more information about a given writer.

The drama listings under individuals' entries include comedy
and tragedy, stage productions, musicals, pageantry, and rituals.

BIOGRAPHY AND CRITICISM: Secondary Sources

Major Writers: Because numerous bibliographies on particular
major writers exist, references to these sources were made where
necessary.   Minor Writers: Bibliographies, as comprehensive as
possible, accompany each author's entry in the dictionary.

Reviews: Whenever they reflect the ideas and attitudes of the
era in which an author wrote, or when they contain pertinent information, offer a critical commentary, or when, as in the case of a
few writers, little criticism exists, only then are they listed.

INTERJECTIONS

These quotations, found at the end of many of the entries,

are from the writers themselves and express their ideas, theories, impressions, and philosophies. Where feasible, in the case of a deceased writer, an interjection may be quoted from another source --a family member, peer, or critic--apropos the author's ideas.

GENERAL BIBLIOGRAPHY

A bibliographical guide to research in the literary genres is located in the back of the book. Consult individual entries in the Dictionary proper and note that abbreviated bibliographical notations are used for all those works most frequently cited. For example, an entry may read: "Mitchell. Black Drama, p. 81." The reader refers to the General Bibliography for the complete citation. ·

While all of the biographical and bibliographical entries are for Black writers only, many of the critics, editors and historians whose works were consulted are non-Blacks. At this time the compilers have been able to provide only a partial listing of Black critic see Appendix A. A partial listing of white critics is provided in Appendix B.

INTRODUCTION

Come Celebrate Me
Jayne Cortez

This directory comes as a partial cure for a 400-year wave of literary amnesia and mis-knowledge. Ignorance abounds. People in crucial places have an overdose of it. Some years ago an aging and ·puzzled white English professor (who was attending a language conference), asked: "Do you mean to tell me that Frank Yerby is a Negro?" More recently, a Black student expressed amazement that Rhodes Scholar Alain Locke was an Afro-American. Admitted the student: "When I read all those impressive credentials... I mean about him getting a Ph. D. way back then and winning all those scholastic awards, I thought that he must have been white." Ludicrous or sad, both encounters are indicators on the time-gauge announcing that this biographical and bibliographical dictionary is long overdue. How many times have we been asked, or have wondered, if so-and-so or the author of such-and-such were Black? And how many times has someone answered, "I think so, but I'm not sure."

Ms. Cortez's epigrammatic invitation, then, restates the vigorousness and robust flavor of Black American survival and creativity--creativity in all areas especially in writing. For while we submit that the Afro-American community (which is quite oral) <u>reeds</u> and <u>rites</u>, there is also a great and glorious <u>reading</u> and <u>writing</u> history. Lucy Terry's "Bars Fight" was written in 1746 as a poetic account of an Indian massacre in Deerfield, Massachusetts. And it is a recorded fact that Africans had been in the Western Hemisphere for well over 200 years before 1746. Black explorers, traders, trappers, settlers and others roamed over North and South America and communed with the Indians prior to, and after, the infamous "sale" of 1619. One of these forerunners was Jean Baptiste Pont du Sable, considered the founder of Chicago. Throughout Colonial and pre-Civil War America, Black writers (freed and escaped slaves) recorded their multifarious experiences. The lengthy list of narrators includes Olaudah Equiano (Gustavus Vassa), Phillis Wheatley, Jupiter Hammon, Benjamin Banneker, Briton Hammon, John Marrant, David Walker, George Moses Horton, James M. Whitfield, William Wells Brown (first published Black novelist and playwright), Sojourner Truth and Frederick Douglass. Then there were the anomalous situations of writers Frances Ellen Watkins and Charlotte Forten, born free during slavery to well-to-do and educated parents. A Pan-African flavor was injected by the arrival in the U.S. of Black activists/writers from the West Indies and the Caribbean. Prominent among them was Jamaican-born John Russwurm (the second Black to graduate from a U.S. college). This trend, continuing throughout modern Black history, would include such figures as Claude McKay, Marcus Garvey and Stokely Carmichael. It would be broadened by the arrival of continental Africans like Ezekiel Mphahlele and Keorapetse Kgositsile.

While a strong literary tradition was developing among freed and educated Blacks of the North, a folk literature tradition, steeped in Africanisms and encasing the longings and philosophies of the Black masses, was evolving from Southern plantations and chain gang The first successful attempt to place this folk material within the context of an English literary tradition was made by Paul Laurence Dunbar who later denounced the fame he derived from his endeavors. The Age of Dunbar, as his time is sometimes called, also witnessed the rise in Black self-help programs, the debut of Charles Chestnutt (first major Black fiction writer) and the coming to power of Booker Taliafero Washington. Washington, an advocate of Black vocational training and social segregation, became a legend in his own day, als earning "The Age of" prefix before his name. His "Accommodationist" policy, however, would come to be challenged in the writings and speeches of W. E. B. Du Bois and others; and Washington's and Dunbar's influence (symbolized by dialect writing) was in decline by the first decade of the twentieth century.

At the dawn of the Harlem Renaissance, or "The New Negro Movement" (of the 1920's), statesman-critic-poet James Weldon Johnson announced (in The Book of American Negro Poetry) that dialect literature, because it was associated with the "happy-go-lucky, singing, shuffling, banjo-picking" Negro, had "but two full stops, humor and pathos." Even so, Johnson noted, dialect paved the way for creation and acceptance of a genuine Black American literature. As he wrote his evaluations of the literature and culture, Black writers of the Renaissance had already begun to fulfill Johnson's prophecy. Langston Hughes, Rudolph Fisher, Claude McKay, Jean Toomer, Countee Cullen, Arna Bontemps and Sterling Brown, among others, were forging new forms or reworking old ones. Johnson was a participant as well as a chronicler of the Renaissance, along with Locke, Charles Johnson and Du Bois, who was editor of the NAACP's Crisis. Correlative events and involvements included renewed interests in all of the arts and the serious treatment of Negro characters by established white writers: Eugene O'Neill, Dubose Heyward, Carl Van Vechten and Sherwood Anderson.

The crash of the stock market in 1929 also knelled the collapse of the Renaissance. But soup lines, high unemployment rates and other defeating aspects of the economic slump did not seriously deter or alter the development of Black literature. Throughout the thirties (when many Black writers worked for WPA programs: Margaret Walker, Richard Wright, Robert E. Hayden), and into (and beyond) World War II, important literature came from Du Bois, Fisher (and other "Renaissance" figures), May Miller, Melvin B. Tolson, Waring Cuney, William Attaway, Owen Dodson, Sterling Brown, Arthur P. Davis (The Negro Caravan, 1941, with Sterling Brown and Ulysses Lee), Saunders Redding (To Make A Poet Black, 1936), Zora Neale Hurston, Chester Himes, William Demby, Gwendolyn Brooks (first Black Pulitzer Prize winner, 1950) and Ralph Ellison. Wright's Native Son (1940) was a Book-of-the-Month Club selection, Ms. Walker's For My People (1942) was a title in the Yale Younger Poets series, and Ellison became in 1950 the first Black writer to win a National Book Award. In spite of all this creative activity,

the post-Renaissance/World War II period witnessed great racial
tension and violence. It witnessed, also, an unprecedented marshall-
ing of Black legal, intellectual and numerical strengths under the
banners of social and racial equality and human justice.

Black men had fought in every U.S. military conflict since
the Revolutionary War, but it was in World War II and Korea that
the racial barriers were relaxed to allow Blacks to die on equal
terms with whites even though they could not so live with them!
Moreover, Black veterans were forbidden to wear their military uni-
forms on the streets of some cities in the South. But Blacks, by
this time having actually or vicariously savored world culture, were
determined to accept nothing less than first-class citizenship. Attending the flaming cries for freedom and equality were the Supreme
Court decision of 1954, the appearance of Martin Luther King, Jr.,
as a new force in social protest, the entry of African nations into
world affairs, and the emergence of massive student protest demon-
strations in the sixties and early seventies. Into this social cauldron
stepped the fiery James Baldwin--from a self-imposed exile in Europe
With passionate accuracy, Baldwin reported on the mood of Black
America and predicted the coming social holocaust. He warned (cor-
rectly) that the student non-violent movement would be Blacks' final
attempt to seek peaceful solutions to the racial nightmare. By this
time most of the major voices of the Harlem Renaissance had been
silenced, but the Venerable Hughes would plod on until 1967, Bontemps until 1973 and Sterling Brown up through this writing.

The landscape of the sixties was one of terror and violence:
Vietnam, assassinations of important Black (and white) spokesmen,
the appearance of Black "militant" groups (some armed in public)
and writers, Black rebellions, police riots, ill-planned social programs, confrontations between police and Black communities, and
commission studies on poverty and violence. From the flame-and-
bullet-gutted horizon, new young writers spoke with tongues of anger
or subdued admonishment: Rolland Snellings (Askia Muhammad Toure)
Ed Spriggs, Austin Black, LeRoi Jones (Imamu Amiri Baraka), Mari
Evans, A. B. Spelman, Etheridge Knight, Larry Neal (Black Fire,

with Baraka) Joe Goncalves (Journal of Black Poetry), Conrad Kent
Rivers, Sonia Sanchez, Nathan Hare, Marvin X, Eldridge Cleaver,
Malcolm X, Henry Dumas and Ronald Stone (Yusef Rahman). And
even younger ones spoke: Stephany Fuller, Don L. Lee, Quincy
Troupe, David Henderson, Nikki Giovanni, Carolyn Rodgers, Sterling
Plump and Arthur Pfister. Still, there were the quiet new and
established writers diligently at work: Dudley Randall (Broadside
Press), Paule Marshall, Ann Petry, Ernest Gaines, William Melvin
Kelley, Samuel Allen (Paul Vesey), Margaret Burroughs (Du Sable
Museum in Chicago), Maya Angelou (of the Harlem Writers Guild),
Bob Kaufman (Solitudes Crowded with Loneliness), Louise Meriweth-
er, John Oliver Killens, Lance Jeffers, John A. Williams, Naomi
Long Madgett, Harold Cruse, John Henrik Clarke (Freedomways)
and Hoyt Fuller (Black World). Plus more and more and more!
The establishment of writing workshops, performing arts troupes,
literary contests, new regional and national journals and underground
newspapers, Black TV talk shows, Black studies programs on college
campuses, and new publishing companies--all these resulted from
or fed the Black Consciousness/Black Power/Black Arts movements.
Important new writers, anthologies and ideologies came from Watts,
Chicago, Harlem, Newark, Atlanta, East St. Louis, Detroit, New
Orleans, Seattle, Philadelphia and Southern Black colleges and universities which began writer-in-residence programs. All moving,
all part of the literary confluence!

   The final analysis of the foregoing achievements, much too
briefly stated here, would not be available to readers if Professors
Rush, Myers and Arata had not spent lions' shares of their public
and private time collecting this important data. Certainly there are
other (not so ambitious or thorough) attempts to which these relentless compilers went for a beginning. But the achievement is theirs
and--because of what they wrote--the writers they have listed herein.
As a writer and teacher, I can only express gratitude and issue a sigh
of relief from the one-way streets, the dead-ends and "missing"
pages that one confronts elsewhere in an attempt to unravel the continuing saga of Black writing--and Black writers--in America. Surely

not every one of these writers has written at the level of a Wheatley, Douglass, Dunbar, Ellison or Brooks. But they all have written--and in most instances, written well. Against this lengthy history of vitality and creativity, one must sadly observe that an almost criminal ignorance of Black writers exists in American educational institutions. Yet the pain of such a glaring contradiction might be salved somewhat by our knowledge that this project is, in part, the brainchild of veteran Black educator Marguerite Randall who has been with the Mott Adult Education Program in Flint, Michigan, since the late fifties; and who, in addition to being a writer herself, has mothered two sons/poets.

Henry Dumas said: "Music and I ... have come at last!" Quite the case! A dictionary of this type and caliber is indeed music to the ears of serious researchers or casual page-flippers looking for either self-reflections or for Hughes' "darker brother"-- the one who asks us, through the sensitive vessel of Ms. Cortez, t

<u>Come Celebrate Me</u>

Eugene B. Redmond
Professor of English, and
Poet-in-Residence in Ethnic Studies
California State University, Sacramento
May 10, 1974

ABRAM, Theresa Williams. Born 7 November 1903 in Magnolia, Arkansas. Education: B. S. in Elementary Education, Langston University, 1941; M. S. in Elementary Education, Oklahoma University, 1954; attended workshops at Union Theological Seminary. Currently living in Oklahoma City. Career: Taught elementary school for a number of years, and is presently tutoring slow readers as well as being employed by Wholesale Tours International, Inc. Has been a public speaker in the fields of religion, education, and poetry. At present and for the past two years, has served as resource person in poetry for Oklahoma University student teachers, and as guest poet in the Oklahoma public schools. Reads poetry locally and nationally for Phi Delta Kappa. Wrote a choral script for an Oklahoma City elementary school musical. Member: St. John Baptist Church; National Sorority,

Theresa Williams Abram

Phi Delta Kappa; International Platform Association; Local and
National Federated Clubs; Oklahoma Poetry Society; Poetry
Society of Illinois; Centro Studie Scambi Internagionli. Awards,
Honors: Named Sorority Woman of the Year by Gamma Epsilon
Chapter of Phi Delta Kappa.

POETRY
    Abram's Treasures.   New York: Vantage, 1967.
    Rhythm and Animals.   Oklahoma City: Best Way, 1971.
    (Anthology):   Stella Craft, ed. Anthology (n.p.: American
        Poets Fellowship Society, 1969.)
    (Periodicals):   Black Voices, March 1971; Krinon (National
        Sorority of Phi Delta Kappa), 1971; Modern Images, 1968.
    (Newspapers):   Black Dispatch (Oklahoma City); Tulsa Eagle.
UNPUBLISHED WORK
    Black-oriented poetry; Black history: "Black Bits and Pieces
BIOGRAPHY ON ABRAM
    International Who's Who in Poetry, 1972-73.

ABRAMS, Robert J. Born March 1924 in Philadelphia.
    POETRY (Anthologies): Hughes, New Negro Poets: USA; Pool,
        Beyond the Blues.

ABRAMSON, Dolores.
    POETRY (Anthologies): Patterson, A Rock Against the Wind;
        Sanchez, 360 Degrees of Blackness Coming at You.

ADAMS, Alger LeRoy (Philip B. Kaye).
    NOVEL
        Taffy, 1950; New York: Avon, 1951.
    CRITICISM ON ADAMS
        Bone.   The Negro Novel in America, p. 159.
    REVIEWS: Taffy
        Petry, Ann.   Saturday Review of Literature, 23 December
            1950, p. 21.
        Redding, Saunders.   New York Herald Tribune Book Review,
            19 November 1950, p. 18.
        Sullivan, Richard.   New York Times, 5 November 1950, p.
            32.

ADAMS, Alvin.
    SHORT STORY (Periodical): Negro Digest, March 1966.

ADAMS, Clayton.
    NOVEL
        Ethiopia, The Land of Promise: The Book with a Purpose.
            New York: Cosmopolitan, 1917.
    BIOGRAPHY AND CRITICISM ON ADAMS
        Gloster.   Negro Voices in American Fiction, pp. 95-97, 117.

ADAMS, Doris B.
    POETRY Longing and Other Poems.   Philadelphia: Dorrance,
        1962.

ADAMS, Jeanette.
    POETRY
        (Anthologies): Patterson, A Rock Against the Wind; Sanchez,
            360 Degrees of Blackness Coming at You.
        (Periodicals): Black Creation, Fall, Winter 1973; Journal of
            Black Poetry, Spring 1969.
    REVIEW BY ADAMS
        (Periodical): Black Books Bulletin, 1973.

ADAMS, Wellington Alexander.
    POETRY Lyrics of an Humble Birth. Washington: Murray
        Brothers Printing Co., 1914.

ADDISON, Lloyd. Born 10 March 1931 in Boston, Massachusetts.
    Education: B.A., University of New Mexico, 1958. Currently
    living in New York City. Career: In Social Service (Welfare)
    in New York City. Editor and publisher of Beau-Cocoa: The
    Biannual Beauti-Force. When asked to describe his field of
    specialization as a writer, Mr. Addison replied: "Historically,
    the concern has been with a delineation of a pervasive black
    aesthetic, to solicit (elicit) the romantic (surromantic) disposi-
    tion of the self--(group) enchanted awakened black--a program-
    matic conditioning of feelings (values), predicated on the idea
    that 'beauty,' like love, is power (beauti-force), that this touch
    of narcissism is vital for the independent spirit. Lately, over-
    hauling the historical intuitional projections that relate to the
    universal man."
    EDITOR
        Beau-Cocoa: The Biannual Beauti-Force, vols. 1-9. New
            York: Beau-Cocoa, Inc., 1969-73.
    POETRY
        The Aura and the Umbra. Heritage Series of Poetry, vol. 8.
            London: P. Breman, 1970; U.S. distributor, Detroit: Broad-
            side†.
        (Anthologies): Pool, Beyond the Blues; Breman, You'd Better
            Believe It.
    INTERJECTIONS
        "One of my most profound impressions is that man so little
    knows, controls, his own mind--his psychic world--is so greatly
    influenced by socio-political forces--that I often wonder if I am
    a deceived self-conflicting genius in limbo--the oblivion of my
    affectiveness."

ADELL, Ilunga (AKA William Adell Stevenson III). Born 27 Novem-
    ber 1948 in Memphis, Tennessee. Education: Studied at Mem-
    phis State University, Morehouse College, Wesleyan University,
    and the University of Massachusetts. Career: Actor, writer,
    director, stage manager. Presently employed as story editor
    for the television production, Sanford & Son. Member: Ameri-
    can Federation of Television and Radio Artists; Writers Guild of
    America; New Dramatist Society; Actors Equity.
    DRAMA
        Bugles.

Bulldogs.
Love, Love.
One: The Two of Us.
UNPUBLISHED WORK
An untitled collection of poetry.
INTERJECTIONS

Dream weavers	Dreamers
With threads of dignity	Dreaming Dreams
Making new clothes	Which unborn beautifuls
For our people	Will use
	To Make
	New Black Realities

AFIF, Fatimah.
POETRY (Periodical): Journal of Black Poetry, Winter-Spring
1970.

AFTON, Effie (pseud.) see HARPER, Frances Ellen Watkins

AHEART, Andrew Norwood.
POETRY Figures of Fantasy: Poems. New York: Exposition,
1949.

AHMAD, Dorothy.
DRAMA Papa's Daughter. In The Drama Review 12 (Summer
1968).

AHMASI.
POETRY The Water of Your Bath...Poems for Black Lovers.
New York: Rannick Amuru, n.d. †

AIKEN, Aaron Eugene. Born 1868.
SHORT STORIES Exposure of Negro Society and Societies...
Twenty Stories Combined. New York: J. P. Wharton
Printer, 1916.

AJAYI, Afolabi.
DRAMA Akokawe, 1970.

AKHNATON, Askia see ECKELS, Jon

ALBA, Nanina. Born 21 November 1917 in Montgomery, Alabama.
Died 1968. Education: attended Haines Institute, Augusta,
Georgia; A.B. Knoxville College, 1935; attended graduate school,
Indiana University. Career: Taught English, French, and mu-
sic in Alabama public schools; became a member of the English
department at Tuskegee Institute. Awards, Honors: Won the
Ester R. Beer Memorial Poetry Prize--2nd place, of the Na-
tional Writers' Club. [1]
POETRY
The Parchments I. n.p.: Merchants Press, 1963.
Parchments II. n.p., n.d.
(Anthologies): Adoff, Poetry of Black America, p. 169;

Hughes and Bontemps, The Poetry of the Negro 1746-
1970; Randall and Burroughs, For Malcolm, p. 39.
(Periodicals): Crisis 75 (November 1968): 321; Negro Digest 12 (September 1963): 58; 13 (February 1964): 76-
79; 13 (September 1964): 62; 14 (September 1965): 69;
15 (August 1966): 63; 16 (January 1967): 74; 17 (December 1967): 48.
SHORT STORIES
(Periodicals): Negro Digest 14 (May 1965): 36-39; 15 (July
1966): 65-68.
BIOGRAPHY AND CRITICISM ON ALBA
Emanuel and Gross, Dark Symphony, p. 373.
INTERJECTIONS
"I long for the day when our fine literary efforts are re-
lieved of the onus of being neglected by that other 'literate.' "[2]
    [1]Dudley Randall and Margaret G. Burroughs, eds.,
    For Malcolm (Detroit: Broadside Press, 1969), p. 95.
    [2]Ibid.

ALBERT, Leslie.
POETRY (Periodical): Negro Digest, November 1963.

ALDEBARAN (D. P. Byer).
POETRY Conquest of Coomassie: An Epic of the Mashanti
Nation. Long Beach, Calif.: Worth While, 1923.

ALEE, Lycurgus J.
POETRY (Anthology): Murphy, Negro Voices.

ALEXANDER, Lewis Grandison. Born 4 July 1900 in Washington,
D.C. Died 1945. Education: attended public schools in
Washington, D.C., Howard University, and the University of
Pennsylvania.[1] Career: He was a bus boy, bundle wrapper,
clerk, cook, costume designer, dishwasher, presser, porter,
shroud-maker, tailor; director of plays, and an actor. He
edited four Negro numbers of The Carolina Magazine, pub-
lished at Chapel Hill, North Carolina.[2] He was also a mem-
ber of the Howard Players, and of the Ethiopian Art Theatre.
He directed two Little Theatre Groups in Washington, the Ira
Aldridge Players of the Grover Cleveland School, and the Ran-
dall Community Center Players.[3]
CRITICISM BY ALEXANDER
"Plays of Negro Life, A Survey." Carolina Magazine 59
(April 1929): 45-47.
POETRY
(Anthologies): Adoff, The Poetry of Black America; Cullen,
Caroling Dusk; Calverton, Anthology of American Negro
Literature; Hughes and Bontemps, Poetry of the Negro
1746-1970; Johnson, Ebony and Topaz; Murphy, Negro
Voices; Nussbaum, Anna, Africa Singt (German Anthology).
(Periodicals): Opportunity 1 (May 1924): 142; 3 (Septem-
ber 1925): 278; 4 (April 1926): 118; 5 (June 1927): 174;

5 (December 1927): 368; 7 (January 1929): 11; <u>Palms</u> 6
(October 1926): 15-16.
BIOGRAPHY AND CRITICISM ON ALEXANDER
Cromwell, Turner, and Dykes. <u>Readings from Negro Au-
thors</u>, pp. 46-47.
Wagner. <u>Black Poets of the United States</u>, p. 163.
[1]Arnold Adoff, ed., <u>The Poetry of Black America:
Anthology of the 20th Century</u> (New York: Harper & Row,
1973), p. 517.
[2]Beatrice Murphy, <u>Negro Voices</u> (New York: Henry
Harrison, 1938), p. 9.
[3]Countee Cullen, <u>Caroling Dusk</u> (New York: Harper,
1927), p. 122.

ALEXANDER, Marion see NICHOLES, Marion

ALHAMISI, Ahmed Akenwale (Ahmed LeGraham Alhamisi). <u>Born</u> 18
February 1940 in Savannah, Tennessee.
EDITOR
With Harun K. Wangara. <u>Black Arts: An Anthology of
Black Creations.</u> Detroit: Broadside, 1969†.
NON-FICTION
(Periodical): <u>Journal of Black Poetry,</u> Fall-Winter, 1971.
POETRY
<u>The Black Narrator.</u> Detroit: Harlo Press, 1966.
<u>Black Spiritual Gods: New Poems.</u> Detroit: Black Arts,
1968.
<u>Guerilla Warfare.</u> New ed. Detroit: Broadside, 1970 †.
<u>Holy Ghosts,</u> 1971. New ed. Detroit: Broadside, 1972†.
(Anthologies): Alhamisi and Wangara, <u>Black Arts;</u> Jones and
Neal, <u>Black Fire;</u> Randall, <u>Black Poetry: A Supplement;</u>
Randall and Burroughs, <u>For Malcolm.</u>
(Periodicals): <u>Journal of Black Poetry,</u> Special Issue 1970;
Fall-Winter 1971.
BIOGRAPHY AND CRITICISM
Kent. "Outstanding Works," pp. 322-323.

ALLEN, George Leonard. <u>Born</u> 1905. <u>Died</u> 1935.
POETRY
(Anthologies): Brown, Davis, and Lee, <u>Negro Caravan;</u>
Cullen, <u>Caroling Dusk.</u>
(Periodicals): <u>Opportunity,</u> January, June 1927; October
1928, July 1930; September 1930.

ALLEN, Junius Mordecai (J. Mord Allen). <u>Born</u> 26 March 1875
in Montgomery, Alabama. <u>Died</u> 1906. <u>Education:</u> Attended
schools in Montgomery. <u>Career:</u> Became a boiler-maker in
St. Louis, Mo., 1892. From 1889 to 1892 he travelled with
a theatrical group for which he wrote a few state pieces.[1]
POETRY
<u>Rhymes, Tales, and Rhymed Tales.</u> Topeka, Kansas:
Crane and Company, 1906.
(Anthologies): Kerlin, <u>Negro Poets and Their Poems</u>, pp.

48-50, 239-242; Robinson, Early Black American Poets,
p. 231; Wagner, Black Poets in the United States, pp.
143-145; White and Jackson, An Anthology of Verse by
American Negroes, pp. 116-132.
BIOGRAPHY AND CRITICISM ON ALLEN
  Butcher. The Negro in American Culture, p. 99.
  Kerlin. Negro Poets and Their Poems, pp. 48-50, 239-242.
  Loggins. The Negro Author in America, pp. 334-335.
  Wagner. Black Poets in the United States, pp. 128-129,
    141-145, 175, 493.
  White and Jackson. An Anthology of Verse by American
    Negroes, pp. 17-18, 23-24.
    [1]William H. Robinson, Early Black American Poets
(Dubuque, Iowa: Wm. C. Brown, 1969), p. 231.

ALLEN, Richard. Born February 1760 in Philadelphia--a slave.
Died 26 March 1831. Career: Was a wood cutter; worked in
a brickyard; served as a wagoner during the Revolutionary War.
Purchased his liberty on September 3, 1783; organized the Free
African Society,[1] became the founder and first Bishop of the
African Methodist Episcopal Church.[2] He was also the first
Negro to write an autobiography.[3]
EDITOR
  The African Methodist Pocket Hymn Book: Selected from
    Different Authors. First Edition. Philadelphia: Published
    by Richard Allen, for the African Methodist Connection in
    the United States, 1818.
NON-FICTION
  Confession of John Joyce, alias Davis, Who Was Executed on
    Monday, the 14th of March, 1808. Philadelphia: Printed
    for the benefit of Bethel Church, 1808.
  With Jacob Tapisco. The Doctrine and Discipline of the Af-
    rican Methodist Episcopal Church. Philadelphia: n. p.,
    1813.
  A Letter on Colonization. Freedom's Journal, 2 November
    1827.
  The Life, Experience, and Gospel Labors of the Right Rev-
    erend Richard Allen. Philadelphia: F. Ford and M. A.
    Ripley, 1880; Philadelphia: A. M. E., 1887.
  With Absalom Jones. A Narrative of the Proceedings of the
    Black People During the Late Awful Calamity in Philadel-
    phia in the Year 1793. Philadelphia: By the Authors,
    1794.
  Late Publications: With Absalom Jones. A Refutation of
    Some Censures Thrown Upon Them in Some Late Publica-
    tions, Philadelphia, 1794.
  (Periodicals): "Some Letters of Richard Allen and Absalom
    Jones to Dorothy Ripley." Journal of Negro History 1
    (October 1961): 436-443.
POETRY
  Spiritual Song. Philadelphia: By the Author, ca. 1800.
    (Broadside.)

BIOGRAPHY AND CRITICISM ON ALLEN

Adams. Great Negroes Past and Present, p. 92.
Bardolph. The Negro Vanguard, pp. 38, 43-48, 51-55.
Baskin and Runes. Dictionary of Black Culture, p. 19.
Bennett. Pioneers in Protest, pp. 41-55.
_____. Before the Mayflower, pp. 68-69, 131.
Bergman. The Chronological History of the Negro in Amer-
    ica, p. 41.
Bragg, George F. Richard Allen and Absalom Jones. n.p.:
    1915, pp. 10-11.
Brawley. Early Negro American Writers, pp. 87-95, 142-144.
_____. History of the Negro Church. Washington, D.C.:
    n.p., 1921, pp. 73-78.
_____. Negro Builders and Heroes, pp. 30-34.
Cain, Alfred E., ed. Winding Road to Freedom. Yonkers:
    Educational Heritage, 1965, pp. 92-94.
Douty, Esther M. Under the New Roof. Chicago: Rand Mc-
    Nally, 1965, pp. 201-234.
Ebony (May 1965): 142-152.
Hughes and Meltzer. A Pictorial History of the Negro in
    America, pp. 34, 61, 62, 64, 67, 82.
Jennifer, Rev. John D. D. "Who Was Richard Allen and
    What Did He Do?" Voice of the Negro 3 (January 1905).
Katz. Eyewitness: The Negro in American History, p. 51.
Kittler, Glen D. Profiles in Faith. New York: Coward Mc-
    Cann, 1962, pp. 233-255.
Loggins. The Negro Author in America, pp. 56-63, 72, 89,
    95, 104, 190, 294.
Meier. Negro Thought in America 1880-1915, p. 52.
Ottley and Weatherby. The Negro in New York, p. 89.
Ploski. Negro Almanac, pp. 4-6.
Porter. Early Negro Writing: 1760-1837, pp. 414, 559.
Robinson. Historical Negro Biographies, pp. 5-6.
Rollins. They Showed the Way, pp. 12-16.
Romero, Patricia. I, Too Am American: Documents from
    1619 to the Present. New York: Publishers, 1968, pp.
    31-32.
Simmons. Men of Mark, pp. 491-497.
Spaulding. Encyclopedia of Black Folklore and Humor, pp.
    160-161.
Toppin. A Biographical History of Blacks in America Since
    1528, pp. 62, 103, 177, 247-248.
Woodson. The Mind of the Negro As Reflected in Letters
    Written During the Crisis, 1800-1860, p. 224.
(Audio-Tape Reel)
    "Richard Allen." Educational Record Sales, New York.
    [1]Richard Bardolph, The Negro Vanguard (New York:
    Vintage Books, 1959), p. 45.
        [2]Benjamin Brawley, Early Negro American Writers
    (Freeport, N.Y.: Books for Libraries Press, 1968), p. 89
        [3]Romeo B. Garrett, Famous First Facts About Negroes
    (New York: Arno Press, 1972), p. 99.

ALLEN, Samuel (Paul Vesey). Born 9 December 1917 in Columbus,
Ohio. Education: A.B. (Sociology), Fisk University, 1938;
J.D., Harvard University Law School, 1941; additional study in
humanities at New School of Social Research, 1947-48; Sorbonne
(Paris), 1949-50. Currently living in Boston, Massachusetts.
Career: Deputy Assistant District Attorney, New York City;
General Practice of Law, New York City; Assistant General
Counsel, United States Information Agency; Chief Counsel, Com-
munity Relations Service, Department of Commerce. Associ-
ate Professor of Law, Texas Southern University, 1958-60;
Avalon Professor of English, Wesleyan University, 1970-71;
Professor of English, Boston University, January 1971 to pres-
ent, specializing in African and Afro-American Literature.
Has served as guest lecturer on Frantz Fanon, African, and
Afro-American Literature at numerous colleges and universities in the United States, Canada, Dakar (Senegal), and Lagos
(Nigeria). In 1972, the Nigerian Broadcasting Company taped
a dramatization of his poems. He has given poetry readings
at United States colleges and universities, and at the Library
of Congress. Member: New York Bar Association; A.A.U.P.;
American Federation of Teachers; College English Association;
African Heritage Studies Association; College Language Association; Southern Education Foundation (Vice President).

CRITICISM
    "Black Writers' Views on Literary Lions and Values."
        Negro Digest 17 (January 1968).
    "Negritude, Agreement and Disagreements." American So-
        ciety of African Culture.
    "Negritude and Its Relevance to the American Negro Writer."
        American Society of African Culture; in Davis and Red-
        ding, Cavalcade; Miller, Backgrounds to Blackamerican
        Literature.
    "Tendencies in African Poetry." Présence Africaine (1958);
        also in Drachler, African Heritage.
    "Two Writers, Senghor and Soyinka." Negro Digest (May
        1967).
EDITOR
    Poems from Africa. Poems of the World Series. New
        York: T. Y. Crowell, 1973*.
    Co-Editor, American Society of African Culture. Pan-Afri-
        canism Reconsidered. Berkeley: University of California
        Press, 1962.
NON-FICTION
    (Anthology): Wright, What Black Educators Are Saying.
    (Periodicals): Journal of Afro-American Studies 2 (1971);
        Black World, January 1971.
POETRY
    Elfenbein-Zahne. Heidelberg: Rothe, 1956. English title:
        Ivory Tusks....
    Ivory Tusks and Other Poems. New York: Poets Press,
        1968.
    Poems. Heritage Series. London: P. Breman, forthcoming.
    (Anthologies): Abdul, The Magic of Black Poetry; Adams,

Samuel Allen (credit: Chester Higgins Jr.)

Afro-American Literature: Poetry; Clark, The Real Imagi
nation; Adoff, I Am the Darker Brother; Adoff, Poetry of
Black America; Barksdale and Kinnamon, Black Writers o
America; Bontemps, American Negro Poetry; Brooks, A
Broadside Treasury; Brown et al., To Gwen With Love;
Christ and Potell, Adventures for Today; Crocker, Young
& Black; Davis and Redding, Cavalcade; Durham et al.,
Directions 2; Eisenberg, Not Quite Twenty; Gordon et al.
American Literature; Gordon, Types of Literature; Greave
Burning Thorn; Hayden, Kaleidoscope; Henderson, Under-
standing the New Black Poetry; Hill, Soon One Morning;

Hogan, Poetry of Relevance; Hughes, New Negro Poets:
USA; Hughes and Bontemps, The Poetry of the Negro:
1746-1970; Jewett, Discovering Literature; Jordan, Soul-
script; Knudson and Ebert, Sports Poems; Koppell, Live
Poetry; Lomax and Abdul, 3000 Years of Black Poetry;
Lowenfels, Poets of Today; McCullough, Earth, Air, Fire,
and Water; McFarland, Moments in Literature; McKay
and MacKenzie, What Does It Take; McMaster, Points of
Light; Marshall and Myers, Designs of Reading Poems;
Michel, Way Out; Miller, Blackamerican Literature;
Pool, Beyond the Blues; Randall, The Black Poets; Ran-
dall, Black Poetry: A Supplement; Robinson, Nommo;
Oliver et al., New Worlds of Reading; Segnitz and Rainey,
Psyche; Walrond and Pool, Black and Unknown Bards;
Weisman and Wright, Black Poetry for All Americans.
  (Periodicals): Negro Digest, October 1969; July 1967; Black
    World, September 1972.
REVIEWS BY ALLEN
  Published in Boston Herald Traveler; The Crisis.
TRANSLATIONS
  (Anthology): "Africa" by Aimee Cesaire. In Voices of the
    Whirlwind and Other Essays. Edited by Ezekiel Mphahlele.
    New York: Hill and Wang, 1972.
  (Periodical): "Elegy for Martin Luther King" by Leopold
    Senghor. Black Orpheus (1973).
BIOGRAPHY AND CRITICISM ON ALLEN
  Cartey, Wilfred. "Dark Voice." Présence Africaine, n.d.,
    pp. 94-97.
  Dickenberger, George. "Paul Vesey." Black Orpheus 4
    (October 1958): 5-8.
  Mphahlele, Ezekiel. "Roots." In Cooke, Modern Black Novel-
    ists, pp. 24-29.
  Valenti. "The Black Diaspora," p. 397.
  Von Eberhard, Horst. "Protest Gegen Unmenschlichkeit,"
    Rheinische Post, 14 September 1957.
REVIEW: Poems from Africa
  Publishers' Weekly, 23 April 1973, p. 72.

ALLEN, Sena.
  DRAMA Song My Father Me (musical).

ALLISON, Hughes.
  DRAMA The Trial of Dr. Beck. In Best Plays of 1937-38.
  SHORT STORIES
    (Periodicals): Challenge, May 1935; Ellery Queen Mystery
      Magazine.

ALLISON, Margaret M.
  POETRY The Sun Looked Upon Me and I Am Black. Madison,
    Wis.: By the Author, 1970.

ALONZO, Cecil.
  DRAMA Black Voices.

Johari Amini

ALVAREZ, Julia. Born 27 March 1950 in New York City.
   POETRY (Anthology): Jordan, Soulscript.

AMINI, Johari (Jewel C. Latimore). Born in Philadelphia, Pennsylvania. Education: A. A., Chicago City College, 1968; studied at University of Chicago, 1972. Career: Instructor in
   Psychology, Black Literature, and Social Science at Kennedy-
   King College Mini Campus, Chicago, 1970-1972. Co-instructed
   a course in The Black Aesthetic at Indiana University, Bloomington, Spring 1971 (the course was designed with four other
   OBAC members). Currently lecturing in Black Literature, Uni-
   versity of Illinois Chicago Circle Campus. Reading appear-
   ances have been held in California, Illinois, Indiana, Maryland,
   Minnesota, Missouri, New York, and Ohio. Two recordings
   (Black Spirits, Motown/Black Forum Records, 1972, and Spec-
   trum in Black, Scott Foresman, 1971) include her poetry.
   Member: Organization of Black American Culture.
   NON-FICTION
      An African Frame of Reference. Chicago: Institute of Posi-
         tive Education, n.d. (Pamphlet.)
   POETRY
      Black Essence. Chicago: Third World, 1968†.
      Images in Black. rev. ed. Chicago: Third World, 1969.
      Let's Go Somewhere. Chicago: Third World, 1970†.
      Folk Fable. Chicago: Third World, forthcoming.
      (Anthologies): Adoff, The Poetry of Black America; Alha-
         misi and Wangara, Black Arts; Brooks, Jump Bad; Brown,
         Lee, and Ward, To Gwen With Love; Coombs, We Speak
         as Liberators; Giovanni, Night Comes Softly; Henderson,
         Understanding the New Black Poetry; King, Black Spirits,
         Patterson, Rock Against the Wind; Perkins, Black Ex-
         pressions Anthology; Randall, The Black Poets; Robinson,
         Nommo; Simmons and Hutchinson, Black Culture.
      (Broadsides):
         A Folk Fable for My People. Chicago: Third World, n.d.
         A Hip Tale in the Death Style. Detroit: Broadside, 1972.
      (Periodicals): Negro Digest, December 1967; September
         1969; Black World, June, August, September 1970; Sep-
         tember 1973; Journal of Black Poetry, Spring 1969; Fall-
         Winter 1971; also published in Pan African Journal.
   REVIEWS BY AMINI
      (Periodicals): Negro Digest, April, June, September, No-
         vember 1969; Black World, October, July 1971.
   REVIEW: Black Essence
      Sanchez, Sonia. Negro Digest 18 (April 1969): 91-92.
   REVIEW: Let's Go Somewhere
      Fabio, Sarah Webster. Black World 20 (December 1970):
         68.

AMIS, Lola Elizabeth Jones.   Born 26 February 1930 in Norfolk,
   Virginia.
   CRITICISM BY AMIS
      "Native Son" Notes. Lincoln, Neb. : Cliff's Notes, n.d.

DRAMA
  Three Plays. New York: Exposition, 1965.
BIOGRAPHY ON AMIS
  Shockley and Chandler. Living Black American Authors,
    pp. 5-6.

ANDERSON, Alice D.
  POETRY (Anthology): Murphy, Ebony Rhythm.

ANDERSON, Alston. Born 1924.
  NOVEL
    All God's Children. Indianapolis: Bobbs-Merrill, 1965.
  SHORT STORY
    Lover Man. Garden City, N.Y.: Doubleday, 1959.
    (Anthology): Hughes, Best Short Stories by Negro Writers.
  REVIEW: Lover Man
    Crisis, November 1959, pp. 580-581.

ANDERSON, Charles L. Born 7 August 1938 in Fullerton, California.
  POETRY
    Frustration: A Negro Poet Looks at America. Puebla,
      Mexico: El Grupo Literario of the "United Nations" School,
      1961.
    (Anthologies): Jones and Neal, Black Fire; Pool, Beyond the
      Blues.
    (Periodical): Présence Africaine, 57.

ANDERSON, Edna.
  POETRY
    Through the Ages: A Book of Poems. Philadelphia: Dor-
      rance, 1946.
    (Anthology): Murphy, Ebony Rhythm.
    (Periodicals): Crisis; Negro Story; New Vistas.

ANDERSON, Edward H. Born in Cleveland.
  POETRY
    (Periodical): Negro History Bulletin, October 1962.
  BIOGRAPHY ON ANDERSON
    Negro History Bulletin, 26 (October 1962): 57.

ANDERSON, Garland.
  DRAMA
    Appearances, 1925.
  BIOGRAPHY AND CRITICISM ON ANDERSON
    Abramson. Negro Playwrights in the American Theatre, pp.
      27-32, 39-40.
    Anderson, Garland. "How I Became a Playwright." In
      Patterson, Anthology of the American Negro in the The-
      atre, pp. 85-86.
    Mitchell. Black Drama, p. 84.

ANDERSON, Henry L. N.   Born 23 May 1934 in Ogeechee, Georgia.
Education: B.S., Cheyney State College, 1958; Ed.D., U.C.
L.A., 1973; additional work at Yale University Divinity School,
California State University at Los Angeles; Pepperdine University.   Currently living in Los Angeles.   Career: Taught in elementary and secondary schools in Los Angeles County, 1961-
1966.   Held various positions in the Los Angeles Unified School
District, teaching English as a Second Language at the Community Adult Center;   an English and Mathematics instructor at
the Neighborhood Youth Corps; Administrative Assistant Director, Saugus Urban Residential Education Center; Administrative
Assistant, Counselor and teacher at the Watt Skill Center; Business instructor, Mathematics and English instructor at Bethune
Junior High; Associate Director, Department of Special Educational Programs; and Director, Project Upward Bound, University of California, Los Angeles, 1968-1969.   Assistant Professor, Graduate School of Education, Loyola University.   Assistant Professor, School of Education, California State University,
Los Angeles.   Director, Child Development Center and Day
School; Vision Elementary Day School and Child Development
Center, Los Angeles.   Professional Consultant in Education:
U.S. Office of Education, HEW, DSSS, 1969-1972; Evaluations
and Management International, Inc., 1970 to present; Help, Inc.
Has published numerous articles in professional education jour-
nals.   Member: Adult Education Association; Cheyney Alumni
Association; Yale Club of Southern California; UCLA Alumni As-
sociation; Black Men Unemployed; National Association of Black
Adult Educators; American Academy of Political and Social Sci-
ences; Common Cause; Center for the Study of Democratic Insti-
tutions; The Fund for the Republic, Inc.; American Academy of
Arts and Sciences; Phi Delta Kappa.
NON-FICTION
     You and Race--A Christian Reflects.   Los Angeles: Western,
          1960.
     Revolutionary Urban Teaching.   Inglewood, Cal.: American
          University Publishers, n.d.
NOVEL
     No Use Cryin'.   Los Angeles: Western, 1961.

ANDERSON, Odie.   Born 25 October 1943 in Chicago, Illinois.
DRAMA
     Trial of God: A Dramatization.   New York: Exposition,
          1970.
BIOGRAPHY ON ANDERSON
     Shockley and Chandler.   Living Black American Authors, p. 4.

ANDERSON, S. E.   Born 1943 in Brooklyn.
CRITICISM BY ANDERSON
     "Black Writer's Views on Literary Lions and Values."   Ne-
          gro Digest 17 (January 1968): 24.
NON-FICTION
     (Periodicals): Negro Digest, September 1967; September-
          October 1968; Black Scholar, September, November 1970;

March 1971; November 1973.
POETRY
(Anthologies): Adoff, The Poetry of Black America; Alhamisi
and Wangara, Black Arts; Coombs, We Speak as Libera-
tors; Jones and Neal, Black Fire; King, Blackspirits; Ma-
jor, The New Black Poetry.
(Periodicals): Negro Digest, December 1967; May, Septem-
ber-October 1968; September 1969; Journal of Black Po-
etry, Winter-Spring 1970; other poetry in The Liberator.
SHORT STORY
(Anthologies): Alhamisi and Wangara, Black Arts; King,
Black Short Story Anthology.
(Periodicals): Black World, June 1970.
SYMPOSIUM
"What Lies Ahead for Black Americans?" Negro Digest 19
(November 1969): 6-8.

ANDERSON, T. Diane.
DRAMA   The Unicorn Died at Dawn.

ANDERSON, William.
POETRY (Anthology): Miller, Dices and Black Bones.

ANDREWS, Henry H.
POETRY Vicious Youth. Boston: Boston Popular Poetry, 1940

ANDREWS, Regina.
DRAMA
Underground (1932).
BIOGRAPHY AND CRITICISM
Mitchell. Black Drama, p. 88.

ANGELOU, Maya. Born 4 April 1928 in St. Louis, Missouri. Cu-
rently living in Berkeley, California. Career: Journalist, lec-
turer, civil rights activist, dancer, teacher, actress, producer
and writer. Northern coordinator of the Southern Christian
Leadership Conference. Journalist and lecturer in Ghana and
Egypt (Editor of Africa Review in Accra, Ghana, and of Arab
Observer in Cairo, Egypt.) Wrote, produced and hosted the
NET series, "Black! Blues! Black!"
AUTOBIOGRAPHY
I Know Why the Caged Bird Sings. New York: Random,
1970*; New York: Bantam, 1971†. Excerpt in Watkins an
David, To Be a Black Woman; Harper (February 1970):
86-98.
Gather Together in My Name. New York: Random, 1974*.
DRAMA
Adjoa Amissah, 1967.
The Best of These, 1966.
The Clawing Within, 1966-67.
POETRY
Just Give Me a Cool Drink of Water 'fore I Diiie. New
York: Random, 1971; New York: Bantam, 1973†.

SHORT STORY
(Anthologies): Clarke, Harlem; Mayfield, Ten Times Black.
(Periodical): Essence, January 1971.
SCREENPLAY
Georgia! Georgia!
BIOGRAPHY AND CRITICISM ON ANGELOU
"I Know Why the Caged Bird Sings." Ebony 25 (April 1970):
62-64.
Julianelli, J. "Angelou: Interview." Harper's Bazaar,
November 1972, p. 124.
Shockley and Chandler. Living Black American Authors, pp.
4-5.
Smith, Sidonie Ann. "The Song of a Caged Bird: Maya
Angelou's Quest for Self-Acceptance." Southern Humani-
ties Review 7 (Fall 1973): 365-374.
Weller, Sheila. "Work in Progress: Maya Angelou." In-
tellectual Digest 3 (June 1973): 1.

ANTARAH, Obi (L. C. Redmond, Jr.). Born 17 March 1943 in Chi-
cago. Education: B.A. (Philosophy), University of Illinois-
Chicago Circle, 1973. Currently living in Chicago. Career:
Presently a student.
NOVEL
The Birth of Benny Young. New York: Emerson Hall, forth-
coming.
NON-FICTION
(Periodical): Black World, October 1973.
INTERJECTIONS
"I believe God has a duty for each of us to perform. Now,
I don't know at present exactly what my duty is, but I try to do
my best in everything that I do; so that, when I learn what my
job on earth is, I'll be better able to do it. I regiment my di-
et and practice yoga so that my body will be healthier and my
mind will be, hopefully, keener. I paint occasionally, I play a
little chess. I study one or two of the occult sciences. And
I do all of these with one overall goal in mind, to become a
better person, i.e. to become the kind of person I'll have to be
in order to do whatever it is God wants me to do."

ANTHONY, David.
POETRY (Periodical): Journal of Black Poetry, Summer 1972.

ANTHONY, Earl.
DRAMA
A Long Way from Here.
EDITOR
With Woodie King. Black Poets and Prophets. New York:
New American Library, 1972†.
NON-FICTION
Picking Up the Gun. New York: Pyramid, 1971†.
Time of the Furnaces: A Case Study of Black Student Re-
volt. New York: Dial, 1971*†.
(Anthology): King and Anthony, Black Poets and Prophets.
(Periodical): Black Scholar, October 1971.

Ray Aranha

ANTHONY, Paul.
    POETRY (Anthology): Watkins, Black Review No. 2.

APOLLON, Gerald.
    DRAMA
        Domingo.
        Oh, Jesus.
        Toussaint L'Ouverture and San.

ARANHA, Ray. Born 1 May 1939 in Miami, Florida. Education:
    A.B., Florida A & M University, 1961. Currently living in

New York City. <u>Career:</u> Actor and Playwright. <u>Member:</u>
<u>Screen Actors Guild; Actors Equity Association. Awards, Hon-</u>
<u>ors: Who's Who in American Universities and Colleges, 1959.</u>
DRAMA
   <u>My Sister; My Sister,</u> 1973.
INTERJECTIONS
   "Black people must learn to look at the past honestly, study-
ing those attributes, both good and bad, which make us human."

ARDRY, Robert.
   <u>DRAMA Jeb.</u>

ARKHURST, Joyce Cooper. <u>Born</u> 20 October 1921 in Seattle, Wash-
ington.
   CHILDREN AND YOUNG ADULTS
      <u>The Adventures of Spider.</u> Boston: Little, Brown, 1964*.
   BIOGRAPHY ON ARKHURST
      Shockley and Chandler. <u>Living Black American Authors</u>, p.
      5.

ARMSTRONG, Henry.
   <u>POETRY Twenty Years of Poem, Moods, and Meditation.</u> Los
      Angeles: By the Author, 1954.

ARNEZ, Nancy L.
   CRITICISM
      "New Black Literature." <u>Negro Education Review</u> 22 (April
      1971): 67-78.
   NON-FICTION
      (Periodical): <u>Journal of Black Studies,</u> September 1971.
   POETRY
      With Beatrice Murphy. <u>The Rocks Cry Out.</u> Detroit:
      Broadside, 1968†.

ARNOLD, Ethel Nishua.
   <u>NOVEL She Knew No Evil.</u> New York: Vantage, 1953.

ARNOLD, Walter G.
   POETRY
      <u>In Quest of Gold: The Negro in America and Other Poems.</u>
         New York: William-Frederick, 1947.
      (Anthology): Murphy, <u>Ebony Rhythm.</u>
      (Periodical): <u>Opportunity,</u> August 1940.

ARTHUR, Barbara.
   <u>POETRY Common Sense Poetry.</u> Berkeley: Respect Interna-
      tional, 1969.

ARTHUR, John see JOSEPH, Arthur

ASCHER, Rhoda G.
   <u>POETRY</u> (Periodical): <u>Journal of Black Poetry,</u> Summer
      1972.

ASHANTI, Baron J.
   POETRY
      (Periodicals): Black World, September 1972; Journal of
      Black Poetry, Winter-Spring 1970.

ASHBURN, Gene Holmes.
   POETRY Dark Gods. New York: William-Frederick, 1952.

ASHBY, William Mobile. Born 1889.
   DRAMA
      The Road to Damascus: A Play in Seven Episodes. Boston:
      Christopher, 1935.
   NON-FICTION
      (Periodicals): Opportunity 18 (March 1940): 18; 20 (June
      1942): 170-71, 188; 20 (December 1942): 369-370, 390;
      25 (September 1947): 76.
   NOVEL
      Redder Blood. New York: Cosmopolitan, 1915.
   SHORT STORY
      (Periodical): Opportunity 16 (November 1938): 329-330.
   BIOGRAPHY AND CRITICISM ON ASHBY
      Gloster. Negro Voices in American Fiction, pp. 89-91, 99.
      Hughes. The Negro Novelist, p. 36.
      Mays. The Negro's God, pp. 177-178, 253.

ASHLEY, Martin.
   FICTION
      Checkmate and Deathmate. New York: Vantage, 1973.

ASHLEY, William.
   DRAMA
      Booker T. Washington (1939).
   BIOGRAPHY AND CRITICISM ON ASHLEY
      Mitchell. Black Drama, p. 107.

ASTWOOD, Alexander Carl.
   POETRY Beauty and the Universe, A Book of Poems. Boston:
      Humphries, 1950.

ATHENS, Ida Gerding.
   POETRY Brethren. Cincinnati: Talaria, 1940.

ATKINS, Russell. Born 25 February 1926 in Cleveland, Ohio.
   Education: Attended Cleveland Institute of Music; Cleveland
   Music School Settlement; Cleveland School of Art (now Institute);
   private study in musical composition with J. H. Bron. Currently living in Cleveland, Ohio. Career: Founder and Co-
   editor of Free Lance magazine; Co-founder and Chairman of
   MUNTU Poet's Workshop; Affiliate of Cleveland State University
   Poetry Forum; Instructor for Karamu House Poetry Lab; Consultant for Cleveland's WVIZ-ETV Station; Consultant in Poetry
   for Cleveland Board of Education and Poets-in-the-School Program under the National Endowment for the Arts; consultant for

various writers conferences; lecturer with Poet Lecturers' Alliance for colleges and universities. Specializes in theory and technique in poetry, using poetry, musical composition and poetic drama as facets of a general experimental aesthetic.

DRAMA
>The Nail: A Three-Act Play Adapted from Pedro de Alarcon's Short Story. Cleveland: Free Lance, 1971.

NON-FICTION
>Psychovisualism. Cleveland: Free Lance, 1956, 1958.

POETRY
>Heretofore. Heritage Series 7. London: Breman, 1968.
>Objects. Eureka, California: Hearse, 1963.
>Objects 2. Cleveland: Renegade Press, 1964.
>Phenomena. Wilberforce, Ohio: Wilberforce University, 1961.
>A Podium Presentation. Cleveland: Free Lance, n.d.
>Two by Atkins: The Abortionist and The Corpse (Two Poetic Dramas to Be Set to Music.) Cleveland: Free Lance, 1963.
>(Anthologies): Abdul, The Magic of Black Poetry; Adoff, The Poetry of Black America; Bontemps, American Negro Poetry; Hughes and Bontemps, The Poetry of the Negro: 1746-1970; Jordan, Soulscript; Major, The New Black Poetry.

SHORT STORY
>Maleficium. Cleveland: Free Lance, 1971.

REVIEW: Heretofore
>Amini, Johari. Negro Digest 18 (September 1969): 94-95.

REVIEW: Maleficium
>Library Journal, 15 June 1972, p. 2191.

ATKINS, Thomas.
>POETRY The Eagle. St. Louis, Mo.: St. Louis Argus, 1936.

ATTAWAY, William.
CHILDREN AND YOUNG ADULTS
>Calypso Song Book. Lyle Kenyon Engel, ed. and comp. New York: McGraw-Hill, 1957.
>Hear America Singing. New York: Lion, 1967*.

NON-FICTION
>Blood on the Forge, 1941; reprint ed., Chatham, N.J.: Chatham Bookseller, 1969*; New York: Macmillan, 1970†.
>Let Me Breathe Thunder, 1939; reprint ed., Chatham, N.J.: Chatham Bookseller, 1969.

SHORT STORY
>(Periodical): Challenge, June 1936.

BIOGRAPHY AND CRITICISM ON ATTAWAY
>Bone. The Negro Novel in America.
>Ellison, Ralph. "Transition." The Negro Quarterly 1 (Spring 1942): 87-92.
>Felgar, Robert. "William Attaway's Unaccommodated Protagonists." Studies in Black Literature 4 (Spring 1973): 1-3.

> Gloster. <u>Negro Voices in American Fiction</u>.
> Margolies. "Migration: William Attaway and <u>Blood on the</u>
>   <u>Forge</u>." In Margolies, <u>Native Sons: A Critical Study</u>,
>   pp. 47-64.

AUBERT, Alvin. <u>Born</u> 12 March 1930 in Lutcher, Louisiana.
<u>Education:</u> A high school dropout who nevertheless liked books
enough to achieve a passing score on the G.E.D. Test. A.B.,
Southern University, 1959; M.A., University of Michigan, 1960;
additional study at the University of Illinois in 16th and 17th
century English literature. <u>Currently living in</u> Fredonia, New
York. <u>Career:</u> Taught at Southern University, 1960-1970;
presently teaching Afro-American literature at State University
College, Fredonia, New York. Has also served as visiting
professor, University of Oregon, and as a regular reviewer for
the <u>Library Journal.</u> "I regard myself as primarily a teacher
since for better or worse that is essentially my mode of being
in the world. But even this, I suspect, is something of a
strategem, enabling my being a poet on my own terms and
somewhat at leisure; I have no program of writing as such.
However, I am convinced that I must write, and that there really isn't any alternative so that in a sense my particular way of
being a poet (or the way of being a poet that claims and binds
me) has survival value." <u>Awards, Honors:</u> Scholar in Poetry,
Bread Loaf Writers' Conference, Summer 1968.
CRITICISM
> "Black American Poetry: Its Language and the Folk Tradi-
>   tion." <u>Black Academy Review 2,</u> pp. 7-80.
POETRY
> <u>Against the Blues</u>. Detroit: Broadside, 1972†.
> (Anthologies): Corrington and Williams, <u>Southern Writing in</u>
>   <u>the Sixties</u>; Williams, <u>Contemporary Poetry in America</u>.
> (Periodicals): <u>The Greenfield Review</u>, Summer 1972; <u>Jour-</u>
>   <u>nal of Black Poetry,</u> Summer 1972; <u>Journal of Human Re-</u>
>   <u>lations,</u> Autumn 1963; other poetry in <u>Motive</u>, <u>The New</u>
>   <u>Orleans Review, Prairie Schooner</u>.
REVIEWS BY AUBERT
> In <u>Black Academy Review</u> and <u>The Library Journal.</u>
INTERJECTIONS
"From the perspective of the moment (11:15 pm CST,
3/14/73) all my life seems to have been and promises to be
sustained effort to resist what many years ago I read in a book
(by Dale Carnegie, I think) that one ought to do: live in day-
tight compartments. A relentless struggle to hold back the en-
circling walls implicit in that insane prescription, which I aimed
at expressing once, albeit unknowingly at the time, in a very
bad poem which I nevertheless like a great deal, titled FOR A
MAN LOST IN INFANCY and which goes in part: "corners van-
ish/Bearing unswept dust of days;/Walls thrust to roundness,
windows disappear/The circular room contracts, binds the cir-
cumference/Of my zodiacal headgear...." Thus emerges what
has been my sustaining philosophy for some time now: that
whatever world view one holds had better be informed by a con-

cept of history, of necessity a dialectically progressive outlay
of time, involving both a short prospect dealing with relatively
immediate means and ends, and a long one, having to do with
events and issues that in the interest of sanity one had better
consign to a realm beyond one's own--God's time as distinct
from man's. In short, one continues to work and write poems,
but with no assurance (and with all assurance) that work and
the writing of poems make anything (everything) happen. And
I report this from the perspective of a recently renascent
Black man whose previous view of history was from the outside of history, cyclical and futile. I now walk upright in the
world and where my body goes so goes my soul."

AUGUSTUS, Timothy Bell.
  The Black Spot in the Sun. Philadelphia: A.M.E. Book Con-
    cern, 1918.

AUSTIN, Edmund.
  FICTION The Black Challenge. New York: Vantage, 1958.

AVOTCJA.
  POETRY (Periodical): Glide In/Out, April 1972.

AWEUSI, Alli.
  DRAMA
    Agent Among the Just. Play Series. New York: Rannick
      Amuru, 1973†.
    The Day Pop Threw Out the Teevee. Play Series. New
      York: Rannick Amuru, 1973†.

AWOONER, Kofi. Born 13 March 1935 in Wheta, Ghana. Educa-
  tion: University of London, A.B., 1960; M.A., University of
  London, 1968; Ph.D., State University of New York-Stony
  Brook. Currently living in Austin, Texas. Career: Profes-
  sor of English, University of Texas.
  EDITOR
    With G. Adali-Morty. Messages: Poems from Ghana.
      New York: Heineman, 1970; reprint ed., New York: Hu-
      manities, 1971†.
    Ewe Poetry. Garden City, N.Y.: Doubleday, 1972*.
    Guardians of the Sacred Word. NOK, 1974*†.
  NOVEL
    This Earth, My Brother. Garden City, N.Y.: Doubleday,
      1972†.
  POETRY
    Night of My Blood: Poetry about Africa and Africans.
      Garden City, N.Y.: Doubleday, 1971*†.
  BIOGRAPHY AND CRITICISM ON AWOONER
    Lindfors, Bernth, et al. "Palaver: Interviews with Five
      African Writers in Texas." Monograph. Occasional Pub-
      lications of the African and Afro-American Research In-
      stitute. Austin: University of Texas, 1972.
    Contemporary Authors, 29/32.

REVIEW: This Earth, My Brother.
New Statesman, 17 March 1972, p. 364.
New York Times Book Review, 2 April 1972, p. 7.

AYBAR, Trudy.
DRAMA Morning Train.

AYERS, Vivian. Born in Chester, South Carolina.
DRAMA
    Bow Boly (musical tragi-comedy).
POETRY
    Hawk. Houston, Texas: Hawk, 1957.
    Spice of Dawns. New York: Exposition, 1953.
    (Anthology): Hughes, New Negro Poets: USA.

-B-

BAILEY, Joseph.
POETRY (Periodical): Black Dialogue.

BAILEY, Richard.
POETRY Soul Blood Poems. Indianapolis: By the Author, 1969.

BAILEY, Roberta.
DRAMA New Life.

BAILEY, William Edgar. Born in Salisbury, Missouri. Education:
Attended Salisbury Public Schools.
POETRY
    The Firstling. n. p. , 1914.
    (Anthology): Kerlin, Negro Poets and Their Poems, pp. 65-
    67, 229-30.

BAIRD, Keith A.
POETRY
    (Periodical): Freedomways, Spring 1962; Fall 1963; Fourth
    Quarter 1971.

BAKER, Augusta. Born 1 April 1911 in Baltimore, Maryland.
CHILDREN AND YOUNG ADULTS
    Golden Lynx and Other Tales. Philadelphia: Lippincott,
    1960*.
    Talking Tree and Other Stories. Philadelphia: Lippincott,
    1955*.
EDITOR
    The Black Experience in Children's Books. New York: New
    York Public Library, 1971.
    Young Years: Anthology of Children's Literature. New York:
    Parents, 1963*.
BIOGRAPHY ON BAKER
    Shockley and Chandler. Living Black American Authors, pp.
    7-8.
    Commire. Something About the Author, vol. 3.

BAKER, Houston A., Jr. Born 22 March 1943 in Louisville, Kentucky. Education: B.A., Howard University, 1965; M.A.,
University of California-Los Angeles, 1966; one year of doctoral work at the University of Edinburgh, Scotland, 1967-1968;
Ph.D., University of California-Los Angeles, 1968. Currently
living in Charlottesville, Virgina. Career: Instructor in English, Howard University, June 1966 to August 1966; Instructor
in English, Yale University, July 1968 to July 1969; Assistant
Professor in English, Yale University, appointed for four-year
term beginning July 1969; Associate Professor and Member of
Center for Advanced Studies for three-year term beginning July
1970, University of Virginia; Professor of English, University
of Virginia, September 1973 to present. Awards, Honors:
Four year competitive scholarship, Howard University, 1961-
1965; John Hay Whitney Foundation Fellowship, 1965-1966;
three year NDEA Fellowship, 1965-1968; magna cum laude
graduate of Howard University, 1965; member of Kappa Delta
Pi, elected 1964; winner of the Alfred Longueil Poetry Award,
UCLA, 1966.

CRITICISM
   "The Achievement of Gwendolyn Brooks," CLA Journal 16
      (September 1972): 23-31.
   "Arna Bontemps." Black World 22 (September 1972): 4-9.
   "Balancing the Perspective, A Look at Early Black Ameri-
      can Literary Artistry." Negro American Literature For-
      um 6 (Fall 1972): 65-70.
   "A Decadent's Nature: The Poetry of Ernest Dawson."
      Victorian Poetry 6 (1968): 21-28.
   "Engaged Literature and Jean Paul Sartre's The Flies."
      The UCLA Graduate Journal 1 (1967): 13-23.
   "The Environment as Enemy in a Black Autobiography:
      Manchild in the Promised Land." Phylon 32 (1971):
      53-59.
   "A Forgotten Prototype: The Autobiography of an Ex-Col-
      ored Man and Invisible Man." Virginia Quarterly Review
      49 (1973): 433-439.
   Long Black Song: Essays in Black American Literature and
      Culture. Charlottesville: University Press of Virginia,
      1972*.
   "Paul Laurence Dunbar: An Evaluation." Black World 21
      (November 1971): 30-37.
   "The Poet's Progress: Rossetti's The House of Life." Vic-
      torian Poetry 8 (1970): 1-14.
   "A Tragedy of the Artist: The Picture of Dorian Gray."
      Nineteenth Century Fiction 24 (1969): 349-355.
   "Utile, Dulce and the Literature of the Black American."
      Black World 21 (September 1972): 30-35.
   "The Western University: Culturocentricism and the Inter-
      disciplinary Ideal." Afro-American Studies 3 (1972):
      111-114.

EDITOR
   Black Literature in America. New York: McGraw-Hill,
      1971.

Twentieth Century Interpretations of Native Son. Englewood
Cliffs, N.J.: Prentice-Hall, 1972†.
ESSAYS
(Anthology): Huggins, et al.
(Periodicals): Liberator, 1969; 1970.
REVIEWS BY BAKER
In The Yale Review, The Liberator, and Black World.
INTERJECTIONS
"The prime task of the Black American critic is to discover
and articulate the traditional bases of art in his sui generis
culture.   To the young Black critic belongs the job of repudiat-
ing a number of the older neocolonial keepers of the keys as
well as the always oppressive white cultural custodians."

BAKER, Robert Milum   see   JOHNSON, Homer Preston

BAKR, Khaula R.
POETRY   Gut and Soul.   New York: Rannick Amuru, 1973†.

BALAGON, Kuwasi.
POETRY   (Anthology): Jones and Neal, Black Fire.

BALDWIN, James A.   Born 2 August 1924 in New York City.   Career: See Barksdale and Kinnamon, Black Writers of America,
pp. 722-723; Butler, Encyclopedia of World Literature in the
Twentieth Century, pp. 91-92; Contemporary Authors, 3; Cur-
rent Biography, 1964; Eckman, The Furious Passage of James
Baldwin; Ploski, Reference Library of Black America.
CRITICISM BY BALDWIN (Selected)
"Everybody's Protest Novel."   The Partisan Review 16 (June
1949): 578-585.   Also in Notes of a Native Son; Hemen-
way, The Black Novelist, pp. 218-226; Barksdale and Kin-
namon, The Black Writer in America.
"Many Thousand Gone."   The Partisan Review 18 (November-
December 1951): 665-680.   Also in Notes of a Native
Son; Chapman, Black Voices.
"The Negro in American Culture."   Bigsby, The Black Amer-
ican Writer, vol. 1.
DRAMA
Amen Corner.   New York: Dial, 1968*; also in Patterson,
Black Theatre.
Blues for Mr. Charlie.   New York: Dial, 1964*; New York:
Dell, n.d.; also in Oliver and Sills, Contemporary Black
Drama; Gassner and Barnes, Best American Plays, 1963-
1967.
ESSAYS
The Fire Next Time.   New York: Dial, 1963*; (large type
edition) New York: Watts, n.d.*; New York: Dell, 1970†.
No Name in the Street.   New York: Dial, 1972*; New York:
Dell, 1973†.
Nobody Knows My Name.   New York: Dial, 1961*; New York:
Dell, n.d.†

Notes of a Native Son.   New York: Dial, 1955*; Boston:
    Beacon, 1957†.
(Anthologies): Davis and Redding, Cavalcade; Ford, Black
    Insights; Gordon and Hills, New York, New York; Gross,
    A Nation of Nations; Gross and Hardy, Images of the Ne-
    gro in American Literature; Hill, Soon One Morning;
    Kearns, The Black Experience; Kendricks, Afro-American
    Voices; Long and Collier, Afro-American Writing; Singh
    and Fellowes, Black Literature in America; Young, Black
    Experience.
(Periodicals): Ebony, August 1965; Negro Digest, July 1961;
    April, October 1963; Liberation, March, October 1963;
    Integrated Education, March-April, 1969.

NON-FICTION

With others. Black Anti-Semitism and Jewish Racism.   In-
    troduction by Nat Hentoff.   New York: R. W. Baron,
    1969.
With Nikki Giovanni.   A Dialogue.   Philadelphia: Lippincott,
    1973*†.
With others. The Negro Protest: James Baldwin, Malcolm
    X and Martin Luther King Talk with Kenneth B. Clark.
    New York: University Place Book Shop, n.d.*
With Richard Avedon. Nothing Personal.   New York: Athen-
    eum, 1964; New York: Dell, 1965. (Photographs by Ave-
    don; text by Baldwin.)
With Margaret Mead. Rap on Race.   Philadelphia: Lippin-
    cott, 1971*.   New York: Dell, 1972†.

NOVELS

Another Country.   New York: Dial, 1962*; New York: Dell,
    1970†.
Giovanni's Room.   New York: Dial, 1956*; New York: Dell,
    n.d.†
Go Tell It on the Mountain.   New York: Knopf, 1953*; New
    York: Dell, 1970†.   See also Virginia F. Allen and Glenn
    Munson, eds., Falcon Books Classroom Library.   New
    York: Noble & Noble, 1968†.   Excerpts in Davis and Red-
    ding, Cavalcade; Faderman and Bradshaw, Speaking for
    Ourselves; Ford, Black Insights; Hill, Soon One Morning;
    Miller, Blackamerican Literature; Watkins and David, To
    Be a Black Woman.
If Beale Street Could Talk.   New York: Dial, 1974†.
Tell Me How Long the Train's Been Gone.   New York: Dial,
    1968*; New York: Dell, 1969†.

SCENARIO

One Day When I Was Lost.   New York: Dial, 1973*; New
    York: Dell, 1973†.   (Based on Alex Haley's The Autobiog-
    raphy of Malcolm X.)

SHORT STORIES

Going to Meet the Man.   New York: Dial, 1965*; New York:
    Dell, 1966†.
(Anthologies): Barksdale and Kinnamon, The Black Writer
    in America; Clarke, American Negro Short Stories;
    Clarke, Harlem; Emanuel and Gross, Dark Symphony;

Foley and Bennett, <u>Best American Short Stories</u>; Gold,
<u>Fiction of the Fifties</u>; Hayden, Burrows, and Lapides,
<u>Afro-American Literature</u>; Hills and Hills, <u>How We Live</u>;
Hughes, <u>The Best Short Stories by Negro Writers</u>; James,
<u>From These Roots</u>; King, <u>Black Short Story Anthology</u>;
Margolies, <u>A Native Sons Reader</u>; Margolies, <u>New World
Writing, 16</u>; Mirer, <u>Modern Black Stories</u>; Singh and
Fellowes, <u>Black Literature in America</u>; Turner, <u>Black
American Literature--Fiction.</u>
(Periodicals): <u>American Mercury</u>, August 1962; <u>Atlantic</u>,
September 1960; <u>Commentary</u>, 1948; 1950; <u>Mademoiselle</u>,
March 1958; <u>Negro Digest</u>, September 1961; <u>Partisan Review</u>, Summer 1957; Spring 1960.

BIBLIOGRAPHIES OF BALDWIN'S WORK

Adelman and Dworkin. <u>The Contemporary Novel</u>, pp. 29-34.

Fischer, Russell G. "James Baldwin: A Bibliography,
1947-1962," <u>Bulletin of Bibliography</u> 24 (January-April
1965): 127-130.

Jones, Mary C. "James Baldwin." <u>CAAS Bibliography No.
5</u>. Atlanta, Georgia: Atlanta University, n.d. (mimeographed).

Kindt, Kathleen A. "James Baldwin: A Checklist, 1947-
1962," <u>Bulletin of Bibliography</u> 24 (January-April 1965):
123-126.

Standley, Fred L. "James Baldwin: A Checklist, 1963-
1967," <u>Bulletin of Bibliography</u> 25 (May-August 1968):
135-137, 160.

Turner, Darwin T. <u>Afro-American Writers</u>, pp. 37-39.

BIOGRAPHY AND CRITICISM ON BALDWIN

(Selected Criticism Prior to 1970)

Alexander, Charlotte. "The 'Stink of Reality': Mothers and
Whores in James Baldwin's Fiction." <u>Literature and Psychology</u> 18 (1968): 9-26.

Bigsby, C. W. E. "The Committee Writer: James Baldwin
as Dramatist." <u>Twentieth Century Literature</u> 13 (1967):
39-48.

Charney, Maurice. "James Baldwin's Quarrel with Richard
Wright." <u>American Quarterly</u> 15 (1963): 65-75.

Eckman, Fern M. <u>The Furious Passage of James Baldwin</u>.
New York: Popular Library, 1967†.

Gayle, Addison, Jr. "A Defense of James Baldwin." <u>CLA
Journal</u> 10 (1967): 201-208.

Gross, Theodore. "The World of James Baldwin." <u>Critique</u>
7 (1965): 139-149.

Levin, David. "Baldwin's Autobiographical Essays: The
Problem of Negro Identity." <u>Massachusetts Review</u> 5
(1964): 239-247.

Mayfield, Julian. "And Then Came Baldwin." <u>Freedomways</u> 3 (1963): 143-155.

Spender, Stephen. "James Baldwin: Voice of a Revolution."
<u>Partisan Review</u> 30 (1963): 256-260.

Thelwell, Mike. "<u>Another Country</u>: Baldwin's New York

Novel." In Bigsby, The Black American Writer.

Watson, Edward A. "The Novels of James Baldwin: Case-Book of a 'Lover's War' with the United States." Massachusetts Review 5 (1964): 239-247.

(Criticism since 1970)

Adams, George R. "Black Militant Drama," American Imago 28 (Summer 1971): 121-128.

Adelson, C. E. "Love Affair: James Baldwin and Istanbul." Ebony 25 (March 1970).

Bennett, Stephen B. and William W. Nichols. "Violence in Afro-American Fiction: An Hypothesis." Modern Fiction Studies 17 (1971): 221-228.

"The Black Scholar Interviews: James Baldwin." Black Scholar 5 (December 1973-January 1974): 33-42.

Bone. "The Novels of James Baldwin." In Hemenway, The Black Novelist, pp. 111-113.

Brudnoy, David. "Blues for Mr. Baldwin." National Review, 7 July 1972, pp. 750-751.

Cohn, Ruby. "James Baldwin." Dialogue in American Drama. Indiana University Press, 1971, pp. 188-192.

Collier, Eugenia. "Thematic Patterns in Baldwin's Essays." Black World 21 (June 1972): 28-34.

DeMott, B. "James Baldwin and the Sixties: Acts and Revelations." Saturday Review 37 May 1972, pp. 63-66.

Dickstein, Morris. "The Black Aesthetic in White America." Partisan Review 38 (Winter 1971-1972): 376-395.

_____. "Wright, Baldwin, Cleaver." New Letters 38 (Winter 1971): 117-124.

Fabre, Michel. "Fathers and Sons in James Baldwin's Go Tell It on the Mountain." In Cooke, Modern Black Novelists, pp. 88-104.

Foster, D. C. "'Cause My House Fell Down: The Theme of the Fall in Baldwin's Novels." Critique 13 (1971): 50-62.

Fuller, Hoyt W. "James Baldwin and the Black-Jewish Conflict." Black World 11 (September 1971): 83.

George, Felice. "Black Woman, Black Man." Harvard Journal of Afro-American Affairs 2 (1971): 1-17.

Gérard, Albert. "The Sons of Ham." Studies in the Novel 3 (1971): 148-164.

Gitlin, Todd. "Yet Will I Maintain My Own Ways Before Him." Nation, 10 April 1972, pp. 469-470.

Gross, Barry. "The 'Uninhabitable Darkness' of Baldwin's Another Country: Image and Theme." Negro American Literature Forum (Winter 1972): 113-121.

Gross. The Heroic Ideal in American Literature, pp. 166-179.

Hall, John. "Interview." Transatlantic Review, nos. 37 and 38, (Autumn-Winter, 1970-1971), pp. 5-14.

Harrison. The Drama of Nommo, pp. 83-84, 138.

Jordan, Jennifer. Cleaver vs. Baldwin: Icing the White Negro." Black Books Bulletin 1 (Winter 1972): 13-15.

Kazin, Alfred. "Brothers Crying Out for More Access to Life." Saturday Review, 2 October 1971, pp. 33-35.

Kent, George. "Baldwin and the Problem of Being." Blackness and the Adventure of Western Culture, pp. 139-151.

_____. "Outstanding Works," pp. 307-309.

Lee, Robert A. "James Baldwin and Matthew Arnold: Thoughts on 'Relevance.' " CLA Journal 14 (March 1971): 324-330.

Macebuh, Stanley. James Baldwin: A Critical Study. New York: Third Press, 1973.

May, John R. "Ellison, Baldwin, and Wright: Vestiges of Christian Apocalypse." Toward a New Earth: Apocalypse in the American Novel. Notre Dame: University of Notre Dame, 1972.

Ognibene, Elaine. "Black Literature Revisited: 'Sonny's Blues.' " English Journal 60 (January 1971).

Ray, Robert. "James Baldwin's Insecurities." Books and Bookman, September 1972, p. 61.

Reilly, John M. " "Sonny's Blues': James Baldwin's Image of Black Community." Negro American Literature Forum 4 (1970): 56-60.

Rupp, Richard H. Celebration in Postwar American Fiction, 1945-1967. Coral Gables: University of Miami, 1970.

Schrero, Elliot M. "Another Country and the Sense of Self." Black Academy Review, 1-2, pp. 91-100. Also in Mezu, Modern Black Literature, pp. 91-100.

Schurer, Mark. The Literature of America: Twentieth Century. New York: McGraw-Hill, 1970, pp. 1075-1092.

Scott, Robert. "Rhetoric, Black Power, and James Baldwin's Another Country." Journal of Black Studies 1 (September 1970): 21-34.

Singh, Raman K. "The Black Novel and Its Tradition." Colorado Quarterly 20 (Summer 1971): 23-29.

Standley, Fred L. "James Baldwin: The Artist as Incorrigible Disturber of the Peace." Southern Humanities Review 4 (1970): 18-30.

Turner, Darwin. "Afro-American Authors: A Full House." College English 34 (January 1972): 15-19.

Wald, Karen, " 'We Are All the Viet Cong!': An Interview with James Baldwin." Nickel Review 4 (February 27, 1970): 5.

Watkins, Mel. New York Times Book Review, 28 May 1972, pp. 17-18.

Whitlow. Black American Literature, pp. 127-130.

Williams. Give Birth to Brightness, pp. 150-166.

REVIEW: No Name in the Street.
New York Times Book Review, 3 December 1972, p. 72.
Black Creation 3 (Summer 1972): 51-53.

REVIEW: One Day When I Was Lost.
National Review, 22 December 1972, p. 1415.

BAMBARA, Toni Cade (Toni Cade). Born 25 March 1939, in New
York City. Education: A.B., Queens College, 1959; University of Florence (Commedia dell'Arte), 1961; Ecole de Mime
Etienne Decroux, Paris, 1961 and New York 1963; M.A., City
University of New York, 1964; additional study at New York Uni-
versity (linguistics); New School for Social Research; Katherine
Dunham Dance Studio, Syvilla Fort School of Dance, Clark Cen-
ter of Performing Arts, 1958-1969; Studio Museum of Harlem
Film Institute, 1970. Currently living in New York City. Ca-
reer: Reviewer of films, plays and books; Associate Professor
of English at Rutgers University-Livingston College, 1965 to
present. Awards, Honors: Received award from the Black
Child Development Institute for Service to Independent Black
School Movement.
CHILDREN AND YOUNG ADULTS
    A Junior Casebook on Racism. New York: Bantam, forth-
        coming.
CRITICISM BY BAMBARA
    "Black Theatre." Gayle, Black Expressions; also in Miller,
        Backgrounds to Blackamerican Literature.
EDITOR
    The Black Woman. New York: New American Library, 1970†.
    Tales and Short Stories for Black Folks. Garden City, New
        York: Doubleday, 1971*; New York: Doubleday, 1971†.
SHORT STORIES
    Gorilla, My Love and Other Stories. New York: Random,
        1972*; New York: Pocket Books, 1973†.
    (Periodicals): Massachusetts Review, Summer 1964; reprinted
        in Chametzky and Kaplan; Black World, October 1971.
BIOGRAPHY AND CRITICISM ON BAMBARA
    Contemporary Authors, 29/32.
    Harrison. The Drama of Nommo, p. 159.
REVIEWS: Gorilla, My Love
    New York Times Book Review, 3 December 1972, p. 76.
    Black World 22 (July 1973): 80.
WORK IN PROGRESS
    Copin Wid de White Folks Tongue: Language as a Political
        Institution.
INTERJECTION
    "Particularly concerned at the moment in the development of
political primers for Black students (pre-school through univer-
sity) both as books and films."

BANKS, Brenda C. Born 6 October 1947 in Sacramento, California.
Education: M.A. in English, University of California, Santa
Barbara, 1972. Currently living in Los Angeles. Career:
Writer, Sacramento Bee newspaper, summers 1965-1969; Coun-
selor-resident-Black literature instructor, summers 1970-1972;
Upward Bound Program, University of California-Davis; Instructor, Black Literature, Reed College, 1970-71; Teaching Assistant, English literature, University of California-Santa Barbara,
1972-73. Presently a staff writer for a small Southern California newspaper.

SHORT STORIES
　(Periodical): Black World, 1970, July 1972, July 1973.
INTERJECTIONS
　"to write for Blackpeople
　to write Black stories
　to write Black stories with heart in them
　　for Blackpeople."

BANKS, William Augustus.
　POETRY
　　Beyond the Rockies and Other Poems. Philadelphia: Dor-
　　　rance, 1926.
　　Lest We Forget. Chattanooga, Tenn.: Central High Press,
　　　1930.
　　"Gathering Dusk." Chattanooga, Tenn.: Wilson Printing Co.,
　　　1935.

BARAKA, Imamu Amiri (Everett LeRoi Jones). Born 7 October
　1934 in Newark, New Jersey. Education: B.A., Howard Uni-
　versity 1954; graduate work at New School of Social Research
　and Columbia University. Currently living in Newark, New
　Jersey. Career: Taught poetry at the New School of Social
　Research, 1967; drama at Columbia University, 1967; and lit-
　erature at the University of Buffalo; served as Visiting Profes-
　sor, San Francisco State College, 1967. Founded the Black
　Arts Repertory Theater School in Harlem, 1964, and Spirit
　House in Newark, New Jersey, 1966. Founded the Black Com-
　munity Development and Defense Organization in 1968. Mem-
　ber: United Brothers, NewArk 1967; Committee for Unified
　NewArk; Chairman, Congress of Afrikan People; Co-Convenor,
　National Black Political Convention; Secretary-General, Nation-
　al Black Assembly, National Political Council of National Black
　Political Convention; Afrikan Liberation Day Support Committee;
　IFCO International Task Force; Black Academy of Arts and Let-
　ters. Awards, Honors: Whitney Fellowship, 1963; Guggen-
　heim Fellowship, 1965; Fellow, Yoruba Academy, 1965; Doctor-
　ate of Humane Letters, 1972, Malcolm X College.
　CRITICISM BY BARAKA
　　"And the New Black Writers of the Sixties." Freedomways
　　　9 (Summer 1969): 232-247.
　　"The Black Aesthetic." Negro Digest 18 (September 1969):
　　　5-6.
　　"Black (Art) Drama Is the Same as Black Life." Ebony 26
　　　(February 1971): 74-76.
　　"Black Revolutionary Poets Should Also Be Playwrights."
　　　Black World 21 (April 1972): 4-7.
　　"In Search of the Revolutionary Theatre." Negro Digest 16
　　　(April 1966): 20-24.
　　"The Myth of a 'Negro Literature,'" Saturday Review, 20
　　　April 1963, pp. 20-21. Also in Davis and Redding, Cav-
　　　alcade; Gayle, Black Expression; Singh and Fellowes,
　　　Black Literature in America.
　　"Philistinism and the Negro Writer." In Hill, Anger and

Beyond, pp. 51-61.
"The Revolutionary Theatre." Liberator 5 (July 1965): 4.
"Technology and Ethos." In Williams, Amistad 2.
"What the Arts Need Now." Negro Digest 14 (April 1967):
    5.

DRAMA
Arm Yourself or Harm Yourself. Newark, N.J.: Jihad,
    196?.
B.P. Chant, 1968.
Baptism and The Toilet. New York: Grove, 1967†.
Black Mass. In Liberator 6 (June 1966): 14.
Bloodrites. In King and Milner, Black Drama Anthology.
Board of Education, 1968.
Columbia, The Gem of the Ocean. 1972.
Dante, 1962.
The Death of Malcolm X. In Bullins, New Plays from the
    Black Theatre.
Dutchman. In Oliver and Sills, Contemporary Black Drama;
    Patterson, Black Theatre; A Treasury of the Theatre,
    vol. 2.
Dutchman and The Slave: Two Plays. New York: Morrow,
    1964*†.
Four Black Revolutionary Plays. New York: Bobbs-Merrill,
    1969*†. (Includes Experimental Death Unit #1, A Black
    Mass, Great Goodness of Life, Madheart.)
Great Goodness of Life (A Coon Show). In Richards, Best
    Short Plays of the World Theatre, 1958-1967.
Home on the Range. In The Drama Review 12 (Summer
    1968).
Insurrection, 1968.
J-E-L-L-O. Newark, N.J.: Jihad, n.d.; Chicago: Third
    World, 1970.
The Kid Poeta Tragical, 1969.
Madheart: A Morality Play. In Jones and Neal, Black Fire;
    Robinson, Nommo.
Police. In The Drama Review 12 (Summer 1968): 112-115.
Slave Ship. In Negro Digest 16 (April 1967): 62; Poland
    and Mailman, The Off Off Broadway Book; Three Negro
    Plays.
The Toilet. In Turner, Black Drama in America.
EDITOR
Afrikan Congress: A Documentary of the First Modern Pan-
    African Congress. New York: Morrow, 1972*.
With Larry Neal. Black Fire: An Anthology of Afro-Amer-
    ican Writing. New York: Morrow, 1968*†.
With Diane DiPrima. Floating Bear, A Newsletter, Nos. 1-
    37, 1961-69: A Complete Annotated, Facsimile Edition.
    LaJolla, Calif.: McGilvery, 1973*.
Four Young Lady Poets. Millerton, N.Y.: Corinth, 1962†.
The Moderns: An Anthology of New Writing in America.
    Millerton; N.Y.: Corinth, 1963*†.
NON-FICTION
Black Music. New York: Morrow, 1967*; New York: Apollo

eds. , 1968†.

Blues People: Negro Music in White America. New York:
Morrow, 1963*†.

Gary and Miami: Before and After. Newark, N. J. : Jihad,
n. d.

Home: Social Essays, 1966; New York: Apollo eds. , 1967*;
New York: Morrow, 1972†.

With Billy Abernathy. In Our Terribleness: Pictures of the
Hip World. New York: Bobbs-Merrill, 1969*.

It's Nationtime. Chicago: Third World, forthcoming.

Kawaida Studies: The New Nationalism. Chicago: Third
World, 1972†.

Raise Race Rays Raze: Essays Since 1965. New York:
Random, 1971*†.

Strategy and Tactics of a Pan Afrikan Nationalist Party.
n. p. , 1972.

(Anthologies): Barbour, The Black Power Revolt; Barksdale
and Kinnamon, Black Writers of America; Gayle, The
Black Aesthetic; King and Anthony, Black Poets and
Prophets; Robinson, Nommo; Williams and Harris, Amistad 2.

(Periodicals): Black Scholar, November 1969; June 1970;
March 1971; September 1972; Black World, July 1970;
March, October 1972; The Drama Review, Summer 1968;
Journal of Black Poetry, 1970; Liberation, February 1964;
Negro Digest, December 1963; also in Downbeat; Jazz
Review; Metronome.

NOVEL

The System of Dante's Hell. New York: Grove, 1965†.
Excerpt in Hill, Soon One Morning.

POETRY

(Collections of Baraka's work)

Preface to a Twenty Volume Suicide Note. Millerton,
N. Y. : Corinth 1961†.

The Dead Lecturer: Poems. New York: Grove, 1964†.

Black Art. Newark, N. J. : Jihad, 1966.

Spirit Reach. Newark, N. J. : Jihad, n. d.

(Anthologies): Adams, Conn and Slepian, Afro-American
Literature: Poetry; Adoff, Black Out Loud; Adoff, I Am the
Darker Brother; Adoff, The Poetry of Black America;
Afro-Arts Anthology; Alhamisi and Wangara, Black Arts;
Allen, The New American Poetry; Austin, Fenderson and
Nelson, The Black Man and the Promise of America;
Baker, Black Literature in America; Barksdale and Kin-
namon, Black Writers of America; Baylor and Stokes,
Fine Frenzy; Bell, Afro-American Poetry; Bontemps,
American Negro Poetry; Brooks, A Broadside Treasury;
Burroughs and Randall, For Malcolm; Chambers and
Moon, Right On!; Chapman, Black Voices; Chapman, New
Black Voices; Davis and Redding, Cavalcade; Eastman, et
al, The Norton Anthology of Poetry; Emanuel and Gross,
Dark Symphony; Faderman and Bradshaw, Speaking for
Ourselves; Foerster, American Prose and Poetry; Ford,

Black Insights; Gleeson, First Reader of Contemporary Po-
etry; Gross, A Nation of Nations; Hayden, Kaleidoscope;
Henderson, Understanding the New Black Poetry; Hill,
Soon One Morning; Hollo, Negro Verse; Hughes, New Ne-
gro Poetry: USA; Hughes and Bontemps, Poetry of the
Negro: 1746-1970; Jones and Neal, Black Fire; Jordan,
Soulscript; Kearns, Black Experience; Kendricks, Afro-
American Voices; King, Black Spirits; Lomax and Abdul,
3000 Years of Black Poetry; Long and Collier, Afro-Amer-
ican Writing; Lowenfels, The Writing on the Wall; Main,
College Book of Verse; Major, The New Black Poetry;
Margolies, A Native Sons Reader; Miller, Blackamerican
Literature; Patterson, An Introduction to Black Literature
in America; Pool, Beyond the Blues; Randall, The Black
Poets; Randall, Black Poetry: A Supplement; Robinson,
Nommo; Rosenthal, 101 Postwar Poems; Rosenthal, The
New Modern Poetry; Rothenberg and Quasha, America: A
Prophecy; Simmons and Hutchinson, Black Culture; Singh
and Fellowes, Black Literature in America; Strand, The
Contemporary American Poets; Turner, Black American
Literature: Poetry; Weisman and Wright, Black Poetry for
All Americans; Oscar Williams, Little Treasury of Mod-
ern Poetry.
(Periodicals): Beloit Poetry Journal, Fall 1963; Big Table,
Spring 1960; Black World, June 1970; May 1973; Black
Theatre, April 1970; 1971; Epos, Winter 1958; Evergreen
Review, March-April 1960; November-December 1960;
July-August, 1961; Harper's, April, June 1965; Journal
of Black Poetry, Winter-Spring 1970; Kulchur, Summer
1963, Winter 1964-65, Spring 1965; The Nation, 23 Febru-
ary, 13 July 1963; 6 January, 29 June 1964; Negro Digest,
September 1964; April, September 1965; April, September
1966; September-October 1968; Outsider, Fall 1961; Paris
Review, Summer 1966; Poetry, April 1962; December
1963; March, December 1964; Writing, 1964; poetry also
in Beat Coast East; Big Table; Black Dialogue; Burning
Deck; Combustion; Floating Bear; Fuck You/A Magazine
of the Arts; Locus Solus; Massachusetts Review; The
Naked Ear; Nomad Outburst; Penny Poems; Provincetown
Review; Quixote; The Seasons; Set; Signal; Trobar; The
Village Voice; Whet; White Dove Review; Umbra.
SHORT STORY
Tales. New York: Grove, 1967†.
(Anthologies): Hicks, Cutting Edges; Patterson, An Introduc-
tion to Black Literature in America; Reed, 19 Necro-
mancers from Now.
(Periodicals): Evergreen Review 36, June 1965; Mutiny 2,
Autumn 1959; GWW2, Fall 1963.
BIBLIOGRAPHIES ON BARAKA
Hudson, Theodore R., comp. An Imamu Amiri Baraka (Le-
Roi Jones) Bibliography, Washington, D.C., 1816 Varnum
Street NE, n.d.
McPherson, James M., et al. Black in America: Biblio-

graphic Essays. pp. 249-250, 260-261, 283.

Schatt, Stanley. "LeRoi Jones: A Checklist to Primary and
Secondary Sources." Bulletin of Bibliography (April-
June 1971): 55-57.

BIOGRAPHY AND CRITICISM ON BARAKA
(Selected Criticism Prior to 1970)

Brodin, Pierre. "LeRoi Jones." Vingt-cinq Américains.
Paris: Nouvelles Editions Debresse, 1969, pp. 93-99.

Coleman, Larry. "Comic-strip Heroes: LeRoi Jones and
the Myth of American Innocence." Journal of Popular
Culture 3 (Fall 1969): 191-204.

Dennison, George. "The Demogogy of LeRoi Jones." Commentary 39 (1965): 67-70.

Gottlieb, Saul. "They Think You're an Airplane and You're
Really a Bird." Evergreen Review 11 (December 1967):
50-58. (Interview.)

Jackson, Kathryn. "LeRoi Jones and the New Black Writers
of the Sixties." Freedomways 9 (1969): 232-247.

Levertov, Denise. "Poets of the Given Ground." The Nation, 14 October 1961, pp. 251-252.

Llorens, David. "Ameer (LeRoi Jones) Baraka." Ebony 24
(August 1969): 75-78, 80-83.

Major, Clarence. "The Poetry of LeRoi Jones." Negro
Digest 14 (March 1965): 54-56.

Mootry, Maria K. "Themes and Symbols in Two Plays by
LeRoi Jones." Negro Digest 18 (April 1969): 42-47.

Nelson, Hugh. "LeRoi Jones' Dutchman: A Brief Ride on
a Doomed Ship." Educational Theatre Journal 20 (February 1968): 53-59.

Phillips, Louis. "LeRoi Jones and Contemporary Black
Drama." The Black American Writer, vol. 2. Edited
by C. W. E. Bigsby, pp. 203-217.

Weales, Gerald. "The Day LeRoi Jones Spoke on Penn
Campus--What Were the Blacks Doing in the Balcony?"
The New York Times Magazine, 4 May 1969, pp. 38-40.

(Selected Criticism Since 1970)

Adams, George R. " 'My Christ' in Dutchman." CLA Journal 15 (September 1971): 54-58.

Bermel, Albert. "Dutchman, Or the Black Stranger in
America." Arts in Society 9 (Fall 1972): 423-433.

"Black and Angry." Newsweek, 10 July 1972, pp. 35-36.

"Black Art Drama Is the Same as Black Life." Ebony 26
(February 1971): 74-76.

Brecht, Stefan. "LeRoi Jones' Slave Ship." The Drama Review 14 (1970): 212-219

Brooks. "Reactionary Trends in Recent Black Drama,"
pp. 44-45.

Brown, C. M. "Black Literature and LeRoi Jones." Black
World 17 (June 1970): 24-31.

Brown, Lloyd W. "Dreamers and Slaves: The Ethos of
Revolution in Walcott and LeRoi Jones." Caribbean Quarterly 17 (September-December): 36-44.

Cargas, Harry J. "LeRoi Jones: The Poetry of Exaggeration." <u>Daniel Berrigan and the Contemporary Poetry of Protest.</u> New Haven, Conn.: College and University Press, 1972.

Cohn, Ruby. "LeRoi Jones." <u>Dialogue in American Drama.</u> Bloomington: Indiana University Press, 1971, pp. 295-302.

Coleman, Larry G. "LeRoi Jones' <u>Tales:</u> Sketches of the Artist as a Young Man Moving Toward a Blacker Art." <u>Black Lines</u> 1 (Winter 1970): 17-26.

Coleman, Michael. "What Is Black Theatre? An Interview with Imamu Amiri Baraka." <u>Black World</u> 20 (April 1971): 32-36.

Conforti, J. M. "Nationalist from Newark." <u>Society</u> 9 (July 1972): 66.

<u>Current Biography,</u> 1970, 204-207.

Dippold, Mary D. "LeRoi Jones: Tramp with Connections." Ph.D. dissertation, University of Maryland, 1971.

Fischer, W. C. "Pre-revolutionary Writing of Imamu Amiri Baraka." <u>Massachusetts Review</u> 14 (Spring 1973): 259-305.

Frost, David. <u>The Americans.</u> Chicago: Stein, 1970, pp. 129-135.

Gallagher, Kathleen. "The Art(s) of Poetry: Jones and MacLeish." <u>Midwest Quarterly</u> 12 (July 1971): 383-392.

Harrison. <u>The Drama of Nommo,</u> pp. xiii, 38, 57, 60, 66, 86, 142, 169, 174, 182, 196, 197, 203, 212-213.

Hudson, Theodore R. <u>From LeRoi Jones to Amiri Baraka: The Literary Work.</u> Durham, N.C.: Duke, 1973*†.

Jackson, Esther M. "LeRoi Jones (Imamu Amiri Baraka): Form and the Progression of Consciousness." <u>CLA Journal</u> 17 (September 1973): 33-56.

Jacobus, Lee A. "Imamu Amiri Baraka: The Quest for Moral Order." In Gibson, <u>Modern Black Poets.</u>

Jeffers, Lance. "Bullins, Baraka, and Elder: The Dawn of Grandeur in Black Drama." <u>CLA Journal</u> 16 (September 1972): 32-48.

Kazin, Alfred. "Brothers Crying Out for More Access to Life." <u>Saturday Review,</u> 2 October 1971, pp. 33-35.

Kempton, Murray. "Newark: Keeping Up with LeRoi Jones." <u>The New York Review of Books,</u> 2 July 1970, pp. 21-23.

Kent. "Struggle for the Image," pp. 313-314, 322.

Kessler, Jascha. <u>Poetry</u> (February 1973): 292-293.

Klotman. "The White Bitch Archetype in Contemporary Black Fiction," pp. 96-110.

Lederer, Richard. "The Language of LeRoi Jones' 'The Slave.'" <u>Studies in Black Literature</u> 4 (Spring 1973): 14-16.

Lindberg, J. "Dutchman." <u>Black Academy Review</u> 2 (Spring-Summer 1971): 11-17. Reprinted in Mezu, <u>Modern Black Literature.</u>

Malkoff. <u>Crowell's Handbook of Contemporary Poetry,</u> pp. 51-57.

May. "Images of Apocalypse in the Black Novel," pp. 31-45.

Miller, Jeanne-Marie A. "The Plays of LeRoi Jones."
CLA Journal 14 (March 1971): 331-339.

Munro, C. Lynn. "LeRoi Jones: A Man in Transition."
CLA Journal 17 (September 1973): 57-78.

O'Brien, John. "Racial Nightmares and the Search for Self:
An Explication of LeRoi Jones' 'A Chase: Alighieri's
Dream).' " Negro American Literature Forum 7 (Fall
1973): 89-90.

Otten, Charlotte F. "LeRoi Jones: Napalm Poet." Con-
cerning Poetry 3 (1970): 5-11.

Pennington-Jones, Paulette. "From Brother LeRoi Jones
Through The System of Dante's Hell to Imamu Ameer Baraka." Journal of Black Studies 4 (December 1973): 195-
214.

Primeau, Ronald. "Richard Wright's Black Boy and LeRoi
Jones' Home." Studies in Black Literature 3 (Summer
1972): 12-18.

"Recent Killing." Nation, 12 February 1973, pp. 218-219.

Rice, Julian C. "LeRoi Jones' Dutchman: A Reading."
Contemporary Literature 12 (Winter 1971): 42-59.

Taylor, Clyde. "Baraka as Poet." In Gibson, Modern
Black Poets, pp. 131-134.

Tener, Robert L. "Role Playing as a Dutchman." Studies
in Black Literature 3 (Autumn 1972): 17-21.

Toppin. A Biographical History of Blacks in America Since
1528, pp. 340-341.

Trillin, C. "U.S. Journal: Newark." New Yorker, 30 December 1972, pp. 62-65.

Turner, Darwin T. "Afro-American Authors: A Full House.'
College English 34 (January 1972): 15-19.

Vickery, Olga W. "The Inferno of the Moderns." The
Shaken Realist. Edited by Melvin J. Friedman and John
B. Vickery. Baton Rouge: Louisiana State University,
1970, pp. 147-164.

Watkins, Mel. "Talk with LeRoi." New York Times Book
Review, 27 June 1971, sec. 7, p. 4.

Weisgram, Dianne H. "Dutchman: Inter-racial Ritual of
Sexual Violence." American Imago 29 (Fall 1972): 215-
232.

Whitlow. Black American Literature, pp. 170-176.

Witherington, Paul. "Exorcism and Baptism in LeRoi Jones's
The Toilet." Modern Drama 15 (September 1972): 159-
163.

BARBER, John.
SHORT STORY (Anthology): Coombs, What We Must See.

BARBOUR, Floyd.
DRAMA
The Bird Cage. Scene in Childress, Black Scenes.
EDITOR
Black Seventies. Extending Horizons Series. Boston: Sar-
gent, 1970*†.

Black Power Revolt. Extending Horizons Series. Boston:
    Sargent, 1969*.

BAREA, Tylon.
    POETRY (Periodicals): Journal of Black Poetry, Fall-Winter
    1971.

BARKSDALE, Richard K. Born 31 October 1915 in Winchester,
    Massachusetts. Education: A.B., cum laude, Bowdoin College,
    1933; A.M., cum laude, Syracuse University, 1938; A.M., Har-
    vard University, 1947; Ph.D., Harvard University, 1951. Ca-
    reer: Instructor, Department of English, Southern University,
    1938-39; Chairman, Department of English, Tougaloo College,
    1939-42; Professor of English, Department of English, North
    Carolina College at Durham (now North Carolina Central Univer-
    sity), 1949-53; Dean, Graduate School, North Carolina College
    at Durham, 1953-58; Chairman, Department of English, More-
    house College, 1962-67; Dean of the Graduate School, Atlanta
    University, 1967-71; Professor of English, University of Illinois
    at Urbana-Champaign, 1971; Director, English Undergraduate
    Studies, Department of English, University of Illinois, 1972 to
    present; also Consultant in Academic Administration for TAC-
    TICS, a program designed to improve the operation of selected
    Black colleges, sponsored by the United Board of College De-
    velopment. Member: Board of Directors, National Council of
    Teachers of English; President, College Language Association;
    Administrative Board of the National Fellowships Fund for Black
    Americans, Atlanta, Georgia; Commission on Institutions of
    Higher Education, North Central Association. Awards, Honors:
    Phi Beta Kappa, Bowdoin, 1937; Outstanding Educator of Amer-
    ica, 1971; Honorary Degree, Doctor of Humane Letters, Bow-
    doin College, June 1972.
CRITICISM
    "Alienation and the Anti-Hero in Recent American Fiction."
        CLA Journal 9 (1966): 1-10.
    "Arnold and Tennyson on Etna." CLA Journal 4 (September
        1960): 40-48.
    "Black American and the Mask of Comedy." The Comic Im-
        agination in American Literature, ed. Louis D. Rubin, Jr.
        New Brunswick, N.J.: Rutgers University, 1973, pp. 349-
        360.
    "Humanistic Protest in Recent Black Poetry." Modern Black
        Poets, ed. Donald Gibson. Englewood Cliffs, N.J.:
        Prentice-Hall, 1973, pp. 157-164.
    "The Nature Poetry of Henry Vaughan." Western Humanities
        Review 9 (Autumn 1955): 341-47.
    "Social Background in the Plays of Miller and Williams."
        CLA Journal 6 (1963): 161-169.
    "Symbolism and Irony in McKay's Home to Harlem. CLA
        Journal 15 (1972): 338-342.
    "Temple of the Fire Baptized." Phylon 14 (1953): 326-327.
        (James Baldwin's Go Tell It on the Mountain.)
    "Thomas Arnold's Attitude Toward Race." Phylon 18 (1957):

George Barlow

174-180.

"Trends in Contemporary Poetry." Phylon 19 (1958): 87-103.

"Urban Crisis and the Black Poetic Avant-Garde." Negro American Literature Forum 3 (1969): 40-44.

"White Tragedy, Black Comedy." Phylon 22 (1961): 226-233.

EDITOR

With Keneth Kinnamon. Black Writers of America, A Comprehensive Anthology. New York: Macmillan, 1972*.

SHORT STORY

(Periodical): Phylon, 1966.

WORK IN PROGRESS

"Langston Hughes: The Poet and His Critics" to be published in 1974 by the American Library Association.

BARLOW, George. Born 23 January 1948 in Berkeley, California. Education: A. A., Contra Costa College, 1968; B. A. (English), California State College at Hayward, 1970; M. F. A. (English and Creative Writing), University of Iowa, 1972. Currently living in Iowa City, Iowa. Career: College teaching in the areas

of Afro-American Literature and Writing (Poetry and Composition). Visiting Lecturer in English, University of California at Berkeley, 1973-74. Awards, Honors: Woodrow Wilson Fellowship, 1970-71; Ford Foundation Advanced-Study Fellowship, 1972-73.
POETRY
>   Gabriel. Detroit: Broadside, 1973†.
>   (Anthologies): Boyd, Broadside Series No. 66; Harper, Heartblows; Nathan and Rose, The Laureate; Shuman, Galaxy of Black Writing; Witherspoon, Broadside Annual 1972.
INTERJECTIONS
"The poems that make-up Gabriel, my first volume, are the articulation of my vision; they are that part of my survival kit I'm willing to reveal and share. I try to write poems that are magical, black and beautiful, since I am black, and since magic and beauty are basic to love, life, and living--things I'm committed to. I also try to tell the truth in my poems, particularly the truth about the American past and present, because I believe psychic and physical liberation can be realized only after one has heightened one's own historical consciousness. If America's past and present is a nightmare, it's only because too many people have refused to see it for what it is; a funky-assed dream that's been wiping everything and everybody out for 400 years. This country wasn't founded on truth and freedom and all those other good things. It was founded on myths; lies that have repeatedly manifested themselves in white racism, oppression, death, and destruction. Nothing short of a real psychic awakening will keep this nightmare from recurring, and I'm fighting, writing, running my mouth, dancing, and singing to facilitate such an awakening."

BARNES, Aubrey.
>   DRAMA   The Superheroes.   New York: Rannick Amuru, n.d.

BARNWELL, Desiree A. (Mrs. Lawrence S. Cumberbatch).   Born in Guyana, South America.
>   POETRY (Anthologies): Coombs, We Speak as Liberators; Shuman, Nine Black Poets.

BARON, Linda.
>   POETRY
>   Black Is Beautiful and.... n.p., 1971.
>   (Anthology): Dee, Glow Child; Street Verses in Some Righteousness (Manna House Anthology, 1971).
>   (Periodicals and Newspapers): Black Creation, 1970; 1971; Hope Journal, March 1970; Hudson Guild, 1972; New Daily News, March 1971; The Village Voice, 1972.
>   UNPUBLISHED WORK
>   With Robert E. Moore.   Rocksteady.

BARRAX, Gerald William.   Born 21 June 1933 in Attalla, Alabama. Education: B.A., Duquesne University, 1963; M.A., University of Pittsburgh, 1969; now enrolled in the Ph.D. program at

University of North Carolina at Chapel Hill. <u>Career</u>: Steel
mill worker, cab driver, mail carrier, and postal clerk, sub-
stitute teacher in public schools, encyclopedia salesman (sold
zero), awning manager; radio mechanic in U.S. Air Force,
1953-57. Taught at North Carolina Central University (Durham), 1969-70, and at North Carolina State University (Raleigh),
1970-72. <u>Awards, Honors</u>: Winner of the 1972 "first published" Broadside Press award.

POETRY
>   <u>Another Kind of Rain.</u>   Pittsburgh: University of Pittsburgh
>   Press, 1970.
>   (Anthologies): Adoff, <u>The Poetry of Black America</u>; Carroll,
>   <u>The Young American Poets</u>; Chapman, <u>New Black Voices</u>;
>   Hayden, <u>Kaleidoscope</u>; Hayden, Burrows and Lapides,
>   <u>Afro-American Literature</u>; Henderson, <u>Understanding the</u>
>   <u>New Black Poetry</u>; Leverton, <u>Out of the War Shadow</u>.
>   (Periodicals): <u>Black World</u>, September 1972; September
>   1973; <u>Journal of Black Poetry</u>, 1969; 1971; other poetry
>   in <u>Colloquy</u>; <u>Four Quarters</u>; <u>Poetry</u>; <u>Poetry Northwest</u>;
>   <u>Southern Poetry Review</u>; <u>World Order</u>.

BARRETT, Lindsay (Eseoghene). <u>Born</u> in Jamaica.
CRITICISM
>   <u>The State of Black Desire</u>. London: New Beacon, forthcom-
>   ing.

DRAMA
>   <u>Sighs of a Slave Dream</u> (one act).

NON-FICTION
>   (Anthologies): Alhamisi and Wangara, <u>Black Arts</u>; Jones and
>   Neal, <u>Black Fire</u>.
>   (Periodicals): <u>Negro Digest,</u> August, October 1969; <u>Black</u>
>   <u>World</u>, October 1970.

POETRY
>   (Anthology): Alhamisi and Wangara, <u>Black Arts</u>.
>   (Periodical): <u>Black Lines</u>.

SHORT STORY
>   (Periodical): <u>Black World,</u> December 1970; August 1971.

BIOGRAPHY AND CRITICISM ON BARRETT
>   "The Fifth Conrad Kent Rivers Memorial Fund Award."
>   <u>Black World</u> 2 (August 1971): 61-66.

BARRETT, Nathan. <u>Born</u> 24 May 1933 in New York City.
DRAMA
>   <u>S-C-A-R-E-W-E-D,</u> 1960.
>   <u>Losers: Weepers</u> (one act), 1962.
>   <u>Lead Ball</u> (one act), 1962.
>   <u>A Room of Roses</u>, 1964.
>   <u>The Aunts of Antioch City</u>, 1964.
>   <u>Engagement in San Dominque</u>, 1964.
>   <u>Evening of Black Comedy,</u> 1965.
>   <u>While Dames Dine</u> (one act), 1965.
>   <u>Sitting and Chipping</u> (one act), 1965.
>   <u>For Love of Mike,</u> 1967.

NOVEL
  Bars of Adamant: A Tropical Novel. New York: Fleet,
    1966*.
POETRY
  Floating World. New York? c 1962.
BIOGRAPHY AND CRITICISM ON BARRETT
  Contemporary Authors, 17/18.
REVIEW: Bars of Adamant.
  Williams, Ronald. Negro Digest 16 (January 1967): 94.

BASS, George Houston. Born 23 April 1938 in Nashville, Tennessee. Education: B.A., Fisk University, 1959; M.A. New
  York University (Film School), 1964; additional work at Columbia University's Graduate School of Business, 1959-1960, and
  at Yale University School of Drama, 1966-1968. Currently living in Providence, Rhode Island. Career: Literary Assistant
  and Secretary to Langston Hughes, 1959-64; Editorial Assistant
  to Daisy Bates for writing of her book, Long Shadow Over Little
  Rock, 1962; Script Writers, VOICES, Inc., 1960-1963; Artistic
  Director, Jacob Riis Amphitheatre, New York City, Summer,
  1966; Teacher-Director, Spanish-English Theatre Arts Schools,
  New York City, Summer, 1967; Director, Black Arts Theatre,
  New Haven, Connecticut, 1967-68; Artistic Director, (Third
  Party) Long Wharf Summer Theatre, New Haven, 1968; Associ-
  ate Producer (Story Editor) and Director for ON BEING BLACK
  series of original teleplays, WGBH-TV, Boston, 1968-69; Associate Director and playwright in residence, Urban Arts Corp.,
  New York City, 1969-70; Associate Professor, English Department, Brown University, 1970 to present; Director, RITES AND
  REASON. a University/Community cultural arts project sponsored by the Afro Arts Center, Inc., Providence, and by the
  Afro-American Studies Program of Brown University, Summer,
  1973. Free Lance Writer, director, producer for television
  and stage, June 1964 to present. Awards, Honors: John Hay
  Whitney Fellow (Foundation Grant), 1963-64; American Society
  of Cinematologists' Rosenthal Award, 1964 (most creative film
  script by young American writer); John Golden Fellow (play-
  wrighting), Yale University School of Drama, 1966-68; Plaque
  of the Lion of St. Marc awarded for The Game, a screen adap-
  tation of the play, 1967, Venice Film Festival, Italy; Artist's
  Grant, Harlem Cultural Council, February 1969.
DRAMA
  Black Blues, 1968.
  Black Masque, 1971.
  The Fun House, 1968.
  Games (one act), 1967. In Patterson, Introduction to Black
    Literature in America.
  The How Long Sweet, 1969.
  The Third Party, 1968.
  A Trio for the Living, 1968.
POETRY
  (Anthology): Lowenfels, Poets of Today.

INTERJECTION
"The primary assumption influencing my work as writer-director-producer-teacher is that the arts and creative expression are intelligent vehicles for the illumination (enunciation and interpretation) of the realities that determine the quality and conditions of our life and the realization of one's own creative potential. I work to help people (and myself) gain the deep recognition that freedom is a quality of action (and being) within each of us that may be discovered and expressed through the arts. It is my responsibility as an artist to master the use of symbols, forms, and vocabularies that are a part of my cultural heritage and use them effectively to communicate with the people with whom I wish to share my visions and ideas. I take on myself the responsibility to help people know and understand the arts as essential realities for intelligent living."

BASS, Kingsley B., Jr. (pseud. attributed to Ed Bullins).
DRAMA "We Righteous Bombers." In Turner, Black Drama in America.

BATES, Arthenia J. (Arthenia Bates Millican). Born 1 June 1920 in Sumter, South Carolina. Education: A.B., Morris College, 1941; M.A., Atlanta University, 1948. Additional study at North Carolina Central University, University of Michigan. Ph.D., Louisiana State University, 1972. Has also participated in writers' workshops: Langston Hughes' workshop at Atlanta University; the McKendre Writers Conference; Chautauqua Institute; Bread Loaf Writer's Conference; Home Study: Writer's Digest Course; Deep South Writer's Conference. Currently living in Baton Rouge, Louisiana. Career: Taught high school at Kershaw, South Carolina, and at Hartsville, South Carolina, 1942-46; Departmental Chairman and English instructor at Morris College, 1947-49; English instructor at Mary Bethune High, Halifax, Virginia; English instructor at Mississippi Valley State College, 1955-56; has taught at Southern University since 1956. Member: Immaculate Conception Catholic Church; Baton Rouge Sigma Alumnae Chapter of Delta Sigma Theta; Gamma Sigma Sigma; Lifetime Member, College Language Association, and a member of the Committee on Creative Writing. Awards, Honors: The Arthenia J. Bates Creative Writing Club was founded in May 1969 by Edward Glenn Jackson of Washington, D.C.
CRITICISM
    James Weldon Johnson: In Quest of an Afrocentric Tradition for Black American Literature. Ann Arbor, Mich.: University Microfilms, 1972.
    (Periodicals):
    "The Higher Fatality in Madame Bovary." The Southern University Creative and Research Bulletin, September 1959.
    Sound of the Lyre Off Main Street U.S.A." The Negro American Literature Forum 2 (Apring 1968).
FOLK TALES
    Folk Tales of Virginia, Part 1 and Part 2. New York: Amuru, n.d.

NON-FICTION
   (Periodical): The American Literature Forum, Winter 1967.
NOVEL
   The Deity Nodded. Detroit: Harlo Press, forthcoming.
POETRY
   (Anthologies): National Poetry Anthology, 1958 and 1962;
      Octagon Poems; Poetry Broadcast: An Anthology Com-
      piled for Radio Programs, 1946.
   (Periodicals): The English Newsletter (Southern University),
      March 1956; Southern University Creative and Research
      Bulletin, Summer 1958; The Southern University Faculty
      News Bulletin; Southern University Digest.
SHORT STORIES
   Seeds Beneath the Snow. New York: Greenwich, 1969.
   (Periodicals): Black World; The Last Cookie; Negro Digest;
      September 1965; Scriptiana Delta.
INTERJECTIONS
   "As a short story writer and novelist, I intend to depict
characters who represent the life styles, hopes and visions of
provincial black life. As a critic, I desire to show that black
writings have values apart from literature in the mainstream.
As an impulse poet, my verse has no central aim. I have
been most impressed about the theory of art for life's sake
when it comes to the matter of artistic purpose. It is my firm
impression that Black writers have not yet learned to use all
of the complexities of Black reality in drama, fiction or poetry."

BATES, Myrtle.
   POETRY (Periodical): Black Lines, Summer 1971.

BATIPPS, Percy Oliver.
   POETRY Lines of Life. Media, Pa.: American, 1924.

BATTLE, Effie T.
   POETRY Gleanings from Dixie-Land in Ten Poems, Okolona,
      Miss.: By the Author, 191?.

BATTLE, Sol. Born 20 November 1934 in Talladega, Alabama.
   Education: B. A., Temple University, 1955; additional work at
   Brooklyn College and New School For Social Research. Currently living in New York City. Career: Free lance photog-
   rapher, 1962-67; Director, Workshop for Young Writers, East
   Harlem, 1967-69; Editor, Panther House, Ltd., 1968-70, and
   Creative Director, 1970 to present; Editor-in-chief of Black
   List, the standard guide to the world black press corps. Free
   lance TV spot script writer, 1968 to present; ghost writer,
   speech writer, advisor on social problems to corporate execu-
   tives, 1971 to present; campaign writer, political candidates,
   1971 to present. Made the film, Harlem Etude. Member:
   Group for Advertising Progress (GAP); Coordinating Council for
   African-American Cinema. Awards, Honors: Grant-in-Aid,
   Mary Roberts Rinehart Foundation, 1969.

EDITOR
    Ghetto '68.   New York: Panther House, 1970*†.
NOVEL
    Mélange in Black.   New York: Panther House, 1970*†.
SCREENPLAYS
    Only 'til Spring.
    With Wale Ogunyemi.   The Vow.
    Underground Man (an adaptation).
UNPUBLISHED NOVEL
    Plastic Man.
BIOGRAPHY ON BATTLE
    Contemporary Authors.
    Who's Who in the East.
INTERJECTIONS
    Sol Battle, a strict vegetarian and follower of C. G. Jung's
school of analytical psychology, is opposed to legalized killing
and violence.   He is strongly influenced by French and Scandi-
navian existentialists, West African juju and ancient Egyptian
philosophy.   He has travelled extensively in South America and
Scandinavia.

BATTLES, Jesse Moore.   Born 1935.
    NOVEL Somebody Please Help Me.   New York: Pageant, 1965.

BAXTER, Joseph Harvey Lowell.
    POETRY
    Sonnets for the Ethiopians and Other Poems.   Roanoke, Va.:
        City Press, 1936.
    That Which Concerneth Me: Sonnets and Other Poems.
        Roanoke, Va.: Magic City Press, 1934.

BAYKIN, R. C.
    Peace of Mind.   n. p.: Doron Inner Prizes, 1972.

BEACH, Marion "Tumbleweed."
    POETRY Come Ride With Me.   Chicago: D. M. A. A. H. Press,
        1970.

BEADLE, Samuel Alfred.   Career: was a successful lawyer in
        Jackson, Miss.
    EDITORIAL
    "First Words."   The Voice of the Negro 1 (January 1904):
        33-36.
    POETRY
    Sketches from Life in Dixie.   Chicago: Scoll Publishing and
        Literary Syndicate, 1899.
    Lyrics of the Underworld.   Jackson, Miss.: W. A. Scott,
        1912.
    (Periodical): The Voice of the Negro 1 (January 1904): 23-
        24; 5 (May 1904): 185.

Robert Beck (credit: Impact Photos, Inc.)

BEAUFORD, Fred.
CRITICISM BY BEAUFORD
"Conversation with Al Murray." Black Creation 3 (Summer 1972): 26-27.
"A Conversation with Black Girl's J. E. Franklin." Black Creation (Fall 1971): 38-40.
"John A. Williams, Agent Provacateur." Black Creation 2 (Summer 1971): 4-6.
"Conversation with Ernest Gaines." Black Creation 4 (Fall 1972): 16-18.
"Conversation with Ishmael Reed." Black Creation 4 (Winter 1973): 12-15.
SHORT STORY
(Periodical): Black Creation, Summer 1973.

BECK, Robert (Iceberg Slim). Born 4 August 1918 in Chicago. Education: The streets of South Side Chicago. Currently living in Los Angeles. Career: A former pimp who has since dedicated his life to the Black movement through his writings. Lecturer at colleges and universities and for civic groups. Two novels, Trick Baby and Pimp, have been made into films.
NOVELS
Pimp: The Story of My Life. Los Angeles, Calif.: Holloway, 1967†. Excerpts in Robinson, Nommo; Young, Black Experience.
Trick Baby. Los Angeles, Calif.: Holloway, 1967†.
Mama Black Widow. Los Angeles, Calif.: Holloway, 1970†.
Naked Soul of Iceberg Slim. Los Angeles, Calif.: Holloway, 1971†.
BIOGRAPHY AND CRITICISM ON BECK
"Portrait of an Ex-pimp Philosopher, Iceberg Slim." Los Angeles Free Press, 25 February 1972, p. 3.
Harrison. The Drama of Nommo, p. 164.

BECKHAM, Barry. Born 19 March 1944 in Philadelphia. Education: A.B., Brown University, 1966; additional study at Columbia University Law School and New York University, School of Continuing Education. Currently living in Providence, Rhode Island. Career: Public Relations writer for the Chase Manhattan Bank, 1966-67; National Council of YMCA's, 1967-68; and the Western Electric Company, 1968-69; Urban Affairs Associate, Chase Manhattan Bank, 1969-70. Lecturer in English and Afro-American Studies, the African novel and creative writing, Brown University, 1970 to present.
NON-FICTION
(Periodicals): Brown Alumni Monthly, March 1970; Esquire, September 1969; New York Magazine, 22 September 1969; New York Sunday Times, 6 September 1970; Social Forces, June 1973.
NOVELS
My Main Mother. New York: Walker, 1969; New York: New American Library, 1971, 1972†.
Runner Mack. New York: Morrow, 1972*; New York: Popular

Library, 1973†.
REVIEWS
    (Periodical): <u>Novel: A Forum for Fiction</u>, vol. 5.
SHORT STORY
    (Anthology): Watkins, <u>Black Review No. 1.</u>
BIOGRAPHY AND CRITICISM ON BECKHAM
    <u>Contemporary Authors</u>, 29/32.
REVIEW: <u>My Main Mother</u>
    Orde Coombs. <u>Negro Digest</u> 19 (February 1970): 77-79.
REVIEW: <u>Runner Mack</u>
    New York Times Book Review, 3 December 1972, p. 78.
    Jim Walker. <u>Black Creation</u> 4 (Winter 1973): 62-63.

BECKINELLA, Janette.
    POETRY <u>Journal of Black Poetry</u>, Fall-Winter 1971.

BEECHER, John.
    POETRY <u>Land of the Free.</u> Oakland, Calif.: Morning Star
        Press, 1956.

BELL, James Madison. <u>Born</u> 3 April 1826 in Gallipolis, Ohio.
    <u>Died</u> 1902. <u>Education:</u> attended elementary and secondary
    schools in denominational institutions, Cleveland, Ohio. <u>Career:</u>
    Lecturer, reformer, [1] plasterer, poet-orator. He was a per-
    sonal friend of John Brown and recruited Negroes for the
    Harper's Ferry Raid, 1859. [2] Later, he became a steward in
    the African-Methodist Episcopal Church in San Francisco, 1863;
    a superintendent of a Sunday School in Toledo, Ohio. Through-
    out his entire life he read his own poetry at various gatherings;
    for this, he received the title, "Bard of Maumee."
    POETRY
        <u>The Poetical Works of James Madison Bell.</u> Lansing, Mich-
            igan: Wyncoop, Hallenbeck, Crawford, 1901 (2nd ed. 1904).
        "Modern Moses," and "Andrew Jackson Swinging Around in a
            Circle," were read most frequently by Bell between 1867
            and 1869 in San Francisco. [3] (Neither poem is printed in
            <u>The Poetical Works</u>, 1st or 2nd edition; nor does either
            appear among those poems listed in the article, "James
            Madison Bell," <u>The Negro History Bulletin</u>, April 1938,
            p. 7. "Modern Moses," however, does appear in William
            H. Robinson's <u>Early Black Poets</u>, Iowa: William C.
            Brown, 1969, p. 83.)
        "The Day and the War," delivered 1 January 1864, at Platt's
            Hill, San Francisco, for the celebration of the First Anni-
            versary of President Lincoln's Emancipation.
        "The Progress of Liberty," an anniversary poem delivered
            for the Celebration of the Third Anniversary of President
            Lincoln's Emancipation Proclamation, San Francisco,
            1866.
        "Triumph of Liberty," delivered 7 April 1870 on the Grand
            Amendment to the Constitution of the United States, De-
            troit, 1870. Later, these three poems, "The Day and the
            War," "The Progress of Liberty," and "Triumph of Lib-

erty" were printed in the 1901 edition of The Poetical
Works.[4]

"Emancipation in the District of Columbia" was read, 16
April 1862.[5]

(Anthologies): Calverton, Anthology of American Negro, p.
176; Davis, The American Negro Reference Book, p. 856;
Robinson, Early Black American Poets, pp. 82-83; White
and Jackson, An Anthology of Verse by American Negroes,
p. 38.

BIOGRAPHY AND CRITICISM ON BELL

Bardolph, Richard. The Negro Vanguard. New York: Vintage Books, 1959, pp. 58, 61, 75.

Butcher. The Negro in American Culture, p. 97.

Brawley. Early Negro American Writers, p. 279.

_____. Negro Genius, pp. 70, 87-89.

Emanuel and Gross. Dark Symphony, p. 9.

Loggins. The Negro Author, pp. 334-335, 454.

Mays. The Negro's God, pp. 146-148.

Saunders. To Make a Poet Black, pp. 44-47.

Thorpe, Earl E. Black Historians. New York: Morrow,
1971, p. 213n.

White and Jackson. An Anthology of Verse by American
Negroes, pp. 9, 37-39, 215, 225.

[1]Allen Johnson, ed., Dictionary of American Biography II (New York: Scribner's, 1929), p. 156.

[2]Benjamin Brawley, Early Negro American Writers
(New York: Dover Publishers, 1970), p. 279. (Republica-
tion of the original by the University of North Carolina
Press, 1935.)

[3]Bishop B. W. Arnett, "Introduction," The Poetical
Works of James Madison Bell. (Michigan: Wyncoop,
Hallenbeck, Crawford, 1904), pp. 8-11.

[4]Vernon Loggins, The Negro Author in America (New
York: Kennikat Press, Inc., 1964), pp. 334-45, 454.

[5]Brawley, p. 289.

BELLINGER, Claudia.
NOVEL Wolf Kitty. New York: Vantage, 1959.

BENFORD, Lawrence. Born 1946 in Texas.
POETRY
(Anthologies): Davis and Redding, Cavalcade; Lomax and
Abdul, 3000 Years of Black Poetry; Major, The New
Black Poetry.
(Periodical): Journal of Black Poetry, 1969.

BENITEZ, Lillie Kate Walker.
POETRY (Anthology): Henderson, Understanding the New Black
Poetry.

BENJAMIN, Joseph Louis
POETRY
Run White Man, Run! New York: Vantage, 1970. (Includes

prose.)

With Anita Honis. And the Truth Shall Make Us Free. New
York: Carlton, 1964.

BENJAMIN, Kathy.
POETRY (Anthology): Black Poets Write On!

BENJAMIN, Paul.
DRAMA
Memoirs of a Junkie.
A Twosome.

BENJAMIN, Robert C. O. Born 1855. Career: First black attorney to be admitted to practice in California (1880). Was
city editor of the Los Angeles Daily Sun.
BIOGRAPHY
Life of Toussaint L. Ouverture. Los Angeles: Evening Express Co., 1888.
POETRY
Poetic Gems. Charlottesville, Va.: Peck and Allan Printers,
1883.

BENNETT, Bob.
POETRY
(Anthologies): Jones and Neal, Black Fire; Watkins and
David, To Be a Black Woman.

BENNETT, Gwendolyn B. Born 8 July 1902 in Giddings, Texas.
Career: See Cullen, Caroling Dusk, pp. 153-155.
CRITICISM
"The Ebony Flute." Opportunity, August 1926-May 1928
(column about writers and writing.)
POETRY
(Anthologies): Adams, Conn and Slepian, Afro-American
Literature; Adoff, The Poetry of Black America; Bon-
temps, American Negro Poetry; Braithwaite, Anthology of
Magazine Verse for 1926; Calverton, Anthology of Ameri-
can Negro Literature; Cullen, Caroling Dusk; Eleazer,
Singers in the Dawn; Hughes and Bontemps, The Poetry
of the Negro: 1746-1970; Johnson, The Book of Ameri-
can Negro Poetry; Patterson, An Anthology of Black Literature in America; Walrond and Pool, Black and Un-
known Bards.
(Periodicals): Opportunity, December 1923; May, November
1924; February, September 1925; June, July, October
1926; October 1927; March 1934; Palms, October 1926.
SHORT STORIES
(Anthology): Johnson, Ebony and Topaz.
(Periodical): FIRE!!, 1926.

BENNETT, Hal. Born 21 April 1930 in Buckingham, Virginia.
NOVELS
The Black Wine. Garden City, N.Y.: Doubleday, 1968.

Lerone Bennett, Jr.

Lord of Dark Places. New York: Norton, 1970; New York:
    Bantam, 1971†.
Wait Until Evening. Garden City, N.Y.: Doubleday, 1974*.
A Wilderness of Vines. Garden City, N.Y.: Doubleday,
    1966; London: Cape, 1967; New York: Pyramid, 1970†.
REVIEW: Lord of Dark Places.
Times Literary Supplement, 12 November 1971, p. 1427.

BENNETT, John. Born 1865.
    FICTION
    Madam Margot: A Grotesque Legend of Old Charleston.
        New York: Century, 1921 (Lettered on Book Cover: The
        Bat Series).
    FOLK LORE
    The Doctor to the Dead: Grotesque Legends and Folk Tales
        of Old Charleston. New York: Rinehart, 1946.

BENNETT, Lerone, Jr. Born 17 October 1928 in Clarksdale, Mis-
    sissippi. Education: A.B., Morehouse College, 1949; addition-
    al work at Atlanta University, 1949. Currently living in Chi-
    cago. Career: Reporter, Atlanta Daily World, 1949-52; City
    Editor, Atlanta Daily World, 1952-53; Associate Editor, Jet
    magazine, 1953; Associate Editor, Ebony magazine, 1954-57;
    Senior Editor, Ebony magazine, 1958 to present; Visiting Pro-
    fessor of History, Northwestern University, 1968-69; Senior
    Fellow, Institute of Black World, 1969. He has travelled in
    Europe and Africa, and has lectured in colleges and universi-
    ties and before audiences in all sections of the country. Mem-
    ber: Fellow, Black Academy of Arts and Letters; Board of Di-
    rectors, Race Relations Information Center, Institute of the
    Black World; Board of Trustees, Martin Luther King Memorial
    Center. Awards, Honors: D.Litt., Morehouse College, 1965.
    CRITICISM
    "Nat's Last White Man." In Clarke, William Styron's Nat
        Turner.
    NON-FICTION
    Before the Mayflower: A History of Black America. Chi-
        cago: Johnson, 1962*; rev. ed. New York: Penguin,
        1966†.
    The Black Mood. New York: Barnes and Noble, 1970†.
    Black Power U.S.A.: The Human Side of Reconstruction,
        1867-1877. Chicago: Johnson, 1967*; New York: Pen-
        guin†.
    The Challenge of Blackness. Chicago: Johnson, 1972*.
    Confrontation: Black and White. Chicago: Johnson, 1965*;
        New York: Penguin, 1965†.
    The Negro Mood. Chicago: Johnson, 1964*.
    Pioneers in Protest. Chicago: Johnson, 1968*; New York:
        Penguin, 1969†.
    Unity in the Black Community. Chicago: Institute of Positive
        Education, n.d. (Pamphlet.)
    What Manner of Man: A Biography of Martin Luther King,
        Jr. 1929-1968. Chicago: Johnson, 1964*; New York:

Pocket Books, 1968†.
Over seventy-five articles, essays, and excerpts from his
books appear in Black World, Ebony, and Negro Digest.
POETRY
(Anthologies): Adoff, The Poetry of Black America; Baylor
and Stokes, Fine Frenzy; Chapman, Black Voices; Hughes,
New Negro Poets: U.S.A.
(Periodicals): Black Lines; Freedomways, Fall 1965; Negro
Digest, January 1962.
SHORT STORIES
(Anthologies): Chambers and Moon, Right On!; Clarke,
American Negro Short Stories; King, Black Short Story
Anthology; Mirer, Modern Black Stories.
(Periodical): Negro Digest, January 1963.
BIOGRAPHY AND CRITICISM ON BENNETT
Clarke, John Henrik. "Lerone Bennett: Social Historian."
Freedomways 5 (Fall 1965).
Llorens, David. "Two Busy Writers Who Are Also Real."
Negro Digest 15 (December 1965): 49-50.
Newquist, Roy, ed. Conversations. New York: Rand Mc-
Nally, 1967.
Who's Who in America.
Who's Who in the Midwest.

BENNETT, Richard.
SHORT STORY (Periodical): Negro Story, December-January
1944-45.

BENNETT, Walter Lee.
POETRY (Periodical): Black Lines, Spring 1973.

BERKLEY, Constance Elaine. Born 12 November 1931 in Washing-
ton, D.C. Education: B.A., Columbia University, 1971; M.A.,
Columbia University, 1972; presently working toward Ph.D. at
New York University. Currently living in Woodstock, New
York. Career: Has lectured at the New School, Brooklyn Col-
lege, Public Library, and other schools--public and private.
Now teaching Afro-American literature in the Vassar Black
Studies program.
POETRY
(Anthologies): Boyd, Poems by Blacks, I; Dee, Glow Child;
Lane, Poems by Blacks, II; People in Poetry (Hunter
College).
(Periodicals): Freedomways, Spring, Summer 1967; Second
Quarter 1973; other poetry in American Dialog; Black
Collegian; The Fiddlehead; New World Review; Penumbra;
Roots.
INTERJECTIONS
"The struggle to maintain life (living forms) and human dig-
nity must be inseparable from the black artist's work and ritu-
al of life. If all men do not soon rise to a never before
reached plateau of moral compassion and daily life based upon
mutual concessions then all people will suffer the dire conse-
quences."

BERNARD, Ruth Thompson.
NOVEL What's Wrong With Lottery? Boston: Meador, 1943.

BERRI, Wilhelm C.
POETRY The Weaning Years Beyond. New York: Vantage,
        1969.

BERRY, Faith. Born 29 May 1939 in Cincinnati, Ohio. Educa-
     tion: attended Fisk University for two years; spent junior year
     in Sweden (Independent Study Abroad): B.A. (History), Colum-
     bia University, 1962; graduate study, Institut des Professeurs
     de Français à l'Etranger, Paris; certificate in French-English
     translation, Georgetown University; M.A. (Comparative Litera-
     ture), Catholic University, 1972. Currently living in Washing-
     ton, D.C. Career: Editor, National Gallery of Art, Washing-
     ton, D.C.
     EDITOR
        Good Morning Revolution: The Uncollected Social Protest
           Writings of Langston Hughes. New York: Lawrence Hill,
           1973*†.
     NON-FICTION
        (Anthologies): Davis and Redding, Cavalcade; Stone and De-
           Nevi, Teaching Multi-Cultural Populations; Davis, The
           Paradox of Poverty in America; Daniels, Southern Africa.
        (Periodicals): Black World 20 (1970); Cosmopolitan, April
           1965; Crisis, June-July 1970; Harper's Bazaar, Septem-
           ber 1966; Jeune Afrique, 1 August 1965; 5 September
           1965; 24 October 1965; Nation, 6 May 1968; New Republic,
           28 May 1966; New York Times Magazine, 7 July 1968.

BERRY, Josie Graig.
     POETRY (Anthology): Murphy, Negro Voices.

BERRY, Kelley-Marie.
     DRAMA
        Baku, or How to Save the Whale's Tale, 1970.
        The Boomp Song, 1973.

BERRY, Lloyd Andrew.
     POETRY Heart Songs and Bygones. Dayton, Ohio: By the
        Author, 1926.

BERTHA, Gus.
     POETRY (Periodical): Journal of Black Poetry, Spring 1969;
        Winter-Spring 1970.

BESS, Olean. Born 23 February 1936 in Florence, South Carolina.
     Education: business and cosmetology courses. Currently liv-
     ing in St. Albans, New York. Career: Hairdresser and book-
     keeper. Poet, writer, actress. Has appeared on cable TV
     and radio programs, and has read her work at various meet-
     ings and other functions. Member: Alma John's Talent Work-
     shop. Awards, Honors: "Literary Highlight" award, presented

by the Foundation for Universal Brotherhood for the collection
of poems, Mixed Feelings.
POETRY
  Mixed Feelings. n.p.: By the Author, 1973.
UNPUBLISHED WORK
  Poems n' Things.
INTERJECTIONS
  "My philosophy is--I can't please all my listeners, but I
hope that the majority is pleased. I write what I feel and
leave it up to my audience to decide its value."

BETHUNE, Lebert.   Born 1937 in Kingston, Jamaica.
  POETRY
    A Juju of My Own. Paris, Imprimerie Union, 1965.
    (Anthologies): Adoff, The Poetry of Black America; Hender-
      son, Understanding the New Black Poetry; Hughes and
      Bontemps, The Poetry of the Negro: 1746-1970; Jones
      and Neal, Black Fire.
  SHORT STORY
    (Anthology): Hughes, The Best Short Stories by Negro
      Writers.

BEVERLY, Katherine.
  POETRY (Anthologies): Murphy, Ebony Rhythm; Murphy,
    Negro Voices.

BIBB, A. Denee.   Born 1885.   Died 1934.   Education: attended
    Lincoln University.
  POETRY (Anthology): Cuney, Hughes, and Wright, Lincoln
    University Poets.

BIBB, Eloise A. (Eloise Bibb Thompson).
  POETRY
    Poems. Boston: Monthly Review Press, 1895.
    (Periodical): Opportunity, March 1924.
  SHORT STORY
    (Periodical): Opportunity, September 1925; October 1927.
  BIOGRAPHY AND CRITICISM ON BIBB
    Loggins. The Negro Author in America, p. 335.

BIBBS, Hart Leroi.   Born 1930, Kansas City, Missouri.
  POETRY
    Cametude, Livre de recettes. Paris: Christian Bourgois
      Editeur, 1969; also in Umbra's Blackworks, Summer 1970,
      under the title, "Diet Book for Junkies."
    Poly Rhythms to Freedom. New York: McNair, 1964.
    (Anthologies): Jones and Neal, Black Fire; Major, The New
      Black Poetry.

BIRCH, McLane.
  POETRY
    The Kandi Man. Detroit: Broadside, 1970†.
    (Periodical): Journal of Black Poetry, Fall-Winter 1971.

BIRCHFIELD, Raymond.
    DRAMA   The Diamond Youth. New York: Rannick Amuru,
        1973†.

BIRD, Bessie Calhoun.
    POETRY Airs from the Woodwinds. Introduction by Arthur
        Huff Fauset. Philadelphia: Alpress, 1935.

BLACK, Austin. Born 1929 in East St. Louis, Illinois.
    NON-FICTION
        (Periodicals): Sepia, March, June, October, 1961; July,
        November 1962; July, August 1963.
    POETRY
        A Tornado in My Mouth: Poems. New York: Exposition,
        1966.
        (Anthology): Major, The New Black Poetry.
    REVIEW: A Tornado in My Mouth: Poems
        Sepia 16 (February 1967): 47.

BLACK, Isaac J.
    POETRY
        (Anthology): Chapman, New Black Voices.
        (Periodicals): Black Creation, Summer, Winter 1973; Black
        Dialogue; Black World, July, September 1970; September
        1972; September 1973; Journal of Black Poetry, Winter-
        Spring 1970; Summer 1972; Negro Digest, September-Oc-
        tober 1968; September 1969.

BLACKMAN, Louis.
    POETRY (Anthology): Murphy, Ebony Rhythm.

BLACKSHEAR, E. J. Education: attended Tabor College, Tabor,
    Iowa. Career: was Principal of Prairie View State Normal
    and Industrial College, Prairie View, Texas; President of the
    Teacher's Association, Texas.[1]
    POETRY
        (Periodical): "Africa--A Medley." Voice of the Negro 1
        (March 1904): 116-117.
    BIOGRAPHY AND CRITICISM ON BLACKSHEAR
        Meier, August. Negro Thought in America: 1880-1915.
        Ann Arbor: The University of Michigan Press, 1966, p.
        267.
        [1]Voice of the Negro, 1 (March 1904), p. 74.

BLACKSON, Lorenzo Dow. Born 9 May 1817 in Christiana, Dela-
    ware. Education: Attended schools in Baltimore and Christi-
    ana. Largely self-taught. Career: Was a Methodist preacher.
    NOVEL
        The Rise and Fall of the Kingdoms of Light and Darkness or
        the Reign of Kings Alpha and Abadon. Philadelphia: J.
        Nicholas, 1867.
    BIOGRAPHY AND CRITICISM ON BLACKSON
        Loggins. The Negro Author, pp. 305-309.

Williams. They Also Spoke, p. 151.
INTERJECTIONS
"Lorenzo Blackson was the first Negro writer to attempt a
story using legend as a background."[1]
    [1]Kenny J. Williams, They Also Spoke (Nashville, Tenn.:
Townsend Press, 1970), p. 218.

BLACKWELL, Dorothy F.
    POETRY (Anthology): Murphy, Ebony Rhythm.

BLACKWELL, James
    DRAMA The Money Game.

BLACKWOOD, Granby. Born 1921.
    NOVEL Un Sang Mal Mele. Paris: Editions Denoel, 1966.

BLAIR, John Paul.
    NOVEL Democracy Reborn. New York: By the Author, 1947.

BLAKE, James.
    Behind the Mask. San Francisco: Julian Richardson, n.d.

BLAKELEY, All Etheered.
    ESSAYS AND POETRY Poetic Facts and Philosophy. New
        York: A. E. Blakeley, 1936.

BLAKELEY, Henry.
    POETRY (Periodical): Crisis, 1940.

BLAKELEY, Nora.
    POETRY (Anthology): Brown, Lee and Ward, To Gwen With
        Love.

BLAND, Alden.
    NOVEL
        Behold--A Cry. New York: Scribner, 1947.
    CRITICISM ON BLAND
        Fleming, Robert E. "Overshadowed by Richard Wright:
            Three Black Chicago Novelists." Negro American Litera-
            ture Forum 7 (Fall 1973): 75-79.

BLANTON, Lorenzo D. Education: State University of Iowa; Uni-
    versity of Chicago.
    With others. Sing, Laugh, Weep. St. Louis, Mo.: The Scribes,
        1944
    POETRY
        In Dreer, American Literature by Negro Authors, p. 54.

BLESSITT, Bernadine.
    POETRY
        (Anthology): Murphy, Negro Voices.
        (Newspapers): Amsterdam News; Chicago Defender; New Or-
            leans Times.
        (Periodical): Opportunity, August 1940.

BLICKER, Seymour.
    Blues Chased a Rabbit. Montreal: Chateau Books, 1971.

BLUE, Cecil A.
    POETRY
        (Anthology): Brown, Davis and Lee, Negro Caravan.
    SHORT STORY
        (Periodical): Opportunity, July 1928.

BOGUS, Diane.
    POETRY I'm Off to See the Goddamn Wizard Alright. Chi-
        cago: By the Author, 7902 South Perry St., n.d.

BOHANAN, Wally.
    SHORT STORIES Wally Bohanan: His Short Stories. New
        York: Amuru, 1973†.

BOHANON, Mary.
    POETRY
        Earth Bosom and Collected Poems. New York: Carlton,
            n.d.
        Poems and Character Sketches. New York: Greenwich, 1967.
        (Anthology): Shuman, A Galaxy of Black Writing.
    REVIEW: Poems and Character Sketches.
        Farrison, W. Edward, CLA Journal 12 (September 1968):
            84-85.

BOHANON, Otto Leland. Born in Washington, D.C.
    POETRY
        (Anthology): James Weldon Johnson, The Book of American
            Negro Poetry; Kerlin, Negro Poets and Their Poems.

BOLES, Robert E. Born 1943.
    NOVELS
        The People One Knows. Boston: Houghton-Mifflin, 1964.
        Curling. Boston: Houghton-Mifflin, 1968.
    SHORT STORY
        (Anthology): Hughes, The Best Short Stories by Negro
            Writers; Patterson, An Introduction to Black Literature
            in America.
    SKETCHES
        Tri-Quarterly 29 (Winter 1974): 144-155.
    BIOGRAPHY AND CRITICISM ON BOLES
        "Black Writer's Views on Literary Lions and Values." Ne-
            gro Digest 17 (January 1968): 28.
        Greenya, John. "A Colorless Sort of Gray." Saturday Re-
            view, 17 February 1968, p. 38.
    REVIEW: Curling.
        Nikki Giovanni. Negro Digest 17 (August 1968): 86-88.
    REVIEW: The People One Knows.
        Woodford, John. Negro Digest 14 (May 1965): 52.

BOND, Frederick Welden.
    CRITICISM
        The Negro and the Drama, 1940; College Park, Md.: Mc-
          Grath, 1969*.
    DRAMA
        Family Affair, 1927.
    NON-FICTION
        Speech Construction. Boston: Christopher, 1936.

BOND, Horace Julian. Born 14 January 1940 in Nashville, Tennes-
    see. Education: attended Morehouse College, 1957-61. Cur-
    rently living in Atlanta, Georgia. Career: Founder of the Com-
    mittee on Appeal for Human Rights, the Atlanta University Cen-
    ter student organization that coordinated anti-segregation pro-
    tests; helped found the Student Nonviolent Coordinating Commit-
    tee (SNCC); reporter and feature writer for the Atlanta Inquirer
    (later becoming managing editor); Communications Director for
    SNCC (1961-66). Elected to office in the Georgia House of Rep-
    resentatives in 1965; finally allowed by U.S. Supreme Court rul-
    ing to become a member of the House in January 1967. Mem-
    ber: Southern Correspondents Reporting Racial Equality Wars
    (SCRREW); Delta Ministry Project of the National Council of
    Churches; Robert Kennedy Memorial Fund; Martin Luther King
    Junior Memorial Center; Center for Community Change; High-
    lander Research and Education Center; The National Sharecrop-
    per's Fund; Southern Regional Council; NAACP Legal Defense
    and Education Fund, Inc.; New Democratic Coalition; Advisory
    Board of the Voter Education Project; Visiting Fellow of the
    Metropolitan Applied Research Center of New York City.
    Awards, Honors: Honorary Trustee of the Institute of Applied
    Politics; B.A., Morehouse College, 1971; other honorary de-
    grees from Dalhousie University, 1969; University of Bridge-
    port, 1969; Wesleyan University, 1969; Syracuse University,
    1970; Eastern Michigan University, 1971; Tuskegee Institute,
    1971; Howard University, 1971; Morgan State University, 1971;
    Wilberforce University, 1971; Lincoln University, 1970.
    NON-FICTION
        A Time to Speak, A Time to Act. New York: Simon Schus-
          ter, 1972†.
        (Anthology): Austin, Fenderson, and Nelson, The Black Man
          and the Promise of America.
        (Periodicals): Black Scholar, November 1970; Ebony, August
          1971; Freedomways, Spring 1963.
    POETRY
        (Anthologies): Bontemps, American Negro Poetry; Hughes,
          New Negro Poets: USA; Hughes and Bontemps, The Po-
          etry of the Negro: 1746-1970; Lomax and Abdul, 3000
          Years of Black Poetry; Pool, Beyond the Blues; Singh and
          Fellowes, Black Literature in America.
        (Periodical): Présence Africaine, No. 57.
    BIOGRAPHY AND CRITICISM
        Llorens, David. "Julian Bond." Ebony 24 (May 1969): 58-
          62.

Neary, John. Julian Bond: Black Rebel. New York: Morrow, 1972†.
Negro History Bulletin 31 (December 1968): 21-22.
"Saving the Seed of Power." Ebony 26 (October 1971): 14-18.

BOND, Jean Carey.
CHILDREN AND YOUNG ADULTS
A Is for Africa. New York: Watts, 1969*.
Brown Is for Beautiful Color. New York: Watts, 1969*.
NON-FICTION
(Periodicals): Freedomways, Winter 1964; Spring 1964; Second Quarter 1971.

BOND, Odessa.
The Double Tragedy. New York: Vantage, 1970.

BONNER, Marita (Marita Bonner Occomy).
DRAMA
Exit on Illusion, 1929.
The Pot Maker. In Opportunity, February 1972.
The Purple Flower, 1928.
POETRY
(Periodical): Opportunity, March 1936.
SHORT STORIES
(Periodicals): Crisis, June, December 1939; March 1940, February 1941; Opportunity, August 1925; August, July, September 1933; August 1934; July 1938; January 1939.

BONTEMPS, Arna. Born 13 October 1902 in Alexandria, Louisiana. Died June 1973. Education: Attended elementary schools in Los Angeles; the San Fernando Academy. Received B.A. from the University of Chicago, 1943; L.H.D., Morgan State College, 1969. Career: Librarian, Fisk University, 1943-65; Professor, University of Illinois, Chicago Circle, 1966-69; Lecturer and Curator, Yale University, 1969-1972. Member: P.E.N., Authors League, Dramatists Guild, Sigma Pi Phi, Omega Psi Phi, Phi Mu Alpha, Council of the American Library Association. Awards, Honors: Julius Rosenwald Fellow, 1938-39; 1942-43; John Simon Guggenheim Fellowship, 1949; National Endowment for the Humanities Grant, 1973. Poetry prize, Crisis, 1926; Alexander Pushkin Poetry Prize, 1926, 1927; Short Story prize, Opportunity, 1932; Jane Addams Children's Book Award for The Story of the Negro, 1956; Dow Award, Society of Midland Authors for Any Place But Here, 1966.[1]
CRITICISM BY BONTEMPS
"American Negro Poetry." The Crisis 70 (1963): 509.
"The Black Renaissance of the Twenties." Black World 20 (November 1970): 5-9.
"Famous WPA Authors." Negro Digest 8 (June 1950): 43-47.
"Harlem: The 'Beautiful' Years: A Memoir." Negro Di-

gest 14 (January 1965):   62-69.

"Harlem in the Twenties." Crisis 73 (October 1966): 431-434†.

"The Harlem Renaissance." Saturday Review 30 (22 March 1947): 12-13, 44; condensed in Negro Digest 5 (June 1947): 20-24.

"The James Weldon Johnson Memorial Collection of Negro Arts and Letters." The Yale University Library Gazette 18 (October 1943): 19-26.

"Most Dangerous Negro in America." Negro Digest 10 (September 1961): 3-8.

"The Negro Contribution to American Letters." In The American Negro Reference Book. Edited by John P. Davis. Englewood Cliffs, N.J.: Prentice-Hall, 1966, pp. 850-878.

"Negro Poets--American." In Encyclopedia of Poetry and Poetics. Edited by Alex Preminger. Princeton, N.J.: Princeton University Press, 1965.

"Negro Poets, Then and Now." Phylon 11 (1950): 355-360.

"The Negro Renaissance: Jean Toomer and the Harlem Writers of the 1920's." In Hemenway, The Black Novelist, pp. 150-165.

"The New Black Renaissance." Negro Digest 11 (November 1961): 52-58.

"Special Collections of Negroana." Library Quarterly 14 (1944): 187-206.

"A Tribute to DuBois." Journal of Human Relations 14 (First Quarter 1966): 112-114; Negro Digest 13 (July 1964): 42-44.

"Unlocking the Negro's Past." Library Quarterly (July 1944); reprinted in Negro Digest 3 (December 1944): 71-75. (About the Schomberg Collection.)

"Why I Returned." In The South Today. Edited by Willie Morris. New York: Harper & Row, 1965.

DRAMA

With Countee Cullen. The Saint Louis Woman, 1946. (Musical adaptation of God Sends Sunday, 1931; printed in Black Theater, Lindsy Patterson, comp. New York: Dodd, Mead, 1971).

With Langston Hughes. When Jack Hollars, (on microfilm, 1936, Schomburg Collection).

EDITOR

With others. American Negro Heritage. San Francisco: Century Schoolbooks Press, 1965.

American Negro Poetry. New York: Hill & Wang, 1963; rev. ed., 1974*†.

With Langston Hughes. The Book of Negro Folklore. New York: Dodd, Mead, 1958.

With W. C. Handy. Father of the Blues, The Autobiography of W. C. Handy. New York: Macmillan, 1941; reissued in paperback, 1970.

Golden Slippers: An Anthology of Negro Poetry for Young People. New York: Harper, 1941*.

Great Slave Narratives. Boston: Beacon Press, 1969*†.
The Harlem Renaissance Remembered: Essays. New York:
    Dodd, Mead, 1972*.
Hold Fast to Dreams. New York: Follett, 1969*. (Poetry)
With Langston Hughes. The Poetry of the Negro: 1746-
    1970. Garden City, N.Y.: Doubleday, 1949.
JUVENILE
(Biography)
    Famous Negro Athletes. New York: Dodd, Mead, 1964*;
      New York: Apollo Editions, 1970†.
    Frederick Douglass: Slave, Fighter, Freeman. New York:
      Knopf, 1958*.
    Free at Last: The Life of Frederick Douglass. New York:
      Dodd, Mead, 1971*; New York: Apollo Editions, 1972†.
    George Washington Carver. New York: Row, Peterson, 1950.
    The Story of George Washington Carver. New York: Grosset
      & Dunlap, 1954.
    Young Booker: The Story of Booker T. Washington's Early
      Days. New York: Dodd, Mead, 1972*.
(Fiction)
    Chariot in the Sky: A Story of the Jubilee Singers, 1951;
      rev. ed. New York: Holt, Rinehart & Winston, 1971*.
    With Jack Conroy. The Fast Sooner Hound. Boston: Hough-
      ton Mifflin, 1942*.
    Lonesome Boy. Boston: Houghton Mifflin, 1955*.
    Mister Kelso's Lion. Philadelphia: Lippincott, 1970*.
    With Langston Hughes. Popo and Fifina: Children of Haiti.
      New York: Macmillan, 1932.
    Sad-Faced Boy. Boston: Houghton Mifflin, 1937*.
    With Jack Conroy. Sam Patch, The High, Wide and Hand-
      some Jumper. Boston: Houghton Mifflin, 1951.
    With Jack Conroy. Slappy Hooper, The Wonderful Sign
      Painter. Boston: Houghton Mifflin, 1946.
    You Can't Pet a Possum. New York: Morrow, 1934.
NON-FICTION
    With Jack Conroy. Anyplace But Here. New York: Hill &
      Wang, 1966 (a revised and enlarged version of They Seek
      a City, 1945)*† excerpt in Negro Digest, August 1945.
    100 Years of Negro Freedom. New York: Dodd, Mead,
      1961*; Apollo Edition, 1966†.
    The Story of the Negro, 1948; New York: Knopf, 1958*; ex-
      cerpt in Negro Digest, July 1948.
    We Have Tomorrow. Boston: Houghton Mifflin, 1945*.
    (Periodicals): Negro Digest, April, June 1945; December
      1947; American Scholar, Spring 1945.
NOVELS
    Black Thunder. New York: Macmillan, 1936; Beacon Press,
      1968†.
    Drums at Dusk. New York: Macmillan, 1939.
    God Sends Sunday. New York: Harcourt Brace, 1931*;
      (dramatized as The Saint Louis Woman, 1946).
    (Anthologies): Excerpts in Brown, Davis, Lee, Cavalcade;
      Hughes, The Book of Negro Humor.

POETRY

Personals. London: Paul Breman, 1964.

(Anthologies): Adams, Conn, Slepian, Afro-American Literature: Poetry; Adoff, The Poetry of Black America; Adoff, I Am the Darker Brother; Baker, Black Literature in America; Barksdale and Kinnamon, Black Writers of America; Bell, Afro-American Poetry; Bigsby, The Black American Writer, vol. 1.; Bontemps, Golden Slippers; Braithwaite, Anthology of Magazine Verse for 1926; Chametzky and Kaplan, Black and White in American Culture; Chapman, Black Voices; Cromwell, Turner, Dykes, Readings from Negro Authors; Cullen, Caroling Dusk; Cunard, Negro Anthology; Davis and Redding, Cavalcade; Emanuel and Gross, Dark Symphony; Ford, Black Insights; Hayden, Burrows, and Lapides, Afro-American Literature; Hill, Soon One Morning; Hughes and Bontemps, The Poetry of the Negro: 1746-1970; Johnson, Ebony and Topaz; Johnson, The Book of American Negro Poetry; Kearns, Black Identity; Kerlin, Negro Poets and Their Poems; Locke, The New Negro; Lomax and Abdul, 3000 Years of Black Poetry; Miller, Blackamerican Literature: 1760 to Present; Pool, Beyond the Blues; Redding, They Came in Chains; Randall, The Black Poets; Randall, Black Poetry: A Supplement; Singh and Fellowes, Black Literature in America; Stanford, I, Too, Sing America; Turner, Black American Literature; Wagner, Black Poets of the United States; Watkins, Anthology of American Negro Poetry.

(Periodicals): Commonweal, 23 May 1928; Crisis May 1926, May 1927; November 1970; Negro Digest, August 1947; September 1964; Opportunity, August, June 1925; January, February, March, June, October 1926; January, July 1927; April, May 1931; December 1932; January 1933; February 1942; Summer 1944.

SHORT STORY

The Old South: "A Summer Tragedy" and Other Stories of the Thirties. New York: Dodd, Mead, 1973*.

(Anthologies): Clarke, American Negro Short Stories; Ford, Black Insights; Hughes, The Best Short Stories by Negro Authors; Jones, From the Roots: Black Short Stories by Black Americans; Pickering, Fiction 100: An Anthology of Short Stories.

(Periodicals): Challenge, March 1934; Classmate, 11 February 1945; Negro Digest, February 1945; Opportunity, 1933.

BIOGRAPHY AND CRITICISM ON BONTEMPS

Baker, Houston A. Jr. "Arna Bontemps: A Memoir." Black World 22 (September 1973): 4-9.

Bardolph. The Negro Vanguard, pp. 202, 206, 209, 290, 373.

Bergman, Peter. The Chronological History of the Negro in America. New York: Harper & Row, 1969, p. 476.

Bone. The Negro Novel in America, pp. 45, 113-117, 120-123.

Brawley. Negro Builders and Heroes, p. 241.
_____. The Negro in Literature and Art, p. 122.
Brown, Lloyd W. "The Expatriate Consciousness in Black
    American Literature." Studies in Black Literature 3
    (Summer 1972): 9-12.
Brown, Sterling A. "Arna Bontemps: Co-Worker, Comrade."
    Black World 22 (September 1973): 11, 91-97.
_____. "The Negro Author and His Publisher." Negro
    Quarterly 1 (Spring 1942): 7.
_____. The Negro in American Fiction.
Butcher. The Negro in American Culture, pp. 140, 198,
    218.
Davis. The American Negro Reference Book, Englewood
    Cliffs, N. J.: Prentice-Hall, 1966, pp. 850-878.
Dickinson, Donald C. A Bio-Bibliography of Langston
    Hughes, New York: Archon Books, 1967, pp. ix-xi, 60-
    63, 106.
Dreer. American Literature by Negro Authors, pp. 82-84,
    269-278.
Frasier, Franklin E. The Negro Church in America. New
    York: Schlochen Books, 1968, p. 73n.
Gayle. Black Expression, pp. 78, 110-111, 118, 222-223,
    242, 254, 277.
Gloster. Negro Voices in American Fiction, pp. 111-117,
    162, 172-173, 194, 208, 216, 251.
Goldstein, Rhoda L. Black Life and Culture in the United
    States. New York: T. Y. Crowell, 1971, pp. 157, 169,
    178.
Hemenway. The Black Novelist, pp. 150-165.
Hickey, LaVerne. "Review of One Hundred Years of Negro
    Freedom." Community 21 (February 1962): 141.
Hill. Anger and Beyond, pp. 201-204, 206-210.
Hornsby, Alton Jr. The Black Almanac. New York: Bar-
    ron's Educational Series, 1973, pp. ix. 8, 10, 12, 16.
Huggins. Harlem Renaissance, pp. 72, 219.
Hughes. The Negro Novelist, pp. 37-39, 210, 221, 228,
    244.
Hughes, Langston and Milton Meltzer. A Pictorial History
    of the Negro in America. New York: Crown, 1966, pp.
    272-275, 286, 300.
Jahn, Janheinz. Neo-African Literature. New York: Grove,
    1968, pp. 151, 201-202, 206-207, 212-213, 230.
Kent. Blackness and the Adventure of Western Culture, pp.
    23-24, 32, 53.
Long and Collier. Afro-American Writing, vol. 1, p. 439.
Margolies. Native Sons, p. 39.
Mitchell. Black Drama, pp. 1, 87, 128, 218, 222.
Mphahlele, Ezekiel. Voices in the Whirlwind and Other Es-
    says. New York: Hill & Wang, 1972, pp. 138-139.
O'Brien. Interviews with Black Writers, pp. 3-16.
Robinson. Historical Biographies. New York: Publishers,
    1968, p. 164-165.
Spalding. Encyclopedia of Black Folklore and Humor, pp. 5,
    9, 444.

Tischler. Black Masks: Negro Characters in Modern
  Southern Fiction, p. 127.
Turner. In a Minor Chord, pp. xix, 5, 92, 95.
Wagner. Black Poets of the United States, pp. 263, 291.
Weil, Dorothy. "Folklore Motifs in the Arna Bontemps'
  Black Thunder." Southern Folklore Quarterly 35: 1-14.
"Young Readers Lose a Friend and a Mentor." Wilson Li-
  brary Bulletin (October 1973).
BIOGRAPHY
  Current Biography, 1946.
  Who's Who in America, 1940.
  World Book Encyclopedia, 1947; 1954.
  (Obituary-Tribute)
  Jet 44 (21 June 1973): 44.
REVIEWS ABOUT WORKS
  American Negro Poetry: Negro Digest 12 (September 1963): 52.
  Any Place But Here: Negro Digest 16 (August 1967): 51;
    Sepia 15 (October 1966): 71.
  Black Thunder: Challenge 1 (June 1936): 45; Opportunity 14
    (July 1936): 213.
  Drums at Dusk: Opportunity 17 (July 1939): 218-219.
  God Sends Sunday: Opportunity 9 (June 1931): 188.
  Golden Slippers: Opportunity 20 (January 1942): 27.
  Sad Faced Boy: Opportunity 15 (August 1937): 247-248.
  They Seek a City: Opportunity 23 (January 1945): 224.
  (Discs)
  "Negro Poetry for Young People." Educational Record Sales:
    1-10", 33 1/3 RPM, N.Y.N.Y.: 1973. (Compiled and
    read by Arna Bontemps whose poetry is also included.)
  (Audio-Tape Reel)
  "Arna Bontemps--Interview: Meet the Authors." Imperial
    International Learning Co., Kankakee, Ill, 1972.
    [1]Arna Bontemps: A biographical sketch was sent to
  the editors shortly before he passed away.

BOOKER, Simeon, Jr.
  NON-FICTION
    (Periodicals): Ebony, May, August, September, November
      1971; Jet, 7 January 1971; 11 February 1971; 25 March
      1971; 1 April 1971; 15 April 1971; 29 April 1971; 3 De-
      cember 1971; 15 April 1973.
  SHORT STORY
    (Anthology): Ford and Faggett, Best Short Stories by Afro-
      American Writers.

BORDER, William Holmes.
  POETRY
    Thunderbolts. Atlanta, Ga.: Morris Brown College Press,
      1942.
  SERMONS
    Seven Minutes at the "Mike" in the Deep South. Atlanta,
      Ga.: B. F. Logan, 1943.

BOSWORTH, William
NOVEL   The Long Search.   Great Barrington, Mass.: Advance,
     1957.

BOWEN, Robert.
   POETRY
      (Anthology): Dee, Glow Child; Troupe, Watts Poets.
      (Periodical): Journal of Black Poetry, Summer 1972.

BOWERS, Lassie
   POETRY Plantation Recipes.   N.Y.: Speller, 1959.

BOYD, Francis A.   Born 1844 in Lexington, Kentucky.
   NON-FICTION
      The Death and Funeral of Elder Richard Sneethen, Pastor of
         the Green Street Baptist Church, of Louisville, Ky., Who
         Died Thursday, April 11th, 1872, and Was Buried Sunday,
         April 14th, 1872.   Louisville, Ky.: Bradley & Gilbert,
         Printers, 1872.
   POETRY
      Columbiana; or, The North Star, Complete in one Volume.
         Chicago: Steam Job and Book Printing House of B. Hand,
         1870; excerpts from Cantos IV and V in Robinson, Early
         Black American Poets.
   BIOGRAPHY AND CRITICISM ON BOYD
      Robinson.   Early Black American Poets, pp. 76-77.

BOYD, John.   Born on New Providence Island.   Education: Large-
   ly self-taught.
   POETRY
      Poems on Various Subjects.   London: Cowie and Strange,
         1829.
      The Vision and Other Poems, in Blank Verse.   London:
         Longman, 1834.   Excerpts in Robinson, Early Black
         American Poets.
   BIOGRAPHY AND CRITICISM ON BOYD
      Robinson.   Early Black American Poets, p. 147.

BOYD, Melba.   Born 2 April 1950 in Detroit, Michigan.   Education: B.A. in English, and Communications, Western Michigan University, 1971; M.A. in English, Western Michigan University, 1972.   Currently living in Detroit.   Career: Presently Assistant Editor at Broadside Press in Detroit, and Instructor at Wayne County Community College.
   POETRY
   (Broadsides)
      With George Barlow, Jose-Angel Figueroa.   No. 66, "To
         Darnell and Johnny," No. 68.   Detroit: Broadside, n.d.
      (Periodicals): Maisha, August 1973.
   REVIEWS BY BOYD
      (Periodicals): Black Books Bulletin, Fall 1973; Black World,
         March 1972.
   WORK IN PROGRESS: a political piece entitled The Stress Af-

Arthur Boze (credit: Linda Brundige)

---

fair, to be published in 1974 by Broadside.
INTERJECTIONS
"In the Black man's quest for liberation all activities of that
quest should reflect an attempt to create a better world in which
to live that liberation.   Art should promote such a world."

BOYD, Raven Freemont.
POETRY Holiday Stanzas. New York: Fortuny's, 1940.

BOYD, Samuel.
POETRY (Anthology): Murphy, Ebony Rhythm.

BOYER, Jill Witherspoon.
EDITOR
The Broadside Annual 1972. Detroit: Broadside, 1972†.
The Broadside Annual 1973. Detroit: Broadside, 1973†.
POETRY
(Periodicals): Journal of Black Poetry, Spring 1969; Fall-
Winter 1971.

BOZE, Arthur Phillip. Born 23 July 1945 in Washington, D.C.
Education: B.A., George Washington University, 1967. Currently living in Los Angeles, California. Career: Director,

Youth Department, YMCA, Washington, D.C., 1967-68. Social
worker Los Angeles County Department of Public Social Serv-
ices, 1968-72. Presently writing poetry, songs and screenplays.
Member: Alpha Kappa Delta, Sociology Honorary. Awards,
Honors: Gold Medal Award, International Poetry Shrine.
POETRY
    Black Words. Detroit: Broadside, 1972†.
    Loving You. Kansas City, Mo.: Hallmark, 1972†.
    In Love with You. Los Angeles: Poetry Co., 1973†.
    (Periodicals): The Archer; Beyond Baroque; Journal of Black
       Poetry; The International Poetry Review; Verdad.

BRADFORD, Walter. Born 27 May 1937 in Chicago.
    POETRY
    (Anthologies): Brooks, A Broadside Treasury; Brooks,
       Jump Bad; Brown, Lee and Ward, To Gwen with Love.
    (Periodicals): Nommo, vols. 1 and 2.
    ESSAY
    (Periodicals): Black World, January 1972; Journal of Black
       Poetry, 1970-71.

BRADLEY, Henry T.
    POETRY Out of the Depths. New York: Avondale Press, 1928.

BRAITHWAITE, William Stanley Beaumont. Born 6 December 1878
in Boston, Massachusetts. Died 8 June 1962. Education:
Mainly self-educated. Received Honorary degree, M.A. from
Atlanta University, 1918; Litt.D. from Talladega College, 1918.[1]
Career: Published a yearly Anthology of Magazine Verse, 1913-
1929; the Golden Treasury of Magazine Verse; compiled a series of articles and wrote book reviews for the Boston Transcript; became editor of the Poetry Review in 1916.[2] In the
1920's he headed the B. J. Brimmer Publishing Company, Boston; in 1924, he first published Confusion, a novel by James
Gould Cozzens. He was Professor of Literature, Atlanta University, 1936-45.[3] He was a member of the Authors Club, the
New England Poetry Society, and the Poetry Society of America.[4] Awards, Honors: awarded the Spingarn Medal for excel-
lence in literature, 1918.[5]
CRITICISM BY BRAITHWAITE
    "Alain Locke's Relationship to the Negroes in American Lit-
      erature," Phylon 18 (Summer 1957): 166-173.
    John Myers O'Hara and the Grecian Influence. Portland,
      Me.: Smith & Sole, 1926.
    "Negro America's First Magazine." Negro Digest 6 (Decem-
      ber 1947): 21-27.
    "The Negro in American Literature." In Locke, The New
      Negro, pp. 29-44.
    "The Negro in Literature," Crisis 22 (September 1924):
      204-210.
    "The Novels of Jessie Fauset." Opportunity 12 (January
      1934): 24-28.
    "Poetry of the Public." The Poetry Journal (December

1915): 152-159.

"Some Contemporary Poets of the Negro Race." <u>Crisis</u> 17
(1919): 275-280.

EDITOR

<u>Anthology of Magazine Verse for 1913-1929 and Yearbook of</u>
<u>American Poetry</u>. New York: Schulte, 1913; 1926.
Sequi-Centennial Edition.

<u>Anthology of Massachusetts Poets</u>. Boston: Small, Maynard,
1922.

<u>The Book of Elizabethan Verse</u>. Boston: H.B. Turner, 1906.

<u>The Book of Georgian Verse</u>. New York: Brentano's, 1909;
London: Duckworth & Co., 1908.

<u>The Book of Modern British Verse</u>. Boston: Small, May-
nard, 1919.

<u>The Book of Restoration Verse</u>. New York: Brentano's,
1910; London: Duckworth, 1909.

<u>The Golden Treasury of Magazine Verse</u>. Boston: Small,
Maynard, 1918.

<u>Our Lady's Choir: A Contemporary Anthology of Verse by</u>
<u>Catholic Sisters</u>. Boston: B. Humphries, 1931.

<u>The Poetic Year for 1916: A Critical Anthology</u>. Boston:
Small, Maynard, 1917.

With Jessie B. Rittenhouse and Edward O'Brien. <u>The Po-</u>
<u>etry of Thomas S. Jones, Jr</u>. New York: G. W. Brown-
ing (privately printed), 1910.

<u>The Poets of the Future: A College Anthology for 1915/16</u>.
Boston: Stratford, 1916.

With Henry Thomas Schmittkind. <u>Representative American</u>
<u>Poetry</u>. Boston: R. G. Badger, 1916.

<u>Victory! Celebrated by Thirty-Eight American Poets</u>. Bos-
ton: Small, Maynard, 1919.

NON-FICTION

(Autobiography)

"The House of Arcturus: An Autobiography." <u>Phylon</u> 2
(First Quarter 1941): 9-26; 2 (Second Quarter 1941): 121-
136; 2 (Third Quarter 1941): 250-259; 3 (First Quarter
1942): 31-44; 3 (Second Quarter 1942): 183-194. Summa-
rized in Barton, <u>Witnesses for Freedom</u>, pp. 93-100.

(Biography)

<u>The Bewitched Parsonage: The Story of the Brontës</u>. New
York: Coward-McCann, 1950.

(History-Juvenile)

<u>The Story of the Great War</u>. New York: Frederick A.
Stokes, 1919.

(Introductions)

Cowdery, Mae V. <u>We Lift Our Voices and Other Poems</u>.
Philadelphia: Alpress, 1936.

Gibson, Charles. <u>The Wounded Eros: Sonnets</u>. Boston:
By the Author, Riverside Press, 1908.

Johnson, Georgia Douglas. <u>The Heart of a Woman and Oth-</u>
<u>er Poems</u>. Boston: Cornhill, 1918.

More, Brookes. <u>The Beggar's Vision</u>. Boston: Cornhill,
1921.

(Preface)
Buchman, Marion. A Voice in Ramah: Poems. New York:
Bookman Assoc. , 1959.
(Anthology): Watkins, Anthology of American Poets.
(Periodicals): Crisis 69 (June-July 1962): 343; Negro Digest
6 (January 1948): 36-39.

NOVELS
The Canadian, a Novel. Boston: Small, Maynard, 1901.
Going Over Tindel, a Novel. Boston: Brimmer, 1924.

POETRY
House of Falling Leaves. Boston: J. W. Luce, 1908.
Lyrics of Life and Love. Boston: H. B. Turner, 1904.
Selected Poems. New York: Coward-McCann, 1948.
A Tale of a Walled Town and Other Verses. Philadelphia:
J. B. Lippincott, 1921.
(Anthologies): Adoff, Poetry of Black America; Barksdale
and Kinnamon, Black Writers of America; Bontemps,
American Negro Poetry; Bontemps, Golden Slippers;
Brawley, The Negro Genius; Brawley, The Negro in Lit-
erature and Art; Brown, Davis and Lee, The Negro Cara-
van; Calverton, Anthology of American Negro Literature;
Chametzky and Kaplan, Black and White in American Cul-
ture; Cullen, Caroling Dusk; Davis and Redding, Caval-
cade; Eleazer, Singers in the Dawn; Hughes and Bontemps,
The Poetry of the Negro: 1746-1970; Johnson, The Book
of American Negro Poetry; Kerlin, Negro Poets and Their
Poems; Locke, The New Negro; Long and Collier, Afro-
American Writing; Patterson, Rock Against the Wind;
Turner, Black American Literature; Wagner, Black Poets
of the United States; Watkins, An Anthology of American
Negro Literature; White and Jackson, An Anthology of
Verse by American Negroes.
(Periodicals): Atlantic, July 1909; Crisis 77 (November
1970): 364; Palms (Negro Poets' Number) 4 (October
1926): 11; Phylon 1 (First Quarter 1940); Voice of the
Negro 3 (December 1906): 586; 4 (January-February 1907):
67; 4 (March 1907): 134; (June 1907): 227; 4 (July 1907):
291.

BIOGRAPHY AND CRITICISM ON BRAITHWAITE
Aiken, Conrad. "Looking Pegasus in the Mouth." The Po-
etry Journal (February 1916): 20-28.
_____. "Prizes and Anthologies." The Poetry Journal (No-
vember 1915): 95-100.
Bardolph. The Negro Vanguard, pp. 202-209, 289, 316,
339, 383-84.
Bergman, Peter M. The Chronological History of the Negro
in America. New York: Harper & Row, 1969; 1878, 1904,
1908, 1913.
Biram, Brenda M. "Paid Servant." Negro Digest 18 (April
1969): 92-93.
Boston Evening Transcript, 30 November 1915.
Brawley. The Negro Genius, pp. 202-206.

Brown, Davis and Lee. The Negro Caravan, p. 773.

Butcher. The Negro in American Culture, pp. 101, 129, 218.

Butcher, Philip. "William Stanley Braithwaite and the College Language Association." CLA Journal 15 (December 1971): 117-125.

Chamberlain, John. "The Negro As Writer." Bookman 70 (February 1930): 610.

Clairmonte, Glenn. "He Made American Writers Famous." Phylon 30 (Summer 1969): 184-190.

Cromwell, Turner and Dykes. Readings from Negro Authors, pp. 30-31, 209-211.

Davis. The American Negro Reference Book, p. 855.

Dickinson, Donald C. A Bio-Bibliography of Langston Hughes, 1902-1967. New York: Archon, 1967, p. 3.

Dreer. American Literature by Negro Authors, p. 43.

Du Bois, W. E. B. The Gift of Black Folk. Boston: Stratford, 1924, pp. 303-304, 307.

Emanuel and Gross. Dark Symphony, pp. 10, 11, 370.

Frances Teresa, Sister. "Poet's Discoverer." Phylon 5 (Fourth Quarter 1944): 375-378.

Gayle. Black Expression, pp. 75, 233, 287.

Isaacs, Harold R. The New World of Negro Americans, London: Phoenix House, 1963, pp. 315-318.

Janheinz, Jahn. Neo-African Literature. New York: Grove Press, 1968, pp. 192-211.

Journal of Negro History 47 (July 1962): 214. (Obituary)

Kerlin. Negro Poets and Their Poems, pp. 105-109.

Pickens, William. "Braithwaite," Voice of the Negro 4 (March 1907): 119-121.

Ploski. Negro Almanac, pp. 279-280.

Randall, D. "White Poet, Black Critic." Negro Digest 14 (February 1965): 46-48.

Redding, Saunders. They Came in Chains. Philadelphia: J. B. Lippincott, 1970, pp. 207, 267.

Spellman, Franzell. "The Twentieth Century's Greatest Negro Anthologist." Negro History Bulletin 26 (January 1963): 137.

Thurman, Wallace. "Negro Poets and Their Poetry." Bookman 67 (March 1928-August 1928): 558.

Turner. In a Minor Chord, p. 2.

REVIEW: Lyrics of Life and Love.
Voice of the Negro 1 (December 1904): 628-629.

REVIEW: Selected Poems.
A. M. S. Saturday Review 32 (12 February 1949): 31.

[1]Newman Ivey White and Walter Clinton Jackson, An Anthology of Verse by American Negroes (Durham, N.C.: Moore Publishing Co., 1968), p. 134.

[2]Thomas Yenser, ed., Who's Who in Colored America, 5th ed. (Brooklyn: Yenser, 1938, 1939, 1940), p. 74.

[3]"Obituary," New York Times, 9 June 1962, 25:4.

[4]Who Was Who in America, vol. 4, (Chicago: Marquis, Inc., 1961-68), p. 111.

[5]Yenser, p. 74.

BRANCH, Edward.
  NOVEL The High Places. New York: Exposition, 1957.

BRANCH, William Blackwell. Born 11 September 1927 in New Hav-
en, Connecticut. Education: B.S., Northwestern University,
1949; M.F.A., Columbia University, 1958; American Broadcasting Fellow at Yale University, 1965-66. Currently living in
New Rochelle, New York. Career: Began a career in theatre
while still a college freshman when he joined the national cast
of the Broadway play, Anna Lucasta. In addition to playwrighting, he writes and produces for television, radio, documentary
films and feature motion pictures as follows: Documentaries--
"What Is Conscience?" CBS-TV, 1955; "Let's Find Out," syndicated documentary TV series for National Council of Churches,
1956; "The Explorers Club," 1963, "Gypsy in My Soul," 1964,
and "Fair Game," 1964, TV documentaries for "The City" series, "Legacy of a Prophet," 1964, for the Educational Broadcasting Corp.; "Still a Brother: Inside the Negro Middle
Class," 1968, for NET; "The Case of the Non-Working Work-
ers," 1972, NBC News; "Build, Baby, Build," 1972, NBC
News; "The 20 Billion Dollar Rip-Off," 1972, NBC News; "No
Room to Run, No Place to Hide," 1972, NBC News; "The Black
Church in New York," 1973, NBC News. TV Drama--"The
Way," 1955, ABC-TV; "Light in the Southern Sky," 1958, NBC-
TV. Radio--"The Alma John Show (1963-65) for Coca Cola,
Inc., Atlanta. Motion Picture Outlines--"Judgment," 1969, for
Harry Belafonte; "Red, White and Black," 1972, for Sidney
Poitier. Screenplay--"Together for Days," 1971, for Olas
Corp. Documentary Drama--"Fifty Steps Toward Freedom,"
1959, for NAACP; "The Man on Meeting Street," 1960, for
Alpha Kappa Alpha Sorority. Filmstrips--"Marcus Garvey,"
1969, for Buckingham Learning Corp. Syndicated newspaper
column--(with Jackie Robinson) for New York Post and other
newspapers. Currently developing independent projects in feature films and television. Awards, Honors: Robert E. Sher-
wood Television Award and Special Citation from National Coun-
cil of Christians and Jews, 1958, for the TV drama, "Light in
the Southern Sky"; Blue Ribbon Award of the American Film
Festival, 1969; "Emmy" Award nominee, 1969, for "Still a
Brother: Inside the Negro Middle Class"; Guggenheim Fellow-
ship for Creative Writing in Drama, 1959; Hannah Del Vecchio
Award for achievement in playwrighting, Trustees of Columbia
University, 1958.
DRAMA
  Baccalaureate, 1954.
  In Splendid Error, 1954. In Patterson, Black Theatre.
  Light in the Southern Sky (one act), 1958.
  A Medal for Willie, 1951. In King and Milner, Black Dra-
    ma Anthology.
  To Follow the Phoenix, 1960. Scene in Childress, Black
    Scenes.

William B. Branch

A Wreath for Udomo, 1961.
NON-FICTION
"Marketing the Products of American Negro Writers."
American Writer and His Roots. New York: American
Society of Africa Culture, 1960.
BIOGRAPHY AND CRITICISM ON BRANCH
Abramson. Negro Playwrights in the American Theatre, pp.
171-188, 255-256, 257-258.
"Black Writer's Views on Literary Lions and Values." Ne-
gro Digest 17 (January 1968): 30.
Harrison. The Drama of Nommo, p. xviii.
Mitchell. Black Drama, pp. 151-154, 167-178.
_____. "Three Writers and a Dream." Crisis 72 (April
1965): 219-223.
REVIEW: A Wreath for Udomo.
Jet, 31 March 1960, p. 60.

BRATH, Cecil E.
POETRY (Periodical): Journal of Black Poetry, Winter-Spring,
1970.

BRAWLEY, Benjamin Griffiths. Born 22 April 1882 in Columbia,
S.C. Died 1 February 1939. Education: A.B., Atlanta Baptist College (now Morehouse College), 1901; A.B., University
of Chicago, 1906; A.M., Harvard University, 1908; Litt.D.,
Shaw University, Raleigh, S.C., 1927.[1] In 1920, studied
abroad on the West Coast of Africa.[2] Career: Professor of
English at Morehouse College, 1902-1910; Harvard University,
1910-1912; Dean at Morehouse, 1912-20; Professor at Shaw,
1923-31.[3] He was president of the Association of Colleges for
Negro Youth, 1918-20; ordained Pastor to the Baptist Ministry,
2 June 1921; became Pastor of the Messiah Baptist Church,
Brockton, Mass., 1921-22.[4] When he wrote The Negro in Art
and Literature, it became the first book devoted exclusively to
this particular aspect of Black History.[5]
BIOGRAPHY
    Dr. Dillard of the Jeanes Fund. New York: Fleming H. Re-
        vell Co., 1930. Reprint of the 1933 edition, Freeport,
        N.Y.: Books for Libraries*.
    Negro Builders and Heroes. Chapel Hill: University of North
        Carolina Press, 1937*.
    Paul Laurence Dunbar, Poet of His People. Chapel Hill:
        University of North Carolina Press, 1936.
    With Arthur Huff Fauset. Sojourner Truth. Chapel Hill:
        University of North Carolina Press, 1938.
    Women of Achievement. Chicago: Women's American Bap-
        tist Home Mission Society, 1919.
CRITICISM BY BRAWLEY
    A History of the English Hymn. New York: Abington Press,
        1932.
    The Negro Genius. New York: Dodd, Mead, 1937; New York:
        Apollo Editions†; reprint ed. New York: Biblo & Tannen*.
    The Negro in Literature and Art in the United States. New
        York: Duffield, 1918 (Based on the author's book of 1910).
        Reprint of 1930 edition, New York: AMS Press, 1971*.
    A New Survey of English Literature. New York: A. A.
        Knopf, 1925.
    A Short History of the English Drama. New York: Harcourt,
        Brace, 1921; facsimile ed., Freeport, N.Y.: Books for
        Libraries*.
    (Periodicals):
    "The Negro in American Fiction." The Dial 60 (1916): 445-
        450.
    "The Negro in American Literature." Bookman 56 (October
        1922): 137-141.
    "The Negro Literary Renaissance." The Southern Workman
        56 (April 1927): 177-180.
    "P. Wheatley." Voice of the Negro 2 (January 1905): 55-59.
    "The Promise of Negro Literature." Journal of Negro His-
        tory 19 (January 1934): 53-59.
    "Three Negro Poets." Journal of Negro History (October
        1917).
EDITOR
    The Best Stories of Paul Laurence Dunbar. New York: Dodd,

Mead, 1938.
Early Negro American Writers. Chapel Hill: University of
   North Carolina Press, 1935; New York: Dover†; Glouces-
   ter, Mass.: Peter Smith*.
New Era Declamations. Sewanee, Tenn.: The University
   Press, 1918.
(Periodical):
The Home Missions Review. May 1927-May 1930, Bi Month-
   ly. Raleigh, N.C.: Shaw University Press.
NON-FICTION
   Africa and the War. New York: Duffield, 1918.
   Desire of the Moth for the Star. Atlanta, Ga.: Franklin-
      Turner, 19--. (Pamphlet)
   Early Effort for Industrial Education. Charlottesville? Va.:
      n.p., 1923.
   Freshman Year English. New York: Noble & Noble, 1929.
   History of Morehouse College. Atlanta, Ga.: Morehouse
      College, 1917; reprint ed. Washington, D.C., McGrath*.
   History of the English Hymn. New York: Cincinnati: Abing-
      don Press, 1932.
   New Survey of English Literature. New York: Crofts, 1930.
   A Short History of the American Negro. New York: Mac-
      millan, 1913. Reprint of 1921 edition, New York: AMS
      Press*.
   A Social History of the American Negro. New York: Mac-
      millan, 1921†; New York: Johnson Reprints, 1969*.
   Studies in English Prose with Exercises in Style. Atlanta,
      Ga.: Atlanta Baptist College Press, 1908. (Pamphlet.)
   Your Negro Neighbor. New York: Macmillan, 1918.
POETRY
   The Problem, and Other Poems. Atlanta, Ga.: Atlanta Bap-
      tist College, 1905.
   The Seven Sleepers of Ephesus; a Lyrical Legend. Atlanta,
      Ga.: Foote & Davies, 1917.
   A Toast to Love and Death. Atlanta, Ga.: Atlanta Baptist
      College Print, 1902.
   (Anthologies): Brown, Davis and Lee, Negro Caravan; Cal-
      verton, Anthology of American Negro Literature; Hughes
      and Bontemps, The Poetry of the Negro: 1746-1970;
      Johnson, The Book of American Negro Poetry; Watkins,
      An Anthology of American Negro Literature; White and
      Jackson, An Anthology of Verse by American Negroes.
   (Periodicals): Crisis 6 (1913): 347; 10 (1915): 37; 77 (De-
      cember 1970): 409-410; Opportunity (December 1926):
      383; 17 (March 1939): 89; Voice of the Negro 1 (February
      1904): 63; 1 (May 1904): 185; 1 (November 1904): 524;
      2 (January 1905): 663; 2 (May 1905): 319; 3 (April 1906):
      265; 4 (July 1907): 294; 4 (October 1907: 355.
SHORT STORY
   (Anthology): In Stories of the South. Edited by Clarence
      Addison Hibbard. Chapel Hill: University of North Caro-
      lina Press, 1931. (Reprinted from Crisis 12 (1916): 145.)

BIOGRAPHY AND CRITICISM ON BRAWLEY
Bardolph. The Negro Vanguard, pp. 126, 160, 164, 168,
179-180, 294, 431.
Brawley. Negro Builders and Heroes, p. 201.
Brown. The Negro in American Fiction.
Butcher. The Negro in American Culture, p. 218.
Chamberlain, John. "The Negro As Writer." Bookman, 70
(February 1930): 608.
Chametzky and Kaplan. Black and White in American Cul-
ture, p. 345.
Cromwell, Turner and Dykes. Readings from Negro Au-
thors, pp. 222-224.
Dickinson, Donald C. A Bio-Bibliography on Langston
Hughes, 1902-1967. New York: Archon Books, 1967, pp.
48, 62.
Du Bois, W. E. B. The Gift of Black Folk. Boston: Strat-
ford Co., 1924, pp. 146, 153, 158, 162-163, 285, 290,
303.
Emanuel and Gross. Dark Symphony, pp. 7, 10, 11, 67, 367.
Garrett, Romeo B. Famous First Facts About Negroes.
New York: Arno Press, 1972, p. 102.
Gayle. Black Expression, p. 240.
Isaacs, Harold R. The New World of Negro Americans.
London: Phoenix House, 1963, p. 183.
Jet, 3 February 1966, p. 11.
Janheinz, Jahn. Neo-African Literature, pp. 41, 48, 187,
208.
Johnson, James W. Black Manhattan. New York: Arno
Press, 1968, p. 33.
Journal of Negro History 24 (April 1939): 242-243.
Mays. The Negro's God, p. 8, 153-154.
Meier, August. Negro Thought in America 1880-1915. Ann
Arbor, Mich.: University of Michigan Press, 1966, pp.
261, 267-268.
"The Negro in Art: A Symposium." Crisis 32 (1926): 71.
Nelson, John Herbert. "Negro Characters in American Lit-
erature." Humanities Studies of the University of Kansas,
vol. 4, Laurence, Kan.: University Publications, 1932,
pp. 130, 134-136.
Parker, John W. "Phylon Profile, XIX: Benjamin Brawley
--Teacher and Scholar." Phylon 10 (First Quarter 1949):
15-23.
_____. "Toward An Appraisal of Benjamin Brawley's Po-
etry." CLA Journal 6 (September 1962): 50-56.
Redding. They Came in Chains, p. 191.
Thorpe, Earl E. Black Historians. New York: Wm. Mor-
row, 1971, pp. 55-60, 207, 212-216, 239.
Turner. In A Minor Chord, xviii, 4.
Watkins. Anthology of American Negro Literature.
Williams, Kenny J. They Also Spoke. Nashville: Town-
send Press, 1970, pp. 18-19, 30, 213, 284.
REVIEWS
Dr. Dillard of the Jeanes Fund: Opportunity 9 (March 1931:

88-89.
Early Negro Writers: Opportunity 13 (September 1935): 282-283.
Negro Genius: Opportunity 15 (September 1937): 280-281.
New Survey of English Literature: The Bookman 63 (March 1926-August 1926): 239; Opportunity 4 (April 1926): 131-132.
Paul Laurence Dunbar, Poet of His People: Opportunity 15 (July 1937): 216-217.

INTERJECTIONS
"The Negro himself as the irony of American Civilization is the supreme challenge to American literature. Like Banquo's ghost, he will not down all faith and hope, all love and longing, all rapture and despair, look out from the eyes of this man who is ever with us and whom we never understand."[6]

[1]Stanley J. Kunitz and Howard Haycraft, eds. Twentieth Century Authors (New York: H. W. Wilson, 1942), pp. 184-185.
[2]Thomas Yenser, ed. Who's Who in Colored America (Brooklyn: T. Yenser, 1938-1939-1940), 5th ed. p. 77.
[3]Kunitz and Haycraft, pp. 184-184.
[4]Yenser, p. 77.
[5]Romeo B. Garrett. Famous First Facts About Negroes (New York: Arno Press, 1972), p. 102.
[6]Kunitz and Haycraft, p. 185.

BRAXTON, Joanne.
POETRY (Periodicals): Black Lines, Fall 1971; Journal of Black Poetry, Summer 1972.

BRAY, Robert L.
POETRY (Periodical): Journal of Black Poetry, 1969.

BRAZIEL, Arthur.
POETRY (Anthology): Murphy, Ebony Rhythm.

BRENNER, Alfred.
DRAMA The Death of Black Jesus.

BREWER, J. Mason. Born 24 March 1896 in Goliad, Texas. Career: See Shockley and Chandler, Living Black American Authors, p. 19; Contemporary Authors, 25/28.
EDITOR
Senior Sentiments and Junior Jottings: A First Book of Verse by the Bellerophon Quill Club of Booker T. Washington High School, Dallas, Texas: n.p., 1935.
Patriotic Moments: A Second Book of Verse by the Bellerphon Quill Club of Booker T. Washington High School. Dallas, Texas: n.p., 1936.
Humorous Folk Tales of the South Carolina Negro. Orangeburg, S.C.: South Carolina Folklore Guild, Claflin College, 1945.
Negro Folktales from Texas. n.p.: Webster, 1942.

Heralding Dawn: An Anthology of Verse, by (!), Selected
  and Edited, with a Historical Summary on The Texas Ne-
  groes' Verse-making by J. Mason Brewer. Dallas, Tex-
  as: June Thomason Printing, 1936.
ESSAYS
  "American Negro Folklore." Phylon (1945); also in Gayle,
    Black Expression.
  "South Carolina Negro Folklore Guide." Journal of Ameri-
    can Folklore 49 (October 1946): 493-494.
  "Afro-American Folklore." Journal of American Folklore
    60 (October 1947): 377-382.
  "Seeker of Negro Folklore." Christian Science Monitor Mag-
    azine Section, 18 November 1950.
FOLK TALES
  "Juneteenth." Tone the Bell Easy. James Frank Dobie, ed.
    Austin, Texas: Texas Folk-lore Society, 1932, pp. 9-54.
  The Word on the Brazos: Negro Preacher Tales from the
    Brazos Bottoms of Texas. Austin: University of Texas,
    1953.
  Aunt Dicey Tales: Snuff-dipping Tales of the Texas Negro.
    Austin, Texas: n.p., 1956.
  Dog Ghosts and Other Texas Negro Folk Tales. Austin,
    Texas: University of Texas, 1958.
  Worser Days and Better Times: The Folklore of the North
    Carolina Negro. Chicago: Quadrangle, 1965.
  (Anthologies): American Negro Folklore; Sterling, Laughing
    on the Outside; Botkin, A Treasury of Southern Folklore;
    Texas Folk and Texas Folklore (Texas Folklore Society);
    A Treasury of American Anecdotes; Withers and Botkins,
    The Illustrated Book of American Folklore; Bontemps,
    The Book of Negro Folklore; Hughes, The Book of Negro
    Humor.
NON-FICTION
  Negro Legislators of Texas, and Their Descendants: A His-
    tory of the Negro in Texas Politics from Reconstruction
    to Disfranchisement. Dallas, Texas: Mathis, 1935.
  An Historical and Pictorial Souvenir of the Negro in Texas
    History in Celebration of the Texas Centennial 1836-1936.
    Dallas, Texas: Mathis, 1935.
POETRY
  The Life of John Wesley Anderson, In Verse. Dallas, Tex-
    as: Printed by C. C. Cockrell & Son, 1938.
  Negrito: Negro Dialect Poems of the Southwest. San Anton-
    io, Texas: Naylor, 1933.
  Echoes of Thought. Fort Worth, Texas: Progressive Print-
    ing Co., 1922.
  Little Dan from Dixieland: A Story in Verse. Bookcraft,
    1940.
  (Periodical): Crisis, May 1941.
GENRES UNKNOWN
  Glimpses of Life. n.p., 1923.
  More Truth than Poetry. n.p.: By the Author, 1947.

BIOGRAPHY ON BREWER
Byrd, James W. J. Mason Brewer: Negro Folklorist.
Austin, Texas: Steck-Vaughn, 1967.
"Negro Folklorist and Professor of English at Livingstone
College." Interracial Review 35 (September 1962): 188-
189.

BREWSTER, Bess E. see CODLING, Bess

BRIDGEFORTH, Med.
NOVEL Another Chance. New York: Exposition, 1951. (Published in 1927 under the title: God's Law and Man's.)

BRIERRE, Jean.
POETRY (Anthology): Murphy, Ebony Rhythm.

BRIGGS, Barbara see KUUMBA

BRIGHT, Hazel.
SHORT STORY (Periodical): Black World, January, October
1973.

BRISTER, Iola M.
POETRY (Anthologies): Murphy, Ebony Rhythm; Murphy, Negro Voices.

BRITT, Nellie.
POETRY My Master and I: Poems that Will Encourage, Inspire and Strengthen. New York: Carlton, 1964.

BROADUS, Robert Deal.
NOVEL Spokes for the Wheel. Muncie: Kingsman Press, 1961.

BROCKET, Joshua Arthur.
NOVEL Zipporah, The Maid of Midian. Zion, Ill.: Zion Printing & Publishing House, 1926.

BROOKS, Edwin.
POETRY (Anthology): Major, The New Black Poetry.

BROOKS, Gwendolyn. Born 7 June 1917 in Topeka, Kansas. Ca-
reer: See Current Biography, 1950, pp. 72-74; Adams, Great
American Negroes, Past and Present, p. 128; Dannett, Pro-
files of Negro Womanhood, pp. 254-259; Drotning and South,
Up from the Ghetto, pp. 170-176; Newquist, Roy, Conversation,
pp. 35-46; Robinson, Donald, 100 Most Important People in the
World Today; Rollins, Famous American Negro Poets.
AUTOBIOGRAPHY
Report from Part One. New ed. Detroit: Broadside, 1972*.
(Excerpt in Black World 21 (September 1972): 4-12; Ebony
(Marcy 1973): 116-120.
BROADSIDES
We Real Cool. Broadside Series #6. Detroit: Broadside,
1966.

The Wall. Broadside Series #19. Detroit: Broadside, 1967.
COLLECTION
The World of Gwendolyn Brooks. New York: Harper & Row,
   1971*. (Includes A Street in Bronzeville, Annie Allen,
   Maud Martha, The Bean Eaters, In the Mecca.)
EDITOR
The Black Position. Detroit: Broadside, 1971.
A Broadside Treasury, 1965-1970. Detroit: Broadside,
   1971*†.
Jump Bad: A New Chicago Anthology. Detroit: Broadside,
   1971*†.
INTRODUCTIONS AND FORWARDS
"Forward." New Negro Poets: USA. ed. Langston Hughes.
"Introduction." The Poetry of Black America: Anthology of
   the 20th Century. ed. Arnold Adoff.
NON-FICTION
(Periodicals and Newspapers): Book Week, The Chicago Sun-
   day Herald Tribune, 18 April 1965; The Chicago American,
   26 February 1958; Chicago Daily News, 14 December 1950;
   11 July 1964; Chicago Sun Times, 12 April 1964; 31 Janu-
   ary 1965; 14 March 1965; Chicago Tribune Magazine, 4
   August 1963; Holiday, October 1951; McCall's Magazine,
   December 1971; Negro Digest, March 1951; Panorama,
   Chicago Daily News, 7 November 1964.
NOVEL
Maud Martha. New York: Harper, 1953. Excerpt in Hill,
   Soon One Morning; Patterson, An Introduction to Black Lit-
   erature in America from 1746 to the Present.
POETRY
A Street in Bronzeville. New York: Harper, 1945.
Annie Allen. New York: Harper, 1949; reprint ed., West-
   port, Conn.: Greenwood, 1972*.
Bronzeville Boys and Girls. New York: Harper, 1956*.
The Bean Eaters. New York: Harper, 1960.
Selected Poems. New York: Harper & Row, 1963*.
With others. Portion of That Field: The Centennial of the
   Burial of Lincoln--Commemorative Sections. Urbana:
   University of Illinois, 1967*.
In the Mecca: Poems. New York: Harper & Row, 1968*.
Riot. Detroit: Broadside, 1970*†.
Family Pictures. Detroit: Broadside, 1970*†.
Aloneness. Detroit: Broadside, 1971†.
The Tiger Who Wore White Gloves, or What You Really Are,
   You Are. Chicago: Third World, forthcoming.
(Anthologies): Abdul, The Magic of Black Poetry; Adams
   and Briscoe, Up Against the Wall, Mother; Adams, Conn
   and Slepian, Black American Literature: Poetry, Adoff,
   Black Out Loud; Adoff, I Am the Darker Brother; Adoff,
   The Poetry of Black America; Austen, Fenderson and
   Nelson, The Black Man and the Promise of America;
   Baker, Black Literature in America; Barksdale and Kin-
   namon, Black Writers in America; Baylor and Stokes, Fine
   Frenzy; Bell, Afro-American Poetry; Bontemps, American

Negro Poetry; Bontemps, Hold Fast to Dreams; Brooks,
A Broadside Treasury; Chambers and Moon, Right On!;
Chapman, Black Voices; Chapman, New Black Voices;
Davis and Redding, Cavalcade; Emanuel and Gross, Dark
Symphony; Faderman and Bradshaw, Speaking for Our-
selves; Ford, Black Insights; Gross, A Nation of Nations;
Hayden, Kaleidoscope; Hayden, Burrow and Lapides, Afro-
American Literature; Henderson, Understanding the New
Black Poetry; Hill, Soon One Morning; Jordan, Soulscript;
Kearns, Black Experience; Kearns, Black Identity; Lomax
and Abdul, 3000 Years of Black Poetry; Long and Collier,
Afro-American Writing; Margolies, A Native Sons Reader;
Miller, Blackamerican Literature; Mirer, Modern Black
Stories; Patterson, Rock Against the Wind; Patterson, An
Introduction to Black Literature in America from 1746 to
the Present; Pool, Beyond the Blues; Randall, The Black
Poets; Randall, Black Poetry, A Supplement; Randall and
Burroughs, For Malcolm; Robinson, Nommo; Rollins,
Christmas Gif'; Simmons, Black Culture; Singh and Fel-
lowes, Black Literature in America; Turner, Black Amer-
ican Literature: Poetry; Walrond and Pool, Black and
Unknown Bards; Watkins and David, To Be a Black Wom-
an; Weisman and Wright, Black Poetry for All Americans;
Williams, Beyond the Angry Black; Williams, Contemporary Poetry in America.

(Periodicals): Black World, November 1971; Chicago Sun
Times, 19 December 1963; Chicago Tribune, 6 December
1953; Common Ground, Spring 1945; Summer 1945; Crisis,
November 1937; March, April 1938; 1939; 1940; Ebony,
September 1963; August 1971; August 1972; Freedomways,
First Quarter 1971; Harper's Magazine, September 1959;
December 1959; Journal of Black Poetry, Fall-Winter
1971; Negro Digest, August 1950; November, June 1951;
June 1967; Opportunity, September 1938; February 1939;
Poetry, November 1944, March 1949; September 1959;
November 1969.

SHORT STORIES

(Anthologies): Hill, New Writings by American Negroes,
1940-1962; Hill, Soon One Morning; Hughes, The Best
Short Stories by Negro Writers; Sanchez, We Be Word
Sorcerers.

(Periodical): Chicago, February 1955.

BIBLIOGRAPHY ON BROOKS

Hoff, Jon N. "Gwendolyn Brooks: A Bibliography." CLA
Journal 17 (September 1973): 21-32.

BIOGRAPHY AND CRITICISM ON BROOKS

Angle, Paul M. We Asked Gwendolyn Brooks. Chicago:
Illinois Bell Telephone Co., n.d.

"Artists, Friends, Admirers Gather in Tribute to Poetess
Gwendolyn Brooks." Jet, 25 February 1971.

Baker, Houston A., Jr. "The Achievement of Gwendolyn
Brooks." CLA Journal 16 (September 1972): 23-31.

Bambara, Toni Cade. "Report from Part One." New York

Times Book Review, 7 January 1973, p. 1.

Barrow, William. "Five Fabulous Females." Negro Digest 12 (July 1963): 78-83.

Bird, Leonard G. "Gwendolyn Brooks: Educator Extraordinaire." Discourse 12: 158-166.

Brooks, Gwendolyn. "I Don't Like to Think of Myself as a Poet." Panorama, Chicago Daily News, 28 September 1963.

_____, and Ida Lewis. "Conversation." Essence (April 1970): 26-31.

Brown, F. L. "Chicago's Great Lady of Poetry." Negro Digest 11 (December 1961): 53-57.

Cherry, Thomas and Willis. Portraits in Color: The Lives of Colorful Negro Women.

Crockett, J. "An Essay on Gwendolyn Brooks." Negro History Bulletin 19 (1955): 37-39.

Cutler, B. "Long Reach, Strong Speech." Poetry 103 (March 1964): 388-389.

Davis, Arthur P. "The Black and Tan Motif in the Poetry of Gwendolyn Brooks." CLA Journal 6 (December 1962): 90-97.

_____. "Gwendolyn Brooks: A Poet of the Unheroic." CLA Journal 7 (December 1963): 114-125.

Emanuel, James A. "A Note on the Future of Negro Poetry." Negro American Literature Forum 1 (Fall 1967): 2-3.

Fuller, Hoyt. "Notes on a Poet." Negro Digest 11 (August 1962): 50.

Furman, Marva Riley. "Gwendolyn Brooks: The 'Unconditioned' Poet." CLA Journal 17 (September 1973): 1-10.

Garland, Phyllis. "Gwendolyn Brooks: Poet Laureate." Ebony 23 (July 1968): 48-50.

Hansell, William H. "Aestheticism Versus Political Militancy in Gwendolyn Brooks' 'The Chicago Picasso' and 'The Wall.'" CLA Journal 17 (September 1973): 11-15.

Harriott, F. "Life of a Pulitzer Poet." Negro Digest 8 (August 1950: 14-16.

Hudson, Clenora F. "Racial Themes in the Poetry of Gwendolyn Brooks." CLA Journal 17 (September 1973): 16-20.

Jaffe, Dan. "Gwendolyn Brooks: An Appreciation from the White Suburbs." In Bigsby, The Black American Writer, vol. 2, pp. 89-98.

Kent. Blackness and the Adventure of Western Culture, pp. 104-138.

_____. "The Poetry of Gwendolyn Brooks, Part I." Black World 2 (September 1971): 30-43.

_____. "The Poetry of Gwendolyn Brooks, Part II." Black World 2 (October 1971): 36-48, 68-71.

_____. "Outstanding Works...," pp. 309-311.

_____. "Review of The World of Gwendolyn Brooks." Black Books Bulletin 1 (Winter 1971): 38-41.

Kunitz, Stanley. "Bronze by Gold." Poetry 76 (April 1950): 52-56.

Lee, Don L. "The Achievement of Gwendolyn Brooks."
Black Scholar 3 (June-Summer 1972): 32-41.

McCluskey, John. "To The Mecca." Studies in Black Literature 4 (Autumn 1973): 25-30.

Malkoff. Crowell's Handbook of Contemporary Poetry, pp.
81-86.

Marr, W. "Black Pulitzer Awardees." Crisis 77 (May
1970): 186-188.

Rivers, Conrad Kent. "Poetry of Gwendolyn Brooks." Negro Digest 3 (June 1964): 67-68.

Stravos, George. "An Interview with Gwendolyn Brooks."
Contemporary Literature 12 (Winter 1970): 1-20.

Untermeyer, Louis, ed. 50 Modern American and British
Poets. McKay, 1973, 300-301.

Whitlow. Black American Literature, pp. 130-133.

BROOKS, Helen Morgan. Born in Reading, Pennsylvania.
POETRY
Against Whatever Sky. Provincetown, Mass.: Advocate,
1955.
From These My Years. n.p., n.d.
(Anthologies): Hughes, New Negro Poets: USA; Hughes and
Bontemps, The Poetry of the Negro: 1746-1970; Patter-
son, Rock Against the Wind.

BROOKS, Janet
POETRY (Anthology): Black Poets Write On!

BROOKS, Jonathan Henderson. Born 1904 in Lexington, Kentucky.
Died 1945. Education: Attended Jackson College; Lincoln Uni-
versity, Missouri, 1925; Tougaloo College. Career: Worked
as a postal clerk; was part-time Pastor of the Second Baptist
Church, Kosciusko, Michigan; taught in Humphrey County.
Awards, Honors: Won 1st Prize in a local contest for his first
short story, "The Bible in the Cornfield."[1]
POETRY
The Resurrection and Other Poems. Dallas: Kaleidograph
Press, 1948. (This his only book, was published post-
humously.)[2]
(Anthologies): Bontemps, American Negro Poetry, p. 95;
Brown, Davis and Lee, The Negro Caravan; Cullen, Car-
oling Dusk, pp. 193-196; Cunard, Negro Anthology, p.
259; Hughes and Bontemps, The Poetry of the Negro:
1746-1970; Johnson, Ebony and Topaz.
(Periodicals): Crisis 36 (1929): 50; 38 (1931): 306; 40
(1933): 106, 200, 238, 281; 41 (1934): 38, 95, 201.
[1]Countee Cullen, ed., Caroling Dusk (New York:
Harper & Row, 1927), p. 192.
[2]Arna Bontemps, American Negro Poetry (New York:
Hill & Wang, 1969), p. 188.

BROOKS, William F. Education: Studied medicine for two years;
S.T.B. from Lincoln University, 1885. Career: Taught at

the Institute for Colored Youth, Philadelphia; Johnson C. Smith
University, Charlotte, N.C. (Formerly Biddle University.)[1]
POETRY
    (Anthology): Cuney, Hughes and Wright, Lincoln University
      Poets.
        [1]Waring Cuney, Langston Hughes, and Bruce Wright.
    Lincoln University Poets (New York: Fine Editions
    Press, 1954), p. 67.

BROWN, Benjamin A.
    UNPUBLISHED NOVEL   Excerpt in Hill, Soon One Morning.

BROWN, Cecil M.
    CRITICISM
      "Bad Writing, or Unclewillieandthebadpoet." Partisan Re-
        view 39 (1972): 406-411.
      "Black Literature and LeRoi Jones." Black World 19 (June
        1970): 24-31.
      "Pimping Blackness." Kenyon Review 31 (1969): 395-400.
      "The White Whale." Partisan Review 36 (1969): 453-459.
    DRAMA
      The African Shades: A Comedy in One Act. In Reed,
        Yardbird Reader, pp. 17-42.
      The Gila Monster.
      Our Sisters Are Pregnant.
    NON-FICTION
      (Periodicals): Evergreen Review, Spring 1973; Negro Digest,
        November 1969.
    NOVEL
      The Life and Loves of Mr. Jiveass Nigger. New York:
        Farrar, Straus Giroud, 1970*; reprint ed., New York:
        Fawcett, 1971†. Excerpts in Chapman, New Black
        Voices; Hicks, Cutting Edges; Reed, 19 Necromancers
        from Now.
    POETRY
      (Periodical): Umbra.
    CRITICISM ON BROWN
      Klotman. "The White Bitch Archetype in Contemporary
        Black Fiction," pp. 96-110.
    REVIEW: The Life and Loves of Mr. Jiveass Nigger.
      Elder, Lonne III. Black World (June 1970): 51-52.

BROWN, Charlotte Hawkins (Mrs. Edward S.). Born 11 June 1882
in Henderson, North Carolina. Died 11 January 1961. Education: Attended Cambridge elementary school; Boston-Alliston
Grammar School; Cambridge English High School; A.B., State
Normal School, Salem, Massachusetts, 1901. Harvard Summer
School, 1901, 1909; Simmons College, 1917. Received Honorary degree, A.M., Livingstone College, 1921; Honorary L.L.D.,
Wilberforce Univesity, 1932.[1] Career: In 1902 became founder and President of the Palmer Memorial Institute, Sedalia,
North Carolina (Negro Junior College). From 1952 to 1955,
became director of finance for the Institute. In 1940, was ap-

pointed to State Council of Defense. Became the first Negro
to be elected to the National Board of YWCA.[2] Was President
of the North Carolina Home for Delinquent Colored Girls; Member of the Federation Council of Churches. Awards, Honors:
Elected to Board of Education State of North Carolina Hall of
Fame; 1926; 1928 elected a member of the 20th Century Club
of Boston--the only Black woman to gain this distinction.[3]
NON-FICTION (Etiquette)
    The Correct Thing to Do, To Say, To Wear. Boston:
        Christopher Publishing House, 1941.
    Hill, Roy L., ed. Rhetoric of Racial Revolt. Denver,
        Colorado: Golden Bell Press, 1964, pp. 84-88.
NOVEL
    Mammy. Boston: Pilgrims Press, 1919.
BIOGRAPHY AND CRITICISM ON BROWN
    Bardolph. The Negro Vanguard, pp. 160, 164, 171, 173,
        312.
    Brawley. Negro Builders and Heroes, pp. 282-284.
    Daniel. Women Builders, pp. 133-163.
    Dannett. Profiles of Negro Womanhood, vol. 1, p. 233.
        _____. Profiles of Negro Womanhood, vol. 2, pp. 59-63.
    Goldstein, Rhoda L., ed. Black Life and Culture in the
        United States. New York: T. Y. Crowell, 1971, p. 186.
    Johnson, Charles Spurgeon. A Preface to Racial Understanding. New York: Friendship Press, 1936, pp. 113-
        121.
    Ovington. The Walls Came Tumbling Down, pp. 72, 229.
        [1]Who's Who in Colored America, pp. 82-83.
        [2]Obituary. New York Times, 12 January 1961, 29:2.
        [3]Who's Who in Colored America, p. 83.

BROWN, Claude. Born 23 February 1937 in New York City. Education: Attended Howard University, 1961-1965. Currently living in New York City. Career: Lecturer and writer, specializing in politics and urban life.
AUTOBIOGRAPHICAL NOVEL
    Manchild in the Promised Land. New York: Macmillan,
        1965*; reprint ed. New York: New American Library†.
        Excerpts in anthologies: Austin, Fenderson and Nelson,
        The Black Man and the Promise of America; Davis and
        Redding, Cavalcade; Demarest and Landin, The Ghetto
        Reader; Faderman and Bradshaw, Speaking for Ourselves;
        Ford, Black Insights; Gross, A Nation of Nations; Simmons et al., Black Culture; Watkins and David, To Be a
        Black Woman.
BIOGRAPHY AND CRITICISM ON BROWN
    Baker, Houston A., Jr. "The Environment as Enemy in a
        Black Autobiography: Manchild in the Promised Land."
        Phylon 32 (Spring 1971): 53-59.
    Brown, Claude. "In Consequence of Manchild." Reed,
        Yardbird Reader, vol. 1.
    Current Biography, 1966, pp. 43-45.

BROWN, Delores A.
POETRY (Anthology): Murphy, Ebony Rhythm.

BROWN, Edna.
POETRY (Periodical): Negro History Bulletin, March 1958.

BROWN, Elaine.
POETRY (Anthologies): Dee, Glow Child; Troupe, Watts Poets.

BROWN, Ellen M.
POETRY (Periodical): Antioch Review, Fall 1967.

BROWN, Fannie Carole.
POETRY (Anthology): Schulberg, From the Ashes.

BROWN, Frank London. Born 1927 or 1928 in Kansas City, Missouri. Died 13 March 1962. Education: B.A., Roosevelt University; M.A. Chicago University;[1] attended Wilberforce University and Chicago Kent College of Law. Career: Machinist, Union Organizer, bartender, government employee, appeared as a jazz singer and musician. Was associate editor of Ebony.[2] Was director of the Union Research Center, University of Chicago and a candidate for a doctorate as a Fellow of the University's Committee on Social Thought.[3] Recipient of the John Hay Whitney Foundation Award for Creative Writing.[4]
CRITICISM BY BROWN
  "Chicago's Great Lady of Poetry (Gwendolyn Brooks)." Negro Digest 11 (December 1961): 53-57.
NOVELS
  The Myth Makers. Chicago: Path Press, 1969.
  Trumbull Park. Chicago: Regnery, 1959. Translated: Marin Dessaner, Frankfurt, Knect, 1961.
POETRY
  (Anthologies): Adams, Conn and Slepian, Afro-American Literature: Fiction; Hughes and Bontemps, The Poetry of the Negro: 1746-1970.
SHORT STORIES
  (Anthologies): Chapman, Black Voices; Clarke, American Negro Short Stories; Hill, Soon One Morning; Hughes, The Best Short Stories by Negro Authors; Margolies, A Native Sons Reader.
  (Periodicals):
  "The Ancient Book." Negro Digest 13 (March 1964): 53-61.
  "A Matter of Time." Negro Digest 11 (March 1962): 58-60.
CRITICISM ABOUT BROWN
  Fleming, Robert E. "Overshadowed by Richard Wright: Three Black Chicago Novelists." Negro American Literature Forum 7 (Fall 1973): 75.
  "Frank London Brown: Courageous Author." Sepia 8 (June 1960): 26-30.
  Gayle. Black Expression, p. 255.
  Hughes. The Negro Novelist, p. 33.

Brown, F. L. (cont.)   106

Pinkney, Alphonso. Black America. New York: Prentice-
Hall, 1969, p. 150.
Stuckey, Sterling. "Frank London Brown." In Chapman,
Black Voices, pp. 669-676.
REVIEW: Trumbull Park
Sepia 8 (June 1960): 26-30.
[1]Obituary. New York Daily Times, 13 March 1962, 32:
2.
[2]Herbert Hill, Soon One Morning: New Writing by
American Negroes, 1940-1962 (New York: Alfred A.
Knopf, 1963), p. 348.
[3]Obituary, 32:2.
[4]Hill, p. 348.

BROWN, Handy Nereus.
The Necromancer; or The Voo-Doo Doctor, Apelika, Ala.:
1904; New York: AMS Press.*

BROWN, Henry "Box." Born 1816, in slavery, Richmond, Virginia. Escaped from slavery enclosed in a box three feet long
and two feet wide,[1] sent express from Richmond, Virginia to
Philadelphia. The story of his romantic escape provided
enough publicity to make him a lecturer on the abolition plat-
form, and inspired some lover of the minstrel song, "Uncle
Ned," to compose a ballad about him.[1]
AUTOBIOGRAPHY
Narrative of the Life of Henry "Box" Brown. Boston: Brown
and Slearns, 1849.
Narrative of the Life of Henry Box Brown, Written by Him-
self. First English Edition, Manchester: Lee and Glynn,
1851.
(Anthology)
Excerpt: Miller, Blackamerican Literature.
BIOGRAPHY AND CRITICISM ON BROWN
Bardolph. Negro Vanguard, pp. 58-59, 68-70.
Fischel, Leslie H. Jr., and Benjamin Quarles. The Black
American. New York: Wm. Morrow, 1970, pp. 152-155.
Hughes, Langston, and Milton Meltzer. A Pictorial History
of the Negro in America. New York: Crown Publ., Inc.,
1963, p. 131.
Loggins, Vernon. The Negro Author in America. Port
Washington, N.Y.: Kennikat Press, 1959, pp. 227, 395,
434.
Still, William. Underground Railroad. Philadelphia: People
Publishing House Co., 1872, pp. 81-85.
Wesley, Charles H. In Freedom's Footsteps. New York:
Publishers Co., Inc., 1968, p. 252.
[1]Vernon Loggins. The Negro Author in America (Port
Washington, N.Y.: Kennikat Press, 1959), p. 227.

BROWN, Herbert G.
POETRY Into the Light. New York: Comet, 1959.

Lennox Brown

BROWN, Isabella Marie. <u>Born</u> 1917 in Natchez, Mississippi.
    <u>POETRY</u> (Anthologies): Hughes, <u>New Negro Poetry: USA;</u>
        Hughes and Bontemps, <u>The Poetry of the Negro: 1746-</u>
        <u>1970.</u>

BROWN, James.
    <u>DRAMA</u> <u>King Shotaway,</u> 1823.

BROWN, James Nelson.
    <u>DRAMA</u> <u>Tomorrow Was Yesterday.</u> New York: Exposition,
        1966.

BROWN, Joe C.
    POETRY
       But Not Like Yesterday. Detroit: Broadside, 1968.
    (Anthology): Murphy, Ebony Rhythm.

BROWN, Juanita.
    POETRY (Anthology): Boyd, Poems by Blacks II.

BROWN, Lennox John. Born 7 February 1934 in Trinidad, West-
    Indies. Education: B.A. (Honours), University of Western On-
    tario, Canada, 1961; M.A., University of Toronto, 1969. Per-
    manent address: Toronto, Canada. Currently living in Hart-
    ford, Connecticut. Career: Government of Trinidad and To-
    bago: Civil servant, 1952-1956; Freelance Journalist, Trini-
    dad Guardian, Evening News, 1952-1956; Freelance Journalist
    for Canadian newspapers and magazines, 1956-1960; Reporter,
    freelance writer for The Globe and Mail, The Toronto Star,
    The Telegram, Financial Post, 1961-1963; Canadian Broadcast-
    ing Corporation (CBC) editor; producer, National Network Radio
    News (assignments in Toronto, Montreal, Ottawa, New York,
    Harlem, Chicago, the United Nations) 1963-1967. His plays
    have been produced as follows: 17 radio productions in Canada,
    U.S., Holland, on television production in Canada, ten play
    publications in Canadian and American magazines. Presently
    visiting playwright-in-residence, University of Hartford. Mem-
    ber: Ebo Society for Black Art; Black Arts of Canada; Nation-
    al Black Coalition of Canada; Canadian Newspaper and Wireless
    Guild; Canadian Association of Radio and Television Actors' and
    Writers' Association. Awards, Honors: Minnesota Mining and
    Manufacturing Undergraduate Fellowship, 1958; Canada Council
    Travel Grant to attend performance of prize-winning play, 1966;
    Canada Council Promising Artist Grant (3 months), 1968; Gov-
    ernment of Ontario Graduate Fellowship (1 year), 1969; Canada
    Council Short Term Promising Artist (3 months), 1969; Winner
    of Canada Council Arts Bursary Contest (1 year plus travel),
    1970; Canada Council Short Term Artist Grant (3 months),1971.
    Prizes for plays: Canadian National One-Act Playwriting Com-
    petition, Yousuf Award, Birk's Medal for The Captive, 1965,
    Night Sun, 1967, Jour Ouvert, 1968, and the Dorothy White
    Award for The Meeting, 1966. (Brown was the first playwright
    in history to win four prizes in four consecutive years.) First
    prize, Canadian National University Drama League Competition
    for I Have to Call My Father, 1969; Runner-up, Shubert Fel-
    lowship, University of Michigan Theatre School for The Voyage
    Tonight, 1970; Runner-up, Norma Epstein National Creative
    Writing Award, University of Toronto, 1969, for The Night
    Class; Eugene O'Neill Memorial Playwriting National Competi-
    tion for Prodigal in Black Stone, 1971.
    CRITICISM
       (Periodicals): Black Orpheus; Ebo Voices; Black Images.
    DRAMA
       A Ballet Behind the Bridge.
       The Captive. In Ottawa Little Theatre. Ranking Play Se-

ries 2, Catalogue No. 43. (Ottawa, Canada), September
1965.

Devil Mas'. In <u>Kuntu Drama</u>. Paul Carter Harrison, ed.
New York: Grove, forthcoming.

<u>Fire for an Ice Age</u>.

<u>Fog Drifts in the Spring</u>.

<u>I Have to Call My Father</u>. In <u>Drama and Theatre</u> 8 (Winter
1969-70).

<u>The Klinti Train</u>. In <u>Black American Drama</u>. New York:
Simon & Schuster, forthcoming.

<u>The Meeting</u> and <u>Jour Ouvert</u> ("Day Break"). In <u>Ottawa Lit-
tle Theatre</u>. Ranking Play Series 2, Catalogue No. 56.
(Ottawa, Canada), October 1966.

<u>The Night Class</u>.

<u>Night Sun</u>.

<u>Prodigal in Black Stone</u>.

<u>Saturday's Druid</u>.

<u>Snow Dark Sunday</u>.

<u>Song of the Spear</u>.

<u>This Scent of Incense</u>.

<u>The Throne in an Autumn Room</u>.

<u>The Trinity of Four</u>. In <u>Caribbean Rhythms</u>. New York:
Simon & Schuster, forthcoming.

<u>The Voyage Tonight</u>.

<u>Wine in Winter</u>.

POETRY

(Periodicals): <u>Alphabet</u> (London), June 1964; <u>Canadian Forum</u>,
February 1964; <u>Canadian Poetry Magazine</u>, August 1963,
November 1963, February 1967; <u>CBC Anthology</u>, February
1970; <u>Ebo Voice</u>, February 1964.

INTERJECTIONS

"I believe that every member of every race carries the collective racial history of that race in his or her subconscious
mind. However, it is given to a few to excavate that subconscious history. These few are called writers or artists. They
re-create the experience of their race's history. They tell
their people who they are, where they have come from, where
they are at the present, and where they are going in the future.
As a Black writer I believe I am doing this for the Black race.
Because of the violent disruptions, physical, spiritual and psy-
chological, caused by slavery, colonialism and segregation in
both the Old and the New Worlds, I believe that there are several gaps in the inner continuum of the Black History of Mythological Consciousness in all Black peoples born outside of Africa.
I believe it is my destiny, my divinely-appointed role and duty
in life to help to fill those gaps. As a result, I am writing two
cycles of plays, twenty of which have already been completed.
One cycle ("Behind the Bridge") deals with Black Mythological
Consciousness in the Caribbean, the other ("West Indian Winter"), with the Consciousness in North America and Europe."

BROWN, Linda (Linda Brown Bragg). <u>Born</u> 14 March 1939 in Akron, Ohio.

POETRY (Anthology): Pool, Beyond the Blues.

BROWN, Lloyd Louis. Born 1913.
CRITICISM
"Which Way for the Negro Writer?" Masses & Mainstream
4 (March 1951): 53-63; 4 (April 1951): 50-59.
NON-FICTION
(Periodical): Freedomways, Spring 1964.
NOVEL
Iron City. New York: Masses & Mainstream, 1951.
Die Eiserne Stadt; Roman. Berlin Dietz, 1954 (Translation
of Iron City).
SHORT STORIES
(Periodicals): Masses and Mainstream, April 1948; Decem-
ber 1953.
REVIEW: Iron City.
Butcher, Margaret Just. Phylon 12 (1951).

BROWN, Lloyd W.
CRITICISM
"Black Entities: Names as Symbols in Afro-American Lit-
erature." Studies in Black Literature 1 (Spring 1970):
16-44.
"The Calypso Tradition in West Indian Literature." Black
Academy Review 2 (Spring-Summer 1971): 127-143.
"Comic-Strip Heroes: Leroi Jones and the Myth of Ameri-
can Innocence." Journal of Popular Culture 3 (Fall
1969): 191-204.
"Dreamers and Slaves: The Ethos of Revolution in Walcott
and LeRoi Jones." Caribbean Quarterly 17 (September-
December): 36-44.
"The Expatriot Consciousness in Black American Literature."
Studies in Black Literature 3 (Summer 1972): 9-11.
"Ralph Ellison's Exhorters: The Role of Rhetoric in Invis-
ible Man.: CLA Journal 13 (1970): 289-303.
"Richard Wright: Stereotypes in Black and White." Black
Academy Review 1 (Fall 1970): 35-44.
"The West Indian as an Ethnic Stereotype in Black American
Literature." Negro American Literature Forum 5 (Spring
1971): 8-14.
EDITOR
The Black Writer in Africa and the Americas. Los Ange-
les: Hennessey and Ingall, 1973*†.

BROWN, Martha.
SHORT STORY (Anthology): Ford and Faggett, Best Short Stories by Afro-American Writers.

BROWN, Mattye Jeanette.
NOVEL The Reign of Terror. New York: Vantage, 1962.

BROWN, Oscar, Jr.
DRAMA

"Kicks and Co." 1961. In Hewes, Best Plays of 1961-1962.
Slave Song.
BIOGRAPHY AND CRITICISM ON BROWN
 "Many Faces of Oscar Brown, Jr." Sepia 11 (September
   1962): 72-74.
 Mitchell. Black Drama, pp. 190-192.
 "Oscar Brown, Jr.: The Flop that Flipped." Sepia 12 (May
   1963): 18-22.

BROWN, Robert H.
 POETRY Wine of Youth. New York: Exposition, 1949.

BROWN, Ruby Berkeley.
 POETRY
  (Anthology): Weisman and Wright, Black Poetry for All
   Americans.

BROWN, Samn.
 SHORT STORY
  (Periodical): Black World, August 1971.

BROWN, Samuel E.
 POETRY Love Letters in Rhyme. New York: By the Author,
   1930.

BROWN, Sarah Lee see FLEMING, Sarah L. B.

BROWN, Sterling A. Born 1 May 1901 in Washington, D.C. Ca-
  reer: See Ploski, Reference Library of Black America.
 CRITICISM BY BROWN
  "The American Race Problem as Reflected in American Lit-
   erature." Journal of Negro Education 8 (July 1939): 275-
   290; reprinted in Baker, Black Literature in America,
   pp. 221-238.
  "Arna Bontemps: Co-Worker, Comrade." Black World 12
   (September 1973): 11, 91-97.
  "The Blues." Phylon 13 (Fourth Quarter 1952): 286-292.
  "The Blues as Folk Poetry." Botkin, Folk-say.
  "A Century of Negro Portraiture in American Literature."
   Massachusetts Review 7 (Winter 1966): 73-96; reprinted in
   Chametzky and Kaplan, Black and White in American Cul-
   ture; Chapman, Black Voices; Hayden, Burrows and La-
   pides, Afro-American Literature; Ford, Black Insights.
  "Contemporary Negro Poetry, 1914-1936." In Watkins, An-
   thology of American Negro Literature, pp. 243-261.
  "The Federal Theatre." (Myrdal-Carnegie Study, 1940);
   reprinted in Patterson, Anthology of the American Negro
   in Theatre.
  With Alain Locke. "Folk Values in New Medium." Botkin,
   Folk-say.
  "Literary Scene--Chronicle and Comment." Opportunity,
   1930-1938.
  "The Negro Author and His Publisher." The Quarterly Re-

view of Higher Education Among Negroes 9 (July 1941): 140 -146.

"Negro Character as Seen by White Authors." Journal of Negro Education 2 (January 1933): 180-201; reprinted in Emanuel and Gross, Dark Symphony.

"Negro Folk Expression." Phylon 11 (Fourth Quarter): 318-327; reprinted in Gayle, Black Expression.

"Negro Folk Expression: Spirituals, Seculars, Ballads and Songs." Phylon 14 (First Quarter 1953): 50-60.

The Negro in American Fiction. Washington, D.C.: The Associates in Negro Folk Education, 1937; reprint ed., New York: Arno Press, 1969*.

The Negro on the Stage, 1937. (Available on microfilm from several university libraries, including California at Berkeley, Chicago, Fisk, Harvard, North Carolina at Chapel Hill.)

Negro Poetry and Drama and the Negro in American Fiction, 1937; reprint ed. Studies in American Negro Life Series. New York: Atheneum, 1969†.

"The New Negro in Literature (1925-1955)." The New Negro Years Afterwards. Edited by Rayford W. Logan et al. Washington, D.C.: Howard University Press, 1955, pp. 57-72; reprinted in Davis and Redding, Cavalcade, pp. 410-427.

Outline for the Study of the Poetry of American Negroes. New York: Harcourt, Brace, 1931. (To be used with James Weldon Johnson's The Book of American Negro Poetry.)

EDITOR

With George E. Haynes. The Negro Newcomers in Detroit Board with the Negro in Washington, 1918; reprint ed., New York: Arno, 1970*.

With Arthur P. Davis and Ulysses Lee. The Negro Caravan: Writings by American Negroes. New York: Dryden, 1941; reprint ed., New York: Arno, 1969†.

American Stuff: An Anthology of Prose and Verse by Members of the Federal Writers' Project. New York: Viking, 1937.

With others. The Reader's Companion to World Literature. New York: Dryden, 1956; rev. ed. New York: New American Library, 1973†.

NON-FICTION

(Anthologies), Gleason, Jam Session: An Anthology of Jazz; Moon, Primer for White Folks; Watkins, Black Review; Francis James Brown, Contribution of the American Negro.

(Periodicals): Black World, February 1974; Crisis, January 1972; Opportunity, December 1938; Phylon, First Quarter 1945.

POETRY

Southern Road. New York: Harcourt, Brace, 1932.

The Last Ride of Wild Bill and Other Narrative Poems. Detroit: Broadside, 1974.

(Anthologies): Adams, Conn and Slepian, Afro-American
Literature: Poetry; Adoff, The Poetry of Black America;
Austin, Fenderson and Nelson, The Black Man and the
Promise of America; Baker, Black Literature in America;
Barksdale and Kinnamon, Black Writers of America; Bell,
Afro-American Poetry; Bontemps, American Negro Poetry;
Bontemps, Golden Slippers; Bontemps, Hold Fast to
Dreams; Botkins, Folk-say; Brown, American Stuff; Brown,
Davis and Lee, Negro Caravan; Calverton, Anthology of
American Negro Literature; Chambers and Moon, Right
On!; Chapman, Black Voices; Cullen, Caroling Dusk;
Cunard, Negro Anthology; Davis and Redding, Caval-
cade; Eleazer, Singers in the Dawn; Hayden, Kaleidoscope;
Henderson, Understanding the New Black Poetry; Hughes
and Bontemps, The Poetry of the Negro: 1746-1970;
Johnson, Ebony and Topaz; Jordan, Soulscript; Lomax and
Abdul, 3000 Years of Black Poetry; Long and Collier,
Afro-American Writing; Miller, Blackamerican Literature;
Patterson, An Introduction to Black Literature from 1746
to the Present; Pool, Beyond the Blues; Randall, The
Black Poets; Simmon, et al., Black Culture; Turner,
Black American Literature: Poetry; Walrond and Pool,
Black and Unknown Bards.
(Periodicals): Crisis, 1927; 1932; 1933; 1939; November
1970; Freedomways, Summer 1953; New Challenge, Fall
1937; Opportunity, July 1927; August 1928; May 1929;
September 1930; January 1932; United Asia, June 1953.

SHORT STORIES
(Anthologies): Clarke, American Negro Short Stories; James,
From These Roots.
(Periodical): Phylon, 1946.

VIGNETTES
(Periodical): Phylon, Third Quarter, Fourth Quarter 1945.

BIOGRAPHY AND CRITICISM ON BROWN
Brawley. Negro Genius, pp. 253-257.
Cullen. Caroling Dusk, pp. 129-130.
Henderson, Stephen A. "A Strong Man Called Sterling
Brown." Black World 19 (September 1970): 5-12.
Huggins. Harlem Renaissance, pp. 221, 222, 225-227.
Jahn. Neo-African Literature, pp. 187-189, 201.
Kerlin. Negro Poets and Their Poems, p. 344.
Mitchell. Black Drama, pp. 16, 26, 31, 95.
Redding. To Make a Poet Black.
Wagner. Black Poets of the United States, pp. 83-421 pas-
sim; 475-503.

BROWN, Tyki.
SHORT STORY (Anthology): Sanchez, We Be Word Sorcerers;
also published in Sanchez, 360° of Blackness Coming at
You.

BROWN, Virginia Suggs. <u>Born</u> 14 July 1924 in St. Louis, Missouri.
   CHILDREN AND YOUNG ADULTS
      With others. <u>Out Jumped Abraham</u>. New York: McGraw-Hill, 1967*.
      <u>Who Cares</u>. New York: McGraw-Hill, 1967*.
   BIOGRAPHY ON BROWN
      Shockley and Chandler. <u>Living Black American Authors</u>, p. 22.

BROWN, Wesley. <u>Born</u> 23 May 1945 in New York. <u>Education</u>: B. A. in Political Science and History, Oswego State University, 1968. <u>Currently living in</u> New York City. <u>Career</u>: Presently working on a novel. <u>Member</u>: John O. Killens Writer's Workshop.
   POETRY
      (Anthologies): Sanchez, <u>360° of Blackness Coming at You</u>; Turco, <u>Poetry</u>.
      (Periodical): <u>Black Creation</u>, Winter 1972.
   SHORT STORY
      (Anthology): Sanchez, <u>We Be Word Sorcerers</u>.

BROWN, William B.
   POETRY
      (Anthology): Murphy, <u>Negro Voices</u>.

BROWN, William Wells. <u>Born</u> March 1815 in Lexington, Kentucky. <u>Died</u> 6 November 1884. <u>Education</u>: Self-educated; apprenticed to Elijah Lovejoy, editor of the <u>St. Louis Times</u>; also studied medicine when abroad.[1] <u>Career</u>: worked on a riverboat in service on the Mississippi; worked as a steward on Lake Erie Ships;[2] served in the Underground Railroad; lectured to the Western New York and the Massachusetts Anti-Slavery Society; was active in the temperance movement; worked for the extension of suffrage to women and for prison reform.[3] He also attended the Peace Conference in England and Paris. After the Civil War, he practiced medicine.[4] He took his name from the Quaker Wells Brown who first befriended him after his escape from slavery.[5] He was the first Black American to publish a novel, a drama, and a travel book,[6] and to earn a living with his writing.[7]
   AUTOBIOGRAPHY
      <u>The Narrative of William W. Brown</u>. Boston: Anti-Slavery Office, 1847.
      <u>Narrative of William W. Brown, A Fugitive Slave</u>, 1847.
         Reading, Mass.: Addison-Wesley, 1969; New York: Johnson Reprint, 1970*.
   COMPILER
      <u>The Anti-Slavery Harp</u>. 2nd ed. Boston: B. Marsh, 1848.
   DRAMA
      <u>Escape or, A Leap for Freedom: A Drama in Five Acts</u>. Boston: R. F. Wallcut, 1858. (Play was written in 1856; first recorded public reading was Salem, Ohio, on 4 Feb-

ruary 1847.)[8]

(Unpublished Plays)

Experience: Escape: Life at the South.

A Southside View of Slavery (read publicly for the first time, 9 April 1856; was eventually titled: Experience, or How to Give a Northern Man a Backbone. Although never published, records indicate that Brown presented it frequently at dramatic readings).[9]

NON-FICTION

The American Fugitive in Europe: Sketches of Places and People Abroad. Boston: J. P. Jewett, 1855; reprint ed., Westport, Conn.: Negro Universities Press*.

The Anti-Southern Lectures. London: 1862.

The Black Man: His Antecedents, His Genius, and His Achievements. New York: Hamilton, 1863; reprint ed., New York: Arno, 1969*; facsimile of 1855 ed., Freeport, N.Y.: Books for Libraries*.

A Lecture Delivered Before the Female Anti-Slavery Society of Salem at Lyceum Hall, 14 November 1847. Reported by Henry M. Parkhurst, Boston: Anti-Slavery Society, 1847.

Levengeschiedenis van den Amerikaanschen slaaf, W. Wells Brown, Amerikaansch Afgevaardigde by het vredescongres te Parys, 1849, door hem zelven heschreven. Naar den 5, Engelschen druk vertoald door M. Keijzer. Z wolle, W.E.J. Tjeenk Wilnik, 1850. (A Narrative of the author's experiences as a slave in St. Louis, Mo., and elsewhere.)

My Southern Home, or The South and Its People. Boston: A. G. Brown and Co., 1880; Boston, Mass.: Gregg*.

The Negro in the American Rebellion: His Heroism and His Fidelity. Boston: Lee & Shepard, 1867; Miami, Fla.: Mnemosyne†.

The Rising Son, or The Antecedents and Advancements of the Colored Race. Boston: A. G. Brown & Co., 1874; Westport, Conn.: Negro Universities Press*.

St. Domingo: Its Revolutions and Its Patriots. (A lecture.) Boston: B. Marsh, 1855.

Sketches of Places and People Abroad, 1854; facsimile ed., Freeport, N.Y.: Books for Libraries*.

Three Years in Europe or Places I Have Seen and People I Have Met. London: C. Gilpin, 1852.

"A Visit of a Fugitive Slave to the Grave of Wilberforce." Autographs for Freedom. Edited by Julia Griffiths. Auburn: Alden, Beardsley, pp. 70-76.

(Anthologies): Davis and Redding, Cavalcade; Sterling, Speak Out in Thunder Tones.

NOVEL

(4 printings)

Clotel: or the President's Daughter. London: Partridge, Oakey, 1853; New York: Arno, 1969*†.

Clotelle: A Tale of the Southern States. Boston: J. Redpath, 1864.

Clotelle: or the Colored Heroine. Boston: Lee & Shepard,
  1867; facsimile ed., Freeport, N.Y.: Books for Libraries*.
Clotelle: A Tale of the Southern States. Philadelphia: A.
  Saifer, 1955; Miami, Fla.: Mnemosyne†. ("At the begin-
  ning of the war in 1861, Clotelle was issued in a Camp-
  fire edition for the soldiers.")
Miralda or, The Beautiful Quadroon. Ran as a serial in
  Anglo-African, 1860-1861. [10]
(Anthologies-Excerpts): Barksdale and Kinnamon, Black
  Writers of America; Brown, Davis and Lee, Negro Cara-
  van; Davis and Redding, Cavalcade; Miller, Blackameri-
  can Literature; Takaki, Violence in the Black Imagination.
BIOGRAPHY AND CRITICISM ON BROWN
  Abramson. Negro Playwrights in the American Theatre, pp.
    8-14, 18-19.
  Adams. Great Negroes Past and Present, pp. 34, 52, 107,
    135, 142, 147.
  Bardolph. The Negro Vanguard, pp. 58-70.
  Biography of an American Bondsman, by His Daughter. Bos-
    ton: Walcutt, 1855.
  Bontemps. 100 Years of Negro Freedom, p. 1.
  Bond. The Negro and The Drama, pp. 25-27, 205.
  Bone. The Negro Novel in America, pp. 26, 30, 212.
  Brawley. Early Negro American Writers, pp. 168-174.
  _____. Negro Builders and Heroes, p. 234.
  _____. The Negro in Literature and Art, pp. 39-40.
  Brown, Josephine. Biography of an American Bondsman.
    Boston: Walcutt 1855.
  Butcher. The Negro in American Culture.
  Cash, W. J. The Mind of the South. Garden City, N.Y.:
    Doubleday.
  Coleman, Edward M. "William Wells Brown as an Histori-
    an." Journal of Negro History 31 (1946): 47-49.
  Cromwell, Turner and Dykes. Readings from Negro Au-
    thors, pp. 181-186.
  Davis. The American Negro Reference Book, 1966, pp. 35,
    867-870.
  Emanuel and Gross. Dark Symphony, pp. 4, 6, 7, 365-366.
  Eppse, Merl R. The Negro, Too, in American History.
    Chicago: National Educational Publishing Co., 1939, p.
    174.
  Farrison, W. Edward. William Wells Brown, Author and
    Reformer. Chicago: University of Chicago Press, 1969.
  _____. "Brown's First Drama." CLA Journal 2 (1958):
    104-110.
  _____. "A Flight Across Ohio: The Escape of William
    Wells Brown from Slavery." Ohio State Archeological
    and Historical Quarterly 61 (1952): 272-282.
  _____. "One Ephemerer After Another." CLA Journal
    13 (December 1969): 192-197.
  _____. "The Origin of Brown's Clotel." Phylon 15 (1954):
    347-354.

_____. "Phylon Profile, XVI: William Wells Brown." Phylon 9 (1948): 13-24.

_____. "A Theologian's Missouri Compromise." Journal of Negro History 48 (1963): 33-43.

_____. "William Wells Brown, America's First Negro Man of Letters." Phylon 9 (1948): 13-23.

_____. "William Wells Brown, Social Reformer." Journal of Negro Education 18 (1949): 29-39.

Fischel and Quarles. The Black American, pp. 119, 170, 227, 229.

Gloster. Negro Voices in American Fiction.

Heermance, Joel. William Wells Brown and Clotelle, A Portrait of the Artist in the First Negro Novel. Hamden, Conn.: Archon, 1969.

Hopkins, Pauline. "William Wells Brown." Colored American Magazine 2 (1901): 232-36.

Hughes. The Negro Novelist, p. 33.

Jahn. Neo-African Literature, pp. 127, 130-131, 136, 138, 140.

Katz. Five Slave Narratives, pp. 1-110.

Loggins. The Negro Author in America, pp. 132-134, 156-173, 176-455 passim.

Margolies, Edward. "Ante-Bellum Slave Narratives: Their Place in American Literature." Studies in Black Literature 4 (Autumn 1973): 1-8.

Meier. Negro Thought in America 1880-1915, pp. 52, 57-58, 78.

Mitchell. Black Drama, p. 34.

Morais, Herbert M. The History of the Negro in Medicine. New York: Publishers Co., Inc., 1969, pp. 23-26, 34.

Murray, Daniel. "Bibliographia Africania." Voice of the Negro 6 (May 1904): 188.

Nelson, John Herbert. "Negro Characters in American Literature." Humanistic Studies of the University of Kansas, IV, Laurence, Ka.: University Publishers, 1932, pp. 64, 133, 583-585.

Pawley, Thomas D. "The First Black Playwrights." Black World (April 1972): 16-24.

Phillips, Porter Williams. W. W. Brown, Host. New York: Fleming H. Revel Co., 1941.

Redding. They Came in Chains, pp. 69, 82, 102, 108, 141, 145, 208.

_____. To Make a Poet Black.

Thorpe, Earl E. Black Historians. New York: Morrow, 1971, pp. 25, 36, 38-43, 67, 132.

Tischler. Black Masks, p. 150.

Trent, Toni. "Stratification Among Blacks by Black Authors." Negro History Bulletin 34 (December 1971): 179-181.

Turner. In a Minor Chord, pp. xv, 116.

Woodson, Carter G. The Mind of the Negro as Reflected in Letters Written During the Crisis, 1800-1860. New York: Negro Universities Press, 1926, pp. 213-216, 349-383.

Yellin, Jean. The Intricate Knot. New York: N.Y. University Press, 1972, p. 1.

[1]Allen Johnson, ed., Dictionary of American Biography, vol. 3 (New York: Charles Scribners' Sons, 1929), p. 161.

[2]Harry A. Ploski and Ernest Kaiser, The Negro Almanac (New York: Bellwether Co., 2nd. ed., 1971), p. 668.

[3]Wilhelmena S. Robinson, Historical Negro Biographies. (New York Publishers Co., Inc., 1969), p. 56.

[4]Dorothy Sterling, Speak Out in Thunder Tones (New York: Doubleday, 1973), p. 472.

[5]John P. Davis, American Negro Reference Book (Englewood Cliffs, N.J.: Prentice-Hall, 1966), p. 868.

[6]Ploski, p. 668.

[7]Davis, p. 870.

[8]Thomas D. Pawley, "The First Black Playwrights," Black World (April 1972): 22.

[9]Ibid.

[10]Daniel Murray, "Bibliographia Africania," Voice of the Negro 6 (May 1904): 188.

BROWNE, Benjamin A.
SHORT STORY (Periodical): Harlem Quarterly, Winter 1949-50.

BROWNE, George B.
POETRY (Anthology): Murphy, Ebony Rhythm.

BROWNE, Patricia Wilkins. Born 6 June 1950 in New York City. Education: B.A., Marymount Manhattan College, 1973; studied with the Negro Ensemble Company and at Theatre Black in New York City. Currently living in Brooklyn. Career: Was a member of Theatre Black from 1968 to 1971. Performed poetry shows with dance and music at churches, schools, and theatres in New York City and in New Jersey. Directed Richard Wesley's Gettin' It Together (A Steady Rap) at BED*STUY Theatre, 1971. Has also performed with numerous workshops as well as serving as technical assistant for productions at Negro Ensemble Company. Directed her own original play, In Search of Unity, at Marymount Manhattan College, 1973. Edits a literary magazine for Third World Coalition, M.M.C. Currently teaching second grade at Public School in Bronx--District 9. Awards, Honors: award for outstanding contribution to the college community, Marymount College, 1973.
DRAMA
In Search of Unity, 1972.

BROWNE, Roscoe Lee.
POETRY (Anthology): Pool, Beyond the Blues.

BROWNE, Theodore.
DRAMA
A Black Woman Called Moses.

Go Down Moses.
Gravy Train, 1940.
Minstrel.
Natural Man. A scene from the play is published in Chil-
    dress, Black Scenes.
NOVEL
    The Band Will Not Play Dixie: A Novel of Suspense. New
        York: Exposition, 1955.
BIOGRAPHY AND CRITICISM ON BROWNE
    Abramson. Negro Playwrights in the American Theatre, pp.
        102-109, 159-160.
    Atkinson, Brooks. New York Times, 8 May 1941.
    Brown, John Mason. New York Post, 8 May 1941.
    Mitchell, Black Drama, pp. 221, 223.
    Warner, Ralph. Daily Worker, 12 May 1941.

BROWNE, William. Born 29 August 1930 in New York City.
    POETRY
        (Anthologies): Bontemps, American Negro Poetry; Pool,
            Beyond the Blues.
        (Periodicals): Présence Africaine No. 57; Phylon, Fourth
            Quarter 1955.

BROWNLEE, Julius Pinkney. Born 1886.
    POETRY Ripples. Anderson, S.C.: Cox Stationery Co., 1914.

BRUCE, John Edward (Pen name "Grit"). Born 22 February 1856.
    Died 7 August 1924. Education: Never progressed beyond the
    grades.[1] Career: Employed as a news writer in the Washing-
    ton Office of the New York Times, 1870.[2] He was the founder
    of the Negro Historical Society of New York.[3] To many, he
    was known as the "Duke of Uganda."[4]
    BIOGRAPHY
        Prince Hall, The Pioneer of Negro Masonry. New York:
            1921.
        Short Biographical Sketches of Eminent Negro Men and Wom-
            en. Yonkers, N.Y.: Gazette Press, 1910.
    NON-FICTION (Addresses, later published)
        The Blot on the Escutcheon given before the Afro-American
            League, Number 1. Second Baptist Church, Washington,
            D.C., 4 April 1890. Published by R. L. Pendleton Print-
            er, 1890.
        Concentration of Energy; Bruce Grit Uses Plain Language in
            Emphasizing the Power of Organization. New York: Edgar
            Printing and Stationery Co., 1899.
        A Defense of Colored Soldiers. Yonkers, N.Y.: n.p., 1906.
        The Making of a Race. New York: n.p., 1922.
        The Mission and the Opportunity of the Negro Mason. (Notes
            on Solomon's Temple address given by J.E.B. Grit before
            the Craftsmen Club, 6 March 1910), New York, 1906.
        The Significance of Brotherhood. New York: Clarion Pub-
            lishers Association, 1919.
        A Tribute for the Negro Soldier. Washington, D.C.: Gov-

ernment Printing Office, 1918.

"Was Othello a Negro?" Articles and Addresses by Negroes. Washington Colored Society, n.p., 1877 (type-
script).

(Periodicals)

"Dusky Kings of Africa." Voice of the Negro 2 (September
1905): 573-575.

"A History of Negro Musicians." The Southern Workman
65 (October 1916): 569-573.

"The Song of Solomon." Voice of the Negro 2 (June 1905):
418-419.

"The Stronger Nations vs. The Weaker Nations." Voice of
the Negro 2 (April 1905): 256-257.

"William Ewart Gladstone." 3 (May 1906): 364-365.

"What Negro Supremacy Means." (a Reply to Senator Wade
Hampton's Article.) Forum, June 1888.

NOVEL

The Awakening of Hezekiah Jones. Hopkinsville, Ky.:
Philip H. Brown, 1916.

POETRY

A Love Song. (Words by J. E. Bruce set to music by H. T.
Burleigh, N.Y. 1919.)

BIOGRAPHY AND CRITICISM ON BRUCE

Bardolph. The Negro Vanguard, pp. 192-193, 294.

Davis. American Negro Reference Book, pp. 676, 752.

Gilbert, Peter, ed. Selected Writings of John Edward
Bruce. New York: Arno, 1971.

Hughes. The Negro Novelist, p. 36.

Meier. Negro Thought in America 1880-1915, pp. 130, 262-
263, 267.

[1]Richard Baldolph, The Negro Vanguard (New York:
Vintage Books, 1959), p. 193.

[2]Obituary, New York Times, 11 August 1924, 13:5.

[3]Earl E. Thorpe, Black Historians (New York: Morrow, 1971), p. 149.

[4]Obituary, p. 13:5.

BRUNO, Joann. Born June 2 in Opelousas, Louisiana. Education:
studied cinema and the performing arts, University of Southern
California-Los Angeles; drama, Little Theater; Watts Writer's
Workshop. Currently living in Los Angeles. Career: Actress
and writer. Her children's story, "My Dog Toe-Toe-Scarey
Scarecrow" was used on Sesame Street T.V. Member: Equity;
Writers Guild, West.

DRAMA

Sister Selena, 1970.

Uncle Bud's No Stranger.

INTERJECTIONS

"Since childhood I was fed a steady stream of Folk Tales by
my father, uncle and aunt. In grade school I was constantly
wondering why I never read about Black Folks. High School
showed me you had to be 'A Big Some Body' as my father used
to say, before people could read about you. So I write with a

smile--doing what I have to do--writing about the little some-
bodies."

BRUNSON, Doris.
DRAMA
    With Roger Furman. Three Shades of Harlem.
BIOGRAPHY AND CRITICISM ON BRUNSON
    Mitchell. Black Drama, p. 208.

BRYAN, Robert.
    POETRY Blacker Tomorrows. New York: Amuru, 1973†.

BRYANT, Franklin Henry.
    POETRY Black Smiles: or, The Sunny Side of Sable Life.
        Nashville, Tenn.: Southern Missionary Society, 1909.

BRYANT, Frederick James, Jr. Born 6 July 1942 in Philadelphia.
    Education: A.B., Lincoln University; presently in the graduate
    program at Temple University (Political Science). Currently
    living in Philadelphia. Career: Casework Supervisor, Penn-
    sylvania Department of Public Welfare; free lance photographer.
    Has given many lectures and poetry readings. Awards, Honors:
    Eichelburger Prize for Prose Writing, Lincoln University; Poet
    Laureate at Lincoln University.
    DRAMA
        Lord of the Mummy Wrappings, 1967.
    POETRY
        While Silence Sleeps.
        (Anthologies): Black Poets Write On!; Brown, Lee and
            Ward, To Gwen with Love; Chapman, New Black Voices;
            Jones and Neal, Black Fire; Major, The New Black Po-
            etry; Rosenberg, Extension.
        (Periodical): Nickel Review.
    UNPUBLISHED WORK
        "Songs from Ragged Streets," 1972.
        "And Who Hears the Sun Rise?"
    INTERJECTIONS
        "I've tried to be singular
        to fit in. Change my style
        each year three months early
        I've tried to keep from bending
        and twisting and stretching,
        being nimble with the wind. I
        wanted to be dependable like others
        But I can't. I'm stuck for
        whatever length of being a poet
        and if not, wanting to be."

BRYANT, Hazel.
    DRAMA
        With Hope Clarke and Hank Johnson. Mae's Amis (musical),
            1969.
        With Beverly Todd and Hank Johnson. Origins (musical), 1969.

With Jimmy Justice. Black Circles 'Round Angela (musical),
1971.
With Jimmy Justice. Sheba (musical), 1972.
With Gertrude Grenidge and Walter Miles. Makin' It (musical), 1972.

BUFORD, Naomi E.
POETRY (Anthology): Murphy, Ebony Rhythm.

BUGGS, George.
POETRY (Periodicals): Black Lines, Summer 1971; Journal
of Black Poetry, Spring 1969; Phylon, Spring 1972; also
published in Evergreen Review.

BULL, John.
POETRY The Slave and Other Poems. London: 1824.

BULLINS, Ed. Born 2 July 1935 in Philadelphia. Education: Attended William Penn Business School in Philadelphia; Los Angeles City College; San Francisco State College. Career: One of
the founders of Black Arts/West in San Francisco; member of
the Black Arts Alliance (an organization of Black Theatre
Groups); editor of Black Theatre. Has assisted LeRoi Jones in
film-making and stage productions on the West Coast. Writer-
in-residence at the New Lafayette and American Place theatres.
Presently involved in writing, producing, editing and teaching.
Awards, Honors: Obie Award for "The Fabulous Miss Marie";
Drama Desk--Vernon Rice Award for "Outstanding achievement
in the Off-Broadway Theatre, 1967-68 Season." Recipient of
grants from the Rockefeller and Guggenheim foundations.
COLLECTION
     The Hungered One: Early Writings. New York: Morrow,
     1971*†.
CRITICISM BY BULLINS
     "Black Theatre Groups: A Directory." The Drama Review
        12 (Summer 1968): 172-175.
     "Black Theatre Notes." Black Theatre No. 1 (1968): p. 4.
     "Short Statements on Street Theatre." The Drama Review 12
        (Summer 1968): 93.
     "The So-Called Western Avant-Garde Drama." Liberator 7
        (December 1967): 16; reprinted in Gayle, Black Expres-
        sion.
     "Theatre of Reality." Negro Digest 15 (April 1966): 60-66.
     "What Lies Ahead for Black Americans." Negro Digest 19
        (November 1968): 8. (Symposium.)
DRAMA
     (Collections of Bullins' plays)
     Five Plays: Goin' a Buffalo; In the Wine Time; A Son,
        Come Home; The Electronic Nigger; Clara's Old Man.
        Indianapolis: Bobbs-Merrill, 1969†.
     Four Dynamite Plays. New York: Morrow, 1972*†. (In-
        cludes "It Bees Dat Way," "Death List," "The Pig Pen,"
        "Night of the Beast.")

Ed Bullins (credit: Doug Harris)

The Theme Is Blackness: The Corner and Other Plays.
New York: Morrow, 1973*†.
(Individual listing of plays) •
Clara's Old Man. In The Drama Review 12 (Summer 1968):
159-171; also in Richards, Best Short Plays of 1969;
Davis and Redding, Cavalcade; Poland and Mailman, The
Off Off Broadway Book.
The Corner. In King and Milner, Black Drama Anthology.
Death List. Black Theatre 5 (1971): 38-43.
Dialect Determinism; or, The Rally. In R. Owens, ed.
Spontaneous Combustion: Eight New American Plays.
New York: Klinter House, 1972.
Duplex: A Black Love Fable in Four Movements. New
York: Morrow, 1971†.
The Electronic Nigger. In Hoffman, New American Plays;
Robinson, Nommo.
The Fabulous Miss Marie.
With Shirley Tarbell. The Game of Adam and Eve (one act),
1966.
The Gentleman Caller. In A Black Quartet; Oliver and Sills,
Contemporary Black Drama; Richards, Best Short Plays
of 1970.
Goin' a Buffalo. In Couch, New Black Playwrights.
The Helper (one act), 1966.
How Do You Do: A Nonsense Drama (one act). Mill Valley,
Calif.: Illuminations Press, 1967; also in Jones and Neal,
Black Fire.
In the Wine Time. In Patterson, Black Theater.
It Has No Choice (one act), 1966.
The Man Who Dug Fish, 1967.
A Minor Scene (one act), 1966.
A Short Play for a Small Theatre. In Black World 2 (April
1971): 39.
A Son, Come Home. In Negro Digest 17 (April 1968): 54-
73; also in Childress, Black Scenes.
You Gonna Let Me Take You Out Tonight, Baby? In Alha-
misi and Wangara, Black Arts, pp. 45-51.
EDITOR
New Plays from Black Theatre. New York: Bantam, 1969†.
The New Lafayette Theatre Presents: Plays and Aes-
thetic Comments by 6 Black Playwrights. Garden City,
N.Y.: Doubleday, 1974†.
NON-FICTION
(Periodicals): Black Dialogue; Negro Digest, November 1969.
NOVEL
The Reluctant Rapist. New York: Harper & Row, 1973*.
POETRY
(Anthologies): Alhamisi and Wangara, Black Arts; King,
Black Spirits; Major, The New Black Poetry.
(Periodicals): Black World, September 1970; Journal of
Black Poetry, Spring 1969; Fall-Winter 1971; Negro Digest;
December 1969.

SHORT STORY
(Anthologies): King, Black Short Story Anthology; Sanchez,
We Be Word Sorcerers; Watkins, Black Review No. 1.
(Periodicals): Negro Digest, May, November 1967; August
1968; other poetry in Citadel; Dust; Illuminations; Man-
hattan Review; Nexus; Wild Dog.

BIOGRAPHY AND CRITICISM ON BULLINS
"Black Theater." Negro Digest 18 (April 1969): 9-16.
(Interview by Marvin X.)

Brooks, Mary E. "Reactionary Trends in Recent Black
Drama." Literature and Ideology 10: 41-48.

Cade, Toni. "Review of Four by Ed Bullins." umbra-
blackworks (Summer 1970).

Evans, Don. "The Theatre of Confrontation: Ed Bullins,
Up Against the Wall." Black World 23 (April 1974): 14-
18.

Gant, Lisbeth. "New Lafayette Theatre," Drama Review
16 (December 1972): 46-55.

Giles, James R. "Tenderness in Brutality: The Plays of
Ed Bullins." Players 48 (October-November 1972): 32-
33.

Goss, Clay. "Review of The Duplex--A Love Fable in Four
Movements." Black Books Bulletin 1 (Spring-Summer
1972): 34-35.

Hay, Samuel A. " 'What Shape Shapes Shapelessness?'
Structural Elements in Ed Bullins' Plays." Black World
23 (April 1974): 20-26.

Harrison. The Drama of Nommo, pp. 169, 177-178, 191,
223-225.

Haslam, Gerald W. "Two Traditions in Afro-American Literature." Research Studies 36 (September 1969): 183-
193.

Jeffers, Lance. "Bullins, Baraka, and Elder: The Dawn
of Grandeur in Black Drama." CLA Journal 16 (September 1972): 32-48.

O'Brien, John. "Interview with Ed Bullins." Negro American Literature Forum 7 (Fall 1973): 108.

Riggins, Linda N. "A Review of Ed Bullins' The Hungered
One." Black Scholar 3 (February 1972): 59-60.

Smitherman, Geneva. "Ed Bullins/Stage One: Everybody
Wants to Know Why I Sing the Blues." Black World 23
(April 1974): 4-13.

Trotta, Geri. "Black Theatre." Harper's Bazaar 101 (August 1968): 150-153.

Wesley, Richard. "An Interview with Playwright Ed Bullins."
Black Creation 4 (Winter 1973): 8-10.

INTERJECTIONS
"A Writer's job is to write."

BUNTON, Frederica Katheryne.
POETRY (Anthology): Murphy, Ebony Rhythm.

Margaret Burroughs

BURBRIDGE, Edward. Education: Attended Talladega College.
    Career: Editor for the Louisiana Weekly.
    POETRY
        (Anthology): Murphy, Negro Voices.
        (Periodicals): Crisis, 1935; 1937; 1940; also published in
            the Chicago Defender and Verse.

BURGESS, Marie Louis.
    FICTION Ave Maria: A Tale.   Boston: Press of the Monthly
        Review, 1895.

BURGHARDT, Arthur.
    DRAMA With Michael Egan.   Frederick Douglass...Through
        His Own Words.

BURLEIGH, Benny (Thomas Hildred Oden).
    POETRY Two Gun Bill. New York: Comet, 1957.

BURNHAM, Frederick Russell.
    NOVEL Taking Chances. Los Angeles: Haynes, 1945.

BURRELL, Benjamin Ebenezer. Born 1892 in Manchester Mountains, Jamaica.
POETRY
   (Anthology): Kerlin, Negro Poets and Their Poems.
   (Periodical): Crusader.

BURRELL, Louis V.
   POETRY The Petals of the Rose: Poems and Epigrams. Morton, Pa. : n. p. , 1917.

BURROUGHS, Margaret Taylor Goss. Born 1 November 1917 in St. Rose, Louisiana. Education: Received teaching certificate from Chicago Normal College, 1937, and Chicago Teacher's College, 1939; B. Art Education, Art Institute of Chicago, 1946; M. Art Education, Art Institute of Chicago, 1948; one year study, Institute of Painting and Sculpture, Mexico City, 1953; graduate study, Teachers College of Columbia University, 1958-60; interne under a grant from the National Endowment for the Humanities, Field Museum of Chicago, 1968; additional courses in Institute of African Studies, Northwestern University, 1968, and at Illinois State University, 1970. Currently living in Chicago, Illinois. Career: Teacher, Chicago school system, 1940-46; Director, Museum of African-American History, Inc. , Chicago, 1961; Assistant Professor, African and African-American Art History, Art Institute of Chicago, 1968; presently Assistant Professor of Humanities, Kennedy-King City College; Founder and Director of the DuSable Museum of African-American History. A frequent lecturer at colleges and universities, churches, civic groups and professional societies. Has travelled extensively in Mexico, U. S. S. R. , Europe, Africa, and the West Indies. A painter and sculptor as well as writer and illustrator: her work has been exhibited at colleges and universities and museums in this country as well as in Mexico City, Poland, Moscow, Leipzig; works were reproduced in Soviet Woman's Magazine (Third Prize Award), in Der Bildener Kunst, and in Time magazine (9 April 1945). Member: National Conference of Negro Artists, Atlanta 1959; Annual Lake Meadows Outdoor Arts and Crafts Fair, 1957; Founder, Ebony Museum of Negro History and Art, Chicago, 1961; The New Crusader--Negro History Hall of Fame, 1960-62; State of Illinois Centennial of Emancipation Commission, 1963; American Forum for International Study at University of Ghana, 1969, and at University of West Indies, Jamaica, 1970; South Side Community Art Center Board; Chicago Council of Foreign Relations Board; Art Council Board; Art Panel (Illinois) Board; American Forum for International Study Abroad Board; Urban Gateways Board; The Governor's Commission on the Financing of the Arts; Better Boys Foundation; Hull House Association of Chicago. Awards, Honors: Honorable Mention, Annual Negro Art Show, Atlanta, 1947; First Water Color Purchase Award, Atlanta University, 1955; Best in Show Award, Hall Mark Prize, Lincoln University, 1966; Better Boys Foundation Award for work with the inner city; South Side Community Art Center Citation, 1953;

Committee for the Negro in the Arts Citation, 1955; Beaux Arts
Guild of Tuskegee, First Annual Art Festival Citation, 1957;
National Conference of Artists Trophy, 1963; Volunteers for
Community Improvement Award, 1966; Prospair Girls Social
and Charitable Club Award, 1968; Doctorate of Honoris Causis,
Lewis College, 1972.

EDITOR

Africa, My Africa. Chicago: DuSable Museum, 1970.

Did You Feed My Cow? New York: Crowell, 1955; rev. ed.
   Chicago: Follette, 1969*. (Street games, chants and
   rhymes.)

Jasper the Drummin' Boy. New York: Viking, 1947; rev.
   ed. Chicago: Follette, 1970*.

With Dudley Randall. For Malcolm: Poems on the Life and
   and Death of Malcolm X. Detroit: Broadside, 1967†.

What Shall I Tell My Children Who Are Black? Chicago:
   DuSable Museum, 1968.

Whip Me Whop Me Pudding and Other Stories of Riley and
   His Fabulous Friends. Praga Press, 1966; Chicago:
   DuSable Museum, n. d.

NON-FICTION

(Anthologies): Barbour, The Black Seventies; Brown, Lee
   and Ward, To Gwen with Love.

(Periodicals): Art Gallery, April 1968; Campus Life, July-
   August 1969; Chicago Schools Journal, 1938; Child Life;
   Crossroads, February 1967; Discovery; Elementary Art;
   Freedomways, 1971; Negro Digest, March 1966; New York
   Public Schools; Phi Delta Kappa magazine; School Arts
   Magazine; Soviet Woman; Urbanite, 1965; Youth magazine;
   July 1968.

POETRY

(Anthologies): Dee, Glow Child; Simmons and Hutchinson,
   Black Culture.

SHORT STORIES

(Periodicals): Negro Digest, December 1962; November
   1963; Black World, July 1970.

BIOGRAPHY AND CRITICISM ON BURROUGHS

Atkinson, J. Edward. Black Dimensions in Contemporary
   Art. New York: New American Library, 1971, 39-40.

Contemporary Authors, 23/24.

BUSH, Joseph Bevans. Born in Philadelphia. Died 1968. Education: Attended Philadelphia public schools. Career: Wrote
for approximately 15 years. Was a member of the Philadelphia Writers' Club. [1]

CRITICISM BY BUSH

"Odetta: American's Foremost Folk Singer." Negro Digest
   14 (May 1965): 45-48.

POETRY

(Anthologies): Alhamisi and Wangara, Black Arts; Coombs,
   We Speak as Liberators; Shuman, A Galaxy of Black Writings.

(Periodicals): Negro American Literature Forum 6 (Spring

1972): n. p. ; Negro Digest 16 (August 1967): 48; 18 (March
1969): 53. Also published in The Liberator, The Philadelphia Tribune, Pride Magazine, The Negro History Bulletin, Philly Talk, and The Philadelphia Independent.
[1]Information provided by son.

BUSH, Olivia Ward. Born 1869.
    POETRY
    Driftwood. Providence, R.I.: Atlantic Printing Co., 1914.
    Memories of Calvary: An Easter Sketch. Philadelphia:
        A.M.E. Book Concern Press, 191?.
    Original Poems. Providence, R.I.: Press of Louis A. Bas-
        inet, 1899.
    (Periodicals): The Voice of the Negro 2 (June 1905): 400;
        (December 1905): 866; also published in Colored Ameri-
        can Magazine.

BUSTER GREENE.
    NOVEL Brighter Sun: An Historical Account of the Struggles
        of a Man to Free Himself and His Family from Human
        Bondage, By His Grandson. New York: Pageant, 1954.

BUTCHER, James W., Jr.
    DRAMA The Seer. In Brown, Davis and Lee, Negro Caravan.

BUTCHER, Philip. Born 1918 in Washington, D.C. Education:
    A.B., Howard University, 1942; M.A., Howard University,
    1947; Ph.D., Columbia University, 1956. Currently living in
    Baltimore, Maryland. Career: Literary Editor, Opportunity:
    Journal of Negro Life, 1947-48; Professor, English Depart-
    ment, Morgan State College, 1947 to date; Dean of the Gradu-
    ate School, Morgan State College, 1972 to date; Visiting Pro-
    fessor, South Carolina State College, Summer, 1958. Has
    served as consultant, panelist and lecturer for university groups
    and professional organizations. Member: College Language
    Association (Associate Editor of CLA Journal), Modern Lan-
    guage Association, Society for the Study of Southern Literature.
    Awards, Honors: General Education Board Fellowship, 1948-
    49; John Hay Whitney Opportunity Fellowship, 1951-52; elected
    by the faculty to two three-year terms as Chairman, Division
    of Humanities, Morgan State College, 1960-66; Creative Schol-
    arship Award, College Language Association, 1964; several re-
    search grants from MSC Faculty Committee on Research; Re-
    search Grant, American Philosophical Society, 1968 to 1969;
    "Outstanding Educators of America" Award, 1972.
    CRITICISM
    "Cable to Boyesen on The Grandissimes." American Litera-
        ture 40 (November 1968): 391-394.
    "Creative Writing in the Negro College." Journal of Negro
        Education 20 (Spring 1951): 160-163.
    "Emerson and the South." Phylon 17 (Third Quarter 1956):
        279-285. Also in Emanuel and Gross, Dark Symphony.
    "Francis Barber, Dr. Samuel Johnson's Negro Servant."

Negro History Bulletin 11 (November 1947): 37-38, 47.

George W. Cable. New York: Twayne Publishers, Inc., 1962 (vol. 24, Twayne's United States Authors Series)*; New York: College & University Press, 1964†.

George W. Cable: The Northampton Years. New York: Columbia University Press, 1959.

"George Washington Cable." A Bibliographical Guide to the Study of Southern Literature. Edited by Louis D. Rubin, Jr., Baton Rouge: Louisiana State University Press, 1969.

"George Washington Cable." American Literary Realism, 1870-1910 1 (Fall 1967): 20-25.

"George W. Cable and Booker T. Washington." Journal of Negro Education 17 (Fall 1948): 462-468.

"George W. Cable and George W. Williams: An Abortive Collaboration." Journal of Negro History, 58 (October 1968): 334-344.

"George W. Cable and Negro Education." Journal of Negro History, 34 (April 1949): 119-134.

"George W. Cable: History and Politics." Phylon 9 (Second Quarter 1948): 137-145.

" 'The Godfathership' of A Connecticut Yankee." CLA Journal 12 (March 1969): 189-198.

"In Print... The Literary Scene." Opportunity: Journal of Negro Life 25 (Fall 1947): 218-222.

"In Print... The Literary Scene." Opportunity: Journal of Negro Life 26 (Winter 1948): 23-26.

"In Print... Pot Pourri." Opportunity: Journal of Negro Life 26 (Summer 1948): 113-115.

"James (Arthur) Baldwin." Encyclopedia of World Literature in the 20th Century. New York: Frederick Ungar Publishing Co., 1967, vol. 1, pp. 91-92.

"Mark Twain Sells Roxy Down the River." CLA Journal 8 (March 1965): 22-33.

"Mark Twain's Installment on the National Debt." Southern Literary Journal 1 (Spring 1969): 48-55. (Item BC-39 in the Bobbs-Merrill Reprint Series in Black Studies, 1970.)

"Mutual Appreciation: Dunbar and Cable." The Free Lance 4 (First Half 1957): 2-3. Reprinted in CLA Journal 1 (March 1958): 101-102.

"Othello's Racial Identity." Shakespeare Quarterly 3 (July 1952): 243-247.

"Two Early Southern Realists in Revival." CLA Journal 14 (September 1970): 91-95.

"W. S. Braithwaite's Southern Exposure: Rescue and Revelation." Southern Literary Journal 3 (Spring 1971): 49-61.

"William Stanley Braithwaite and the College Language Association." CLA Journal 15 (December 1971): 117-125.

The William Stanley Braithwaite Reader. Ann Arbor: University of Michigan Press, 1972*.

"The Younger Novelists and the Urban Negro." CLA Journal 4 (March 1961): 196-203.

NON-FICTION
> (Periodicals): Afro-American Magazine Section, 21 January
> 1961; CLA Journal, March 1959; Journal of Human Rela-
> tions, Winter 1956.

POETRY
> (Anthologies): National Poetry Anthology; Russell, Ted Ma-
> lone's Scrapbook.
> (Periodicals): Driftwood: A Magazine of Verse, January
> 1948; Midwest Journal, Winter 1951-52; Phylon, Third
> Quarter 1949; Prairie Wings, January-February 1948;
> University of Kansas Review, Summer 1949.

REVIEWS
> Over fifty book reviews have been published in American Lit-
> erature; CLA Journal; Crisis; Journal of Negro Education;
> Journal of Negro Life; Midwest Journal; Negro Quarterly;
> Opportunity; Phylon; Shakespeare Quarterly; The Sun.

BIOGRAPHY ON BUTCHER
> Contemporary Authors, 4.

BUTLER, Anna Land. Born 7 October 1901 in Philadelphia. Education: Attended Trenton State Teachers College, 1920-22,
1936; Temple University, 1953; University of Maryland, 1942-
45. Currently living in Atlantic City, New Jersey. Career:
Elementary School teacher, 1922-64; Head Teacher-Director,
Morris Child Care Center, 1969-72. Editor-reporter for the
Philadelphia Tribune, 1965-72; newspaper correspondent, Pittsburgh Courier, 1936-65. Editor, Magazine Responsibility, Official Organ, National Negro Business and Professional Women's
Clubs, 1955-59. Member: Charter Member and Board Director, Philadelphia Cotillion Society; Charter Member, Phi Delta
Kappa, Iota Chapter; Education Council, Human Resources Atlantic County Anti-Poverty Program, 1965; President, Seaboard
Council Heritage House, 1954--; Atlantic City Study Center,
1959--; Episcopal Women Diocese of New Jersey; New Jersey
Federation of Colored Women's Clubs; New Jersey Organization
of Teachers; National Association of Negro Business and Professional Women; Catholic Poetry Society; American Poets Fellowship Society; Atlantic Teachers Association; National Links,
Inc.; Atlantic City Chamber of Commerce; International Biographical Association. Awards, Honors: Versatile Teachers
Award, 1953; Legion of Honor Award--Chapel of Four Chap-
lains, 1963; "Teacher of Year" Awarded by New Jersey Organization of Teachers, 1961; Northside Business and Professional
Women's Achievement Award, 1963; Theta Phi Lambda Sorority
Women's Showcase Award of Merit, 1964; National Link Inc.
Creative Arts Achievement Award, 1960 in Nassau; Citation--
Creative Writing, New Orleans, 1972; National Association Ne-
gro Business and Professional Women's Sojourner; Truth Award
for Meritorious Service, 1966; Certificate of Merit--The United
States Jaycees, 1967; Sach's Certificate of Recognition for Out-
standing Community Services, New York, 1963; Certificate of
Award of Achievement, Outstanding Negro Women, Imperial
Court, Daughters of Isis, 1972; Certificate of Appreciation, Na-
tional Links, 1972.

Anna Land Butler

POETRY
Album of Love Letters--Unsent. New York: Margent, 1952.
Touchstone. Provincetown, Mass.: The Advocate Press for
the Delaware Poetry Center, 1961.
High Noon. n.p.: Prairie Press Books, 1971.
(Anthologies): Spring Anthologies, London: Mitre, 1962-65;
Today Poets, America Poets Fellowship Society, 1965;
American Poets Best, Los Angeles: Swordsman, 1962-
65; Jewels on a Willow Tree, Mabelle A. Lyon, ed.,
Charleston, Ill.: Prairie Press.
(Periodicals): United Poets, January-March, 1971.

INTERJECTIONS
"That God has given each of us at least one talent. If you
don't use or share it, you lose it! Those so endowed have a
purpose in life to perpetuate the beauty and wonder of God's
creations. Accepting this role we help others grow and experience a realization that God directs the lives of those who pause
to listen and do His will. By serving others in love we grow
as a person, and help others appreciate God's universe in some
media here, manifested through effort and achievement. Be
thankful for life, the opportunity to serve others in whatever
way is possible. Little kindnesses go far too. Count your
blessings with your woes. Be grateful always."

BUTLER, Glen Anthony see RAVELOMANANTSOA, Glen Anthony

BUTLER, Hood C. Born in the Philippines.
POETRY (Anthology): Murphy, Ebony Rhythm.

BUTLER, James Alpheus. Born 22 August 1905 in Miami, Florida.
Education: A.B., University of Denver, 1929; M.A., Fisk University. Workshops in English Literary Movements and in Philosophy, University of California--Berkeley; workshop in Higher
Education and Teacher Education, University of Minnesota; workshop in The Community College, Teachers College, Columbia
University. Career: Founder, Paths in Philosophy and Tower
by the Sea symposiums, colloquiums and tutorials in English,
Violin Music, Education and Global Philosophy (affiliated with
the Foundation for the Advancement of the Cultural Arts and the
Laurel Lore Workshops in Creative Writing, Melody Writing,
and Voice Recording). Editor and Publisher, Tower by the Sea,
the Laurel Publishers Poetry Symposium International Souvenir
Booklet. Official Critic (elected) for the United Amateur Press
Association of America. Co-author of more than forty volumes
of inspirational-philosophical poetry. Several of his song po-
ems have been recorded; his song sonnet, "The Lyric Hour"
was published in sheet music form. Member: Major Poets
Chapter, American Poets Fellowship Association; International
Songwriters Club; Life Member, International Clover Poetry As-
sociation; Speech Association of America. Awards, Honors:
First Prize Award, New York World Fair Anthology Poetry
Award; Golden Medallion for Achievement in Creative Writing,
Fine Art Crafts Foundation; Honorary Ph.D., awarded by the
Laurel College of Authors and Voice Recording, 1955.
EDITOR
    The Parnassian: Prose and Poetry by 16 Members of the
        Younger Generation. New York and Chicago: Laurel,
        1930.
    Tower by the Sea: Souvenir Poems by Members of the
        Laurel Publishers Poetry Symposium. Tampa, Florida:
        Laurel, 1973.
POETRY
    Make Way for Happiness. Boston: Christopher, 1932.
    Sepia Vistas. New York: Exposition, 1939.
    Philosopher and Saint. New York: Exposition, 1951.
    20th Century Song Sonnets: Sphere of the Sprite and the
        Sage. Tampa, Fla.: Laurel, 1973.
    (Periodicals): Opportunity, June 1927; July 1928; September
        1928; August 1929; January 1930.
INTERJECTIONS
    "Life can become Art, and Poetry and Music can become its
Medium of Assertion. Emotion created by Poetry and Music in
the Soul is Relaxation and from that Pleasure we obtain complete Consolation, complete Fruition for Wishes, Needs, De-
sires, Visions.
    "No one was ever yet a Great Poet without being at the same
time a profound Philosopher. For Poetry is the Blossom and

the Fragrance of all Human Knowledge, Human Thoughts, Emotion, Language.
"One Poet has said that a Poem begins in Delight and ends in Wisdom. Let us, then, make Lyric Lore, Songs and Music for the Globe."
CRITICISM ON BUTLER
   Brown. Negro Poetry and Drama, pp. 78-79.

BUTLER, Reginald.
   POETRY (Anthology): Henderson, Understanding the New
      Black Poetry.

BYRON, Asaman B. W. Born in Trinidad.
   POETRY To Be Black Is to Be Equal (=) to God. New York:
      By the Author, 1971.

-C-

CADE, Toni see BAMBARA, Toni Cade

CAIN, Brother.
   DRAMA Epitaph to a Triangulated Trinity.

CAIN, George.
   NOVEL
      Blueschild Baby. New York: McGraw-Hill, 1971*; New
         York: Dell, 1972†.
   BIOGRAPHY AND CRITICISM ON CAIN
      Kent, George. "Struggle for the Image," p. 308.
   REVIEWS: Blueschild Baby.
      McCluskey, John. Black World 2 (September 1971): 93-95.
      Meaddough, R. J. Freedomways 11 (1971): 27-28.

CAIN, Johnnie Mae.
   FICTION
      White Bastards. New York: Vantage, 1973*.
   POETRY
      Do You Remember. Philadelphia: Dorrance, 1973*.

CAINES, Jeannette. Born in Harlem. Currently living in Freeport, Long Island. Career: Works at a publishing house.
   Member: Council on Adoptable Children.
   CHILDREN AND YOUNG ADULTS
      Abby. New York: Harper-Row, 1973*.

CALDWELL, Ben.
   DRAMA
      All White Caste. King and Milner, Black Drama Anthology.
      Family Portrait, or My Son the Black Nationalist. In Bul-
         lins, New Plays from the Black Theater.
      The Fanatic (one act), 1968.
      The First Militant Preacher. Newark, N.J.: Jihad, 1967.

Hypnotism (one act), 1966. In Afro-Arts Anthology; also in
    Simmons and Hutchinson, Black Culture.
The Job (one act), 1966. In The Drama Review 12 (Sum-
    mer 1968); also in Robinson, Nommo; Kearns, Black
    Identity.
The King of Soul or The Devil and Otis Redding. Black
    Theatre, 3 (1969): also in Bullins, New Plays from Black
    Theatre.
Mission Accomplished. In The Drama Review 12 (Summer
    1968).
Prayer Meeting or The First Militant Minister. In Jones
    and Neal, Black Fire; A Black Quartet.
Recognition (one act), 1968.
Riot Sale or Dollar Psyche Fake Out. In The Drama Re-
    view 12 (Summer 1968); also in Simmons and Hutchinson,
    Black Culture.
Top Secret or a Few Million After B.C. In The Drama Re-
    view 12 (Summer 1968).
Unpresidented (one act), 1968.
The Wall (one act), 1967.
BIOGRAPHY AND CRITICISM ON CALDWELL
    Bigsby. The Black American Writer, vol. 2, pp. 201-202.
    Harrison. The Drama of Nommo, p. 205.
    Peavy. "Satire and Contemporary Black Drama," pp. 42-45.

CALDWELL, Gwendolyn D.
    POETRY (Periodical): Negro History Bulletin, April 1971.

CALDWELL, Lewis A. H. (Abe Noel).
    NOVEL The Policy King. Chicago: New Vistas, 1945.

CALOMEE, Lindsay.
    POETRY (Periodical): Black Scholar, April-May, 1971.

CAMPBELL, Alfred Gibbs.
    POETRY Poems. Newark, N.J.: Advertiser Prtg. House, 1883.

CAMPBELL, Herbert.
    DRAMA Goin' Home to Papa.

CAMPBELL, James E.
    NON-FICTION
        (Periodical): Freedomways, Fall 1968.
    SHORT STORY
        (Periodical): Freedomways, Spring 1962.

CAMPBELL, James Edwin. Born 1867 in Pomeroy, Ohio. Died
    1895.[1] Education: graduated from the local academy in 1884;
    attended Miami College (Ohio). Career: Taught two years at
    Buck Ridge (Ohio); became principal of the Langston School,
    Point Pleasant, Ohio; principal of the West Virginia Colored
    Institute, Charleston (now Virginia State College).[2] From
    1890-1900 [see 1], he was a journalist for the Chicago Times-

Herald.[3] He worked with the Black coal miners.[4] He was also one of a group who issued the Four O'Clock Magazine,[5] and was one of the first Blacks to write dialect poetry.[6]

POETRY
Driftings and Gleanings. Chicago: Donohue and Henneberry, 1888, Charleston, W. Va.: 1887.
Echoes from the Cabin and Elsewhere. Chicago: Donohue and Henneberry, 1895. (Robinson, Early Black American Poets, p. 231, cites: Echoes from the Plantation and Elsewhere.)
(Anthologies): Barksdale and Kinnamon, Black Writers of America; Brown, Davis and Lee, Negro Caravan; Brown, Negro Poetry and Drama; Johnson, The Book of American Negro Poetry; Patterson, Introduction to Black Literature in America; Redding, To Make a Poet Black; Robinson, Early Black American Poets; Wagner, Black Poets of the United States.

BIOGRAPHY AND CRITICISM ON CAMPBELL
Bergman. A Chronological History of the Negro in America, p. 321.
Johnson. The Book of American Negro Poetry, pp. 64-65.
Williams. They Also Spoke, pp. 194-197.

CRITICISM ON CAMPBELL
Woodson, Carter G. "James Edwin Campbell: A Forgotten Man of Letter." Negro History Bulletin (November 1938): 11.

[1]Sterling Brown, Arthur Davis and Ulysses Lee in Negro Caravan, p. 316, and Harry Ploski and Ernest Kaiser in The Negro Almanac, 1971, p. 700, cite Campbell's dates as 1860-1905.
[2]Wilhelmena S. Robinson, Historical Negro Biographies (New York: Publishers Co., Inc., 1969), pp. 59-60.
[3]Sterling Brown, Arthur P. Davis and Ulysses Lee, Negro Caravan (New York: Arno Press, 1969), p. 316.
[4]Robinson, p. 60.
[5]James Weldon Johnson, The Book of American Negro Poetry (New York: Harcourt, Brace & World, 1959), p. 64.
[6]Brown, Davis and Lee, p. 316.

CAMPBELL, Ralph.
DRAMA Death of a Crow.

CANNON, C. E.
POETRY Nigger. Detroit: Broadside, 1972†.

CANNON, David Wadsworth, Jr. Born 1911. Died 14 December 1938. Education: B.S. Hillside College, Michigan, 1931; M.A., University of Michigan, 1932; candidate for Ph.D., Columbia University, 1937-39. Career: Instructor of psychology at Junior State College, Cranford, N.J., 1932-36. He was a member of the Board of Directors of the National Council of Religious Education, 1937-39. Awards, Honors: Received a

fellowship to the University of Michigan, 1932[1] and the Rosen-
feld Fellowship for further study at Columbia University.
POETRY
    Black Labor Chant and Other Poems. New York: The As-
        sociation Press, 1940.
    (Anthologies): Hughes and Bontemps, The Poetry of the Ne-
        gro: 1746-1970; Murphy, Ebony Rhythm.
BIOGRAPHY AND CRITICISM ON CANNON
    Emanuel and Gross. Dark Symphony, p. 370.
    Gayle. Black Expression, p. 92.
REVIEW
    "Book of the Month." Negro History Bulletin (April 1940):
        112.
            [1]Obituary, New York Times, 16 December 1938, sec.
    4, p. 25.

CANNON, Steve. Born 10 April 1935 in New Orleans, Louisiana.
Education: self-taught. Career: Radio-television technician;
book publisher, school teacher. Specializes in American folk-
lore and American art.
INTERVIEW
    With Lennox Raphael and James Thompson. "A Very Stern
        Discipline." Harper's Magazine 234 (March 1967): 76-
        95. (An exchange with Ralph Ellison.)
NOVEL
    Groove, Bang, and Jive Around. New York: Olympia, 1971.
        Excerpt in Reed, 19 Necromancers from Now.
REVIEW BY CANNON
    (Anthology): Reed, Yardbird Reader I.
WORK IN PROGRESS
    "The Shadow Boxer Scores."
    "Dealing from the Top," an anthology of American poetry
        from then to now.
INTERJECTIONS
    "An Artist is a juggler, a master manipulator of forms, who
    informs, and creates forms, thereby demonstrating new possi-
    bilities of perceiving the so-called concrete world...A Master
    Magician."

CANTON, Cal.
    POETRY (Periodical): Journal of Black Poetry, Winter-Spring
        1970.

CANTY, Emma.
    POETRY (Periodical): Journal of Black Poetry, Summer 1972.

CAPEL, Sharon.
    DRAMA Dreams Are For the Dead.

CARLIN X.
    POETRY (Periodical): Journal of Black Poetry, Summer 1972.

CARMICHAEL, Waverly Turner. <u>Born</u> in Snow Hill, Alabama.
  <u>Education:</u> Attended the Snow Hill Institute; Harvard University.
  <u>Career</u>: Served in W.W. I, France, the 37th Regiment, "The
  Buffaloes."[1]
  POETRY
      <u>From the Heart of a Folk: A Book of Songs</u>. Boston:
          Cornhill, 1918.
      (Anthologies): Eleazer, <u>Singers in the Dawn</u>; Johnson, <u>The
          Book of American Negro Poetry</u>.
      (Periodical): <u>Crisis</u> 15 (1918): 133.
  BIOGRAPHY AND CRITICISM ON CARMICHAEL
      Johnson. <u>The Book of American Negro Poetry</u>, p. 162.
      Kerlin. <u>Negro Poets and Their Poems</u>, pp. 53, 235-236.
          [1]James Weldon Johnson, <u>The Book of American Negro
          Poetry</u> (New York: Harcourt, Brace & World, 1959), p.
          162.

CARPENTER, Howard.
  POETRY (Anthology): Murphy, <u>Ebony Rhythm</u>.

CARPENTER, Pete.
  POETRY (Periodical): <u>Journal of Black Poetry</u>, Summer 1972.

CARR, Clarence F. <u>Born</u> 26 February 1880 in Crockett, Texas.
  <u>Education:</u> Attended elementary schools in Crockett; received
  B.A. from Wilberforce University; Honorary Degree, M.A.,
  from Wilberforce University, 1918. <u>Career</u>: Became principal of Palestine High School and of various schools in Dallas,
  including the Booker T. Washington High School. Was president of the State Teachers Association, Texas.[1]
  POETRY
      (Anthology): Brewer, <u>Heralding Dawn</u>.
  CRITICISM ON CARR
      <u>Palestine Daily Herald</u>, 1918; Cf. <u>Heralding Dawn</u>, p. 7.
          [1]J. Mason Brewer, <u>Heralding Dawn</u> (Dallas, Texas:
          June Thomason Printing, 1936), p. 7.

CARRERE, Mentis.
  NOVEL <u>Man in the Cane</u>. New York: Vantage, 1956.

CARRIGAN, Nettie W.
  CHILDREN AND YOUNG ADULTS
      <u>Rhymes and Jingles for the Children's Hour</u>. Boston: Chris-
          topher, 1940.

CARRINGTON, Harold.
  POETRY <u>Drive Suite</u>. Heritage Series. London: Breman,
      1970†. Distributed in the U.S. by Broadside Press of De-
      troit.

CARROLL, Vinnette. <u>Born</u> New York City. <u>Education:</u> B.A.,
  Long Island University, 1944; M.A., New York University,
  1946; post graduate work, New School of Social Research, 1948-

50; Ph.D. candidate, Columbia University. Currently living in New York City. Career: Actress in various stage productions, including Caesar and Cleopatra, 1955; Small War on Murray Hill, 1956; Jolly's Progress, 1959; Moon on a Rainbow Shawl (London), 1959; 1962; Prodigal Son (London), Black Nativity (London). Appearances in films include One Potato, Two Potato; Up the Down Staircase; Alice's Restaurant. Appearances on TV include Member of the Wedding, Granada TV (London), numerous talk shows and documentaries. Has directed Dark of the Moon, 1960; Ondine, 1961; The Disenchanted, 1962; Black Nativity, 1962; Spoleto Festival of Two Worlds, 1963; The Prodigal Son, 1965; The Flies, 1966 (Los Angeles), 1967; Slow Dance on the Killing Ground, 1967; Old Judge Mose Is Dead, 1967; The Lottery, 1967; But Never Jam Today, 1969; Moon on a Rainbow Shawl, 1969; Bury the Dead, 1971; Don't Bother Me I Can't Cope, 1971, Los Angeles and Chicago, 1972, Toronto and San Francisco, 1973; Step Lively, Boy, 1973; Croesus and the Witch, 1973. Directed the TV show, Beyond the Blues, 1964, Prodigal Son, Jubilation Tempo. Has taught drama at the High School of the Performing Arts, New York City; and has directed the Ghetto Arts Program for the New York State Council on the Arts. Is currently Artistic Director for Urban Arts Corps. Member: Directors Unit, Actors Studio. Awards, Honors: Obie Award for distinguished performance, 1962; Emmy Award for directing "Beyond the Blues," 1964; Outer Critics Circle Award for Directing, 1971-72; NAACP Image Award (Los Angeles), 1972; Los Angeles Drama Critics Circle Award, distinguished directing, 1972; Harold Jackman Memorial Award, 1973; Tony nomination, directing, 1973.

DRAMA

With Micki Grant. But Never Jam Today, 1969.
With Micki Grant. Croesus and the Witch, 1972.
With Micki Grant. Don't Bother Me, I Can't Cope, 1972.
With Micki Grant. Step Lively, Boy, 1972.

POETRY

Trumpets of the Lord, An Anthology of Afro-American Poetry, 1968.

BIOGRAPHY AND CRITICISM ON CARROLL

Mitchell. Black Drama, pp. 191, 205.
"Woman on the Run." Sepia, October 1961, pp. 57-60.

CARSON, Dwight.

POETRY What the Hell Does All Beef Pork Gotta Do with the Revolution. New York: Amuru, 1973†.

CARSON, Lular L. Born 15 April 1921 in Blackstone, Virginia. Career: See Shockley and Chandler, Living Black American Authors, p. 25.

The Priceless Gift. New York: Vantage, 1970.

CARTER, Herman J.

POETRY (Anthology): Murphy, Ebony Rhythm.

CARTER, Jean (Emma Loyal Lexa).
DRAMA Country Gentleman. New York: Exposition, 1950.

CARTER, John D.
DRAMA The Assassin, 1971.

CARTER, Karl W. Born 25 February 1944 in New Orleans, Louisi-
ana. Education: B.A., Tennessee State University, 1967; J.D.,
Howard University Law School, 1970. Currently living in Wash-
ington, D.C. Career: Specializes in Administrative Law, Con-
stitutional Law and Employment Law. Presently employed with
Neighborhood Legal Services in Washington, D.C. Member:
District of Columbia Bar. Awards, Honors: Sigma Rho Sigma;
I.S.S.P. Scholarship, Columbia University.
POETRY
    (Broadside): Three Poems. Detroit: Broadside, 1972.
    (Anthologies): Henderson, Understanding the New Black Po-
        etry.
    (Periodicals): Black World, September 1970; Présence Afri-
        caine.
INTERJECTIONS
"Basically I believe the function of the poet is to draw his
ideas and material from the everyday life of Black people.
Since poetry is a limited medium in relation to the novel, the
Black poet must use his talents to capsulize the essence of the
spirit of Black people; his poetry must be not only political but
also capture the emotions and feelings of his subjects."

CARTER, Lillie Mae.
POETRY (Periodicals): Negro American Literature Forum,
        Spring 1972; Negro History Bulletin, April 1971.

CARTER, Steve.
DRAMA
        As You Can See (one act), 1968.
        One Last Look, 1971, Scene in Childress, Black Scenes.
        The Terraced Apartment (one act), 1972.

CARVALHO, Grimaldo. Born 2 April 1919 in Miracema, Rio de
Janeiro, Brazil. Education: M.D., Escola de Medicina e
Cirurgia do Rio de Janeiro, 1948. Currently living in Littleton,
Maine. Career: A cytopathologist who has held numerous positions as cancer research scientist in Rio de Janeiro and in
the United States; University professor at the Medical College
of Virginia, 1963-69; Chariman of Cytopathology at Escola de
Medicine de Cirurgia do Rio de Janeiro, 1969-72; has published prolifically in his field (including three textbooks on cytology) and has lectured in Brazil and the United States as well
as other countries. Currently, Associate Professor at Tufts
University, New England Medical Center Hospital in Boston.
Member: International Academy of Cytology; American Society
of Cytology; Brazilian Society of Cytology as well as many other professional organizations and societies.

CHILDREN AND YOUNG ADULTS
   The Modern Witches.   New York: Vantage, 1969.
NOVEL
   The Negro Messiah.   New York: Vantage, 1969.
POETRY
   Folhas Secas (Dry Leaves).   Brazil: Editora Vozes, n.d.
INTERJECTIONS
   "Patrocinio, a Black maestro, says in a discussion, 'I'm
not against miscegenation, but I don't believe that it would absorb a race as numerous as ours.   It is only a social occur-
rence, which may not be pointed out as a people's rule or a
government program.'   In the end of the book Messiah talks to
his grandson, '...You can be a doctor if you really want to be
one.   However, do not plan to acquire a title like that only because you feel inferior due to the color of your skin.   That
will make you very unhappy too.   Do not look for social com-
pensations because that would be a great mistake.   Look for
personal satisfaction, for that will be true happiness.' "

CASEY, Bernie.
   POETRY
      Look at the People.   New York: Doubleday, 1969*.
   BIOGRAPHY ON CASEY
      Atkinson, J. Edward.   Black Dimensions in Contemporary
         Art.   New York: New American Library, 1971, pp. 42-43.
   REVIEW: Look at the People.
      Plumpp, Sterling.   Black World, 19 (September 1970): 51-
         52.

CASEY, Raymond O.   see SHABAZZ, Turhan Abdul

CASON, P. Martin.
   POETRY Book of Fifty Poems: Our Brave Heroes.   n.p.,
      n.d.

CASSELLE, Corene Flowerette.   Born 26 January 1943 in Chicago.
   Education: B.A., Northern Illinois University, 1965; M.E.,
   University of Illinois--Champaigne/Urbana, 1970.   Currently
   living in Chicago.   Career: Served as a Volunteer in the
   Peace Corps; taught grades K-5 in the public schools.
   CHILDREN AND YOUNG ADULTS
      Country of the Black People.   Chicago: Third World, n.d.
   INTERJECTIONS
      "Black awareness + Black Knowledge will equal Black re-
   spect + Afrikan values of dignity and universal being."

CATER, Catherine.   Born 1917.
   POETRY
      (Anthologies): Bontemps, American Negro Poetry; Hughes
         and Bontemps, The Poetry of the Negro: 1746-1970.
      (Periodical): Phylon, 1943.

CHAMBERS, Stephen A.
   POETRY
      Forms, on #3.   New York: Afro-Arts, 1968.
      (Periodical): Journal of Black Poetry, Spring 1969.

CHANDLER, Len. Born 1935 in Akron, Ohio.
   POETRY (Anthology): Major, The New Black Poetry.

CHANTAL, Berry. Born 10 March 1948 in Newark, New Jersey.
   POETRY (Anthology): Boyer, Broadside Annual 1973.

CHANTRELLE, Seginald.
   NOVEL Not Without Dust.   New York: Exposition, 1954.

CHAPMAN, Nell.
   POETRY (Anthology): Murphy, Ebony Rhythm.

CHAPPELL, Helen F.
   POETRY (Anthology): Murphy, Negro Voices.

CHARLES, Martha Evans (Marte Charles).
   DRAMA
      Black Cycle. In King and Milner, Black Drama Anthology.
      Jamimma, 1971.
      Where We At, 1969.
      Job Security, 1970.

CHASTAIN, Thomas.
   NOVEL Judgment Day.   Garden City, N.Y.: Doubleday, 1962.

CHEATHAM, Modell.
   POETRY (Anthology): Alhamisi and Wangara, Black Arts.

CHENAULT, John.
   POETRY
      Blue Blackness. Cincinnati; Seven Hills Neighborhood House,
         1969.
      (Anthology): Brown, Lee and Ward, To Gwen with Love.

CHERIOT, Henri.
   POETRY Black Ink, by the Author of Variant Verse.   Orlando,
      Fla.: H. Cheriot Publishing Co., 1917.

CHESNUTT, Charles Waddell. Born 20 June 1858 in Cleveland,
   Ohio. Died 15 November 1932. Education: Attended Howard
   School, Fayetteville, N.C.; took independent courses and tutor-
   ial instructions in German, French, and Greek; [1] studied law,
   passed the Ohio Bar examinations, and was admitted to the bar
   in 1887. [2] After his mother's death, when his father planned to
   withdraw Charles from the school so that he could help support
   the family, Robert Harris, principal of Howard School, hired
   Chesnutt, then fourteen, to teach while he continued with his
   studies. Later, he went to Charlotte, N.C., as assistant prin-

cipal to Cicero Harris.   After Harris's death he became principal. [3] During his term in Charlotte, he continued his studies.
In 1877, he returned to Fayetteville and became an English
teacher and first assistant to Robert Harris in the new Fayetteville State Normal School.   After Harris's death in 1880, Chesnutt succeeded him as principal, and remained at State Normal
School until his resignation in 1883. [4]

Frustrated with the limitations imposed upon Blacks in North
Carolina, he taught himself stenography and then moved to New
York City in 1883, with his wife and children. [5] He worked as
a stenographer for Dow Jones and Company, and as a reporter
for a daily column, The Wall Street Gossip, and for the New
York Mail and Express.   Six months later, however, he left
New York City and moved to Cleveland, Ohio, where he re-
sided for nearly half a century. [6] He became a legal stenographer in the accounting department for the Nickel Plate Railroad.
It was at this time that Chesnutt studied law and later joined
the law firm of Henderson, Kline, and Tolles. [7] For several
years he lived four lives simultaneously: court-room stenographer, lawyer, author and lecturer.   (He was now succeeding
professionally with his writing, and father to a growing family.)
He also participated in civic affairs, promoted civil and political rights and opportunities for Afro-Americans, and travelled
in Europe. [8] Awards, Honors: On 4 March 1887 in the "State
Capital Gossip" column in The Cleveland Leader a reporter
noted that: "Mr. Charles W. Chesnutt stood at the head of his
class (bar examinations, Columbus, Ohio) having made the high-
est percent in the thorough examination, which was one of the
hardest to which a class of students was ever subjected."[9] On
July 1928, he received the Spingarn Achievement Award for his
pioneer work as a literary artist depicting the life and struggle
of Americans of Negro descent, and for his long and useful career as scholar, worker, and freeman of one of America's
greatest cities."[10] His final novel, The Quarry, was rejected.
He was unable to revise the novel because his health was fail-
ing.   It remained unpublished when he died on 15 November
1932.[11]

BIOGRAPHY
    Frederick Douglass.   Boston: Small, Maynard, 1899; Lon-
        don: K. Paul, French, Trubner & Co., 1899; reprint ed.
        New York: Johnson, 1971*.
    (Periodical):
        "Short Life of Frederick Douglass."   Negro History Bulle-
        tin (December 1938): 19.
CRITICISM BY CHESNUTT
    "A Defamer of His Race."   The Critic 38 (April 1901): 350-
        351.
    "A Plea for the American Negro."   Critic 36 (February 1900):
        160-163.
    "Superstition and Folk-lore of the South."   Modern Culture
        13 (May 1901): 231-235.
NON-FICTION
    The Disfranchisement of the Negro.   New York: J. Pott &

Co., 1903.

(Anthology): Kearns, Black Identity.

(Periodicals)

"Peonage: or the New Slavery." Voice of the Negro 1 (September 1904): 394-397.

"Post Bellum--Pre-Harlem." Part 5 of the Colophon, February 1931, (A Book Collection Quarterly, 1930-37), a lost literary production, an essay. Was later edited by Elmer Adler as Breaking Into Print. New York: Simon Schuster, 1937. Chesnutt's essay was one of twenty by writers of international reputation telling how their first books were published.

"Post-Bellum--Pre-Harlem." Crisis 38 (1931): 193-194.

"Sketch." Current Literature 29 (October 1900): 416.

"A Visit to Tuskegee." Cleveland Leader, 31 March 1901.

"The White and the Black." Boston Transcript, 20 March 1901.

NOVELS

The Colonel's Dream. New York: Doubleday, Page & Co., 1905; reprints are presently available in both hardbound and paperback.

The House Behind the Cedars. Boston: Houghton, Mifflin, 1900; 1901; reprint of 1900 ed., Boston: Gregg, 1968*.

The Marrow of Tradition. Boston: Houghton, Mifflin, 1901. (Several reprints are presently available.) Excerpt in Brown, Davis and Lee, Negro Caravan.

SHORT STORIES

The Conjure Woman. Boston: Houghton, Mifflin, 1899. (Cambridge: Riverside Press, 1899), 1900; 1928; reprint of 1899 ed., Boston: Gregg, 1968*; Ann Arbor: University of Michigan Press, 1969*†.

Render, Sylvia Lyons, ed. The Short Fiction of Charles W. Chesnutt. Washington, D.C.: Howard University Press, 1974*.

The Wife of His Youth, and Other Stories of the Color Line. Boston: Houghton, Mifflin, 1899; 1901; Ann Arbor: University of Michigan Press, 1968*†; Boston: Gregg, 1967*.

(Anthologies): Baker, Black Literature in America; Barksdale and Kinnamon, Black Writers of America; Brown, Davis and Lee, The Negro Caravan; Calverton, An Anthology of American Negro Literature; Chambers and Moon, Right On!; Chapman, Black Voices; Clarke, American Negro Short Stories; Davis and Redding, Cavalcade; Emanuel and Gross, Dark Symphony; Ford, Black Insights; Haslam, Forgotten Pages of American Literature; Hibbard, Addison Clarence, ed., Stories of the South, Old and New (Chapel Hill: University of North Carolina Press, 1931); Hughes, The Best Short Stories of Negro Writers; James, From These Roots; Kearns, Black Identity; Kendricks and Levitt, Afro-American Voices; Long and Collier, Afro-American Writing; Margolies, A Native Sons Reader; Miller, Blackamerican Literature; Simon, Ethnic Writers in America; Singh and Fellowes, Black

Literature in America; Stanford, I Too Sing America;
Turner, Black American Literature: Fiction; Walser,
Gaither, ed. North Carolina in the Short Story (Chapel
Hill: University of North Carolina Press, 1948).
(Periodicals): Atlantic Monthly 60 (August 1887): 254-260;
    64 (October 1889): 500-508; 82 (July 1898): 55-61; 93
    (June 1904): 823-830; Century 61 (January 1901): 422-
    428; Cleveland News and Herald, December 1885; Crisis,
    3 (1912): 248; 9 (1915): 313; 10 (1915): 34; 29 (1924):
    59; 29 (1925): 110; 37 (1930): 153; 77 (November 1970):
    357-361 From Crisis (April-May 1915), Family Fiction,
    The Great Inter-National Weekly Story Paper, 27 Novem-
    ber 1886; Family Fiction, November 1887, n. p.; Outlook
    66 (3 November 1900): 588-593; Two Tales 5 (11 March
    1893): 1-8.
POETRY
    (Periodical): The Cleveland Voice, 1885, n. p.
BIOGRAPHY AND CRITICISM ON CHESNUTT
    Adams. Great Negroes Past and Present, pp. 147-151.
    Allaback, Steven. Black American Literature, 16 (June/
        Fall 1969): 18-20.
    Ames, Russell. "Social Realism in Charles Chesnutt."
        Phylon 14 (1953): 199-206.
    Andrews, William L. "Chesnutt's Patesville: The Presence
        and Influence of the Past in The House Behind the Cedars."
        CLA Journal 15 (March 1972): 284-294.
    Baldwin, R. E. "Art of the Conjure Woman." American
        Literature 43 (November 1971): 385-398.
    Bardolph. The Negro Vanguard, pp. 127, 223.
    Barksdale and Kinnamon. Black Writers of America, pp.
        324-328.
    Bell, Bernard W. "Afro-American Poetry as Folk Art."
        Black World 22 (March 1973): 16-26, 74-83.
    Bone. The Negro Novel in America, pp. 14, 18, 26, 29,
        35-38, 58, 174.
    Bontemps. 100 Years of Freedom, pp. 183-196, 209, 211,
        229, 262.
    Brawley. Negro Builders and Heroes, pp. 64, 234-235, 240.
    _____. Negro Genius, pp. 145-151.
    _____. The Negro in Literature and Art in the United
        States, pp. 76-81.
    Britt, David D. "Chesnutt's Conjure Tales: What You See
        Is What You Get." CLA Journal 5 (March 1972): 269-
        283.
    Brown, Sterling. "In Memorium: Charles Chesnutt." Op-
        portunity 10 (December 1932): 387.
    Burris, A. M. "America's First Edition: Charles Waddell
        Chesnutt." Publisher's Weekly, 131:2033, 1937.
    Butcher. The Negro in American Culture, pp. 129, 216.
    Chametzky and Kaplan. Black and White in American Cul-
        ture, pp. 335, 356, 381.
    Chesnutt, Helen M. Charles Waddell Chesnutt: Pioneer of
        the Color-Line. Chapel Hill: University of North Caro-

lina Press, 1952.

"Chesnutt Marker (Looking and Listening)." Crisis 68 (October 1961): 494-495.

Davis. The American Negro Reference Book, pp. 55, 871-872.

Davis and Redding. Cavalcade.

Dreer, Herman. American Literature by Negro Authors. New York: Macmillan, 1950, pp. 230-241.

Drotning, Phillip P. A Guide to Negro History in America. New York: Doubleday and Co., 1968, p. 145.

DuBois, W. E. B. "Chesnutt." (Postscript) Crisis 40 (1933): 20.

Farnsworth, Robert M. "A New Introduction to The Marrow of Tradition." Ann Arbor: University of Michigan Press, 1969, pp. v-xvii.

_____. "Testing the Color Line--Dunbar and Chesnutt." In Bigsby, The Black American Writer, vol. 1, pp. 111-124, 218.

Gayle. Black Expression, pp. 8, 180-181, 190-191, 229, 231, 234, 260.

"Politics of Revolution: Afro-American Literature." Black World 21 (June 1972): 4-12.

Gloster, Hugh M. "Charles W. Chesnutt: Pioneer in the Fiction of Negro Life." Phylon 2 (First Quarter 1941): 57-66.

Gross. The Heroic Ideal in American Literature, pp. 130, 132, 135.

Hatcher, Harlan. Creating the Modern American Writing. New York: Farrar, Rinehart, 1935, p. 149.

Heermance, J. Noel. Charles W. Chesnutt: America's First Great Black Novelist. Hamden, Conn.: Shoe String Press, forthcoming.

Hemenway. The Black Novelist, pp. 25-32.

Hill. Anger and Beyond, p. 35.

Hovit, Theodore R. "Chesnutt's 'The Goophered Grapevine' as Social Criticism." Negro American Literature Forum 7 (Fall 1973): 86-90.

Howells, William Dean. "Charles W. Chesnutt's Stories." The Atlantic Monthly 85 (May 1900): 699-701. Same condition in Current Literature 28 (June 1900): 277-278.

Huggins. Harlem Renaissance, pp. 200, 232.

Hughes. The Negro Novelist, pp. 34, 39, 42-44, 131, 138, 196, 235.

Hughes and Meltzer. A Pictorial History of the Negro in America, p. 255.

Hugley, G. "Charles Waddell Chesnutt." Negro History Bulletin 19 (December 1955): 54-55.

Jackson, Blyden. "The Negro's Image of the Universe as Reflected in His Fiction." CLA Journal 4 (September 1960): 23-31.

Jahn. Neo-African Literature, pp. 131, 141, 150-151, 154, 204.

Jarrett, D. C. "A Negro Novelist Remembered." Negro

Digest 13 (October 1964): 38-45.

Johnson. _Black Manhattan_, pp. 273, 275, 278.

Jones, LeRoi. _Blues People_. New York: Morrow House, 1963, pp. 58-59, 132.

Kaiser, Ernest. "Literature on the South." _Freedomways_ 4 (Winter 1964): 159.

Keller, Dean H. "Charles Waddell Chesnutt (1858-1932)." _American Literary Realism_ No. 3 (Summer 1968): 1-4.

Kent. _Blackness and the Adventure of Western Culture_, pp. 12-13, 18, 185.

_____. "Patterns of the Renaissance." _Black World_ 21 (June 1972): 13.

Loggins. _The Negro Author in America_, pp. 256, 259, 270-271, 310-315, 318-320, 324, 326-331, 352-353, 360, 398, 400, 403, 405, 440, 443, 452-453.

Margolies. _Native Sons_, pp. 24, 25, 30.

Masare, Julian D., Jr. "Charles W. Chesnutt as Southern Author." _Mississippi Quarterly_ 20 (1967): 77-89.

Mays. _The Negro's God_, pp. 149-151.

Meier. _Negro Thought in America_, pp. 110, 155-156, 243-244, 264-266, 268-269, 275, 277.

Nelson, John H. "Negro Characters in American Literature." _Humanistic Studies at the University of Kansas_, vol. 4. Laurence, Ka.: University Publishers, 1932, pp. 134-136.

Ovington, Mary W. _The Walls Came Tumbling Down_. New York: Schocken Books, 1970, pp. 19, 214, 238.

Parker, John W. "Chesnutt as a Southern Town Remembered Him." _Crisis_ 56 (1949): 205-206, 221.

Pinkney, Alphonso. _Black Americans_. Englewood Cliffs, N.J.: Prentice-Hall, 1969, p. 148.

Redding. _They Came in Chains_, pp. 206, 210.

Rees, Robert A., and Earl N. Harbert, eds. _Fifteen American Authors Before 1900_. Madison: University of Wisconsin Press, 1971, pp. 402-408.

Render, S. L. "North Carolina Dialect: Chesnutt Style." _North Carolina Folklore_ 15 (1967): 67-70.

_____. "Preface." Charles W. Chesnutt, _The Marrow of Tradition_. New York: Houghton Mifflin, 1901, pp. i-vii.

_____. "Tar Heelia in Chesnutt." _CLA Journal_ 9 (September 1965): 39-50.

Reilly, J. M. "Dilemma in Chesnutt's _The Marrow of Tradition_." _Phylon_ 32 (Spring 1971): 31-38.

Shipman, Carolyn. "The Author of _The Conjure Woman_, Charles W. Chesnutt." _The Critic_ 35 (July 1899): 632-634.

Simon, Myron. _Ethnic Writers in America_. New York: Harcourt, Brace Jovanovich, 1972, pp. 79-80.

Sillen, Samuel. "Charles W. Chesnutt: A Pioneer Negro Novelist." _Masses and Mainstream_ 6 (February 1953): 8-14.

Smith, R. A. "Note on the Folktales of Charles W. Chesnutt." _CLA Journal_ 5 (March 1962): 229-232.

Teller, Walter. "Charles W. Chesnutt's Conjuring and Color-

Line Stories." _American Scholar_ 42 (Winter 1972-73):
125-127.

Turner, D. In a Minor Chord, pp. xvi, 2, 117.

_____. "Introduction" to Charles Chesnutt's The House Be-
yond the Cedars. Toronto: Collier-Macmillan, 1969,
pp. xii-xx.

_____. "The Negro Novel in America: In Rebuttal." CLA
Journal 10 (December 1966): pp. 122-134.

Walcott, Ronald. "Chesnutt's 'The Sheriff's Children' as
Parable." Negro American Literature Forum 7 (Fall
1973): pp. 84-85.

Watkins. An Anthology of American Negro Literature, pp.
295-310.

Wideman, John. "Charles W. Chesnutt: The Marrow of
Tradition." American Scholar 42 (Winter 1972-73): 128-
134.

Williams. They Also Spoke, pp. 218-219, 223-225, 238,
248, 262, 270, 276.

REVIEWS: The Conjure Woman
Morgan, Florence. The Bookman 9 (June 1899): 373.
Anon. CLA Journal 36 (1929): 125.
Anon. The Critic 35 (July 1899): 646.
Anon. "Recent Novels." Nation 72 (28 February 1901):
182.

REVIEW: House Behind the Cedars
Nation 72 (28 February 1901): 182.

REVIEWS: The Marrow of Tradition
Bookman 14 (January 1902): 533.
Nation 74 (2 March 1902): 232.

REVIEW: Wife of His Youth
Banks, N. H. Bookman 10 (February 1900): 597-598.

OTHER SOURCES OF PUBLICATIONS[12]

Poetry
1885, several poems in The Cleveland Voice, a weekly.

Sketches
1886 Tidbits.
      Puck.
      Chicago Ledger.
      Household Realm (a paper).

Short Stories
Cleveland News and Herald, December 1885.
Independent, 7 November 1889.
McClure Syndicate, 1885-1888.
Overland Monthly, June 1889.

MEMORIAL
Charles Waddell Chesnutt Collection at the Erastus Milo Cro-
vath Memorial Library, Fisk University, Nashville, Tennessee.
The Collection contains published works, manuscripts, corre-
spondence, journals and scrapbooks.

[1]Richard Barksdale and Keneth Kinnamon, Black
Writers of America (New York: Macmillan, 1972), p.
324.

[2]Abraham Chapman, ed., Black Voices (New York:

The New American Library, 1968): p. 51.
[3]Darwin T. Turner, "Introduction," Charles W. Chesnutt. The House Behind the Cedars (New York: Macmillan Co., 1969), pp. ix-x.
[4]Edgar A. Toppin, A Biographical History of Blacks in America (New York: David McKay, 1971), p. 269.
[5]Turner, pp. x-xi.
[6]Helen Chesnutt, Charles Waddell Chesnutt: Pioneer of the Color-Line (Chapel Hill: University of North Carolina Press, 1952), p. 34.
[7]Ibid., p. 41.
[8]Turner, pp. xi-xii.
[9]Helen Chesnutt, p. 40.
[10]Turner, p. xii.
[11]Ibid., p. xii.
[12]Helen Chesnutt, pp. 39, 40, 49.

CHEW, Birdell see MOORE, Birdell Chew

CHIANESE, Merle Molofsky.
   Writings from the Lower Sonoran Region. n.p.: Awareness Press, 1973.

CHILDRESS, Alice. Born in Charleston, South Carolina. Education: A Radcliffe Alumna through Harvard appointment. Currently living in New York City. Career: Has acted in teleplays, radio, film and stage productions, and was a member of the original American Negro Theatre for ten years. Has directed many plays, beginning with her own one-act play, Florence, in 1951. Wrote a weekly column, "Here's Mildred," published by Afro-American Newspapers, 1956-58. Was a writer-observer with the original companies of "The Sound of Music" and "A Thousand Clowns" on a Rockefeller Grant administered through The New Dramatists. Participated in a British Broadcasting Company presentation of A Roundtable Discussion on Black Theatre with James Baldwin, Imamu Baraka and Langston Hughes. Has lectured at numerous universities, for theatre groups and at public schools, and is well-known for her community volunteer work. Visited Russia in 1971 to study Soviet life and art; visited Mainland China in 1973 to observe the theatre arts in Peking and Shanghai. Member: The Authors League of Actors Equity, American Federation of Television and Radio Artists, community-elected member of Advisory Board of Frances Delafield Community City Hospital, Society of Choreographers and Stage Directors, The Radcliffe Club of New York. Awards, Honors: The Obie Award for the Best Original Off-Broadway production (Trouble in Mind), 1956; Grant, The John Golden Fund for Playwrights, 1957; Harvard Appointment to the Radcliffe Institute as scholar-writer, 1966-1968.
CHILDREN AND YOUNG ADULTS
   A Hero Ain't Nothin' But a Sandwich. New York: Coward, McCann & Geoghegan, 1973*.

CRITICISM BY CHILDRESS
   "Black Writer's Views on Literary Lions and Values." Ne-
      gro Digest, 17 (January 1968): 36.
   "A Negro Playwright Speaks Her Mind." Freedomways 6
      (Winter 1966): 14-19; reprinted in Patterson, Anthology
      of the American Negro in the Theatre.
   "Why Talk About That." Negro Digest 14 (April 1967):   17.
DRAMA
   The African Garden. Scene in Childress, Black Scenes.
   Florence: A One-Act Drama. In Masses and Mainstream
      31 (October 1950):   34-47.
   The Freedom Drum.
   Gold Through the Trees, 1952.
   Just a Little Simple, 1953. (Adaptation of Hughes' Just a
      Little Simple.)
   A Man Bearing a Pitcher.
   Mojo: A Black Love Story. In Black World 2 (April 1971):
      53-82.
   "String" and "Mojo: A Black Love Story." New York: Dra-
      matists Play Service, 1971.
   Trouble in Mind. In Patterson, Black Theater.
   Wedding Band. New York: Samuel French, 1973*.
   Wine in the Wilderness. New York: Dramatists Play Serv-
      ice, 1969*; reprinted in Major Black Writers, Scholastic
      Black Literature Series; Richards, Best Short Plays of
      1972; Sullivan and Hatch, Plays by and about Women.
   The World on a Hill.
   Young Martin Luther King, Jr., 1969.
EDITOR
   Black Scenes: Collection of Scenes from Plays Written by
      Black People about Black Experience. Garden City,
      N.Y.: Doubleday, 1971*†.
NON-FICTION
   (Periodicals): Freedomways 11 (First Quarter 1971); Es-
      sence, May 1971.
SHORT STORIES
   Like One of the Family. Brooklyn, N.Y.: Independence,
      1956. Excerpt in Hughes, The Book of Negro Humor.
   (Anthologies): Clarke, Harlem U.S.A.; Hughes, The Best
      Short Stories by Negro Writers; Miller, Blackamerican
      Literature; The Young America Basic Reading Program
      (Chicago: Lyons and Carnahan, 1972); Success in Reading
      (Morristown, N.J.: Silver-Burdette General Learning
      Corp., 1972.
   (Periodical): Essence, June 1970.
BIOGRAPHY AND CRITICISM ON CHILDRESS
   Abramson. The Negro Playwrights in the American Theatre,
      pp. 187-204, 258-259.
   Harrison. The Drama of Nommo, p. xviii.
   Hughes and Bontemps. Black Magic, pp. 199, 209, 211,
      214, 220, 222, 223.
   Mitchell. Black Drama, pp. 122-127, 130, 145-147, 154,
      168-169, 215-217, 218, 224.

_____. "Three Writers and a Dream." Crisis 72 (April 1965): 219-223.

REVIEWS: Wedding Band

Gottfried, Martin. Women's Wear Daily, 10 October 1972.

Watt, Douglas. Daily News, 27 November 1972.

INTERJECTIONS

"A part of the Black Liberation struggle is to constantly evaluate, or to re-evaluate ground we have covered, making sure that we are not judging our struggle by appearances; substituting appearance for struggle...dashiki, jewelry, language, stance, attitudes, music preferences, soul food,...used in place of concrete action, or used as delaying action because we may not know exactly what to do at the moment. Knowing we are in trouble and knowing we do not exactly know what to do ...is true knowledge and gives us a clean slate to start with. We are a varied people and our ideas are bound to clash...but I remind myself frequently that symbols may trick us."

CHILDRESS, Alvin.
DRAMA With Alice Herndon. Hell's Alley.

CHIMBAMUL. (Jeri Fowler).
DRAMA How the Spider Became the Hero of Folk Tales, 1971. (Children's play).

CHIPASULA, Frank.
POETRY (Anthology): Journal of Black Poetry, Summer 1972.

CHIRI, Ruwa.
POETRY An Acknowledgment of My Afro-American Brother. Chicago: Free Black Press, 1968.

CHISHOLM, Earle.
DRAMA
Black Manhood, 1970.
Two in the Back Room, 1971.

CHISHOLM, William Mason.
POETRY Splintered Darkness. Brooklyn: Trilon Press, 1953.

CHITTICK, Conrad.
POETRY (Anthology): Murphy, Negro Voices.

CHRISTIAN, Marcus. Born 8 March 1900 in Houma, Louisiana. Education: Self-educated since the age of 13. Currently living in New Orleans. Career: Former newspaper writer and frequent contributor to Opportunity and the Louisiana Weekly. Lecturer and librarian at Dillard University for many years, and supervisor of Dillard University's Negro History unit. An authority on the folklore and history of the Black man in Louisiana, he began collecting material during the Depression when working on the Federal Writer's Project. He is presently a Special Lecturer in History and English at Louisiana State Uni-

versity. Awards, Honors: Rosenwald Fellowship, 1943.
NON-FICTION
    Negro Ironworkers of Louisiana, 1718-1900. Gretna, La.:
      Pelican, 1972.
    (Periodical): Phylon, Third Quarter, 1945.
POETRY
    The Common Peoples' Manifesto of World War II. New Or-
      leans: Les Cenelles Society of Arts & Letters, 1948.
    High Ground; a Collection of Poems Published in Commem-
      oration of the United States Supreme Court's Decision of
      May 17, 1954, and Its Final Decree of May 31, 1955,
      Abolishing Racial Segregation in the Nation's Public
      Schools. New Orleans: Southern, 1958.
    In Memoriam, Franklin Delano Roosevelt, 1882-1945. By
      the Author, n.d.
    (Anthologies): Bontemps, American Negro Poetry; Bon-
      temps, Golden Slippers; Hughes and Bontemps, The Po-
      etry of the Negro: 1746-1970; Murphy, Ebony Rhythm;
      Murphy, Negro Poetry. Also published in Cernošská
      Poesie (Edited by Knihovna Vojaka. Praha: Nase Vojski,
      1958).
    (Periodicals): Crisis, June, December 1933; May, June,
      July, September 1934; Opportunity, February, May, July,
      August, September 1937; February 1938; February 1939;
      September, November, December 1941.
BIOGRAPHY AND CRITICISM ON CHRISTIAN
    Peterson, Betsy. "Marcus Christian: Portrait of a Poet."
      Dixie 18 (January 1970).

CHRISTOPHER, James (Nakisaki). Born in Chicago.
    POETRY (Anthology): Murphy, Ebony Rhythm.

CLARK, Benjamin P. Born in a slave state, which he refused to
    identify. Education: One year's tuition at school. Career:
    Was a delegate from his adopted home town, York, to the 1835
    Annual Convention of Free People of Color, in Philadelphia.[1]
    PROSE AND POETRY
    The Past, The Present, The Future. Toronto: n.p., 1867.
    (Anthology): Robinson, Early Black American Poets, 177-
    184.
    BIOGRAPHY AND CRITICISM ON CLARK
    Loggins. The Negro Author, pp. 332-333.
    Robinson. Early Black American Poets, pp. 177-184.
        [1]Wm. N. Robinson, Early Black American Poets, Du-
    buque, Iowa: Brown, 1969, p. 176.

CLARK, Carl. Born 21 November 1932 in Brinkley, Arkansas.
    POETRY (Anthology): Brooks, Jump Bad.

CLARK, China Debra. Born 11 September 1949 in Pennsylvania.
    Education: Studied at Central State University; American Acad-

emy of Dramatic Arts; Martha Graham's School of Dance; The
American Mime Theatre; Al Fann Theatrical Ensemble; New
Lafayette Theater. Currently living in Englewood, New Jersey.
Career: Has written plays for television, stage and screen.
Has given poetry readings and concerts at the Lincoln Center
for the Performing Arts, The Negro Ensemble Company, Tuum
Est Drug Rehabilitation Center, Hilly's, The Poet's Bookshop,
The Other Side, The Black House, The National Urban League,
The Soul! (television show), and at colleges and universities.
Currently coordinator of "Behind the Black Intellect" series at
Columbia University.
DRAMA
     In Madwoman's Room.
     Neffie.
     Perfection in Black, 1972.
     The Sabian.
     Why God Hates Rev. Chandler.
     The Willow Lottery.
POETRY
     Poems from China.   Valveadies, Calif.: California Institute
          of Arts, 1971.
     (Anthologies): Lev, HNY Anthology; Reed, The Yardbird
          Reader, vol. 1.
     (Periodicals): Essence, July 1973; other poetry in The Black
          American; The Black Collegian; San Francisco Intersec-
          tion; The Sunday Sun; The Velvet Glove.
UNPUBLISHED WORK
     Poetry: "Brown Sugar."
WORK IN PROGRESS
     Preparation of play, "In Sorrow's Room," to be presented by
          New Federal Theatre's Workshop in New York City.

CLARK, George W.
     POETRY AND SONGS
          The Harp of Freedom.   New York: Miller, Orton & Mulli-
               gan, 1956.
          The Liberty Minstrel, 1844; New York: Leavit & Alden,
               1845. (Includes original compositions and arrangements
               by G. W. Clark.)

CLARK, John.
     POETRY (Periodical): Journal of Black Poetry, Summer
          1972.

CLARK, Mazie Earhart.
     POETRY
          Life's Sunshine and Shadows.   Cincinnati, Ohio: Eaton, 1940.
          Garden of Memories...Dedicated to My Friends in Memory
               of My Husband Sgt. George J. Clark.   Cincinnati, Ohio:
               Eaton, 1932.

CLARK, Peter Wellington.
POETRY (Anthology): Murphy, Ebony Rhythm.

CLARKE, Helen F.
POETRY (Anthology): Murphy, Ebony Rhythm.

CLARKE, John Henrik. Born 1915 in Union Springs, Alabama.
Career: See "John Henrik Clarke, Writer and Lecturer."
Negro History Bulletin (January 1960): 91-92; Shockley and
Chandler, Living Black American Authors.
CRITICISM BY CLARKE
    "The Alienation of James Baldwin." Journal of Human Re-
        lations 12 (First Quarter 1964): 30-33; reprinted in Gayle,
        Black Expression.
    "Langston Hughes and Jesse B. Semple." Freedomways 8
        (Spring 1968): 167-169.
    "The Neglected Dimensions of the Harlem Renaissance."
        Black World 20 (November 1970): 118-129.
    "Ngugi Wa Thiong'o (James Ngugi)." Freedomways 13
        (Third Quarter 1973): 246-251.
    "The Origin and Growth of Afro-American Literature." Ne-
        gro Digest 17 (December 1967): 54-67; also in Hayden,
        Burrows and Lapides, Afro-American Literature.
    "Paul Laurence Dunbar." Freedomways 12 (Fourth Quarter
        1972): 316-318.
    "Reclaiming the Lost African Heritage." The American Ne-
        gro Writer and His Roots; reprinted in Patterson, An In-
        troduction to Black Literature in America.
    "Transition in the American Negro Short Story." Phylon
        21 (1960): 360-366.
    "The Visible Dimensions of Invisible Man." Black World 20
        (December 1970): 27-30.
EDITOR
    American Negro Short Stories. New York: Hill & Wang,
        1966*†.
    Black Titan: W. E. B. DuBois. Boston: Beacon, 1970.
    Harlem, U.S.A. New York: Macmillan, 1971†.
    Malcolm X. New York: Macmillan, 1969*†.
    William Styron's Nat Turner: Ten Black Writers Respond.
        Boston: Beacon, 1968*†.
NON-FICTION
    Harlem: A Community in Transition. New York: Citadel,
        1969†.
    (Anthologies): Haskins, Manifesto for Black Education;
        Jones and Neal, Black Fire.
    (Periodicals): Black Scholar, February 1973; Black World,
        October, November, 1970; February 1971; February 1973;
        February 1974; March 1974; Essence, May, June, July
        1971; Freedomways, Spring, Fall 1961; Spring 1962; Fall
        1965; 1971; Présence Africaine 87; Harlem Quarterly,
        Winter 1949-50; Journal of Black Poetry, Summer 1973;
        Journal of Human Relations, Autumn 1960; Summer 1962;
        Third Quarter 1970; Journal of Negro Education, Winter

1961; Fall 1962; Spring 1964; Negro Digest, June 1966;
February, March 1967; February, Fall 1968; February,
May, November 1969; February, Fall 1970; Negro History
Bulletin, February 1950; Phylon, Spring, Fall 1962.
POETRY
  Rebellion in Rhyme. Prairie City, Ill.: Decker, 1948.
  (Anthologies): Adoff, The Poetry of Black America; Dee,
    Glow Child; Murphy, Ebony Rhythm; Weisman and Wright,
    Poetry for All Americans.
  (Periodical): Crisis, December 1940.
SHORT STORIES
  (Anthologies): Adoff, Brothers and Sisters; Chambers and
    Moon, Right On!; Clarke, American Negro Short Stories;
    Clarke, Harlem; Hughes, The Best Short Stories by Ne-
    gro Writers; James, From These Roots; Sanchez, We Be
    Word Sorcerers; Simmons and Hutchinson, Black Culture;
    Singh and Fellowes, Black Literature in America.
  (Periodicals): Crisis, September 1941; Freedomways, Sum-
    mer 1963; Summer 1964; Harlem Quarterly, Winter 1949-
    50; Spring 1950; Midwest Journal, September 1952; Op-
    portunity, September, October, December 1939; Septem-
    ber, November 1940.
BIOGRAPHY AND CRITICISM ON CLARKE
  Cruse. The Crisis of the Negro Intellectual, pp. 246-247,
    340-344, 373-374, 506-510.
  Larrabee, Harold A. "The Varieties of Black Experience."
    New England Quarterly 43 (December 1970): 638-645.

CLARKE, Sebastian.
  CRITICISM BY CLARKE
    "Sonia Sanchez and Her Work."   Black World 2 (June 1971):
      44-46†.
  DRAMA
    Heliocentric World.
    Lower Earth.
  POETRY
    (Periodicals): Black World, May 1971; Black Theatre, Ap-
      ril 1970; also published in Journal of Black Poetry.
  REVIEWS BY CLARKE
    (Periodical): Black Theatre 5 (1971).
  SHORT STORY
    (Anthology): Sanchez, We Be Word Sorcerers.
    Also published in Black Creation and Présence Africaine.

CLAY, Buriel II. Born 11 November 1943 in Abilene, Texas.
  Education: B.A., (English) California State University-San
  Francisco; presently a graduate candidate in Film at California
  State University-San Francisco. Has travelled extensively in
  Europe, North Africa, the Virgin Islands, Mexico and Canada.
  Currently living in San Francisco. Career: A film/drama
  critic for local television program (Black Renaissance), Ch.
  44; contributes reviews to San Francisco Sun Reporter (Black
  news weekly); has produced over thirty dramatic productions

Buriel Clay II

in California and one production at the Lincoln Center in New
York City--plays produced include The Creation of the World
(an African ballet); Buy a Little Tenderness (a tragicomedy;
X's (a love story); Jezebelle (a satire).   Also: Artistic Director, West Coast Black Theater Alliance; Regional Editor, Black
Creation; Director, The Black Arts Writer's Workshop in San
Francisco Foundation and the Douglas House Foundation, and
holds classes in creative writing, poetry, playwrighting, art,
history, and Swahili for adults and children).   Recently produced a 45-minute film of Ben Caldwell's play, The Job, for
the San Francisco Neighborhood Arts Program.   Instructor in
film writing at Laney College.   Presently putting together a
text on Blacks in California before 1900 for a television series.
Awards, Honors: Awarded a California State Senate Resolution
for outstanding work in organizing Black Quake 72 (the largest
Black Artistic and Cultural Exposition ever held on the West
Coast); has also received scholarships to writer's conferences;
the play, Buy a Little Tenderness, was chosen to be a part
of New York's Library and Museum of the Performing Arts
Permanent Theatre Collection.
DRAMA
     Buy a Little Tenderness, 1973.
     San Francisco.
     X's (Bridges Over Troubled Waters), 1973.

POETRY
  Broken Pieces of Clay. San Francisco: Black Writer's
    Workshop, n.d.
  (Periodical): Black Art Writer's Workshop Literary Maga-
    zine.
INTERJECTIONS
  "I am very much concerned about the total neglect given by
  the mainstream communication media to West Coast perform-
  ing artists and writers, especially Black Theatre and playwrights.
  The San Francisco Bay Area probably houses more excellent
  theatres and writers than anywhere on the West Coast, and I
  feel we are not receiving proper credit."

CLEAGE, Pearl see LOMAX, Pearl Cleage

CLEAVER, Eldridge. Born 1935 in Wabbaseka, Arkansas. Career:
  See Barksdale and Kinnamon, The Black Writer in America;
  Contemporary Authors 21/22; Ploski, Reference Library of
  Black America, pp. 8-9.
NON-FICTION
  Post-Prison Writings and Speeches. Edited by Robert Scheer.
    New York: Random, 1969†.
  Soul on Ice. New York: McGraw-Hill, 1968*†. Excerpts in
    Austin, Fenderson and Nelson, The Black Man and the
    Promise of America; Davis and Redding, Cavalcade;
    Ford, Black Insights; Gayle, Black Expression; Hemenway,
    The Black Novelist; Kearns, Black Identity; Kendricks,
    Afro-American Writing; Margolies, A Native Sons Reader;
    Miller, Blackamerican Literature; Robinson, Nommo, Sim-
    mons and Hutchinson, Black Culture; Singh and Fellowes,
    Black Literature in America; Watkins and David, To Be a
    Black Woman.
  (Periodicals): Black Scholar, November 1969; October 1971;
    November-December 1972; January 1973; Commonweal, 14
    June 1968; also published in Black Dialogue.
SHORT STORY
  (Periodical): Playboy, December 1969; reprinted in Prize
    Stories 1971: The O'Henry Awards.
BIOGRAPHY AND CRITICISM ON CLEAVER
  Anderson, Jervis. "Race, Rage, and Eldridge Cleaver."
    Commentary 46 (December 1968): 63-69.
  Cunningham, James. "The Case of the Severed Lifeline."
    Negro Digest 18 (October 1969): 23-28.
  Dickstein, Morris. "Wright, Baldwin, Cleaver." New Let-
    ters 38 (Winter 1971): 117-124.
  Hedgepeth, W. "Radicals--Are They Poles Apart," Look, 7
    January 1969, p. 35.
  Jordan, Jennifer. "Cleaver vs. Baldwin: Icing the White
    Negro." Black Books Bulletin 1 (Winter 1972): 13-15.
  Larrabee, Harold A. "The Varieties of Black Experience."
    New England Quarterly 42 (December 1970): 630-645.
  Lockwood, Lee. Conversation with Eldridge Cleaver: Al-
    giers. New York: McGraw-Hill, 1970.

Nower, Joyce. "Cleaver's Vision of America and the New White Radical: A Legacy of Malcolm X." Negro American Literature Forum 4 (March 1970): 12-21.

Pacion, Stanley. "Soul Still on Ice? The Talents and Troubles of Eldridge Cleaver." Dissent 16 (July-August 1969): 310-316.

Parks, Gordon. "Eldridge Cleaver in Algiers, a Visit with Papa Rage." Life, 6 February 1970, pp. 20-23.

Swados, Harvey. "Old Con, Black Panther, Brilliant Writer and Quintessential American." The New York Times Magazine, 7 September 1969, pp. 38-39.

Weinstein, H. E., ed. "Conversation with Cleaver." The Nation, 20 January 1969, pp. 74-77.

CLEAVES, Mary Wilkerson.
POETRY (Anthology): Murphy, Ebony Rhythm.

CLEM, Charles Douglass. Born 10 July 1876 in Johnson City, Tennessee. Died 1934. Education: Attended schools in Kentucky, Oklahoma, and Tennessee. About 1891 he completed a "Common school course" in Oklahoma. Although he supposedly graduated from Greeneville College (now Tusculum), 1898, no attendance record can be found.[1] Career: worked in Kentucky Coal mines; taught two years in Oklahoma; edited Western World (Oklahoma) 1901-02; was assistant steward of the Elks Club in Chanute; was editor of the Coffeyville Vindicator (Kansas), 1904-07;[2] worked for the Santa Fe Railway; became head of the linoleum and rug department of the Rosenthal Department Store, Chanute, 1909-26; and finally, in 1929, did janitorial work for the Rosenthal Mercantile Company. For a time, he travelled through Colorado, Kansas, and Oklahoma lecturing on "metaphysical science"; and also gave poetry recitals. Member: President of the Chanute Chapter, N.A.A.C.P.; an officer in the Masonic Lodge--Prince Hall.[3]
NON-FICTION[4]
Fourteen Years in Metaphysics, 1913.
Oklahoma, Her People and Professions, 1892.
POETRY[5]
"Booker T. Washington." n.p., n.d. (Broadside.)
A Little Souvenir. n.p., 1908.
Rhymes of a Rhymster. Edmond, Okla.: By the Author, 1901.
PROSE AND POETRY
The Upas Tree of Kansas. Chanute, Ka.: Tribune Publ. Co., 1917.
BIOGRAPHY AND CRITICISM ON CLEM
Sherman, Joan R. "A Poet with a Purpose." Negro History Bulletin 34 (November 1971): 163-164.
     [1]Joan R. Sherman, "A Poet with a Purpose: Charles Douglass Clem," Negro History Bulletin 34 (November 1971): 163.
     [2]Ibid., p. 164.
     [3]Ibid., p. 163.

[4]Ibid., p. 164 (cf. author's note under Prose).
[5]Ibid., (cf. author's note under Poetry).

CLEMMONS, Bob.
POETRY (Periodical): Journal of Black Poetry.

CLEMMONS, Carole Gregory. Born 1945 in Youngstown, Ohio.
POETRY
(Anthologies): Adams, Conn and Slepian, Afro-American
Literature: Poetry; Adoff, The Poetry of Black America;
Brown, Lee and Ward, To Gwen with Love; Major, The
New Black Poetry; Shuman, Nine Black Writers; Shuman,
A Galaxy of Black Writing; Watkins, Black Review No. 1.
(Periodical): Black World, September 1971.

CLEMMONS, François.
POETRY
(Anthology): Shuman, A Galaxy of Black Writing.
(Periodicals): Black World, September 1970; September
1971; Negro American Literature Forum, Spring 1972.

CLIFFORD, Carrie Williams. Born in Chillicothe, Ohio. Educa-
tion: at Columbus, Ohio. Career: Editorial and Club Work. [1]
POETRY
Race Rhymes. Washington, D.C.: R. L. Pendleton, 1911.
The Widening Light. Boston: Walter Reid Co., 1922.
(Anthology): Cunard, Negro Anthology, p. 261.
(Periodicals): Crisis 10 (1915): 136; 19 (1920): 193, 336;
34 (1927): 123; Opportunity, July, December 1925.
BIOGRAPHY AND CRITICISM ON CLIFFORD
Kerlin. Negro Poets and Their Poems, p. 272.
REVIEW: The Widening Light
Crisis 29 (1924): 80.
[1]Robert T. Kerlin, Negro Poets and Their Poems,
3rd ed. (Washington, D.C.: Associated Publishers, 1935):
p. 272.

CLIFTON, Lucille. Born 27 June 1936 in Depew, New York. Edu-
cation: Howard University, Fredonia State Teacher's College.
Currently living in Baltimore, Maryland. Career: Participant,
YW-YMCA Poetry Center's Discovery Series, 1969; poetry read-
er at numerous colleges and universities; mother of six chil-
dren.
CHILDREN AND YOUNG ADULTS
The Black B C's. New York: Dutton, 1970*.
Some of the Days in the Life of Everett Anderson. New
York: Holt, Rinehart Winston, 1970*; 1971†.
Everett Anderson's Christmas Coming. New York: Holt,
Rinehart & Winston, 1971*; 1972†.
All Us Come Cross the Water. New York: Holt, Rinehart
& Winston, 1973*.
The Boy Who Didn't Believe in Spring. New York: Dutton,
1973*. Also in Ms. magazine, August 1973.

Don't You Remember?　New York: Dutton, 1973*.
Good, Says Jerome.　New York: Dutton, 1973*.
POETRY
Good Times.　New York: Random, 1970†.
Good News About the Earth.　New York: Random, 1972*†.
(Anthologies): Adoff, The Poetry of Black America; Bell,
　　Afro-American Poetry; Chametzky and Kaplan, Black and
　　White in American Culture; Colley and Moore, Starting
　　with Poetry; Hayden, Burrows & Lapides, Afro-American
　　Literature; Miller, Dices and Black Bones; Randall, The
　　Black Poets; Watkins and David, To Be a Black Woman.
(Periodicals): Black World, August 1970, September 1973;
　　Massachusetts Review, Winter-Spring 1972; Summer 1973;
　　Negro Digest, August 1966.
REVIEW: Good Times.
　　Amini, Johari.　Black World (July 1970): 51-53.
REVIEW: Good News About the Earth.
　　Black World, 12 (February 1973): 77.
INTERJECTIONS
　　"The artist is supposed to tell the truth."

CLIMMONS, Artie.
DRAMA　My Troubled Soul, 1970?

CLINTON, Delores.
POETRY　(Anthology): Murphy, Ebony Rhythm.

CLINTON, Dorothy Randle.
NOVEL　The Maddening Scar: A Mystery Novel.　Boston:
　　Christopher, 1962.

CLINTON, Gloria.
POETRY　Trees Along the Highway.　New York: Comet, 1953.

COBB, Bessie A.
POETRY　(Anthology): Murphy, Negro Voices.

COBB, Charlie.　Born 1944 in Washington, D.C.
NON-FICTION
　　African Notebook: Views on Returning "Home."　Chicago:
　　　　Third World, 1971.　(Pamphlet.)
　　(Periodicals): Black Books Bulletin, No. 4, 1973; Journal
　　　　of Black Poetry, Special Issue 1970-71.
POETRY
　　Everywhere Is Yours.　Chicago: Third World. 1971†.
　　In the Furrows of the World.　Tougaloo, Miss.: Flute Pro-
　　　　ductions, 1967.
　　(Anthology): Adoff, The Poetry of Black America.
　　(Periodicals): Journal of Black Poetry, Special Issue 1970-
　　　　71; Liberation, August 1965.

COBB, Janice.　Born 19 May 1952 in St. Louis, Missouri.　Educa-
　　tion: A pre-med senior at California State University-San Fran-

Janice Cobb (credit: Ralph Flynn)

cisco.   Currently living in San Francisco.   Career: Plans to
enter medical school in 1975.   Has served as women's editor,
San Francisco Sun Reporter.   Member: Black Women Organ-
ized for Action; Community Advisory Board Westside; Community Mental Health.   Awards, Honors: Youth of the Year, 1973;
Greyhound Corporation "Woman of Tomorrow," 1973; San Francisco Representative, National White House Conference for
Youth, 1970.
POETRY
    Yesterdays: The Poems of Janice Cobb.   San Francisco:
        Julian Richardson, n.d.
UNPUBLISHED WORK
    "No Need for Crutches."
INTERJECTIONS
    "I write for Black people.   My poetry is a product of the
environment out of which it and I have evolved--and my poetry
reflects that environment.   It is a complete expression.   Like
the gamut of my emotions, my writings reflect happiness, sad-
ness, joy and anger of my existence."

CODLING, Bess.
    DRAMA
        The Assassin.

Elegy to X (two acts). New York: Amuru, 1973†.
Mama's Crazyhorse Rockin Again. New York: Amuru, 1973†.

COFFEY, John.
POETRY A Negro Speaks of Life: Poetry. Karlsruhe, Germany: n.p., 1961.

COFFIN, Frank Barbour. Born 1871.
POETRY
   Coffin's Poems, with Ajax' Ordeals. Little Rock, Ark.:
     The Colored Advocate, Printers, 1897.
   Factum Factorum. Little Rock, Ark.: n.p., 1947.
BIOGRAPHY AND CRITICISM
   White and Jackson. An Anthology of Verse by American Negroes, p. 217.

COFFMAN, Steven.
DRAMA Black Sabbath. In Negro American Literature Forum
     7 (Fall 1973): 91-102.

COLE, Robert, "Bob." Born 1868 in Athens, Ga. Died 1911.
   Education: Graduated from Atlanta University. Although he
   danced, sang, joked and acted in shows,[1] Cole also wrote dialogue, sketches, lyrics and music; played several musical in-
   struments; frequently directed the shows.[2] He headed a Negro
   stock company in New York from 1901-09. In 1898, with Billy
   Johnson, Cole wrote, produced and directed A Trip to Coon-
   town, the first show ever to be planned, directed, managed,
   and promoted entirely by Blacks. The show opened in New
   York; April 1898, and ran for three years.[3] He wrote the hit
   songs, "The Maiden with the Dreamy Eyes," "Oh, Didn't He
   Ramble," and "Under the Bamboo Tree."
DRAMA (Produced in New York)
   With Glen MacDonough. Belle of Bridgeport, 1900.
   Black Patti's Troubadours, 1897.
   With John S. McNally. Humpty Dumpty, 1904.
   With James Weldon Johnson and John J. McNally. In New-
     port, 1904.
   With Billy Johnson. A Trip to Coontown, 1896.
OPERATTAS
   With Rosamund Johnson. Red Moon, 1908.
   With Rosamund Johnson. The Shoofly Regiment, 1906.
BIOGRAPHY AND CRITICISM ON COLE
   Abramson. Negro Playwrights in the American Theatre, p.
     19.
   Bardolph. The Negro Vanguard, p. 236.
   Butcher. The Negro in American Culture, pp. 56-59.
   Hughes and Meltzer. Black Magic, pp. 48, 52, 53, 70, 71.
   Johnson. Black Manhattan, pp. 90-187 passim.
   Isaacs. The Negro in the American Theatre, p. 31.
   Mitchell. Black Drama, pp. 141, 146-147.
   Toppin. A Biographical History of Blacks in America, pp.
     271-272.

[1]Edgar A. Toppin, A Biographical History of Blacks in America (New York: David McKay, 1971), p. 271.
[2]James Weldon Johnson, Black Manhattan (New York: Alfred A. Knopf, 1940), p. 98.
[3]Toppin, p. 271.

COLEMAN, Anita Scott.
  POETRY
    (Anthologies): Murphy, Negro Voices; Murphy, Ebony Rhythm.
    (Periodicals): Crisis 30 (1925): 224; 36 (1929): 85, 232, 302; 37 (1930): 56, 93; 38 (1931): 199.
  SHORT STORY
    (Periodical): The Crisis, May 1933.

COLEMAN, Carolyn.
  POETRY (Anthology): Boyd, Poems by Blacks, II.

COLEMAN, Ethel.
  POETRY (Anthology): Murphy, Negro Voices.

COLEMAN, Horace Wendell, Jr. (Chaka Shango). Born 4 May 1943 in Dayton, Ohio. Education: B.A. (English), Bowling Green University, 1965; M.F.A. (Creative Writing), Bowling Green University, 1972; additional education--twenty-nine years of blackness in America. Currently living in Athens, Ohio. Career: Assistant Professor of English, Ohio University, teaching creative writing (poetry) and Black literature. As a poet, he is working toward the creation of a "high art" Black poetry which is simple and accessible but rich in poetic materials and Black lore and style. Black poetry (the kind he makes) is "to be dug now and savored later." Has given poetry readings at universities and high schools in Ohio, New York, and Michigan, and edited the little magazine, Black Swamp Review (now defunct).
  CRITICISM
    "Melvin Van Peebles." Journal of Popular Culture 5 (Fall 1972): 368-384.
  POETRY
    (Anthology): Sun Flower Queen, Broadside No. 74. Detroit: Broadside, August 1973.
    (Periodicals), Afro-American Affairs, December 1972; Amython, May 1972; Confrontation, No. 3 (1974); Greenfield Review, Summer 1973; Journal of Black Poetry, Summer 1972; Journal of Popular Culture, Summer 1971; Spring 1973; Mwendo, Fall 1973; Negro American Literature Forum, Winter 1972; Shenandoah, Fall 1973; Stooge, May 1972; Vagabond, May 1972; Wisconsin Review, Summer 1972.
  SHORT STORY
    (Periodical): Black Swamp Review, No. 5 (1970).
  TRANSLATION
    (Periodical): Contemporary Literature in Translation,

Summer 1972.
WORK IN PROGRESS
    Editing a collection of poetry by Black students at Bowling
        Green University; writing a novel: "Black Angel Flying."
INTERJECTIONS
"We are all God--i.e., we struggle to become that good,
honest, etc. There is more struggle than mastery to life--
mastering the struggle is coming to grace--this explains the
'soul' of Black people, Jews, hillbillies, etc. Clarity, brevity,
wit and passion--these are the soul of poetry. Black poetry
should be pro-<u>Black</u> not anti-white."

COLEMAN, James Nelson.
  SCIENCE FICTION
    <u>The Null-Frequency Impulser</u>. New York: Berkley, 1969.
    <u>Seeker from the Stars.</u> New York: Berkley, 1967.

COLEMAN, Jamye H.
  POETRY (Anthology): Murphy, <u>Ebony Rhythm</u>.

COLEMAN, Larry G. <u>Born</u> 8 March 1946 in Gulfport, Mississippi.
<u>Education:</u> A.B., University of Buffalo, 1967; M.A., Indiana
University, 1969; Ph.D., University of Pittsburgh, 1973. <u>Cur-</u>
<u>rently living in</u> Pittsburgh, Pennsylvania. <u>Career:</u> Instructor
in Literature and Drama, Indiana University Upward Bound Program, Summer 1969; Teaching Associate in English, Indiana
University (Bloomington), 1968-69; Instructor in Literature and
Folklore, Division of Culture and Art, Department of Black Studies, University of Pittsburgh, 1969-. Film critic for the <u>Pitts-</u>
<u>burgh Courier.</u> Editor of <u>Black Lines</u>, a journal of Black Stud-
ies published quarterly by the University of Pittsburgh's Black
Studies Department. Also an actor (member of the Indiana University Black Theatre Workshop, Summer 1968) and lecturer (on
Drama and Black Communication, Westminster College, 1970,
and the University of Virginia, 1972). <u>Awards, Honors:</u> New
York State Scholarship Incentive Award, 1963; Cedric Major
Award (Mathematics), 1963; Teaching Fellowship, Indiana University, 1968; Ford Foundation Fellowship for Doctoral Study, and
Provost's Development Fellow, 1971 and 1972; National News-
paper Publishers Award for column on Black film and mass
media.
CRITICISM
    "Comic Strip Heroes: LeRoi Jones and the Myth of Ameri-
        can Innocence." <u>Journal of Popular Culture</u> 3 (Fall 1969):
        191-204.
    "LeRoi Jones' <u>Tales:</u> Sketches of the Artist." <u>Black Lines</u>
        1 (Winter 1970): 17-26.
    "The Bad Nigger Social Type: His Essence and Importance
        in the Black Community." Doctoral Dissertation, Univer-
        sity of Pittsburgh, 1973.
INTERJECTIONS
"It is imperative that many of us who are sensitive to the
kind of communicating power residing in the works of any black

artist must try to integrate that power into a carefully woven edifying tapestry. We must be mindful that black peoples' understanding of themselves and their direction may well proceed from an understanding of their thought and feeling, the circumstances and possibilities expressed within their art and an exact awareness of the nature and operations of structures and institutions from which their experience, hence their art, derives." (Black Lines.)

COLEMAN, Wanda. Career: Apprentice at Studio Watts (Los Angeles) for three years, and Editorial Coordinator, Studio Watts Publications. Wrote a television script for "Name of the Game," 1970, and contracted with Levy-Gardner-Laven to do a screenplay of The Girl.
DRAMA
   Black Girl in Search of God.
   The Girl.
   With Lee Williams and Frank Joseph. The Product.
   Song/Dance of Nommo (The Magic Power of Words).
NON-FICTION
   (Periodical): Black Theater, 1972.
POETRY
   (Periodical): Journal of Black Poetry (Winter-Spring 1970).
SHORT STORY
   (Periodical): Negro Digest, February 1970.
INTERJECTIONS
   "I have one desire--to write. And, through writing control, destroy, and create social institutions. I want to weld the power that belongs to the pen."

COLLIER, Eugenia. Born 6 April 1928 in Baltimore, Maryland. Career: See Shockley and Chandler, Living Black American Authors, p. 32.
CRITICISM
   "The Endless Journey of an Ex-Colored Man." Phylon 32 (Fourth Quarter 1971): 365-373.
   "Heritage from Harlem." Black World 19 (November 1970): 52-59.
   "I Do Not Marvel, Countee Cullen." CLA Journal 11 (September 1967): 73-87; also in Gibson, Modern Black Poets.
   "James Weldon Johnson: Mirror of Change." Phylon 21 (Winter 1960): 351-359.
   "The Nightmare Truth of an Invisible Man." Black World 21 (June 1972): 28-34.
   "A Pain in His Soul: Simple as Epic Hero." In Langston Hughes: Black Genius. Edited by Therman O'Daniel. New York: Morrow, 1971.
   "The Phrase Unbearably Repeated." Phylon 25 (1964): 288-296.
EDITOR
   With Richard A. Long. Afro-American Writing: An Anthology of Prose and Poetry. New York: New York University, 1972†.

With Ruth T. Sheffey. <u>Impressions in Asphalt: Images of Urban America in Literature</u>. Scribner, 1969†.
POETRY
(Periodical): <u>Black World</u>, November 1971; September 1970.
REVIEWS BY COLLIER
Published in <u>Black World</u>.
SHORT STORIES
(Anthology): Adoff, <u>Brothers and Sisters</u>.
(Periodicals): <u>Black World</u>, July 1971; <u>Negro Digest</u>, November 1969; August 1972.
TEXTBOOK
With Joel Glasser, Edward Meyers, George Steele, and Thomas L. Wolf. <u>A Bridge to Saying It Well</u>. Springfield, Va.: Norvec, 1970.

COLLIER, Simone.
DRAMA
<u>In a City</u>.
<u>Straw/Baby with Hay Feet</u>.

COLLINS, Durward. <u>Born</u> 11 July 1937 in Houston, Texas. <u>Education</u>: B.A., University of Michigan, 1959; M.S. in Education, City College of New York, 1973. <u>Currently living in</u> Nyack, New York. <u>Career</u>: Educational Consultant for Wiltwyck School for Boys and for the Union Free School District #11 (North Westchester County). Wrote song lyrics to "G'won Train" and "It's the Truth...Nothing But the Truth" published by Duchess Music Corp. (subsidiary of Leeds Music Corp.). <u>Awards, Honors</u>: Recipient, Jules and Avery Hopwood Poetry Grant, University of Michigan, 1959.
POETRY
(Anthology): Pool, <u>Beyond the Blues</u>.
(Periodicals): <u>Chelsea</u>, vols. 8 and 29; <u>The Sixties</u>, Spring 1962; <u>Quadrant</u>.
INTERJECTIONS
"I am not a poet, but I do write poems occasionally; enjoy counseling delinquent boys and also minority-group college students; I will most probably write poems 'off and on' for the rest of my life, no matter what efforts I employ to earn my livelihood."

COLLINS, Harry Jones.
POETRY <u>From Shadow to Sunshine</u>. Indianapolis: The Indianapolis Recorder Print, 1918.

COLLINS, Helen Johnson. <u>Born</u> 1918 in Hampton, Virginia.
POETRY (Anthologies): Hughes and Bontemps, <u>The Poetry of the Negro: 1746-1970</u>; Murphy, <u>Negro Voices</u>.

COLLINS, Leslie Morgan. <u>Born</u> 1914 in Alexandria, Louisiana.
POETRY (Anthologies): Bontemps, <u>American Negro Poetry</u>; Hughes and Bontemps, <u>The Poetry of the Negro: 1746-1790</u>; Pool, <u>Beyond the Blues</u>; Walrond and Pool, <u>Black and Unknown Bards</u>.

COLLINS, Pauline. <u>Born</u> 4 April 1930 in Youngstown, Ohio. <u>Cur-</u>
<u>rently living in</u> Fort Worth, Texas. <u>Career:</u> Presently a stu-
dent of poetry with a special interest in modern works and existentialism. Has given original poetry readings on television
and a recital at Canturbury House in Fort Worth.
POETRY
    (Periodicals): <u>American Scholar</u>, Fall 1971; also published
       in <u>Black Scholar.</u>
INTERJECTIONS
    "Writing or any of the other art-forms should never be a
retreat from, but rather an expression of, the times.... Man
has always received his enlightenment while in a dark and dis-
mal crypt.... The Empire is indeed Dying! There is time to
save it, but not much."

COLTER, Cyrus. <u>Born</u> 8 January 1910 in Noblesville, Indiana.
<u>Education:</u> Attended Youngstown College and Ohio State Univer-
sity; LL.B., Chicago Kent College of Law, 1940. <u>Currently</u>
<u>living in</u> Chicago, Illinois. <u>Career:</u> Worked with YMCA's in
Youngstown and Chicago, 1932 to 1940. Admitted to the practice of law in 1940. Served as Deputy Collector of Internal
Revenue until 1942. Entered military service where he at-
tained rank of captain. After four years of military service returned to law practice in Chicago. Appointed Assistant Commissioner of the Illinois Commerce Commission in 1950; full
Commissioner from 1951 to the present. <u>Member:</u> Chairman
of the Illinois Emergency Transport Board; member of the Illinois Resources Planning Committee; member of the Committee
on Railroads of the National Association of Regulatory Utility
Commissions. Also a member of Kappa Alpha Psi fraternity,
NAACP, Chicago Urban League; former member of the Friends
of the Chicago Schools Committee and member of the Board of
Directors; former member of the Board of Trustees of Illinois
Children's Home and Aid Society; Vice Chairman of the Citi-
zen's Committee for the Chicago Public Library; Chicago Bar
Association; The Cliff Dwellers Club; Board of Trustees of the
Chicago Symphony Orchestra; Commercial Club of Chicago.
<u>Awards, Honors:</u> Received award from The Friends of Litera-
ture, Chicago; Patron Saints Award of the Society of Midland
Authors; $1000 Iowa School of Letters Award for short fiction,
1970.
NOVELS
    <u>River of Eros.</u> Chicago: Swallow, 1972*; Philadelphia:
      Curtis, 1973†.
    <u>The Hippodrome.</u> Chicago: Swallow, 1973*.
POETRY
    (Periodical): <u>Chicago Review</u>, 1973.
SHORT STORIES
    <u>The Beach Umbrella.</u> Iowa City: University of Iowa Press,
      1970*; Chicago: Swallow, 1971†.
    (Anthologies): Chapman, <u>New Black Voices</u>; Hill, <u>Soon One</u>
      <u>Morning</u>; Hughes, <u>The Best Short Stories by Negro Writers</u>;
      Morgan, <u>Here and Now II.</u>

(Periodicals): Chicago Review; Epoch; Prairie Schooner.
BIOGRAPHY AND CRITICISM ON COLTER
"Black Writer's Views on Literary Lions and Values." Negro Digest 17 (January 1968): 34.
Kent. "Outstanding Works," pp. 314-317.
O'Brien, John. "Forms of Determinism in the Fiction of Cyrus Colter." Studies in Black Literature 4 (Summer 1973): 24-28.
_____. Interviews with Black Writers, pp. 17-33.
REVIEW: The Beach Umbrella.
Randall, Dudley. Black World (November 1970): 67-68.
REVIEW: The River of Eros.
Choice 10 (March 1973): 90.
Watkins, Mel. New York Times Book Review, 14 July 1972, p. 32.

CONLEY, Cynthia see ZUBENA, Sister

CONNER, Charles H. Born 1864 in Grafton, New York. Education: Self-educated. Career: Worked in the shipyards of Philadelphia; became a preacher.[1]
WORKS
The Enchanted Valley: A Series of Three Sermonettes that Have Helped Me to Understand Life, Death and Destiny. Philadelphia: C. H. Conner, 1917.
BIOGRAPHY AND CRITICISM ON CONNER
Kerlin. Negro Poets and Their Poems, pp. 225-229.
    [1]Robert T. Kerlin, Negro Poets and Their Poems, 3rd ed. (Washington, D.C.: Associated Publishers, 1935), p. 335.

CONYUS. Born 2 November 1942 in Detroit. Education: public school graduate, a college senior dropout; educated in prison. Currently living in San Francisco.
POETRY
(Anthologies): Adoff, The Poetry of Black America; Chapman, New Black Voices; Harper, Heartblows; Miller, Dices and Black Bones; Wilentz and Weatherly, Natural Process.
(Periodicals): Beatitude; Black Dialogue; North Dakota Review; Ramparts; Scanlan's Monthly; Soul Book.
INTERJECTIONS "(for Michael's violin)"
"the universe is infinite,
the earth is a circle.
everything is a cycle,
birth, death, love, hate,
evolution and destruction.
. . .

the sensitive absorb and collect.
they create beauty and balance.
they use their tools of annexation
with emotion, sensibility and a deep
commitment for peace, some expand

the void and fill it with tranquility,
while shadows of others direct you to the sun.
peace and tranquility communicate frequency.
music is compassionate voltage infinitely powerful.
music is magic, juju, and a spiritual source of love.
it can destroy moon vehicals and automotive pressures.
it can erase the judas of social warfare and
internal darkness; there is a direction to the light,
perspective of spiritual change and consciousness of harmony
. . .

    everything is a cycle
    land
    spirit
    light. "

CONYUS, James.
   POETRY (Periodical): Black Scholar, April-May 1971.

COOK, Douglas. Born 1927.
   Choker's Son. New York: Comet, 1959.

COOK, Gayla.
   POETRY (Periodical): Journal of Black Poetry, Special Issue
     1970-71.

COOK, Mercer. Born 30 March 1903 in Washington, D.C. Career:
   See Shockley and Chandler, Living Black American Authors, p.
   34; Ploski and Kaiser, The Negro Almanac, 1971, p. 287.
   CRITICISM
     Five French Negro Authors. Washington, D.C.: Associated,
      1943.
     The Haitian Novel. New York: Gordon, n.d.
     "The Literary Contribution of the French West Indian Ne-
      gro." Journal of Negro History 25 (October 1940): 520-
      530.
     With Stephen Henderson. The Militant Black Writer in Af-
      rica and the United States. Madison: University of Wis-
      consin Press, 1969†.
     "Trends in Recent Haitian Literature." Journal of Negro
      History 32 (January 1947): 220-231.
   EDITOR
     The Haitian-American Anthology: Haitian Readings from
      American Authors. Port-au-Prince, Haiti: Imprimerie
      de l'état, 1944.
     An Introduction to Haiti. Washington, D.C.: Department of
      Cultural Affairs, Pan American Union, 1951.
     Le Noir: Morceaux Choisis de Vingt-Neuf Français Célèbres.
      New York: American Book Co., 1934.
     Portraits Américains. Boston, New York: D. C. Heath,
      1939.
   NON-FICTION
     Education in Haiti. Washington, D.C.: Federal Security
      Agency, Office of Education, 1948.

Handbook for Haitian Teachers of English.   Port-au-Prince:
     H. Deschamps, 1944?
(Anthologies): Cook and Bellegarde, The Haitian-American
     Anthology.
(Periodicals): Journal of Human Relations, Spring-Summer
     1960; Negro Digest, September, November 1943; Novem-
     ber 1944; Opportunity, April, October 1939; February,
     September, November 1941; Phylon, Third Quarter 1941;
     Third Quarter, 1943; Fourth Quarter, 1948; Second
     Quarter 1954.
POETRY
(Periodicals): Phylon, Second Quarter, Third Quarter 1942.
BIOGRAPHY ON COOK
     "Ambassador Mercer Cook (Looking and Listening)." Crisis
          70 (December 1963): 603-605.
     Christmas. Negroes in Public Affairs and Government, pp.
          213-214.
     "Haiti's Youngest Ambassador." Crisis 64 (April 1957):
          215-218.
     Ploski. Negro Almanac, pp. 606-607.
     Robinson. Historical Negro Biographies, p. 176.

COOK, Mike. Born March 1939 in Chicago.
     POETRY
     (Anthology): Brooks, Jump Bad.
     (Periodical): Journal of Black Poetry, Fall-Winter 1971;
          Nommo.

COOK, Will Marion. Born 1869 in Washington, D.C. Died 1944.
     Education: Attended Oberlin Preparatory School;[1] studied the
     violin at Hochschule, Berlin, Germany.[2] Returning to the
     United States, he continued his musical career at the New York
     Conservatory of Music.[3] Later, he pioneered with jazz orches-
     tras, trained and directed the Memphis Students band. It be-
     came the first jazz band to play a theatre engagement, appear-
     ing at Proctor's Theatre in New York, 1905, before going on
     tour to Europe. He also formed the American Syncopated Or-
     chestra which played a long engagement at New York's 44th
     Street Theatre; he gave concerts in Berlin, London, and Paris.[4]
     DRAMA
          (Musicals)
          With George Walker. Abyssinia, 1906.
          With George Walker. Bandanna Land, 1907.
          With Paul Laurence Dunbar. Clorindy--The Origin of the
               Cake-Walk, 1898.
          With George Walker. In Dahomey, 1902.
          Jes Lak White Folk: A Musical Playlet, 1899.
          With J. A. Shipp. The Policy Players, 1900.
     POPULAR SONGS
          "Bon Bon Buddy."
          "I May Be Crazy But I Ain't No Fool."
     BIOGRAPHY AND CRITICISM ON COOK
          Bardolph. The Negro Vanguard, pp. 236, 294-295, 319.

Butcher. The Negro in American Culture, pp. 57-59, 66,
    70, 152.
Johnson. Black Manhattan, pp. 102-103, 107, 115-119, 121.
Mitchell. Black Drama, pp. 47, 49, 50, 61.
Negro History Bulletin (February 1939): 35.
Robinson. Historical Negro Biographies, pp. 66-67.
Toppin. A Biographical History of Blacks in America, pp.
    271-272.
    [1]Richard Bardolph, Negro Vanguard (New York: Vin-
tage Books, 1959), p. 236.
    [2]James Weldon Johnson, Black Manhattan (New York:
Alfred A. Knopf, 1940), p. 117.
    [3]Wilhelmena S. Robinson, Historical Negro Biogra-
phies (New York: Publishers Co., 1969), p. 66.
    [4]Edgar A. Toppin, A Biographical History of Blacks
in America (New York: David McKay Co., Inc., 1971),
p. 272.

COOLIDGE, Fay Liddle.
    NOVEL Black Is White. New York: Vantage, 1958.

COOMBS, Orde M. Born in St. Vincent, West Indies. Education:
    B.A., Yale University, 1965; M.A., New York University,
    1971; also studied at Clare College, Cambridge (England) 1965-
    66. Currently living in New York City. Career: Producer
    of several photo-theatrical documentaries examining the dynam-
    ics of social change in West Indian society (including Carib
    Lives and The Hill), 1958-61. Associate Editor, Doubleday and
    Company, 1966-68. Senior Public Relations Specialist, West-
    ern Electric Company, New York City, 1968-69. Senior Edi-
    tor, The McCall Publishing Company, New York City. Pres-
    ently writing several screenplays and a novel.
    EDITOR
        Is Massa Day Dead? Black Moods in the Caribbean. Gar-
            den City, N.Y.: Doubleday, 1974.
        We Speak as Liberators: Young Black Poets. New York:
            Dodd, 1970*; New York: Apollo, 1971†.
        What We Must See: Young Black Storytellers. New York:
            Dodd, Mead, 1971*; New York: Apollo, 1971†.
    NON-FICTION
        Do You See My Love for You Growing? New York: Dodd,
            Mead, 1972*.
        With John H. Garabedian. Eastern Religions in the Electric
            Age. New York: Grosset and Dunlap, 1968*.
        With Chester Higgins, Jr. Drums of Life. Garden City,
            N.Y.: Doubleday, 1974. (Photographic Essay.)
    (Anthology): Watkins, Black Review No. 2.
    (Periodicals): Black World, May 1972; Change; Cosmopoli-
        tan; Encore; Esquire, February 1974; Harper's, January
        1972; McCall's, September 1973; New York, 20 November
        1972; New York Times, 27 January 1971; Redbook, No-
        vember 1972, March 1972.

Orde Coombs (credit: Chester Higgins, Jr.)

SHORT STORY
    (Periodical): Essence, May 1971.
INTERJECTIONS
    "I believe in optimism. I do not relish despair. I see the
lives of black Americans as thundering affirmations of the abil-
ity of the human spirit to prevail. I see black American history as a history of triumph, a chapter written in blood and
resilience and scattered in the wind for the world to look at and
marvel that man, finally, never can accept the debasement of
himself."

COOPER, Alvin Carlos. Born 1925.
NOVEL Stroke of Midnight. Nashville, Tenn.: Hemphill, 1949.

COOPER, Dr. Anna Julia. Born 10 August 1859 in Raleigh, North
    Carolina. Died 27[1] February 1964. Education: St. Augustine
    N. and C. Institute, 1881; B.A., Oberlin College, 1884; M.A.,
    1887; took Extension course from Columbia University, 1913-16;
    studied at Guilde Internationale, Paris, 1911-12; Ph.D., Sor-
    bonne University, Paris, 1925. Career: Taught at Oberlin
    Academy, 1882-84; taught French and German at Wilberforce
    University, 1884-85; Latin, Greek and Mathematics, St. Augus-
    tine N. and C. Institute, 1885-87; taught summer schools in Cot-
    tage City, Mass., Wilberforce, Ohio, Raleigh, N.C.; State
    Teachers Association, Hampton, Va.; Jefferson City, Mo.; Indi-
    anapolis, Ind.; Wheeling, W.Va.; Principal of M. Street High
    School, Washington, D.C., 1901-06; Professor of Languages,
    Ancient and Modern, Lincoln University, Mo., 1906-11; Super-
    visor, Colored Social Settlement, 1906-07; 1911-17; Teacher at
    Dunbar High School, Washington, D.C., 1911-30; retired June
    1930.[2] She was President of Frelinghuysen University, a school
    for employed Negroes, which she ran from her own home. She
    was 104 when she died.[3]
EDITOR
    Charlemagne. Voyage à Jérusalem et à Constantinople. Le
        pèlerinage de charlemagne, publié avec un glossaire par
        Anna J. Cooper; Paris: A. Lahure, 1925 (old French and
        modern French verse).
    The Life and Writings of the Grimké Family. Cooper, 1951.
NON-FICTION
    L'Attitude de la France a l'égard l'Esclavage pendant la
        Révolution. Paris: Imprimerie de la Cour d'Appel, 1925.
        (Measures concerning Slavery in the United States, 1787-
        1850. Equality in the Democratic Movement.)
    "Social Settlement." Reprint. Oberlin Alumni Journal.
    A Voice from the South--By a Black Woman of the South.
        Xenia, Ohio: Aldine Printers, 1892.
BIOGRAPHY AND CRITICISM ON COOPER
    Dannett. Profiles of Negro Womanhood, p. 245.
    Majors. Noted Negro Women, 1971, pp. 284-287.
    Ploski and Kaiser. The Negro Almanac. 2nd ed., pp. 873-
        874.
    Yenser. Who's Who in Colored America. 5th ed., p. 133.

(Periodical): <u>Jet,</u> 12 August 1965, p. 11.
    [1]Editors of <u>Ebony,</u> Compilers for the <u>Negro Handbook</u>
Chicago: Johnson Publishing Co., 1966, p. 422, list February 29 as the day Dr. Anna Cooper died.
    [2]Thomas Yenser, ed., <u>Who's Who in Colored America,</u>
5th ed. (New York: Yenser, 1938-1940), p. 133.
    [3]Harry A. Ploski and Ernest Kaiser, <u>The Negro Al-</u>
<u>manac,</u> 2nd ed. (New York: Bellwether Co., 1971), p.
874.

COOPER, Charles B. <u>Born</u> 1948 in Oakland, California.
    POETRY (Anthologies): Adoff, <u>The Poetry of Black America;</u>
        Adoff, <u>Black Out Loud;</u> Shuman, <u>A Galaxy of Black Writ-</u>
        <u>ing.</u>

COOPER, Clarence L., Jr.
    NOVELS
        <u>Black! Two Short Novels.</u> Evanston, Ill.: Regency, 1963.
        <u>The Dark Messenger.</u> Evanston, Ill.: Regency, 1962.
        <u>The Farm.</u> New York: Crown, 1967; New York: Universal
            Publishing & Distributing Corp., 1970†.
        <u>The Scene.</u> New York: Crown, 1960.
        <u>Weed.</u> Evanston, Ill.: Regency, 1961.
    SHORT STORY
        (Anthology): King, <u>Black Short Story Anthology.</u>
    REVIEW: <u>The Farm</u>
        Barrow, William. <u>Negro Digest</u> 17 (May 1968): 94-95.

COOPER, John L.
    NOVEL <u>Opus One.</u> New York: Maelstrom, 1966.

COOPER, William.
    NOVEL
        <u>Thank God for a Song: A Novel of Negro Church Life in</u>
        <u>the Rural South.</u> New York: Exposition, 1962.
    REVIEW: <u>Thank God for a Song.</u>
        Abernathy, Dorothy. <u>Community</u> 23 (October 1963): 11.

COPELAND, Josephine.
    POETRY (Anthology): Bontemps, <u>Golden Slippers.</u>

CORBETT, Maurice Nathaniel. <u>Born</u> 1859 in Yanceville, N.C.
    <u>Education:</u> Common schools; Shaw University. <u>Career:</u> Clerk
    in the Census Bureau, then in the Government Printing Office,
    Washington, D.C.[1]
    POETRY
        <u>The Harp of Ethiopia.</u> Nashville, Tenn.: The National Bap-
        tist Publishing Board, 1914.
        [1]Robert T. Kerlin, <u>Negro Poets and Their Poems</u>
    (Washington, D.C.: Associated Pub., Inc., 1935).

CORBIN, Lloyd. (Djangatolum.) <u>Born</u> 1949 in Harlem, New York.
    <u>Education:</u> B.A., Brandeis University, 1973; Ed.M., Harvard

University, 1974. Currently living in New York City. Career:
An educational media specialist. His song, "The White Horse,"
was recorded on The Me Nobody Knows musical album (Atlantic
Recording Corp., 1970). His poem, "The White Horse," ap-
peared in the off-Broadway, Broadway, and international pro-
ductions of the play, The Me Nobody Knows. Awards, Honors:
Langston Hughes Poetry Scholarship, 1968; Eugene M. Warren
Poetry Prize, 1973.
POETRY
    (Anthologies): Adoff, Black Out Loud; Adoff, The Poetry of
        Black America; Jordan, Soulscript; Joseph, The Me No-
        body Knows.
    (Newspaper): The Boston Globe.
    (Periodicals): Black at Brandeis; Black Reflection; C.A.W.;
        Look Magazine; What's Happening Magazine; The Writer's
        Workshop Anthology.

CORBO, Dominic R., Jr.
    NOVEL Hard Ground. New York: Vantage, 1954.

CORNELL, Adrienne.
    SHORT STORY (Anthology): Beier, Black Orpheus.

CORNISH, Sam. Born 1938 in Baltimore, Maryland. Career: See
    Shockley and Chandler, Living Black American Authors, pp. 34-
    35.
    CHILDREN AND YOUNG ADULTS
        Your Hand in Mine. New York: Harcourt, Brace & World,
            1970*.
    EDITOR
        With Lucien W. Dixon. Chicory: Young Voices from the
            Black Ghetto. New York: Association, 1969†.
        With Hugh Fox. The Living Underground. East Lansing,
            Mich.: Ghost Dance Press, 1969. (Poetry.)
    POETRY
        Angles. Baltimore: n.p., 1967.
        Generations. 2nd Printing. Baltimore: Multi-Service, 1967;
            Boston: Beacon, 1971*.
        In This Corner: Sam Cornish and Verses. n.p.: Fleming-
            McAllister, 1964.
        People Beneath the Window. Baltimore: Sacco, 1965?
        Winters. Cambridge, Mass.: Sans Souci, 1967.
        (Anthologies): Adoff, The Poetry of Black America; Jones
            and Neal, Black Fire; Major, The New Black Poetry;
            Wilentz and Weatherly, Natural Process.
        (Periodicals): Journal of Black Poetry; Massachusetts Re-
            view; New American Review.

CORROTHERS, James David. Born 2 July 1869 in Chain Lakes
    Settlement, Michigan. Died 12 February 1917.[1] Education:
    Attended school at South Haven, Michigan from 1874-83; attended
    Northwestern University, 1890-93; Bennett College, Greensboro,
    N.C. Career: Worked in lumber camps, sawmills, hotels,

sailed the lakes a season; was a bootblack, coachman, boxing
instructor, and a janitor in a newspaper office. He also
worked on the Chicago Record; Daily News and Journal. In
1893 he became minister of a Methodist Church; later an ordained minister of the Baptist Church. In 1914 became a minister in the Presbyterian Church. [2]

FICTION
>The Black Cat Club: Negro Humor and Folk-Lore. New
>York: Funk and Wagnalls Co., 1902. (The Sketches con-
>tributed as articles first appeared in a series of News-
>paper Sketches and in the Chicago Daily Newspapers.)
>Reprint ed., New York: AMS Press*.

NON-FICTION
>In Spite of the Handicap: An Autobiography. New York:
>George H. Doran Co., 1916; reprint ed. New York:
>Negro Universities Press*.

POETRY
>The Dream and the Song, 1914. [3]
>Selected Poems, 1907. [4]
>(Anthologies): Brown, Davis and Lee, Negro Caravan; Calver-
>ton, Anthology of American Negro Literature; Davis and
>Redding, Cavalcade; Hughes and Bontemps, The Poetry
>of the Negro: 1746-1970; Johnson, The Book of Ameri-
>can Negro Poetry; Kendricks and Levitt, Afro-American
>Voices; Kerlin, Negro Poets and Their Poems; Robinson,
>Early Black American Poets; Singh and Fellowes, Black
>Literature in America; Wagner, Black Poets in the
>United States; Walrond and Pool, Black and Unknown
>Bards; White and Jackson, An Anthology of Verse By
>American Negroes.
>(Periodicals): Crisis 5 (1913): 121; 6 (1913): 39, 8 (1914):
>79, 80; 9 (1915): 138; 10 (1915): 304; Voice of the Negro
>6 (April 1904): 156; 6 (June 1904): 247; 7 (January 1905):
>686; 7 (March 1905): 186; 9 (June 1907): 264. Also pub-
>lished in Century Magazine.

SHORT STORIES
>(Periodicals): Crisis 7 (1913): 85; 7 (1914), 136; 41 (1934):
>159.

BIOGRAPHY AND CRITICISM ON CORROTHERS
>Anon. "J. D. Corrothers." Crisis 9 (1915); 116.
>Bardolph. The Negro Vanguard, pp. 202-203, 206.
>Barton. Witnesses for Freedom, pp. 18-23.
>Brawley. Negro Genius, pp. 167-168.
>Eleazer, Robert B. Singers in the Dawn, pp. 6-7.
>Emanuel and Gross. Dark Symphony, p. 10.
>Gayle. Black Expression, pp. 111, 222.
>Gross. The Heroic Ideal in American Literature, p. 129.
>Kerlin. Negro Poets and Their Poems, pp. 37, 85-89.
>White and Jackson. An Anthology of Verse By American
>Negroes, pp. 21, 217-218.
>Wagner. Black Poets of the United States, p. 76.

REVIEWS ON CORROTHERS' WORKS
>Anon. "In Spite of the Handicap." Crisis 13 (1917): 133.

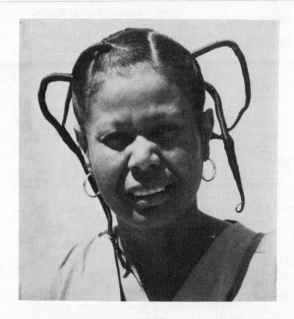

Jayne Cortez

[1] Vernon Calverton in Anthology of American Negro Literature, p. 530, and Robert T. Kerlin in Negro Poets and Their Poems, p. 335, cite 1919 as the year of Corrothers' death.

[2] Newman Ivey White and Walter Clinton Jackson, An Anthology of Verse By American Negroes (Durham, N.C.: Moore, 1924), p. 163.

[3] Ibid.

[4] Ibid.

CORTEZ, Jayne. Born 10 May 1936 in Arizona. Currently living in Arizona. Career: A co-founder of the Watts Repertory Theater in Los Angeles; a jazz singer and an actress. Has travelled within the Third World (India, Japan, Africa) and has given poetry readings and lectures at numerous colleges and universities as well as at the Chicago Art Institute, Countee Cullen Library (Harlem), Liberty House (Harlem), The East (Brooklyn), Lincoln Center, Public Theatre (N.Y.C.), The Billie Holiday Theatre, "The Soul Show" (NET Television). She also read her poetry to an accompaniment by the Clifford Thornton New Art Ensemble at Carnegie Hall, 1970. Awards, Honors: New York State Council on the Arts Creative Artist Award for Poetry, 1973.

POETRY
<u>Pissstained Stairs and the Monkey Man's Wares</u>.   New York:
      Phrase Text. 1969.
<u>Festivals and Funerals</u>.   New York: Phrase Text, 1971.
(Anthologies):   Adoff, <u>The Poetry of Black America;</u> Coombs,
      <u>We Speak as Liberators</u>; Patterson, <u>A Rock Against the</u>
      <u>Wind</u>; Chapman, <u>New Black Voices; Discourses on Poetry</u>,
      Vol. 6.
(Periodicals):   <u>Black World</u>, September 1971; <u>Negro Ameri-</u>
      <u>can Literature Forum,</u> Spring 1972; <u>Negro Digest</u>, Sep-
      tember 1969; other poems in <u>American Dialog</u>; <u>Black Dia-</u>
      <u>logue; Confrontation; Mundus Artium; Pan African Journal</u>;
      <u>Umbra; Works</u>.
REVIEW
<u>Pissstained Stairs and the Monkey Man's Wares</u>.
Giovanni, Nikki.   <u>Negro Digest</u> 19 (December 1969): 97.

COTTER, Joseph Seamon, Jr.   <u>Born</u> 2 September 1895 in Louis-
      ville, Kentucky. <u>Died</u> 3 February 1919. <u>Education:</u> Graduated
      1911 from Louisville Central High School, winning 2nd honors
      in his graduating class; attended Fisk University.[1]
POETRY
<u>The Band of Gideon and Other Lyrics</u>.   Boston: Cornhill,
      1918.
(Anthologies):   Calverton, <u>Anthology of American Negro Po-</u>
      <u>etry</u>, p. 178; Cullen, <u>Caroling Dusk</u>, pp. 100-105; John-
      son, <u>The Book of American Negro Poetry</u>, pp. 185-189.
UNPUBLISHED WORKS
"Book of Poems."
"Book of One Act Plays."[2]
BIOGRAPHY AND CRITICISM ON COTTER
Brawley.   <u>The Negro in Literature and Art</u>, p. 110.
Kerlin.   <u>Negro Poets and Their Poems</u>, pp. 67-68, 70, 80-
      84.
            [1]Countee Cullen, <u>Caroling Dusk</u> (New York: Harper,
      1927), p. 100.
            [2]Ibid.

COTTER, Joseph Seamon, Sr. <u>Born</u> 2 February 1861 in Nelson
      County, Kentucky. <u>Died</u> 1949. <u>Education:</u> Attended a private
      school; quit school at the age of eight, and did not return to
      the classroom until he was 22 years old. He then attended a
      Louisville public night school, continued his education, and
      earned a high school diploma. <u>Career:</u> He began to work at
      the age of eight as a rag picker. Later, he worked in tobacco
      factories and brick yards. At 19, he became a distiller in one
      of Kentucky's largest distilleries. He then became a teamster;
      hauled cotton and tobacco; became a prize fighter. After he
      received his diploma, he taught school and wrote.[1] When he
      became principal of the Colored Ward School in Louisville, he
      also taught English literature and composition.[2] Later, he
      taught in a public school in Cloverport, Kentucky, 1885-1887;
      conducted a private school, 1887-1889; taught in the Western

Colored School, Louisville, Kentucky, 1889-1893; was the
Founder and principal of the Paul L. Dunbar School, 1893-1911;
Founder-Principal of the Samuel Coleridge-Taylor School in
1911. Member: National Story Teller's League; Author's
League of America; NAACP.[3] Awards, Honors: His first po-
em appeared in the Louisville, Kentucky Courier Journal about
1894.[4] His short story, "Tragedy of Pete," won a prize in
the Opportunity contest, during the Harlem Renaissance.[5]
DRAMA
    Caleb, The Degenerate. Louisville, Ky.: The Bradley &
        Gilbert Co., 1903; reprint, New York: H. Harrison, 1940;
        New York: AMS Press*.
    (Periodicals): Crisis 20 (June 1920); Saturday Evening Quill,
        June 1913.
NON-FICTION
    Negroes and Others at Work and Play. Narratives, Plays,
        Sketches. New York: Paeber Co., 1947.
    Negro Tales. New York: Cosmopolitan Press, 1912; fac-
        simile ed., Freeport, N.Y.: Books for Libraries*.
    (Anthology): Kerlin, Negro Poets and Their Poems.
POETRY
    Collected Poems of Joseph S. Cotter, Sr. New York: H.
        Harrison, 1938; facsimile ed., Freeport, N.Y.: Books
        for Libraries*.
    Links of Friendship IV (Poetry). Louisville, Ky.: Bradley
        & Gilbert, 1898.
    A Rhyming. Louisville, Ky.: New South, 1895.
    Sequel to the "Pied Piper of Hamelin," and Other Poems.
        New York: H. Harrison, 1939.
    A White Song and a Black One. Louisville, Ky.: Bradley
        & Gilbert, 1909.
    (Songs)
    I'm Wondering and Other Songs. Dedicated to Myra Shar-
        low, 1921.
    (Anthologies): Adams, Conn and Slepian, Afro-American
        Literature: Poetry; Brown, Davis and Lee, Negro Cara-
        van; Calverton, An Anthology of American Negro Litera-
        ture; Cullen, Caroling Dusk; Emanuel and Gross, Dark
        Symphony; Kerlin, Negro Poets and Their Poems; White
        and Jackson, An Anthology of Verse by American Negroes.
    (Periodicals): Crisis 16 (1918): 64; 17 (1919): 125; 20 (1920):
        22; 20 (1920): 173; 26 (1923): 213; Opportunity 3 (June
        1925): 186, 179; 3 (December 1925): 357; 4 (June 1926):
        180, 188, 189; 4 (July 1926): 214; 5 (August 1927): 227;
        5 (November 1927): 325; 13 (April 1935): 120; 15 (Janu-
        ary 1937): 22.
BIOGRAPHY AND CRITICISM ON COTTER, SR.
    Abramson. Negro Playwrights in the American Theatre,
        pp. 14-21.
    Anon. "Joseph S. Cotter, Sr." Crisis 19 (1920): 126.
    Bardolph. The Negro Vanguard, pp. 202-203.
    Bergman. A Chronological History of the Negro in Amer-
        ica, p. 1903.

Brawley. The Negro Genius, p. 168.
_____. The Negro in Literature and Art.
Butcher. The Negro in American Culture, p. 153.
Chametzky and Kaplan. Black and White in American Culture, p. 381.
Eleazer. Singers in the Dawn, p. 6.
Gloster. Negro Voices in American Fiction, p. 84.
Gross. The Heroic Ideal in American Literature, p. 129.
Jahn. Neo-African Literature, pp. 183, 211.
Jones, Paul W. L. "Two Kentucky Poets." Voice of the Negro 8 (1906): 583-588.
Kerlin. Negro Poets and Their Poems, pp. 52, 70-80, 236-237, 302-303.
Mitchell. Black Drama, p. 239.
Molette, Carlton W. III. "First Afro-American Theatre." Negro Digest 19 (April 1970): 4-9.
Redding. To Make a Poet Black.
White and Jackson. An Anthology of Verse by American Negroes, pp. 25, 146.
UNPUBLISHED WORKS[6]
Ceasar Driftwood and Other One Act Plays.
Life's Dawn and Dusk. (Poems.)
My Mother and Her Family.
　　　[1]Countee Cullen, Caroling Dusk (New York: Harper & Brothers, 1927), pp. 10-11.
　　　[2]William H. Robinson, Early Black American Poets (Dubuque, Ia.: Wm. C. Brown, 1969), p. 185.
　　　[3]Thomas Yenser, ed., Who's Who in Colored America, 5th ed. (New York: Yenser, 1938-1939-1940), p. 140.
　　　[4]Paul W. L. Jones, "Two Kentucky Poets." Voice of the Negro 8 (1906): 586.
　　　[5]Harry A. Ploski and Ernest Kaiser, The Negro Almanac, rev. ed. (New York: Bellwether, 1971), p. 671.
　　　[6]Cullen, p. 11.

COTTON, Ella Earls.
NOVEL Queen of Persia: The Story of Esther Who Saved Her People. New York: Exposition, 1960.

COTTON, Walter.
DRAMA Monday Morning of Homing Brown.

COUCH, William, Jr.
CRITICISM
"The Problem of Negro Character and Dramatic Incident." Phylon 11 (Second Quarter 1959): 127-133.
"Sinclair Lewis: Crisis in the American Dream." CLA Journal 7 (March 1964): 222-234.
EDITOR
New Black Playwrights. New York: Avon, 1970†.
POETRY
(Periodicals): Negro Story, July-August, October-November 1944; December-January 1944-45.

COUSINS, L. S.
POETRY (Periodical): Journal of Black Poetry, Fall-Winter 1971.

COUSINS, Linda.
POETRY (Anthologies): Patterson, A Rock Against the Wind; Sanchez, 360° of Blackness Coming at You.

COUSINS, William.
POETRY (Anthology): Murphy, Ebony Rhythm.

COWDERY, Mae V.
POETRY
We Lift Our Voices and Other Poems. Introduction by William Stanley Braithwaite. Philadelphia: Alpress, 1936.
(Anthology): Johnson, Ebony and Topaz.
(Periodicals): Crisis 34 (1927): 337; 35 (1928): 300, 372; 36 (1929): 50; 37 (1930): 207, 235, 273; Opportunity, October 1927; September 1928.
BIOGRAPHY AND CRITICISM ON COWDERY
Brawley. The Negro Genius, p. 265.

COWDERY, Mincy.
POETRY (Anthology): Black Poets Write On!

COX, Joseph Mason Andrew. Born 12 July 1923 in Boston, Mass.
Education: B. A., Columbia University, 1945; L. L. B., LaSalle Law School, 1949; Doctorate (Art Psychology), World University, Hong Kong, British Crown Colony, 1972. Currently living in New York City. Career: Reporter and feature writer, New York Age, 1955-1957; reporter and feature writer, New York Post, 1958-60; President, Afro-Asian Purchasing Commission, 1961-68; Consultant, New York City Board of Education, 1969-71; Lecturer, City University of New York (Medgar Evans College), 1972 to present. Served as U. S. A. representative to the World Poetry Conference, Expo 67, Montreal, Quebec.
His poetry was set to music and ballet by Dr. J. Brooks Dendy III and the Creatadrama Society of Pittsburgh, and was televised nationwide on "Together" by Charles Wiggfall, on KDKA-TV, Pittsburgh. Member: The Authors League of America; The Poetry Society of America (former Executive Board member); The Poetry Society of London; International Who's Who in Poetry; International Poets Shrine; United Poet Laureate International; Academy of American Poets. Awards, Honors: Daniel S. Mean International Essay Award, 1964; President Johnson's Great Society Writer's Award, 1965; Master Poets Award, 1970; World Poets Award, 1971; P. E. N. Grant, 1972; International Poet Laureate, 1973.
DRAMA
Ode to Dr. Martin Luther King (three acts).
NOVEL
The Search. New York: Daniel S. Mead, 1960.

POETRY
>   The Collected Poetry of Joseph Mason Andrew Cox. Fran-
>   cestown, N. H. : Golden Quill, 1970.
>   Shore Dimly Seen. New York: Daniel S. Mead, 1963.
>   (Anthologies): The Golden Quill Anthology, 1968, 1969,
>   1970, 1971; World Poets Anthology; Spring Anthology
>   (Great Britain); Boyd, Poems by Blacks II; Lane, Poems
>   by Blacks III. Poetry also in: Moon Age Poets (Charles-
>   ton, Ill. : Prairie Press, 1970; McCarthy, New and Better
>   World Poets (Charleston, Ill. : Prairie Press, 1971); Lin-
>   coln Log (n. p. : Illinois State Poetry Society, 1973); The
>   First International Poetry Society Anthology (Youlgrave,
>   England: HUB, forthcoming).

WORK IN PROGRESS
>   Novel: "Indestructible Monument."

INTERJECTIONS
>   "My art (poetry and writing) is a sword to fight the dehuman-
>   izer and beast of civilization and for a one world concept.
>   "Therefore, I must make it plain with the whole truth. Half-
>   truths have proven inadequate to awaken a mass of unaware
>   people."

COX, Ollie H.
>   CRITICISM BY COX
>   "The Sport of Joy in 'My Last Duchess.' " CLA Jour-
>   nal 12 (September 1968): 70-76.
>   POETRY
>   Last Call for Peace. New York: Arlain Printing Co. , 1959.
>   (Anthologies): Shuman, A Galaxy of Black Writing.

COX, Sandra. Born 13 April 1949 in Greenville, South Carolina.
>   POETRY (Anthology): Boyer, Broadside Annual 1973.

COX, Walter. Born 1952 in Detroit.
>   POETRY
>   (Anthology): Boyer, Broadside Annual 1973.
>   (Periodical): Journal of Black Poetry, Fall-Winter, 1971.

CRAWFORD, Isaac.
>   POETRY Weeds and Other Poems. Brooklyn, N. Y. : By the
>   Author, 1953.

CRAWFORD, Marc.
>   SHORT STORY (Periodical): Black World, May 1972.

CRAYTON, Pearl.
>   SHORT STORIES
>   (Anthologies): Adoff, Brothers and Sisters; Bambara, Tales
>   and Stories; Hughes, The Best Short Stories by Negro
>   Writers.
>   (Periodicals): Negro Digest, August 1965; August 1966.
>   Also published in The Texas Quarterly.

CREWS, Stella Louise. Born 1950 in Port Huron, Michigan.
POETRY (Anthology): Boyer, Broadside Annual 1973.

CRITTENDEN, Annie R.
SHORT STORY (Periodical): Essence, June 1972.

CROUCH, Stanley. Born 1945 in Los Angeles, California.
POETRY
Ain't No Ambulances for No Nigguhs Tonight. New York:
R. W. Baron, 1972†.
(Anthologies): Coombs, We Speak as Liberators; Jones and
Neal, Black Fire; King, Blackspirits; Major, The New
Black Poetry; Troupe, Watts Poets.
(Periodicals): Black World, December 1970; August 1971;
Essence, March 1971, February 1974; Journal of Black
Poetry, Spring 1969; Fall-Winter 1971; Negro Digest, De-
cember 1967; September-October 1968; February, July,
August 1969; also published in Black Dialogue and The
Liberator.

CRUMP, George Peter, Jr.
NOVEL From Bondage They Came. New York: Vantage, 1954.

CRUMP, Paul.
NOVEL
Burn, Killer, Burn. Chicago: Johnson, 1962; excerpt in Ne-
gro Digest, October 1962.
POETRY
(Periodical): Negro Digest, September 1962.
BIOGRAPHY ON CRUMP
Crump, Paul. "Fifteen Dates with the Electric Chair."
Ebony, July 1962, pp. 31-34.
_____. "How a Prisoner Became a Writer." Ebony, No-
vember 1962, pp. 88-90.
"Justification for Living." Negro Digest 11 (October 1962):
50.
Nizer, Louis. The Jury Returns. Garden City, N.Y.:
Doubleday, 1966, pp. 1-137.

CRUSE, Harold. Born in Virginia. Education: High school education; learned administration in military service, 1941-45;
attended army courses in journalism and languages; studied
cinematography. Currently living in Ann Arbor, Michigan. Career: Has had a varied career as film editor, political activist
in Harlem, journalist (a trainee on a labor union newspaper after World War I), clerk for the Veterans Administration, writer,
director and stage manager in theatre, and as an independent
writer, researcher and historian. Currently Professor in
American and Afro-American History, University of Michigan,
specializing in Black developments since 1890.
CRITICISM AND NON-FICTION
Crisis of the Negro Intellectual. New York: Morrow, 1967*†.
Rebellion or Revolution. New York: Apollo, 1969†. New York:

Morrow, 1972†.

(Anthologies): Davis and Redding, Cavalcade; Robinson, Nommo; Jones and Neal, Black Fire.

(Periodicals); Black World 2 (January, March and May 1971), excerpts from book tentatively entitled Black and White: Outlines of the Next Stage; Negro Digest, July 1967; January 1968.

BIOGRAPHY AND CRITICISM ON CRUSE

Bigsby. The Black American Writer, vol. 2, pp. 227-239.

Chrisman, Robert. "Response to Black and White: Outlines of the Next Stage: The Contradictions of Harold Cruse." Black World 20 (May 1971): 90-98.

"The Crisis of Harold Cruse." Black Scholar 1 (November 1969): 77-84.

Harrison. The Drama of Nommo, pp. 167-168.

Mayfield, Julian. "Crisis or Crusade? An Article-Review of Harold Cruse's Crisis of the Negro Intellectual." Negro Digest 18 (June 1968): 10-24.

Mitchell. Black Drama, pp. 161-162.

CUESTAS, Katherine L. Born 19 July 1944 in Brooklyn.

POETRY

(Anthologies): Jordan, Soulscript; Pool, Beyond the Blues.

(Periodical): Présence Africaine, No. 57.

CULLEN, Countée Porter. Born 30 May 1903 in New York City. Died 9 January 1946. Education: Attended New York City public schools; graduated from DeWitt Clinton High School in 1922; B.A., New York University, 1925; M.A., Harvard, 1926.[1] He studied in Paris on a Guggenheim Scholarship, 1928.[2] Career: He wrote his first free verse at the age of 14;[3] became an editor in high school, working for the Clinton News, his school paper, and for the Magpie, the school's literary magazine. He worked as a bus boy at the Traymore Hotel, Atlantic City. In 1925 he published his first book, Color. From 1926-28, he was the assistant editor of Opportunity. June 1928, Cullen travelled to Paris to study on a scholarship.[4] When he returned from France, he taught in the public school system of New York City. He also continued to write until his death.[5] Cullen found time to read his poetry, to lecture on the role of "The American Negro in Literature," and to even investigate, and offer solutions to ameliorate the racial problems stemming from the Harlem riots of 1935.[6] Member: Phi Beta Kappa; Alpha Delta Phi; the New York Civic Club. Awards, Honors: He won prizes in the following poetry contests: 2nd prizes, 1923 and 1924, and 1st prize in 1925 in the Witter Bynner undergraduate poetry contest sponsored by the Poetry Society of America; in 1925, May issue of Opportunity, he received 2nd prize; won the John Reed Memorial prize, the same year, awarded by Poetry magazine. In 1926, he again won 2nd prize in the Crisis contest.[8] He received the Guggenheim Fellowship in 1928.

CHILDREN AND YOUNG ADULTS
    The Lost Zoo. Chicago: Follett, 1969*.
    My Lives and How I Lost Them. By Christopher Cat in
       collaboration with Countee Cullen, 1942; Chicago: Follett*;
       Curtis, 1973†.
DRAMA
    Byword for Evil (Medea). Manuscript. Yale University Li-
       brary.
    Medea. New York: Harper, 1935.
    One Way to Heaven, 1936. Manuscript. Yale University
       Library.
    With Arna Bontemps. St. Louis Woman. Presented at Mar-
       tin Beck Theatre, 30 March 1946.
    With Arven Dodson. The Third Fourth of July. In Theatre
       Magazine 30 (1946): 488-493.
EDITOR
    Caroling Dusk. New York: Harper, 1927. (Poetry Anthol-
       ogy.)
NON-FICTION
    "Introduction." The House of Vanity, Frank Ankenbrand and
       Benjamin Isaac. Philadelphia: Leibman Press, 1928.
    "The Dark Tower." Opportunity (a monthly column), 1926-
       1928.
    Writers Take Sides: Letters about the War in Spain from
       418 American Authors. New York: League of American
       Writers, 1938.
    (Periodicals): Crisis 28 (1924): 31; 29 (1924): 8-1; 32 (1926):
       193.
NOVEL
    One Way to Heaven. New York: Harper, 1932.
POETRY
    Ballad of a Brown Girl. New York: Harper, 1927.
    The Black Christ. New York: Harper, 1929.
    Color. New York: Harper, 1925; reprint ed., New York:
       Arno, 1970*.
    Copper Sun. New York: Harper, 1927.
    The Medea and Other Poems. New York: Harper, 1935.
    On These I Stand. New York: Harper & Row, 1947*.
    (Anthologies): Abdul, The Magic of Black Poetry; Adams,
       Conn and Slepian, Afro-American Poetry; Adoff, I Am the
       Darker Brother; Adoff, Poetry of Black America; Baker,
       Black Literature in America; Barksdale and Kinnamon,
       Black Writers of America; Bell, Afro-American Poetry;
       Bontemps, American Negro Poetry; Braithwaite, Anthol-
       ogy of Magazine Verse of 1926; Breman, You Better Be-
       lieve It; Chapman, Black Voices; Cullen, Caroling Dusk;
       Cunard, Negro Anthology; Davis and Redding, Cavalcade;
       Eastman, The Norton Anthology of Poetry; Eleazer,
       Singers in the Dawn; Ellman and O'Claire, The Norton
       Anthology of Modern Poetry; Emanuel and Gross, Dark
       Symphony; Eastman, et al., The Norton Anthology of Po-
       etry, 1970 ed.; Faderman and Bradshaw, Speaking for
       Ourselves; Fishel and Quarles, The Black American;

Ford, Black Insights; Graham, An Anthology of Revolu-
tionary Poetry; Gross, A Nation of Nations; Hayden, Ka-
leidoscope; Henderson, Understanding the New Black Po-
etry; Hughes, The Book of Negro Humor; Hughes and
Bontemps, The Poetry of the Negro: 1746-1970; Johnson,
Ebony and Topaz; Johnson, The Bond of American Negro
Poetry; Jones, Blues People; Jordan, Soulscript; Kearns,
The Black Experience; Kendricks and Levitt, Afro-Ameri-
can Voices; Kerlin, Negro Poets and Their Poems; Locke,
The New Negro; Lomax and Abdul, 3000 Years of Black
Poetry; Long and Collier, Afro-American Writing, vol. 1;
Margolies, A Native Sons Reader; Miller, Blackamerican
Literature; Patterson, An Introduction to Black Literature;
Patterson, A Rock Against the Wind; Pool, Beyond the
Blues; Quarles, Benjamin, Blacks on John Brown (Urbana:
University of Illinois Press, 1972); Randall, The Black
Poets; Rollins, Christmas Gif'; Simmons and Hutchinson,
Black Culture; Simon, Ethnic Writers in America; Singh
and Fellowes, Black Literature in America; Stanford, I,
Too, Sing America; Turner, Black American Literature:
Essays, Poetry, Fiction and Drama; Wagner, Black Po-
ets of the United States; Walrond and Pool, Black and Un-
known Bards.
(Periodicals): Bookman 58 (September 1923-February 1924):
245; (September 1924-February 1925): 285; Century 108
(May-October 1924): 713; 118 (May-August 1929): 375;
The Clintonian (Clinton High School, New York City)
(1921): 77; Crisis 25 (1922): 26; 26 (1923): 64; 27 (1924):
274; 28 (1925): 165; 29 (1926): 78; 30 (1927): 13; 34
(1931): 222; 77 (November 1970): 366 (from Crisis May
1927); Jet (11 January 1962): 11; Opportunity (January
1942): 7; Phylon (Fourth Quarter 1942); Tuesday Magazine
(February 1969): 14-15.

BIOGRAPHY AND CRITICISM ON CULLEN

Adams. Great Negroes Past and Present, pp. 147, 154,
159.
Adoff, Poetry of Black Americans, p. 521.
Arden, Eugene. "The Early Harlem Novel." Phylon 20
(September 1959): 25-31.
Austin, Fenderson and Nelson. The Black Man and the
Promise of America, p. 429.
Baker. Black Literature in America, p. 430.
Bardolph. The Negro Vanguard, pp. 202-207, 209, 295.
Barksdale and Kinnamon. Black Writers of America, pp.
529-530.
Bell, Bernard W. "Teaching Contemporary Afro-American
Poetry as Folk Art." Black World 22 (March 1973):
16-26, 74-83.
Bergman. The Chronological History of the Negro in Amer-
ica, year 1922.
Bigsby. The Black American Writers, vol. 1, pp. 10-11,
60.

Bone. The Negro Novel in America, pp. 56, 60, 78-80,
    248.
Bontemps, Arna. "Countee Cullen, American Poet. " The
    People's Voice 5 (26 January 1946): 52-53.
    _____. "The Harlem Renaissance. " The Saturday Review
    of Literature 30 (March 1947): 12-13, 44.
    _____. The Harlem Renaissance Remembered, pp. 1-6,
    11, 12, 17-21, 36, 40-43, 46, 65, 91, 101, 103-125, 150,
    194, 223-225, 227, 229, 231, 234, 240, 247, 256, 258,
    261, 273.
    _____. 100 Years of Negro Freedom, pp. 227, 229, 233,
    235.
Brawley. Negro Builders and Heroes, p. 239.
    _____. Negro Genius, pp. 224-227, 263.
    _____. The Negro in Literature and Art, pp. 117, 121-123.
Bronz, Stephen H. Roots of Negro Racial Consciousness,
    New York: Libra, 1964.
Butcher. The Negro in American Culture, pp. 103, 106-
    107, 140.
Chametzky and Kaplan. Black and White in American Cul-
    ture, pp. 346, 364.
Collier, E. W. "I Do Not Marvel, Countee Cullen. " Crisis
    11 (September 1967): 73-87.
Cook and Henderson. The Militant Black Writer, pp. 12,
    114.
Cromwell, Turner and Dykes. Readings from Negro Au-
    thors, pp. 24, 313, 318-325.
Daniel, Walter C. "Countee Cullen as Literary Critic. "
    CLA Journal 14 (March 1971): 281-290.
Davis, Arthur. "The Alien and Exile Theme in Countee Cul-
    len. " Phylon (Fourth Quarter 1953): 390-400.
Davis. The American Negro Reference Book, pp. 861-862,
    858, 874.
Dickinson, Donald C. A Bio-Bibliography of Langston
    Hughes 1902-1967. New York: Archon Books, 1967, pp.
    x, 14, 22, 24, 28, 34, 106.
Dodson, Owen. "Countée Cullen (1903-1946). " Phylon 7
    (January-March 1946): 19-20.
Dorsey, D. F. Jr. "Countee Cullen's Use of Greek Myths. "
    Crisis 13 (October 1969): 68-77.
Dreer. American Literature by Negro Authors, pp. 67-72,
    263-268.
Drotning, Phillip T. A Guide to Negro History in America.
    New York: Doubleday, 1968, p. 136.
Emanuel and Gross. Dark Symphony, pp. 63-66, 172-175,
    361, 517.
Faderman and Bradshaw. Speaking for Ourselves, p. 72.
Ferguson, Blanche. Countee Cullen and the Negro Renais-
    sance. New York: Dodd, Mead & Co. , 1966.
Fishel and Quarles. The Black American, pp. 402-403, 440.
Ford. Black Insights, p. xiv-xv, 59, 78-79, 137.

Frazier, E. Franklin. Black Bourgeoisie. New York: Collier Books, 1966, p. 106.

Gayle. Black Expression, pp. 59, 76, 79, 82, 86, 221-222, 230, 236, 241-242, 248, 254.

Gloster. Negro Voices in American Fiction, pp. 111, 117, 162.

Goldstein. Black Life and Culture in the United States, pp. 166-169, 176-177, 298.

Gregory H., and M. Zaturenaka. "History of American Poetry." New York Times, 10 January 1946.

Gross. The Heroic Ideal in American Literature, p. 138.

Huggins. Harlem Renaissance, pp. 69-70, 102, 108, 148-149, 171, 189, 197, 205-214, 217, 220-221, 228-231, 306.

Hughes. The Negro Novelist, p. 37.

Hughes and Meltzer. A Pictorial History of the Negro in America, pp. 274-275, 277, 300.

Isaacs, Harold. The New World of Negro Americans. London: Phoenix House, 1963, pp. 58, 146, 232, 235, 265, 284.

Jackson, Miles M. "A Bio-Bibliography of Countee Cullen." Freedomways 12 (First Quarter).

Jahnheinz. Neo-African Literature, pp. 189, 191, 196, 207, 212-213, 217.

Johnson. Black Manhattan, pp. 266-271.

_____. The Book of American Negro Poetry, pp. 219-231.

Kent. Blackness and the Adventure of Western Culture, pp. 24, 28-29.

_____. "Struggle for the Image: Selected Books By or About Blacks during 1971." Phylon 33 (Winter 1972): 304-323.

Killam, G. D. African Writers on African Writings. Evanston, Ill.: Northwestern University Press, 1973, p. 101.

Killens, John O. "Another Time When Black Was Beautiful." Black World 20 (November 1970): 20-36.

Kunitz, Stanley, and Howard Haycroft, eds. Twentieth Century Authors. New York: H. W. Wilson, 1942, p. 337.

Larson, Charles R. "African Afro-American Relationships." Negro Digest 19 (December 1969): 35-42.

_____. "Three Harlem Novels of the Jazz Age." Critique 11 (1969): 66-78.

Locke. Four Negro Poets.

Loggins. The Negro Author in America, p. 352.

Lomax, Michael. "Fantasies of Affirmation: The 1920's Novel of Negro Life." CLA Journal 16 (December 1972): 232-246.

Lyons, Thomas T. Black Leadership in American History. Mass.: Addison-Wesley Publ. Co., 1971, p. 121.

Margolies. A Native Sons Reader, p. 6.

_____. Native Sons, pp. 31, 42-43.

Mays. The Negro's God, pp. 219-220, 227-231.

Mitchell. Black Drama, p. 128-129.

Mitchell, L. "Harlem My Harlem." Black World 20 (November 1970): 91-97.

Mphalele, Ezekiel. Voices in the Whirlwind. New York: Hill & Wang, 1972, p. 139.

"Obituary." New York Times, 10 January 1946, 23:1.

Ottley, Roi and Wm. J. Weatherby. The Negro in New York. Dobbs Ferry, N.Y.: Oceana, 1967, pp. 256-258, 278.

Ovington, Mary White. The Walls Came Tumbling Down. New York: Schocken Books, 1970, pp. 190-193.

Patterson. Black Theatre, pp. i-42.

_____. An Introduction to Black Literature in America, pp. 150-151.

Perry, Margaret. A Bio-Bibliography of Countée P. Cullen, 1903-1946. Westport, Conn.: Greenwood, 1971, 134 pp. (An excellent source.)

Pinkney, Alphonso. Black Americans. Englewood Cliffs, N.J.: Prentice-Hall, 1969, p. 147.

Ploski and Kaiser. The Negro Almanac, pp. 671-672.

Pool. Beyond the Blues, p. 78.

Quarles, Benjamin. Blacks on John Brown. Urbana: University of Illinois Press, 1972, p. 119.

Redding, Saunders. The Lonesome Road. New York: Doubleday, 1958, pp. 243-245.

_____. They Came in Chains, pp. 263-267, 285.

_____. To Make a Poet Black, pp. 108-112.

Redmond, Eugene B. "The Black American Epic: Its Roots Its Writers." Black Scholar 2 (January 1971): pp. 15-22.

Reimherr, Beulah. "Race Consciousness in Countée Cullen's Poetry." Susquehanna University Studies 7 (1963): 65-82.

Richardson. Great American Negroes, pp. 174-184.

Robb, Izetta W. "From the Darker Side." Opportunity 5 (1926): 381-382.

Robinson. Historical Negro Biographies, p. 176.

Rollins, Charlemae. Christmas Gif'. New York: Follette, 1964, p. 101.

Simmons and Hutchinson, Black Culture, pp. 66, 129, 151, 278.

Smith, R. A. "The Poetry of Countée Cullen." Phylon 11 (Third Quarter 1940): 213-223.

Turner. In a Minor Chord, pp. 60-88.

Wagner. Black Poets of the United States, pp. 15, 42, 97, 149, 173-176, 184, 264, 283-347, 393, 395, 399, 440, 511.

Waldron, Edw. E. "Walter White and the Harlem Renaissance." CLA Journal 15 (June 1973): 438-457.

Ward, Francis and Val Gray. "The Black Artist--His Role in the Struggle." Black Scholar 2 (January 1971): 23-32.

Webster, Harvey. "A Difficult Career." Poetry 70 (1947): 222-225.

White and Jackson. An Anthology of Verse by American Negroes, p. 210.

Williams. They Also Spoke, pp. 244-245, 255, 259, 265-268.

Woodruff, Bertram. "The Poetic Philosophy of Countée Cullen." Phylon 1 (1940): 213-223.

Yenser, Thomas, ed. Who's Who in Colored America, 5th ed., New York: Yenser, 1938-1939-1940, p. 140.

Young. Black Writers of the Thirties, pp. 141, 167-172, 196, 202, 205-211,240.

[1]Stanley Kunitz and Howard Haycraft, eds. Twentieth Century Authors (New York: H. W. Wilson, 1942), p. 337.

[2]Thomas Yenser, ed., Who's Who in Colored America, 5th ed. (New York: Yenser, 1938-1939-1940), p. 140.

[3]Margaret Perry, A Bio-Bibliography of Countée Cullen, 1903-1946 (Westport, Conn.: Greenwood, 1971), p. 3.

[4]Ibid., pp. 4-10.

[5]Harry A. Ploski and Ernest Kaiser, eds., The Negro Almanac (New York: Bellwether, 1971), p. 672.

[6]Perry, p. 16.

[7]Kunitz and Haycraft, p. 337.

[8]Perry, pp. 5-8.

CULVER, Eloise Crosby. Born 7 July 1915 in Tennessee. Died 29 December 1972. Education: B.S. (Education), Wayne State University, 1938; M.A., Wayne State University, 1968. Career: Taught school for more than thirty years. Awards, Honors: Was honored on many occasions for her contribution towards Black Awareness. She was responsible for naming a Detroit Elementary School after Dr. Drew. She wrote short stories of great American Negroes for the Mott Foundation.[1]
POETRY
    Christmas Around the World. n.p., n.d.
    Great American Negroes in Verse, 1723-1966. Washington, D.C.: Associated, 1966.
    (Periodical): Negro History Bulletin 34 (March 1971): 58.
INTERJECTIONS
    "Black children must be taught of their worth by presenting famous Negroes to be proud of--and a rich and noble past beginning with Africa. This awareness must begin in the home and continue in school. If every person searches for knowledge and passes such knowledge on to others, the Contribution will be great. (To this she devoted her life.)"[2]

[1]Information supplied by Deborah A. Culver, daughter of Eloise C. Culver.

[2]Ibid.

CUMBERBATCH, Lawrence S. Born 1946 in Brooklyn.
POETRY (Anthology): Coombs, We Speak as Liberators.

CUMBO, Kattie M. Born 3 November 1938 in the U.S.A. Education: Long Island University, 1955-58 (dropped out because of "the oppression that kills black ambition"). Returned in 1967 to receive an A.A. in Eduation, 1969, and a B.A. in Journalism, 1970. Received a Certificate in Afro-Caribbean Studies, University of West Indies; presently completing an M.A. in

Urban Studies at Long Island University. ~~Currently living in~~
Brooklyn, New York. Career: During the past fifteen years,
she has been Assistant to the Bursar at Columbia University;
secretary to a Long Island University dean; editor of a magazine; editor and administrative assistant at the African American Institute. She has lectured at numerous high schools,
universities and conferences, and has given poetry readings as
well as conducting seminars. Member: Harlem's Writing
Guild; Women in Communications.

NON-FICTION
   Published in Hep magazine; Ghanian Times; Muhammad
      Speaks; Africa Opinions; The Liberator.
POETRY
   (Anthologies): Black Works; Shuman, A Galaxy of Black
      Writing; Shuman, Nine Black Poets.
   (Periodicals): Afro-American; African Opinion; Angel Crow;
      The Liberator; Morning Post (poetry column); Negro
      American Literature Forum; Rights and Review.
REVIEWS BY CUMBO
   Published in Freedomways.
WORK IN PROGRESS
   A book of poetry.

CUMMINS, Cecil.
DRAMA Young Blood, Young Breed, 1969.

CUNEY, Waring. Born 6 May 1906 in Washington, D.C. Education: Attended public schools in Washington, D.C.; Howard
   University; Lincoln University (Pennsylvania). He studied music at the New England Conservatory, Boston,[1] and the Conservatory in Rome, Italy. Career: Musician; poet and song-
   writer. He served more than three years in the South Pacific,
   and held various military distinctions.[3] After World War II,
   he disappeared from society until March 1971, when he appeared in Black World, criticizing John O'Killens for labeling
   his early religious verse "irrelevant." Since that time, he has
   been actively engaged on a new volume of poetry, to appear in
   the Heritage Series under the title, Storefront Church. Awards,
   Honors: Poem, "No Images" won a national poetry contest--
   the Opportunity Prize in 1926. The poem is one of the most
   complete and reprinted pictures of the philosophy of the Renaissance and was translated into more languages than even the
   work of Langston Hughes.[4]
CRITICISM BY CUNEY
   "Letter to J. O. Killens." Black World 20 (March 1971):
      98.
EDITOR
   With Langston Hughes and Bruce McM. Wright. Lincoln
      University Poets: Centennial Anthology 1854-1954. New
      York: Fine Editions, 1954.
POETRY
   Chain Gang Chant. Norman, Okla.: n.p., 1930.
   Puzzles. Utrecht, Holland: DeRoos, 1960. (Selected and

introduced by Paul Breman.)

(Anthologies): Bontemps, American Negro Poetry; Braithwaite, An Anthology of Magazine Verse for 1926; Breman, You Better Believe It; Brown, Davis and Lee, Negro Caravan; Cullen, Caroling Dusk; Cuney, Hughes and Wright, Lincoln University Poets; Davis and Redding, Cavalcade; Johnson, Book of American Negro Poetry; Kerlin, Negro Poets and Their Poems; Lomax and Abdul, 3000 Years of Black Poetry; O'Donnell, Eva Herse and Paridam von dem Knesebeck, eds., Meine dunklen Hände (My Dark Hands) Munich, 1953. A translation of Waring Cuney's poetry is included in this anthology of Eva Hesse O'Donnell. These translations first appeared in German newspapers, Die Meue Zeitung, Munich, 1950;[5] Pool, Beyond the Blues; Walrond and Pool, Black and Unknown Bards.

(Periodicals): Crisis 1 (April-May 1971): 81; Harlem Quarterly, Spring 1950; Negro Quarterly 1 (Spring 1942): 40-41; Opportunity 4 (June 1926); 180, 188; 5 (August 1927): 227; 5 (November 1927): 325; 13 (April 1935): 120; 15 (January 1937): 22; Palms: Negro Poets Number 4 (October 1926): 12.

(Broadsides): The Alley Cat Brushed His Whiskers, n.p., 1955?; Two Poems: "Darkness Hides His Throne" and "We Make Supplication," n.p., By the Author, 1955?; Women and Kitchens, n.p., 1955?

SONGS

"Shiny Cooking Children," recorded by Balladeer, Josh White.
"Southern Exposure" texts done for John White's album; verse "Hard Times Blues" is included.[6]
"This Time Tomorrow" (Albert Hague, Burl Ives, Waring Cuney) Phonodisc: Decca 28079, 1952. (Ballads by Cuney.)

BIOGRAPHY AND CRITICISM ON CUNEY

Abdul. The Magic of Poetry, pp. 70, 90.
Bell, Bernard W. "Afro-American Poetry as Folk Art." Black World 22 (March 1973): 16-26, 74-83.
Bontemps. The Harlem Renaissance Remembered, pp. 234, 248, 260-262.
Brawley. The Negro in Art and Literature, p. 122.
Breman. You Better Believe It, p. 99.
Chametzky and Kaplan. Black and White in American Culture, p. 346.
Collier, Eugenia. "Heritage from Harlem." Black World 20 (November 1970): 52-58.
Cromwell, Turner and Dykes. Readings from Negro Authors, p. 51.
Davis. The American Negro Reference Book, p. 862.
Gayle. Black Experience, pp. 84, 217, 248.
Killens, John O. "Another Time When Black Was Beautiful." Black World 20 (November 1970): 20-36.
Lovell, John J. Black Song: The Forge and the Flame. New York: Macmillan, 1972, p. 570.
Pool. Beyond the Blues, p. 81.
Williams. They Also Spoke, pp. 259-260.

[1]Robert T. Kerlin, Negro Poets and Their Poems (Washington, D.C.: Associated, 1935), p. 336.
[2]Arna Bontemps, American Negro Poetry (New York: Hill & Wang, 1963), p. 189.
[3]Rosey E. Pool, ed., Beyond the Blues (London: Headley Bros., 1962), p. 81.
[4]Paul Breman, ed., You Better Believe It (Baltimore, Md.: Penguin Books, 1973), p. 99.
[5]John J. Lovell, Black Song: The Forge and the Flame (New York: Macmillan, 1972), p. 570.
[6]Breman, p. 81.

CUNEY-HARE, Maud.   Born 1874 in Galveston, Texas.   Died 1936.
Education: Graduated from Galveston Central High School, 1890; studied music at the New England Conservatory, Boston. Career: Became Director of Music for the Deaf, Dumb and Blind Institute of Texas; Prairie View State College, Texas; was also a concert pianist and lecturer; writer and collector. Later, she established the Musical Art Studio, Boston; sponsored a Little Theatre movement among Blacks.   She directed plays and appeared in recitals in the New England area.   She travelled in Mexico, and the Caribbean Islands.[1]
CRITICISM BY CUNEY-HARE
   "Afro-American Folk Song Contributions."   The Musical Observer 15 (February 1917): 13, 21, 51.
   "History of Song in the Virgin Islands."   Crisis 40 (1933): 83, 108.
DRAMA
   (Anthology): Richardson, W., ed.   Plays and Pageants from the Life of the Negro.   Washington, D.C.: 1929 (1930), p. 27.
   (Periodical):   Negro Quarterly 1 (Spring 1942): 27-74.
NON-FICTION
   (Biography)
   Norris Wright Cuney: A Tribune of the Black People.   New York: Crisis, 1913.
   Negro Musicians and Their Music.   Washington, D.C.: Associated, 1936.
POETRY
   The Message of the Trees: An Anthology of Leaves and Branches.   Boston: Cornhill, 1918.
SONGS
   Six Creole Folk Songs: With Original Creole and Translated English Text.   Boston: Fisher, 1921.
BIOGRAPHY AND CRITICISM ON CUNEY-HARE
   Ayars, Christine Herrick.   Contribution to the Art of Music in America by the Music Industries of Boston.   New York: H. W. Wilson, 1937, p. 50.
   Chametzky and Kaplan.   Black and White in American Culture, p. 124.
   "The Cuney Family."   Negro History Bulletin 11 (March 1948).
   Jones, LeRoi.   Blues People.   New York: Wm. Morrow &

Co., 1963, pp. 44-45.

Journal of Negro History 21 (April 1936): 239-240. (Obituary.)

Lovell, John Jr. Black Song: The Forge and the Flame. New York: Macmillan, 1972, pp. 25, 66.

COLLECTIONS

Maud Cuney-Hare Private Collection of Negro-American Music: sheet music, pictures, clippings.[2]

[1]Sylvia G. Dannett, Profiles of Negro Womanhood, vol. 1 (Yonkers: Educational Heritage, 1964), p. 265.

[2]Maud Cuney-Hare, Negro Musicians and Their Music (Washington, D.C.: Associated, 1936), p. 422.

CUNNINGHAM, George Jr. Born 1927.

NOVEL Lily-Skin Lover: His Passion for Light-Complexioned Women Leads Him to Destruction. New York: Exposition, 1960.

CUNNINGHAM, James (olumo). Born 4 January 1936 in Webster Groves, Missouri.

CRITICISM

"The Case of the Severed Lifeline." Negro Digest 18 (October 1969): 23-28.

NON-FICTION

(Anthology): Chapman, New Black Voices.

POETRY

The Blue Narrator. n.p., n.d.

(Anthology): Brooks, Jump Bad; Brown, Lee and Ward, To Gwen with Love.

(Periodical): Journal of Black Poetry. Spring 1969.

CURRY, Andrew.

POETRY 17th Tractatus on Words: Selected Poems. Paradise, Calif.: Dustbooks, 1969.

CURRY, Linda. Born 1953 in Harlem.

POETRY

(Anthologies): Baron, Here I Am; Jordan and Bush, Voice of the Children.

(Periodicals): The Teachers College Record; Uhuru.

CURTWRIGHT, Wesley. Born 30 November 1910 in Brunswick, Georgia. Education: Attended numerous schools in several states in the North and the South, including Harlem Academy, New York and Pacific Union College in Angwin, California.[1] Career: Worked as a clerk in the New York State Civil Service.[2]

POETRY

(Anthologies): Bontemps, Golden Slippers; Cullen, Caroling Dusk; Hughes and Bontemps, The Poetry of the Negro: 1746-1970; Murphy, Negro Voices.

(Periodicals): Opportunity, September 1926, February 1927; also published in The African; The Crisis; The Messenger.

[1]Countée Cullen, Caroling Dusk (New York: Harper, 1927), p. 224.

[2]Arna Bontemps, comp., Golden Slippers (New York: Harper, 1941), p. 20.

CUTHBERT, Marion Vera.
NON-FICTION
(Periodical): Opportunity, February 1936.
POETRY
Songs of Creation. New York: Woman's Press, 1949.
SHORT STORY
(Periodical): Crisis 1 (April 1936).

-D-

DAFORA, Asadata.
DRAMA Kykunkor, 1934.

DALE, La Afrique (pseud.)
POETRY (Periodical): Black Scholar, April-May 1971.

DALY, Victor. Career: Industrial secretary for the New York Urban League; business manager for The Journal of Negro History.
CRITICISM
"Green Pastures and Black Washington." Crisis 40 (1933): 106.
NON-FICTION
(Periodical): Crisis, June 1939.
NOVEL
Not Only War: A Story of Two Great Conflicts, 1932; reprint ed., New York: AMS Press, 1970*; Washington, D.C.: McGrath, 1969.
SHORT STORIES
(Periodicals): Crisis 37 (1930): 199; 39 (1932): 91; 41 (1934): 44.
CRITICISM ON DALY
Gloster. Negro Voices in American Fiction, pp. 217-218.
REVIEW
Not Only War.
DuBois, W. E. B. Crisis 39 (1932): 138.

DANCER, William E.
POETRY
Facts, Fun and Fiction. 4th ed. Jacksonville, Fla.: By the Author, 1917.
Today and Yistiday: Poems in Dialect. Tuskegee, Ala.: Tuskegee Institute, 1914.

DANCY, Walter. Born 24 April 1946.
POETRY (Anthologies): Coombs, We Speak as Liberators; Henderson, Understanding the New Black Poetry.

DANDRIDGE, Raymond Garfield. Born 1882 in Cincinnati, Ohio.
  Died 1930. Education: Cincinnati grammar and high schools.
  Career: A painter and decorator until the paralytic stroke of
  1912. Continued to write with left hand while lying down, and
  served as Literary Editor, Cincinnati Journal.[1]
  POETRY
      Penciled Poems. Cincinnati, O.: Powell & White, Printers,
        1917.
      The Poet and Other Poems. Cincinnati, O.: Powell &
        White, 1920.
      Zalka Peetruza and Other Poems. Cincinnati, O.: McDon-
        ald, 1928.
      (Anthologies): Adoff, The Poetry of Black America; Eleazer,
        Singers in the Dawn; Johnson, Book of American Negro
        Poetry; Kerlin, Negro Poets and Their Poems; White and
        Jackson, An Anthology of Verse by American Negroes.
  BIOGRAPHY AND CRITICISM ON DANDRIDGE
      Kerlin. Negro Poets and Their Poems, pp. 169-172.
      Wagner. Black Poets of the United States, p. 179.
          [1]Newman Ivey White and Walter Clinton Jackson, An
      Anthology of Verse by American Negroes (Durham, N.C.:
      Moore, 1924), p. 191.

DANGERFIELD, Abner Walker. Born 1883.
  NON-FICTION
      Extracts on Religious and Industrial Training. Washington,
        D.C.: Murray Brown, Printing, 1909.
  POETRY
      Musings. Washington, D.C.: Triangle Printing Co., 1914.

DANIEL, Gloria.
  DRAMA The Male Bag.

DANIEL, Portia Bird.
  POETRY (Anthology):   Murphy, Negro Voices.

DANIELS, Ionia.
  POETRY (Anthology):   Murphy, Negro Voices.

DANNER, James.
  POETRY (Anthology):   Jones and Neal, Black Fire.

DANNER, Margaret. Born 12 January 1915 in Chicago, Illinois.
  Career: See Shockley and Chandler, Living Black American
  Authors, pp. 36-37.
  POETRY
      Impressions of African Art Forms, 1960; Detroit: Broad-
        side, 1969†.
      To Flower: Poems. Nashville, Tenn.: Hemphill, 1963.
      With Dudley Randall. Poem Counterpoem. Detroit: Broad-
        side, 1966; 2nd ed., 1969†.
      Iron Lace. Millbrook, N.Y.: Poets Press, 1968.
      (Anthologies): Adoff, Poetry of Black America; Barksdale

and Kinnamon, Black Writers of America; Bell, Afro-
American Poetry; Bontemps, American Negro Poetry;
Brooks, A Broadside Treasury; Brown, Lee and Ward,
To Gwen with Love; Davis and Redding, Cavalcade;
Hayden, Kaleidoscope; Hayden, Burrows, and Lapides,
Afro-American Literature; Henderson, Understanding the
New Black Poetry; Hughes, New Negro Poets: USA;
Hughes and Bontemps, The Poetry of the Negro: 1746-
1970; Long and Collier, Afro-American Writing; Lowen-
fels, Poets of Today; Patterson, An Introduction to Black
Literature in America; Pool, Beyond the Blues; Randall,
The Black Poets; Randall, Black Poetry: A Supplement;
Randall and Burroughs, For Malcolm; Weisman and
Wright, Black Poetry for All Americans.
(Periodicals): Journal of Black Poetry, Special Issue, 1970-
1971; Negro Digest, August 1961; September 1963; July,
September 1966; January 1968; September-October 1968;
Negro History Bulletin, October 1962; October 1964; also
published in Chicago Review; Quicksilver; Browning Let-
ters; Poetry Digest; Voices.
BIOGRAPHY AND CRITICISM ON DANNER
Lee. Dynamite Voices, p. 41.
"Negro Woman Poet of Detroit, Michigan." Negro History
Bulletin 26 (October 1964): 53-54.
Redding. "Since Richard Wright," pp. 29-30.

DANTE see GRAHAM, D. L.

DAVENPORT, Jennette.
POETRY (Periodical): Journal of Black Poetry, Winter-
Spring 1970.

DAVIDSON, Norbert R., Jr. Born 1940 in New Orleans.
DRAMA
El Haji Malik, 1968. In Bullins, New Plays from the Black
Theatre, pp. 201-246.
Falling Scarlet, 1971.
The Further Emasculation of..., 1970.
Jammer, 1970.
Short Fun, 1970.
Window, 1970.

DAVIDSON, William F.
DRAMA Learn, Baby, Learn, 1969.

DAVIS, A. I. Born in Harlem, U.S.A. Birthdate: Everyday.
Education: "A listener of Black conversations and explanations,
an observer of the 'changes' people make, a striver in the tradition of Black folk ever since our incarceration." Currently
living in Bronx, New York. Career: Working as a writer to
dramatize and to record the Black existence--its relation to the
world--life--living--and the pursuit of being. Presently "at-
tempting to seduce Black folk with literature without resorting

to 'Superfly.' " Wrote a P.B.A. radio script for WHA/Ear-
play of the University of Wisconsin. Awards, Honors: 1972
Grant, New York Council on the Arts.
DRAMA
    Better Make Do, 1971.
    Cirema the Beautiful.
    The Cock Crows, 1971.
    Man, I Really Am, 1969.
    A Man Talking, 1971.
SHORT STORY
    (Periodical): Essence, 1972; 1973.
INTERJECTIONS
    "Impressions: The rhetoric is futile and gone / Do we real-
ly want to read? Ideas: American MONEY is irrelevant in relation to meaningful presentations of Blackness--sweet and sour.
Philosophy: We are separate people--Blacks, Whites--distor-
tion is greatest when we struggle to meld! Theories: The future of Black folk is what we've always been--survivors. Intellectual rhetoric is unnecessary, we just have to remember
what went down, in order to go on."

DAVIS, Arthur P. Born 21 November 1904 in Hampton, Virginia.
Education: Attended Hampton Institute and Howard University;
A.B., Columbia College, 1927; A.M., Columbia University,
1929; Ph.D., Columbia University, 1942. Currently living in
Washington, D.C. Career: Professor of English: North Carolina College, 1927-28, Virginia Union University, 1929-44; Professor of Graduate English, Hampton Institute, Summer School,
1943-49; Professor of English, Howard University, 1944-70;
University Professor, Howard University, since 1970. Conducted a weekly column for the Norfolk Journal and Guide from
1933 to 1950. Wrote numerous English Units for use in secondary schools for Educational Services, Inc. During 1972-73,
presented 26 radio talks in a WAMU-FM series called "Ebony
Harvest"; after April 1973 the series was distributed to about
one hundred public radio stations all over the country (included
in the series are lectures spanning the time from the pioneer
writers to the revolutionary poets of the early seventies). Member: Modern Language Association, College Language Association, English Graduate Union (Columbia University).
Awards, Honors: Phi Beta Kappa; General Education
Board Fellowship, 1932-33 and 1936-37 for study in England;
Proudfit Fellowship (Columbia University), 1937; National
Hampton Alumni Award, 1947.
AUTOBIOGRAPHY
    "Growing Up in the New Negro Renaissance: 1920-1935."
      Negro American Literature Forum 2 (1968): 53-59.
    "I Go to Whittier School." Phylon 21 (Summer 1960): 155-
    166.
    "My Most Humiliating Jim Crow Experience." Negro Digest
    2 (May 1944): 61-62.
    "When I Was in Knee Pants." Common Ground (Winter
    1944): 47-52.

BIOGRAPHY
"My Grandfather." The Southern Workman 51 (August 1922): 368-373.
"William Roscoe Davis and His Descendants." Negro History Bulletin (January 1950): 75-90.

CRITICISM
"The Alien-and-Exile Theme in Countée Cullen's Racial Poems." Phylon 14 (1953): 390-400.
"American Negro Literature," Encyclopedia of the Arts, pp. 39-45. Edited by Runes and Schrickel. New York, 1946.
"The Black-and-Tan Motif in the Poetry of Gwendolyn Brooks." CLA Journal 6 (December 1962): 90-97.
"A Blueprint for Negro Writers." Alpha Kappa Mu Journal 3 (1947): 8-13.
"E. Franklin Frazier (1894-1962): A Profile." The Journal of Negro Education 31 (Fall 1962): 90-97.
With Eugenia Collier. From the Dark Tower: Afro-American Writers from 1900 to 1960. Washington, D.C.: Howard University Press, 1974*.
"The Garies and Their Friends: A Neglected Pioneer Novel." CLA Journal 13 (September 1969): 27-34.
"Gwendolyn Brooks: Poet of the Unheroic." CLA Journal 7 (December 1963): 114-125; reprinted in Miller, Backgrounds to Blackamerican Literature.
"The Harlem of Langston Hughes' Poetry." Phylon 13 (1952): 276-283; reprinted in Gross and Hardy, Images of the Negro in American Literature; Singh and Fellowes, The Literature of Black America.
"Integration and Race Literature." Phylon 17 (1956): 141-146; reprinted in Chapman, Black Voices.
"Isaac Watts: Late Puritan Rebel." The Journal of Religious Thought 13 (Spring-Summer 1956): 123-130.
"Isaac Watts and 18th Century New England." Alpha Kappa Mu Journal 14 (1953): 9-17.
"Jesse B. Semple: Negro American." Phylon 15 (1954): 21-28.
"Langston Hughes: Cool Poet." CLA Journal 11 (June 1968); reprinted by Bobbs-Merrill Reprint Series in Black Studies.
"Negro American Literature: 1941-46." Negro Year Book (Tuskegee, 1947), pp. 456-472.
"Negro American Literature: 1951." Negro Year Book. New York, 1952.
"The New Poetry of Black Hate." CLA Journal 12 (June 1970): reprinted in Gibson, Modern Black Poets.
"The Outsider as a Novel of Race." The Mid-West Journal 2 (Winter 1956).
"Personal Elements in the Poetry of Phillis Wheatley." Phylon 13 (1953): 191-198.
"The Tragic Mulatto Theme in Six Works of Langston Hughes." Phylon 16 (1955): 195-204; reprinted in Gibson, Five Black Writers.
"Trends in Negro American Literature: 1940-65." The

Promethean (May 1967, Howard University Student Magazine); reprinted in Emanuel and Gross, Dark Symphony, pp. 519-526; Altenbernd, Exploring Literature.

EDITOR
With Sterling Brown and Ulysses Lee. The Negro Caravan. New York: Dryden, 1941.
With Saunders Redding. Cavalcade: Negro American Writers from 1760 to the Present. Boston: Houghton Mifflin, 1971.

INTRODUCTIONS
Clotel; or The President's Daughter by William Wells Brown. New York: Collier, 1970.
The Garies and Their Friends by Frank J. Webb. New York: Arno, 1969.
William Wells Brown and Clotelle by J. Noel Heermance. Hampden, Conn.: Shoe String Press, 1969.

NON-FICTION
(Periodicals): Crisis, August 1930; August 1931; April 1936; August 1946; Headlines, March 1945; Kappa Alpha Psi Journal, May 1948; Journal of Negro Education 12 (1943); North Carolina Teachers Record, May 1947; Negro Digest, April 1943; November 1943; May 1944; August 1945; February 1947; The Southern Workman (high school valedictorian address, August 1922); Virginia Union Bulletin, February 1941.
(Newspapers): Norfolk Journal Guide, 27 February 1943.

REVIEWS BY DAVIS
Published in CLA Journal; Journal of Negro Education; Journal of Negro History; Midwest Journal; Opportunity; Washington Post.

SHORT STORIES
(Anthologies): Anselment and Gibson, Black and White: Stories of American Life; Clarke, American Negro Short Stories; Garner, The Negro Hero; Gordon et al., The Study of Literature; Hoopes, Stories to Enjoy; Murray and Thomas, The Scene.

DAVIS, Barbara (Thulani Nkabinde). Born 19 July 1949 in Hampton, Virginia. Education: B.A., Barnard College. Currently living in Montclair, New Jersey. Career: Has done some newspaper work, but specializes in poetry (to be heard) and in projects combining the word and music, the word and dance, the word and film. Has done a number of writing workshops, including the Black Writer's Workshop in San Francisco, 1972. Currently teaching Afro-American literature, basic writing and research at Seton Hall University, while working on a volume of writing and photographs.

POETRY
(Anthologies): Monaco, New American Poetry; Third World Woman.

INTERJECTIONS
"Art for me is about colors, rhythms, change, perceptions of moments--their color rhythms and the change that happens --and hopefully it is about vision (a very pressing need). Po-

etry, like music, is to be heard/felt--not so cerebral--under-
standable--by all--a chemical change--like love."

DAVIS, Charles.
    NOVEL Two Weeks to Find a Killer. New York: Carlton,
        1966.

DAVIS, Cheryl.
    POETRY Imani. Madison, Wis.: By the Author, 1969?

DAVIS, Daniel Webster. Born 25 March 1862 on a farm in North
    Carolina.[1] Died 1913. Education: Attended Richmond public
    schools; graduated from Richmond High School, with honors in
    1878.[2] He was awarded an honorary[3] M.A. from Guadalupe
    College, Sequin, Texas.[4] Sometime in his life, he attended
    what is known as the "Swamp University."[5] Career: Began to
    teach in the Richmond Colored Public Schools, 1880;[6] was or-
    dained a Baptist Minister in 1895,[7] and accepted the pastorate
    of a Church in Manchester, Va. Later, in 1900, he became
    a lecturer under the management of the Central Lyceum Bureau.
    Awards, Honors: At graduation from the Richmond High and
    Normal School, 1878, he received the "Essayist Medal."[8]
    BIOGRAPHY
        The Life and Public Services of Reverend William Washing-
            ton Browne. Richmond, Va.: Mrs. M. A. Browne-Smith,
            1910.
    NON-FICTION
        With Giles B. Jackson. An Industrial History of the Negro
            Race in the United States. Richmond, Va.: Negro Educa-
            tional Association, 1911; facsimile of 1908 ed., Freeport,
            N.Y.: Books for Libraries*.
        Speech Delivered.
        "The Sunday-School and Church as a Solution of the Negro
            Problem." Masterpieces of Negro Eloquence. Edited by
            Alice Moore Dunbar. New York: Bockery Pub. Co.,
            1914; reprint ed. New York: Johnson Reprint, 1970, pp.
            291-304.
    POETRY
        Idle Moments, 2 vols. Baltimore: The Educator of Morgan
            College, 1895.
        'Weh Down Souf and Other Poems." Cleveland: Hellman-Tay-
            lor Co., 1897.
        Wrote "Exposition Ode," read at the opening of the Negro
            Building, Atlanta Exposition, 1895.[9]
        (Anthologies): Adoff, The Poetry of Black America; Ford,
            Black Insights; Johnson, The Book of American Negro
            Poetry; Robinson, Early Black American Poets; White and
            Jackson, An Anthology of Verse by American Negroes.
        (Periodicals): Voice of the Negro 1 (February 1904): 39; 1
            (July 1904): 308; 2 (November 1905): 779.
    BIOGRAPHY AND CRITICISM ON DAVIS
        Bergman. The Chronological History of the Negro in Amer-
            ica, cf. 1897, p. 321.

Butcher. The Negro in American Culture, p. 99.
Johnson. The Book of American Negro Poetry, p. 81.
Robinson. Early Black American Poets, p. 230.
Wagner. Black Poets of the United States, pp. 129, 138-
141, 357.
White and Jackson. An Anthology of Verse by American Ne-
groes, pp. 98, 218-219.
Voice of the Negro 1 (February 1904): 39.
      [1]While Johnson [note 2] and White and Jackson [note 8]
are in agreement that Davis was born in North Carolina,
Robinson [note 4] cites Richmond, Va., as his birthplace.
Johnson, White and Jackson, however, add that after the
war, the Davis family moved to Richmond, Virginia.
      [2]James Weldon Johnson, ed., The Book of American
Negro Poetry (New York: Harcourt, Brace & World, 1959):
p. 81.
      [3]Whereas Robinson [note 1] claims that Davis' M.A.
was an honorary degree, White and Jackson [note8]
claim that the M.A. degree was conferred.
      [4]William H. Robinson, ed., Early Black American Po-
ets (Dubuque, Iowa: Wm. C. Brown, 1959), p. 230.
      [5]"Biography," Voice of the Negro 1 (February 1904):
39.
      [6]Johnson, p. 81.
      [7]A difference of 10 years exists in the dates given by
Johnson [note 2], White and Jackson [note 8] for Davis'
entry into the Church; Johnson gives 1885 as the date for
Davis' entry into the ministry; White and Jackson cite the
year 1895 as the date he was ordained a Baptist minister.
      [8]Newman Ivey White and Walter Clinton Jackson, An
Anthology of Verse by American Negroes (Durham, N.C.:
Moore, 1968), p. 98.
      [9]Ibid., p. 219.

DAVIS, Frank Marshall. Born 1905 in Arkansas City, Kansas.
   AUTOBIOGRAPHY
      "My Most Humiliating Jim Crow Experience." Negro Digest
         2 (September 1944): 57-58.
   NON-FICTION
      (Periodicals): Crisis, February 1941; Negro Digest, Novem-
         ber 1946.
   POETRY
      Black Man's Verse. Chicago: Black Cat Press, 1935.
      47th Street: Poems. Prairie City, Ill.: Decker, 1948.
      I Am the American Negro. Chicago: Black Cat Press, 1937;
         facsimile ed. Black Heritage Library Collection. Free-
         port, N.Y.: Books for Libraries*.
      Through Sepia Eyes. Chicago: Black Cat Press, 1938.
      (Anthologies): Abdul, The Magic of Black Poetry; Adams,
         Conn and Slepian, Afro-American Literature: Poetry;
         Adoff, I Am the Darker Brother; Adoff, Poetry of Black
         America; Bell, Afro-American Poetry; Bontemps, Ameri-
         can Negro Poetry; Brown, Davis and Lee, Negro Caravan;

Faderman and Bradshaw, Speaking for Ourselves; Ford,
Black Insights; Hayden, Kaleidoscope; Henderson, Under-
standing the New Black Poetry; Hughes and Bontemps,
The Poetry of the Negro: 1746-1970; Miller, Blackamer-
ican Literature; Murphy, Ebony Rhythm; Simmons and
Hutchinson, Black Culture.
(Periodicals): Crisis 34 (1927): 48; 35 (1928): 272; 36
(1929): 232; 37 (1930): 307; (1935); also in April issue,
1944; The Negro Quarterly, Summer 1942; Negro Story,
July-August 1944; New Challenge, Fall 1937; Opportunity,
January 1939.

BIOGRAPHY AND CRITICISM ON DAVIS
Brawley. The Negro Genius, pp. 266-267.
Brown. Negro Poetry and Drama, pp. 77-78; also in Wat-
kins, An Anthology of American Negro Literature, pp.
259-260.
_____. "Two Negro Poets." Opportunity (July 1936):
216, 220.
Kloder, Helena. "The Film and Canvas of Frank Marshall
Davis." CLA Journal 15 (September 1971): 59-63.
Randall, Dudley. "An Interview with Frank Marshall Davis."
Black World 23 (January 1974): 37-48.
Wagner. Black Poets of the United States, pp. 172, 187-
190.
Young. Black Writers of the Thirties, pp. 167-168, 188-
193.
REVIEWS
Black Man's Verse.
Brown, Sterling A. Opportunity 26 (February 1948): 145.
47th Street: Poems.
Korn, Albert Ralph. Opportunity 26 (Fall 1948): 145.

DAVIS, Gene.
SHORT STORY (Anthology): Ford and Faggett, The Best Short
Stories by Afro-American Writers.

DAVIS, George B.
ESSAY
"The Howard University Conference." Negro Digest 18
(March 1969): 44-48.
NOVEL
Coming Home. New York: Random, 1971*.
SHORT STORIES
(Anthologies): King, Black Short Story Anthology; Watkins,
Black Review No. 1.
(Periodical): Negro Digest, July 1967.
BIOGRAPHY AND CRITICISM ON DAVIS
Kent. "Struggle for the Image," p. 309.
REVIEWS
Coming Home.
Black World 22 (January 1973): 79.
New York Times Book Review, 3 December 1972, p. 74.

DAVIS, Gene.
SHORT STORY (Anthology): Ford and Faggett, The Best Short
Stories by Afro-American Writers.

DAVIS, George B.
ESSAY
"The Howard University Conference." Negro Digest 18
(March 1969): 44-48.
NOVEL
Coming Home. New York: Random, 1971*.
SHORT STORIES
(Anthologies): King, Black Short Story Anthology; Watkins,
Black Review No. 1.
(Periodical): Negro Digest, July 1967.
BIOGRAPHY AND CRITICISM ON DAVIS
Kent. "Struggle for the Image," p. 309.
REVIEWS
Coming Home.
Black World 22 (January 1973): 79.
New York Times Book Review, 3 December 1972, p. 74.

DAVIS, Geri Turner.
DRAMA A Cat Called Jesus (one act).

DAVIS, Gloria.
POETRY
(Anthology): Major, The New Black Poetry.
(Periodical): Negro Digest, September 1963; September
1964; February 1965.
SHORT STORY
(Periodical): Negro Digest, August 1966.

DAVIS, John P.
EDITOR
The American Negro Reference Book, Englewood Cliffs,
N. J.: Prentice-Hall, 1966.
SHORT STORIES
(Anthologies): Clarke, American Negro Short Stories; Clarke,
Harlem.
(Periodicals): Opportunity, November 1927; December 1928;
January 1929; March 1930.

DAVIS, Joseph A. Born 1919.
NOVEL Black Bondage: A Novel of a Doomed Negro in Today's South. New York: Exposition, 1959.

DAVIS, Milburn.
DRAMA
Nightmare.
The 100,000 Nigger, 1969.
Sometimes a Switchblade Helps, 1969.

Nolan Davis (credit: Roland M. Charles)

DAVIS, Nolan. <u>Born</u> 23 July 1942 in Kansas City, Missouri. <u>Edu-cation:</u> A.B., U.S. Navy Journalist School, 1960; M.A., Stan-ford University, 1968. <u>Currently living in</u> Los Angeles, Cali-fornia. <u>Career:</u> Circulation specialist, troubleshooter and di-rector of Media Research for Fleet Home Town News Center, USNTC, 1961-62; editor of the Navy's largest force newspaper, <u>The Amphibian,</u> 1962-63; staff writer, rewriteman, aerospace editor, assistant city editor for <u>The Evening Tribune</u> (San Diego), 1963-66; director of Public Information/Communications for the Economic Opportunities Commission of San Diego County, Inc., 1966-67; Staff Correspondent, <u>Newsweek</u>, 1967-70; senior writer and producer, KNXT-TV (CBS), 1970; writer and producer of "The Stellar Story," Stellar Industries Corp., 1970; story writer, "Grave Undertaking," for Tandem Productions (<u>Sanford & Son,</u> NBC), 1970; writer, producer, director of the film, <u>Men (and Women) Managing Money</u>, Shareholders Management Co., 1971; Chief Newswriter for KABC-TV, 1971; newswriter for NBC, "KNBC Newsservice," 1971; scriptwriter, <u>The Jazz Show with Billy Eckstein</u>, NBC, 1972; writer and producer, <u>Fur-ther Than the Pulpit</u>, NBC-TV, 1972; presently a full-time in-dependent writer and producer. Specializes in writing novels, stories and screenplays exploring the universal myths of man-kind: death, religion, money, politics, fame, sex, science and

history. "My work seeks to convey an understanding of the
effects of men's personal myths upon their societies and the
effects of those societies' myths upon selected individuals."
Awards, Honors: Fellowship in communications, Stanford University, 1967-68. Member: Authors League of America;
Writers Guild of America, West; Sigma Delta Chi.

NON-FICTION
    (Periodicals): National Catholic Reporter, 7 September
        1971; oui, 7 November 1972; Race Relations Report, 4
        December 1972; TV Radio Mirror, 13 June 1971; west;
        23 December 1971; 23 June 1972.

NOVEL
    Six Black Horses. New York: Putnam, 1971.

WORK IN PROGRESS
    Biography: "O'Grady" a biography of Hollywood's leading
        private eye, to be published in 1974 by the Tarcher Co.
        of Los Angeles.

BIOGRAPHY AND CRITICISM ON DAVIS
    Land, I. S. "First Novelists." Library Journal, 1 Oc-
        tober 1971, pp. 3164-3165.

INTERJECTIONS
    Davis believes "that all matter is in a state of motion to-
wards resolution in the Absolute, assisted by positive and neg-
ative forces which often appear to be the opposite of what they
really are." He has dedicated his life to advancing positive
evolution by writing about the interplay of the forces, with emphasis on their mythological symbolism as it affects the destiny of whole societies.

DAVIS, Ossie. Born 18 December 1917 in Cogsdell, Georgia.
Education: Attended Howard University. Currently living in
New Rochelle, New York. Career: At the suggestion of Dr.
Alain Locke, Davis left Howard to explore the possibilities of
a career in theatre in New York City. He began an acting career with the Rose McClendon Players in Harlem, and has
played leading Broadway roles, beginning at the Martin Beck
Theatre in Jeb, 1946; other roles include: Anna Lucasta,
1947; Wisteria Trees, 1950; Green Pastures, 1951; Jamaica,
1957; A Raisin in the Sun, 1959; Purlie Victorious (playing the
lead role opposite his wife, Ruby Dee, 1962); The Zulu and
the Zada, 1966. He has also played in innumerable motion
picture productions: The Joe Louis Story; No Way Out, 1949;
The Cardinal, 1963; The Slaves, 1969. He has not only acted
in many television productions, but has written scripts for
Bonanza, N.Y.P.D., Name of the Game, East Side/West Side,
1963, The Eleventh Hour, 1963. He wrote, directed and produced The Annual Negro History Week Show for Local 1199,
the Retail Drug Employees Union. He has more recently become a motion picture director (Cotton Comes to Harlem,
Kongi's Harvest, Black Girl, The Hit). He has given lectures
and dramatic readings for educational, religious and civic
groups, and is well-known as a dedicated civil rights activist.
He was master of ceremonies for the March on Washington,

Ossie Davis

1963, and for the Solidarity Poor People's Campaign, 1968.
He is North American Zone Chairman for the Second World
Black and African Festival of Arts and Culture (January 1975).
Member: Actors Equity; Director's Guild of America Advisory
Board, CORE. NAACP; Urban League; Student Non-Violent Co-
ordinating Committee; Southern Christian Leadership Confer-
ence. Awards, Honors: Emmy Award for his role in "Teacher,
Teacher," a Hallmark Hall of Fame production, 1969; Frede-
rick Douglass award of the New York Urban League, 1970.
CRITICISM BY DAVIS
 "The English Language Is My Enemy!" Negro History Bul-
  letin 30 (April 1967): 18.
 "Flight from Broadway." Negro Digest 15 (April 1966):
  14-19.
 "Nat Turner: Hero Reclaimed." Freedomways 8 (Summer
  1968): 230-232.
 "Purlie Told Me." Freedomways 2 (Spring 1962): 155-159;
  also in Patterson, Anthology of the American Negro in
  the Theatre.
 "The Significance of Lorraine Hansberry." Freedomways 5
  (Summer 1965): 396-402.
 "Why I Eulogized Malcolm X." Negro Digest 15 (February
  1966): 64-66; also in The Autobiography of Malcolm X,
  edited by Alex Haley; Randall and Burroughs, For Malcolm.

"The Wonderful World of Law and Order." In Hill, <u>Anger and Beyond</u>, pp. 153-180.

DRAMA
<u>Alice in Wonder</u> (one act), 1953.
<u>The Big Deal</u>, 1953.
<u>Clay's Rebellion</u>, 1951.
<u>Curtain Call Mr. Aldrich Sir</u> (one act), 1963. In Reardon and Pawley, <u>The Black Teacher and the Dramatic Arts</u>.
<u>Alexis Is Fallen</u>, 1974.
<u>The Mayor of Harlem</u>, 1949.
<u>Point Blank</u>, 1949.
<u>Purlie Victorious: A Comedy in Three Acts</u>. New York: French, 1961; also in Adams, Conn and Slepian, <u>Afro-American Literature: Drama</u>; Brasmer and Consolo, <u>Black Drama</u>; Disch and Schwartz, <u>Killing Time; A Guide to Life in the Happy Valley</u>; Faderman and Bradshaw, <u>Speaking for Ourselves</u>; Oliver and Sills, <u>Contemporary Black Drama</u>; Patterson, <u>Black Theatre</u>; Turner, <u>Black Drama in America</u>. Excerpts in Childress, <u>Black Scenes</u>; Davis and Redding, <u>Cavalcade</u>.
<u>Purlie</u> (a musical based on the play, with lyrics by Peter Udell, music by Gary Geld, book by Davis, Rose and Udell). New York: Samuel French, 1971.
<u>They Seek a City</u>, 1947.
<u>What Can You Say to Mississippi?</u> (one act), 1955.

NON-FICTION
(Anthology): Clarke, <u>Harlem U.S.A.</u>
(Periodicals): <u>Freedomways</u>, Winter 1967; Summer 1968; Winter, Spring 1971; <u>Negro Digest</u>, February 1966.

POETRY
(Anthologies): Dee, <u>Glow Child</u>; Hill, <u>Soon One Morning</u>; Hughes and Bontemps, <u>The Poetry of the Negro: 1746-1970</u>.

BIOGRAPHY AND CRITICISM ON DAVIS
Abramson. <u>Negro Playwrights in the American Theatre</u>, pp. 273-274.
Adams, A. John, and Joan Martin Burke. <u>Civil Rights: A Current Guide to the People, Organization and Events</u>. New York and London: Bowker, 1970, pp. 34-35.
Bennett, J. "First African Movie By and About Africans Made by Ossie Davis." <u>Sepia</u> 2 (September 1971): 59-63.
Cruse. <u>Crisis of the Negro Intellectual</u>, pp. 10-531 passim.
<u>Current Biography</u> 1969, pp. 115-117.
Funke, Lewis. <u>Curtain Rises: The Story of Ossie Davis</u>. New York: Grossett & Dunlap, 1971.
Hentoff, Nat. <u>The New York Times</u>, 5 May 1968, sec. 2, p. 15 (interview).
Hughes and Bontemps. <u>Black Magic</u>, pp. 125-339 passim.
Hurd, Laura E. "Director Ossie Davis Talks About <u>Black Girl</u>." <u>Black Creation</u> 4 (Winter 1973): 38-40.
Mapp, Edward. <u>Blacks in American Films: Today and Yesterday</u>. Metuchen, N.J.: Scarecrow, 1972, pp. 74, 75, 77, 87, 180-182, 210-211, 248.
"Mr. and Mrs. Broadway: Ruby Dee, Ossie Davis Blend

Stage, Marriage." Ebony 16 (February 1961): 111-114.
Mitchell. Black Drama, pp. 125, 144, 155-156, 181, 188-
190, 194, 197, 211.
Peterson, Maurice. "Being about Ossie Davis." Essence
3 (February 1973): 20.
"Purlie Victorious." Ebony 17 (March 1962): 55-56.
Whitlow. Black American Literature, pp. 148-151.
Who's Who in the Theatre.
REVIEW
Purlie Victorious.
Leaks, Sylvester. Freedomways 1 (February 1961): 347.

DAVIS, Robert A. Born 1917 in Mobile, Alabama.
POETRY
(Anthology): Adoff, I Am the Darker Brother.
(Periodicals): Negro Story, July-August 1944; New Challenge,
Fall 1937.

DAVIS, Ronda Marie. Born 31 October 1940 in Chicago.
POETRY
(Anthologies): Brooks, A Broadside Treasury; Brooks, Jump
Bad; King, Blackspirits.
(Periodicals): Negro Digest, May 1969; September 1969;
other poetry in Nommo, Juggernaut, the Broadside Series
"Sister Songs."

DAVIS, Russell F.
NOVEL Anything for a Friend. New York: Crown, 1963.

DAWLEY, Jack H.
POETRY (Anthology): Lincoln University Poets.

DEAN, Barbara J.
POETRY The Key. Chicago: n.p., 1970.

DEAN, Corinne.
SHORT STORIES
Cocoanut Suite: Stories of the West Indies. Boston:
Meador, 1944.
(Periodical): Crisis, January 1940.

DEAN, Michael.
POETRY (Periodical): Journal of Black Poetry, Summer 1972.

DEAN, Phillip Hayes. Born in Chicago.
DRAMA
Every Night When the Sun Goes Down, 1969.
Freeman, 1971.
Johnny Ghost, 1969 (television play).
The Owl Killer. In King and Milner, Black Drama Anthology.
Sty of the Blind Pig and An American Night Cry: A Trilogy.
New York: Bobbs, 1972*†. (An American Night Cry in-
cludes The Minstrel Boy and The Thunder in the Index.)

This Bird of Dawning Singeth All Night Long.   New York:
        Dramatists, 1971†.
REVIEW
    Sty of the Blind Pig.
        Kalem, T. E.   Time, 6 December 1971.
        Kroll, Jack.   Newsweek, 6 December 1971.

DE ANDA, Peter.   Born in Pittsburgh.
    DRAMA   Ladies in Waiting.   In King and Milner, Black Drama
        Anthology.

DEAS, Katherine.
    POETRY   Life Line Poems.   Chicago: Edward C. Deas, n.d.

DEASE, Ruth Roseman.   Born 9 November 1911 in Jackson, Mis-
    sissippi.   Education: B.S., Jackson State College, 1946; M.A.,
    Atlanta University, 1952.   Currently living in Jackson, Missis-
    sippi.   Career: Director of the Nursery-Kindergarten at Jack-
    son State College for 13 years; Instructor in the English De-
    partment, Summer School and Extension School, Jackson State
    College, for six years; Director, Virden Presbyterian Church
    Pre-School for three years; Assistant Professor of Child Devel-
    opment, Alcorn A & M College, 1961 to present.   Also served
    as church organist.   Member: Pearl Street A. M. E. Church in
    Jackson; Delta Sigma Theta Sorority; Young Women's Christian
    Association, American Vocation Association; National Associa-
    tion for the Education of Young Children.   Awards, Honors:
    Two autograph parties; citation from Jackson Chapter of Delta
    Sigma Theta upon publication of SCAN-SPANS.
    POETRY
        SCAN-SPANS.   New York: Vantage, 1967.
        (Anthologies): National Poetry Anthology; Poetry Broadcast.
        (Periodicals): The Christian Recorder of the African Meth-
            odist Episcopal Church; Delta Journal; Mississippi
            Teachers' Educational Journal.
        (Newspapers): The Mississippi Enterprise.
    UNPUBLISHED WORK
        "Footprints of JRC, a Biography of Jessie R. Chambliss,
            Sr., a Distinguished Pioneer Citizen of Jackson, Miss.";
            "The History of Pearl Street Methodist Episcopal Church."
    INTERJECTIONS
        "Because of my early Christian training and my continuous
    study of Truth, I am a firm believer in the Fatherhood of God
    and the Brotherhood of Man.   I believe that man plays a strong
    role in controlling his destiny in life by demonstrating Truth in
    his affairs, as he strives to achieve some worthy goal in spite
    of the many obstacles he may encounter.   In any age and espe-
    cially in the present one, when there has been a decline in the
    values of society, man needs a power higher than himself.   Es-
    cape mechanisms are not the answer to the search for peace
    and the abundant life.
        "I have written and published my volume of Poems, SCAN-
    SPANS, not for literary recognition.   As I have been inspired

Robert H. DeCoy (credit: painting by A. L. Evans)

---

by poems and prose selections written by others, I, too, want
to make a contribution toward illuminating the pathway of others.
If for anyone I have achieved this goal, I shall always be grateful for sharing my thoughts and feelings."

DeCOY, Robert H. Born 11 October 1920 in New Orleans, Louisi-
  ana. Education: M.A., Tillotson College. 1948; M.F.A.,
  Yale University, 1951. Currently living in Carson, California.
  Career: Creator, writer and narrator of "This Is Progress,"
  a radio documentary on the contributions of Black Americans
  Broadcaster for over eleven years; Writer and consultant for
  CBC and ABC networks; Co-founder and Supervisor of the In-
  stitute of Nigritian Studies; President of Nigratian, Inc., Pub-
  lishers. Also a performer of stage, screen and radio.
  Awards, Honors: Certificate of Merit in four categories:
  Author, Actor, Historian, Philosopher. Dictionary of Interna-
  tional Biography, London, 1971.
  DRAMA
      The Castration, 1970.
  NON-FICTION
      The Big Black Fire. Los Angeles: Holloway, 1969†. (Bi-
        ography of Jack Johnson).
      Cold Black Preach. Los Angeles: Holloway, 1971†.

Nigger Bible. Los Angeles: Holloway, 1967†. Excerpt in
    Simmons and Hutchinson, Black Culture.
This Is Progress: The Blue Book Manual. Carson, Ca.:
    Nigritian, 1969 (History).
SCREENPLAY
    The Black Prodigal and the Priest, 1971.
INTERJECTIONS
    "I am recently cited as 're-discoverer' of 'NIGRITIA' (pres-
ently the area of The Sudan, Africa, where the original pure
'negroes' or blacks emerged). 'NEGRO,' as a racial title, was
abandoned in America after The Nigger Bible illuminated the
fact that 'negro' was listed as 'ADVERB' by dictionaries prior
to the 1930's. 'People, persons and places' are nouns.
'Black,' presently employed in America, is an ADJECTIVE of
color. A people cannot be an Adverb, much less an Adjective.
People are NOUNS and Nigritian is that noun--the correct ethnic title for the present day American of African origin. NI-
GRITIAN is the one singular racial title which can and does allow the variances of our group as a Nation. Nationalism is impossible without this singular collective title. Begrudgingly,
the 'Blacks' and white scholars are being forced into agreement."

DEDEAUX, Richard A. Born 24 September 1940 in New Orleans.
    Education: City College, two years. Currently living in Los
    Angeles. Career: Poet, playwright, lecturer and actor. One
    of the three Watts Prophets (the Watts Prophets are a group of
    Los Angeles poets whose album, Rappin' Black in a White
    World, received an N. A. A. C. P. Image Award nomination in
    1971; their television documentary, "Victory Will Be My Moan,"
    received an Emmy Award nomination; they have given concerts
    and appearances at numerous colleges and universities, clubs,
    festivals and conferences). Editor of Mafundi Institute Newspa-
    per; Founder/Instructor of Creative Writing Workshop, Mafundi
    Institute; Community Advisor for Stax Records; Associate Pro-
    ducer of "Doin' It at the Storefront," a KCET weekly series.
    Member: A. F. T. R. A. Awards, Honors: See above.
DRAMA
    And Baby Makes Three.
    The Decision.
    A Duel with Destiny (teleplay).
    The Rip Off (screenplay).
POETRY
    The Rising Sons: Wisdom and Knowledge. Los Angeles:
        Morgan Enterprises, 1973.
WORK IN PROGRESS
    Two novels--"Me Tiger" and "The Other Side of the Circle"
        (autobiographical).
INTERJECTIONS
    "My writings depict the soul of both young and old Black in-
ner-city America--its wailing sirens, and Ghetto sounds--as
everyday people go at life trying to make it bend, if only for a
while. And looking for beauty in spite of the Bitterness."

DEE, Ruby (Ruby Ann Wallace). Born 27 October 1923 in Cleveland, Ohio. Education: B.A., Hunter College, 1945; apprentice, American Negro Theatre, 1941-44; studied with Morris
Carnovsky, 1958-60; Actors Workshop. Currently living in
New Rochelle, New York. Career: In 1942, she appeared in
South Pacific (a drama by Howard Rigsby and Dorothy Heyward). Since that time she has played lead roles in A Raisin
in the Sun, 1959; Purlie Victorious, 1961; Jeb, 1946; Anna
Lucasta, 1946, as well as many others. Off-Broadway productions include Alice in Wonder, 1952; Boesman and Lena, 1970;
American Shakespeare Festival at Stratford, Connecticut, 1965;
Greek Theatre, Ypsilanti, Michigan, 1966. Her career in motion pictures began with The Jackie Robinson Story, 1950; fol-
lowed by Edge of the City, 1957; Take a Giant Step, 1961; St.
Louis Blues, 1958; A Raisin in the Sun, 1961; The Balcony,
1963; Up Tight, 1969; Gone Are the Days (film version of Purlie Victorious, 1963, re-released the following year under the
original title); Buck and the Preacher, 1972. She collaborated
with Jules Dassin and Julian Mayfield in writing the script for
Up Tight, in which she starred. She has given numerous poetry and dramatic readings, as well as appearing in television
productions. Member: N.A.A.C.P., CORE; Student Non-Violent Coordinating Committee; Southern Christian Leadership
Conference; Urban League. Awards, Honors: Frederick Douglass Award, New York Urban League, 1970.

EDITOR
   Glow Child and Other Poems. New York: Third Press,
      1973.
NON-FICTION
   (Periodical): Freedomways, Winter 1965.
POETRY
   (Anthology): Dee, Glow Child.
REVIEWS BY DEE
   Published in Freedomways.
BIOGRAPHY ON DEE
   Adams, A. John and Joan Martin Burke. Civil Rights: A
      Current Guide to the People, Organizations and Events.
      New York and London: Bowker, 1970, pp. 34-35.
   Cruse. The Crisis of the Negro Intellectual, pp. 68-531
      passim.
   Current Biography 1970, pp. 107-110.
   Dee, Ruby. "The Tattered Queens: Negro Actresses."
      Negro Digest 15 (April 1966): 32-36; also in Patterson,
      Anthology of the American Negro in the Theatre.
   Mayfield, Julian. Interview in Freedom, September, 1952.
   Mitchell. Black Drama, pp. 122-224.
   "Ossie Davis, Wife Starring in New Movie." Jet, 7 Janu-
      ary 1971, p. 59.
   Ploski, Reference Library of Black America, p. 61.
   Weales, G. Commonweal, 9 October 1970, pp. 47-48.
   Who's Who of American Women.
   Who's Who in the Theatre.

DELANY, Clarissa Scott. Born 1901 in Tuskegee Institute, Ala-
bama. Died 1927. Education: Attended Bradford Academy
for three years; was graduated from Wellesley College. Career:
Taught at Dunbar High School in Washington, D.C., for three
years. Completed a study of delinquency and neglect among
Negro children in New York City.[1]
DRAMA
     Dixie to Broadway, 1924.
POETRY
     (Anthologies): Adoff, The Poetry of Black America; Bon-
          temps, American Negro Poetry; Cullen, Caroling Dusk;
          Kerlin, Negro Poets and Their Poems.
     (Periodicals): Opportunity, June, December 1925; October
          1926; November 1927; Palms, October 1926.
          [1]Robert T. Kerlin, Negro Poets and Their Poems
     (Washington, D.C.: Associated, 1923), p. 336.

DELANY, Martin R. Born 6 May 1812 in Charles Town, Old Virginia. Died 24 January 1885. Education: He was taught by
his mother, Pati, from the New York Primer and Spelling Book
which was a basic "bootlegging item" among Blacks all through
the South.[1] After the family moved to Chambersburg, Pa.,
he attended school managed by a clergyman employed by a society of free Blacks[2]--the A.M.E. Church.[3] He began the
study of medicine and applied for entrance to the University of
Pennsylvania Medical School, and was denied admittance. Later,
he applied and gained admittance to the Harvard Medical School,
from which he was graduated.[4] Career: He founded the The-
ban Literary Society in 1832. Later, in 1837, the society
changed its name to the Young Men's Literary and Moral Reform Society of Pittsburgh. In 1837 he founded another group
called the Philanthropic Society.[5] He began a new career as
a journalist and in 1843 started the publication of a newspaper,
The Mystery.[6] Then, on 3 December 1847, he teamed up with
Frederick Douglass and launched another newspaper, The North
Star, in Rochester, N.Y.; the weekly lasted until 1849. Delany was admitted to Harvard Medical School in 1849 and received his M.D. degree from Harvard in 1852. Between 1852
and the Civil War, he practiced medicine in Illinois, Canada,
and Pennsylvania. When cholera broke out in Philadelphia, he
was instrumental in helping to put down the epidemic. During
the Civil War, he served the Union as a surgeon.
     Because he had been commissioned to explore and study the
Niger Valley, he was able to write and publish his Official Report of the Niger Valley Exploring Party. After he wrote his
report on the Niger Valley, he read a paper on his studies before the Royal Geographical Society in London. While in Europe, he was a member of the International Statistical Congress
of the National (British) Association for the Promotion of the
Social Science Congress, Glasgow, Scotland.[7]
     When Delany returned to the States, he served as a Major
of the 104th Regiment at Charleston. He became the first Black
man to serve in the war as a Field Officer.[8]

After the war, he worked for the Freedman's Bureau; became a justice of the peace in South Carolina, and ran as a
candidate for lieutenant governor in South Carolina. Before he
died in 1885, he wrote three more essays on the Civil War,
the international policy towards Africa, and the political destiny
of the Black man in America. [9]

FICTION
Blake, or the Huts of America; A Tale of the Mississippi
      Valley, the Southern United States and Cuba. Boston:
      Beacon, 1970*†. (The novel was begun as a series of
      chapters in the Anglo-African, a magazine established in
      New York City by Negroes in 1859. The work was never
      completed because the magazine suspended publication with-
      in a year. [10] Victor Ullman, however, claims that Blake
      was serialized in 30 chapters, in the Anglo-African Maga-
      zine, January-July 1859. The balance of 80 chapters were
      serialized in 1861-62 in the Weekly Anglo-African. Sup-
      posedly 8 more chapters do exist in unfound issues of the
      Weekly. [11]

NON-FICTION
The Condition, Elevation, Emigration and Destiny of the Col-
      ored People of the United States Politically Considered.
      Philadelphia: Delany, 1852. Reprinted by Arno Press,
      1968; by George Ducas and Charles Van Doren, eds.,
      Great Documents in Black American History. New York:
      Praeger, 1970*.
Official Report of the Niger Valley Exploring Party. New
      York and London: 1861. Reprinted in Search for a Place.
      Edited by Howard Bed. Ann Arbor: University of Michi-
      gan Press, 1969.
Principia of Ethnology: The Origin of Races and Color with
      an Archeological Compendium and Egyptian Civilization,
      From Years of Careful Examination and Enquiry. Phila-
      delphia: 1879.
(Anthologies): Barksdale and Kinnamon, Black Writers of
      America; Brawley, Early Negro American Writers; Brown,
      Davis and Lee, Negro Caravan; Davis and Redding, Caval-
      cade; Miller, Blackamerican Literature.
(Articles)
"Comets," and "The Attraction of the Planets," ran concur-
      rently with the last 30 chapters in the Anglo-African Maga-
      zine, February-August 1859.
(Pamphlets)
Booklet--Freemasonry is in the Western Reserve Historical
      Collection, Cleveland, Ohio; National Policy, Number 4,
      is in the Dawson Pamphlet Collection at the University of
      North Carolina; Homes for the Freedman, printed in
      Charleston, S.C., 1871, is in the Boston Public Library.[12]

BIOGRAPHY AND CRITICISM ON DELANY
Adams. Great Negroes Past and Present, pp. 14, 52-59,
      66.
Bardolph. The Negro Vanguard, pp. 58-61, 63-67, 75-76.
_____. "Some Origins of Distinguished Negroes, 1770-

1865." Journal of Negro History 40 (1955): 211-249.

Barksdale and Kinnamon. Black Writers of America, pp. 192-194.

Bone. The Negro Novel in America, pp. 30-31.

Brawley. Early Negro American Writers, pp. 216-219.

Butcher. The Negro in American Culture, pp. 97, 117.

Chametzky and Kaplan. Black and White in American Culture, pp. 335, 355-356.

Cobb, William Montague. "Martin Robinson Delany." Journal of National Medical Association (May 1952): 232-238.

Cruse. The Crisis of the Negro Intellectual, pp. 129, 341, 344, 431.

Davis. The American Negro Reference Book, pp. 550-553, 609, 870.

Davis and Redding. Cavalcade, pp. 65-66.

Eppse, Merl R. The Negro, Too, in American History. Chicago: National Educational Publishing Co., 1939, p. 161.

Fleming, Robert E. "Delany's Blake." Negro History Bulletin 36 (February 1973): 37-40.

Ford. Black Insights, p. xix.

Gayle, Addison, Jr. "Politics of Revolution: Afro-American Literature." Black World 21 (November 1971-October 1972): 4-12.

Gloster. Negro Voices in American Fiction, pp. 25, 27-29.

Goldstein. Black Life and Culture in the United States, pp. 81, 342, 361-362, 366.

"Great Men in Negro History: Union Army Doctor was Advocate of Education." Sepia 8 (February 1960): 61.

Isaacs. The New World of Negro Americans, pp. 38, 117-118, 120.

Jahn. Neo-African Literature, pp. 129, 137-138, 140-141.

Kent. "Struggle for the Image," pp. 304-323.

Kirk-Greene, A. H. M. "America in the Niger Valley." Phylon 23 (Fall 1962): 225-239.

Loggins. The Negro Author, pp. 94, 129, 152, 182-188, 198, 209, 211, 242, 249, 358, 377, 389, 395-396, 427-428.

McPherson, James M. The Negro's Civil War. New York: Pantheon, 1965.

Malveaux, Julianne. "Revolutionary Themes in Martin Delany's Blake." Black Scholar 4 (July-August 1973): 52-56.

Miller, K. "The Historical Background of the Negro Physician." Journal of Negro History 1 (1916): 99-109.

Negro History Bulletin 4 (May 1941): 170-171, 182.

"Negro Novelists Blazing the Way in Fiction." Negro History Bulletin 3 (December 1938): 17.

"Obituary Notices." Charleston News and Courier, 13 February, 2 and 15 September, 2 and 3 October, 1885.

Quarles, Benjamin. Black Abolitionists, pp. 140-141, 162.

Redding. They Came in Chains, pp. 103, 144-145.

Rollins, Frank A. Life and Public Services of Martin Rob-

inson Delany. Boston: Lee & Shepard, 1883. (née Francis Rollins.)

Sterling. Speak Out in Thunder Tones, pp. 134-136, 154,
198-204, 232-239; 224-225, 275-277, 292-296, 360, 374.

Takaki, Ronald T. Violence in the Black Imagination. New
York: Putnam's Sons, 1972, pp. 79-214.

Tischler. Black Masks, p. 150.

Trent, Toni. "Stratification Among Blacks by Black Authors." Negro History Bulletin 34 (1971): 179-181.

Ullman, Victor. Martin Delany: The Beginning of Black
Nationalism. Boston: Beacon Press, 1971. p. 3.

Williams. They Also Spoke, pp. 222-223, 255.

Woodson, Carter G. The Negro in Our History. rev. ed.
Washington, D.C.: Associated Press 1941, p. 297.

Yellin. The Intricate Knot, pp. 185, 187-211.

Yeugner, John. "A Note on Martin Delany's Blake and
Black Militancy." Phylon 32 (Spring 1971): 98-105.

[1]Victor Ullman, Martin Delany: The Beginning of
Black Nationalism (Boston: Beacon Press, 1971), p. 3.

[2]"Martin R. Delany," Negro Heritage 3 (1964): 48.

[3]Ullman, p. 25.

[4]"Martin R. Delany," p. 48.

[5]Ullman, pp. 25-26.

[6]Benjamin Brawley, Negro Builders and Heroes (Chapel Hill: The University of North Carolina Press, 1937),
p. 91.

[7]Richard Barksdale and Keneth Kinnamon, Black
Writers of America (New York: Macmillan, 1972), pp.
192-193.

[8]"Martin R. Delany," p. 48.

[9]Barksdale and Kinnamon, p. 193.

DELANY, Samuel R. Born 1942.
  EDITOR (Science Fiction)
    Quark, No. 1. New York: Popular Library, n.d.
    Quark, No. 2. New York: Popular Library, n.d.
    With Marilyn Hacker. Quark, No. 3. New York: Popular
      Library, n.d.
    Quark, No. 4. New York: Popular Library, n.d.
  SCIENCE FICTION
    Babel - 1.7, 1966; 2nd ed. New York: Ace, 1973†.
    The Ballad of Beta-2, 1965; New York: Ace, 1971†. (Is-
      sued with this is Petaja, Emil. Alpha Yes, Terra No.)
    Captives of the Flame. New York: Ace, 1963†. (Issued
      with this is Woodcott, Keith. The Psionic Menace.)
    City of a Thousand Suns. New York: Ace, 1965.
    Driftglass: Ten Tales of Speculative Fiction. New York:
      New American Library, 1971†.
    The Einstein Intersection, 1967; New York: Ace, 1971†.
    Empire Star. New York: Ace, 1966. (Issued with Purdom,
      Tom. The Tree Lord of Imeten.)
    The Fall of the Towers, 1971; New York: Ace, 1972†.
      Originally published in three volumes: Out of the Dead

City. London: Sphere, 1968; The Towers of Torn. New
    York: Ace, 1964; City of a Thousand Suns. London:
    Sphere, 1969.
The Jewels of Aptor, 1962; New York: Ace, 1972†.
Nova. New York: Doubleday, 1968.
The Tides of Lust. New York: Lancer, 1973†.
The Towers of Toron. New York: Ace, 1964. (Issued with
    this is Williams, Robert M., The Lunar Eye.)
(Anthologies): Ellison, Harlan, ed. Dangerous Visions
    (Garden City, N.Y.: Doubleday, 1967); Ferman, Edward
    L., ed. The Best from Fantasy and Science Fiction
    (Garden City, N.Y.: Doubleday, 1968); Meril, Judith, ed.
    SF 12 (New York: Delacorte, 1968).
(Periodicals): Fantasy and Science Fiction, October 1967;
    Worlds of Science Fiction, June 1967; Worlds of Tomor-
    row, February 1967.
CRITICISM ON DELANY
    Scobie, Stephen. "Different Mazes: Mythology in Samuel
        R. Delaney's [sic] The Einstein Intersection." Riverside
        Quarterly (Saskatchewan) 5: 12-18.
REVIEW
    The Tides of Lust.
        Publisher's Weekly, 19 February 1973, p. 82.

DE LEGALL, Walter. Born 13 June 1936 in Philadelphia. Educa-
    tion: B.A., (Mathematics) Howard University. Columbia Uni-
    versity Graduate School of Business. Currently living in New
    York City. Career: President of compatibility processing cor-
    poration--a data processing services center. Served as editor
    of Dasein literary journal for five years, and as editor of
    Burning Spear, an anthology of Afro-Saxon verse. Has given
    poetry readings at various colleges and universities in the U.S.,
    and has recorded with the Howard Poets at the Library of Con-
    gress.
POETRY
    (Anthologies): Burning Spear; Henderson, Understanding the
        New Black Poetry; Jones and Neal, Black Fire; Pool, Be-
        yond the Blues; Lowenfels, Poets of Today.
INTERJECTIONS
    "While art in my life is as natural and compelling as a bio-
    logical function, it, nevertheless, must be channeled and di-
    rected. As a Black artist I cannot afford the luxury of art for
    art's sake. The importance of my work will have to be judged
    in relation to how well it succeeds in satisfying the cultural im-
    peratives of our Black Nation."

DEMBY, William. Born 1922 in Pittsburgh, Pennsylvania. Ca-
    reer: See Barksdale and Kinnamon, The Black Writer in
    America, pp. 767-768; Shockley and Chandler, Living Black
    American Authors.
NOVELS
    Beetlecreek. New York: Rinehart, 1967; Chatham, N.J.:
        Chatham Booksellers, 1972*; New York: Avon, 1967; ex-

cerpts in Hill, Soon One Morning; Davis and Redding,
Cavalcade; Miller, Blackamerican Literature.
The Catacombs. New York: Pantheon Books, 1965; New
York: Perennial, 1970. Excerpts in Margolies, A Native
Sons Reader.
BIOGRAPHY AND CRITICISM ON DEMBY
Bayliss, John F. "Beetlecreek: Existential or Human Docu-
ment." Negro Digest 19 (November 1969): 70-74. (Re-
buttal to Bone article.)
Bigsby. "From Protest to Paradox: The Black Writer at
Mid Century," pp. 217-240.
Bone, Robert. "William Demby's Dance of Life." Tri-
Quarterly 9 (1969): 127-141.
_____. The Negro Novel in America, pp. 191-196.
Hoffman, Nancy Y. "The Annunciation of William Demby."
Studies in Black Literature 2 (Spring 1972): 8-13.
_____. "Technique in Demby's The Catacombs." Studies
in Black Literature 2 (Summer 1971): 10-13.
"Interview." Black Creation, Spring 1972.
Littlejohn. Black on White, pp. 153-154.
Margolies, Edward. "The Expatriate as Novelist: William
Demby." In Margolies, Native Sons: A Critical Study of
Twentieth Century Negro American Authors, pp. 173-189.
O'Brien, John. "Interview with William Demby." Studies
in Black Literature 3 (Autumn 1972): 1-6.
_____. Interviews with Black Writers, pp. 35-53.
Singh, Raman K. "The Black Novel and Its Tradition."
Colorado Quarterly 20 (Summer 1971): 23-29.
Whitlow. Black American Literature, pp. 122-124.

DENNIS, R. M.
POETRY (Anthology): Brown, Lee and Ward, To Gwen with
Love.

DENT, Thomas C. (Kush). Born in New Orleans, Louisiana. Edu-
cation: Morehouse College. Currently living in New Orleans,
Louisiana. Career: Free lance writer in New Orleans and Co-
editor of NKUMBO. Founder of Umbra.
CRITICISM
(Periodicals)
"The Free Southern Theatre, An Evaluation." Freedomways
6 (Winter 1966): 26; reprinted in Patterson, Anthology of
the American Negro in the Theatre.
"The Free Southern Theatre." Negro Digest 14 (April 1967):
40.
"Report on Black Theater." Negro Digest 18 (April 1969):
24-26.
"Beyond Rhetoric Toward a Black Southern Theatre." Black
World 2 (April 1971): 14-24.
DRAMA
Feathers and Stuff, 1970.
Negro Study #34A (one act), 1969.
Riot Duty (one act), 1969.

Ritual Murder (one act), 1967.

Snapshot (one act), 1969.

With Val Ferdinand. Song of Survival (one act), 1969.

EDITOR

With Richard Schechner and Gilbert Moses. The Free Southern Theater by the Free Southern Theater. Indianapolis:
Bobbs-Merrill, 1969†.

NON-FICTION

(Periodical): Freedomways, Fall 1698; Winter 1971.

POETRY

(Anthologies): Chapman, New Black Voices; Hughes, New
Negro Poets: USA; Simmons and Hutchinson, Black Cul-
ture; Patterson, An Introduction to Black Literature in
America.

REVIEWS BY DENT

Published in Black World and Freedomways.

DE RAMUS, Betty.

DRAMA

That's Just What I Said, 1971.

NON-FICTION

(Periodical): Negro Digest, November 1967.

SHORT STORY

(Periodical): Black World, June 1972.

DE SAAVEDRA, Guadalupe.

POETRY (Anthology): Schulberg, From the Ashes.

DESBROSSES, Nelson. Career: Well-known as a successful medium who studied with Valmour.[1]

POETRY

(Anthology): Coleman, Creole Voices.
[1]Charles Hamlin Good, "The First American Literary
Movement," Opportunity 10 (March 1932): 77-79.

DESDUNES, P. A. 19th Century Creole. Education: His writings
indicate that he was well-educated. Career: Served on the
board of directors of the Orphanage of Negro Children, which
was appropriate for a man with his concern for humanity. The
writings of the Creole poets of Les Cenelles were preserved in
his ledgers.[1]

POETRY

(Anthology): Coleman, Creole Voices.

BIOGRAPHY ON DESDUNES

Coleman. Creole Voices, p. xxv.

Desdunes. Nos Hommes et Notre Histoire, p. 145.
[1]Edward Maceo Coleman, ed., Creole Voices: Poems
in French by Free Men of Color (Washington, D.C.: Associated, 1945), p. xxv.

DE SHANDS, Lottie Belle.

POETRY

Golden Gems of a New Civilization: Poems. New York: Exposition, 1955.

DETT, Robert Nathaniel. Born 1882 in Drummondsville, Ontario.
Died 2 October 1943. Education: B. Mus., Oberlin College,
1908; additional study at Harvard University, 1920-21. Career:
Taught at Lane College and Lincoln Institute before joining the
faculty at Hampton Institute where he was director of music
from 1913 to 1931, conducting the Hampton Institute Choir on
its national and international tours;[1] accepted the directorship
at Bennett College in 1937. At the time of his death, he was
working with the USO chorus. He was not only an outstanding
teacher and choirmaster, but an arranger and composer.[2]
Awards, Honors: D. Mus., Harvard University, 1924; D. Mus.,
Oberlin College, 1926. While at Harvard, he was awarded the
Bowdoin essay prize and the Francis Boott prize in composi-
tion.
MISCELLANEOUS WRITINGS
   "As the Negro School Sings." Southern Workman 56 (July
      1927).
   The Dett Collection of Negro Spirituals. Chicago: Hall &
      McCreary, 1936.
   "The Emancipation of Negro Music." The Southern Work-
      man 47 (April 1918).
   "Ethnologist Aids Composer to Draw Inspiration from Heart
      of People." Musical America, 31 May 1919.
   "Negro Music of the Present." Southern Workman 47 (May
      1918).
   Religious Folk Songs of the Negro, 1927; reprint ed., New
      York: AMS Press*.
POETRY
   The Album of a Heart. Jackson, Tenn.: Mocowat-Mercer,
      1911.
   (Anthologies): Johnson, The Book of American Negro Po-
      etry; Kerlin, Negro Poets and Their Poems.
   (Periodical): Opportunity, January 1929.
BIOGRAPHY AND CRITICISM ON DETT
   Adams. Great Negroes Past and Present.
   Brawley. The Negro Genius, pp. 202-203.
   _____. The Negro in Literature and Art, pp. 168-169.
   Grove's Dictionary of Music and Musicians, p. 679.
   Guzman. Negro Yearbook (1941-1946), pp. 426-427.
   Kerlin. Negro Poets and Their Poems, pp. 230-233.
   Lovell, John, Jr. Black Song. New York: Macmillan,
      1972, pp. 446-447.
   Lovingood, Penman. Famous Modern Negro Musicians.
      Brooklyn, N.Y.: Press Forum Co., 1921.
   Negro History Bulletin 2 (February 1939): 36, 46.
   New York Times, 4 October 1943, p. 17. (Obituary.)
   Pope, Marguerite. "A Brief Biography of Dr. Robert Na-
      thaniel Dett." Hampton, Va.: Hampton Institute Press,
      1945. The Hampton Bulletin 42 (October 1945).
   "Robert Nathaniel Dett." Negro History Bulletin 7 (No-
      vember 1943): 45, 47.
   Robinson. Historical Negro Biographies, pp. 182-183.

INTERJECTIONS

"Dett was a firm believer in the religious significance and power of the spirituals. Not only was he sure that religion was the primary motivation of the slaves who created songs; he believed they were right. The term spiritual he derived from the fact that the creators and singers were moved by 'the Spirit.' He felt the spiritual 'became very sincerely the voice of a divine power, as wonderful as that which wakens the magnolias into their gorgeous bloom, hurls a Niagara over thundering precipice, wakens the trill of the morning bird or paints the glories of a sunset sky.' "[3]

[1]Benjamin Brawley, The Negro Genius (New York: Dodd, Mead, 1937), pp. 302-303.

[2]Refer to The National Union Catalog Pre-1956 Imprints for a listing of many of his compositions.

[3]John Lovell, Jr., Black Song (New York: Macmillan, 1972), p. 447.

DETTER, Thomas.
SKETCHES Nellie Brown; or, The Jealous Wife, with Other Sketches, written and published by Thomas Detter, (colored) of Elko, Nevada. San Francisco: Cuddy & Hughes, Printers, 1871.

DE WINDT, Hal.
DRAMA Us Versus Nobody, 1972.

DICKENS, Dorothy Lee.
NOVEL Black on the Rainbow. New York: Pageant Press, 1952.

DICKERSON, Glenda.
DRAMA
Jesus Christ--Lawd Today, 1971.
The Torture of Mothers, 1973.

DICKERSON, Juanita M.
POETRY (Anthology): Murphy, Negro Voices.

DICKINSON, Blanche Taylor. Born 15 April 1896 in Franklin, Kentucky. Education: Attended Bowling Green Academy, Simmon's University, and summer schools. Career: Taught school in Kentucky for many years.[1]
POETRY
(Anthologies): Cullen, Caroling Dusk; Johnson, Ebony and Topaz; Patterson, A Rock Against the Wind.
(Periodicals): Crisis, 1927; 1928; Opportunity, February, July 1927; June 1929.
Also published in Franklin Favorite; Chicago Defender; Louisville Leader; Pittsburgh Courier; Wayfarer.
BIOGRAPHY ON DICKINSON
Opportunity 5 (July 1927): 213.
[1]Countée Cullen, ed., Caroling Dusk (New York: Harper & Row, 1927), p. 105.

DIGGS, Arthur.
    POETRY
        Black Children, Black and Beautiful. Chicago: By the Au-
          thor, P.O. Box 6862, 1969. (Poems for Black Children.)
        Black Woman. New York: Exposition, 1954.
        Naturally Black. Chicago: By the Author, 1968. (Revised edi-
          tion of The Plain Poet.)
        (Anthology): Brown, Lee and Ward, To Gwen with Love.
        (Periodicals): Journal of Black Poetry, Spring 1969; Negro
          History Bulletin, April 1971.

DINGANE see GONCALVES, Joe

DINKINS, Rev. Charles R. Career: Minister of the A.M.E. Zion
    Church.
    POETRY
        Lyrics of Love, Sacred and Secular. Columbia, S.C.: State
          Co., 1904.
        (Anthology): White and Jackson, An Anthology of Verse by
          American Negroes.

DISMOND, Henry Binga. Born 27 December 1891 in Richmond,
    Virginia. Education: Virginia Union University; Howard Uni-
    versity; B.S., University of Chicago, 1917; M.D., Rush Medi-
    cal College, 1921. Career: Physician, specializing in electro-
    therapy and x-ray. Awards, Honors: His record for the quar-
    ter-mile sprint, in 1916, equalled the world's record.[1] He
    was a Chevalier of the National Order of Honor and Merit,
    Haiti, having been cited by President Stenio Vincent for his
    work following the Dominican Massacre of 1937.[2]
    POETRY
        We Who Would Die, and Other Poems, including Haitian Vign-
          ettes. New York: Associated, 1945.
        (Anthologies): Adams, Conn and Slepian, Afro-American Lit-
          erature: Poetry; Murphy, Ebony Rhythm.
          [1]Who's Who in Colored America, 3rd ed. (1933).
          [2]Beatrice Murphy, Ebony Rhythm (Freeport, N.Y.:
        Books for Libraries, 1968), p. 58.

DIXON, Edwina.
    SHORT STORY (Anthology): Ford and Faggett, Best Short
        Stories by Afro-American Writers.

DIXON, Melvin.
    DRAMA
        Confrontation, 1969.
        Kingdom, or The Last Promise, 1972.
        Ritual: For Malcolm, 1970.

DIXON, Sam.
    POETRY (Periodical): Negro American Literature Forum,
        Fall 1973.

DJANGATOLUM see CORBIN, Lloyd McMillan, Jr.

DODSON, Owen. <u>Born</u> 28 November 1914 in Brooklyn. <u>Education:</u>
B.A., Bates College, 1936; M.F.A. in Drama, Yale University, 1939. <u>Currently living in</u> New York City. <u>Career:</u> Former head of the Department of Drama, College of Fine Arts,
Howard University; Drama Director at Atlanta University, Spelman College, and Hampton Institute; director of a morale-build-
ing program, U.S. Navy; tour director for a three-month tour
of the Howard Players in Denmark, Sweden, and Germany; lecturer and poetry reader at a number of colleges and universities; director of summer theatre at Atlanta University, Hampton Institute, The Theater Lobby, Lincoln University, and Howard University; poet-in-residence, Ruth Stephen Poetry Center,
University of Arizona; executive secretary for the Committee
for Mass Education in Race Relations of the American Film Center, New York City; artistic consultant, Harlem School of the
Arts Community Theatre. His new opera, "A Christmas Miracle," had its premiere performance sponsored by Phi Kappa
Lambda, the national music organization; another opera, " 'Til
Victory Is Won," is scheduled for a New York City performance; "The Confession Stone," a song cycle, was sung by
Maureen Forrester in Carnegie Hall, 1968. James Earle Jones
narrates "The Dream Awake" (dramatic poem) on a Spoken Arts
recording. <u>Member:</u> Phi Beta Kappa; Charter Member, The
Negro Playwrights Company. <u>Awards, Honors:</u> Rosenwald and
General Education Board Fellowships; Guggenheim Fellowship,
1953; Rockefeller Grant, 1968; received the <u>Paris Review</u> international prize for the short story, "The Summer Fire." Received the Doctor of Letters degree from Bates College, 1967.

<u>CRITICISM</u>
    "Countée Cullen (1903-1946)." <u>Phylon</u> 7 (First Quarter 1946):
        19-20.
    "Oedipus Rex at Howard University." <u>World Theatre,</u> n.d.
    "Personal Impressions of Richard Wright." <u>New Letters</u> (a
        publication of the University of Missouri), n.d.
    "Playwrights in Dark Glasses." <u>Negro Digest</u> 16 (April
        1968).
    "The Special Wonder of the Theatre." <u>The Washingtonian</u>
        5 (February 1966).
    "The World Seemed Wide and Open." <u>Theatre Arts</u> (March
        1950).

<u>DRAMA</u>
    <u>Bayou Legend,</u> 1946 In Turner, <u>Black Drama in America.</u>
    <u>The Christmas Miracle.</u>[1]
    <u>Divine Comedy,</u> 1938. New York: Harper & Row, forthcom-
        ing; excerpt in Brown, Davis and Lee, <u>The Negro Cara-</u>
        <u>van.</u>
    <u>Dorie Miller.</u> In <u>Theatre Arts</u> (July 1943).
    <u>Everybody Join Hands.</u> In <u>Theatre Arts</u> 28 (1942).
    <u>Medea in Africa,</u> 1964.
    <u>Someday We're Gonna Tear the Pillars Down.</u> In <u>The Ne-</u>
        <u>gro Quarterly</u> 1 (Summer 1942): 161-166.
    With Countée Cullen. <u>The Third Fourth of July.</u> In <u>The-</u>
        <u>atre Arts</u> 30 (1946).[2]

New World A-Coming.[3]
With Mark Fax. Till Victory Is Won, 1967.
MANUSCRIPTS IN THE YALE UNIVERSITY LIBRARY
Americus.
Amistad, 1939.[4]
The Ballad of Dorie Miller, 1942.
Climbing to the Soul.
Divine Comedy, 1938.
Don't Give Up the Ship.
Doomsdale Tale, 1941?
Freedom the Banner, 1942.
The Garden of Time, 1939.
Gargoyles in Florida, 1936.
Heroes on Parade, No. 3.
Including Laughter, 1936.
Jonathan's Song.
Lord Nelson, Naval Hero.
The Southern Star, 1940.
NON-FICTION
   (Periodicals): Color, USA, Fall-Winter 1946-47; Harlem
   Quarterly, Fall-Winter 1950; The New Republic, 27 July
   1953; Negro Digest, March 1947; Common Ground, Winter
   1947.
NOVELS
   Boy at the Window, 1951; New York: Chatham Bookseller,
   1972*; published under the title, When Trees Were Green,
   New York: Popular Library. Excerpt in Davis and Red-
   ding, Cavalcade. Also published in Japan (Tokyo: Haya-
   kawa Shobo and Co., 1961).
POETRY
   Cages. New York: Popular Library, forthcoming.
   The Confession Stone: A Song Cycle by Mary about Jesus.
   London: Paul Breman, 1970. Distributed in U.S. by
   Broadside Press, Detroit.
   Powerful Long Ladder, 1946. New York: Farrar, Straus &
   Giroux, 1970*†.
   (Anthologies): Abdul, The Magic of Black Poetry; Adams,
   Conn and Slepian, Afro-American Literature: Poetry;
   Adoff, I Am the Darker Brother; Adoff, The Poetry of
   Black America; Austin, Fenderson and Nelson, The Black
   Man and the Promise of America; Baker, Black Litera-
   ture in America; Barksdale and Kinnamon, The Black
   Writer in America; Bontemps, American Negro Poetry;
   Chambers and Moon, Right On!; Brown, Davis and Lee,
   Negro Caravan; Chapman, Black Voices; Davis and Red-
   ding, Cavalcade; Faderman and Bradshaw, Speaking for
   Ourselves; Hayden, Kaleidoscope; Hayden, Burrow and
   Lapides, Afro-American Literature: An Introduction;
   Henderson, Understanding the New Black Poetry; Hughes,
   and Bontemps, Poetry of the Negro: 1746-1970; Jordan,
   Soulscript; Lomax and Abdul, 3000 Years of Black Poetry;
   Long and Collier, Afro-American Writing; Michel, Way
   Out; Miller, Blackamerican Literature; Morgan, Here and

Now II; Pool, Beyond the Blues; Pool, Ik bende Nieuwe
Neger; Pool, Ik ZagHoe ZwartIk Way; Sweetkind, Getting
Into Poetry; Turner, Black American Literature--Poetry;
Walrond and Pool, Black and Unknown Bards.
(Periodicals): Black Creation, Summer 1972; Cavalcade,
November 1941; Challenge, Spring 1937; Christian Century
(Boston), 7 January 1942; Common Ground, Winter 1943;
Life and Letters Today (London), September 1940; Negro
Digest, April 1950; April, August 1951; Negro Quarterly,
1942; New Challenge, Fall 1937; Opportunity, November
1934; December 1935; August 1936; July 1937; February
1942; Phylon, Second Quarter 1940; Third Quarter 1941;
Third Quarter 1943; Fourth Quarter 1946; Theatre Arts,
January 1943; September, December 1944.

SHORT STORIES
(Anthologies): Hill, Soon One Morning; Hughes, The Best
Short Stories by Negro Writers; Hughes and Bontemps,
Book of Negro Folklore; Schulman, Come Out the Wilder-
ness; Best Short Stories of the Paris Review.

WORK IN PROGRESS
Novel: "A Bent House," to be published by Curtis Books.
Three plays under the title, "Justice Blindfolded"; a book
on "Black and White Writers I Have Known."

BIOGRAPHY AND CRITICISM ON DODSON
Bergman. The Chronological History of the Negro in Amer-
ica, p. 374.
Bone. The Negro Novel in America, pp. 185-186.
Kerlin. Negro Poets and Their Poems, p. 331.
Mitchell. Black Drama, pp. 8-9, 105, 113, 114, 123.
O'Brien. Interviews with Black Writers, pp. 55-61.
Opportunity. See the following items: July 1934, pp. 220-
221; August 1936, p. 250; May 1942, p. 150; December
1942, p. 392; Fall 1946, p. 200.
"Poets." Ebony 4 (February 1949): 41.

REVIEW
Powerful Long Ladder.
Braithwaite, William Stanley. Phylon 7 (1946).

INTERJECTIONS
"I write the best I can from my personal experiences and ob-
servations. I believe art can shape and change lives, can make
living bearable."
    [1]A libretto performed twice at Howard University.
    [2]Commissioned by the Drama Division of the New
School for Social Research.
    [3]A pageant performed at Madison Square Garden dur-
ing World War II to help the Blacks gain equality in the
Armed Forces.
    [4]Commissioned by Talladega College and performed
there in 1939.

DOLAN, Harry.
CRITICISM
"On Black Theater in America: A Report." Negro Digest

19 (April 1970): 31-34.
DRAMA
The Iron Hand of Nat Turner, 1970.
Losers Weepers (one act). In Schulberg, From the Ashes.
NON-FICTION
(Anthologies): Ford, Black Insights; Simmons and Hutchin-
son, Black Culture.
SCREENPLAY
Losers Weepers, 1966 (NBC television production under the
title, "Love Song for a Delinquent.")
SHORT STORIES
(Anthology): Schulberg, From the Ashes.
(Periodical): Esquire.
BIOGRAPHY AND CRITICISM ON DOLAN
Wilkerson, Margaret. "Black Theater in California," pp.
35-38.

DOMINIQUE, Otis G.
CHILDREN AND YOUNG ADULTS Poems for Boys and Girls.
Philadelphia: Dorrance, 1966.

DONEGAN, Pamela.
POETRY (Anthology): Troupe, Watts Poets.

DONGO, Malika.
POETRY
To You...Black Man with Love. Chicago: 5000 S. Indiana
Ave: n.d.
(Periodical): Black World, December 1973.

DONOGHUE, Dennis.
DRAMA
The Black Messiah, 1939.
Legal Murder.
BIOGRAPHY AND CRITICISM ON DONOGHUE
Mitchell. Black Drama, p. 4.

DOOLEY, Tom (Dooley, Ebon) see EBON

DORSEY, John T.
NOVEL The Lion of Judah. Chicago: Fouche Co., 1924.

DOUGLAS, Elroy.
POETRY (Anthology): Murphy, Ebony Rhythm.

DOUGLAS, Prentice Perry.
POETRY Leaves in the Wind. New York: Exposition, 1944.

DOUGLAS, Rodney K.
DRAMA
The Marijuana Trap.
The Voice of the Ghetto, 1968.

DOUGLASS, Frederick (Frederick Augustus Washington Baily). [1]
  Born a slave in February 1817 in Talbot County, Maryland.
  Died 1895. [2] Education: Learned to read and write from his
  mistress, who had to desist in her instructions when her husband told her that she was making Frederick unfit to be a slave.
  Career: Became a house servant at the age of eight, worked
  as a field hand, and was apprenticed to a calker until 1838,
  when he borrowed a free Black seaman's identification papers
  and rode public transportation to freedom. In 1841 he spoke
  out so admirably at an abolitionist meeting, that he was accepted as an agent for the Massachusetts Anti-Slavery Society. [3]
  After publishing his Narrative, 1845, he was forced to go to
  England to avoid re-enslavement. During his time in England
  he lectured on slavery and women's rights, raising enough
  money to buy his freedom. [4] Upon his return to the United
  States he founded his famous newspaper, The North Star, (published in Rochester, New York, from 1847 to 1963, renamed
  Frederick Douglass's Newspaper in the early 1850's). [5] At the
  outbreak of the Civil War he met with President Lincoln and
  was instrumental in the creation of the celebrated 54th and
  55th Massachusetts Negro regiments. In 1871, he was appointed to the territorial legislature of the District of Columbia; in
  1872 he served as one of the presidential electors-at-large for
  New York and, shortly thereafter, became secretary of the
  Santo Domingo Commission; in 1877 he was appointed police
  commissioner of the District of Columbia, eventually becoming
  Marshal; in 1881 he was named Recorder of Deeds. From
  1889 to 1891 he was U.S. Minister of Haiti. His government
  career was concluded as Chargé d'Affaires for Santo Domingo. [6]
  Douglass' influence is considered a major factor in the emancipation of the slaves, in the passage of the 14th and 15th
  Amendments to the Constitution, and in the struggle for en-
  franchisement following the Civil War. His speeches and writings are included in literary anthologies not only because of the
  significant role he played in the history of the United States,
  but also because of his fine blending of style with content. [7]
  AUTOBIOGRAPHY (Three Versions.)
      Narrative of the Life of Frederick Douglass, an American
        Slave. Boston, 1845; reissue edited by Benjamin Quarles.
        Cambridge: Harvard University Press, 1960*†. Garden
        City, N.Y.: Doubleday*.
      (Anthologies): Adams, Conn and Slepian, Afro-American
        Literature: Non Fiction; Austin, Fenderson and Nelson,
        The Black Man and The Promise of America; Baker,
        Black Literature in America; Barksdale and Kinnamon,
        Black Writers of America; Brown, Davis and Lee, The
        Negro Caravan; Chapman, Black Voices; David, Black
        Joy; Davis and Redding, Cavalcade; Emanuel and Gross,
        Dark Symphony; Katz, Eyewitness; Miller, Blackamerican
        Literature; Turner and Bright, Images of the Negro in
        American Literature.
      My Bondage and My Freedom. New York, 1855; New York:
        Dover, 1969†; Chicago: Johnson*.

(Anthologies): Brawley, <u>Early Negro American Writers;</u>
Katz, <u>Eyewitness;</u> Kendricks and Levitt, <u>Afro-American</u>
<u>Voices;</u> Long and Collier, <u>Afro-American Writing.</u>
<u>The Life and Times of Frederick Douglass.</u> Hartford, 1881;
New York: Pathway Press, 1941; New York: Macmillan,
1962†; abridged edition, <u>From Slave to Statesman: The</u>
<u>Life and Times of Frederick Douglass.</u> Edited by Philip
S. Foner. New York: Noble & Noble, 1972†.
(Anthology): Stanford, <u>I, Too, Sing America.</u>
See also:
(Anthologies): Quarles, <u>Blacks on John Brown;</u> Takaki, <u>Vio-</u>
<u>lence in the Black Imagination;</u> Woodson, <u>The Mind of the</u>
<u>Negro as Reflected in His Letters.</u>
(Reference Sources): <u>The Dictionary of the Schomburg Col-</u>
<u>lection of Negro Literature and History; The National Un-</u>
<u>ion Catalog Pre-1956 Imprints.</u>
COLLECTED WORKS
Foner, Philip S. <u>Life and Writings of Frederick Douglass.</u>
4 vols. New York: International, 1950-55*†.
SPEECHES
(Refer to Foner's <u>Life and Writings of Frederick Douglass,</u>
listed above; <u>The Dictionary of the Schomburg Collection</u>
<u>of Negro Literature and History; The National Catalog</u>
<u>Pre-1956 Imprints;</u> Sutton, Roberta Briggs. <u>Speech Index.</u>
New York: Scarecrow, 1966, p. 240.)
<u>The Mind and Heart of Frederick Douglass: Excerpts from</u>
<u>Speeches of the Great Negro Orator.</u> Edited by Barbara
Ritchie. New York: T. Y. Crowell, 1968.
(Anthologies): Barksdale and Kinnamon, <u>Black Writers of</u>
<u>America;</u> Brawley, <u>Early Negro American Writers;</u> Chace
and Collier, <u>Justice Denied;</u> Fishel and Quarles, <u>The</u>
<u>Black American: A Documentary History;</u> Ford, <u>Black</u>
<u>Insights;</u> Hill, <u>Rhetoric of Racial Revolt;</u> Long and Collier,
<u>Afro-American Writing;</u> Miller, <u>Blackamerican Literature;</u>
Turner and Bright, <u>Images of the Negro in America.</u>
BIOGRAPHY AND CRITICISM ON DOUGLASS
Abramson. <u>Negro Playwrights in the American Theatre,</u> pp.
8, 9, 12, 117, 224, 300 n.21, 179-188, 256, 257, 260.
Adams. <u>Great Negroes Past and Present,</u> p. 26.
Armour, Anobel. <u>Freedom from Bondage.</u> Scottdale, Pa.:
Herald, 1970. (Children and Young Adults.)
Baker, Houston A., Jr. "Revolution and Reform: Walker,
Douglass, and the Road to Freedom." In Baker, <u>The</u>
<u>Long Black Song,</u> pp. 58-83.
Bardolph. <u>The Negro Vanguard,</u> pp. 21-374 passim.
Bennett, Lerone, Jr. <u>Before the Mayflower,</u> pp. 75-316
passim.
_____. "Father of the Protest Movement." <u>Negro Digest</u>
14 (February 1965): 12-20.
_____. "Frederick Douglass: Father of the Protest Move-
ment." <u>Ebony</u> 18 (September 1963): 50-52.
_____. "Pioneers in Protest: The Up-to-Date Frederick
Douglass." <u>Ebony</u> 19 (June 1964): 70-72.

Bontemps, Arna. "The Dilemma of Frederick Douglass in the Civil War Years." Sepia 2 (August 1971): 68-74.

_____. Frederick Douglass: Slave--Fighter--Freeman. New York: Knopf, 1959. (Children.)

_____. Free at Last: The Life of Frederick Douglass. New York: Dodd, Mead, 1971.

_____. 100 Years of Negro Freedom, pp. 106-124.

Brawley. Early Negro American Writers, pp. 175-179.

_____. Negro Builders and Negroes, pp. 61-66.

_____. The Negro Genius, pp. 51-58.

_____. The Negro in Literature and Art, pp. 4, 39, 53, 55-58, 62-63.

Butcher. The Negro in American Culture, 19, 37, 97, 117-120, 122, 123, 216.

Cain, Alfred E. Winding Road to Freedom. Yonkers: Educational Heritage, pp. 133-136.

Chesnutt, Charles W. Frederick Douglass, 1899; reprint ed., New York: Johnson Reprint, 1971.

Child, Lydia M. Freedmen's Book, pp. 156-176.

Christmas. Negroes in Public Affairs and Government, pp. 166-168.

Davidson, Margaret. Frederick Douglass Rights for Freedom. Scholastic Book Service, 1971. (Children.)

Davis. The American Negro Reference Book, pp. 35-866 passim.

Dictionary of American Biography, vol. 5 (1930).

Factor, Robert. Black Response to America: Men, Ideals and Organization. Reading, Mass.: Addison-Wesley, 1970.

Fishel and Quarles. The Black American: A Documentary History, 82-305 passim.

Foner, Philip S. Frederick Douglass, A Biography. New York: Citadel, 1964*.

Gara, Larry. "The Professional Fugitive in the Abolition Movement." Wisconsin Magazine of History 48 (1965): 196-204.

Gloster. Negro Voices in American Fiction, pp. 17, 18, 38, 211, 212, 252.

Graham, Shirley. There Was Once a Slave: The Heroic Story of Frederick Douglass. New York: Messner, 1947. (Children.)

Gregory, James M. Frederick Douglass the Orator, 1893; reprint ed., Metro Books, 1969.

Hale, Frank W. "Frederick Douglass: Antislavery Crusader and Lecturer." Journal of Human Relations 14 (First Quarter 1966): 100-111.

Haley, James T., ed. Afro-American Encyclopedia; or, the Thoughts, Doings and Sayings of the Race. Nashville, Tenn.: Haley & Florida, 1896, pp. 579-610.

Hoexter, Corinne K. Black Crusader: Frederick Douglass. Chicago: Rand McNally, 1970.

Holland, Frederic M. Frederick Douglass: The Colored Orator, 1891; Westport, Conn. Negro Universities Press.*

Hughes, Langston. Famous Negro Heroes of America, pp. 79-100.

Hunt, I. G. "Recollections of Frederick Douglass." Negro History Bulletin 16 (June 1953): 202-203.

In Memoriam: Frederick Douglass, 1897; facsimile ed., Freeport, N.Y.: Books for Libraries.

Jahn. Neo-African Literature, pp. 127, 136, 140.

Johnson. Black Manhattan, pp. 54-57.

Katz. Eyewitness: The Negro in American History, pp. 95-339 passim.

Logan, Rayford Whittingham. Two Bronze Titans: Frederick Douglass and W. E. B. DuBois. Washington, D.C.: History Department, Howard University, 1972.

Loggins. The Negro Author pp. 41-429 passim.

Lovell. Black Song, pp. 115-497 passim.

Lyons, Thomas T. Black Leadership in American History. Menlo Park, Ca.: Addison-Wesley, 1971, pp. 13-52.

Mays. The Negro's God, pp. 121-126, 128.

Meier. Negro Thought in America 1880-1915, pp. 3-306 passim.

Ottley and Weatherby. The Negro in New York, pp. 84-85, 90, 98-99, 110, 114, 123-125.

Patterson, Lillie. Frederick Douglass. New York: Dell, n.d.

_____. Frederick Douglass, Freedom Fighter. Scarsdale, N.Y.: Garrard, 1965.

Perry, Patsy Brewington. "Before The North Star: Frederick Douglass' Early Journalistic Career." Phylon 35 (March 1974): 96-107.

Quarles. Blacks on John Brown, pp. 75-77.

_____. "Frederick Douglass: Black Imperishable." Quarterly Journal of the Library of Congress 29 (1972): 159-162.

_____. "Frederick Douglass: Bridge-Building in Human Relations." Negro History Bulletin 29 (1966): 99-100, 112.

_____, ed. Frederick Douglass. Englewood Cliffs, N.J.: Prentice-Hall, 1968.

_____. Frederick Douglass. New York: Atheneum, 1968.

_____. "Frederick Douglass as Hero." Midwest Journal 1 (Winter 1948): 50-56.

Redding. The Lonesome Road, pp. 44-62.

_____. They Came in Chains, pp. 35-322 passim.

Robinson. Historical Negro Biographies, p. 74.

Rollins. They Showed the Way, pp. 46-52.

Takaki. Violence in the Black Imagination, pp. 18-35.

"Ten Greats of Black History." Ebony 27 (August 1972): 36.

Thorpe. Black Historians, pp. 6, 12, 28, 37,39, 41, 54, 82, 171, 179, 180, 199-200.

Yellin. The Intricate Knot, pp. 85, 99, 160-167, 169, 196.

[1]He assumed the name of Douglass after his escape from slavery.

[2]Harry A. Ploski and Ernest Kaiser, eds., The Negro

Almanac (New York: Bellwether, 1971), p. 287.
[3]Edgar A. Toppin, A Biographical History of Blacks
in America Since 1528 (New York: McKay, 1969), p. 282.
[4]Ploski and Kaiser, p. 287.
[5]Toppin, p. 282.
[6]Ploski and Kaiser, pp. 287-288.
[7]Richard Barksdale and Keneth Kinnamon, Black
Writers of America (New York: Macmillan, 1972), p. 68.

DOWNING, Henry Francis. Born 1851.
  DRAMA
    The Arabian Lovers; or, The Sacred Jar, an Eastern Tale
      in Four Acts. London: F. Griffiths, 1913.
    Human Nature; or, The Traduced Wife (An Original English
      Domestic Drama, in four acts). London: F. Griffiths,
      1913.
    Incentive, 1914.
    Lord Eldred's Other Daughter. London: F. Griffiths, 1913.
    A New Coon in Town, 1914.
    Placing Paul's Play. London: F. Griffiths, 1913.
    The Shuttlecock; or, Israel in Russia. London: F. Griffiths,
      1913.
    Voodoo. London: F. Griffiths, 1914.
  NON-FICTION
    Liberia and Her People. New York, 1925.
    A Short History of Liberia (1816-1908). New York: Amos
      M. Gailliard, n.d.
  NOVEL
    The American Cavalryman: A Liberian Romance. New
      York: Neale, 1917; reprint ed., Washington, D.C.: Mc-
      Grath, 1969*; New York: AMS Press, 1969*.
  CRITICISM ON DOWNING
    Bone. The Negro Novel in America, p. 49.
    Gloster. Negro Voices in American Fiction, pp. 94-95.
  REVIEWS
    The American Cavalry Man:
      Crisis 15 (1918): 186.
      Hunt, Ida Gibbs. Journal of Negro History 3 (October
      1918): 444-445.

DOZIER, Arthur, Jr.
  POETRY (Periodical): Journal of Black Poetry, Winter-
    Spring 1970.

DRAKE, Sandra.
  SHORT STORY (Anthology): Mayfield, Ten Times Black.

DRAYTON, Ronald.
  DRAMA
    Black Chaos, 1966.
    The Conquest of Africa, 1968.
    Nocturne on the Rhine. In Jones and Neal, Black Fire.
    Notes from a Savage God. In Jones and Neal, Black Fire.

DRAYTON, Thomas.
POETRY Looking It Over. n.p., 1967.

DREER, Herman. Born 12 September 1889 in Washington, D.C.
Education: Attended the Elementary School and the M. Street
High School in Washington, D.C. He received an A.B. from
Bowdoin College, 1910, and graduated magna cum laude. He
attended Virginia Theological Seminary, Lynchburg, 1911-1914;
earned A.M. from University of Illinois, 1916 and from Columbia University, 1919; studied at the University of Chicago, summer 1930, 1931; received D.D. from Douglass University, St.
Louis, Mo., 1938. Career: Professor of Latin and Science,
Virginia Theological Seminary, Lynchburg, 1910-1914; taught
English and Drama, Sumner High School, St. Louis, Mo., 1914-
26; Professor of English, Stowe Teacher's College, 1926-30;
became Assistant High School Principal 1930-. He was president of the St. Louis Welfare Association; treasurer of the National Pan-Hellenic Council; director of the Carter Woodson
School of Negro History, St. Louis, Mo.; President of Doug-
lass University, St. Louis. Professor Dreer's activities were
not limited only to teaching and academic activities. He was
campaign speaker for the Liberty League; Editor-in-Chief of
Oracle, Omega Psi Phi Magazine, and Director of its Negro
Achievement Project; director of Sumner High School's Drama
Club. Member: Elected to Phi Beta Kappa at Bowdoin Col-
lege.[1]
DRAMA[2]
    Historical Plays and Religious Plays of Negro Life.
NON-FICTION
    American Literature by Negro Authors. New York: Macmil-
        lan, 1950.
    The History of the Omega Psi Phi Fraternity. Washington,
        D.C.: The Fraternity, 1940.
    Negro Leadership in St. Louis: A Study in Race Relations.
        Chicago: Library of Photographic Reproductions, Univer-
        sity of Chicago, 1955.
NOVELS
    The Immediate Jewel of His Soul. St. Louis, Mo.: Argus,
        1919; reprint ed., Washington, D.C.: McGrath, 1969*.
        New York: AMS Press, 1969*.
    The Tie that Binds. Boston: Meador, 1958.
    Out of the Night, 1916.
BIOGRAPHY AND CRITICISM ON DREER
    Bone. The Negro Novel in America, p. 35.
    Gayle. Black Expression, p. 110.
    Gloster. Negro Voices in American Fiction, pp. 118-122.
    Hughes. The Negro Novelist, p. 36.
    Rees, Robert A. and Earl N. Harbert, eds. Fifteen Amer-
        ican Authors Before 1900. Madison: University of Wiscon-
        sin Press, 1971. p. 410.
    Yenser, Thomas, ed. Who's Who in Colored America, 3rd
        ed. New York: Yenser, 1930-31-32, p. 135.
        [1]Thomas Yenser, ed., Who's Who in Colored America,

3rd ed. (New York: Yenser, 1930-31-32), p. 135.
²Ibid.
³Ibid.

DU BOIS, Shirley Graham (Shirley Lola Graham).   Born 11 November 1907 in Indianapolis, Indiana.   Career: See Ploski, Reference Library of Black America; Shockley and Chandler, Living Black American Authors, p. 59; Current Biography, 1946, pp. 221-222.

BIOGRAPHY
Booker T. Washington: Educator of Hand, Head, and Heart. New York: Messner, 1955.
With George D. Lipscomb. Dr. George Washington Carver, Scientist.   New York: Messner, 1944*; New York: Pocket Books†. Excerpt in Negro Digest, July 1944.
Gamal Abdel Nasser: Son of the Nile.   New York: Third Press, 1972*.
His Day Is Marching On: A Memoir of W. E. B. Du Bois. Philadelphia: J. B. Lippincott, 1971*.
Jean Baptiste Pointe de Sable: Founder of Chicago.   New York: Messner, 1953*.
Paul Robeson, Citizen of the World.   Introduction by Carl Van Doren.   New York: Messner, 1946; reprint ed., New York: Negro Universities Press, n.d.*; rev. ed., New York: Messner, 1971*.
The Story of Phyllis Wheatley: Poetess of the American Revolution.   New York: Messner, 1949*; New York: Pocket Books†.
The Story of Pocahontas.   New York: Grosset & Dunlap, 1953*.
There Once Was a Slave: The Heroic Story of Frederick Douglass.   New York: Messner, 1966*.
Your Most Humble Servant: The Story of Benjamin Banneker.   New York: Messner, 1949*.

CRITICISM BY DU BOIS
"Towards an American Theatre." The Arts Quarterly 1 (October-December 1937): 18-20.

DRAMA
Coal Dust.
Dust to Earth.   Princeton: Yale Drama School, 1941.
Elijah's Ravens, 1941.
I Gotta Home, 1942.
It's Morning.
Tom-Tom.   Cleveland: n.p., 1932 (opera).
Track Thirteen.   Boston: Expression Co., 1940.

NON-FICTION
(Periodicals): Black Scholar, May, September, November 1970; February 1971; January 1972; November 1973; Crisis, 1933; Etude, November 1936; Freedomways, Spring, Summer 1961; Fall 1962; Fall 1963; Summer 1966; First Quarter 1971; Harlem Quarterly, Spring 1950.

POETRY
(Periodical): Crisis, 1935.

SHORT STORY
   (Periodical): Negro Story, March-April 1945.
BIOGRAPHY ON DU BOIS
   Blackburn, H. B. "Born Storyteller." Negro Digest 8 (September 1950): 13-15.
   Brawley. The Negro Genius, p. 305.
   Chrisman, Robert. "The Black Scholar Hosts Shirley Graham Du Bois." Black Scholar 2 (December 1970): 50-52.
   "Conversation: Ida Lewis and Shirley Graham Du Bois." Essence 1 (January 1971): 22-27.
   Du Bois, Shirley Graham. "Return After Ten Years." Freedomways 11 (Second Quarter 1971): 158-169.

Du BOIS, William Edward Burghardt. Born 23 February 1868 in Great Barrington, Massachusetts. Died 27 August 1963 in Accra, and was buried on a Ghana coast. Education: B.A., Fisk University, 1888; Ph.D., Harvard University, 1895 (First Black Ph.D. from Harvard University). Also studied at the University of Berlin for two years on a Slater Fund fellowship. Career: Correspondent for New York and Springfield, Massachusetts, papers while a student in high school; instructor in Greek and Latin at Wilberforce University, 1894-1896; instructor in sociology at the University of Pennsylvania, 1896-97; professor of economics and history at Atlanta University, 1897-1910.[1] Organized the Niagara Movement in 1905, merging with an organization of white liberals to form the N. A. A. C. P. in 1909. In 1919 he organized a Pan-African Conference which lasted until 1929. In 1934 he came out for Negro autonomy and "non-discriminatory segregation" alienating the other leaders of the N. A. A. C. P.; he was forced to resign. He then returned to Atlanta University and served as Chairman, Department of Sociology, until he was fired in 1944. He again worked with the N. A. A. C. P. until another schism developed in 1948. During the 1950's he was active in the world peace movement, forming the Peace Information Service in 1950, working to ban nuclear weapons. During this period, he rejected all Negro rights groups, joined the Communist Party and, in 1960, accepted President Kwame Nkrumah's invitation to live in Ghana; he became a citizen of Ghana in 1962.[2] Founder and editor of numerous periodicals: The Moon, 1905-06; The Horizon, 1908-10; The Brownies' Book, 1920-21; The Crisis, organ of the N. A. A. C. P., 1910-35; Phylon Quarterly, 1940; also edited the Fisk Herald for a period of time. Awards, Honors: First Black man elected to the National Institute of Arts and Letters, 22 December 1943. LL.D., Howard University, 1930; LL.D., Atlanta University, 1938; Litt.D., Fisk University, 1938; L.H.D., Wilberforce University, 1940; Knight Commander of the Liberian Humane Order of African Redemption, conferred by the Liberian Government; Minister Plenipotentiary and Envoy Extraordinary, conferred by President Calvin Coolidge.[3]
COLLECTIONS OF DU BOIS'S WORK
   Foner, Philip S., ed. W. E. B. Du Bois Speaks: Speeches and Addresses, 1920-1963. Pathfinder Press, 1970.

Killens, John O. , ed. An ABC of Color: Selections from
over a Half-Century of the Writings of W. E. B. Du Bois.
Berlin, E. Germany: Seven Seas, 1963. New York: International, 1970†.

Lester, Julius, ed. Seventh Son: The Thought and Writings
of W. E. B. Du Bois. New York: Random House, 1971.

Paschal, Andrew G. , ed. W. E. B. Du Bois Reader. New
York: Collier, 1971.

Weinberg, Meyer, ed. W. E. B. Du Bois: A Reader. New
York: Harper, 1970.

Wright, Stephen J. , ed. Selected Writings of W. E. B. Du
Bois. New York: New American Library, 1970.

CRITICISM BY DU BOIS

"Can the Negro Save the Drama?" Theatre Magazine 38
(July 1923): 12, 68.

"The Donor of the Du Bois Literary Prize." Crisis 39
(1931): 157.

"The Drama Among Black Folk." Crisis 12 (August 1916):
169-173.

"The Du Bois Literary Prize." Crisis 39 (1931): 117.

"Dunbar." Crisis 19 (1920): 234.

"The Ethiopian Art Theatre." Crisis 26 (1923): 103.

"Garland Anderson." Crisis 31 (1926): 112.

"The Krigwa Players Little Negro Theatre." Amsterdam
News, 5 October 1927.

"The Negro in Literature and Art." Annals of the American Academy of Political and Social Science 49 (September 1913): 233-237.

"Negro Literature." The Encyclopaedia Britannica. 13th
ed. New York: Encyclopaedia Britannica, 1926, pp. 110-
111.

"A Negro Theatre." Crisis 25 (1923): 251.

"A Poet's Wail." Crisis 36 (1929): 349.

"Postscript." Crisis, 1910-1934. (A monthly column.)

With Alain Locke. "The Younger Literary Movement."
Crisis 27 (1924): 161-163.

DRAMA

The Christ of the Andes. In Horizon 4 (November-December
1908): 1-14. (two scenes.)

"George Washington and Black Folk: A Pageant for the Cen-
tenary, 1732-1932." Crisis 39 (1932): 121-124.

Haiti.

The Star of Ethiopia, 1911. (A four-page leaflet issued in
November (?) 1915; and again in 1925 in program form:
The Star of Ethiopia: A Pageant. Hollywood Bowl, 15
and 18 June 1925.)[1]

EDITOR

Atlanta University Publications; New York: Arno, 1968, 1969*.
(Du Bois edited the proceedings of the Atlanta University
Conferences from 1898-1913, Nos. 3-18.

NON-FICTION

Africa: An Essay Toward a History of the Continent of Africa and Its Inhabitants. Moscow, 1961.

Africa, Its Geography, People and Products. Girard, Ka.:
  Haldeman-Julius, 1930.
Africa--Its Place in Modern History. Girard, Ka.: Halde-
  man-Julius, 1930. (Repetitious of The Negro.[4])
The Autobiography of W. E. B. Du Bois: A Soliloquy on
  Viewing My Life from the Last Decade of Its First Cen-
  tury. New York: International, 1968†.
Black Folk Then and Now: An Essay in the History and
  Sociology of the Negro Race. New York: Holt, 1939; re-
  print ed., New York: Octagon, 1970*.
Black Reconstruction in America: 1860-1900, An Essay To-
  ward a History of the Part which Black Folk Played in
  the Attempt to Construct Democracy in America. New
  York: Harcourt, Brace, 1935; New York: Russell & Rus-
  sell, 1956*. New York: Atheneum, 1969†.
Color and Democracy: Colonies and Peace. New York:
  Harcourt, Brace, 1945.
Darkwater: Voices from within the Veil. New York: Har-
  court, Brace & How, 1921. Reprint of 1920 ed., New
  York: AMS Press, 1969*; New York: Schocken, 1969†.
Dusk of Dawn: An Essay Toward an Autobiography of a
  Race Concept. New York: Harcourt, Brace, 1940; New
  York: Schocken, 1968*†.
The Gift of Black Folk: Negroes in the Making of America.
  Boston: Stratford, 1924; reprint ed., New York: Johnson
  Reprint, 1969*; New York: Washington Square Press,
  1970†; New York: AMS Press, 1972*.
In Battle for Peace: The Story of My 83rd Birthday. With
  Comment by Shirley Graham. New York: Masses and
  Mainstream, 1952.
John Brown, A Biography. Philadelphia: G. W. Jacobs,
  1909; rev. ed., New York: International, 1962†; reprint
  of 1909 ed., Northbrook, Ill.: Metro Books, 1972*.
The Negro. New York: Holt, 1915; New York: Oxford Uni-
  versity Press, 1970†.
The Philadelphia Negro: A Social Study, 1899. New York:
  Schocken, 1967*†; Millwood, N.Y.: Kraus Reprint, 1973*.
The Souls of Black Folk: Essays and Sketches. Chicago:
  A. C. McClurg 1903; Blue Heron, 1953; New York: Dodd,
  Mead, 1970*; New York: Washington Square, 1970†; New
  York: New American Library, 1969†; Millwood, N.Y.:
  Kraus Reprints, 1973*.
The Suppression of the African Slave Trade to the United
  States of America, 1638-1870. New York: Longmans,
  Green, 1896; Gloucester, Mass.: Peter Smith*; Williams-
  town, Mass.: Corner House, 1970*; Baton Rouge: Louisi-
  ana State University Press, 1970†; New York: Dover,
  1970†; reprint of 1898 edition; New York: Russell & Rus-
  sell*; New York: Schocken, 1969†.
The World and Africa: An Inquiry into the Part which Africa
  Has Played in World History. New York: Viking, 1947;
  New York: International, 1965†.

NOVELS
  The Black Flame: A Trilogy. New York: Mainstream,
    1957-1961. (Book One: The Ordeal of Mansart, 1957;
    Book Two: Mansart Builds a School, 1959; Book Three:
    Worlds of Color, 1961.)
  Dark Princess: A Romance. New York: Harcourt, Brace,
    1928. AMS Press*.
  The Quest of the Silver Fleece: A Novel. Chicago: Mc-
    Clurg, 1911; facsimile ed., Freeport, N.Y.: Books for
    Libraries*; reprint ed., New York: Arno, 1970*; New
    York: Negro Universities Press*; New York: AMS Press*;
    Washington, D.C.: McGrath, 1969*; Florida: Mnemosyne†.
POETRY
  Selected Poems. Accra, Ghana: Ghana University Press,
    1965; New York: Panther House, 1971†.
  "Selected Poems of W. E. B. Du Bois." Freedomways 5
    (1965): 88-102.
  (Periodicals): Crisis 2 (1911): 209; 3 (1912): 235; 19
    (1920): 274; New York Herald Tribune, 10 October 1926;
    Masses & Mainstream 6 (July 1953): 10-12; 9 (Decem-
    ber 1956): 42-43; China Reconstructs 8 (June 1959):
    6; Palms 4 (October 1926): 18-19. Poems are also in-
    terspersed among the essays of Darkwater, and published
    in The Horizon and The Independent.
SHORT STORIES
  (Periodicals): Crisis 6 (1913): 285; also published in Hori-
    zon.
REVIEWS BY DU BOIS
  Published in Amsterdam News; Book Review; Crisis; Liberty
    Book Club News; Masses & Mainstream; New York Herald
    Tribune; Phylon; Political Affairs.
WRITINGS PUBLISHED IN ANTHOLOGIES
  Du Bois's work may be found in most anthologies of Black
    literature. A partial listing is provided below.
  (Autobiographical excerpts): Adams, Conn and Slepian, Afro-
    American Literature: Non-Fiction; Barksdale and Kinna-
    mon, The Black Writers of America; Brown, Davis and
    Lee, Negro Caravan; Chambers and Moon, Right On!;
    Watkins, Anthology of American Negro Literature.
  (Essays): Barksdale and Kinnamon, Black Writers of Amer-
    ica; Calverton, Anthology of American Negro Literature;
    Davis and Redding, Cavalcade; Ford, Black Insights; Gayle,
    Black Expression; Long and Collier, Afro-American Writ-
    ing; Margolies, A Native Sons Reader.
  (Poetry): Adoff, The Poetry of Black America; Baker, Black
    Literature in America; Brown, Davis and Lee, Negro
    Caravan; Cullen, Caroling Dusk; Emanuel and Gross, Dark
    Symphony; Ford, Black Insights; Hughes and Bontemps,
    The Poetry of the Negro: 1746-1970; James, From These
    Roots; Johnson, Book of American Negro Poetry; Long and
    Collier, Afro-American Writing; Pool, Beyond the Blues;
    Simmons and Hutchinson, Black Culture.
  (Short Stories): Larson, Prejudice; Simmons and Hutchinson,

Black Culture.
BIBLIOGRAPHIES ON DU BOIS
Aptheker, Herbert. Annotated Bibliography of the Writings
 of W. E. B. Du Bois. Milwood, N.Y.: Kraus-Thomson,
 1973.
 _____. "Some Unpublished Writings of W. E. B. Du Bois."
 Freedomways 5 (First Quarter 1965): 103-128.
Kaiser, Ernest. "A Selected Bibliography of the Published
 Writings of W. E. B. Du Bois." Freedomways 5 (Winter
 1965): 207-213; also in Clarke, Black Titan, pp. 309-
 330.
Lester, Julius, ed. The Seventh Son, pp. 739-767. (See
 "Collections of Du Bois's Work" for complete bibliograph-
 ical notation.)
Libman, Valentina A., comp. Russian Studies of American
 Literature: A Bibliography. Chapel Hill: University of
 North Carolina Press, 1969, pp. 76-77.
Yellin, Jean Fagan. "An Index of Literary Materials in The
 Crisis, 1910-1934: Articles, Belles Lettres, and Book
 Reviews." CLA Journal 14 (June 1971): 452-465; 15 (De-
 cember 1971): 197-234.
BIOGRAPHY AND CRITICISM ON DU BOIS: For a more com-
plete listing, refer to one of the bibliographies above. This
check list emphasizes literary criticism and pertinent essays
providing background information.
(Books)
Broderick, Francis L. W. E. B. Du Bois, Negro Leader at
 a Time of Crisis. Stanford, Ca.: Stanford University
 Press, 1959.
Clarke, John Henrik, et al. Black Titan: W. E. B. Du Bois,
 an Anthology by the Editors of Freedomways. Boston:
 Beacon, 1970. (Special Issue of Freedomways, Winter
 1971.
Graham, Shirley. His Day Is Marching on: A Memoir of
 W. E. B. Du Bois. Philadelphia: Lippincott, 1971.
Hamilton, Virginia. W. E. B. Du Bois: A Biography. New
 York: T. Y. Crowell, 1972. (Children and Young Adults.)
Lacy, Leslie Alexander. Cheer the Lonesome Traveler:
 The Life of W. E. B. Du Bois. New York: Dial, 1970.
 (Children and Young Adults.)
Logan, Rayford Whittingham. Two Bronze Titans: Fred-
 erick Douglass and W. E. B. Du Bois. Washington, D.C.:
 History Department, Howard University, 1972.
 _____, ed. W. E. B. Du Bois: A Profile. New York:
 Hill & Wang, 1971.
Rudwick, Elliott M. W. E. B. Du Bois: A Study in Minor-
 ity Group Leadership. Philadelphia: University of Penn-
 sylvania Press; reprinted as W. E. B. Du Bois: Propa-
 gandist of the Negro Protest. New York: Atheneum, 1968.
 _____. "W. E. B. Du Bois on the Role of Crisis Editor."
 Journal of Negro History 43 (July 1948): 214-240.
Tuttle, William M., ed. W. E. B. Du Bois. Englewood
 Cliffs, N.J.: Prentice-Hall, 1973.

(Essays in Books and Periodicals)

Adams, John Henry. "Rough Sketches: William Edward Burghardt Du Bois, Ph. D." Voice of the Negro 2 (March 1905): 176-181.

Amann, Clarence A. "Three Negro Classics--An Estimate." Negro American Literature Forum 4 (Winter 1970): 113-119.

Aptheker, J. "Du Bois: The Final Years." Journal of Human Relations 14 (First Quarter 1966): 149-155.

Baker, H. A. Long Black Song, pp. 96-108. (About The Souls of Black Folk.)

Barksdale and Kinnamon. Black Writers of America, pp. 363-368.

Bond, Horace M. "The Legacy of W. E. B. Du Bois." Freedomways 5 (1965): 16-40.

Bone. The Negro Novel in America, pp. 5, 6-7, 13n. 20, 29, 34, 43-45, 57, 91, 97, 99-100.

Bontemps, Arna. "Tribute to Du Bois." Negro Digest 13 (July 1964): 42-44.

Brawley. The Negro in Art and Literature in the United States, pp. 82-87.

_____. The Negro Genius, pp. 195-202.

Cruse. The Crisis of the Negro Intellectual, pp. 5-565 passim.

Downs, R. B. "Black Man in a White Man's World." Famous American Books. New York: McGraw, 1972, pp. 220-226. (About The Souls of Black Folk.)

Finkelstein, Sidney. "W. E. B. Du Bois' Trilogy: A Literary Triumph." Mainstream 14 (October 1961): 6-17.

Ford. The Contemporary Negro Novel.

Gloster. Negro Voices in American Fiction, pp. 74-79, 151-155.

Gross, T. L. "The Two Traditions: Booker T. Washington and W. E. B. Du Bois." In Gross, The Heroic Ideal in American Literature, pp. 127-136.

Harding, Vincent. "W. E. B. Du Bois and the Black Messianic Vision." Freedomways 9 (1969): 44-58.

Henderson, Lenneal J. "W. E. B. Du Bois: Black Scholar and Prophet." The Black Scholar 1 (January-February 1970): 48-57.

Howe, Irving. "Remarkable Man, Ambiguous Legacy." Harper's Magazine 236 (March 1968): 143-149.

Huggins. Harlem Renaissance, pp. 23-306 passim.

Kerlin. Negro Poets and Their Poems, pp. 217-222.

Kostelanetz, Richard. "Fiction of a Negro Politics: The Neglected Novels of W. E. B. Du Bois." Xavier University Studies 7 (1968): 5-39.

Lee, Everett S. "W. E. B. Du Bois: The Souls of Black Folk." In Landmarks of American Writing. Edited by Hennig Cohen. New York: Basic Books, 1969.

Loggins. The Negro Author, pp. 255, 281-284, 298, 392, 397, 398, 442, 444, 449.

Margolies. Native Sons, pp. 21-23.

Mays. <u>The Negro's God as Reflected in His Literature</u>, pp. 173-174, 231-232.

Paschal, A. G. "The Spirit of W. E. B. Du Bois." <u>Black Scholar</u> 2 (October 1970): 17-28.

Ploski. <u>The Negro Almanac</u>, pp. 682-683.

Savory, Jerold J. "The Rending of the Veil in W. E. B. Du Bois's <u>The Souls of Black Folk</u>." <u>CLA Journal</u> 15 (March 1972): 334-337.

Shaw, Peter. "The Uses of Autobiography." <u>The American Scholar</u> 38 (1969): 136, 138, 140, 142, 144.

Thorpe, Earl E. "W. E. B. Du Bois: Writing with a Sword in His Hand." <u>Black Historians</u>. New York: William Morrow, 1971, pp. 72-107.

Wagner. <u>Black Poets of the United States</u>, pp. 177-178.

Whitlow. <u>Black American Literature</u>, pp. 67-70.

"William Edward Burghardt Du Bois." <u>Crisis</u> 70 (1963): 468-470.

_____. <u>Negro Digest</u> 13 (November 1963): 65.

REVIEWS

    <u>Dark Princess</u>:
        Davis, Allison. <u>Crisis</u> 35 (1928): 339.
        Locke, Alain. <u>New York Herald Tribune Books</u>, 20 May 1928, p. 12.
        Whipple, Leon. <u>Opportunity</u> 6 (1928): 244.
    <u>Ordeal of Mansart</u> (Book Two of the trilogy):
        A. B. S., <u>Crisis</u> 64 (August-September 1957): 454-455.
    <u>The Quest of the Silver Fleece</u>:
        Braithwaite, William S. <u>Crisis</u> 3 (1911): 77.
        <u>Opportunity</u> 6 (1928): 244.
    <u>Worlds of Color</u> (Book Three of the Trilogy):
        Graham, Lorenz. <u>Freedomways</u> 1 (Summer 1961): 211-214.
        Ivy, J. W. <u>Crisis</u> 68 (June-July 1961): 378-379.

DUBONEE, Ylessa.
    POETRY (Anthology): Murphy, <u>Ebony Rhythm</u>.

Du CILLE, Ann. <u>Born</u> 17 February 1949 in Brooklyn, New York. <u>Education</u>: B. A. in English, Bridgewater State College, 1971; M. A. in Creative Writing, Brown University, 1973. <u>Currently living in</u> Brockton, Massachusetts. <u>Career</u>: Instructor of English Composition, Brown University, Summer 1972; Director of poetry workshops for elderly Black women, Providence, Rhode Island, Spring 1973; their anthology, <u>Bannister House</u>, published by the Rhode Island State Council on the Arts. E. S. L. instructor, Latin American Center, Providence. Girl Friday, East Side Senior Citizens Center, 1973. Presently Director, South Providence Girls' Club. Readings were given at Brown University, Bryant College, Bannister House, and Olney Street Baptist Church. <u>Awards, Honors</u>: N. A. A. C. P. Scholarship 1967; P. T. A. Scholarship, 1967; Teacher's Memorial Scholarship, 1967; South Shore Citizen's Club Scholarship, 1967; Ella Brown Scholarship, 1967; J. McCarthy Award, 1967;

Katherine Ann Hill Prize for Writing, 1971; University Fellowship, Brown University, 1971 and 1972.
POETRY
(Anthologies): Harper, <u>Black Veils</u>; Welburn, <u>Dues.</u>
UNPUBLISHED WORK
Poems and Prose: "All I Ask Is That You Hold Me."
INTERJECTIONS
"I have always wished that I could sing, but I'm one of those rare children born Black, beautiful, and tone deaf. Poetry, however, has become my music. I believe that life is art and that living can and should be the most poignant of poems."

DUCKETT, Alfred. <u>Born</u> 1918 in Brooklyn, New York.
CHILDREN AND YOUNG ADULTS
<u>Changing of the Guard: The New Breed of Black Politicians.</u>
New York: Coward-McCann & Geoghegan, 1972*.
NON-FICTION
<u>Soul in Type: The Romance and History of the Black American Press.</u> Chicago: Nelson-Hall, n.d.*
<u>I Never Had It Made</u>, by John Roosevelt Robinson as told to Alfred Duckett. New York: Putnam, 1972*.
POETRY
<u>Raps.</u> Chicago: The Little Black Library Press, 1972; Chicago: Nelson-Hall, 1973.
(Anthologies): Adoff, <u>The Poetry of Black America;</u> Bontemps, <u>American Negro Poetry;</u> Dee, <u>Glow Child;</u> Hughes and Bontemps, <u>The Poetry of the Negro: 1746-1970;</u> Jordan, <u>Soulscript.</u>
VIGNETTE
(Anthology): Hughes, <u>The Book of Negro Humor.</u>

DUDLEY, S. H.
DRAMA
With Henry Troy. <u>Dr. Beans from Boston,</u> 1911.
<u>The Smart Set</u>, 1896.

DUKE, Bill.
DRAMA
<u>An Adaption: Dream,</u> 1972.
POETRY
(Periodicals): <u>Black Creation,</u> Summer 1972; Winter 1973.

DULOCK, Jerre A.
CRITICISM (Anthology): Boyd, <u>Poems by Blacks</u> II.

DUMAS, Aaron.
DRAMA <u>Poor Willie,</u> 1970.

DUMAS, Gerald.
CHILDREN AND YOUNG ADULTS
<u>Rabbits Rafferty.</u> Boston: Houghton Mifflin, 1968*.
POETRY
<u>An Afternoon in Waterloo Park: A Narrative Poem.</u>
Boston: Houghton-Mifflin, 1972*.

DUMAS, Henry L. Born 20 July 1934 in Sweet Home, Arkansas.
Died 23 May 1968. Education: Attended the public schools of
New York City; was graduated from Commerce High; studied
at Rutgers University, 1958-61, and at New York City College
in the mid-fifties; studied in-residence with the Musician-phi-
losopher Sun Ra in the late sixties. Career: U.S. Air Force
(including a year in the Arabian Peninsula and two years in
Texas, 1953-57); operator of printing machines at IBM (New
York City), 1963-64; Social Worker for the State of New York
(New York City), 1965-66; Assistant Director of Upward Bound,
Hiram College, 1967; Teacher-Counselor and Director of Language Workshops, Southern Illinois University's Experiment in
Higher Education, 1967-68. Was active on the "little magazine" circuit, editing, publishing and distributing them from
1953-68 (some of the magazines were The Anthologist, Untitled, Camel, Hiram Poetry Review, Collection). Awards,
Honors: Received several awards between 1953-57 for creative writing published in various Air Force newspapers and
magazines; received the 1963 Editors Award for Creative Writing from Untitled magazine; received an award for creative
writing from The Anthologist in the mid-sixties. An Annual
Henry Dumas Memorial Poetry Contest is sponsored for college students through the Hiram Poetry Review. There is also a Henry Dumas Memorial Library at Southern Illinois Uni-
versity's Experiment in Higher Education.[1]
NON-FICTION
  Several articles, interviews and unpublished studies are
    presently being edited for publication.[2]
POETRY
  Play Ebony Play Ivory. Edited by Eugene Redmond. New
    York: Random House, 1974*.
  Poetry for My People. Edited by Hale Chatfield and Eugene
    Redmond. Carbondale: Southern Illinois University, 1970.
  (Anthologies): Adoff, Black Out Loud; Adoff, Brothers and
    Sisters; Adoff, The Poetry of Black America; Gross, et
    al. Open Poetry; Gershmehl, Words Among America;
    Henderson, Understanding the New Black Poetry; Hicks,
    Cutting Edges; Jones and Neal, Black Fire; Schulte and
    Troupe, Sunbursts: Third World Voices.
  (Periodicals): Negro Digest, June 1965; September 1966;
    May 1967; also published in Freedomways, Umbra, Trace,
    The Anthologist, Hiram Poetry Review, and American
    Weave.
SHORT STORIES
  "Ark of Bones" and Other Stories. Edited by Hale Chat-
    field and Eugene Redmond. Carbondale: Southern Illinois
    University Press, 1970; new ed., edited by Eugene Red-
    mond. New York: Random House, 1974*.
  (Periodical): Negro Digest, November 1965; January 1968.
    [1]Information on Dumas was provided by his literary
  executor, Eugene Redmond.
    [2]Ibid.

DUNBAR, Paul Laurence. <u>Born</u> 27 June 1872 in Dayton, Ohio.
<u>Died</u> 9 February 1906. <u>Education</u>: Attended the public schools
in Dayton; graduated, with honors, from Steele High School,
1891. The class song composed by him was sung at the com-
mencement exercises.[1] <u>Career</u>: He began writing poems at
the age of six; at 13 he gave a public recital of his verse.[2]
He was 16 years old when his first published poem appeared
in the <u>Dayton Herald</u>.[3] After his father's death, too poor to
go on to college, Paul helped his mother delivering her laundry
bundles, working part-time in hotels, and as an elevator operator. Although he sought employment in journalism or clerical
work, newspapers and offices had nothing to offer a black boy.[4]
After reading one of his poems at a session of the Western
Writers Association in Dayton, one of the members encouraged
him to enter the publishing field.[5] He struggled to publish his
works. Late in 1892, when a local publisher demanded $125
to cover the cost of printing his first book, he may have turned
away from writing had not an executive advanced him the money.
Thus, <u>Oak and Ivy</u> was published.[6] When he went to Chicago
to seek a job at the World's Columbian Exposition, he met
Frederick Douglass. Douglass helped Dunbar secure a job.
At this time, the young poet wrote "The Columbian Ode," to
commemorate the exposition.[7] His overnight fame, as a poet,
occurred after William Dean Howells reviewed his volume of
verse, <u>Majors and Minors</u>. In 1897, Dunbar toured Europe.
After his return, he took a job in the reading room of the Library of Congress. By 1897 his health began to fail. Although
he continued to write, he gave fewer and fewer readings.[8]
Forty of his poems were set to music by famous musicians of
his time, including the Black composers J. Rosamond Johnson,
and Samuel Coleridge-Taylor. Fifteen of his short stories appeared in such publications as <u>Lippincott's</u>, <u>The Saturday Evening Post</u>, <u>Independent</u>, <u>Dayton Tattler</u>, <u>Harper's Weekly</u>, <u>Cen-
tury</u>, <u>Denver Post</u>, <u>Smart Set</u>,[9] <u>Outlook</u>, <u>Bookman</u>, and <u>Cur-
rent Literature</u>. After a long illness, for he was always frail,
he died on 9 February 1906.
DRAMA
    Uncle Eph's Christmas: A One Act Musical Sketch, 1900;
        music by W. M. Cook.
NON-FICTION
    "Introduction." Thoughts for True Americans by Richard
        E. Toomey, Washington, D.C.: Neale, 1901.
    The Negro Problem. "Representative American Negroes."
        New York: J. Pott & Co., 1903.
    (Periodicals)
    "Unpublished Letters of Paul Laurence Dunbar to a Friend."
        Crisis 20 (1920): 73.
NOVELS
    The Fanatics. New York: Dodd, Mead, 1901; facsimile ed.,
        Freeport, N.Y.: Books for Libraries, 1971*; reprint ed.
        Gregg, 1971*; Miami: Mnemosyne†; New York: Negro Uni-
        versities Press*.
    The Heart of Happy Hollow. New York: Dodd, Mead, 1904;

facsimile ed., Freeport, N.Y.: Books for Libraries*.
The Love of Landry. New York: Dodd, Mead, 1900; facsimile ed., Freeport, N.Y.: Books for Libraries*; Bos-
 ton: Gregg, 1970*; Miami: Mnemosyne†; Westport, Conn.:
 Negro Universities Press*.
The Sport of the Gods. New York: Dodd, Mead, 1902.
 (Originally published in Lippincott's Mag. 67 (May 1901):
 515-594); facsimile ed., Freeport, N.Y.: Books for Li-
 braries*; New York: Macmillan†; New York: AMS Press*;
 Miami: Mnemosyne†.
The Uncalled. New York: Dodd, Mead, 1898. (Originally
 published in Lippincott's Magazine, 64 (May 1898): 579-
 669); facsimile ed., Freeport, N.Y.: Books for Libraries*;
 New York: AMS Press*; reprint ed., Boston: Gregg*;
 Washington, D.C.: McGrath, 1969*; Miami: Mnemosyne†;
 New York: Panther House*; Westport, Conn.: Negro Uni-
 versities Press*.
(Anthologies-Excerpts): Kendricks and Levitt, American
 Voices.

POETRY
Candle-Lightin' Time. New York: Dodd, Mead, 1901; fac-
 simile ed., Freeport, N.Y.: Books for Libraries*; New
 York: AMS Press*.
Chris'mus' Is a Comin' and Other Poems. New York: Dodd,
 Mead, 1905.
The Complete Poems of Paul Laurence Dunbar. New York:
 Dodd, Mead, 1913*† (reprints from 1913-1952).
Howdy, Honey, Howdy. Toronto: Musson, 1905; New York:
 Dodd, Mead, 1905; facsimile ed., Freeport, N.Y.: Books
 for Libraries*; New York: AMS Press*.
Joggin' erlong. New York: Dodd, Mead, 1906; facsimile
 ed., Freeport, N.Y.: Books for Libraries*.
Li'l Gal. New York: Dodd, Mead, 1904; facsimile ed.,
 Freeport, N.Y.: Books for Libraries*; New York: AMS
 Press*.
Little Brown Baby. New York: Dodd, Mead, 1940*.
Lyrics of the Hearthside. New York: Dodd, Mead, 1899;
 facsimile ed., Freeport, N.Y.: Books for Libraries*;
 New York: AMS Press*.
Lyrics of Love and Laughter. New York: Dodd, Mead,
 1903.
Lyrics of Lowly Life. New York: Dodd, Mead, 1896; New
 York: Arno, 1969*; facsimile ed., Freeport, N.Y.:
 Books for Libraries*; Boston: Gregg*.
Lyrics of Sunshine and Shadow. New York: Dodd, Mead,
 1905; facsimile ed., Freeport; N.Y.: Books for Li-
 braries*; New York: AMS Press*.
Majors and Minors. Toledo, O.: Hadley & Hadley, 1895;
 facsimile ed., Freeport, N.Y.: Books for Libraries*.
Oak and Ivy. Dayton, O.: United Brethren Publishing House,
 1893.
A Plantation Portrait. New York: Dodd, Mead, 1905.
Poems of Cabin and Field. New York: Dodd, Mead, 1899;

facsimile ed., Freeport, N.Y.: Books for Libraries*; New York: AMS Press*.

Speakin' O' Christmas, and Other Christmas and Special Poems. New York: Dodd, Mead, 1914.

When Malindy Sings. New York: Dodd, Mead, 1903; facsimile ed., Freeport, N.Y.: Books for Libraries*; New York: AMS Press*.

(Anthologies): Abcarian and Klotz, Literature: The Human Experience; Abdul, The Magic of Poetry; Adams, Conn and Slepian, Afro-American Literature: Poetry; Adoff, I Am the Darker Brother; Adoff, Poetry of Black America; Barksdale and Kinnamon, Black Writers of America; Barnes, Ruth, I Hear America Singing; Benét, The Poetry of Freedom; Breman, You Better Believe It; Brown, Davis and Lee, Negro Caravan; Bontemps, American Negro Poetry; Bontemps, Golden Slippers; Calverton, An Anthology of American Negro Literature; Chambers and Moon, Right On!; Chapman, Black Voices; Cullen, Caroling Dusk; Davis, and Redding, Cavalcade; Emanuel and Gross, Dark Symphony; Eastman, et al., The Norton Anthology of Poetry; Eleazer, Singers in the Dawn; Faderman and Bradshaw, Speaking for Ourselves; Ford, Black Insights; Haslam, Forgotten Pages of American Literature; Hayden, Kaleidoscope; Henderson, Understanding the New Black Poetry; Hughes, The Book of Negro Humor; Hughes and Bontemps, The Poetry of the Negro: 1746-1970; Johnson, Ebony and Topaz; Jordan, Soulscript; Kearns, Black Identity; Kendricks and Levitt, Afro-American Voices; Lomax and Abdul, 3000 Years of Black Poetry; Margolies, A Native Sons Reader; Miller, Blackamerican Literature; Patterson, An Introduction to Black Literature; Randall, The Black Poets; Robinson, Early Black American Poetry; Shmuel, An Anthology of Revolutionary Poetry; Simmons and Hutchinson, Black Culture; Singh and Fellowes, Black Literature in America; Turner, Black American Literaature; Wagner, Black Poets of the United States; Walrond and Pool, Black and Unknown Bards; White and Jackson, An Anthology of Verse by American Negroes; Young, Black Experience.

(Periodicals): Century 49 (November 1894-April 1895): 960; 162; Half-Century, June 1919; Opportunity 2 (June 1924): 162; Outlook, 3 November 1900; Reedy's Mirror 13 (25 June 1903): 7; 15 (14 September 1911): Voice of the Negro 4 (March 1906): 210; 4 (August 1906): 578.

SHORT STORIES

The Best Stories of Paul Laurence Dunbar. Edited by B. G. Brawley. New York: Dodd, Mead, 1938.

Folks from Dixie. New York: Dodd, Mead, 1898; London: J. Bowden; facsimile ed., Freeport, N.Y.: Books for Libraries*; Boston: Gregg*; Westport, Conn.: Negro Universities Press*.

In Old Plantation Days. New York: Dodd, Mead, 1903;
    Westport, Conn.: Negro Universities Press*.
The Strength of Gideon and Other Stories. New York: Dodd,
    Mead, 1900; facsimile ed., New York: Freeport, N.Y.:
    Books for Libraries*; New York: Arno*.
(Anthologies): Clarke, American Negro Short Stories; Davis
    and Redding, Cavalcade; Hughes, The Best Short Stories
    by Negro Writers; Patterson, An Introduction to Black
    Literature in America; Turner, Black American Fiction.
(Periodicals): Reedy's Mirror 12 (27 March 1902): 24.
SONGS
    "Candle Lightin' Time" (words, P. L. Dunbar; Music Sam-
        uel Coleridge-Taylor). Cincinnati, O.: Church, 1911.
    Clorindy--Origin of the Cake Walk (lyrics, Dunbar; script
        Wm. M. Cook)
    "A Corn Son" (words, P. L. Dunbar; music, Harry Thacker
        Burleigh), New York: Ricordi, 1970.
    "A Corn Song" (words, P. L. Dunbar; music, Samuel Cole-
        ridge-Taylor), New York: Bosey, 1897.
    "A Death Song" (words, P. L. Dunbar; music, Howard Swan-
        son), New York: Leads Music Corp., 1951. Also re-
        corded by Laurence Winters on Columbia Records.
    "Down De Lovers Lane: Plantation Croon" (words, P. L.
        Dunbar; music, Marion Cook), New York: Schirmer, 1900.
    In Dahomey: Play (lyrics, Dunbar; text, J. A. Shipp; music,
        Wm. M. Cook), London: Keith, Prowse, 1902.
    Jes Lak White Folk (lyrics, Dunbar; script, Wm. M.
        Cook)
    "Plantation Melodies, Old and New" (words, Dunbar; R. E.
        Phillips and J. E. Campbell; music, Harry Thacker Bur-
        leigh), New York: Schirmer, 1901.
    "Who Knows?" (words, Dunbar; music, Ernest Ball), New
        York: M. Witmark, 1909.
BIBLIOGRAPHIES ON DUNBAR
    Blanck, Jacob. Bibliography of American Literature, II.
        New Haven, Conn.: Yale University Press, 1957.
    Brawley, Benjamin G. Paul Laurence Dunbar: Poet of His
        People. Chapel Hill: University of North Carolina Press,
        1936.
    Burris, Andrew M. "Bibliography of Works by Paul Laur-
        ence Dunbar...," American Collector 5 (1927): 68-73.
BIOGRAPHY AND CRITICISM ON DUNBAR
    Abramson. Negro Playwrights in the American Theatre,
        p. 188.
    Abramowitz, Jack. "The Negro in the Populist Movement."
        Journal of Negro History 38 (July 1953): 83, 284-285.
    Achille, L. T. "Paul Laurence Dunbar: Poète nègre."
        Revue Anglo-Américaine 12 (August 1934): 504-520.
    Adams. Great Negroes Past and Present, pp. 111, 152,
        173.
    Anon. "Dunbar--Negro Poet." Christian Science Monitor,
        29 (26 July 1937): 141.
    Arden, Eugene. "The Early Harlem Novel." Phylon 20

(September 1959): 25-31.

Arnold, Edw. F. "Some Personal Reminiscences of Paul Laurence Dunbar." Journal of Negro History 17 (October 1932): 400-408.

Baker, Houston A., Jr. "Paul Laurence Dunbar: An Evaluation." Black World 21 (November 1971): 30-37.

_____. "Report on a Celebration: Paul Laurence Dunbars' One-Hundredth Year." Black World 22 (February 1973): 81-85.

Bardolph. The Negro Vanguard, pp. 93-95.

Barksdale and Kinnamon. Black Writers of America, pp. 349-352.

Breman. You Better Believe It, pp. 36-37.

Bigsby. The Black American Writer, vol. 1, pp. 111-124, 218.

Blair, Walter, et al. The Literature of the United States. Chicago: Scott, Foresman, 1966, vol. 2, p. 30.

Bone. The Negro Novel in America, pp. 29, 35-43, 58.

Bontemps. The Harlem Renaissance Remembered, pp. 7, 9, 27-28, 114, 225, 261.

Boyd, Rubie. An Appreciation of Paul Laurence Dunbar. n.p., 1930.

Brawley. Negro Builders and Heroes, pp. 158-166, 170, 234-235, 243, 291.

_____. The Negro in Literature and Art, pp. 4, 64-75, 109, 182.

_____. Negro Genius, pp. 1, 9, 12-13, 110, 144, 151-161, 176-177, 213, 216, 249, 290.

_____. Paul Laurence Dunbar: Poet of His People. Chapel Hill: University of North Carolina Press, 1936.

_____. "Thirty Years After." Southern Workman, 1930.

Brooks, Van Wyck. The Confident Years. New York: E. P. Dutton, 1957, pp. 41-42, 54, 142-143.

Brown. Negro Poetry and Drama.

Burch, Charles E. "The Plantation Negro in Dunbar's Poetry." Southern Workman 50 (October 1921): 469-473.

Burris, A.M. "Bibliography of Works by Paul Laurence Dunbar." American Collector 5 (November 1927): 69-71.

_____. "Dunbar's Poetry in Literary English." The Southern Workman, October 1921.

Butcher. The Negro in American Culture, pp. 57, 99-100, 129, 175, 225.

Butcher, Philip. "Mutual Appreciation: Dunbar and Cable." CLA Journal 1 (March 1958): 101-102. Also in Free Lance 4 (First Half, 1957): 2-3.

Cady, Edwin Harrison. The Realist at War. Syracuse, N.Y.: Syracuse University Press, 1958, pp. 161-163.

Chamberlain, John. "The Negro as Writer." Bookman 70 (February 1930): 603-611.

Chametzky and Kaplin. Black and White in American Culture, pp. 341-343, 362-365.

Chapman. Black Voices, pp. 354-355.

Clark, David Wasgatt. Paul Laurence Dunbar: Laurel
Decked. Boston? Published by the Commissioners, Paul
Laurence Dunbar Scholarship Fund, for private circula-
tion, 1909? (cf. Schomburg.)

Colbron, Grace Isabel. "Across the Color Line." Bookman
8 (December 1898): 338-341.

Collier, Eugenia W. "Heritage from Harlem." Black World
20 (November 1970): 52-59.

_____. "James Weldon Johnson: Mirror of Change."
Phylon 21 (Winter 1960): 351-359.

Cromwell, Turner and Dykes. Readings from Negro Authors,
pp. 7-11, 85, 90.

Cromwell, J. Wesley. The Negro in American History.
Washington, D.C.: The American Negro Academy, 1914.

Cullen. Caroling Dusk, pp. 1-2.

Cunningham, Virginia. Paul Laurence Dunbar and His Song.
New York: Dodd, Mead, 1947.

Curti, Merle. The Growth of American Thought. New York:
Harper, 1943, pp. 428-433, 488-491.

Daniel, T. W. "Paul Laurence Dunbar and the Democratic
Ideal." Negro History Bulletin 6 (June 1943): 206-208.

Dickinson, Donald C. A Bio-Bibliography of Langston Hughes.
New York: Archon Books, 1967, pp. 3, 10, 21, 35, 106.

Dreer. American Literature by Negro Authors, pp. 27-36,
218.

Dunaway, Philip and George de Kay. Turning Point. New
York: Random House, 1958, p. 920.

Dunbar, Alice, et al. Paul Laurence Dunbar: Poet Laureate of the Negro Race. Philadelphia: A. M. E. Church Review, 1914.

Dunbar, Wil to Matilda Dunbar. 30 December 1899, Dunbar
Papers, Ohio Historical Society.

Du Bois, W. E. B. "Dunbar" in Opinion Column. Crisis 19
(1920): 234.

_____. The Gift of Black Folks. Boston: Stratford, 1924,
pp. 304-305.

Emanuel and Gross. Dark Symphony, pp. 2-4, 10, 36-37,
192, 199.

Faderman and Bradshaw. Speaking for Ourselves, pp. 53-
55.

Fishel and Quarles. The Black American, pp. 314-364.

Fauset, Arthur Huff. For Freedom. Philadelphia: Franklin,
1927.

Fossan, William H. The Story of Ohio. New York: Macmillan Co., 1932, pp. 133, 160.

Fox, Allan B. "Behind the Mask: Paul Laurence Dunbar's
Poetry in Literary English." Texas Quarterly 14 (Summer 1971): 7-19.

Gayle. Black Expression, pp. 36. 72-75, 80, 86, 88, 96,
110, 116-117, 175-177, 180, 190, 208-209, 229-231, 260-
261.

Gintzburg, Ralph. 100 Years of Lynchings. New York:

Lance Books, 1969, pp. 253-270.

Gould, Jean. That Dunbar Boy: The Story of America's Famous Negro Poet. New York: Dodd, Mead, 1958.

Gross. The Heroic Ideal in American Literature, pp. 114, 130-132, 135.

Haynes, Mrs. Elizabeth Ross. Unsung Heroes. New York: Du Bois & Dill, 1921.

Henderson, Julia. A Child's Story of Dunbar. New York: Crisis, 1913.

Heydrick, B. A., ed. Americans All. New York: Harcourt, Brace, 1941.

Hibbard, Clarence A., ed. Stories of the South, Old and New. Chapel Hill: University of North Carolina Press, 1931, pp. 288-293.

Howells, Dean. The Complete Poems of Paul Laurence Dunbar. New York: Dodd, Mead, 1967, p. 356.
_____. "Paul Laurence Dunbar." North American Review 23 (April 1906): 185-186.
_____. "Paul Laurence Dunbar's Majors and Minors." Harper's Weekly 27 June 1897.

Hudson, Gossie Harold. "Paul Laurence Dunbar: Dialect et la Negritude." Phylon 34 (September 1973): 236-247.
_____. "Poem and Essay 'Emancipation,' an Unpublished Poem by Paul Laurence Dunbar." Negro History Bulletin 36 (February 1973): 41-42.

Hughes, John Milton. Black Magic, p. 50.

Hughes, Langston. Famous American Negroes. New York: Dodd, Mead, 1954.
_____. The Negro Novelist, pp. 34, 39.

Hundley, Mary Gibson. The Dunbar Story. New York: Vantage Press, 1965. (Bibliography.)

Isaacs, Harold L. The New World of Negro Americans. London: Phoenix House, 1963, p. 58.

Jahn. Neo-African Literature, pp. 131, 141, 149-150, 154, 183, 193, 197, 217.

James, Charles. From These Roots, pp. 28-30.

Jeer, Fred J. Census of Ohio. Columbus, O.: 1901, p. 7, 56.

Johnson, J. W. Along This Way. New York: Viking, 1947, p. 58. (Originally published in 1933.)
_____. Black Manhattan, pp. 102, 119, 262, 270, 273.
_____. The Book of American Negro Poetry, pp. 49-52.

Johnson, Ralph Glassgow. The Poetry of Dunbar and McKay. Pittsburgh: M.A. Thesis, 1950.

Katz. Eyewitness: The Negro in American History, pp. 126-127, 344-345.

Kent. Blackness and the Adventures of Western Culture, pp. 7, 17-18, 39, 108, 114, 185.
_____. "Patterns of the Renaissance." Black World 21 (June 1972): 13.

Larsen, Charles R. "The Novels of Paul Laurence Dunbar." Phylon 29 (Fall 1968): 257-271.

Lawson, Edward H. "Paul Laurence Dunbar." Alexander's

Magazine 1 (March 1906): 47-50.

Lawson, Victor. Dunbar Critically Examined. Washington,
D.C.: Associated, 1941.

Lindley, Harlow. Ohio in the Twentieth Century 1900-1936.
Columbus, O.: Ohio State Archeological Historical Society, 1942, vol. 4, p. 275.

Logan, Rayford W. The Negro in the United States. New
York: D. Van Nostrand, 1957, pp. 57-61, 90.

Loggins. The Negro Author, pp. 256, 298, 313-317, 320-
324, 331-336, 342-353, 360, 404-407, 444, 453-456.

Long, Richard A. "Poem to Paul Laurence Dunbar."
Phylon 33 (Winter 1972): 368.

Lotz, Phillip Henry. Rising Above Color. New York: Associated Press; New York: Fleming Revell Co., 1943,
pp. 90-97.

Lovell. Black Song, pp. 425, 445, 512.

McGinnis, Charl. "Paul Laurence Dunbar." Negro History
Bulletin 5 (May 1942): 170, 182.

Manuscripts, Box 7. Dunbar Papers, Columbus, O.: Ohio
Historical Society.

Margolies. Native Sons, pp. 27-30.

Martin, Jay. "'Jump Back Honey': Paul Laurence Dunbar
and the Rediscovery of American Political Traditions."
The Bulletin of the Midwest Modern Language Association
7 (Spring 1974): 40-51. (Bibliography.)

_____, ed. A Singer in the Dawn: A Reinterpretation of
Paul Laurence Dunbar. New York: Dodd, Mead, 1974.

_____ and Gossie Hudson, eds. The Paul Laurence Dunbar
Reader. New York: Dial, 1974.

Meier, August. Negro Thought in America. Ann Arbor:
University of Michigan Press, 1966, pp. 266-269.

Mitchell, Loften. Black Drama. New York: Hawthorne
Books, 1958, pp. 150-151, 158, 165.

Morrison, Samuel Eliot. The Oxford History of the American People. New York: Oxford University Press, 1950,
p. 723.

New York Times, 10 February 1906, 1:4. (Obituary.)

Ottley, Roi, and William Weatherly. The Negro in New
York. Dobbs Ferry, N.Y.: Oceana, 1967, pp. 157, 164,
167, 259.

Ovington, Mary White. The Walls Came Tumbling Down.
New York: Schocken Books, 1960, p. 187.

Oxley, Thomas L. G. "Survey of Negro Literature." The
Messenger 9 (February 1927): 37-39.

Park, Robert Ezra. Race and Culture. New York: Macmillan, 1950, p. 291.

Parrington, Vernon C. Main Currents in American Thought.
New York: Harcourt, Brace & World, 1927, vol. 4, p.
372.

Pinkney, Alphonso. Black Americans. Englewood Cliffs,
N.J.: Prentice-Hall, 1969, pp. 146-148.

Ploski and Kaiser. The Negro Almanac, pp. 199, 675, 714.

Quillan, Frank V. The Color Line in Ohio. New York:

Negro Universities Press, 1913, pp. 134-139, 166, 289.

Redding. They Came in Chains, pp. 42, 206-207.

_____. To Make a Poet Black.

Robinson. Historical Negro Biographies, p. 77.

Rollins, Charlemae H. They Showed the Way. New York: T. Y. Crowell, 1964, pp. 59-62.

Scarborough, William Saunders. The Poet Laureate of the Negro Race. Philadelphia: A. M. E. Publ. House, 1914, (in A. M. E. Church Review, 31 (October 1914). (Bibliography.)

Stronks, J. B. "PLD and William Dean Howells." Oregon Historical Quarterly 67 (April 1958): 95-108.

Terrell, Mary Church. "Paul Laurence Dunbar." Voice of the Negro (April 1906): 271-278.

Thorpe, Earl E. Black Historians. New York: Morrow, 1971, pp. 12, 67, 214, 220.

Tischler, Nancy M. Black Masks, University Park: Pennsylvania State University Press, 1969, pp. 11, 15.

Turner, Darwin. In a Minor Chord, pp. xvii, 1, 68-69, 110.

_____. "Paul Laurence Dunbar: The Rejected Symbol." Journal of Negro History 52 (January 1967): 1-13. (cf. Robert Hemenway, The Black Novelist, pp. 33-45.)

Turpin, Waters E. "The Contemporary American Negro Playwright." CLA Journal 9 (September 1965): 12-24.

Wagner, Jean. Black Poets of the United States. Chicago: University of Illinois Press, 1973, pp. 73-149.

Waldo, Phillips. "Paul Laurence Dunbar: A New Perspective." Negro History Bulletin 29 (October 1965), 7-8.

Wells, Ida B. A Red Record. Chicago: Scott, Foresman, 1894, p. 97.

Wesley, Charles Harris. The Quest for Equality. New York: Publishers, 1968, p. 60.

Wiggins, Linda Keck. "Den of a Literary Lion." Voice of the Negro 3 (January 1905): 50-53.

_____. The Life and Works of Paul Laurence Dunbar. New York: Dodd, Mead, 1907.

Williams. They Also Spoke, pp. 108, 120, 122, 152-194, 197-215, 218-219, 222-225, 243, 247-249, 276, 290-291.

MULTIMEDIA

Guide to Films (16 mm) About Negroes. 1st ed. Alexandria, Va.: Serina Press, 1970.

Johnson, Dr. Harry A. Multimedia Materials for Afro-American Studies. New York: R. R. Bowker, 1971, pp. 66, 150, 181, 219, 232, 235-236, 259.

[1]Linda Keck Wiggins, The Life and Works of Paul Laurence Dunbar. (Naperville, Ill.: J. L. Nichols, 1907), p. 29.

[2]Edgar A. Toppin, A Biographical History of Blacks in America (New York: David McKay, 1971), p. 286.

[3]Charlemae Rollins, They Showed the Way (New York: T. Y. Crowell, 1964), p. 59.

[4]Toppin, p. 286.

[5]Rollins, p. 59.
[6]Toppin, pp. 286-287.
[7]Rollins, p. 60.
[8]Toppin, p. 287.
[9]Rollins, p. 61.

DUNBAR-NELSON, Alice Moore. Born 19 July 1875 in New Orleans, La. Died 1935. Education: Attended Straight College,
New Orleans; University of Pennsylvania; Cornell University;
School of Industrial Arts in Philadelphia.[1] Career: Taught
school in the New Orleans public school system until 1896, and
then moved to New York and taught in Brooklyn, 1897. She also conducted evening classes in Manual Training and did Mission work on the East Side of New York.[2] From 1902-1920,
she was head of the English Department at Howard School, Wilmington, Delaware. From 1920-24, she became a parole worker and an instructor at the Industrial School for Colored Girls,
Delaware.[3] At this time, she also was the associate editor of
the African Methodist Review, and the editor of the Wilmington
Advocate. While working for these publications, she found
time to contribute articles and short stories to various newspapers and magazines.[4] She was active in the Women's division
of the Council of National Defense, Loan Drives, Red Cross,
YMCA, and the War Work Council.[5] From 1928-31, she was
elected as Executive Secretary of the American Interracial
Peace Commission of Philadelphia.[6] Member: National Feder-
ation of Colored Women's Clubs, League of Independent Politi-
cal Action, Women's International League of Peace and Free-
dom, Delta Sigma Theta, N. A. A. C. P. , I. B. P. O. E. W. , and the
Delaware State Republican Campaign, 1920-22.[7]
DRAMA
  (Periodical): Crisis 15 (1918): 271.
MISCELLANEOUS (Poems, essays and narrative sketches)
  Violets and Other Tales. Boston: Monthly Review, 1895.
NON-FICTION (as Alice Dunbar Nelson, Compiler)
  "David Livingstone," Speech delivered at Lincoln University
    (Pennsylvania) Centenary of the Birth of D. Livingstone,
    7 March 1913, Masterpieces of Negro Eloquence. Edited
    by A. M. Dunbar. The Basic Afro-American Reprint
    Library, 1970; Bookery Publishing Co. , 1914, pp. 425-
    444.
  The Dunbar Speaker and Entertainer. Napierville, Ill. :
    J. L. Nichols, 1920.
  Journal of Negro History, Part I, 1 (October 1961): 361-376;
    Part II, 2 (January 1917): 51-78.
  Masterpieces of Negro Eloquence. New York: The Bookery
    Pub. Co. , 1914; New York: Johnson Reprint, 1970*.
  With Prof. Scarborough and Reverdy C. Random. Paul
    Laurence Dunbar, Poet Laureate of the Negro Race.
    Philadelphia, 191? (cf. Schomburg, p. 2070). Also, re-
    print from A. M. E. Church Review.
  "People of Color in Louisiana. " Journal of Negro History
    2: 75.

POETRY
>The Poet and His Song. <u>A.M.E. Church Review</u>, v. 13, 1914.
>(Anthologies): Eleazer, <u>Singers in the Dawn</u>; Johnson, <u>Book of American Negro Poetry</u>; Johnson, <u>Ebony and Topaz</u>.
>(Periodicals): <u>Crisis</u> 18 (1919): 193; 36 (1929): 378; 39 (1932): 458; 77 (November 1970): 365; <u>Negro History Bulletin</u> 31 (April 1968): on the <u>Cover</u>.

SHORT STORIES (as Alice Dunbar)
>The Goodness of St. Rocque and Other Stories. New York: Dodd, Mead, 1899.
>(Periodicals): <u>Crisis</u> 8 (1914): 238; <u>Opportunity</u> 2 (November 1924): 339-340; 3 (July 1925): 216.

BIOGRAPHY AND CRITICISM ON ALICE DUNBAR
>"Alice Dunbar Nelson." <u>Negro History Bulletin</u> 31 (April 1968): 5-6 (Editorial.)
>Anon. "Biography of Alice Dunbar-Nelson." <u>Negro History Bulletin</u> 31 (April 1968): 5.
>Anon. "Personal: The Passing of Distinguished Persons, Alice Dunbar Nelson." <u>Journal of Negro History</u> 21 (January 1936): 95-96.
>Bardolph. <u>The Negro Vanguard</u>, p. 202.
>Chametzky and Kaplan. <u>Black and White in American Culture</u>, p. 362.
>Cromwell, Turner and Dykes. <u>Readings from Negro Authors</u>, p. 32.
>Dannett. <u>Profiles of Negro Womanhood</u>, vol. 1, p. 299.
>Du Bois, W.E.B. <u>The Gift of Black Folk</u>. Boston: Stratford, 1924, pp. 68-69, 83, 87, 97, 100, 145, 155, 267, 268-289.
>Eleazer. <u>Singers in the Dawn</u>, p. 10.
>Gayle. <u>Black Expression</u>, p. 233.
>Huggins. <u>Harlem Renaissance</u>, pp. 196, 261, 276.
><u>Journal of Negro History</u> 21 (January 1936): 95-96. (Obituary.)
>Loggins. <u>The Negro Author</u>, pp. 317-318, 453.
>Redding. <u>They Came in Chains</u>, pp. 207-249.
>Young. <u>Black Writers of the Thirties</u>, p. 135.

REVIEWS
>The Dunbar Speaker and Entertainer:
>>Crisis 22 (1921): 218.
>Masterpieces of Negro Eloquence:
>>Crisis 7 (1914): 253.

[1]Anon., "Alice Dunbar Nelson," <u>Negro History Bulletin</u> 31 (April 1968): 5.

[2]D. W. Culp, <u>Twentieth Century Negro Literature</u> (Miami, Fla.: Mnemosyne, 1969), p. 138.

[3]"Alice Dunbar Nelson," p. 5.

[4]Sylvia Dannett, <u>Profiles of Negro Womanhood</u>, vol. 1 (Yonkers, N.Y.: Educational Heritage, 1964), p. 299.

[5]Saunders Redding, <u>They Came in Chains</u> (New York: Lippincott, 1915 (1973)), p. 249.

[6]"Alice Dunbar Nelson," p. 5.

DUNCAN, Thelma.
  DRAMA
    The Death Dance. In Locke and Gregory, Plays of Negro
      Life.
    Sacrifice. In Richardson, Plays and Pageants.

DUNHAM, Katherine. Born in Chicago, Illinois. Education: Ph.B.,
  University of Chicago; M.S., University of Chicago, 1939.
  Currently divides her time between New York City, East. St.
  Louis, and Port-au-Prince, Haiti. Career: Choreographer,
  choreographer-performer and guest star for theatrical produc-
  tions, playing Pins and Needles, 1939; Tropics and le Jazz Hot,
  1939; Cabin in the Sky, 1940-41; Tropical Review, 1943-44;
  Carib Song, 1945; Bal Negre, 1946; toured with Caribbean
  Rhapsody in Europe, 1948-49, 1954, 1963; in South America
  1950-51, 1954-55; in North Africa, 1952-53; in the U.S. and
  Mexico, 1953; and in Australia. Personal appearances in the
  motion pictures include the following: Carnival of Rhythm
  Hollywood's first dance film in color, 1939); Star Spangled
  Rhythm, 1941; Stormy Weather, 1943; Casbah, 1949; Botta e
  Risposta, Paris, 1952; Mambo, 1954; Musica en la Noche,
  Mexico, 1957; and in other films in Germany, Argentina, Ja-
  pan, and Rome. She has made night club appearances in the
  U.S., as well as in Mexico City, Monte Carlo, Nice, Cannes,
  Tokyo and Argentina. She has done the choreography and stag-
  ing for numerous films, including the 1951 Argentina production
  of Native Son, and for opera, theatre and television productions.
  She has lectured in Singapore, Salzburg, Dakar, Montreal, Mex-
  ico, London, Brussels, Paris, Brazil, New Zealand and the
  U.S. She has composed songs for stage and films, and exhib-
  ited paintings in Paris, Milan, London, Sidney, Lima and
  Buenos Aires. She served as supervisor for the WPA Writers'
  Project in Chicago; as director and teacher of her own schools
  of dance, theatre and cultural arts in Chicago, New York, St.
  Louis, Haiti, Stockholm, Paris, Italy; as State Department Specialist in Dakar, Senegal, 1965-66; as Technical Cultural Advisor to the Presidency, Republic of Senegal, Dakar, 1966.
  She is presently a university professor at Southern Illinois University, and Director of Performing Arts Training Center and
  Dynamic Museum, Southern Illinois University. She is founder
  of the Foundation for the Development and Preservation of Cultural Arts, Inc.; and the Dunham Fund for Research and Development of Cultural Arts, Inc. Member: American Guild of
  Musical Artist, Board of Governors, 1943-49; American Guild
  of Variety Artists, American Federation of Radio Artists; Sigma Epsilon Honorary Women's Scientific Fraternity; Royal Society of Anthropology, London; American Society of Composers
  and Publishers; Screen Actors Guild; Actors' Equity; The Authors Guild, Inc.; Italian Authors and Composers' Union.
  Awards, Honors: Rosenwald and Guggenheim fellowships; Art-
  ist-in-Residence, Southern Illinois University; Visiting Mather
  Scholar, Case Western Reserve University; Honorary Women's
  Scientific Fraternity, University of Chicago, 1937; Chevalier

of Haitian Legion of Honor and Merit, 1952; Commander, Haitian Legion of Honor and Merit, 1958; Grand Officer, Haitian Legion of Honor and Merit, 1968; Honorary Citizen, Port au Prince, Haiti, 1957; Laureate and Member, Lincoln Academy, 1968; Key to the City of East St. Louis, 1968; Professional Achievement Award; Alumni Association, University of Chicago, 1968; Dance Magazine Award, 1969; Eight Lively Arts Award, 1969; Certificate of Merit-Improved Benevolent and Protective Order of Elks of the World, 1969; Southern Illinois University, Distinguished Service Award, 1969; St. Louis Argus Award, 1970; East St. Louis Monitor Award, 1970; Katherine Dunham Day Award, Detroit 1970; Certificate of Merit, International Who's Who in Poetry, 1970-71; Dance Division Heritage Award, AAHPER, Detroit, 1971; East St. Louis Pro-8 Award, 1971; Contribution to the Arts Award, Black Academy of Arts and Letters, 1972; National Center of Afro-American Artists Award, Elma Lewis School of Fine Arts, 1972; Honorary Doctor of Humane Letters Degree, MacMurray College, Jacksonville, Illinois, May 1972; Black Merit Academy Award, 1972; Woman for a Day, Radio Station WRTH, 1973.

AUTOBIOGRAPHY
    Katherine Dunham's Journey to Accompong, 1946; New York:
        Greenwood, 1972*.
NON-FICTION
    Island Possessed. Garden City, N.Y.: Doubleday, 1969.
    Las Danzas de Haiti. Mexico: Acta Anthropologica 114,
        1947; also published in Paris: Le Danses d'Haiti. Paris:
        Fasquelle, 1950.
    (Anthologies): Brown, Davis and Lee, The Negro Caravan;
        Chametsky and Kaplan, Black and White in American Culture; Seven Arts (Garden City, N.Y.: Doubleday, 1954.
    (Periodicals): Ballet (Argentina), January 1955; California
        Arts and Architecture, August 1941; Educational Dance,
        October 1941; Esquire, September 1939 (published under
        the pseud. Kaye Dunn); Mademoiselle, November 1945;
        Manuscripts, 1939; Massachusetts Review, Show, 1963;
        Travel, 1963; also published in Realities.
NOVEL
    A Touch of Innocence. New York: Harcourt Brace, 1959;
        London: Cassell, 1960; New York: Harcourt Brace Jovanovich, 1969†.
POETRY
    (Anthology): Shuman, A Galaxy of Black Writing.
SHORT STORIES
    (Anthologies): Hill, Soon One Morning; Hughes, Best Short
        Stories by Negro Writers.
    (Periodicals): Bandwagon (London), June 1952; Ellery Queen's
        Mystery Magazine, 1964.
VIGNETTE
    (Periodical): Phylon, Second Quarter 1953.
BIOGRAPHY AND CRITICISM ON DUNHAM
    Biemiller, Ruth. Dance: The Story of Katherine Dunham.
        Garden City, N.Y.: Doubleday, 1969*.

"Black Academy of Arts and Letters." Black World 21
(November 1971): 68-71.
Buckle, Richard, ed. Katherine Dunham, Her Dancers,
Singers, Musicians. London: Ballet, 1949.
Cluzel, Magdeleine E. Glimpses of the Theatre and Dance.
New York: Kamin, 1953.
Ebony (January 1947): 14-18; (March 1948): 36; (December
1954): 83-86.
Hughes and Meltzer. Black Magic, pp. 186-339 passim.
"Katherine Dunham." Crisis 57 (June 1950): 344.
"Katherine Dunham, Negro Dancer." Stage and Screen (Lon-
don, Winter 1946-47).
Leaf, Earl. Isles of Rhythm. New York: A. S. Barnes,
1948.
Lloyd, Margaret. The Borzoi Book of Modern Dance. New
York: Knopf, 1949, pp. 243-253.
Mitchell. Black Drama, pp. 109, 130, 144.
Noble, Peter. The Negro in Films. London: Skelton Rob-
inson, 1969, pp. 91-97.
Opportunity, April 1941; Winter 1947.
Richardson, Great American Negroes, pp. 87-96.
REVIEW
A Touch of Innocence:
Winslow, Henry F. Crisis 67 (February 1960): 118.
INTERJECTIONS
"The period of being embedded only in one's own culture
has passed, I believe, for the young American Black. It is
now time, in this interval between stages of action, to take in-
to account the other cultures of the world, to know and to
penetrate them whether for guides or for pre-cautions. The
comparative is always a safe path for knowledge."

DUNJEE, Roscoe. Born 21 June 1883 in Harper's Ferry, West
Virginia. Education: Attended Langston University. Career:
Publisher and Editor of Black Dispatch, an Oklahoma City
newspaper, for several decades, beginning in 1915. Awards,
Honors: N.A.A.C.P. Merit Award, 1935. [1]
POETRY
(Anthology): Kerlin, Negro Poets and Their Poems.
[1]Who's Who in Colored America, 5th ed. (1938-1939-
1940).

DUNSTER, Mark.
DRAMA Sojourner.

DURANT, E. Elliott.
NOVEL The Princess of Naragpur, or a Daughter of Allah.
New York: Grafton Press, 1928.

DUREM, Ray. Born 1915 in Seattle, Washington. Died December
1963 in Los Angeles. Career: Joined the Navy at 14. Fought
as a member of the International Brigades during the Spanish
Civil War. Lived for many years in Mexico. [1]

POETRY
Take No Prisoners. London: Breman, 1962†; distributed in
   the U.S. by Broadside Press.
(Anthologies): Adams, Conn and Slepian, Afro-American Lit-
   erature; Adoff, Black Out Loud; Adoff, I Am the Darker
   Brother; Adoff, The Poetry of Black America; Colley and
   Moore, Starting with Poetry; Hughes, The Book of Negro
   Humor; Hughes, New Negro Poets: U.S.A.; Hughes and
   Bontemps, The Poetry of the Negro: 1746-1970; Jordan,
   Soulscript; Lomax and Abdul, 3000 Years of Black Poetry;
   Major, The New Black Poetry; Pool, Beyond the Blues;
   Randall, The Black Poets; Walrond and Pool, Black and
   Unknown Bards.
(Periodicals): Crisis, April-May 1971; Negro Digest; Phylon,
   Third Quarter, 1955.
   [1]Arnold Adoff, ed., I Am the Darker Brother (New
York: Macmillan, 1968), p. 119.

DURHAM, John Stephens. Born 1861 in Philadelphia. Died 1919.
   Education: B.S., Toune Scientific School of the University of
   Pennsylvania, 1886; B.C.E., 1888. Career: Taught school in
   Delaware, New Jersey and Pennsylvania. Free lance reporter
   for the Philadelphia Times; assistant editor for the Philadelphia
   Evening Bulletin. Appointed by President Harrison to serve as
   U.S. Minister to Haiti, 1891.[1]
   NON-FICTION
   To Teach the Negro History: A Suggestion. Philadelphia:
      n.p., 1897.
   ROMANCE
   "Diane, Priestess of Haiti." Lippincott's Monthly Magazine,
      April 1902.
   BIOGRAPHY ON DURHAM
   Christmas. Negroes in Public Affairs, pp. 168-169.
      [1]Wilhelmina Robinson, Historical Negro Biographies
   (New York: Publishers, 1967): p. 78.

DURHAM, Richard V. Born 1817.
   POETRY
   (Anthology): Bontemps, Golden Slippers.

DURRAH, Jim.
   DRAMA The Ho-Hum Revolution.

DUST, (Welvin Stroud). Born 29 January 1937 in Colorado Springs,
   Colorado. Education: B.A., San José State, 1958; M.A.,
   Stanford University, 1964. Learned how to teach as a Sunday
   School teacher. Currently living in San Francisco, California.
   Career: Teacher. Presently "working on SELF and a Ph.D.
   in Architecture Environmental Design at the University of Cali-
   fornia."
   POETRY
   Poems by Dust. San Francisco: Julian Richardson, 1969.

Jacqueline Earley

INTERJECTIONS
"The Lesson"

Life is circular
Triangles and squares come and go--
But one must find a
Mellow groove
And Live.

DYKES, James.
POETRY
(Periodicals): Opportunity, July 1936; October 1938; February, April, 1939; May, November 1941.
BIOGRAPHY AND CRITICISM ON DYKES
Opportunity 14 (July 1936): 198.

-E-

EARLE, Victoria (Victoria Earle Matthews).
NOVEL Aunt Lindy, A Story Founded on Real Life. New York: Press of J. J. Little, 1893.

EARLEY, Jacqueline. Born 17 December 1939 in Buffalo, New York. Education: Attended three semesters of college in Cleveland, Ohio; trained in dance and theater at Karamu Theater in Cleveland; trained in dance at Connecticut College School of Dance. Currently living in New York City. Career: An actress appearing in many stage plays as well as on television and the screen; also a dancer and a choreographer. During 1967-68, she conducted dance workshops for the Free Southern Theater. She directed "The Smokers" at the Dillard University Afro Arts Festival, and created the poetry and music concert, "Third World Trio," at Louisiana State University New Orleans, and at Tulane University. She published a Harlem newsletter entitled "Celebrated Blackness." She has given numerous lectures on Black literature and has read her poetry at schools and community centers in the New York area. She is the author of The Black West, a poetry narration commissioned by the Afro-American Singing Theater and performed at City Center Theater. Awards, Honors: Harlem Writer's Grant.
NON-FICTION
(Periodicals): Black Dialogue; The Feet.
POETRY
(Anthologies): Abdul, The Magic of Black Poetry; Coombs, We Speak as Liberators; Giovanni, Night Comes Softly; Jordan, Soulscript; King, Blackspirits; Patterson, A Rock Against the Wind.
(Periodicals): Journal of Black Poetry, Spring 1969; Winter-Spring 1970; Summer 1972; also in Black Culture Weekly, Liberator, Revolt.

EASTMOND, Claude T.
  POETRY Light and Shadows. Boston: Christopher, 1934.

EASTON, Sidney.
  DRAMA
    Miss Trudie Fair, 1953.
  BIOGRAPHY AND CRITICISM ON EASTON
    Mitchell. Black Drama, pp. 44-45, 46, 93, 159-162.

EASTON, William Edgar.
  DRAMA
    Christophe, 1911.
    Dessalines, 1893.

EATON, Estelle Atley.
  POETRY Out of My Dreams and Other Verses. Boston:
    Christopher, 1959.

EBON (Tom Dooley). Born 1942.
  POETRY
    Revolution: A Poem. Chicago: Third World, 1968†.
    (Anthologies): Adoff, The Poetry of Black America; Brooks,
      A Broadside Treasury; Henderson, Understanding the New
      Black Poetry; Randall, Black Poetry: A Supplement.
  CRITICISM ON EBON
    Lee. Dynamite Voices, pp. 41-43.

ECHOLS, Carl.
  POETRY (Anthology): Murphy, Negro Voices.

ECKELS, Jon B. Born in Indianapolis, Indiana. Education:
  "From Elementary, P.S. 83 to Stanford's Ph.D., but mainly
  the world--theirs, ours, mine." B.A., Indiana Central College, 1961; B.D., Pacific School of Religion, 1966; Ph.D.,
  Stanford University, 1974. Career: Held miscellaneous jobs
  in Indianapolis until 1961. Pacific Maritime Association, San
  Francisco, 1961-1962; The United Methodist Church, Oakland,
  California, 1966-68; Merritt College, 1969-70; Mills College,
  1968-73; Stanford University, 1971-73. As a writer, teacher,
  and speaker, he is interested in "freedom, spiritual/internal
  and social/external, and in the fullest development of the human spirit." Member: many Black community and cultural
  organizations. Awards, Honors: received prizes for art work.
  POETRY
    Black Dawn. Berkeley, Ca.: By the Author, 1966.
    Black Right On. San Francisco: Julian Richardson, 1969.
    Firesign. San Jose, Ca.: Firesign, 1973.
    Home Is Where the Soul Is. Detroit: Broadside, 1969†.
    Our Business in the Streets. Detroit: Broadside, 1971†.
    This Time Tomorrow. San Francisco: Julian Richardson,
      1966.
    (Anthologies): Brooks, A Broadside Treasury; Brown, Lee
      and Ward, To Gwen With Love; Patterson, A Rock

Against the Wind; Ashland College, 60 of the 60's; Reed, Yardbird Reader I.
(Periodicals): Black Dialogue; Journal of Black Poetry; Negro Digest, September 1969.

BIOGRAPHY AND CRITICISM ON ECKELS

Kent. "Struggle for the Image," pp. 314-315.

INTERJECTIONS

"Today, we need free people, women and men--and not more celebrities; we have enough football, baseball, basketball and player-players to last a lifetime. We are glutted with comedians, singers, musicians, boxers, 'leaders,' pimps, and now, moving actors and cool pusher men, who all buck and swing to the tune of white entrepreneurs under a self-perpetuating exploitative system. We need poets who are free and who will stir our deepest identities, needs and possibilities as human beings; poets who will challenge our abilities to imagine, to live creatively and courageously. I think now is the time for us to flee from, or re-educate those poets who say niggers got rhythm/ nice naturals/ and the white boy is a girl/ and white girls are all powerful/ most niggers/ ain't shit--still, while showing us nothing of the true nature of the phantasmagoria of horror, the system of adversary and the new world that can be. (Perhaps I am in the unpopular minority, the real minority, but I do not think that poets and teachers, etc. should deal in opiates.) Life inspires me to write of life for life.

"We can create, we can love--we can be free. I believe we can. I know we must."

EDMONDS, Randolph. Born 1900 in Lawrenceville, Virginia.

CRITICISM BY EDMONDS

"Black Drama in the American Theatre: 1700-1970." The American Theatre: A Sum of Its Parts. New York: Samuel French, 1971, pp. 379-426.

"Some Reflections on the Negro in American Drama." Opportunity 8 (October 1930): 303-305.

DRAMA

The Land of Cotton and Other Plays. Washington, D.C.: Associated Publishers, 1942. (Includes "Gangsters Over Harlem," "The High Court of Historia," "Silas Brown," "Yellow Death.")

Shades and Shadows. Boston: Meador, 1930. (Includes "The Call of Jubah," "Everyman's Land," "Hewers of the Wood," "The Phantom Treasure," "Shades and Shadows," "The Tribal Chief.")

Six Plays for a Negro Theater. Boston: Baker, 1934. (Includes "Bad Man," "Bleeding Hearts," "The Breeders," "Nat Turner," "The New Window," "Old Man Pete.")

Bad Man. In Brown, Davis and Lee, Negro Caravan.

Career or College, 1956.

Christmas Gift (one act), 1923.

Denmark Vesey (one act), 1929.

The Devil's Price, 1930.

Doom (one act), 1924.

Drama Enters the Curriculum: A Purpose Play (one act),
      1930.
Earth and Stars, 1946; revised 1961; In Turner, Black Dra-
      ma in America.
For Fatherland (one act), 1934.
G.I. Rhapsody, 1943.
The Highwayman (one act), 1934.
Illicit Love, 1927.
Job Hunting (one act), 1922.
The Land of Cotton, 1942.
The Man of God, 1931.
A Merchant of Dixie (one act), 1923.
Nat Turner. In Richardson and Miller, Negro History in
      Thirteen Plays.
One Side of Harlem, 1928.
The Outer Room (one act), 1935.
Peter Stith (one act), 1933.
Prometheus and the Atom, 1955.
Rocky Roads, 1926.
The Shadow Across the Path (one act), 1943.
The Shape of Wars to Come (one act), 1943.
Simon in Cyrene, 1939.
Sirlock Bones (one act), 1928.
Stock Exchange (musical), 1927.
Takazee: A Pageant of Ethiopia, 1928.
The Trial and Banishment of Uncle Tom (one act), 1945.
The Virginia Politician (one act), 1927.
Whatever the Battle Be: A Symphonic Drama, 1950.
Wives and Blues, 1938.
NON-FICTION
   (Periodicals): Crisis, August, November 1938; Negro His-
      tory Bulletin, Fall 1961.
REVIEWS
   Published in Phylon.
BIOGRAPHY AND CRITICISM ON EDMONDS
   Brawley. Negro Genius, pp. 285-287.
   Bond. The Negro's God, pp. 123-128, 136.
   Mitchell. Black Drama, p. 9.

EDWARDS, Harry.
   POETRY (Anthologies): Chambers and Moon, Right On!; The
      New Black Poetry.

EDWARDS, Junius. Born 1929 in Alexandria, Louisiana.
   NOVEL
      If We Must Die. New York: Doubleday, 1963.
   SHORT STORIES
      (Anthologies): Hughes, The Best Short Stories by Negro
         Writers; King, Black Short Story Anthology; Margolies,
         A Native Sons Reader; Williams, Beyond the Angry Black.
   REVIEW: If We Must Die
      Berry, Faith. Crisis 70 (October 1963): 508-509.
      Interracial Review 36 (Summer 1963): 177.

EDWARDS, S. W.   see SUBLETTE, Walter

EDWARDS, Solomon.   Born 1932 in Indianapolis.
   POETRY
      (Anthologies): Hughes, New Negro Poets: USA; Hughes and
        Bontemps, The Poetry of the Negro: 1746-1970.
      (Periodicals): Cornucopia; Présence Africaine, No. 57;
        Voices.

EDWIN, Walter Lewis.
   POETRY Songs in the Desert.   London: Frank H. Morland,
      1909.

EKULONA, Ademola (Ronald Floyd).
   DRAMA
      Last Hot Summer.
      Mother of the House.
      Three Black Comedies.

EL, Leatrice.
   DRAMA Black Magic, Anyone? 1972.

ELDER, Eleanor Hardee.
   POETRY Me n' de Chillun.   New York: Praegar, 1948.

ELDER, Lonne III.   Born in Americus, Georgia.
   DRAMA
      Ceremonies in Dark Old Men.   New York: Farrar, Straus
        & Giroux, 1969*†; New York: Samuel French, n.d. †; al-
        so in Patterson, Black Theater.
      Charades on East Fourth Street.   In King and Milner,
        Black Drama Anthology.
      A Hysterical Turtle in a Rabbit Race, 1961.
      Kissin' Rattlesnakes Can Be Fun (one act), 1966.
      Seven Comes Up, Seven Comes Down (one act), 1966.
      The Terrible Veil, 1963.
   NON-FICTION
      (Periodical): Black Creation, Summer 1973.
   TELEPLAY
      Deadly Circle of Violence.
   BIOGRAPHY AND CRITICISM ON ELDER
      Bigsby.   The Black Writer in America, vol. 2, pp. 219-
        226.
      Gant, Liz. "An Interview with Lonne Elder III." Black
        World (April 1973).
      Harrison.   The Drama of Nommo, p. 27.
      Jeffers, Lance. "Bullins, Baraka, and Elder: The Dawn
        of Grandeur in Black Drama." CLA Journal 16 (Septem-
        ber 1972): 32-48.
      Mitchell.   Black Drama, pp. 215, 216.
      Rosenberg, Harold. "The Artist as Perceiver of Social Re-
        alities: The Post-Art Artist." Arts in Society 8 (Sum-
        mer 1971): 509-510.

ELLETT, M. Deborah. Born 14 October 1949 in Kansas. Education: Attended Central Missouri State and Penn Valley College. Currently living in Kansas City, Missouri. Career:
Works for T.W.A. Is active in community, cultural, athletic
and editorial affairs. Presently is poetry editor of City Inner
& Outer magazine.
POETRY
    From Them I Come. n.p.: A Free Will Publication, 1973.

ELLIOTT, Emily.
    POETRY Still Waters and Other Poems. Cambridge: By the
        Author, 1949.

ELLIS, George Washington. Born 1875. Died 1919.
    NOVEL The Leopard's Claw. New York: International Au-
        thor's Assoc., 1917; reprint ed. AMS Press, 1970.

ELLIS, Teresa.
    NOVELLA No Way Back: A Novella. New York: Exposition,
        1973.

ELLISON, Ralph Waldo. Born 1 March 1914 in Oklahoma City,
    Oklahoma. Education: Studied music at Tuskegee Institute,
    1933-1936; also studied sculpture. Currently living in New
    York City. Career: Worked with the New York City Federal
    Writers Project before serving in the U.S. Merchant Marines
    during World War II. Edited the Negro Quarterly for a short
    time. Taught Russian and American literature, Bard College,
    1958-61; served as Alexander White Visiting Professor, Uni-
    versity of Chicago, 1961, and as Visiting Professor of Writing,
    Rutgers University, 1963-64. Has lectured at numerous col-
    leges and universities in the U.S. as well as at the Salzburg
    Seminar in American Studies, Austria, 1954. Appointed by
    USIA (Department of State) for tour of Italian cities, 1956.
    Member: Charter member, National Council on the Arts; Char-
    ter member, Carnegie Commission on Educational Television;
    member of Author's Guild, Century Association, Institute for
    Jazz Studies; Board member, American P.E.N.; National Ad-
    visory Council, Hampshire College; Trustee, John F. Kennedy
    Center for Performing Arts, 1967-77; Board member, WNDT,
    Channel 13; Board member, Associated Council of the Arts;
    Trustee, New School for Social Research; Trustee, Bennington
    College; Honorary Consultant, Library of Congress, 1966-72;
    Fellow, National Institute of Arts and Letters, American Acad-
    emy of Arts and Sciences, and Silliman College of Yale Univer-
    sity. Awards, Honors: Grants: Rosenwald Fellowship, 1945-
    47; American Academy in Rome, 1955-57; Rockefeller Founda-
    tion, 1964. National Book Award for Invisible Man, 1953;
    Russwurm Award (National Newspapers Publishers Award),
    1953; New York Herald Tribune Book Week Consensus of Au-
    thors and Critics Poll--"Book most cited in 1965." Medal of
    Freedom, civilian award from President Lyndon B. Johnson,
    1969. Chevalier de l'Ordre Arts et Lettres, awarded by the

Ralph Ellison (credit: Bob Adelman)

Minister of Cultural Affairs, France, 1960. Honorary degrees
--Doctor of Philosophy in Humane Letters, Tuskegee Institute,
1963; Doctor of Letters, Rutgers University, 1966; Doctor of
Letters, University of Michigan, 1967; Doctor of Humane Letters, Grinnel College, 1967.

CRITICISM BY ELLISON

"The Art of Fiction: An Interview." Paris Review 8 (Spring
    1955): 55-71; also in Writers at Work: The Paris Review
    Interviews, no. 2, pp. 317-338; Shadow and Act; Hemen-
    way, The Black Novelist, pp. 205-217; Kearns, The Black
    Experience.

"Beating That Boy." The New Republic, 22 October 1945;
    also in Shadow and Act.

"Brave Words for a Startling Occasion: Address for Pre-
    sentation Ceremony: National Book Award, 1956." In
    Shadow and Act; Long and Collier, Afro-American Writing,
    pp. 603-606; Ford, Black Insights, pp. 185-186.

"Harlem Is Nowhere." Harper's 229 (August 1964); also in
    Shadow and Act.

"Hidden Name and Complex Fate." (Address sponsored by
    the Gertrude Clarke Whittall Foundation, Library of Con-
    gress, 6 January 1964.) Also in Shadow and Act; Miller,
    Backgrounds to Black American Literature.

"Light on Invisible Man." Crisis 60 (1953): 157-158.

"The Negro Writer in America: An Exchange." Partisan

Review 25 (Spring 1958): 212; published as "Change the Joke and Slip the Yoke," in Shadow and Act; also in Singh and Fellowes, Black Literature in America, pp. 228-237.

"Philippine Writers Report." Direction 4 (Summer 1941): 13.

"Recent Negro Fiction." New Masses, 5 August 1941, pp. 22-26.

"Richard Wright and Negro Fiction." Direction 4 (Summer 1941): 12-13.

"Richard Wright's Blues." Antioch Review 5 (Summer 1945): 198-211; also in Shadow and Act; Gayle, Black Expression, Ford, Black Insights; Bixler, The Antioch Review Anthology (c1953).

Shadow and Act. New York: Random, 1964*; New York: New American Library†; New York: Random, 1972†.

"The Shadow and the Act." The Reporter, 6 December 1949, pp. 17-18; also in Shadow and Act.

"Society, Morality, and the Novel." In The Living Novel, pp. 58-91. Edited by Granville Hicks. New York: Macmillan, 1957.

"Some Questions and Some Answers." Préuves (May 1958): also in Shadow and Act.

"Stephen Crane and the Mainstream of American Fiction." An introduction to The Red Badge of Courage and Four Great Stories by Stephen Crane; also in Shadow and Act.

"That Same Pain, That Same Pleasure: An Interview." December 3 (Winter 1961); also in Shadow and Act; Gross, and Hardy, Images of the Negro in American Literature.

With others. "The Uses of History in Fiction." Southern Literary Journal 1 (1969): 57-90.

"The Way It Is." New Masses, 20 October 1942; also in Shadow and Act.

"The World and the Jug." Shadow and Act. Includes "The Writer and the Critic," The New Leader, 3 February 1964, pp. 12-22, and "A Rejoinder," The New Leader, 9 December 1963; also in Gibson, Five Black Writers, pp. 271-295.

NON-FICTION

Crisis, March, 1970; Esquire, 1968; High Fidelity, December, 1955; Negro Digest, September 1944, New Leader, 26 September 1966; New Masses, 15 August 1939; New York Post, 2 August 1943; New York Review; Prevues, May 1958; Saturday Review, 26 April, 17 May, 27 September, 1958, 28 June 1962.

NOVEL

Invisible Man. New York: Random, 1952*†; New York: Modern Library, 1963. Excerpts in Chapman, Black Voices; Davis and Redding, Cavalcade; Ford, Black Insights; Gross, A Nation of Nations; Kendricks, Afro-American Writing; Margolies, A Native Sons Reader; Miller, Blackamerican Literature; Patterson, An Introduction to Black Literature in America from 1746 to the

Present.

SHORT STORIES

(Anthologies): Angus and Angus, Contemporary American Short Stories; Baker, Black Literature of America; Barksdale, and Kinnamon, Black Writers of America; Emanuel and Gross, Dark Symphony; Faderman and Bradshaw, Speaking for Ourselves; Fenton, Best Short Stories of World War II; Gold, The Human Commitment; Gold and Stevenson, Stories of Modern America; Hayden, Burrows and Lapides, Afro-American Literature; Hills and Hills, How We Live; Hughes, The Best Short Stories by Negro Writers; James, From These Roots; Kearns, Black Identity; King, Black Short Story Anthology; Klein and Pack, Short Stories; New World Writing #5; New World Writing #9; Seaver, Cross-Section; Singh and Fellowes, Black Literature in America; Sterling, I Have Seen War; Turner, Black Black American Literature: Fiction.

(Periodicals): Common Ground, Summer 1943; Direction, September 1938; Iowa Review, Spring 1970; Negro Story, July-August 1944; March-April 1945; May-June 1945; October-November 1944; New Masses, 4 November 1941; Partisan Review, Spring 1963; Tomorrow, July, November 1944.

REVIEWS BY ELLISON

Published in The New Challenge; New Masses, The Negro Quarterly; Tomorrow; Saturday Review; The New York Review; New York Herald Tribune.

UNPUBLISHED NOVEL EXCERPTS

(Anthology): Hill, Soon One Morning.

(Periodicals): Direction, September 1939; The Noble Savage, 1960; Quarterly Review of Literature, 1960; 1965; Partisan Review, Spring 1963.

"Cadillac Flambé." In American Review 16, pp. 249-269. (Excerpt from forthcoming novel.)

VIGNETTES

(Anthology): Storm and others, American Writing.

(Periodicals): Negro World Digest, July, November 1940; Negro Story, 1945; New Masses, 2 July 1940.

BIBLIOGRAPHIES ON ELLISON

Adelman and Dworkin. The Contemporary Novel, pp. 126-129.

Benoit, Bernard and Michel Fabre. "A Bibliography of Ralph Ellison's Published Writings." Stories in Black Literature 2 (Autumn 1971): 25-28.

Covo, Jacqueline. "Ralph Waldo Ellison: Bibliographic Essays and Finding List of American Criticism 1952-1964." CLA Journal 15 (December 1971): 171-196.

_____. "Ralph Ellison in France: Bibliographic Essay and Checklist of French Criticism, 1954-1971." CLA Journal 16 (June 1973): 519-526.

_____. The Blinking Eye: Ralph Waldo Ellison and His American, French, German and Italian Critics, 1952-1971: Bibliographic Essays and a Checklist. Metuchen,

N. J. : Scarecrow, 1974*.

Leary, L. , ed. Articles on American Literature: 1950-1967. Durham, N.C. : Duke University Press, 1970, pp. 146-147.

Lillard, R. W. "A Ralph Waldo Ellison Bibliography (1914-1967). The American Book Collector 19 (November 1968): 18-22.

Moorer, Frank E. and Lugene Baily. "A Selected Check List of Materials By and About Ralph Ellison." Black World 20 (December 1970): 126-127.

Polsgrove, Carol. "Addenda to 'A Ralph Waldo Ellison Bibliography 1914-1968'." The American Book Collector 20 (November-December 1969): 11-12.

Tischler, Nancy M. "Ralph Ellison (1914-)." In A Bibliographic Guide to the Study of Southern Literature, pp. 191-192. Edited by Louis D. Rubin, Jr. Baton Rouge: Louisiana State University Press, 1969.

Turner, Darwin T. Afro-American Writers. New York: Appleton-Century-Crofts, 1970. pp. 52-53, 112.

BIOGRAPHY AND CRITICISM ON ELLISON
(Selected Criticism Prior to 1970)

Baumbach, Jonathan. "Nightmare of a Native Son: Ellison's Invisible Man." Critique 6 (1963): 48-65; also in Cooke, Modern Black Novelists, pp. 64-78; Gibson, Five Black Writers, pp. 73-87.

Bone, Robert. "Ralph Ellison and the Uses of Imagination." Tri-Quarterly 6 (1966): 39-54; in Hersey, Ralph Ellison, pp. 95-114; Cooke, Modern Black Novelists, pp. 45-63; Reilly, Twentieth Century Interpretations of "Invisible Man."

Cannon, Steve, Lennox Raphael and James Thompson. "A Very Stern Discipline." Harper's Magazine 234 (March 1967): 76-95.

Corry, John. "An American Novelist Who Sometimes Teaches." The New York Times Sunday Magazine, 20 November 1966, pp. 54-55, 179-180.

Ellison, Ralph. "February." Saturday Review 38 (1 January 1955): 25.

_____. " 'Tell It Like It Is, Baby.' " Nation, 20 (September 1965, pp. 129-136.

Fraiberg, Selma. "Two Modern Incest Heroes." Partisan Review, (September-October 1961): 646-661; also in Reilly, Twentieth Century Interpretations of "Invisible Man."

Geller, Allen. "An Interview with Ralph Ellison." Tamarack Review no. 32 (Summer 1964): 3-24; also in Bigsby The Black American Writer, vol. 1.

Glicksberg, Charles I. "The Symbolism of Vision." Southwest Review 39 (1954): 259-265; also in Reilly, Twentieth Century Interpretations of "Invisible Man."

Griffin, Edward N. "Notes from a Clean, Well Lighted Place: Ralph Ellison's Invisible Man." Twentieth Century Literature 15 (October 1969): 129-144.

Hassan, Ihab. Radical Innocence: Studies in the Contemporary Novel. Princeton, N.J.: Princeton University Press, 1961, pp. 168-178.

Hays, Peter L. "The Incest Theme in Invisible Man." The Western Humanities Review 23 (Autumn 1969): 142-159.

Heermance, J. Noel. "A White Critic's Viewpoint: The Modern Negro Jove." Negro Digest 13 (May 1964): 66-76.

Horowitz, Ellin. "The Rebirth of the Artist." In On Contemporary Literature, pp. 330-346. Edited by Richard Kostelanetz. New York: Avon, 1964; also in Reilly, Twentieth Century Interpretations of "Invisible Man."

Horowitz, F. R. "Enigma of Ellison's Intellectual Man." CLA Journal 7 (December 1963): 126-132.

_____. "Ralph Ellison's Modern Version of Brer Bear and Brer Rabbit in Invisible Man." Midcontinental American Studies Journal 4 (1963): 21-27; also in Reilly, Twentieth Century Interpretations of "Invisible Man."

Howe, Irving. "Black Boys and Native Sons." Dissent 10 (1963): 353-368; also in Gibson, Five Black Writers, pp. 254-270; Reilly, Twentieth Century Interpretations of "Invisible Man."

Jackson, Esther Merle. "The American Negro and the Image of the Absurd." Phylon 23 (1962): 359-371; also in Reilly, Twentieth Century Interpretations of "Invisible Man."

Klein, Marcus. "Ralph Ellison." After Alienation: American Novels in Mid Century. Cleveland: World, 1964, pp. 71-146.

Knox, George. "The Negro Novelist's Sensibility and the Outsider Theme." Western Humanities Review 11 (Spring 1957): 137-148.

Kostelanetz, Richard. "Ralph Ellison as Brown Skinned Aristocrat." Shenandoah 20 (Summer 1969): 56-57.

Lehan, Richard. "Existentialism in Recent American Fiction: The Demonic Quest." Texas Studies in Literature and Language 1 (1959): 181-202.

_____. "The Strange Silence of Ralph Ellison." In Reilly, Twentieth Century Interpretations of "Invisible Man."

O'Daniel, Thurman B. "Image of Man as Portrayed by Ralph Ellison." CLA Journal 10 (June 1967): 277-284; also in Gibson, Five Black Writers, pp. 102-107.

Olderman, Raymond M. "Ralph Ellison's Blues and Invisible Man." Wisconsin Studies in Contemporary Literature 7 (Summer 1966): 142-159.

Rodnon, S. "Invisible Man: Six Tentative Approaches." CLA Journal 12 (March 1969): 244-256.

Rovit, E. H. "Ralph Ellison and the American Comic Condition." Wisconsin Studies in Contemporary Literature 1 (1960): 34-42; also in Gibson, Five Black Writers, pp. 108-115; Hersey, Ralph Ellison, pp. 151-159.

Schafer, William J. "Irony from Underground: Satiric Elements in Invisible Man." Satire Newsletter 7 (Fall 1969):

22-28; in Hersey, Ralph Ellison; Reilly, Twentieth Century Interpretations of "Invisible Man."

Stanford, Raney. "The Return of Trickster: When a Not-a-Hero Is a Hero." Journal of Popular Culture 1 (1967): 228-242.

Tischler, Nancy M. "Negro Literature and Classic Form." Contemporary Literature 10 (Summer 1969): 252-265.

Warren, Robert Penn. "The Unity of Experience." Commentary 39 (1965): 91-96; also in Hersey, Ralph Ellison, pp. 21-26.

(Selected Criticism Since 1970)

Baker, H. A. "Forgotten Prototype." Virginia Quarterly 49 (Summer 1973): 433-449.

Bell, J. D. "Ellison's Invisible Man." Explicator 29 (1970): Item 19.

Bennett, Stephen B., and William W. Nicols. "Violence in Afro-American Fiction: An Hypothesis." Modern Fiction Studies 17 (1971): 221-228; also in Hersey, Ralph Ellison, pp. 171-176.

Boulgar, James D. "Puritan Allegory in Four Modern Novels." Thought 40 (1969): 413-432.

Brown, L.L. "The Deep Pit." In Reilly, Twentieth Century Interpretations of "Invisible Man."

Brown, Lloyd W. "Ralph Ellison's Exhorters: The Role of Rhetoric in Invisible Man." CLA Journal 13 (March 1970): 289-303.

Cash, Earl A. "The Narrators in Invisible Man and Notes from Underground: Brothers in Spirit." CLA Journal 16 (June 1973): 505-507.

Clarke, John Henrik. "The Visible Dimensions of Invisible Man." Black World 20 (December 1970): 27-30.

Clipper, Lawrence J. "Folklore and Mythic Elements in Invisible Man." CLA Journal 13 (March 1970): 229-241.

Cooke, M. G., ed. Modern Black Novelists: A Collection of Critical Essays. Englewood Cliffs, N.J.: Prentice-Hall, 1971, pp. 45-78.

Corry, J. "Profile of an American Novelist." Black World 20 (December 1970): 116-125.

Deutsch, Leonard J. "Ellison's Early Fiction." Negro American Literature Forum 7 (Summer 1973): 53-59.

Fass, B. "Rejection of Paternalism: Hawthorne's My Kinsman Major Molineaux and Ellison's Invisible Man." CLA Journal 14 (March 1971): 317-323.

Ford, Nick Aron. "The Ambivalence of Ralph Ellison." Black World 20 (December 1970): 5-9.

Forrest, Leon. "Racial History as a Clue to the Action in Invisible Man. Muhammad Speaks 12 (15 September 1972): 28-30.

_____. "A Conversation with Ralph Ellison." Muhammad Speaks 12 (15 December 1972): 29-31.

Foster, Frances S. "The Black and White Masks of Frantz Fanon and Ralph Ellison." Black Academy Review 1 (1970): 46-58.

Gibson, Donald B. _Five Black Writers_. New York: New York University Press, Gotham Library, 1970.

Goede, William. "On Lower Frequencies: The Buried Men in Wright and Ellison." _Modern Fiction Studies_ 15 (Winter 1969-1970): 483-501.

Graham, John. _Writer's Voice_. New York: Morrow, 1973, pp. 221-227.

Greenberg, Alvin. "Ironic Alternatives in the World of the Contemporary Novel." In _American Dreams, American Nightmares_, pp. 177-186. Edited by David Madden. Carbondale and Edwardsville: Southern Illinois University Press, 1970; London and Amsterdam: Feffer & Simons, 1970.

Gross. _The Heroic Ideal in American Literature_, pp. 157-166.

Guttman, Allen. "Focus on Ralph Ellison's _Invisible Man_." In _American Dreams, American Nightmares_, pp. 188-196. Edited by David Madden. Carbondale and Edwardsville: Southern Illinois University Press, 1970; London and Amsterdam: Feffer & Simons, 1970.

Gvereschi, Edward. "Anticipations of _Invisible Man_: Ralph Ellison's 'King of the Bingo Game.'" _Negro American Literature Forum_ 6 (Winter 1972): 122-124.

Hays, Peter L. _The Limping Hero: Grotesques in Literature_. New York: New York University, 1971.

Hersey, John, ed. _Ralph Ellison: A Collection of Critical Essays_. Twentieth Century Views Series. Englewood Cliffs, N.J.: Prentice-Hall, 1974.

Horowitz, Floyd R. "An Experimental Confession from a Reader of _Invisible Man_." _CLA Journal_ 13 (March 1970): 304-314.

Howard, David C. "Points in Defense of Ellison's _Invisible Man_." _Notes on Contemporary Literature_ 1: 13-14.

Kaiser, Ernest. "A Critical Look at Ellison's Fiction and at Social and Literary Criticism By and About the Author." _Black World_ 20 (December 1970): 53-59.

_____. "Negro Images in American Writing." In Reilly, _Twentieth Century Interpretations of "Invisible Man."_

Kazin, Alfred. "Brothers Crying Out for More Access to Life." _Saturday Review_, 2 October 1971, pp. 33-35.

Kent, George. "Before Ideology: Reflections on Ralph Ellison and the Sensibility of Young Black Writers." _Blackness and the Adventure of Western Culture_, pp. 183-200.

_____. "Ralph Ellison and Afro-American Folk and Cultural Tradition." _CLA Journal_ 13 (March 1970): 265-276; also in Kent, _Blackness and the Adventure of Western Culture_, pp. 152-163; Hersey, _Ralph Ellison_, pp. 160-170.

Klotman, Phyllis R. "The Running Man as Metaphor in Ellison's _Invisible Man_." _CLA Journal_ 13 (March 1970): 277-288.

Kostelanetz, Richard. "The Politics of Ellison's Booker: _Invisible Man_ as Symbolic History." _Chicago Review_ 19 (1967): 5-26; also in Hemenway, _The Black Novelist_, pp. 88-110.

Lane, James B. "Underground to Manhood: Ralph Ellison's Invisible Man." Negro American Literature Forum 7 (Summer 1973): 64.

LeClair, Thomas. "The Blind Leading the Blind: Wright's Native Son and a Brief Reference to Ellison's Invisible Man." CLA Journal 13 (March 1970): 315-320.

Lehan, Richard. "Man and His Fictions: Ellison, Pynchon, Heller, and Barth." A Dangerous Crossing. Carbondale: Southern Illinois University, 1973, pp. 146-184.

Lieber, T. M. "Ralph Ellison and the Metaphor of Invisibility in Black Literary Tradition." American Quarterly 24 (March 1972): 86-100.

Lieberman, M. R. "Moral Innocents: Ellison's Invisible Man and Candide." CLA Journal 14 (September 1971): 64-79.

Ludington, Charles T., Jr. "Protest and Anti-Protest: Ralph Ellison." Southern Humanities Review 4 (Winter 1970): 31-39.

McPherson, James Alan. "Invisible Man." Atlantic 226 (December 1970): 45-60 (interview); also in Hersey, Ralph Ellison.

Mason, C. "Ralph Ellison and the Underground Man." Black World 20 (December 1970): 20-26.

May, John R. "Ellison, Baldwin and Wright: Vestiges of Christian Apocalypse." Toward a New Earth: Apocalypse in the American Novel. Notre Dame: University of Notre Dame, 1972.

Neal, Larry. "Ellison's Zoot Suit." Black World 20 (December 1970): 31-52; also in Hersey, Ralph Ellison, pp. 58-79.

Nichols, William W. "Ralph Ellison's Black American Scholar." Phylon 31 (Spring 1970): 70-75.

O'Brien. Interviews with Black Writers, pp. 63-77.

Pearce, Richard. Stages of the Clown: Perspectives on Modern Fiction from Dostoevsky to Beckett. Carbondale: Southern Illinois University, 1970, pp. 118-123.

Radford, Frederick L. "The Journey Towards Castration: Interracial Sexual Stereotypes in Ellison's Invisible Man." Journal of American Studies 4 (February 1971): 227-231.

Reilly, John M. Twentieth Century Interpretations of "Invisible Man": A Collection of Critical Essays. Englewood, Cliffs, N.J.: Prentice-Hall, 1970.

Rollins, Ronald G. "Ellison's Invisible Man." Explicator 30 (November 1971): Item 22.

Rovit, Earl H. "Ralph Ellison and the American Comic Tradition." Wisconsin Studies in Contemporary Literature 1 (1960): 34-42; also in Reilly, Twentieth Century Interpretations of "Invisible Man."

Ruotolo, Lucio P. Six Existential Heroes: The Politics of Faith. Cambridge, Mass.: Harvard University Press, 1973.

Sanders, A. D. "Odysseus in Black: An Analysis of the

Structure of Invisible Man." CLA Journal 13 (March 1970): 217-228.

Singh, Raman K. "The Black Novel and Its Tradition." Colorado Quarterly 20 (Summer 1971): 23-29.

Singleton, M. K. "Leadership Mirages as Antagonists in Invisible Man." In Reilly, Twentieth Century Interpretations of "Invisible Man."

Stark, John. "Invisible Man: Ellison's Black Odyssey." Negro American Literature Forum 7 (Summer 1973): 60-63.

Tanner, Tony. "The Music of Invisibility." City of Words: American Fiction 1950-1970, pp. 50-63.

Toppin. Biographical History of Blacks in America Since 1528, pp. 292-293.

Trimmer, Joseph F. "Ralph Ellison's Flying Home." Studies in Short Fiction 9 (Spring 1972): 175-182.

Turner, Darwin T. "Afro-American Authors: A Full House." College English 34 (January 1972): 15-19.

_____. "Sight in Invisible Man." CLA Journal 13 (March 1970): 258-264.

Vogler, T. A. "An Ellison Controversy." Contemporary Literature 11 (Winter 1970): 130-135.

_____. "Invisible Man: Somebody's Protest Novel." The Iowa Review 1 (Spring 1970): 64-82; also in Hersey, Ralph Ellison, pp. 127-150.

Walcott, Ronald. "Ellison, Gordone and Tolson: Some Notes on the Blues, Style and Space." Black World 22 (December 1972): 4-29.

Walling, William. " 'Art' and 'Protest': Ralph Ellison's Invisible Man Twenty Years After." Phylon 34 (June 1973): 120-134.

_____. "Ralph Ellison's Invisible Man: 'It Goes a Long Way Back, Some Twenty Years.' " Phylon 34 (March 1973): 4-16.

Weinstein, Sharon Rosenbaum. "Comedy and the Absurd in Ellison's Invisible Man." Studies in Black Literature 3 (Autumn 1972): 12-16.

_____. "Comedy and Nightmare Fiction of John Hawkes, Kurt Vonnegut, Jr., Jerzy Kozinski, Ralph Ellison." Dissertation Abstracts International 32:3336 (Utah).

Whitlow. Black American Literature, pp. 125-127.

Williams, J. A. "Ralph Ellison and Invisible Man: Their Place in American Letters." Black World 20 (December 1970): 10-11.

Williams, Sherley Ann. Give Birth to Brightness, pp. 87-98, 146-150.

Wilner, Eleanor R. "The Invisible Black Thread: Identity and Nonentity in Invisible Man." CLA Journal 13 (March 1970): 242-257.

ELLISTON, Bobbretta M.
   POETRY (Anthology): Boyd, Poems by Blacks, II.

ELLISTON, Maxine Hall.
   POETRY (Anthology): Brown, Lee and Ward, To Gwen with
   Love.

EMANUEL, James A., Sr. Born 14 June 1921 in Alliance, Ne-
   braska. Education: B.A., Howard University (summa cum
   laude), 1950; M.A., Northwestern University, 1953; Ph.D.,
   Columbia University, 1962. Currently living in Westchester County of New York. Career: Professor, American and English Literature, City College, 1957 to present. He has held poetry readings and presented lectures at numerous schools and universities in America and abroad. Awards, Honors: John Hay Whitney Foundation Opportunity Fellow, 1952-54; Eugene F. Saxton
   Memorial Trust Fellow, 1965; Fulbright Professor of Ameri-
   can Literature, upon invitation, University of Grenoble, France,
   1968-69.
CRITICISM BY EMANUEL
   "America Before 1950: Black Writers' Views." Negro Di-
      gest 18 (August 1969): 26-34, 67-69.
   "Black Writer's Views on Literary Lions and Values."
      Negro Digest 17 (January 1968): 37.
   "Blackness Can: A Quest for Aesthetics." In Gayle, The
      Black Aesthetic.
   " 'Bodies in the Moonlight': A Critical Analysis." Readers
      and Writers (November-January 1968): 38-39, 42.
   "The Challenge of Black Literature: Notes on Interpreta-
      tion." In Brown, The Black Writer in Africa and the
      Americas, pp. 85-100.
   "Christ in Alabama: Religion in the Poetry of Langston
      Hughes." In Gibson, Modern Black Poets, pp. 57-68.
   "Emersonian Virtue: A Definition." American Speech 36
      (May 1961): 117-122.
   "Fever and Feeling: Notes on the Imagery in Native Son."
      Negro Digest 18 (December 1968): 16-24. Also in Ab-
      carian, Richard Wright's Native Son: A Critical Hand-
      book.
   "The Future of Negro Poetry: A Challenge for Critics."
      In Gayle, Black Expression, pp. 100-108.
   "The Invisible Men of American Literature." Books Abroad
      37 (Autumn 1963): 391-394.
   Langston Hughes. Twayne's United States Authors Series.
      New York: Twayne Publishers, 1967†; Translated into
      French by Jacques Eymesse. Paris: Nouveaux Horizons,
      1970.
   "Langston Hughes' First Short Story: 'Mary Winosky.' "
      Phylon 22 (Fall 1961): 267-272.
   "The Literary Experiments of Langston Hughes." CLA Jour-
      nal 11 (June 1968): 335-344; also in O'Daniel, Langston
      Hughes, Black Genius.
   "The Short Fiction of Langston Hughes." Freedomways 8
      (Spring 1968): 170-178; also in O'Daniel, Langston
      Hughes, Black Genius.
   " 'Soul' in the Works of Langston Hughes." Negro Digest

16 (September 1967): 25-30.

See also <u>Contemporary Novelists.</u> Edited by James Vinson. Includes essays by Emanuel on Baldwin, Baraka, Mayfield, Petry, and Walker.

EDITOR

With Theodore L. Gross. <u>Dark Symphony: Negro Literature in America.</u> New York: Free Press, 1968*†.

(As General Editor of the Broadside Critics Series)

<u>Dynamite Voices 1: Black Poets of the 1960's,</u> by Don L. Lee. Detroit: Broadside, 1971.

<u>Claude McKay: The Black Poet at War,</u> by Addison Gayle. Detroit: Broadside.

POETRY

<u>Panther Man.</u> Detroit: Broadside, 1970†.

<u>The Treehouse and Other Poems.</u> Detroit: Broadside, 1968†.

(Anthologies): Abcarian, <u>Words in Flight: An Introduction to Poetry;</u> Abdul, <u>The Magic of Black Poetry;</u> Adoff, <u>Black Out Loud;</u> Adoff, <u>The Poetry of Black America;</u> Bank Street College of Education, <u>Don't Read This;</u> Baylor and Stokes, <u>Fine Frenzy;</u> Bontemps, <u>American Negro Poetry;</u> Breman, <u>Sixes and Sevens;</u> Breman, <u>You'd Better Believe It;</u> Brooks, <u>A Broadside Treasury;</u> Carlsen and Tovatt, <u>Insights: Themes in Literature;</u> Chapman, <u>New Black Voices;</u> Contemporary English II; Crafts, <u>Our Own Thing: Contemporary Thought in Poetry;</u> De Silva and Neuschulz, <u>Frameworks: Activities in Contemporary English;</u> Dickenson, <u>Channel One: Reading for Subject and Form;</u> Durham, Graham, and Graser, <u>Directions 2;</u> Emanuel and Gross, <u>Dark Symphony;</u> Fay, Coulter and Lloyd, <u>The Young America Basic Reading Program;</u> Gillespie and Stanley, <u>Someone Like Me: Images for Writing;</u> Guerin, Labor, Morgan, and Willingham, <u>Mandala: Literature for Critical Analysis;</u> Hayden, <u>Kaleidoscope;</u> Henderson, <u>Understanding the New Black Poetry;</u> Hughes, <u>La Poesie Negro Americaine;</u> Hughes, <u>New Negro Poets, USA;</u> Hughes and Bontemps, <u>The Poetry of the Negro: 1746-1970;</u> Jones, <u>Images;</u> Lask, <u>New York Times Book of Verse;</u> Lee and Lee, <u>Wish and Nightmare;</u> Livingston, <u>Listen, Children, Listen;</u> McMaster, <u>Points of Light;</u> Menarini, <u>Negri U.S.A.: Nuove Poesie e Canti;</u> Montel, <u>Change 9: Violence 11;</u> Murphy, <u>Ebony Rhythm;</u> Parry, <u>Words and Beyond;</u> Purves, <u>Rhetoric Book 9;</u> Randall, <u>The Black Poets;</u> Stanford, <u>I, Too, Sing America;</u> Warren, Barbara, <u>The Feminine Image in Literature;</u> Weisman and Wright, <u>Black Poetry for All Americans.</u>

(Periodicals): <u>Freedomways,</u> Fall 1964; <u>Journal of Black Poetry,</u> Fall-Winter 1971; <u>Negro Digest,</u> September 1962; September 1963; September 1964; March, September, November 1965; January, September-October 1968; August, September 1969; June 1970; <u>Phylon,</u> Second Quarter 1958; also published in <u>Midwest Quarterly.</u>

BIOGRAPHY AND CRITICISM ON EMANUEL[1]

Bailey, Leaonead. <u>Broadside Authors and Artists.</u> Detroit:

Broadside, forthcoming.
Baker, Houston A., Jr. Road Apple Review 3 (Winter
    1971-72): 24-30. (Interview.)
Contemporary Authors
Contemporary Poets of the English Language.
Directory of American Scholars.
Kantor, Mackinley, Lawrence Osgood and James Emanuel.
    How I Write/2. New York: Harcourt Brace Jovanovich,
    1972. (Includes a section by Emanuel on how he writes
    poetry.)
Men of Achievement, 1973.
Shockley and Chandler. Living Black American Authors.
Who's Who in the East.
REVIEWS
    The Treehouse and Other Poems, Turner, Darwin T.
        CLA Journal 12 (March 1969): 273.
    Panther Man: Hollis, Burney J. Road Apple Review 3
        (Winter 1971-72): 42-44.
        [1]Four master's theses have been done on Emanuel's
    poetry: Adele Trolin (Columbia University, 1966); others
    completed at Indiana University and at the University of
    Toulouse, France.

EMERUWA, Leatrice.
    CRITICISM
        "Reports on Black Theatre: Cleveland, Ohio." Black World,
            April 1973, pp. 19-26.
    DRAMA
        Black Magic Anyone? 1971.
    POETRY
        Black Girl, Black Girl: Variations on a Theme. n.p., n.d.
        Black Venus in Gemini. n.p., n.d.

EMMONS, Ronald. Born 11 November 1948 in Chicago.
    POETRY
        (Anthology): Witherspoon, Broadside Annual 1972.
        (Periodical): Black Scholar, October 1972.

ENGLAND, Jay Raymond.
    POETRY (Anthology): Murphy, Negro Voices.

ENGLISH, Rubynn M., Sr.
    NOVEL Citizen U.S.A. New York: Pageant, 1957.

ENNIS, Willie, Jr.
    POETRY Poetically Speaking. New York: Exposition, 1957.

EPHRAIM, Joseph L.
    POETRY (Periodical): Journal of Black Poetry, Winter-
        Spring 1970.

EPPERSON, Aloise Barbour.
    POETRY Unto My Heart, and Other Poems. Boston: Chris-
        topher, 1953.

EQUIANO, Olaudah (Gustavus Vassa). Born c.1745 in Benin.
Died c.1797.[1] Education: Attended school in England and ac-
quired skills to become an amateur navigator. Career: Was
captured at age 11 and became a slave. Served on a plantation in Virginia, but purchased his freedom by working for a
Philadelphia merchant in 1766. Became involved in anti-slavery work in England; traveled through the British Isles lecturing against slavery; appointed to assist in colonizing freed
slaves in Africa in 1786, but was fired after he discovered the
dishonesty of some of the officials.[2]
AUTOBIOGRAPHY
    The Interesting Narrative of the Life of Olaudah Equiano or
       Gustavus Vassa, The African. Halifax: Printed at the
       office of J. Nicholson, 1813. (Includes poems on various
       subjects by Phillis Wheatley.)
    The Life of Olaudah Equiano, or Gustavus Vassa, the Afri-
       can. Boston: I. Knapp, 1837.
    (Anthologies): Davis and Redding, Cavalcade; Levitt, Afro-
       American Voices; Miller, Backgrounds to Blackamerican
       Literature.
BIOGRAPHY AND CRITICISM ON EQUIANO
    Ahuma, S. R. B. Memoirs of West African Celebrities.
       Liverpool: D. Marples, 1905.
    Brawley. Early Negro American Writers.
    Davis and Redding. Cavalcade, pp. 17-32.
    Edwards, Paul. Equiano's Travels. New York: Praeger,
       1966.
    Johnson, Augusta Juanita. An Introduction to the Autobiog-
       raphy of Gustavus Vassa. Atlanta, Ga.; 1936. (Type-
       script.)
    Loggins. The Negro Author, pp. 40-47.
    Mays. The Negro's God, pp. 109-110.
    Whitlow. Black American Literature, pp. 24-25.
       [1]Arthur P. Davis and Saunders Redding. Cavalcade
    (Boston: Houghton Mifflin, 1971), p. 17. Conflicting
    dates are found in Brawley's Early Negro American
    Writers, p. 56.
       [2]Davis and Redding, p. 17.

ERROL, John.
    DRAMA Moon on a Rainbow Shawl. New York: Grove, 1962;
       New York: Samuel French, n.d.

ESCALERA, Belen.
    POETRY (Periodical): Journal of Black Poetry, Winter-
       Spring 1970.

ESEOGHENE see BARRETT, Lindsay

ESTE, Charles H.
    POETRY (Anthology): Kerlin, Negro Poets and Their Poems.

Don Evans

EVANS, Don. Born 27 April 1938 in Philadelphia, Pennsylvania.
Education: (Formal): B.S., Cheyney State College, 1962;
M.A., Temple University, 1968; additional study in Business
Administration at Penn Business College, 1958-59; in English
at Temple University, 1960-62; in acting and directing, Berg-
hof Studios in New York City. (Informal education): through
association with Ron Milner, Alice Childress, and many strug-
gling brothers and sisters. Currently living in Trenton, New
Jersey. Career: Teacher, Secondary English, Bristol Town-
ship Schools, 1962-65; consultant and teacher in Theatre Arts,
Princeton Regional Schools, 1965-70; Executive Director of
Princeton Youth Center/Hansberry Arts Workshop, 1970-72.
Also: Visiting Lecturer in Afro-American Studies, Princeton
University, 1972; Assistant Professor of Theatre Arts, Rutgers
University, Douglass College, 1971-72; Director of Drama,
Cheyney State College, 1969-70; Consultant in Theatre Arts,
Philadelphia Board of Education, 1968-69; Visiting Lecturer,
Trenton State College, 1972. Organized four (still operating)
theatres. Presently a professor of Black Studies at Trenton
State College. Director of numerous Black plays by high school,
community and college groups, and has acted in both college
and community productions. Theatre columnist for The Packet,
a New Jersey newspaper. Awards, Honors: "Outstanding Edu-

cator of 1970," Princeton Junior Chamber of Commerce; Black Students Union "Service Award," Princeton Regional Schools, 1969; "Best Director" Award, Rider College Drama Festivals, 1966 and 1968.

CRITICISM BY EVANS
"Bring It All Back Home." Black World 20 (February 1971): 41-45.
"Segregated Drama in Integrated Schools." English Journal 60 (Fall 1971): 260-263.
"The Theater of Confrontation: Ed Bullins, Up Against the Wall." Black World 23 (April 1974): 14-18.

DRAMA
Orrin (one act), 1973.
Nothin But the Blues.
Sugar Mouth Don't Dance No More. In Black World 22 (April 1973): 54-77.

NON-FICTION
(Periodicals): Pride Magazine, March 1972.

SHORT STORY
(Periodical): Essence, November 1973.

INTERJECTIONS
"The Black man is the result of a multiplicity of experiences, some barely remembered, but all sensed in some mysterious manner when the loneliness is deep enough or the togetherness is strong enough. The Black artist (and there must always be such a creature--politics aside) must always struggle to tap and manifest those sometimes distant strains of his world. He must struggle to keep alive those things which are common to all Black men--those things which unite us."

EVANS, Emmery. Born 19 January 1943 at High Point, North Carolina. Education: spent three years in Junior College at East Los Angeles; studied under Jayne Cortez, Kathleen Freeman, Yaphett Kotto. Other educational experiences involved a myriad of people, including a grandmother, Meher Baba, and the folks of Watts, California. Career: Actor, teacher, director. Served as director of Studio Watts, 1967, and of the NBC Special "From the Ashes: Voices of Watts," 1967; as actor, director and playwright for the Lincoln Center Summer Festival of Arts, 1971. Made a poetry tour of the East Coast, 1971. Awards, Honors: Fellowship, International Writing Program, Iowa City, 1968.

POETRY
Emmery the Love Poet. Long Beach, Ca.: By the Author, 1971. (Includes a short drama.)
(Anthology): Schulberg, From the Ashes.
(Periodicals): Negro American Literature Forum, Fall 1970; Negro Digest, July 1966.

INTERJECTIONS
"All that exists is God and God is love. Meher Baba says, 'There is no difference between the lover and the beloved.' "

EVANS, Mari. Born in Toledo, Ohio. Career: See Ploski, Reference Library of Black America.

CHILDREN AND YOUNG ADULTS
  J. D. Garden City, N.Y.: Doubleday, 1973*.
CRITICISM
  "Black Writer's Views on Literary Lions and Values." Ne-
    gro Digest 17 (January 1968): 22.
  "Contemporary Black Literature." Black World 19 (June
    1970): 4.
POETRY
  I Am a Black Woman. Poetry Series. New York: Morrow,
    1970†.
  Where Is All the Music? London: Breman, 1968.
  (Anthologies): Abdul, The Magic of Black Poetry; Adoff,
    Black Out Loud; Adoff, The Poetry of Black America;
    Baker, Black Literature of America; Barksdale and Kin-
    namon, Black Writers of America; Bontemps, American
    Negro Poetry; Cahill and Cooper, The Urban Reader;
    Chambers and Moon, Right On!; Chapman, Black Voices;
    Chapman, New Black Voices; Coombs, We Speak as Lib-
    erators; Davis and Redding, Cavalcade; Emanuel and
    Gross, Dark Symphony; Faderman and Bradshaw, Speak-
    ing for Ourselves; Gold, The Rebel Culture; Goss, A Na-
    tion of Nations; Hayden, Kaleidoscope; Henderson, Under-
    standing the New Black Poetry; Hughes, New Negro Poets:
    USA; Hughes and Bontemps, The Poetry of the Negro:
    1746-1970; King, Blackspirits; Lomax and Abdul, 3000
    Years of Black Poetry; Long and Collier, Afro-American
    Writing; Lowelfels, Poets of Today; Margolies, A Native
    Sons Reader; Miller, Blackamerican Literature; Patter-
    son, A Rock Against the Wind; Pool, Beyond the Blues;
    Randall, The Black Poets; Randall and Burroughs, For
    Malcolm; Segnitz and Rainey, Psyche; Simmons and Hutch-
    inson, Black Culture; Watkins and David, To Be a Black
    Woman; Weisman and Wright, Black Poetry for All Amer-
    icans.
  (Periodicals): Black World, September 1970; September
    1972; Negro Digest, September 1965; January, September,
    1966; February 1967; May 1968; September-October 1968;
    July 1969; April 1970.
BIOGRAPHY AND CRITICISM ON EVANS
  Lee. Dynamite Voices, pp. 40-41.
  Malkoff. Crowell's Handbook of Contemporary American Po-
    etry, pp. 119-120.
  Sedlack, Robert T. "Mari Evans: Consciousness and Craft."
    CLA Journal 15 (June 1972): 465-476.
REVIEWS: I Am a Black Woman.
  Gow, P. Freedomways 11 (Third Quarter 1971): 311-314.
  Henderson, S. E. Black World 2 (July 1971): 51-52.
  Latimore, Jewel. Black World 2 (July 1971): 92-94.

EVERETT, Ron.
  DRAMA The Babbler, 1970. (Includes three one-act plays:
    The Babbler, A Cup of Time, Wash Your Back.

EZILIE.
>   DRAMA   Have You Seen Sunshine?

-F-

FABIO, Sarah Webster.   Born 20 January 1928 in Nashville, Ten-
>   nessee.   Career: See Shockley and Chandler, Living Black
>   American Authors, p. 48.
>   DRAMA
>   >   M. L. King Pageant, 1967.
>   CRITICISM BY FABIO
>   >   "Black Writer's Views on Literary Lions and Values."   Ne-
>   >   >   gro Digest 17 (January 1968):   39.
>   >   "Tripping with Black Writing."   In Gayle, The Black Aes-
>   >   >   thetic.
>   >   "Who Speaks Negro?   What Is Black?"   Negro Digest 17
>   >   >   (September-October 1968):   33-37; reprinted in Gayle,
>   >   >   Black Expression.
>   POETRY
>   >   Black Images/Black Resurrection.   San Francisco: Julian
>   >   >   Richardson, n.d.
>   >   Black Is/A Panther Caged.   San Francisco: Julian Richard-
>   >   >   son, n.d.
>   >   A Mirror: A Soul, a Two-Part Volume of Poems.   San
>   >   >   Francisco: Julian Richardson, n.d.
>   >   (Anthologies):   Adoff, The Poetry of Black America; Brooks,
>   >   >   A Broadside Treasury; Brown, Lee and Ward, To Gwen
>   >   >   with Love; Henderson, Understanding the New Black Po-
>   >   >   etry; Hughes and Bontemps, The Poetry of the Negro:
>   >   >   1746-1970; Miller, Dices and Black Bones; Reed, Yard-
>   >   >   bird Reader I; Simmons and Hutchinson, Black Culture.
>   >   (Periodicals):   Black World, January, November 1971; Jour-
>   >   >   nal of Black Poetry, Winter-Spring 1970; Negro Digest,
>   >   >   July, September 1966; September-October 1968.

FAGGETT, H. L.
>   EDITOR
>   >   With Nick Aron Ford.   Best Short Stories of Afro-American
>   >   >   Writers, 1925-1950.   Boston: Meador, 1950.
>   SHORT STORY
>   >   (Anthology):   Ford and Faggett, Best Short Stories by Afro-
>   >   >   American Writers.

FAIR, Ronald L.   Born 27 October 1932 in Chicago, Illinois.
>   DRAMA
>   >   Sails and Sinkers, 1969.
>   NOVELS
>   >   Hog Butcher.   New York: Harcourt Brace Jovanovich, 1966*;
>   >   >   New York: Bantam, 1973†.
>   >   Many Thousand Gone: An American Fable.   New York: Har-
>   >   >   court, 1965; Chatham, N.J.: Chatham Bookseller, 1973*;
>   >   >   excerpt in Ebony (April 1965):   57-58.

We Can't Breathe. New York: Harper-Row, 1971*; excerpt
  in Reed, 19 Necromancers from Now; Chapman, New
  Black Voices.
SHORT STORIES
  (Anthologies): Hughes, The Best Short Stories by Negro
    Writers; Jones and Neal, Black Fire.
  (Periodicals): Essence, July 1971; Negro Digest, July 1965.
BIOGRAPHY AND CRITICISM ON FAIR
  Fleming, Robert E. "The Novels of Ronald L. Fair."
    CLA Journal 15 (June 1972).
  Kent. "Struggle for the Image," pp. 309-310.
  Klotman, Phyllis A. "The Passive Resistant in A Different
    Drummer, Day of Absence, and Many Thousand Gone."
    Studies in Black Literature 3 (Autumn 1972): 7-11.
REVIEWS
  Many Thousand Gone:
    Janeway, Elizabeth. The Christian Science Monitor, 4
    February 1965, p. 11.
    Levin, Martin. New York Times Book Review, 10 Jan-
    uary 1965, p. 27.

FAIRLEY, Ruth Ann. Born 15 April 1924 in Hattiesburg, Mississippi. Education: B.S., Lane College, 1946; M.S., Texas
  Southern University, 1958; also studied at Tennessee A & I and
  at the University of Southern Mississippi. Currently living in
  Hattiesburg, Mississippi. Career: Has taught in the fields
  of Elementary Education and Home Economics for many years
  in the Clarksdale Public Schools.
  NOVEL
    Rocks and Roses. New York: Vantage, 1970.
  INTERJECTIONS
    "The Golden Rule sums up my beliefs and ideas about many
    things."

FALCONER, Harriet.
  POETRY With Marie Falconer. Poems on Slavery. London:
    n.p., 1788.

FALCONER, Marie.
  POETRY With Harriet Falconer. Poems of Slavery. Lon-
    don: n.p., 1788.

FANITA.
  POETRY (Anthology): Troupe, Watts Poets.

FANN, Al.
  DRAMA King Heroin, 1970.

FANN, Ernie.
  DRAMA Colors, 1972.

FARMER, Clarence.
  Soul on Fire. New York: Belmost, 1969.

FARR, Ronald Lewis.
POETRY (Anthology): Boyd, Poems by Blacks, II.

FARRELL, John T.
NOVEL The Naked Truth. New York: Vantage, 1961.

FARRIS, John.
POETRY (Periodical): Black Dialogue.

FARRISON, William Edward. Born 1902. Career: See Directory of American Scholars, vol. 2; Directory of American Scholars, 5th ed. (1969).
CRITICISM BY FARRISON
"Brown's First Drama." CLA Journal 2 (December 1958): 104-110.
"Coleridge's Christabel, 'The Conclusion to Part II.'" CLA Journal 5 (December 1961): 83-94.
"A Flight Across Ohio: The Escape of William Wells Brown from Slavery." Ohio State Archaeological and Historical Quarterly 61 (July 1952): 272-282.
"George Moses Horton: Poet for Freedom." CLA Journal 14 (March 1971): 227-241.
"Lorraine Hansberry's Last Drama." CLA Journal 16 (December 1972).
"Phylon Profile, XVI: William Wells Brown." Phylon 9 (First Quarter 1948): 13-24.
"The Origin of Brown's Clotel." Phylon 15 (Fourth Quarter 1954): 347-354.
"What American Negro Literature Exists and Who Should Teach It." CLA Journal 13 (June 1970): 374-381.
"William Wells Brown in Buffalo." Journal of Negro History 39 (October 1954): 298-314.
"William Wells Brown, America's First Negro Man of Letters." Phylon 9 (First Quarter 1948): 13-24.
William Wells Brown: Author and Reformer. Chicago: University of Chicago Press, 1969*.
"William Wells Brown, Social Reformer." Journal of Negro Education 18 (1949): 29-39.
EDITOR
With Hugh Morris Gloster and Nathaniel Tillman. My Life, My Country, My World: College Readings for Modern Living. New York: Prentice-Hall, 1952.
NON-FICTION
(Periodicals): CLA Journal, March 1967; December 1969; October 1971; Journal of Negro History, 1963; Negro Digest, November 1942; Phylon, Fourth Quarter 1944; Fourth Quarter 1945; South Atlantic Quarterly, July 1942.
REVIEWS BY FARRISON
Published in CLA Journal.

FATISHA see THOMAS, Fatisha

FAUSET, Arthur Huff. Born 20 January 1899 in Flemington, New
    Jersey. Career: See Shockley and Chandler, Living Black
    American Authors, pp. 48-49.
CHILDREN AND YOUNG ADULTS
    With Nellie R. Bright. America Red White Black Yellow.
        Philadelphia: Franklin, 1969*.
CRITICISM
    "American Negro Folk Literature." In Locke, The New Ne-
        gro.
NON-FICTION
    Black Gods of the Metropolis: Negro Religious Cults of the
        Urban North. New York: Octagon, 1970*; Philadelphia:
        University of Pennsylvania Press, 1971†.
    For Freedom: A Biographical Story of the American Negro,
        1927; reprint ed. West Port, Conn.: Negro Universities
        Press†.
    Sojourner Truth: God's Faithful Pilgrim, 1938; New York:
        Russell & Russell, 1971*.
    (Periodicals): Crisis, May 1944; FIRE!!, 1926; also in Op-
        portunity.
SHORT STORIES
    (Anthologies): Johnson, Ebony and Topaz; O'Brien, Best
        Short Stories of 1926.
    (Periodicals): Crisis 23 (1922): 111; Opportunity 4 (June
        1926): 178-180; 7 (April 1929): 124-128.
BIOGRAPHY AND CRITICISM ON FAUSET
    Brawley. The Negro Genius, p. 261.
    Huggins. Harlem Renaissance, pp. 146-148, 160, 237.
    Opportunity 4 (June 1926): 189.

FAUSET, Jessie Redmond. Born 1886 in Philadelphia.[1] Died
    1961. Education: Received a B.A. degree from Cornell Uni-
    versity, 1905; A.M., University of Pennsylvania, 1906; attend-
    ed Columbia University, 1931;[2] then went to study at the Sor-
    bonne in Paris.[3] Career: She returned to the states in 1920
    and accepted a teaching position at the Dunbar High School in
    Washington, D.C. She also taught at Douglass High School,
    Baltimore, and at DeWitt Clinton High School in New York
    City.[4] She resigned from teaching in the New York City school
    system in 1944. In 1949, however, she accepted the honor as
    Visiting Professor at Hampton Institute, Hampton, Va.[5] For
    awhile, she taught languages at Tuskegee Institute.[6] She
    worked for the N.A.A.C.P. and for Crisis. In January 1920,
    she worked on The Brownie's Book, a monthly publication for
    children from 6-16. This literary publication was Du Bois'
    dream. The publication closed down, December 1921.[7] Aside
    from her various duties, Fauset found time to translate the
    works of a few French Indian Negro Poets.[8] Awards, Honors:
    Phi Beta Kappa.[9]
DRAMA
    (Anthology): Locke, The New Negro.
NON-FICTION
    (Periodicals): Crisis 10 (1915): 247; 19 (1919): 228; 22

(1921): 154; 23 (1922): 162; 25 (1922): 61; 29 (1925): 161; 29 (1925): 107; 29 (1925): 216; 29 (1925): 255; 30 (1925): 16; 31 (1926): 116; 32 (1926): 71; Ebony 4 (February 1949): 41.

NOVELS

The Chinaberry Tree. New York: Frederick A. Stokes, 1931; New York: AMS Press*; Washington, D.C.: McGrath, 1969*; New York: Negro Universities Press*.

Comedy: American Style. New York: Frederick Stokes, 1933; New York: Frederick Stokes, 1933; New York: AMS Press*; Washington, D.C.: McGrath, 1969*; New York: Negro Universities Press*.

Plum Bun. London: E. Mathews & Marrot Ltd., 1928. New York: Frederick A. Stokes, 1929. (Was first published in London in 1928.)

There Is Confusion. New York: Boni and Liveright, 1924.

(Anthologies-Novel Excerpts): Brown, Davis and Lee, Negro Caravan; Calverton, An Anthology of American Negro Literature; Davis and Redding, Cavalcade; Kendricks and Levitt, Afro-American Voices.

POETRY

(Anthologies): Adoff, Poetry of Black America; Bontemps, Golden Slippers; Brown, Davis and Lee, Negro Caravan; Cullen, Caroling Dusk; Davis and Redding, Cavalcade; Eleazer, Singers in the Dawn; Ford, Black Insights; Johnson, Ebony and Topaz; Johnson, Book of American Negro Poetry; Kerlin, Negro Poets and Their Poems; Hughes and Bontemps, Poetry of the Negro: 1746-1970; Patterson, A Rock Against the Wind; White and Jackson, An Anthology of Verse by American Negroes.

(Periodicals): Crisis 3 (1912): 252; 14 (1917): 248; 17 (1919): 118; 19 (1920): 128; 20 (1920): 42; 24 (1922): 124; 24 (1922): 167; 25 (1922): 22; 27 (1924): 122; 27 (1924): 277; 28 (1924): 155; 34 (1927): 303; 35 (1928): 14; 36 (1929): 378; Palms 4 (October 1926): 17-18.

SHORT STORIES

(Anthologies): Kendrick and Levitt, Afro-American Voices; Porter, Edna, Double Blossoms: Helen Keller Anthology.

(Periodicals): American Life Magazine 1 (June 1926); Crisis 5 (1912): 79; 5 (1913): 134; 8 (1914): 143; 13 (1917): 272; 14 (1917): 11; 19 (1919): 51; 20 (1920): 168, 226, 267; 26 (1923): 155, 205; Opportunity 7 (April 1929): 124-128, 133.

REVIEWS BY FAUSET

"L. Hughes, 'The Big Sea'." Negro History Bulletin 2 (December 1938): 20, 23.

SONGS

"Fragments of a Song" (words, Jessie Fauset; music, Harry Thacker Burleigh, New York: Ricordi, 1919).

TRANSLATIONS

Anon. "Joseph and Mary Come to Bethlehem." Crisis 21 (1920): 72.

BIOGRAPHY AND CRITICISM ON FAUSET

Adams. Great Negroes Past and Present, pp. 147, 149.
Bardolph. The Negro Vanguard, pp. 202, 207, 382.
Bigsby. The Black American Writer, vol. 1 p. 234.
Bone. The Negro Novel in America, pp. 58, 65, 77, 101-
102.
Bontemps. The Harlem Renaissance Remembered, pp. 11-
19, 36, 42, 63-83, 91, 213, 223, 225, 227, 236, 238.
Braithwaite, William S. "The Novels of Jessie Fauset."
In Hemenway, The Black Novelist, pp. 46-54.
_____. "The Novels of Jessie Fauset." Opportunity 6
(1928): 346.
Brawley. Negro Builders and Heroes, p. 241.
_____. Negro Genius, pp. 222, 224.
_____. The Negro in Literature and Art, pp. 113, 123-124.
Butcher. The Negro in American Culture, p. 140.
Chametzky and Kaplan. Black and White in American Cul-
ture, pp. 345-362.
Cromwell. Readings from Negro Authors, pp. 38, 212-221.
Cullen. Caroling Dusk, pp. 64-65.
Dannett. Profiles of Negro Womanhood, p. 226.
Dreer. American Literature by Negro Authors, pp. 255-262.
Du Bois, W. E. B. The Gift of Black Folk, pp. 304, 308.
Franklin, John Hope. From Slavery to Freedom. New York:
Knopf, 1963.
Gayle. Black Expression, pp. 88, 133, 181.
Gloster. Negro Voices in American Fiction, pp. 83, 90, 111,
113-114, 117, 131-139, 143, 194.
Huggins. Harlem Renaissance, pp. 146-148, 160, 237.
Hughes. The Negro Novel, pp. 37-38.
Hughes, Langston. Fight for Freedom. New York: Berkley,
1962.
Hughes and Meltzer. A Pictorial History of the Negro in
America, pp. 260, 274-275.
Jahn. Neo-African Literature, pp. 211-212, 217.
"Jessie Fauset." Negro History Bulletin, (December 1938):
19.
Johnson. Black Manhattan, p. 275.
Journal of Negro History 46 (July 1961): 204 (Obituary.)
Lomax, Michael A. "Fantasies of Affirmation: The 1920
Novel of Negro Life." CLA Journal 16 (December 1972):
232-246.
Kent. Blackness and the Adventure of Western Culture, pp.
24, 29.
Mays. The Negro's God, p. 225.
Negro History Bulletin 2 (December 1938): 20-23.
New York Times. 3 May 1961, 37:3 (Obituary.)
Ottley and Weatherby. The Negro in New York, pp. 255-
257.
Ovington. The Walls Came Tumbling Down, p. 192.
Pinkney, Alphonso. Black Americans. Englewood, N.J.:
Prentice-Hall, 1969, p. 149.
Ploski and Kaiser. The Negro Almanac, p. 684.

Redding. They Came in Chains, p. 285.

Sinnette, Elinor. "The Brownie's Book." Freedomways 5 (Winter 1965): 133.

Starkey, Marion L. "Je Fauset." The Southern Workman 61 (May 1932): 217-220.

Tischler. Black Masks, p. 87.

Turner. In a Minor Chord, pp. xviii-xix.

Williams. They Also Spoke, pp. 268-271.

Young. Black Writers of the Thirties, pp. 136-137, 147, 203, 205-207.

REVIEWS
Chinaberry Tree:
Du Bois, W. E. B. Crisis 39 (1932): 38.
Plum Bun:
Crisis 36 (1929): 125.
There Is Confusion:
Locke, Alain. Crisis 37 (1924): 161.

INTERJECTIONS
"The dedication of her life also sums up her attitude and ambition--not attained--to write a book of Plutarch's Lives for Black People."[8]

[1]Dannett [note 2] offers Philadelphia as Fauset's birthplace; James Weldon Johnson in The Book of American Negro Poetry, p. 205, and Robert B. Eleazer in Singers in the Dawn, p. 14, both cite Snow Hill, New Jersey as her birthplace.

[2]Sylvia Dannett, Profiles of Negro Womanhood (Yonkers, N.Y.: Educational Heritage, vol. 2, 1964), p. 226.

[3]Arthur P. Davis and Saunders Redding. Cavalcade (Boston: Houghton Mifflin, 1971), p. 354.

[4]"Jessie R. Fauset," Negro History Bulletin (December 1938): 19.

[5]Dannett, p. 226.

[6]Obituary, New York Times, 3 May 1961, p. 37, sec. 3.

[7]Dannett, p. 231.

[8]Ibid., p. 226.

[9]Ibid., p. 228.

FAUST, Naomi F.
POETRY (Anthology): Boyd, Poems by Blacks II.

FEDDOES, Sadie Clothil. Born 30 September 1931 in St. Vincent, West Indies. Education: Diploma, Teacher Training Center, St. Vincent, West Indies; Brooklyn College. Currently living in Brooklyn, New York. Career: Actress, Off-Broadway; Production Assistant; Radio Commentator. Played featured roles in television plays, Channel 2 and Channel 13. Talent Co-ordinator for benefit shows for the N.A.A.C.P., CORE, Free Southern Theatre, Willa Hardgrow Mental Health Center, Medical Committee for Human Rights, Concerned Mothers, Bedford YMCA, Iota Phi Lambda Sorority. Has also co-ordinated numerous special projects for Brooklyn Heights Youth

Sadie Feddoes

Center, Bedford Stuyvesant Restoration Corporation, testimonial
dinners, Harlem Homecoming. Taught elementary school, Brit-
ish West Indies, 1950-1955. Presently an official at the First
National City Bank in Brooklyn, and a columnist for the New
York Amsterdam News. Member: American Federation of
Radio and TV Artists; Executive Board, Willing Workers for Hu-
man Rights; Vice President and Public Relations Office for
Cross-Country Service for Negro Women's Organizations, Inc.;

Board of Directors, Willa Hardgrow Mental Health Clinic; Advisory Board, "The Women's Diary," Ladies Magazine; Omicron Chapter, Iota Phi Lambda Sorority; National Council of Negro Women, Inc.; Advisory Board, Dance Theatre of Harlem; New York Urban League; Friends of Billie Holiday Theatre; New York State Conference N.A.A.C.P. Awards, Honors: Special Community Award, North Philadelphia, 1964; Outstanding Performance Award, First National Bank, 1970; Award to Women in News Media, Service Organization for Sickle Cell Anemia; Honorary Certificate of Life Membership, Caribbean House; Journalism Award, Bethany United Methodist Church, 1973.

REVIEWS
Published in Westchester Observer; The Bronze Raven (Toledo); Town Talk; The Voice.

INTERJECTIONS
"I am not an American by birth but by choice, and so I am very grateful to relatives and many friends here who helped and encouraged me. These are the people who said to me, 'Yes, you can' even when I said I couldn't. My dream is to see a world of love and peace among all people, and will continue as long as I can to work to make my dream come true."

FEELINGS, Muriel. Born 31 July 1938 in Philadelphia. Career: See Shockley and Chandler, Living Black American Writers, p. 49.

CHILDREN AND YOUNG ADULTS
Moja Means One: The Swahili Counting Book. New York: Dial, 1971*.
Zamini Goes to Market. New York: Seabury, 1970*.

FELTON, James A.
NOVEL Fruits of Enduring Faith. New York: Exposition, 1969.

FENDERSON, Harold. Born 1910.
SHORT STORIES
The Phony and Other Stories. New York: Exposition, 1959.

FENNER, John J., Jr.
POETRY (Anthology): Kerlin, Negro Poets and Their Poems. (Poem reprinted from a Virginia magazine, The Praiseworthy Muse.)

FENNER, Lanon A., Jr.
POETRY (Anthology): Coombs, We Speak as Liberators.

FENTRESS, John W.
POETRY (Anthology): Murphy, Ebony Rhythm.

FERDINAND, Val see SALAAM, Kalamu Ya

FERGUSON, Blanche E.   Born 7 July 1906 in New York City.
Career: See Shockley and Chandler, Living Black American
Authors, p. 50.
CRITICISM
Countée Cullen and the Negro Renaissance.   New York:
Dodd, Mead, 1966*.

FERGUSON, Ira Lunan.   Born 27 January 1904 in Jamaica, British
West Indies. Education: Graduate, Derrick Business College,
1922; B.S., Howard University, 1931; attended Howard University College of Medicine, 1931-34 (had to discontinue due to
lack of tuition funds during the Great Depression); B.A., University of Minnesota, 1937; M. Sc., University of Minnesota,
1941; M.A., Columbia University, 1949; Ph.D., Columbia University, 1950; LL.B., LaSalle Extension University, 1970.
Currently living in San Francisco, California. Career: Taught
at CCC Camps during the depression of the 1930's, and as a
WPA teacher in the Adult Education Program in Washington.
Served as Associate Professor of Health Education and Psychology, Southern University, 1944-48.   Taught at Tuskegee Institute, 1950-57.   Presently a licensed psychologist and marriage
counselor in San Francisco, Associate Editor of the International Journal of Law and Science, and Professional Consultant for
the San Francisco Suicide Prevention Center. Member: International Academy of Law and Science; California State Psycho-
logical Association; American Association of University Professors; California Academy of Sciences; The Gerontological Society; The Royal Society of Health; American Association of Marriage and Family Counselors; American Medical Writers Association; American Public Health Association; New York Academy
of Sciences; Intercontinental Biographical Association. Awards,
Honors: Phi Delta Kappa, Kappa Delta Pi, Beta Kappa Chi;
President's Scholar, Columbia University, 1949-50; Papers and
memorabilia repose in the University of Wyoming's Archive of
Contemporary History.
AUTOBIOGRAPHY
I Dug Graves at Night, to Attend College by Day.   3 vols.
San Francisco: Lunan-Ferguson Library, 1968, 1970.
NOVELS
Ocee McRae, Texas.   San Francisco: Lunan-Ferguson Li-
brary, 1962.
The Biography of G. Wash Carter, White.   San Francisco:
Lunan-Ferguson Library, 1969.
SHORT STORY
Which One of You Is Interracial? and Other Stories.   San
Francisco: Lunan-Ferguson Library, 1969.
BIOGRAPHY ON FERGUSON
American Men of Science; Dictionary of International Biogra-
phy; Intercontinental Biographical Association Directory;
Leaders in Education; Personalities of the West and Mid-
west; Who's Who in American Education; Who's Who in
the South and Southwest; Who's Who in the West.

I. L. Ferguson

INTERJECTIONS

"Blacks should read and study Black History, but should now
be more concerned with creative activities, making contributions, and 'making Black History' for future generations to
read, study, and gain inspiration from. Blacks should stop
blaming God and/or blaming the white man for all our ills and
inadequacies. We need to be more self-reliant, more aggres-
sively industrious, more ambitious, getting all the education we
possibly can, and acquiring skills and competencies that will
make us economically independent, and win us the respect of
other peoples. Entirely too many blacks are making public welfare a way of life, expecting the Great White Father to give
them handouts, and to give them their daily bread, instead of
striving to work and earn their own livelihood. No able-bodied
young man or woman should be willing to accept handouts, depending on the labor of other people who have to work to earn
the money that goes to pay taxes which in turn goes to provide
free welfare for the lazy and irresponsible. The aged, handi-
capped, dependent children should of course be provided for by

society, but able-bodied people should be made to work and earn their bread and butter. Everyone who is not a moron can learn a skill or trade or profession, and should do so."

FERNANDEZ, Ronaldo.
POETRY
The Impatient Rebel. New Orleans: BlkArt South, 1969.
(Anthology): Chapman, New Black Voices.

FERNANDIS, Sarah Collins. Born 8 March 1863 in Baltimore. Education: was graduated from Hampton Institute in 1882; also studied at the New York School of Social Work. Career: Taught for several years in Tennessee, Florida, and at Hampton Institute before joining the Baltimore public school system;[1] then, with her husband, established "a model home" in Bloodfield, the worst Negro district in Baltimore, and eventually renovated the entire community. She was also successful in improving living conditions in the Negro slums of East Greenwich, Rhode Island. She subsequently became a social investigator in the public health clinic in the Provident Hospital, Baltimore.[2]
POETRY
Vision. Boston: Gorham, 1925.
(Anthology): White and Jackson, An Anthology of Verse by American Negroes.
(Periodical): The Southern Workman.
    [1]Who's Who in Colored America (Brooklyn, N.Y.: Thomas Yenser, 1932), p. 150.
    [2]Newman Ivey White and Walter Clinton Jackson, An Anthology of Verse by American Negroes (Durham, N.C.: Moore, 1924), p. 212.

FIELDS, Julia. Born 18 January 1938 in Bessemer, Alabama.
POETRY
Poems. Millbrook, N.Y.: Poets Press, 1968.
(Anthologies): Adoff, Black Out Loud, Adoff, City in All Directions; Adoff, The Poetry of Black America; Bell, Afro-American Poetry; Bontemps, American Negro Poetry; Hayden, Kaleidoscope; Hughes, New Negro Poets: USA; Hughes and Bontemps, The Poetry of the Negro: 1746-1970; Major, The New Black Poetry; Miller, Blackamerican Literature; Patterson, An Introduction to Black Literature in America; Patterson, A Rock Against the Wind; Pool, Beyond the Blues; Randall and Burroughs, For Malcolm; Shuman, A Galaxy of Black Writing.
(Periodicals): Black World, November 1970; September 1972; September 1973; Essence, August 1973; Negro Digest, August, September 1965; June, September, October 1966; February, December 1967; January, September-October 1968; April, September 1969; April 1970; Présence Africaine, No. 57.
SHORT STORIES
(Anthologies): Jones and Neal, Black Fire; King, Black Short Story Anthology.

(Periodicals): Black World, June 1970; August 1973; Negro
Digest, July 1966, February 1967.
CRITICISM ON FIELDS
Lee. Dynamite Voices, pp. 63-65.

FIELDS, Maurice C.
POETRY
The Collected Poems of Maurice C. Fields. New York: Ex-
position, 1940.
Testament of Youth. New York: Pegasus, 1940.

FIGGS, Carrie Law Morgan.
DRAMA
Select Plays: Santa Claus Land, Jepthah's Daughter, The
Prince of Peace, Bachelor's Convention. Chicago: By the
Author, 1923.
POETRY
Nuggets of Gold. Chicago: Jaxon Printing Co., 1921.
Poetic Pearls. Jacksonville, Fla.: Edward Waters College
Press, 1920.

FIGUEROA, Jose-Angel.
POETRY
East 110th Street. Detroit: Broadside, 1973†.
(Periodical): Black Creation, Winter 1973.

FINCH, Amanda.
NOVEL Back Trail. New York: William-Frederick, 1951.

FINLEY, Catherine L.
POETRY (Anthology): Murphy, Ebony Rhythm.

FIOFORI, Tam.
POETRY (Periodical): Journal of Black Poetry, Spring 1969.

FIORE, Carmen Anthony.
NOVEL The Barrier. New York: Pageant, 1965.

FISHER, Gertrude Arquene.
POETRY Original Poems. Parsons, Kans.: Foley Railway
Printing Co., 1910.

FISHER, J. Randolph. Born 6 November 1906 in Norfolk, Virginia.
Education: B.A., Howard University, 1931; M.A., Howard University, 1932; additional graduate work at Ohio State University,
1938-39, 1942, and 1952, and at the University of Oslo, Nor-
way, 1954. Currently living in Savannah, Georgia. Career:
Chairman, Department of Language and Literature, Rust College, 1935-38; Professor, Allen University, 1940-43; Professor,
Tennessee State College, 1945-47; Associate Professor of English, Savannah State College, 1947 to present. Has also served
as: workshop coordinator, Savannah State College, 1949-53;
Lecturer, CLA Conference, St. Louis, 1954; Book Review edi-

tor and member of the advisory editorial board, Negro College Quarterly, 1945-47; Lecturer at numerous professional conferences. Presently serving as Book Review Editor and Advisory Editor for CLA Journal, and as Chairman of the Committee on Academic Representation for CLA. Member: College Language Association; Georgia Association of Educators; National Council of Teachers of English, Modern Language Association of America; Milton Society of America; South Atlantic Modern Language Association; Modern Humanities Research Association of England; American Association of University Professors. Awards, Honors: Freedom Foundation Award for his essay, "What the American Credo Means to Me," 1956; Cash award and George Washington Honor Medal for his essay, "What Is the American Way of Life?" 1962; Freedom Foundation's Award for his essay, "The American Credo: The Hope of a War-Weary World," 1963.

NON-FICTION

    (Periodicals): Voices: A Quarterly of Poetry; The Midwest Journal; Negro College Quarterly; The Quarterly Review of Higher Education; Freedoms Foundation Bulletin; The Quarterly Journal; The Journal of Higher Education; CLA Journal; and The CEA Critic.

BIOGRAPHY ON FISHER

    Who's Who in American Education; The Directory of American Scholars; The Dictionary of International Biography; The International Scholars Directory, Strasbourg, France.

INTERJECTIONS

    "Although no one has all the answers here on earth, one thing seems undeniable: to live life satisfactorily one must do the very best that he can and hope for the best results."

FISHER, James A., Jr. Born 15 May 1933 in Philadelphia. Education: Was graduated from the Franklin High School, 1952. Currently living in Philadelphia. Career: Winner of the Diamond Belt in 1950 and Golden Gloves in 1951 while a high school student. (He was called the "Battling Bard of Benjamin Franklin High.") He served eight years in the U.S. Armed Forces. The poems in Of Love, Life and Childhood Days were selected by GIs serving in Korea with the author. He returned to boxing for a time, but was forced to forsake a fistic career after receiving an injury. He is presently working on a novel.

POETRY

    Ebony Words of Poetry. Appalachia, Va.: Young Publications, 1965.

    Of Love, Life and Childhood Days. New York: Vantage, 1969.

INTERJECTIONS

    "The origin of 'unity' is loving pride! Loving yourself and what you stand for. Loving your skin, not allowing anyone to harm or disgrace it or its reality among your brothers or sisters! Its loving the 'pride' of all your people because you are the same, the good and the bad: one color! So this is 'racism'? Seemingly so to an extent. But can Blacks learn this? My God! Why can't we have a 'tight' race??"

FISHER, John. Born 14 September 1926 in Goose Creek, Texas.
Education: A.B., San Francisco State College; additional graduate work in Vocational Counseling at San Francisco State. Currently living in San Francisco. Career: Presently Managing
Editor of The Grapevine, a community health newspaper in
Watts. Has had four years of experience in acting at the Mission Neighborhood Playhouse (San Francisco) as well as serving
as its publicity chairman, as set designer, and as a member of
the Board of Directors.
DRAMA
    Beyond the Closet.
POETRY
    (Periodicals): Journal of Black Poetry, 1969; other poetry in
        Black Dialogue, Black Journal, Correlator, Nexus, The
        Grapevine, and the U.C. literary magazine.
INTERJECTIONS
    "An artist is a person of extraordinary powers of observa-
tion, concentration, insight and sensitivity in the area of his
endowment, with regard to the relationship of things and people
to each other. He is a person who can assume multiple personalities and is able to serve humanity best when uncircum-
scribed by political considerations from without. Because he is
best qualified to help people communicate across dualistic ideo-
logical, sectarian lines, to make him anything less is to make
him a prostitute. He can be a propagandist, but in my mind
there is a difference between art, and propaganda which tamp-
ers with the people's sanity."

FISHER, Leland Milton. Born 1875 in Humbolt, Tennessee. Died
before 30 years of age in Evansville, Indiana, where he was
editor of a newspaper.[1]
POETRY
    Kerlin. Negro Poets and Their Poems, pp. 189-190.
        [1]Robert T. Kerlin, Negro Poets and Their Poems
(Washington, D.C.: Associated, 1923), p. 338.

FISHER, Rudolph. Born 9 May 1897 in Washington, D.C. Died
1934. Education: B.A., Brown University, 1919; M.A.,
Brown University, 1920; M.D. (with honors), Howard University, 1924. Career: Interned at Freedmen's Hospital in Washington, D.C., for one year before registering at Columbia University to do research in biology; worked with the x-ray division of the New York Department of Health;[1] operated his own
x-ray laboratory in Manhattan; served as superintendent of New
York's International Hospital; contributed numerous scientific
articles to professional journals. Also arranged a number of
Negro Spirituals, and performed in concerts with singer, Paul
Robeson.[2] Awards, Honors: Phi Beta Kappa; Sigma Xi; Delta
Sigma Pho; Amy Spingarn Short Story Prize Contest, 1925.
DRAMA
    The Conjure Man Dies, 1936. (In Schomburg Collection,
        mimeographed.)

NOVEL

The Conjure-Man Dies: A Mystery Tale of Dark Harlem.
New York: Covici-Friede, 1932; reprint ed. New York:
Arno*. (First detective novel by a Black.)[3]

The Walls of Jericho. New York: Knopf, 1928; New York:
Arno, 1969*†. Excerpt in Calverton, An Anthology of
American Negro Literature.

SHORT STORIES

(Anthologies): Baker, Black Literature in America; Brown,
Davis and Lee, The Negro Caravan; Calverton, An An-
thology of American Negro Literature; Clarke, American
Negro Short Stories; Clarke, Harlem; Davis and Redding,
Cavalcade; Emanuel and Gross, Dark Symphony; Ford and
Faggett, Best Short Stories by Afro-American Authors;
Hughes, The Book of Negro Humor; Hughes, Best Short
Stories by Negro Writers; James, From These Roots;
Locke, The New Negro; Long and Collier, Afro-American
Writers; O'Brien, Best Short Stories of 1934; Watkins,
An Anthology of American Negro Literature.

(Periodicals): Atlantic Monthly, February 1925; August 1927;
Crisis 30 (1925); Opportunity, February 1931; March 1933;
Story Magazine, June 1933.

Also published in American Mercury; The Book League
Monthly; Books, New York Herald Tribune; The Journal of
Infectious Diseases; McClure's; Survey Graphic.

BIOGRAPHY AND CRITICISM ON FISHER

Abramson. The Negro Playwrights in the American Theatre,
pp. 59-63.

Bond. The Negro and the Drama, pp. 118-119.

Bone. The Negro Novel in America, pp. 89, 96.

Botkin, B.A. "The Lighter Touch in Harlem." Opportunity
6 (1928): 346.

Brawley. The Negro Genius, pp. 251-252.

Calverton. Anthology of American Negro Literature, p. 531.

Davis. The American Negro Reference Book, pp. 835, 874.

Emanuel and Gross. Dark Symphony, pp. 110-111.

Gloster. Negro Voices in American Fiction, pp. 174-177.

Gross. The Heroic Ideal in American Literature, pp. 138-
139.

Henry, O. L. "Rudolph Fisher, An Evaluation." Crisis
78 (July 1971): 149-154.

Huggins. Harlem Renaissance, pp. 118-121, 127, 172, 200,
243.

Hughes. The Big Sea, pp. 240-241.

Isaacs. The Negro in the American Theatre, pp. 102-105.

Lomax, Michael L. "Fantasies of Affirmation: The 1920's
Novel of Negro Life." CLA Journal 16 (December 1972):
232-246.

Mitchell. Black Drama, p. 102.

Opportunity 13 (January 1935): 38-39. (Editorial.)

Robinson. Historical Negro Biographies, p. 191.

Robinson, William H., Jr. "Introduction." The Walls of
Jericho. New York: Arno Press, 1969.

"Rudolph Fisher." Negro History Bulletin 2 (December
1938): 19, 23.
Redding. They Came in Chains, pp. 108, 112, 118.
Schmuhl, Robert. "Treating the Harlem Human Condition."
Negro History Bulletin 37 (January 1974): 196-197.
Turpin, Waters Edward. "Four Short Fiction Writers of the
Harlem Renaissance: Their Legacy of Achievement."
CLA Journal 11 (September 1967): 59-72.
Who's Who in Colored America, 1932, p. 153.
REVIEWS
The Conjure-Man Dies:
Anon. Crisis 39 (1932): 293.
Davis, Arthur P. Opportunity 10 (October 1932): 320.
The Walls of Jericho:
Du Bois, W. E. B. Crisis 35 (1928): 374.
Times Literary Supplement, 6 September 1928, p. 630.
Walrond, Eric. New York Herald Tribune Books, 26
August 1938, p. 5.
White, W. F. New York World, 5 August 1928, p. 7.
[1]Benjamin Brawley, The Negro Genius (New York:
Dodd, Mead, 1937), pp. 251-252.
[2]Robert Schmuhl, "Treating the Harlem Human Condi-
tion," Negro History Bulletin 37 (January 1974): 196-197.
[3]Romeo B. Garrett, Famous First Facts About Ne-
groes (New York: Arno, 1972), p. 102.

FISHER, William. Born 1909.
NOVEL
The Waiters. Cleveland: World, 1950.

FITZ, A. W., Sr. Born in Kansas. Currently living in Council
Bluffs, Iowa. Career: Manager, Multi-Lingual Greeting Cards.
As Director and Founder of the Constructive Citizenship League,
he has worked for world peace and constitutional government.
Many readers know him as "The Bible Poet." A song, "Crea-
tion and I" (with music by Betty Casey), has been published and
made into a recording. Member: Iowa Poetry Association;
Midwest Federation of Chaparrae Poets.
POETRY
Poems of Protest. Council Bluffs, Ia.; By the Author, 1949.
Try It. n.p., n.d.

FLAGG, Ann.
DRAMA Great Gittin' Up Mornin', 1964.

FLANAGAN, Thomas Jefferson. Born 7 April 1890 in Stewart
County, Georgia. Education: Morris Brown College; A.B.,
Atlanta University. Career: Contributor to numerous newspapers and magazines. Principal, Lumpkin High School, Lumpkin, Georgia.[1] Awards, Honors: Received an honorary Ph.D.
degree from Paul Quinn College.
POETRY
By the Pine Knot Torches. Atlanta, Ga.: The Dickert Co.,
1921.

The Canyons at Providence (The Lay of the Clay Minstrel).
    Atlanta, Ga.: Morris Brown College Press, 1940.
Harvest Hymns. Atlanta, Ga.? By the Author, n.d.
The Road to Mount McKeithan. Atlanta, Ga.: Independent,
    1927.
Smilin' Thru the Corn, and Other Verse. Atlanta, Ga.:
    Independent, 1927.
(Anthology): Southern Literature, published by Georgia State
    College.
(Newspapers): published frequently in the Atlanta Constitution.
(Periodicals): Crisis 35 (1928): 300, 408; 38 (1931): 199,
    306.
BIOGRAPHY ON FLANAGAN
    Opportunity 6 (August 1928): 250.
        [1]Who's Who in Colored America, 3rd ed. (1932), pp.
    153-154.

FLEMING, James C.
    POETRY (Periodical): Black Dialogue.

FLEMING, Ray. Born 27 February 1945 in Cleveland.
    POETRY
        (Anthology): Witherspoon, Broadside Annual 1972.

FLEMING, Sarah Lee Brown.
    NON-FICTION
    (Biographical sketches)
        "Eliza A. Gardner" and "Josephine St. P. Ruffin" in Home-
        spun Heroines. Hallie Q. Brown, comp., Freeport, N.Y.:
        Books for Libraries Press, 1971, p. 17 and p. 151.
    POETRY
        Clouds and Sunshine. Boston: Cornhill, 1920.
        Hope's Highway. New York: Neale, 1918.
    CRITICISM ON FLEMING
        Gloster. Negro Voices in American Fiction, pp. 97-98.
        Kerlin. Negro Poets and Their Poems, p. 338.

FLEMISTER, John T.
    NOVEL
        Furlough from Hell: A Fantasy. New York: Exposition,
        1964.

FLETCHER, Bob. Born 12 December 1938 in Detroit, Michigan.
    Education: B.A., (History and English), 1961; Experimental
    Post Degree Program in Education, 1962; one year towards
    Masters (M.A.) in English, 1963. Currently living in New
    York City. Career: Former teacher of high school English.
    Presently a photographer, photo journalist, and filmmaker.
    Recently spent six weeks making a film in Mozambique (see
    Ebony magazine, February 1973).
    POETRY
        (Anthology): Major, The New Black Poetry.
        (Periodical): Umbra, 1967.

INTERJECTIONS
"There is no such thing as 'Art for Art's Sake': all art is
social and political commentary, though some is less direct.
All art functions to either advance or thwart the interests of a
given social class."

FLETCHER, T. Thomas Fortune.
    NON-FICTION
        (Periodical): Opportunity.
    POETRY
        (Anthology): Cunard, Negro Anthology.

FLOYD, Ronald see EKULONA, Ademola

FLOYD, Silas Xavier. Born 1869. Education: Was graduated from
    Atlanta University in 1891. Career: According to Max Barber,
    not only was Floyd a good teacher, but he was also a gifted lec-
    turer who abounded in wit and humor. Floyd conducted "The
    Wayside" column, from 1904-1907, in The Voice of the Negro.
    NON-FICTION
        The Life of Charles T. Walker, D.D., 1902; reprint ed.
            New York: Negro Universities Press*.
    POETRY
        (Periodical): see Voice of the Negro, 1904 to 1907, every
            issue.
    SERMONS
        The Gospel of Service, and Other Sermons. Philadelphia:
            American Baptist Society, 1902.
        Prodigal Young Man. Augusta, Ga.: Georgia Baptist Printers,
            1900.
    SHORT STORIES
        Charming Stories for Young and Old. Washington, D.C.:
            Austin Jenkins Co., 1925 (enlarged version of Floyd's
            Flowers.)
        Floyd's Flowers; or Duty and Beauty for Colored Children.
            Atlanta: Hertel, Jenkins, 1905; reprint ed. New York:
            AMS Press, 1970*.
        The New Floyd's Flowers: Short Stories for Colored People
            Old and Young. Washington, D.C.: A. Jenkins, 1922.
        Short Stories for Colored People, Both Old and Young.
            Washington, D.C.: Austin Jenkins Co., 1920.
        (Periodicals): Voice of the Negro, December 1904; June,
            September, October 1906.
            [1]Max Barber, "Our Monthly Review" Voice of the Ne-
            gro, 1 (1904): 9.

FLYNN, George M.
    SHORT STORY (Periodical): Negro American Literature For-
        um, Summer 1971.

FOLANI, Femi.
    DRAMA A Play for Zubena, 1972.

FOLLY, Dennis Wilson. Born 12 March 1954 in Hanover, Virginia.
    POETRY
        (Anthology): Boyer, Broadside Annual 1973.
        (Periodical): The Humanities Journal.

FORBES, Calvin. Born 6 May 1945 in Newark, New Jersey. Edu-
    cation: Attended Rutgers, The New School, and Stanford. Cur-
    rently living in Medford, Massachusetts. Career: Taught at
    Emerson College in Boston. Presently teaching at Tufts Uni-
    versity and working on a critical study of James Baldwin.
    POETRY
        Blue Monday. Middletown, Conn.: Wesleyan University
            Press, forthcoming.
        (Anthologies): Adoff, The Poetry of Black America; Chap-
            man, New Black Voices.
        (Periodicals): American Scholar, Summer 1972; Black World,
            September 1973; Poetry, October 1969; June 1970; also
            published in the Yale Review; Survival (Urban League pub-
            lication, Boston).
    WORK IN PROGRESS
        A novel and several plays.
    INTERJECTIONS
        "I just write and hope to live long enough to finish my work."

FORD, Nick Aaron. Born 4 August 1904 in Ridgeway, South Caro-
    lina. Education: A.B., Benedict College, 1926; M.A., Univer-
    sity of Iowa, 1934; Ph.D., University of Iowa, 1945. Current-
    ly living in Baltimore, Maryland. Career: Has taught in col-
    leges and universities in Florida, Texas, Oklahoma, New York,
    Massachusetts, and Maryland; professor and former chairman
    of the Department of English, 1947-70, at Morgan State Col-
    lege; has done considerable research in Afro-American litera-
    ture, in literature and society, and in improving the reading
    and writing skills of disadvantaged college freshmen; has served
    as consultant for the U.S. Office of Education, The Ford Foun-
    dation, and The National Endowment for the Humanities. Mem-
    ber: President, College English Association: Middle Atlantic
    Group, 1971-73; member of the Advisory Panel for Ethnic Stud-
    ies of the American Association of State Colleges and Universi-
    ties; a former member of the Executive Committee of the As-
    sociation of Departments of English; past president of the Col-
    lege Language Association and of the English Council of Greater
    Baltimore; former director for Maryland of the National Council
    of Teachers of English Achievement Awards Program; a former
    member of the College Section, Board of Directors of NCTE,
    and of the Executive Committee of College Composition and
    Communication. Awards, Honors: Research grant, U.S. Office
    of Education, 1964, to conduct a three-year experiment in im-
    proving the reading and writing skills of disadvantaged college
    freshmen; grant received from the National Endowment for the
    Humanities to evaluate Black Studies in American colleges and
    universities, 1970-71; recipient of the Outstanding Service
    Award of the Maryland Council of Teachers of English, 1971;

selected as "Outstanding Educator of America for 1971."
CRITICISM BY FORD
"The Ambivalence of Ralph Ellison." Black World 20 (December 1970): 5-9.
"Battle of the Books: A Critical Survey of Significant Books by and about Negroes Published in 1960." Phylon 22 (1961): 119-124.
"Black Literature: Problems and Opportunities." CLA Journal 13 (September 1969): 10-20.
"Black Literature and the Problem of Evaluation." In Lloyd W. Brown, The Black Writer.
"A Blueprint for Negro Authors." Phylon 11 (1950): 374-377; reprinted in Gayle, Black Expression, 276-279.
"Confessions of a Black Critic." Black World 2 (June 1971): 3.
"Contemporary Negro Fiction." Southwest Review 50 (1965): 321-335.
The Contemporary Negro Novel: A Study in Race Relations, 1936; reprint ed. College Park, Md.: McGrath, 1968.
"Cultural Integration Through Literature." In Ford, Black Insights.
"Four Popular Negro Novelists." Phylon 15 (1954): 29-39.
"The Fire Next Time? A Critical Survey of Belles Lettres by and about Negroes Published in 1963." Phylon 25 (1964): 123-134.
"How Genuine Is The Green Pastures?" Phylon 24 (October 1963): 123-134.
"Language and Literature as Aids to Cultural Integration." CLA Journal 7 (September 1963): 13-21.
"The Ordeal of Richard Wright." In Ford, Black Insights.
"Search for Identity: A Critical Survey of Significant Belles-Lettres by and about Negroes Published in 1961." Phylon 23 (1962): 128-38.
"Walls Do a Prison Make: A Critical Survey of Significant Belles-Lettres by and about Negroes Published in 1962." Phylon 24 (October 1963): 123-134.
"Walt Whitman's Conception of Democracy." Phylon 11 (1950): 201-206.
EDITOR
American Culture in Literature. New York: Rand McNally, 1967.
With H. L. Faggett. Best Short Stories by Afro-American Writers, 1925-1950. Boston: Meador, 1950.
Black Insights: Significant Literature by Afro-Americans, 1760 to the Present. Boston: Ginn, 1971†.
Extending Horizons. New York: Random House, 1969†.
Language in Uniform: A Reader on Propaganda. Indianapolis: Odyssey, 1967†.
NON-FICTION
With Waters Turpin. Better Skills for Better Writing. n.p., G. P. Putnam's, 1959†.
Black Studies: Threat or Challenge? Port Washington, N.Y.: Kennikat Press, 1973.

(Periodicals): <u>CLA Journal,</u> March 1973; <u>Phylon,</u> September 1954; <u>New England Quarterly</u>, September 1946. Other articles appear in <u>College English</u>, <u>English Journal</u>, <u>Quarterly Review of Higher Education</u>, <u>The Teachers College Record</u>, <u>Vital Speeches</u>, <u>Progressive Education</u>, <u>Bulletin of the Association of Departments of English</u>, <u>Baltimore Bulletin of Education</u>, <u>Journal of Higher Education</u>, <u>Christian Century</u>, <u>New Republic</u>, <u>Chicago Jewish Forum</u>, <u>Afro-American Magazine</u>.

POETRY
(Anthology): Murphy, <u>Negro Voices.</u>

SHORT STORIES
(Anthologies): Ford, <u>Black Insights</u>; Ford and Faggett, <u>Best Short Stories by Afro-American Writers.</u>
(Periodicals): <u>Negro Story,</u> May-June, July-August 1944.

REVIEWS
Published in <u>CLA Journal.</u>

BIOGRAPHY ON FORD
<u>Contemporary Authors,</u> 25/28.

INTERJECTIONS
"I believe that there should be one set of standards for evaluating all literature, but estheticism must no longer be accepted as the chief standard; it must be only one of several standards including historical, racial, sociological, and cultural."

FORD, Patricia.
POETRY (Anthology): Boyd, <u>Poems by Blacks,</u> II.

FORD, Robert Edgar.
POETRY
<u>Brown Chapel: A Story in Verse.</u> Baltimore? By the Author, 1905.

CRITICISM ON FORD
White and Jackson. <u>An Anthology of Verse by American Negroes,</u> pp. 219-220.

FORD, Wally. <u>Born</u> 13 January 1950 in New York City.
POETRY
(Anthology): Coombs, <u>We Speak as Liberators.</u>
(Periodical): <u>Black World</u>, September 1971.

FORDHAM, Mary Weston.
POETRY
<u>Magnolia Leaves.</u> Introduction by Booker T. Washington. Charleston, S.C.: Walker, Evans & Cogswell, 1897; 2nd ed., 1898.

CRITICISM ON FORD
Loggins. <u>The Negro Author in America,</u> p. 335.

FOREMAN, Kent.
POETRY (Anthologies): Brooks, <u>A Broadside Treasury</u>; Randall and Burroughs, <u>For Malcolm.</u>

FORREST, Leon.
> EDITOR
>> Muhammad Speaks.
> NOVEL
>> There Is a Tree More Ancient Than Eden. New York: Ran-
>> dom, 1973*.
> REVIEW
>> There Is a Tree More Ancient Than Eden:
>>> Baker, Houston. Black World 23 (January 1974): 66-69.
>>> Gilbert, Zack. Black World 23 (January 1974): 70.

FORTE, Christine (Christine Forster). Born 23 November 1906 in
the West Indies. Education: A graduate of Famous Writers
School, Inc., Westport, Connecticut. Currently living in Bronx,
New York. Career: Active in Girl Scouts and church activities as well as with writing.
> NOVELS
>> A View from the Hill. New York: Vantage, 1964.
>> Young Tim O'Hare. New York: Vantage, 1966.
> UNPUBLISHED WORKS
>> Novel: "The Violent Man."
> INTERJECTIONS
>> "I have just one bit of advice to relay to our young Black
>> youths of today: So many great opportunities are open to you--
>> grasp, hold, and by all means make the most of them. If one
>> door closes in your face, try another. The size of your life
>> is determined by the size of your thoughts; therefore, make no
>> small plans. For the size of your life will be determined by
>> the size of your plans. Utilize what you have learned. If giv-
>> en the tools, use them wisely and carve a place for yourself
>> in this big world.
>> "Education is the only solid bridge you can rely on to trans-
>> port you over your troubled waters. So, on that premise, I'll
>> say to you: 'Use that bridge to get on the other side where
>> you can stand up and be counted, thereby leaving your footsteps
>> in the sand of time for others to follow.' "

FORTEN, Charlotte L. (Mrs. Francis Grimké). Born 1838 in
Philadelphia. Died 23 July 1914. Education: She was private-
ly tutored; attended Higginson Grammar School in Salem, Mas-
sachusetts.[1] She graduated from Higginson Grammar School in
July, 1856. Career: She taught school for two years at Epes
Grammar School. Later, she taught on St. Helena's Island,
South Carolina. She continued to teach school until the Civil
War when she served as an agent with the Freedman's Aid So-
ciety at Port Royal, St. Helena Island.[2] Besides teaching, she
worked in the Church and Sabbath School on the Island.[3]
Awards, Honors: She won early honors for her poetry while
at Higginson Grammar School.[4]
> NON-FICTION
>> Erckmann, Emilie and Alexander Chatrian, Madame Thérèse;
>> or the Volunteers of '92. Translated from the 13th ed.
>> by Charlotte Forten Grimké. New York: Scribner, 1869.

The Journal of Charlotte L. Forten. New York: Dryden
    Press, 1953. Her diary lay in the Manuscript Collection
    of Moorland Library, Howard University until 1953 when
    Ray Allen Billington edited and published it.[5] New York:
    Macmillan, 1961†.
"Interesting Letter from Miss Charlotte L. Forten." Lib-
    erator, 19 December 1862.
"Life on the Sea Island." Atlantic Monthly, May-June,
    1864.
"Personal Recollections of Whittier." New England Maga-
    zine 8 (June 1893): 472.

POETRY
    (Anthologies): William Wells Brown, The Rising Sun (Bos-
    ton: A.G. Brown, 187-); Calverton, An Anthology of Amer-
    ican Negro Literature; Davis and Redding, Cavalcade;
    Kerlin, Negro Poets and Their Poems.

BIOGRAPHY AND CRITICISM ON FORTEN
    Cooper, Anna Julia, ed., Life and Writing of the Grimké
        Family. n.p., 1951.
    Fishel and Quarles. The Black in America, pp. 199, 219.
    Grimke, Angelina W. "To Keep the Memory of Charlotte
        Forten Grimké--A Poem." Negro History Bulletin (Janu-
        ary 1947): 79, 95. (The cover of the Bulletin is a fam-
        ily photo of the Forten Family.)
    Kerlin. Negro Poets and Their Poems, p. 338.
    Negro History Bulletin 4 (1941): 64-65; 10 (January 1947):
        47.

DISCS
    "Black Pioneers in American History." Educational Record
        Sales, New York.

INTERJECTIONS
    "Let us take Courage; never ceasing to work--hoping and be-
    lieving that, if not for us, for another generation there is a bet-
    ter, brighter day in store--when slavery and prejudice shall
    vanish before the glorious light of Liberty and Truth; when the
    rights of every colored man shall everywhere be acknowledged
    and respected, and he shall be treated as a MAN and a BROTH-
    ER."[6]
        [1]Sylvia Dannett, Profiles of Negro Womanhood.
    (Yonkers, N.Y.: Educational Heritage, Vol. I, 1964): pp.
    87-89.
        [2]Harry A. Ploski and Ernest Kaiser, Negro Almanac.
    (New York: Bellwether, 1971): p. 676.
        [3]Monroe Majors, Noted Negro Women. (Freeport,
    N.Y.: Books for Libraries, 1971): p. 213.
        [4]Ploski and Kaiser, p. 676.
        [5]Dannett, p. 93.
        [6]Ibid.

FORTSON, Bettiola Heloise. Born 1890.
    POETRY
        Original Poems and Essays. Chicago: n.p., 1915.

FORTUNE, Timothy Thomas. Born 3 December 1856[1] in Marianna,
Florida. Died 1928. Education: Attended Staunton Institute,
and Harvard University for two years. Career: Began a newspaper career as a compositor on the New York Witness. Founded the New York Globe in 1879 (later named the New York Age.)
Served as editor and publisher of the Washington Sun; as correspondent for the Washington Eagle and the New York Amsterdam
News. Also established the Negro Outlook, 1921 (Memphis,
Tennessee).[2] Was considered the leading Negro journalist from
the middle 1880's into the 1900's.[3]

NON-FICTION
> Black and White: Land, Labor and Politics in the South.
> > New York: Fords, Howard & Hulbert, 1884; reprint ed.,
> > New York: Johnson reprint, 1970*; New York: Arno,
> > 1968*†.
> The Negro in Politics. New York: Ogilvie & Rowntree, 1885.
> (Anthologies): Haley, The Afro-American Encyclopedia
> > (1896): Miller, Background to Blackamerican Literature.
> (Periodicals): Opportunity, November 1942; Voice of the Ne-
> > gro, February, August 1904; March-June 1906.

POETRY
> Dreams of Life: Miscellaneous Poems. New York: Fortune
> > & Peterson, 1905; facsimile ed., Freeport, N.Y.: Books
> > for Libraries*; reprint ed., New York: AMS Press*.
> (Periodicals): Opportunity, June 1929; June 1931.

BIOGRAPHY AND CRITICISM ON FORTUNE
> Bontemps. 100 Years of Negro Freedom, pp. 158-164.
> Brawley. The Negro Genius, p. 122.
> Loggins. The Negro Author in America, pp. 284-287, 335-
> > 336.
> Meier. Negro Thought in America 1880-1915, pp. 30-32,
> > 34, 36-39, 45-47, 54, 67, 70-74, 94, 111, 128-130, 226-
> > 229.
> Redkey. Black Exodus, pp. 40, 66, 122, 123, 124, 201,
> > 220.
> Robinson. Historical Negro Biographies, pp. 81-83.
> Simmons. Men of Mark, pp. 785-791.
> White and Jackson. An Anthology of Verse by American Ne-
> > groes, pp. 114, 220.

REVIEW
Dreams of Life:
> Daniels, John. Alexander's Magazine, 15 September 1905,
> > pp. 11-12.

> [1]Birth date is given as 6 October 1956 by the Rev.
William J. Simmons, Men of Mark (Cleveland, O.: Geo.
M. Rewell, 1887), p. 785.
> [2]Newman Ivey White and Walter Clinton Jackson, eds.,
An Anthology of Verse by Negro Americans (Durham,
N.C.: Moore, 1924), p. 114.
> [3]August Meier, Negro Thought in America 1880-1915
(Ann Arbor: University of Michigan Press, 1966), p. 31.

FOSTER, Francis M.
POETRY
(Anthology): Murphy, Ebony Rhythm.
(Newspapers): Pittsburgh Courier; People's Voice.

FOX, Mamie Eloise. Born 10 April 1871 in Chilicothe, Ohio.
Education: Graduated from Chilicothe High School, June 1891.
Career: Began to write verse at the age of nine. Was a
writer of both prose and verse. She worked for the church
and for some time held the position of Secretary for the Church
Sunday School.[1]
POETRY
(Anthology): Majors, Noted Negro Women, pp. 126-128,
    365; also contributed to Ringwood's Journal.
    [1]Monroe A. Majors, Noted Negro Women (Chicago:
    Dunahue & Henneberry, 1893), pp. 124-128, rpt. 1971.

FOXWORTH, Nilene Elizabeth. Born 10 July 1936 in Atchinson,
Kansas. Education: Attended Omaha University. Career:
Bookkeeper and accountant. Has given poetry readings for high
schools, colleges, community groups. Writes a weekly column
for the Denver Weekly News. Member: Co-founder, Black
Adults for Youth; Board of Directors, Legal Aid Services; In-
ternational House; Advisory Board for Ethnic Education Pro-
gram.
POETRY
If I Were a Miracle Hen. New York: Amuru, 1973†.
INTERJECTIONS
"My basic idea in writing is expressing true feelings of
blackness--disclosing true pictures, and leaving all delusive abstracts nil."

FRANKLIN, Carl.
POETRY Portrait of Man: A Love Poem. New York: Exposi-
    tion, 1952.

FRANKLIN, Clarence. Born 1932 near Jackson, Mississippi.
DRAMA
    Copper Pig.
POETRY
(Anthologies): Jones and Neal, Black Fire; Patterson, A
    Rock Against the Wind.

FRANKLIN, J. E. Born in Houston, Texas. Education: B.A.,
University of Texas. Currently living in Bronx, New York.
Career: A lecturer at Lehman College (Bronx), involved in
Art-centric Education. (Art-centric education is a process
which views education as an art form rather than a science.
It views art as the encapsulator of all the cultural ideologies
and begins with art as a vehicle for creating a transition process to connect the ideas of the Artist with those of the scholar
with the end in mind of communicating the view that the Tree
of Knowledge and the Tree of Life are simply Branches of the

Franklin, J.E. (cont.)   308

same seed.) <u>Awards, Honors</u>: Media Workshop Award, 1971;
Drama Desk Award, 1972; New York State Council on the Arts
Public Service Grant, 1972.
DRAMA
   <u>Black Girl</u>. New York: Dramatists Play Service, n.d. †
   <u>Cut Out the Lights and Call the Law</u>, 1972.
   <u>First Step to Freedom</u>, 1964.
   <u>Four Women</u>.
   <u>The In-Crowd</u>, 1967.
   <u>Mau-Mau Room</u>.
   <u>Prodigal Daughter</u>.
   <u>Two Flowers</u>.
SHORT STORY
   (Anthology): King, <u>Black Short Story Anthology</u>.
BIOGRAPHY AND CRITICISM ON FRANKLIN
   Beauford, Fred. "A Conversation with <u>Black Girl</u>'s J. E.
     Franklin.
   <u>Black Creation</u> 3 (Fall 1971): 38-40.
   <u>Ebony</u> 28 (April 1973): 108.
REVIEWS: <u>Black Girl</u>
   Kalem, T. E. <u>Time</u>, 28 June 1971.
   Tallmer, Jerry. <u>New York Post</u>, 17 June 1971.

FRANKLIN, James Thomas.
NON-FICTION
   <u>Depth of the Infinite</u>. Memphis: By the Author, 1935.
NOVEL
   <u>Crimson Altars, or A Minister's Sin</u>. Memphis: Great South
     Press, 1895.
POETRY
   <u>Jessamine</u>. Memphis: n.p., 1900.
   <u>Mid-day Gleanings: A Book for Home and Holiday Readings</u>.
     Memphis: Tracy Printing, 1893.

FRASER, W. Alfred.
POETRY
   (Anthologies): Jones and Neal, <u>Black Fire</u>; <u>Burning Spear</u>.

FRAZIER, Levi, Jr.
DRAMA <u>A Tribute to Richard Wright</u>, 1972.

FRAZIER, Max Yergan.
POETRY <u>Fifteen Familiar Faces in Verse</u>. New York: Vantage, 1959.

FRAZIER, Ruby Primus.
POETRY <u>Ruby's Black Emeralds</u>. New York: Amuru, 1973†.

FREEMAN, Carol S. <u>Born</u> 1941 in Rayville, Louisiana. <u>Educa-
tion</u>: B.A., (English), Mills College. <u>Currently living in</u>
Oakland, California. <u>Career</u>: A teacher of pre-school and elementary school children. Presently "in pursuit of a dream--
more or less working towards a Master's Degree in English

Literature--completing a series of stories and poems for urban
youth." One of her poems was included in the NBC television
production Christmas Special in New York, 19 December 1972.
Awards, Honors: Mary Merritt Henry Prize in poetry and
verse for 1971-1972.
DRAMA
    "The Suicide." In Jones and Neal, Black Fire.
POETRY
    The Poetry of Carol Freeman. San Francisco: Julian Rich-
        ardson, n.d.
    (Anthologies): Abdul, The Magic of Black Poetry; Adoff, The
        Poetry of Black America; Colley and Moore, Starting with
        Poetry; Hughes and Bontemps, The Poetry of the Negro:
        1746-1970; Lomax and Abdul, 3000 Years of Black Poetry;
        Miller, Blackamerican Literature; Simmons and Hutchinson,
        Black Culture.
    (Periodicals): Soul Book.
INTERJECTIONS
    "I am pleased to be alive. I will probably be sorry to die."

FREEMAN, Harry Lawrence.
DRAMA
    An African Kraal.
    The Tryst, 1909.

FREEMAN, Lorrain.
SHORT STORY (Anthology): Clark, Harlem.

FRENCH, James Edgar. Born in Kentucky.
POETRY (Anthology): Kerlin, Negro Poets and Their Poems.

FRIEND, Robert C.
POETRY (Periodical): Freedomways, Summer 1962.

FULGER, Willie E.
POETRY Truth Is Beauty. New York: Vantage, 1963.

FULLER, Charles H., Jr. Born 5 March 1939 in Philadelphia.
Education: Studied at Villanova University and LaSalle College.
Career: Co-founder and Co-director, Afro-American Arts The-
atre, Philadelphia, 1967-71; Instructor in Black Literature, La-
Salle College, 1970; Lecturer in Black Literature, seven-uni-
versity tour, 1970-71. Several of his television scripts have
been produced: "Roots, Resistance and Renaissance," a 12-
week series for WHYY-TV (Channel 12), Philadelphia, 1967;
"Mitchell," teleplay, WCAU-TV (Channel 10), Philadelphia, 1968;
"Black America," a one-half hour show, WKYW-TV (Channel 3),
Philadelphia, 1970-71. Was writer-director for "The Black Experience," WIP Radio, Philadelphia, 1970-71; Consultant and
format designer, "Speak Out," 90-minute talk show, WKYW-TV
(Channel 3) Philadelphia, 1971; Story editor, "J.T.," WABC-
TV pilot, New York City, 1972; writer, additional dialogue for
play, "The Selling of the President," Franklin Robert Produc-

Hoyt Fuller

tions, 1972. Awards, Honors: Rockefeller Grant for Play-
writing. Member: Dramatist Guild; Consultant, Philadelphia
Bicentennial Committee, 1969-72; Advisory Committee, Nation-
al Endowment for the Arts, 1970.
CRITICISM
"Black Writing Is Socio-Creative Art." Liberator 7 (April
1967): 8.
DRAMA
Ain't Nobody, Sarah, But Me, 1969.
Cabin, 1969.
Indian Givers, 1969.
JJ's Game, 1969.
Love Song for Robert Lee, 1967.
The Perfect Party, or The Village, A Party, 1969.
The Rise. In Bullins, New Plays from the Black Theatre.
Three Plays: "Sunflower," Untitled Play, and "First Love,"
1971.
Two Plays: "The Layout" and "Emma," 1970.
NON-FICTION
(Periodicals): Liberator; Negro Digest, 1965; Philly Talk,
1970.
SHORT STORIES
(Anthologies): Adoff, Brothers and Sisters; Alhamisi and
Wangara, Black Arts; Chambers and Moon, Right On!;
Jones and Neal, Black Fire; King, Black Short Story An-
thology.
(Periodicals): Black Dialogue, 1965; Liberator, 1965.

FULLER, Hoyt W. Born 10 September 1927 in Atlanta, Georgia.
Education: B.A., Wayne State University, 1950; advanced study
at Wayne State University. Career: Assistant editor, Collier's
Encyclopedia, New York City; West African Correspondent,
Haagse Post, Amsterdam, Holland; Associate Editor, Ebony
Magazine, Chicago; Feature Editor, Michigan Chronicle, De-
troit; Reporter, Detroit Tribune. Currently Executive Editor,
Black World (formerly Negro Digest). Has also taught a Fic-
tion Writing Seminar Columbia College, Chicago; Afro-Ameri-
can Literature, at Northwestern University and Indiana Univer-
sity. Member: Organization of Black American Culture.
Awards, Honors: John Hay Whitney Opportunity Fellowship,
1965-66 for travel and study in Africa.
CRITICISM BY FULLER
"About The Toilet and The Slave." Negro Digest 14 (July
1965): 49-50.
"Arna Bontemps: Bibliography." Black World 2 (September
1971): 78-79.
"Assembly at Asilomar: The Negro Writer in the United
States." Negro Digest 13 (September 1964): 42-48.
"Black Theater in America: An Informal Survey." Negro
Digest 17 (April 1968): 83-93.
"Contemporary Negro Fiction." Southwest Review, 1965; re-
printed in Bigsby, The Black American Writer, vol. 1.
"Famous Writer Faces the Challenge." Ebony 21 (June

1966): 188-190†.

"General Theatre Round-Up." Black World 2 (April 1971): 24-26†.

"Identity, Reality and Responsibility: Elusive Poles in the World of Black Literature." Journal of Negro History 57 (January 1972): 83-98.

"James Baldwin and the Black-Jewish Conflict." Black World 2 (September 1971): 83.

"Negro Writer in the United States." Ebony 20 (November 1964): 126-128†.

"Negro Writers and the Critics." Negro Digest 14 (May 1965): 50†.

"Notes on a Poet (Gwendolyn Brooks)." Negro Digest 11 (August 1962): 50.

"Notes on Writers and Writing." Negro Digest 12 (November 1962): 49.

"Of Integrity, Hope and Dead Dialogue." New School Bulletin 23 (12 May 1966): 1.

"On Black Theater in America: A Report." Negro Digest (April 1970): 34-37†.

"Perspectives." Negro Digest and Black World, monthly columns.

"Perspectives--Two Different Worlds." Negro Digest 14 (March 1967): 49. (Douglas Turner Ward's Happy Ending and Day of Absence.)

"Report on Black Theater." Negro Digest 18 (April 1969): 26†.

"Reverberations from a Writers' Conference." African Forum 1 (1966): 11-20.

"Role of the Negro Writer in an Era of Struggle." Negro Digest 13 (June 1964): 62-66; reprinted in Baker, Black Literature in America, pp. 389-391.

"The So-Called Harlem Renaissance." Black World 20 (November 1970): 4, 65, 130.

"Towards a Black Aesthetic." The Critic, April-May 1967; reprinted in Gayle, Black Expression, pp. 263-270.

NON-FICTION

Journey to Africa. Chicago: Third World, 1971*†.

(Periodicals): Numerous articles have been published in Black World, Negro Digest and Ebony; also published in Nation, The New Yorker, North American Review, Jet, Journal of Black Poetry.

POETRY

(Periodicals): Essence, November 1971; Negro Digest, November 1963; March 1965.

SHORT STORIES

(Anthologies): Adoff, The Poetry of Black America; Clarke, American Negro Short Stories; Williams, Beyond the Angry Black.

(Periodicals): Negro Digest, June 1961; February, March 1962; January 1963.

REVIEWS BY FULLER

Published in Black World.

BIOGRAPHY AND CRITICISM ON FULLER
    Interview. Arts in Society 5 (1968): 275-278.
    Interview. Black Books Bulletin 1 (Fall 1971): 19-23, 40-
    43.
    Llorens, David. "Two Busy Writers Who Also are 'Real.'"
    Negro Digest 15 (December 1965): 49-50.

FULLER, Stephany. Born 23 October 1947 in Chicago. Education:
Attended University of Illinois at Chicago Circle. Currently living in Chicago. Career: Full-time student, and part-time
secretary for the Citizens Committee of Juvenile Court. Two
poems ("That I Am Yours" and "Let Me Be Held") were used
in a dramatic presentation, Many Moods of the Black Experience, jointly sponsored by The Artist Collective, Inc., Wadsworth Atheneum, and Connecticut Public Television, November
1972. Her paintings have been exhibited at local Chicago gal-
leries, at Turnover Bookstore in Berkeley, California, and at
summer art shows at 53rd Street & Lake Meadows; Chicago
School Review (University of Chicago) printed her ink drawings
in their May 1973 issue on Black Women. Awards, Honors:
Scholarship, Art Institute of Chicago, 1960-61; Honorable Mention, Art Institute of Chicago Art Contest, 1965.
POETRY
    Moving Deep. Detroit: Broadside, 1969.
    (Anthologies): Brooks, A Broadside Treasury; Chapman,
        New Black Voices; Randall, The Black Poets.
    (Periodicals): Black America Magazine, April 1971; Es-
        sence, November 1971; Negro American Literature Forum,
        Spring 1972.
REVIEW: Moving Deep:
    Amini, Johari. Black World 19 (May 1970): 52.
INTERJECTIONS
    "Many of my early ideas and theories about life were acted
upon and I suffered the consequences and gained experience.
Life has much to teach, but understanding is not without pain.
The structure of American society, with its emphasis on ma-
terialism and individuality distorts and obscures the very essence of existence. There is a mystique surrounding art and
artists, as though art is separate from life and artists, in all
their variety of expression, a unique breed of beings. The result is a great deal of posturing, striving for recognition
and insistent attempt to turn art into a commodity.
    "I believe it is essential for the individual to know who he
is. I have heard poetry described as that which attempts to
express the inexpressable. I believe that poetry (and other art
forms) expresses what is basic and true in the human experience. This is what the artist must strive for, talent is not
enough. Growth, experience and understanding are the intan-
gibles that determine those tangible forms called the final product. Yet these are continuous and there is in reality no final
product, there is only striving.
    "I feel the responsibility of the artist is to communicate the
possible...to articulate the relatedness and continuity of our

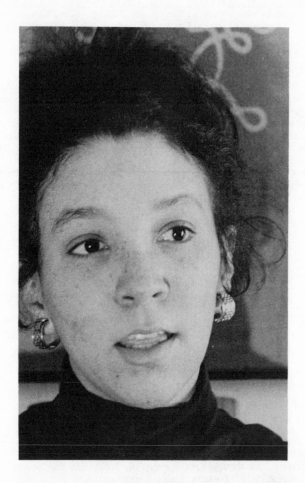

Stephany Fuller

condition in such a way that dispels confusion, that motivates
thought and reflection and that uplifts the spirit.   The artist
must demand much of himself and of his art...creating art for
the sake of humanity, that is a beacon of light in this often-
times dark world."

FULLILOVE, Maggie Shaw.
    NOVEL
        Who Was Responsible.   Cincinnati, O.: Abingdon Press,
            1919.

SHORT STORIES
>   (Periodicals): Half Century, February, March, November,
>   December 1917; April, May, June 1918.

FULTON, David Bryant.   (Jack Thorne, pseud.) Born 1863.
>   NON-FICTION
>>   "Eagle Clippings," a Collection of His Writings to Various
>>   Newspapers. Brooklyn: D.B. Fulton, 1907.
>>   A Plea for Social Justice for the Negro Woman.   Yonkers,
>>   N.Y.: Negro Society for Historical Research, 1912.
>>   Recollections of a Sleeping Car Porter.   Jersey City: Doan
>>   & Pilson, 1892.
>   NOVEL
>>   Hanover; or, The Persecution of the Lowly.   n.p.; M.C.L.
>>   Hill, 1901.
>   SHORT STORY
>>   (Periodical): Voice of the Negro, January-February 1907.

FURMAN, Roger.
>   DRAMA
>>   Fool's Paradise (one act), 1952.
>>   The Gimmick, 1970.
>>   The Long Black Block, 1972.
>>   The Quiet Laughter (one act), 1952.
>>   To Kill a Devil.   Scene in Childress, Black Scenes.
>>   With Doris Brunson.   Three Shades of Harlem, 1964?.
>   BIOGRAPHY AND CRITICISM ON FURMAN
>>   Mitchell.   Black Drama, pp. 154-155, 207-208, 221.

-G-

GABUGAH, O. O.   Born 2 December 1945 in Harlem.
>   DRAMA
>>   Transistor Willie and Latrine Lil.
>>   Go All the Way Down and Come Up Shakin'.
>   POETRY
>>   (Anthology): Reed, Yardbird Reader, vol. 1.

GADSDEN, Janice Marie.   Born 8 September 1952 in Manhattan,
>   New York.   Education: B.A. (English), Queens College, 1973.
>   Currently living in New York City.   Career: Presently teach-
>   ing seventh grade language arts at I.S. 201, Manhattan.   Also
>   writing lyrics to the music of Leon Pendarvis (pianist with
>   Aretha Franklin) and to the music of Andrew Gadsden.
>   POETRY
>>   (Anthology): Coombs, We Speak as Liberators.
>>   (Periodicals): Whereas (Queens College Literary and Arts
>>   Magazine), Winter 1969; Winter 1970.
>   INTERJECTIONS
>>   "No matter what I do, I am a poet at heart.   To write a
>   poem is to sing; to sing is to make music; to make music is
>   to be tuned in to the rhythms of the universe.   We know about

rhythms, about the gut, funk pulsations of the spirit. This is
what my poetry tries to be about."

GAFFNEY, Floyd.
CRITICISM
"The Black Actor in Central Park." Negro Digest 16 (Ap-
ril 1967): 28-34.
"Black Theatre: Commitment and Communication." Black
Scholar 1 (June 1970): 10-15.
"The Free Southern Theater: What Price Freedom." Black
World 2 (April 1971); 11-14.
"In the Dark: King Henry V." Negro Digest 18 (April 1969):
36-41.

GAINES, Ernest J. Born 1933 in Oscar, Louisiana. Career: See
Contemporary Authors 11/12; Ploski, Reference Library of
Black America.
CHILDREN AND YOUNG ADULTS
A Long Day in November. New York: Dial 1971*; New York:
Dell, 1973†.
NOVELS
Catherine Carmier. New York: Atheneum, 1954; Chatham,
N. J.: Chatham Bookseller, 1972*.
Of Love and Dust. New York: Dial, 1967*; New York: Ban-
tam, 1969.
The Autobiography of Miss Jane Pittman. New York: Dial,
1971*; New York: Bantam, 1972†. Excerpt in Negro Di-
gest (February 1971).
"Chapter One of The House and the Field: A Novel." The
Iowa Review, 3 (Winter 1972): 121-25.
SHORT STORIES
Bloodline. New York: Dial, 1968*.
(Anthologies): Adoff, Brothers and Sisters; Bambara, Tales
and Stories; Chapman, New Black Voices; Clarke, Ameri-
can Negro Short Stories; Corrington and Williams, South-
ern Writing in the Sixties: Fiction; Davis and Redding,
Cavalcade; Emanuel and Gross, Dark Symphony; Hicks
Cutting Edges; Hughes, The Best Short Stories By Negro
Writers; James, From These Roots; King, Black Short
Story Anthology; Long and Collier, Afro-American Writ-
ing; Singh and Fellows, Black Literature in America.
(Periodical): Negro Digest, August 1963.
CRITICISM ON GAINES
Beauford, Fred. "Conversation with Ernest Gaines." Black
Creation, 4 (Fall 1972): 16-18.
"Black Writer's Views on Literary Lions and Values." Ne-
gro Digest 17 (January 1968): 27.
Bryant, Jerry. "Politics and the Black Novel." The Na-
tion, 5 April 1971, pp. 436-438.
_____. "From Death to Life: The Fiction of Ernest J.
Gaines." The Iowa Review 3 (Winter 1972): 106-120.
Fuller. "Contemporary Negro Fiction." Southwest Review
50 (1965): 321-335.

Kent. "Struggle for the Image," pp. 307-308, 310.
O'Brien. Interviews with Black Writers, pp. 79-93.
Stoelting, Winifred L. "Human Dignity and Pride in the
    Novels of Ernest Gaines." CLA Journal 14 (March 1971):
    340-358.
Williams. Give Birth to Brightness, pp. 167-209.

GAINES, J. E.
  DRAMA
    Don't Let It Go to Your Head, 1970.
    It's Colored, It's Negro, It's Black Man? 1970.
    Sometimes a Hard Head Makes a Soft Behind, 1972.
    What If It Turns Up Heads (or What If It Had Turned Up
      Heads), 1970.

GAIRY, Richardson A.
  POETRY
    The Poet's Vision, and the Noblest Struggle: Poems. New
      York: New York Age, 1909.

GAMBLE, Quo Vadis Gex see GEX, Quo Vadis

GANT, Lisbeth A. Born 16 April 1948 in Chicago. Education:
  B.A. (with honors), Kalamazoo College, 1968; M.A., Columbia
  University, 1970. Currently living in New York City. Career:
  Specializes in African, Caribbean, and Black American Litera-
  ture as well as Black Children's Literature; free lance writer
  for Afro World Associates (U.N.); West Coast Editor of Es-
  sence magazine, September 1973-. Awards, Honors: The
  Coretta Scott King Award, American Association of University
  Women, 1969; Nomination, Outstanding Young Women of Amer-
  ica, 1969; Richard Wright-Amiri Baraka Award for Literary
  Criticism, Black World magazine, 1972.
  BIBLIOGRAPHY
    A Bibliography of Black American Literature, 1746-1971.
      Washington, D.C.: African Bibliographic Center, forth-
      coming.
  CHILDREN AND YOUNG ADULTS
    They Will Be Free--Resistance to the African Slave Trade.
      New York: Doubleday, forthcoming.
  CRITICISM
    "Charles Chesnutt--Forgotten Mastermind." Freedomways
      (Fourth Quarter 1970).
    "The Black Woman in American Literature." The New York
      Amsterdam News, 27 November 1971.
    "The Black Woman in African Literature." The New York
      Amsterdam News, 1 January 1972.
    " 'That One's Me!'--New Books for Black Children That Mir-
      ror Their World." Redbook 139 (August 1972): 52.
    "New Lafayette Theatre." Drama Review 16 (December
      1972): 46-55.
    "Lonne Elder." Black World (April 1973); (Interview.)

Lisbeth Gant

NON-FICTION
  (Periodical): Black World, January 1973; Essence, March 1974.
REVIEWS BY GANT
  Published in Black Scholar, Black Theatre, Black World, A Current Bibliography on African Affairs; The New York Amsterdam News.
SHORT STORIES
  (Anthologies): Coombs, What We Must See; Sanchez, We Be Word Sorcerers.

GARDNER, Benjamin Franklin. Born 1900.
  POETRY Black. Caldwell, Ida.: Caxton, 1933.

GARDNER, Carl. Born 27 July 1931 in Washington, D.C.
  POETRY (Anthologies): Adoff, The Poetry of Black America; Hughes, New Negro Poets: USA; Lowenfels, In a Time of Revolution; Pool, Beyond the Blues.

GARDNER, G. Ray.
  POETRY (Periodical): Journal of Black Poetry (Fall-Winter 1971).

GARRETT, Jimmy.
DRAMA
And We Own the Night. In The Drama Review 12 (Summer
1968): 62-69; also in Chambers and Moon, Right On!;
Jones and Neal, Black Fire; Simmons and Hutchinson,
Black Culture; Singh and Fellowes, Black Literature in
America.
BIOGRAPHY AND CRITICISM ON GARRETT
Bigsby. The Black American Writer, vol. 2, pp. 200-201.

GARY, Madeleine Sophie. Born 28 July 1923 in Chicago, Illinois.
Education: Attended University of Cincy-NYA extension; John
Marshall Law School; Wilson Junior College; Jones Commercial
College; University of Wisconsin-Madison (Certificate, 1951);
Los Angeles Trade Tech.; Santa Monica City College (Certificate, 1963); various adult education schools. Currently living
in Los Angeles, California. Career: Has had a varied career
as clerk; self-styled social case worker; chauffeurette; laund-
ress; volunteer nurse; truck driver; interior decorator; legal
aide; dental assistant; nurses' aide; double seamer; machine
assistant-drill press operator; auto mechanic helper-attendant;
beauty salon service helper; housemaid; janitress; salad girl;
waitress; short order cook. Presently a career employee with
the U.S. Postal Service; assistant to Bill Mahan, Entertainment Columnist; operator/owner, Snip'n'Clip. Has appeared
in Chicago theatres and on numerous radio and television shows
(including the Joe Pyne Show, Ira Blue Show, Al Jarvis Show,
Fare for Ladies; Groucho Marx; Stairway to Stars; Rocket to
Stardom; Queen for a Day; On the Go; The Other Side of the
Day; Joker's Wild; What's News.) Most important, she is fos-
ter mother of forty-four children. Member: Roman Catholic
Church; Local 1238 APWU; #590 Grand Duchess of Hobo Soci-
ety of America (recognized by Congress) Knights of the Road;
Founder, Mama Soul-Operation Male/Mail Call; Snip'n'Clip
Apostulate of Smiles and Cheers, 1943.
WRITINGS
Philosophical Essays: Vignettes of the Beam in a Nigger's
Eye. New York: Exposition, 1970*.
UNPUBLISHED WORKS
Twenty-two novels and 10 books of poetry.
INTERJECTIONS
"If everyone who condemns welfare, or calls themselves
Christian or believes in One Supreme Being, adopted just one
somebody we'd have no need for institutions because a bootstrap
is just another thong without a boot.... Four hundred years
can't be abolished by a few openings for a few years. Black
people must be set free and those who so desire set apart from
whites--right here and right now.... Black people must unite
if we are to live in an integrated society for the goals of all."

GATES, Betty.
POETRY (Anthology): Henderson, Understanding the New
Black Poetry.

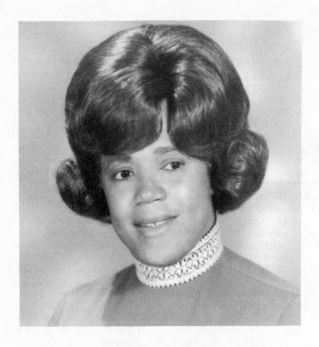

Madeleine Sophie Gary

GATES, Eddie.
POETRY The Poet's Doorway: Poems. New York: Carlton,
1964.

GATEWOOD, L. A.
DRAMA Ghetto: A Place, 1970.

GATOR, E. Z.
POETRY (Periodical): Journal of Black Poetry, Winter-Spring
1970.

GAY, Henry A.
SHORT STORY (Anthology): Mayfield, Ten Times Black.

GAYLE, Addison, Jr. Born 2 June 1932 in New York City. Education: A.B., New York City College, 1964; M.A., University
of California-Los Angeles, 1965. Currently living in New York
City. Career: Lecturer in English, City College of New York,
1965-69; Professor of English at Bernard Baruch College, 1969
to present.
BIOGRAPHY
Oak and Ivy: A Biography of Paul Laurence Dunbar. New

Addison Gayle, Jr.

York: Doubleday, 1971*†.
Claude McKay: The Black Poet at War. Detroit: Broadside, 1972†.
CRITICISM
  "Black Writer's Views on Literary Lions and Values." Negro Digest 17 (January 1968): 32.
  "The Critic, the University and the Negro Writer." Negro Digest 17 (January 1967): 32.
  "Cultural Nationalism: The Black Novel and the City." Liberator 9 (July 1969): 14-17.
  "Cultural Strangulation: Black Literature and the White Aesthetic." Negro Digest 18 (July 1969): 32-39; reprinted in Baker, Black Literature in America, pp. 369-373; Gayle, The Black Aesthetic.
  "A Defense of James Baldwin." CLA Journal 10 (March 1967): 201-208.
  "The Function of Black Literature at the Present Time." In Gayle, The Black Aesthetic.
  "The Harlem Renaissance: Towards a Black Aesthetic." Midcontinent American Studies Journal 11 (Fall 1970): 78-87.
  "Langston Hughes, a Simple Commentary." Negro Digest 16 (September 1967): 53-57.

"The Negro Critic: Invisible Man in American Literature."
  Record 70 (November 1968): 165-171.
"An Open Letter to the Editor of The New York Times Book
  Review." Reprinted in Black World 21 (May 1972): 92-
  94.
"Perhaps Not So Soon One Morning. Phylon (1968): reprinted
  in Gayle, Black Expression, pp. 280-287.
"The Politics of Revolution: Afro-American Literature."
  Black World 21 (June 1972): 4-12.
"Under Western Eyes: A Review--Essay." Black World 22
  (July 1973): 40-48 (Ezekiel Mphahlele).

EDITOR
  The Black Aesthetic. Garden City, N.Y.: Doubleday, 1971†.
  Black Expression: Essays By and About Black Americans in
    the Creative Arts. New York: Weybright & Talley, 1969*.
  Bondage, Freedom and Beyond: The Prose of Black Ameri-
    cans. New York: Doubleday, 1971*†.

NON-FICTION
  The Black Situation. New York: Dell, 1972.
  (Anthology): Gayle, Bondage, Freedom and Beyond.
  (Periodicals): Black World, January 1971; July 1973; Jour-
    nal of Human Relations, Second Quarter 1967; Negro Di-
    gest, July 1969.

SHORT STORIES
  (Periodicals): Black World, May 1970; Negro Digest, May
    1967.

INTERJECTIONS
  "Art must be functional and relevant to the lives of Black
  people. I am a black man first and a black writer second, and
  my life and my writing have no greater guide than the history
  of courage and heroism of Black peoples in this country."

GEARY, Efton F. Born 5 February 1940 in Klondike, Texas. Education: B.A., Prairie View A & M, 1962. Currently living in
San Antonio, Texas. Career: Presently studying for an M.A.
degree at the University of Texas, and working with minorities
in employment. Member: Alamo Area Council of Governments.

POETRY
  Reflections of a Black Man. 1970; 2nd ed.; San Antonio,
    Texas: Naylor, 1972.

WORK IN PROGRESS
  Poetry: "Reflections of a Black Man," vol. 2.

INTERJECTIONS
  "Since inspirations come from the warmth of the human spirit, we as Blacks must endeavor to bring forth this spirit of inspiration in solving problems in our daily lives. For too long
  we as Blacks have allowed our spirits to diminish by looking
  beyond ourselves. I write to help rekindle this spirit. My
  duty as a poet is to reflect upon the lives of Blacks in an attempt to show where the spirit of inspiration can be found. The
  spirit is within ourselves."

GEE, Lethonia. (Lee Gee)
POETRY (Anthologies): Jones and Neal, Black Fire; Patterson, A Rock Against the Wind; Watkins and David, To Be a Black Woman.

GERALD, Carolyn Fowler. Born 27 January 1937 in Lafayette, Louisiana. Education: A.B., University of California-Berkeley, 1960; M.A., University of California-Berkeley, 1965; Ph.D., University of Pennsylvania, 1972. Currently living in Atlanta, Georgia. Career: Social Worker, Alameda County Welfare Department, Oakland, Ca., 1960-63; Instructor of Spanish, Summer School, Bethune-Cookman College, 1965; Instructor French and Spanish, South Carolina State College, 1965-66; Teaching Fellow in French, University of Pennsylvania, 1966-69; Associate Professor of Black Literature, Atlanta University, 1972 to present. Has travelled in Mexico (while attending the Universidad Nacional Autonoma de Mexico, 1958), Paris, (while attending the Universite de Paris-Sorbonne, 1966), and in Santo Domingo, Dominican Republic (as visiting lecturer for a seminar in Afro-American Literature, under the auspices of the U.S. State Department). Has also travelled in Haiti, Martinique, and Puerto Rico. Member: College Language Association; Modern Language Association; Association for the Study of Afro-American Life and History. Awards, Honors: Conrad Kent Rivers Memorial Award, 1971.
CRITICISM BY GERALD
"The Black Writer and His Role." Negro Digest 18 (January 1969): 42-48; also in Gayle, The Black Aesthetic.
"Recent African Poetry in French." Princeton Encyclopedia of Poetry and Poetics, ed. Alex Preminger, et al.
NON-FICTION
(Periodical): Negro Digest, November 1969 (symposium).
POETRY
(Periodical): Journal of Black Poetry, Winter-Spring, 1970.
REVIEWS BY GERALD
Published in Negro Digest; Black World.
UNPUBLISHED WORK
"A Knot in the Thread: The Life and Work of Jacques Roumain." Ph.D. dissertation, University of Pennsylvania, 1972. Also, two plays and numerous poems.

GEX, Quo Vadis. Born 27 October 1950 in New Orleans. Education: Attended Boston University and Radio Engineering Institute (First Class Radio Telephone Operators License). Currently living in Atlanta, Georgia. Career: Secretary for BLKARTSOUTH of the Free Southern Theatre, 1969; Program Coordinator, Harriet Tubman House, South End, Mass., 1969; Clerk, Boston University Student Information Office, 1969; Co-Host, WHRB FM "Sane Society Show," 1970; Announcer, Instructor, DRUM-WBUR Boston University Radio, 1970-71; News Journalist and Director, WYLD Radio, New Orleans, 1972-73; presently employed at Clark College as an Instructor in Radio News and as Program Director for WCLK, Clark College's radio station. Has given

many readings in the South and in the Boston area; has appeared on various TV shows in New Orleans. Member: Media Women. Awards, Honors: Merit Award, Housing Authority of New Orleans, 1972.
POETRY
   Dark Waters. New Orleans: BLKARTSOUTH, 1969.
   (Periodicals): NKOMBO; States Item.
SHORT STORIES
   (Periodical): NKOMBO.
UNPUBLISHED WORK
   "Notebook on New Orleans."

GHOLSON, Rev. Edward. Born 1889.
   APHORISMS
      Aphorisms of Wit and Wisdom. New York: Fortuny's, 1941.
   FICTION
      From Jerusalem to Jericho. Boston: Chapman & Grimes, 1943.
   NON-FICTION
      The Negro Looks Into the South. Boston: Chapman & Grimes, 1947; Ann Arbor, Mich.: University Microfilms, 1970.
      The Philosophy of Ignorance. Boston: Christopher, 1951.
   POETRY
      Musings of a Minister. Boston: Christopher, 1943.

GIBSON, Powell Willard. Born 1875.
   DRAMA
      Jake Among the Indians: A Serio-comic Play Depicting the Trials of an Indian Maid with Her Father. Winchester, Va.: W. P. Gibson, 1931.
   POETRY
      Aida. Winchester, Va.? 193?.
      Grave and Comic Rhymes. Alexandria, Va.: Murray Bros., Printers, 1904.

GIBSON, Rufus.
   POETRY Lyrics of Life and Love. New York: Carlton, 1964.

GIDDINGS, Paula.
   CRITICISM
      " 'A Shoulder Hunched Against a Sharp Concern': Some Themes in the Poetry of Margaret Walker." Black World 21 (December 1971): 2-25.
      "From a Black Perspective: The Poetry of Don L. Lee." Amistad 2, Edited by Williams and Harris, pp. 297-318.
   POETRY
      (Anthologies): Coombs, We Speak as Liberators; Patterson, A Rock Against the Wind.

GILBERT, Herman Cromwell.
   NOVEL That Uncertain Sound. Chicago: Path, 1969.

GILBERT, Mercedes. Born in Jacksonville, Florida. Died 1
March 1952 in Jamaica, New York. Education: Attended Edward Waters College. Career: Prepared to be a nurse, but
turned to songwriting when unable to obtain a nursing position.
Played in silent films, The Call of His People, Secret Sorrow,
Body and Soul (starring Paul Robeson). Appeared in the Broad-
way productions of The Lace Petticoat, Lost, Bamboola, Green
Pastures (five-year run), and Mulatto. Wrote many songs, in-
cluding "Decatur Street Blues" and "Also Ran Blues." Also
wrote for the Associated Negro Press.[1]
DRAMA
    Environment (one act). In Selected Gems of Poetry, Comedy
       and Drama, (see below).
    In Greener Pastures.
    Ma Johnson's Harlem Rooming House (serial), 1938.
NOVEL
    Aunt Sara's Wooden God. Boston: Christopher, 1938; re-
       print ed., Washington, D.C.: 1969*; New York: AMS
       Press*.
POETRY
    Selected Gems of Poetry, Comedy, and Drama. Boston:
       Christopher, 1931.
    (Periodical): Education: A Journal of Reputation, September
       1936.
BIOGRAPHY AND CRITICISM ON GILBERT
    Gloster. Negro Voices in American Fiction, pp. 208, 209,
       235, 241, 251.
    New York Times, 6 March 1952, p. 31 (Obituary.)
    Opportunity 9 (September 1931): 287.
       [1]Harry T. Stewart, "The Poet-Actress: A Personal In-
    terview with Miss Mercedes Gilbert," Education: A Jour-
    nal of Reputation 2 (September 1936): 7.

GILBERT, Zack. Born 21 April 1925 in McMullen, Missouri. Education: High School, Secretarial courses at Peters Business
College, Creative Writing at Parkways Writers' Forum; Insurance Management at Purdue University. Currently living in
Chicago. Career: Licensed insurance agent and broker employed at the transportation department of the B&O-C&O Railroad, in charge of piggy-back trailer movement contracts. Also a free-lance writer and editor for Path Press, a Black publishing company in Chicago.
POETRY
    My Own Hallelujahs. Chicago: Third World, 1971†.
    (Anthologies): Adoff, The Poetry of Black America; Brown,
       Lee and Ward, To Gwen with Love; Hughes and Bontemps,
       The Poetry of the Negro: 1746-1970; Murphy; Ebony
       Rhythm; Randall and Burroughs, For Malcolm.
    (Periodicals): Black World. September 1970; September
       1972; September 1973; January 1974; Negro Digest, July
       1963; January, July, September 1964; April, June, August,
       September, December 1965; April, September 1966; May
       1968; September 1969; also published in The Liberator.

UNPUBLISHED WORK
Novel: "The Way Out World of Hooks and Nails."
WORKS IN PROGRESS
Play: "The Ramp at Swanee" (three act).
Poetry: "Songs Without Music."
CRITICISM ON GILBERT
Kent. "Struggle for the Image," p. 314.
INTERJECTIONS
"The Black writer should have nothing to do with that 'art
for art sake' myth.   Although he may create in several tradi-
tional forms his paramount aim should be to promote Black
Love and to help change the Black man's secondary status in
this country and world.   He should be teacher and leader as
well as artist."

GILLISON, Lenora.
POETRY (Anthology): Murphy, Ebony Rhythm.

GIMENEZ, Joseph Patrick.
POETRY Voice of the Virgin Islands.   Philadelphia: Dorrance,
1952.

GIOVANNI, Nikki.   Born 7 June 1943 in Knoxville, Tennessee.
Education: B.A. (with honors), Fisk University, 1967; additional work at the School of Social Work at the University of Pennsylvania; School of Fine Arts, Columbia University.   Currently
living in New York City.   Career: Founded a chapter of SNCC
at Fisk University, 1964.   Founded the publishing cooperative
TomNik Ltd., in 1970.   Appeared on Soul!, the hour-long television program devoted to Black music, drama, dance, and literature.   Has given poetry readings and lectures in many cities
and on college campuses.   Associate Professor of English, Livingston College of Rutgers University, and Assistant Professor,
SEEK Program, Queens College.   Made two albums, Truth Is
On Its Way (Right On Records, 1971), and Like a Ripple on a
Pond, 1973.   Awards, Honors: Ford Foundation grant, 1967;
National Foundation of the Arts grant, 1968; Harlem Cultural
Council on the Arts grant, 1969; Doctor of Humanities, Wilberforce University, 1972.   Boston University has established a
special Nikki Giovanni collection.   Has also received the Made-
moiselle magazine Award for Outstanding Achievement, 1971;
Omega Psi Phi Fraternity award for Outstanding Contributions
to Arts and Letters; Plaque from the Cook County Jail, 1971;
keys to the cities of Gary, Indiana, 1972, and Lincoln Heights,
Ohio, 1972; National Association of Radio and Television An-
nouncers (N.A.T.R.A.) Award, Best Spoken Word Album, 1972;
National Book Award Nomination for Gemini, 1973; Ladies'
Home Journal award, Woman of the Year--Youth Leadership,
1973.   Member: National Council of Negro Women; Society of
Magazine Writers.
AUTOBIOGRAPHY
Gemini: Extended Biographical Statement on My First Twen-
ty-Five Years of Being a Black Poet.   Indianapolis: Bobbs-

Merrill, 1971*; reprint ed. New York: Viking, 1973.

CHILDREN AND YOUNG ADULTS

Ego Tripping and Other Poems for Young Readers. Westport, Conn.: Lawrence Hill, 1973*†.

Spin a Soft Black Song: Poems for Children. New York: Hill & Wang, 1971*.

CRITICISM

"Black Poems, Poseurs and Power." Negro Digest 18 (June 1969): 30-34.

EDITOR

Night Comes Softly. Detroit: TomNik Ltd., 1970. (Poetry.)

NON-FICTION

With James Baldwin. A Dialogue: James Baldwin and Nikki Giovanni. Philadelphia: Lippincott, 1973*†.

With Margaret Walker. A Poetic Equation: Conversations Between Nikki Giovanni and Margaret Walker. Washington, D.C.: Howard University Press, forthcoming.

POETRY

Black Feeling Black Talk. Detroit: Broadside, 1968; rev. ed., 3rd ed., 1970†.

Black Feeling Black Talk/Black Judgement. Morrow Poetry Series. New York: Morrow, 1970†.

Black Judgement. Detroit: Broadside, 1968†.

My House. New York: Morrow, 1972*†.

Poem of Angela Davis. Detroit: TomNik, 1970.

Re: Creation. Detroit: Broadside, 1970*†.

(Anthologies): Adoff, Black Out Loud; Adoff, The Poetry of Black America; Alhamisi and Wangara, Black Arts; Bell, Afro-American Poetry; Brooks, A Broadside Treasury; Brown, Lee and Ward, To Gwen with Love; Chambers and Moon, Right On!; Chapman, New Black Voices; Colley and Moore, Starting with Poetry; Coombs, We Speak as Liberators; Ellman and O'Claire, The Norton Anthology of Modern Poetry; Henderson, Understanding the New Black Poetry; Jordan, Soulscript; King, Black Short Story Anthology; King, Blackspirits; Lomax and Abdul, 3000 Years of Black Poetry; Long and Collier, Afro-American Writing; Major, The New Black Poetry; Miller, Blackamerican Literature; Patterson, A Rock Against the Wind; Randall, Black Poetry; Randall, Black Poetry: A Supplement; Segnitz and Rainey, Psyche; Wilentz and Weatherly, Natural Process.

(Periodicals): Black Creation, Fall 1971; Black World, September 1970; Ebony, August 1972; Essence, February 1971; Freedomways, 1971; Journal of Black Poetry, Spring 1969; Negro Digest, June 1968. Other poetry in Umbra.

REVIEWS BY GIOVANNI

Published in Black World.

SHORT STORY

(Anthology): Mayfield, Ten Times Black.

WORK IN PROGRESS

A Biography of Nina Simone.

BIOGRAPHY AND CRITICISM ON GIOVANNI

Bailey, P. "Nikki Giovanni: I Am Black, Female, Polite." _Ebony_ (February 1972): 48-50.

Dusky, Lorraine. "Fascinating Woman." _Ingenue_, February 1973.

Lee. _Dynamite Voices_, pp. 68-74.

Malkoff. _Crowell's Handbook of Contemporary American Poetry_.

Nazer, G. "Lifestyle." _Harper's Bazaar_, July 1972, pp. 50-51.

Palmer, R. Roderick. "The Poetry of Three Revolutionists: Don L. Lee, Sonia Sanchez, and Nikki Giovanni." _CLA Journal_ 15 (September 1971): 25-36. Also in Gibson, _Modern Black Poets_.

Whitlow. _Black American Literature_, pp. 177-179.

GLADDEN, Frank A.
DRAMA

The Distant Brother, 1972.

SHORT STORY

(Periodical): _Black World_, June 1972.

GLOSTER, Hugh Morris. Born 11 May 1911 in Brownsville, Tennessee. Career: See Shockley and Chandler, _Living Black American Authors_, pp. 56-57; _Directory of American Scholars_, vol. 2, p. 196.
CRITICISM

"Charles W. Chesnutt, Pioneer in Fiction of Negro Life." _Phylon_ 2 (First Quarter 1941): 57-66; also in Watkins, _Anthology of American Negro Literature_.

Negro Voices in American Fiction. Chapel Hill: University of North Carolina, 1948*.

"The Negro Writer and the Southern Scene." _The Southern Packet_ 4 (January 1948): 1-3.

"Race and the Negro Writer." _Phylon_ 11 (1950): 369-371.

"Sutton E. Griggs, Novelist of the New Negro." _Phylon_ 4 (Fourth Quarter 1943): 335-344.

"The Van Vechten Vogue." _Phylon_ 6 (Fourth Quarter 1945): 310-314.

"Zora Neal Hurston, Novelist and Folklorist." _Phylon_ 4 (Second Quarter 1943): 153-156.

EDITOR

With Helen M. O'Brien and Lillian W. Voorhees. _The Brown Thrush: An Anthology of Verse by Negro Students_. Memphis, Tenn.: Malcolm Roberts, 1935.

With William Edward Farrison and Nathaniel Tillman. _My Life, My Country, My World: College Readings for Modern Living_. New York: Prentice-Hall, 1952.

REVIEWS BY GLOSTER

Published in _Phylon_.

GLOVER, Leonard Horace.
CHILDREN AND YOUNG ADULTS

Paper and Pencil: An Allegory for Young People. New
York: Exposition, 1957.

GOINES, Donald. Born 15 December 1937 in Detroit, Michigan.
Education: Self-taught beyond ninth grade. Currently living in
Los Angeles, California. Career: Writer.
NOVELS
Black Gangster. Los Angeles: Holloway House, 1972†.
Dopefiend, The Story of a Black Junkie. Los Angeles: Hol-
loway House, 1972†.
Street Players. Los Angeles: Holloway House, 1973†.
White Man's Justice, Black Man's Grief. Los Angeles: Hol-
loway House, 1973†.
Whoreson, The Story of a Black Pimp. Los Angeles: Hol-
loway House, 1972†.

GONCALVES, Joe (Dingane). Born 1937 in Boston, Massachusetts.
CRITICISM
"The Mysterious Disappearance of Black Arts West." Black
Theatre No. 2 (1969): 23-25.
"West Coast Drama." Black Theatre No. 4 (1970): 27.
NON-FICTION
(Periodicals): Negro Digest, November 1969 (symposium);
also published in Journal of Black Poetry.
POETRY
(Anthologies): Alhamisi and Wangara, Black Arts; Brown,
Lee and Ward, To Gwen with Love; Colley and Moore,
Starting with Poetry; Jones and Neal, Black Fire.
(Periodicals): Black Dialogue; Journal of Black Poetry,
Spring 1969; Negro Digest, June 1968.
REVIEWS BY GONCALVES
Published in Journal of Black Poetry.

GOODE, Michael. Born 27 December 1954 in Brooklyn.
POETRY (Anthology): Jordan, Soulscript.

GOODWIN, LeRoy. Born in Los Angeles.
POETRY
"Inside Poems"--But Not Jokes. Los Angeles: Bean Bag
Press, 1967.
(Anthology): Jones and Neal, Black Fire.

GOODWIN, Ruby Berkley. Born 17 October 1903 in DuQuoin, Illi-
nois. Education: A.B., San Gabriel College, 1949. Career:
Writer of a syndicated column, "Hollywood in Bronze." Publi-
cist and secretary for Hattie McDaniel, 1936-52. Member:
Los Angeles Urban League; Fullerton Council of Churchwomen;
Fullerton Y.W.C.A.; Chaparrel Poetry Society; Screen Actors
Guild; Actors Equity Association; Negro Actors Guild. Awards,
Honors: Gold Medal, Commonwealth Award for Best Non-Fic-
tion Book by California Author, 1953.[1]
AUTOBIOGRAPHY
It's Good to Be Black. Garden City, N.Y.: Doubleday, 1953.

POETRY
From My Kitchen Window. Introduction by Margaret Widde-
   mer. New York: W. Malliet, 1942.
A Gold Star Mother Speaks. n.p., 1944.
(Anthology): Murphy, Ebony Rhythm; Murphy, Negro Voices.
SHORT STORIES
Still, William Grant. Twelve Negro Spirituals (with Stories
   of Negro Life by Ruby Berkley Goodwin). New York:
Handy Brothers Music Co., 1937.
      [1]Who's Who of American Women, vol. 1 (Chicago: A.
N. Marquis, 1958), p. 491.

GORDON, Charles see OYAMO

GORDON, Edyth Mae.
POETRY (Anthology): Murphy, Negro Voices.

GORDON, Eugene. Born 23 November 1890 in Oviedo, Florida.
Education: Attended Howard University Academy and College,
1910-17; Officers Training Camps; Boston University 1921-23.
Career: Reporter on the Boston Post, May-July 1919; then
joined the Feature Department, editing copy. In 1923, he began
editing short stories and serials in the Daily Post, and con-
tributed editorials to the Sunday Post and to the Daily Post.
Founded and edited The Bayonet, an official publication of the
Second Separate Battalion, Massachusetts National Guard. Mem-
ber: Inter-Racial Commission in Boston; Boston Society of Nat-
ural History; N.A.A.C.P.; Saturday Evening Quill Club.[1]
NON-FICTION
   (Periodicals): Opportunity.
SHORT STORIES
   (Periodicals): Opportunity, September 1926; September 1927;
      November 1928; December 1933; January 1934.
         [1]Who's Who in Colored America, vol. 1 (1927), p. 76.

GORDON, Ken.
DRAMA Black Fog Poem.

GORDON, Taylor. Born 29 April 1893 in White Sulphur Springs,
Montana. Died 7 May 1971. Education: Self-educated. Career:
Mechanic, chauffeur, railroad porter, theatre doorman, porter
and cook on the private railroad for John Ringling; agent in the
West Indies for the United States Immigration Service; whiskey
maker, brick layer, dock worker, and gadgetry inventor; pro-
fessional singer in a vaudeville act; travelled in concert to
France and England. Collaborated with Rosamond and James
Weldon Johnson and sang the spirituals found in The Book of
American Negro Spirituals, 1925.[1]
AUTOBIOGRAPHY
   Born to Be. New York: Covici-Friede, 1929; reprint ed.,
      Seattle: University of Washington Press, 1974*. At his
      death, Gordon left a 131-page manuscript intended as a
      sequel to Born to Be, dated 2 December 1970.[2]

NON-FICTION
Pamphlet of The Local History of White Sulphur Springs,
1967, to take advantage of the tourist trade during the
town's Centennial Celebration.
ESSAY
Nancy Cunard's Negro Anthology.
BIOGRAPHY AND CRITICISM ON GORDON
Chalmers. Witnesses for Freedom, pp. 115-122.
REVIEW: Born to Be.
Gordon, Eugene. Opportunity 8 (January 1930): 22-23.
[1]Robert Hemenway. "Taylor Gordon's Born to Be:
A Lost Autobiography." A paper delivered at the 1973
Midwest Modern Language Association, Illinois, Novem-
ber 1-3, pp. 1-4.
[2]Ibid.

GORDON, William Henry Barefield. Born 1906 in Augusta, Geor-
gia.
POETRY
(Anthology): Lincoln University Poets.
(Periodicals): Opportunity, March 1929; November 1930.
SHORT STORY
(Periodical): Opportunity, March 1929.

GORDONE, Charles. Born 12 October 1925 in Cleveland, Ohio.
Education: B.A. in Drama, Los Angeles State College, 1952.
Career: Has worked in all phases of the entertainment media.
Presently filming the feature film, Coon Skin (playing the lead
role), for Paramount Pictures. Also finishing a three-act play
scheduled for Broadway for Bill Cosby Productions, and direct-
ing a newly written long, one-act play, "The Cowmen."
Awards, Honors: Pulitzer Prize for No Place to Be Somebody,
1970; Best Actor Award of the Year (Off-Broadway); Drama
Desk Award, New York City; Critics Circle Award, Los Ange-
les.
DRAMA
No Place to Be Somebody. Indianapolis: Bobbs-Merrill,
1969*†; reprinted in Oliver and Sills, Contemporary Black
Drama; Patterson, Black Theater.
Worl's Champeen Lip Dansuh an' Wahtah Mellon Jooglah,
1969.
DRAMA/POETRY
"A Quiet Talk with Myself." In Ford, Black Insights.
BIOGRAPHY AND CRITICISM ON GORDONE
"Behind the Pulitzer: An Interview with Charles Gordoné."
Sepia 2 (February 1971): 14-17.
"Black Pulitzer Prize Awardees." Crisis 77 (May 1970):
186-188.
Contemporary Authors
Gill, Brendan. The New Yorker, 10 January 1970, p. 64.
Kerr, Walter. "Not Since Edward Albee." New York Times,
18 May 1969.
Riley, Clayton. New York Times, 18 May 1969.

Charles Gordoné

Simon, John. "Underwriting, Overreaching." New York,
    9 June 1969, p. 56.
Walcott, Ronald. "Ellison, Gordoné and Tolson: Some
    Notes on the Blues." Black World 22 (December 1972):
    4-29.
Wetzsteon, Ross. "Theatre Journal." The Village Voice,
    22 May 1969.

INTERJECTIONS
    " 'Oh, What a piece of work is man, how like a God!' To me,
life and art are synonymous. Man himself is a work of art.
Certainly, if he be worth his salt, his living of life will be,
must be, a work of art. We do not enter this world, literally
or 'to the letter,' biblically speaking, as Adam did, to find ourselves irresponsibly ensconced in the Paradise of some Garden
of Eden. And most certainly, Adam had his rib. Didn't he?
    "We are, all of us, falling down. In many instances, that
can be very easy to do. But it is the getting up to go 'toe to
toe,' that is the most challenging. I use the word challenging
instead of like hard or difficult, because something very creative almost invariably comes out of challenge, don't you think?
    "George Bernard Shaw said that any true work of art re-
quires that one wrestle and struggle with what would appear to
be frustrating, disappointing, and excruciatingly painful, to the
point of intolerability.
    "If one is obsessed, perhaps demonic, in his effort to cre-
ate and to create anew, the rewards are manifold."

GORE, Anthony.
    POETRY (Periodical): Journal of Black Poetry, Fall-Winter,
        1971.

GORHAM, Myrtle Campbell.
    POETRY (Anthology): Murphy, Ebony Rhythm.

GOSS, Clay. Born 26 May 1946 in North Philadelphia, Pennsyl-
    vania.
    CHILDREN AND YOUNG ADULTS
        Bill Pickett: Black Bulldogger. New York: Hill & Wang,
            1970.
    DRAMA
        Andrew (one act), 1972.
        Homecookin (one act), 1972.
        Mars.
        Of Being Hit, 1970.
        Ornette.
        Oursides (one act).
        Spaces in Time.
    POETRY
        (Anthology): Coombs, We Speak as Liberators.
    BIOGRAPHY AND CRITICISM ON GOSS
        Harrison. The Drama of Nommo, pp. 63, 86, 204-207.

GOSS, Linda.
POETRY (Anthologies): Coombs, We Speak as Liberators;
Patterson, A Rock Against the Wind.

GOSS, William Thompson.
POETRY (Anthology): Murphy, Ebony Rhythm.

GOULBOURNE, Carmin Auld. Born 22 February 1912 in El Cristo,
Cuba.
POETRY
(Anthology): Randall and Burroughs, For Malcolm.
(Periodicals): Chicago Jewish Forum; The Hilltop (Howard
University); Negro Digest.

GOVAN, Donald D. Born 1945 in Minot, North Dakota.
POETRY (Anthology): Major, The New Black Poetry.

GOVAN, Oswald. Born in New York City.
POETRY
(Anthologies): Burning Spear; Henderson, Understanding the
New Black Poetry.
(Periodical): Dasein.

GOVERN, Rena Greenlee.
POETRY Democracy's Task. New York: By the Author, 1945.

GOWARD, Gladys McFadden.
POETRY See How They Play: A Pictorial Tour Through the
Orchestra. New York: Exposition, 1953.

GRAHAM, Arthur.
DRAMA The Last Shine, 1969.

GRAHAM, D. L. (Donald L. Graham). Born 1944 in Gary, Indiana.
Died in an automobile accident, summer 1970. Education:
Studied at Fisk University under John Killens.[1]
POETRY
Black Song. n.p., 1966.
Soul Motion I and Soul Motion II. Fisk University, Division
of Cultural Research, Department of Art, 1969.
(Anthologies): Adoff, The Poetry of Black America; Hayden,
Kaleidoscope; Jones and Neal, Black Fire; Umbra: An-
thology 1967-1968.
CRITICISM ON GRAHAM
Lee. Dynamite Voices, pp. 60-63.
[1]Arnold Adoff, ed., The Poetry of Black America (New
York: Harper & Row, 1972), p. 524.

GRAHAM, Le see ALHAMISI, Ahmed LeGraham

GRAHAM, Linda. Born 1958.
POETRY (Anthology): Shuman, A Galaxy of Black Writing.

Lorenz Graham (credit: Warren Williams)

GRAHAM, Lorenz. <u>Born</u> 27 January 1902 in New Orleans. <u>Education</u>: University of California-Los Angeles, 1923-24; University of Washington, 1921; B.A., Virginia Union University, 1936; additional work at New York School of Social Work; Columbia University and New York University. <u>Currently living in</u> Claremont, California. <u>Career</u>: Taught at Monrovia College in Liberia, West Africa, 1924-28; lecturer and fund raiser, United States Foreign Mission Board, National Baptist Convention, 1929-32; teacher in Richmond, Virginia, 1933-35; camp education advisor, U.S. Civilian Conservation Corps, 1936-42; manager of public housing, Newport News, Virginia, 1943-45; free lance writer, real estate salesman, building contractor, Long Island, N.Y., 1946-49; social worker, 1950-57; Los Angeles County (California) probation officer, 1958-66;[1] professor, Department of English, California State University at Pomona. <u>Member</u>: Authors League of America; McCarty Christian Church, Los Angeles; P.E.N. International, Los Angeles; Southern California Writers Guild; United Professors of California. <u>Awards, Honors</u>: Thomas Alva Edison, Citation, 1956; Queens Federation of Churches, Citation, 1957; Charles W. Follett, Award, 1958; Child Study Association of America, Award, 1958; Association for the Study of Negro Life and History, Citation, 1959; Los Angeles City Council on Literature for Children and

Young People, Award, 1968; Book World, First Prize, 1969.
CHILDREN AND YOUNG ADULTS
  David He No Fear. New York: T. Y. Crowell, 1971.
  Every Man Heart Lay Down. New York: T. Y. Crowell,
    1970*.
  God Wash the World and Start Again. New York: T. Y.
    Crowell, 1971*.
  Hongry Catch the Foolish Boy. New York: T. Y. Crowell,
    1971*.
  How God Fix Jonah. New York: Reynal & Hitchcock, 1946.
  I, Momolu. New York: T. Y. Crowell, 1966*.
  John Brown's Raid. New York: Scholastic, 1972*.
  North Town. New York: T. Y. Crowell, 1965*.
  A Road Down in the Sea. New York: T. Y. Crowell, 1971*.
  South Town. Chicago: Follett, 1958; New York: New Ameri-
    can Library, 1966†.
  The Story of Jesus. New York: Gilberton, 1955.
  Tales of Momolu. New York: Reynal & Hitchcock, 1947.
  The Ten Commandments. New York: Gilberton, 1956.
  Whose Town? New York: T. Y. Crowell, 1969*.
CRITICISM
  "An Author Speaks." Elementary English 50 (February 1973).
POETRY
  (Anthologies): Rollins, Christmas Gif', Thompson, Jean, ed.,
    Our Own Christmas (Boston: Beacon, 1967).
SHORT STORIES
  (Anthologies): Directions I, II, III, IV (Boston: Houghton
    Mifflin, 1972); Olsen and Swinburne, eds. Crossroad Se-
    ries: Level Two, He Who Dares (New York: Noble &
    Noble, 1969); Stull and Greenfield, eds., Cities (Holt,
    Rinehart & Winston, 1968); Happenings (Los Angeles City
    Schools, 1967); Cavalcades (Scott-Foresman, 1967, 1971);
    The Sun That Warms Us (Boston: Ginn, 1970, 1972).
BIOGRAPHY AND CRITICISM ON GRAHAM
  Contemporary Authors, 9/10.
  Small, Robert C., Jr. "South Town: A Junior Novel of
    Prejudice." Negro American Literature Forum 4 (Winter
    1970): 136-141.
INTERJECTIONS
  "Writing for children and young people should be of the high-
est possible quality and that which deals with black people should
develop respect and inspire hope."
          [1]Anne Commire, Something about the Author, vol. 2
    (Detroit: Gale Research, 1971), p. 122.

GRAHAM, Rudy Bee. Born 1947 in Winston-Salem, North Carolina.
  POETRY (Anthologies): Hughes and Bontemps, The Poetry of
    the Negro: 1746-1970; Jones and Neal, Black Fire.

GRAHAM, Ruth Morris.
  CHILDREN AND YOUNG ADULTS The Happy Sound. Chicago:
    Follett, 1970*.

Claude D. Grant

GRAHAM, Shirley see DuBOIS, Shirley Graham

GRAINGER, Porter.
DRAMA
With Leigh Whipper. De Board Meetin, 1925.
With Freddie Johnson. Lucky Sambo, 1925.
With Leigh Whipper. We's Risin: A Story of the Simple
Life in the Souls of Black Folk, 1927. (A musical com-
edy in two acts and ten scenes.)
BIOGRAPHY ON GRAINGER
Hughes and Meltzer. Black Magic, p. 97.

GRANT, Claude D. Born 20 December 1944 in Harlem. Education:
A.B., Hunter College, 1974; working toward Ph.D. at City University of New York. Currently lives in Bronx, New York.
Career: A qualified paraprofessional psychologist who has
taught in elementary school and college; a lecturer in Black music and psychology and their applications to Black people; a free
lance writer; musical editor for Essence magazine; editor-in-
chief of Black Voice, 1970-72; poet and musical director for
the Unity Brothers (a poetry and music group whose aim is "to
enlighten those who need it and to bring together as many Black
people as possible.") Has acted in Off-Broadway productions.

DRAMA
   Where Is the Sky, 1972.
POETRY
   Epitaph for My Self. New York: Amuru, 1973†. Also published
   in New York Times; Amsterdam News; Players magazine.
WORK IN PROGRESS
   A book which will postulate a theory of psychology for Blacks
   (non-fiction) and an epic poem with Gary Johnston and
   Reggie McLaurin which will include original music and
   choreography.
INTERJECTIONS
   "The Black artist must strive for a type of artistic freedom
   which will allow him to express the Black experience in a way
   which anyone and everyone can understand--not just tolerate!"

GRANT, John Wesley. Born 1850.
   NOVEL
      Out of the Darkness; or, Diabolism and Destiny. Nashville,
         National Baptist Publishing Board, 1909.
   CRITICISM ON GRANT
      Gloster. Negro Voices in American Fiction, pp. 71-73.

GRANT, Micki. Born 30 June in Chicago, Illinois. Education:
   University of Illinois; Roosevelt and DePaul University. Currently living in New York City. Career: Specializes in theatre, television, and songwriting. Has published numerous songs
   with Fiddleback Music Co., including "Don't Bother Me, I Can't
   Cope"; a recording of "Cope" was released by Polydor Records
   in 1972. Presently composing, writing lyrics and acting. Mem-
   ber: Actors Equity. Life Member, N.A.A.C.P.; Dramatist's
   Guild. Awards, Honors: Drama Desk--Outer Circle--Grammy,
   1972; Mademoiselle Achievement Award, 1972; Girl Friends
   Achievement, 1972; Two Tony Nominations, 1972; N.A.A.C.P.
   Image Award, 1972.
   DRAMA
      Don't Bother Me, I Can't Cope (musical).
   BIOGRAPHY ON GRANT
      Ebony 4 (February 1973): 100-109.
   INTERJECTIONS
      "I've come to realize that important things can be said through
      words set to music. More than being a diversion, songs can be
      an important and accessible form of communication, hence, my
      interest in musical theatre."

GRANT, Richard E. Born 1949 in Gary, Indiana.
   POETRY
      (Anthology): Adoff, The Poetry of Black America.

GRAY, Alfred Rudolf, Jr. Born 26 June 1933 in New York City.
   Education: B.A., City College of New York, 1956; M.A., Hunt-
   er College, 1974. Currently living in New York City. Career:
   Has taught art, science, and mathematics at the Junior High
   School level; presently teaching Junior High School English while

Micki Grant

writing for stage, screen and television. His plays have been
produced by Hunter College Playwrights; American Community
Theater; New Lafayette Players; Company in Black. Member:
Harlem Writers Guild; Negro Ensemble Company Playwrights
Group; Director of Company in Black. Awards, Honors: John
Golden Playwrighting Fellowship, 1972 and 1973.
DRAMA
  With Maxwell Glanville. Dance to a Nosepicker's Drum.
  The Dean.
  Eye for an Eye (revised).
  Lucy, My Rose Petal.
  Open School Night.
  Peeling to the Pain.
  The Revenge.
  Tryout.
WORK IN PROGRESS
  Novel: "Crackup in Slow Motion."
INTERJECTIONS
  "For an American Black to deny either his Africanness or
his American-Europeanness is to deny an important vital part
of his total being. The interaction, fusion of the two cultural
forces, within the psyche of the American Black forms the
uniqueness of his blackness, thus giving him 'soul' no other

Donald Greaves

---

personality in the Western World has. No part of his history, past or present, should be denied. Contrary to current popular belief, The Uncle Tom of the past may have been more militant within his historical context than the black militant is today within the present context."

GRAY, Wade.
    NOVEL Her Last Performance. Omaha, Neb.: Rapid Printing
        & Publishing Co., 1944.

GREANE, David.
    DRAMA Martin Luther King--Man of God.

GREAVES, Donald. Born 1943 in Harlem.
    DRAMA The Marriage. In King and Milner, Black Drama An-
        thology.

GREEN, Donald.
    POETRY (Anthology): Coombs, We Speak as Liberators.

GREEN, Johnny L.
    DRAMA
        Black on Black. New York: Amuru, 1973†. (one act).

The Night of Judgment (one act). New York: Amuru, 1973†.
The Sign (two acts). New York: Amuru, 1973†.
SHORT STORIES
Johnny L. Green's Short Stories. New York: Amuru, 1973†.

GREEN, Ulysses.
POETRY
A Nigger's Thoughts. Carbondale, Ill.: By the Author,
208 E. Willow, n.d.

GREENE, Carl H. Born 2 February 1945 in Philadelphia.
POETRY (Anthologies): Chapman, New Black Voices; Fisher,
The Best in Poetry; Kaplan, Voices of the Revolution;
Shuman, A Galaxy of Black Writing; Witherspoon, Broad-
side Annual 1972.

GREENE, Emily Jane.
POETRY (Anthology): Murphy, Ebony Rhythm.

GREENE, Joe see JOHNSON, B. B.

GREENE, Otis.
DRAMA A Different Part of the World, 1967.

GREENFIELD, Eloise. Born 17 May 1929 in Parmele, North Caro-
lina.
CHILDREN AND YOUNG ADULTS
Bubbles. Washington, D.C.: Drum & Spear, 1972†.
Rosa Parks. New York: T. Y. Crowell, 1973*.
ESSAY
(Periodicals): Negro Digest, June, November 1965.
SHORT STORIES
(Periodicals): Black World, June 1970; June 1972; Negro
Digest, January, July 1966; August 1969; January 1970;
June 1970.

GREENLEE, Sam. Born 13 July 1930 in Chicago, Illinois. Education: B.S., University of Wisconsin-Madison (Political Science), 1952; University of Chicago (Political Science and International Relations), 1954-57; University of Thessalonikki,
Greece (Ancient Greek History, Modern Greek Language), 1963-
64. Currently living in Chicago, Illinois.
CRITICISM
"Report on Black Theater." Negro Digest 18 (April 1969):
23-24.
NOVEL
The Spook Who Sat by the Door. R. W. Baron, 1969*; re-
print ed. New York: Bantam, 1970†. (Adapted for stage
at Southside Center for Performing Arts, Chicago.)
Bagdad Blues. New York: Emerson Hall, 1973*.
"The D.C. Blues." Negro Digest 18 (June 1969): 86-92.
(Novel excerpt.)

POETRY
    Blues for an African Princess. Introduction by Nikki Giovan-
    ni. Chicago: Third World, 1971†.
    (Anthology): Patterson, A Rock Against the Wind.
SHORT STORIES
    (Anthologies): King, Black Short Story Anthology; Mayfield,
    Ten Times Black; Sanchez, We Be Word Sorcerers.
    (Periodicals): Black World, August 1973; Negro Digest, De-
    cember 1965; February 1966; September 1966; January
    1967; October 1970.
BIOGRAPHY AND CRITICISM ON GREENLEE
    Burrell, W. "Rappin with Sam Greenlee." Black World 2
    (July 1971): 42-47. (Interview.)
REVIEW
    Blues for an African Princess.
    Jackson, A. Black World 21 (December 1971): 88-89.

GREENWOOD, Frank.
    DRAMA
        Burn, Baby, Burn.
    BIOGRAPHY AND CRITICISM ON GREENWOOD
        Greenwood, Frank. "Comment on Burn, Baby, Burn!"
        Freedomways 7 (Summer 1967): 244-246.
        Wheeldin, Donald. "The Situation in Watts Today." Free-
        domways 7 (Winter 1967): 57.

GREENWOOD, Theresa (Winfrey). Born 28 December 1936 in Cairo,
    Illinois. Education: B.M.E., Millikin University, 1959; M.A.,
    Ball State University, 1963; D.Ed. (Early Childhood and Social
    Psychology) now in progress at Ball State University. Currently
    living in Muncie, Indiana. Career: Elementary music teacher,
    East Chicago Public Schools, 1959-61; Elementary teacher,
    Muncie Public Schools, 1962-65; Teacher, Kindergarten and
    Headstart, Muncie, 1967-68; Academic Counselor, Fellowship
    assignment, Living Learning Laboratory, Ball State, 1970-71.
    Writes a weekly education column for the Muncie Evening Press.
    Her poetry and articles have appeared in many church-spon-
    sored periodicals. Member: College Avenue Methodist Church;
    Sigma Alpha Iota (Music Honorary); American Red Cross Board
    of Directors; EICTV Public Television Board; United Fund Board
    of Directors (Delaware County); professional organizations.
    Awards, Honors: Tri Delta Scholarship; Kappa Delta Pi (educa-
    tional honorary); Semi-finalist, Mrs. U.S. Savings Bond Pageant;
    Mother of Indiana All-American Family, 1971-72.
    NON-FICTION
        (Periodicals): Indian Social Science Quarterly, 1964; Young
        World, April 1973.
    POETRY
        Psalms of a Black Mother. Anderson, Indiana: Warner
        Press, 1970†.
    INTERJECTIONS
    "Because of my particular penchant for beautiful prose I be-
lieve an author's exacting words can help make men aware and

proud of their unique individualities, yet cognizant of the golden
as well as the brittle threads which link all humanity together.

"To me, writing provides the means with which to examine
the prosaic as well as the phenomenon and at the same time to
mirror the past, the now, and to catch a glimpse of realities
yet untold.

"In my writings, I strive also to help people realize that God
is in all of us, and if we deny His existence we may live--only
for a day.   But if we seek to praise and obey, through Him we
can realize true brotherhood and live forever."

GREGG, Ernest.
   POETRY (Periodical): Journal of Black Poetry, Winter-Spring
      1970.

GREGGS, Herbert D. Born in 1931.
   DRAMA
      The Ballad of a Riverboat Town, 1968.
   POETRY
      (Anthology): Abdul, The Magic of Black Poetry.

GREGORY, Carole see CLEMMONS, Carole G.

GREGORY, Yvonne.
   POETRY (Anthology): Bontemps, American Negro Poetry.

GRIFFIN, Amos.
   POETRY (Anthology): Murphy, Ebony Rhythm.

GRIFFIN, Judith Berry.
   CHILDREN AND YOUNG ADULTS
      The Magic Mirrors. New York: Coward McCann, 1971*.
      Nat Turner. New York: Coward McCann, 1970*.

GRIGGS, Sutton Elbert. Born 1872 in Chatfield, Texas. Died 1930.
   Education: Attended Bishop College; completed a theological
   course at Richmond Theological Seminary (now a part of Virginia Union University), 1893.   After his ordination, he served
   as pastor in Berkley, Virginia, for two years.   From 1895 to
   1915 he was corresponding Secretary of the Education Department of the National Baptist Convention in Nashville, Tennessee.
   He held several pastorates before going to Texas, and died
   while working to establish a National Religious and Civic Institute.[1]
   NON-FICTION
      According to Law. Memphis, Tenn.: National Public Wel-
         fare League, 1916.
      Guide to Racial Greatness, or, The Science of Collective Ef-
         ficiency. Memphis, Tenn.: National Public Welfare
         League, 1923.
      How to Rise. Memphis, Tenn.: National Public Welfare
         League, 1915.
      Kingdom Builders' Manual. Companion Book to Guide to

Racial Greatness. Memphis, Tenn.: National Public Welfare League, 1924.

Light on Racial Issues. Memphis, Tenn.: National Public Welfare League, 1921.

Needs of the South. Nashville, Tenn.: The Orion Publishing Co., 1909.

The Negro's Next Stop. Memphis, Tenn.: National Public Welfare League, 1923.

The One Great Question... Philadelphia: Orion Publishing Co., 1907.

Paths of Progress: or, Co-operation between the Races. Memphis, Tenn.: National Public Welfare League, 1925.

The Race Question in a New Light. Nashville, Tenn.: The Orion Publishing Co., 1909.

The Reconstruction of a Race. Memphis, Tenn.: National Public Welfare League, 1917.

Science of Collective Efficiency. Memphis, Tenn.: National Public Welfare League, 1921.

The Story of My Struggles. Memphis, Tenn.: National Public Welfare League, 1914.

Triumph of the Simple Virtues, or, The Life Story of John L. Webb. Hot Springs, Ark.: The Messenger Publishing Co., 1926.

The Winning Policy. Memphis, Tenn.: National Public Welfare League, 1927.

NOVELS

The Hindered Hand; or, The Reign of the Repressionist. Nashville, Tenn.: Orion, 1902; reprint ed., New York: AMS Press, 1970*; Miami: Mnemosyne*†; New York: AMS Press*†; facsimile ed., Freeport, N.Y.: Books for Libraries. Excerpt in Davis and Redding, Cavalcade.

Imperium In Imperio. Cincinnati: Editor, 1899; reprint ed., Miami: Mnemosyne, 1969*†; New York: Arno, 1969*†; New York: Panther House*†; New York: AMS Press*; facsimile ed., Freeport, N.Y.: Books for Libraries*.

Overshadowed. Nashville: Orion, 1901; reprint ed. New York: AMS Press, 1970*; facsimile ed., Freeport, N.Y.: Books for Libraries*.

Pointing the Way. Nashville: Orion, 1908; reprint ed., New York: AMS Press, 1970*.

Unfettered, A Novel. Nashville: Orion, 1902; reprint ed. New York: AMS Press, 1970.

Wisdom's Call. Nashville: Orion, 1911; reprint ed., Miami: Mnemosyne, 1969*; facsimile ed., Freeport, N.Y.: Books for Libraries*.

BIOGRAPHY AND CRITICISM ON GRIGGS

Bone. The Negro Novel in America, pp. 6, 17, 26, 29, 32-35, 174.

Davis and Redding. Cavalcade, p. 163.

Fleming, Robert E. "Sutton E. Griggs: Militant Black Novelist." Phylon 34 (March 1973): 73-77.

Gloster. Negro Voices in American Fiction, pp. 56-67.

_____. "Sutton E. Griggs, Novelist of the New Negro."
Phylon 4 (1943): 335-345; also in Hemenway, The Black
Novelist, pp. 9-22.
Tatham, Campbell. "Reflections: Sutton Grigg's Imperium
in Imperio." Studies in Black Literature 5 (Winter 1974):
7-15.
REVIEW: The Hindered Hand.
Daniels, John. Alexander's Magazine 1 (15 October 1905):
31-32.
[1]Arthur P. Davis and J. Saunders Redding, Cavalcade
(Boston: Houghton Mifflin, 1971), p. 163.

GRIMES, Nikki. Born 20 October 1950 in New York City. Education: J.H.S. 164; William Howard Taft High School, Class of
1969. Currently living in New York City. Career: "My present involvement includes establishing myself as a community
artist and gaining the financial and spiritual support of the Black
community." (1971) She has given numerous poetry readings
at colleges, universities and for community groups.
POETRY
    Poems by Nikki. New York: Celebrated Blackness, 1970.
    (Periodicals): Black Creation, Summer 1972; Journal of
        Black Poetry, Winter-Spring 1970; Celebrated Blackness
        (a Harlem newsletter).
REVIEW: Poems by Nikki.
    Giovanni, Nikki. Black World 2 (March 1971): 87-88.
INTERJECTIONS
"I cannot conceive of art as being an essential part of life or
culture, but rather view it as a 'prophecy' of life! The main
function of a prophet (artist) being not only to bring the masses
closer to the past and present, but to also enlighten them on
the future, immediate and/or ultimate."

GRIMKE, Angelina Weld. Born 27 February 1880 in Boston, Mas-
sachusetts. Died 10 June 1958. Education: Attended Carleton
Academy, Minnesota; Cushing Academy, Massachusetts; Girls'
Latin School, Boston; Boston Normal School of Gymnastics in
1902. Career: Taught at Armstrong Manual Training School,
1902; Dunbar High School, Washington, D.C.[1]
DRAMA
    Rachel. Boston: Cornhill, 1921; (produced by the N.A.A.
        C.P. at the Neighborhood Theatre in New York);[2] reprint
        ed., Washington, D.C.: McGrath, 1969*.
NON-FICTION
    (Anthology): Brown, Davis and Lee, Negro Caravan.
    (Periodical): Opportunity 3 (February 1925): 44-47.
POETRY
    (Anthologies): Adams, Conn, and Slepian, Afro-American
        Literature: Poetry; Adoff, The Poetry of Black America;
        Barksdale and Kinnamon, Black Writers of America; Bon-
        temps, American Negro Poets; Brown, Davis and Lee,
        Negro Caravan; Byars, Black and White: An Anthology

of Washington Verse; Calverton, An Anthology of American Negro Literature; Cullen, Caroling Dusk; David, Black Joy; Hughes and Bontemps, The Poetry of the Negro: 1746-1970; Johnson, Ebony and Topaz; Kerlin, Negro Poets and Their Poems; Locke, The New Negro; Patterson, A Rock Against the Wind; Simmons and Hutchinson, Black Culture.

(Periodicals): Crisis 9 (1915): 134; 13 (1917): 222; 38 (1931): 380; Opportunity 1 (November 1923): 343; 2 (January 1924): 20; 2 (April 1924): 99; 2 (July 1924): 196; 3 (March 1925): 68.

RADIO PROGRAM
  "Let There Be Light." Lincoln Centennial Phonodisc, New York: National Council of the Churches of Christ in the United States of America Broadcasting and Film Commission, 1954 TV 21802.

BIOGRAPHY AND CRITICISM ON GRIMKE
  Bardolph. Negro Vanguard, pp. 117, 202-203, 206-207, 294.
  Barnes, Gilbert H. and Dwight L. Dumond, eds. Letters of Theodore Dwight Weld. New York: Appleton Century, 1934.
  Bontemps. The Harlem Renaissance Remembered, pp. 248, 261.
  Butcher. The Negro in American Culture, p. 101.
  Chametzky and Kaplan. Black and White in American Culture, p. 346.
  Cromwell. Readings from Negro Authors, pp. 24-25.
  Davis. The American Negro Reference Book, p. 834.
  Du Bois, W. E. B. The Gift of Black Folk, pp. 156, 302.
  Fishel and Quarles. The Black in America, p. 171.
  Gayle, Black Expression, pp. 124, 175, 178.
  Grimké, Angelina W. "Struggle Against Race Prejudice." (Biography.) Journal of Negro History 48 (October 1963): 277-291
  Jahn. Neo-African Literature, p. 211.
  Johnson, Allen and Dumas Malone. Dictionary of American Biography. New York: Chas. Scribners' Sons, 1931, p. 632.
  New York Times, 11 June 1958, 36:1. (Obituary.)
  O'Connor, Lillian. Pioneer Women Orators. New York: Columbia University Press, 1954, pp. 56-57.
  Parton, James, Horace Greeley, T. W. Higginson. Eminent Women of the Age. Hartford, Conn.: S.M. Betts, 1868, pp. 363-364.
  Pinkney, Alphonso. Black Americans. Englewood Cliffs, N.J.: Prentice-Hall, 1969, p. 147.
  Redding. They Came in Chains, p. 75.
  Stanton, E. C. et al. History of Woman Suffrage, vol. 1, 1881.
  Sterling. Speak Out in Thunder Tones, pp. 86-87.
  Weld, Theodore. "In Memory: Angelina Grimké Weld." South Carolina History and Genealogy Magazine (January

1906).
Whitton, Mary Ormsbee. These Were the Women, U.S.A.:
   1776-1860. New York: Hastings House, Inc. 1954, pp.
   126-127.
Williams. They Also Spoke, pp. 259-260.
Yenser, Thomas. Who's Who in Colored America. Brook-
   lyn, N.Y.: Yenser, 1930-1931-1932, 3rd ed., p. 180.
REVIEW: Rachel:
Fauset, Jessie. "Angelina W. Grimké's Rachel." Crisis
   21 (1920): 64.
   [1]Thomas Yenser, Who's Who in Colored America
   (Brooklyn, N.Y.: Yenser, 1930-1931-1932), p. 180.

GROSS, Werter L.
   NOVEL The Golden Recovery. Reno, Nev.: By the Author,
      1946.

GROSVENOR, Kali.
   POETRY
      Poems by Kali. Introduction by William Melvin Kelley. New
         York: Doubleday, 1970.
      (Anthology): King, Blackspirits.

GROSVENOR, Verta Mae (Verta Mae). Born 4 April 1938 in Fair-
   fax, Allendale County, South Carolina. Career: See Shockley
   and Chandler, Living Black American Authors, pp. 62-63.
   AUTOBIOGRAPHY
      Vibration Cooking: Travels of a Geechee Girl. Garden City,
         N.Y.: Doubleday, 1970.
   NON-FICTION
      Thursdays and Every Other Sunday Off: A Domestic Rap.
         Garden City, N.Y.: Doubleday, 1972.
   SHORT STORY
      (Anthology): Sanchez, We Be Word Sorcerers.
   BIOGRAPHY AND CRITICISM ON GROSVENOR
      Garland, P. "Vibes from Verta Mae." Ebony 26 (March
         1971): 86-88.

GUILLAUME, Bob.
   DRAMA Montezuma's Revenge, 1971.

GULLINS, D. Edna.
   POETRY (Anthology): Murphy, Negro Voices.

GUMEDE.
   POETRY (Periodical): Journal of Black Poetry, Summer 1972.

GUNN, Bill.
   DRAMA
      Johnnas. In The Drama Review 12 (Summer 1968). (one act).
      Marcus in the High Grass, 1960.

BIOGRAPHY AND CRITICISM ON GUNN
  Hughes and Meltzer. Black Magic, pp. 203, 214.
  "Interview with Bill Gunn." Essence 4 (October 1973): 27,
    96.

GUY, Rosa. Born 1 September 1925 in Trinidad.
  CHILDREN AND YOUNG ADULTS
    The Friends. New York: Holt, Rinehart & Winston, 1973*.
  DRAMA
    Venetian Blinds (one act), 1954.
  EDITOR
    Children of Longing. New York: Bantam, 1971†. (Non-fic-
      tion.)
  NOVEL
    Bird at My Window. Philadelphia: Lippincott, 1966.
  SHORT STORY
    (Anthology): Mayfield, Ten Times Black.
    Also published in Cosmopolitan and Freedomways.
  BIOGRAPHY AND CRITICISM ON GUY
    Contemporary Authors.

-H-

HAGOOD, Barbara Simmons. Born 18 February 1938 in Washington, D.C. Education: B.A., Howard University, 1960. Currently living in New York City. Career: Founder, President
  and Creative Director of Eden Advertising and Communications,
  Inc. Member: African American Advertising Agency Associa-
  tions; N.A.A.C.P.; Urban League; Operation Push; Media Wom-
  en. Awards, Honors: House of Kuumba Black Communications Award; New York Art Directors Award; Advertising and
  Sales Promotions Magazine Award.
  POETRY
    (Anthologies): Jones and Neal, Black Fire; Simmons and
      Hutchinson, Black Culture.
    (Periodical): Présence Africaine.
  INTERJECTIONS
    "A word fitly spoken is like apples of gold in pictures of
    silver."

HAIRSTON, Loyle. Born 1926 in Mississippi.
  CRITICISM BY HAIRSTON
    "Is Black Writing American Literature?" Freedomways 13
      (1973): 50-54.
    "William Styron's Dilemma." Freedomways 8 (Winter 1968):
      7-11.
    "William Styron's Nat Turner--Rogue-Nigger." In Clarke,
      William Styron's Nat Turner, pp. 68-72.
  REVIEWS BY HAIRSTON
    Published in Freedomways.
  SHORT STORIES
    (Anthologies): Clarke, American Negro Short Stories; Clarke,

Barbara Simmons Hagood

Harlem.
(Periodicals): <u>Freedomways</u>, Winter 1963; Spring 1969; excerpt from an unfinished novel, Summer 1967.

HAIRSTON, William.
 DRAMA
  The Honeymooners, 1967.
  Walk in Darkness, 1963.
 BIOGRAPHY AND CRITICISM ON HAIRSTON
  Mitchell. Black Drama, p. 197.

HALL, Carlyle B. Born in Washington, D.C.
 POETRY (Anthology): Murphy, Ebony Rhythm.

HALL, Douglas.
 SHORT STORY (Anthology): Ford and Faggett, Best Short Stories by Afro-American Writers.

HALL, John. Born 1943 in Cleveland, Ohio.
 POETRY (Anthology): Major, The New Black Poetry.

HALL, John E.
 POETRY (Anthology): Murphy, Negro Voices.

HALL, Kirkwood M. Born 13 May 1944 in Montclair, New Jersey.
Education: B.A. (Sociology), Virginia Union University, 1967;
graduate work at the University of Pittsburgh and Allegheny
Community College; Graduate School of Public Health, University of Pittsburgh; a candidate for the Doctor of Ministry degree at Pittsburgh Theological Seminary. Currently living in
Pittsburgh, Pennsylvania. Career: Campus Traveler and Project Director, Student Non-violent Co-ordinating Committee; Director of the Jazz-Art Society for Social Research; Consultant
to Project Woman Power of the National Council of Negro Wom-
en; Caseworker for the Department of Social Services, New
York City; Assistant Director and Director of the Ujama Circle
Cultural Center for Upper Harlem youth; Social Work Associate
II at the Community Mental Health Center, Western Psychiatric
Institute and Clinic, Pittsburgh; Group Leader at the Mount Ar-
arat Baptist Church Youth Center; Assistant Director of Black
Campus Ministries, Inc.; Campus Minister, California State Col-
lege, California, Pa.; Assistant Director of the Hill Mental
Health Team of the Community Mental Health Center, Western
Psychiatric Institute and Clinic. Member: Pennsylvania Com-
mission for United Ministries in Higher Education; Neighborhood
Advisory Board, Mercy Hospital, Pittsburgh; Create Community
Organization for Media Change; St. Francis Community Mental
Health Center, Citizen Advisory Board, Pittsburgh; Virginia Un-
ion University Alumni Association, co-chairman, Pittsburgh
chapter; National Association for the Advancement of Colored
People; Association of Black Social Workers; Association of
Black Seminarians; Pre-Trial Justice Federation of the Ameri-
can Friends Service Committee; American Orthopsychiatric As-
sociation.
POETRY
    (Anthologies): Chapman, New Black Voices; Davis, Spectrum
        in Black; Haynes, Voices of the Revolution; Jones and
        Neal, Black Fire; Porter, Connections.
    (Periodical): Journal of Black Poetry.

HALSEY, William.
    DRAMA Judgement. In Black Dialogue 4 (Spring 1969): 40-43.

HAMER, Martin J. Born 24 November 1931 in New York City.
    POETRY
        (Periodical): Negro Digest, September 1962.
    SHORT STORIES
        (Anthologies): Adoff, Brothers and Sisters; Clarke, Ameri-
            can Negro Short Stories; Foley, Best American Short Sto-
            ries of 1965; Patterson, An Introduction to Black Litera-
            ture in America.
        (Periodicals): Negro Digest, June 1962; also published in
            The Atlantic.

HAMILTON, Bobb. Born 16 December 1928 in Cleveland, Ohio.
    Career: See Shockley and Chandler, Living Black American
    Authors, pp. 66-67.

POETRY
  (Anthologies): Adoff, Black Out Loud; Alhamisi and Wangara,
    Black Arts; Brooks, A Broadside Treasury; Jones and
    Neal, Black Fire; Lomax and Abdul, 3000 Years of Black
    Poetry; Pool, Beyond the Blues; Randall and Burroughs,
    For Malcolm.
  (Periodical): Negro Digest, September-October 1968.
SHORT STORY
  (Periodical): Negro Digest, March 1965.

HAMILTON, Kiilu Anthony.
  DRAMA
    With Otis Smith and Richard Dedeaux. The Rising Sons--
      Wisdom and Knowledge. Los Angeles: The Watts Proph-
      ets, 1973.

HAMILTON, Roland T.
  SHORT STORY (Anthology): Ford and Faggett, Best Short
    Stories by Afro-American Writers.

HAMILTON, Sarah B. Edmonds.
  POETRY Out of My Heart: Poems. New York: Exposition,
    1961.

HAMILTON, Richard T. Born 31 March 1869 in Montgomery, Alabama. Education: Attended Alabama State Normal School and
  was graduated Valedictorian, 1890. Received M.D., Howard
  University, 1893. Career: Taught elementary school; became
  a clerk in the U.S. Department of the Interior; in 1901, practiced medicine in Dallas. Was president of the National Association of Life Insurance Medical Examiners.[1]
  POETRY
    (Anthology): Brewer, Heralding Dawn.
      [1]J. Mason Brewer, Heralding Dawn (Dallas, Texas:
    June Tomason Printing, 1936), p. 7.

HAMILTON, Virginia. Born in Yellow Springs, Ohio. Education:
  Attended Antioch College, Ohio State University, and the New
  School for Social Research. Currently living in Ohio. Career:
  Mrs. Hamilton describes herself as "a writer of 'books for
  children'--a rather arbitrary category in which books 'children'
  are the main characters. Juvenile fiction and biography is in
  no way a lesser category than its adult counterpart, but one of
  stringent and specific requirements." Awards, Honors: John
  Newbery Honor Book Award for The Planet of Junior Brown,
  1971; Edgar Award for Best Juvenile Mystery of 1968 for The
  House of Dies Drear; five of her books are ALA Notable Books.
  CHILDREN AND YOUNG ADULTS
    House of Dies Drear. New York: Macmillan, 1970*†.
    Planet of Junior Brown. New York: Macmillan, 1971*.
    Tales of Jahdu. New York: Macmillan, 1969.
    Time-Ago Lost: More Tales of Jahdu. New York: Macmil-
      lan, 1969*.

W. E. B. Du Bois: A Biography. New York: T. Y. Crowell,
   1972*.
Zeely. New York: Macmillan, 1971†.
BIOGRAPHY ON HAMILTON
   Commire. Something About the Author, vol. 4, pp. 97-98.
INTERJECTIONS
   "I am rather committed to the written word and its impor-
   tance to freedom of thought. I do not believe that life is a re-
   flection of art; or that art mirrors life. Rather, that art must
   be the essence of how and why we live."

HAMMON, Briton. Nothing is known about this prose writer who
   bore the same surname as that of the poet, Jupiter. The only
   information found in a 14-page pamphlet, ascribed to him, gives
   an account of a Negro who left Plymouth, Massachusetts at the
   end of the year 1747 to go to Jamaica. His tale involves a
   shipwreck, captivity among Florida Indians, imprisonment, escape to England, and an accidental meeting with his master in
   1760.[1] According to Maria Whitman Bryant, Hammon's owner
   may have been General John Winslow (1703-1774).[2] Baskin and
   Runes hold that his only piece of writing is of historical rather
   than literary interest, foreshadowing a fact of black literary history. The autobiographical narrative became the first genre of
   prose writing of literary importance to Black writings.[3]
AUTOBIOGRAPHY
   A Narrative of the Uncommon Sufferings, and Surprising De-
      liverance of Briton Hammon, a Negro Man-Servant to Gen-
      eral Winslow. Boston.
NON-FICTION
   (Anthologies): Patterson, An Introduction to Black Literature
      in America; Porter, Early Negro Writing 1760-1837.
BIOGRAPHY AND CRITICISM ON HAMMON
   Baskin and Runes. Dictionary of Black Culture, p. 197.
   Bergman, Peter. The Negro in America, p. 28.
   Brawley. The Negro Genius, p. 16.
   Emanuel and Gross. Dark Symphony, pp. 7, 365.
   Hornsby, Alton, Jr. The Black Almanac, pp. 4-5.
   Jahn. Neo-African Literature, pp. 40, 48.
   Loggins. The Negro Author in America, pp. 30-31, 95, 271,
      373, 411.
   Wesley, Charles H. In Freedom's Footsteps, p. 122.
         [1]Vernon Loggins, The Negro Author (Port Washington,
      New York: Kennikat Press, 1959), pp. 30-31.
         [2]Ibid., p. 373 (cf. f.n. 85).
         [3]Wade Baskin and Richard Runes, Dictionary of Black
      Culture (New York: Philosophical Library, 1973), p. 197.

HAMMON, Jupiter. Born 1720, an African slave held in the services of the Lloyd family of Lloyd's Neck, Long Island. Died
   1806. Jupiter Hammon's name may have been selected and associated with the ancient Egyptian-African Deity called "Jupiter
   Ammon."[1] Career: He lived his entire life with the Lloyds.
   In Hammon's later years, the slave holder helped him place his

verse before the public. "His first poem antedated several years that of Phyllis Wheatley who is commonly regarded as the first Negro author in American literature. Only one original copy, that of the Connecticut Historical Society is now known to exist."[2] The last definitive reference to Hammon bears the date, 6 October 1770, when he was sent by his master with money to pay a debt. The most accessible source, and at this time, practically the sole authority on Hammon is Oscar Weglin's Jupiter Hammon, American Negro Poet: Selections from His Writings and a Bibliography.[3]

COLLECTION

America's First Negro Poet: The Complete Works of Jupiter Hammon of Long Island. Edited by Stanley A. Ransom. Port Washington, N.Y.: Kennikat, 1969*.

NON-FICTION

An Address to the Negroes of the State of New York. New York: Gordon*.

Phillis Wheatley (Six broadsides). New York: C. F. Heartman, 1915.

(Anthologies): Bergman. The Negro in America, Kendricks and Levitt, Afro-American Voices, Davis, The American Negro Reference Book; Woodson, Carter G., ed. The Mind of the Negro as Reflected in Letters Written During the Crisis 1800-1860.

EXTANT POEMS

An Evening Thought, 1760.
An Address to Miss Phillis Wheatley, 1778.
A Poem for Children with Thoughts on Death, 1782.
The Kind Master and Dutiful Servant (date unknown).
These are included in Oscar Weglin's Jupiter Hammon, American Negro Poet. cf. section on Biography and Criticism in this entry.[4]

POETRY

(Anthologies): Barksdale and Kinnamon, Black Writers of America; Brawley, Early Negro American Writing; Long and Collier, Afro-American Writing; Miller, Blackamerican Literature; Robinson, Early Black American Poets; Rollins, Famous American Negro Poets.

BIOGRAPHY AND CRITICISM ON HAMMON

Adams. Great Negroes Past and Present, p. 147.
Barksdale and Kinnamon. Black Writers of America, pp. 45-46.
Bardolph. The Negro Vanguard, pp. 32-33.
Baskin and Runes. Dictionary of Black Culture, p. 197.
Bergman. The Negro in America, p. 28.
Brawley. Early Negro American Writers, pp. 20-21.
_____. The Negro Genius, pp. 16-19, 30.
_____. The Negro in Literature and Art, pp. 12-14.
Butcher. The Negro in American Culture, p. 96.
Davis. The American Negro Reference Book, p. 851.
Du Bois. The Gift of Black Folk, p. 304.
Gayle. Black Expression, pp. 59-63, 66, 70-71, 109.
Greene. The Negro in Colonial New England, p. 242.

Hornsby. The Black Almanac, pp. 4-5.
Jahn. Neo-African Literature, pp. 41, 48, 51.
Kerlin. Negro Poets and Their Poems, pp. 20-23, 338-339.
Loggins. The Negro Author in America, pp. 9-16, 25, 27,
    110, 115, 248, 282, 332, 354, 369, 374, 393, 408-409,
    411.
Malone, Dumas, ed. Dictionary of American Biography.
    New York: Scribner's Sons, 1932, pp. 201-202.
Mays. The Negro's God, pp. 97, 100-102, 246, 248.
Negroes of New York: Biographical Sketches. Compiled by
    Members of Writer's Workshop. New York. 1938-41.
Oxley, Thomas L. G. "Survey of Negro Literature, 1760-
    1926," The Messenger 9 (February 1927): 37-39.
Patterson. An Introduction to Black Literature in America,
    p. 27.
Ploski and Kaiser. The Negro Almanac, pp. 3, 196, 678.
Porter. Early Negro Writing 1760-1837, pp. 313, 529, 535.
Redding. They Came in Chains, p. 145.
Robinson. Early Black American Poets, pp. 5-7.
Robinson. Historical Negro Biographies, p. 7.
Rollin, Frank A. (Mrs. Francis Whipper). Life and Public
    Services of Martin R. Delany. Boston, 1883, p. 16.
Thorpe. Black Historians. New York: Wm. Morrow, 1971,
    p. 32.
Weglin, Oscar. Jupiter Hammon, American Negro Poet.
    New York: C. F. Heartman, 1915. (Bibliography.)
White and Jackson. An Anthology of Verse by American Ne-
    groes, pp. 3-4, 220-221, 235.
Williams. They Also Spoke, pp. 8-17, 30-36, 48-49, 107,
    115-116, 120, 122, 276, 284.
Woodson. The Mind of the Negro as Reflected in Letters
    Written During the Crisis. p. vi.
Woodson, Carter G. and Charles H. Wesley. The Negro in
    Our History. Washington: Associated, 1966, p. 469.
    [1]William H. Robinson, Jr., Early Black American Po-
    ets (Dubuque, Iowa: William C. Brown, 1969), p. 5.
    [2]Dumas Malone, ed., Dictionary of American Biogra-
    phy, vol. 8 (New York: Scribner's Sons, 1932), p. 201.
    [3]Ibid., p. 202.
    [4]Robert T. Kerlin, Negro Poets and Their Poems
    (Washington, D.C.: Associated, 1935), p. 338.

HAMMOND, Basil Calvin.
    POETRY Something to Remember: Poems. New York: Exposi-
    tion, 1960.

HAMMOND, Mrs. J. W. Education: Self-taught. Career: Trained
    nurse.
    POETRY
        (Anthology): Kerlin, Negro Poets and Their Poems.
        (Newspaper): The Monitor (Omaha, Nebraska).

HANCOCK, Dorothy.
    POETRY (Periodical): Journal of Black Poetry, Summer 1972.

HAND, Q. R., Jr. Born 1937 in Brooklyn.
    POETRY (Anthologies): Afro-Arts Anthology; Jones and Neal,
       Black Fire.

HANKINS, Paula.
    SHORT STORY (Anthology): King, Black Short Story Anthology.

HANNIBAL, Gregor.
    POETRY (Anthology): Henderson, Understanding the New Black
       Poetry.

HANSBERRY, Lorraine. Born May 1930 in Chicago. Died 16 Janu-
    ary 1965. Education: Studied painting at the Art Institute of
    Chicago, and in Guadalajara, Mexico; also studied at the Univer-
    sity of Wisconsin for two years, and at the New School for So-
    cial Research. Career: Moved to New York City in 1950 where
    she worked at an assortment of jobs and began writing plays and
    short stories. Raisin in the Sun was completed in 1957, and re-
    ceived the New York Drama Critics' Circle Award for the Best
    American Play of 1958-59 when it went on Broadway that season.
    Raisin was the first Broadway play to be written by a Black
    woman, and it was the first time a Black director had worked
    on Broadway since 1907.[1] After her death, her husband, Ro-
    bert Nemiroff, and Burton D'Lugoff adapted many of her person-
    al notes, unpublished works, and parts of published works for
    the production, To Be Young, Gifted and Black, which opened
    on Broadway in November 1969.[2] Miss Hansberry was an ac-
    tive member of the Association of Artists for Freedom and the
    Harlem Writers' Guild.[3]
    AUTOBIOGRAPHY
       To Be Young, Gifted and Black: A Portrait of Lorraine Hans-
          berry in Her Own Words. Edited by Robert Nemiroff.
          Englewood Cliffs, N.J.: Prentice-Hall, 1969*; New York:
          New American Library, 1970†; New York: Samuel French,
          1971†.
    CRITICISM BY HANSBERRY
       "American Theatre Needs Desegregating Too." Negro Digest
          10 (June 1961): 28-33.
       "A Challenge to Artists." Freedomways 3 (Winter 1963):
          33-35. (Speech for the abolition of the House UnAmeri-
          can Activities Committee.)
       "Genet, Mailer and the New Paternalism." Village Voice 1
          June 1961, p. 10-15.
       "The Legacy of W. E. B. Du Bois." In Black Titan: W.E.
          B. Du Bois.
       "A Letter from Lorraine Hansberry on Porgy and Bess."
          The Theater (August 1959): 10.
       "Me Tink Me Hear Sounds in De Night." Theatre Arts 44
          (October 19): 9-11, 69-70. Reprinted as "The Negro in
          the American Theater" in American Playwrights on Drama.

Edited by Horst Frenz. New York: Hill & Wang, 1965.

"The Nation Needs Your Gifts." Negro Digest 13 (August 1964): 26-29.

"The Negro in American Culture." In Bigsby, The Black American Writer, vol. 1. (Symposium.)

DRAMA

Les Blancs: The Last Collected Plays of Lorraine Hansberry Edited by Robert Nemiroff. New York: Random House, 1972*†. (Includes the television play "The Drinking Gourd"; "Les Blancs"; "What Use Are Flowers?")

A Raisin in the Sun. New York: Random House, 1961*; New American Library, 1961†; New York: Samuel French, 1961†. Also in Adams, Conn and Slepian, Afro-American Literature: Drama; Cerf, Plays of Our Time, Cerf, Six American Plays for Today; Kronenberger, The Best Plays of 1958-59 (condensed); Oliver and Sills, Black Drama; Patterson, Black Theater; excerpts in Childress, Black Scenes; Chambers and Moon, Right On!; Kendricks and Levitt, Afro-American Voices.

This play was also published in Theatre Arts 44 (October 1960).

The Sign in Sidney Brustein's Window. New York: Random House, 1965*; New York: Samuel French, 1965†. Included in Three Negro Plays. Harmondsworth, England: Penguin, 1969. Also in Gassner and Barnes, Best American Plays, 6th Ser.

NON-FICTION

The Movement: Documentary of a Struggle for Equality. New York: Simon & Schuster, 1964*†.

(Periodicals): Ebony, August 1960; Freedomways, Winter 1963; Negro Digest, August 1964; National Guardian, 4 July 1964, pp. 5-9; New York Times Magazine, 26 March 1961, p. 4; The Urbanite, May 1961; The Village Voice, 12 August 1959, p. 8; 23 July 1964, pp. 10-16.

POETRY

(Anthology): Hansberry, To Be Young, Gifted and Black.

(Periodical): Masses and Mainstream, September 1950; July 1951.

BIBLIOGRAPHIES ON HANSBERRY

Gordon, Carolyn. "Lorraine Hansberry." CAAS Bibliography No. 1, Atlanta, Ga.: Center for African and African-American Studies, n.d. (Mimeographed.)

Williams, Ora. American Black Women in the Arts and Social Sciences. Metuchen, N.J.: Scarecrow, 1973.

BIOGRAPHY AND CRITICISM ON HANSBERRY

Abramson. The Negro Playwrights in the American Theatre, pp. 239-254.

Adams, George R. "Black Militant Drama." American Imago 28: 107-128.

Alvarez, A. "That Evening Sun." New Statesman 58 (15 August 1959): 190.

Baldwin, James. "Sweet Lorraine." Esquire 72 (November 1969): 139-140.

Bigsby. Confrontation and Commitment, pp. 54, 122-123, 138, 154, 156-173.

Brien, Alan. "Suspected Persons." Spectator 203 (14 August 1959): 189, 191.

Clurman, Harold. "Theatre." Nation, 4 April 1959, p. 301.

Cruse. The Crisis of the Negro Intellectual, pp. 10-252, passim, 268-283, 409-413, 418-525 passim.

Current Biography, 1959.

Dannett. Profiles of Negro Womanhood, p. 190.

Davis, Ossie. "The Significance of Lorraine Hansberry." Freedomways 5 (Summer 1965): 396-402.

Driver, Tom F. "A Raisin in the Sun." New Republic, 13 April 1959, p. 21.

Farrison, W. Edward. "Lorraine Hansberry's Last Dramas." CLA Journal 16 (December 1972).

Fleming, Alice. Pioneers in Print. Chicago: Reilly & Lee, 1971, pp. 100-113.

Gassner, John. Dramatic Soundings: Evaluations and Retractions culled from Thirty Years of Dramatic Criticism. New York: Crown, 1968, pp. 579-580.

Harrison. The Drama of Nommo, pp. 6-7, 200-202.

Hays, Peter L. "Raisin in the Sun and Juno and the Paycock." Phylon 33 (Summer 1972): 175-176.

Holtan, Orley I. "Sidney Brustein and the Plight of the American Intellectual." Players 46: 222-225.

Hughes and Meltzer. Black Magic, pp. 228-231.

Isaacs, Harold R. "Five Writers and Their African Ancestors." Phylon 28 (Fourth Quarter 1960): 329-336.

_____. The New World of Negro Americans, pp. 277-287.

Killens, John O. "Broadway in Black and White." African Forum 1 (1965): 66-70.

Laufe, Abe. Anatomy of a Hit: Long Run Plays on Broadway from 1900 to the Present Day, pp. 297-302.

Lerner, Max. "A Dream Deferred." New York Post, 5 April 1959.

Lewis, Theophilus. "Social Protest in A Raisin in the Sun?" Catholic World (October 1959): 31-35.

"Liberalism and the Negro--a Round-Table Discussion." Commentary (March 1964): 25-42.

Littlejohn. Black on White, pp. 68-72.

"Lorraine Hansberry's World." Liberator (December 1964): 9. (Also a review of The Sign in Sidney Brustein's Window, p. 25.)

Lumley, Frederick. New Trends in 20th Century Drama. London: Barrie & Rockliff, 1960, p. 339.

Miller, Jordan. "Lorraine Hansberry." In Bigsby, The Black American Writer, vol. 2, pp. 157-170.

Mitchell. Black Drama, pp. 29, 180-182, 191, 202-204.

"Negro Playwrights." Ebony 14 (April 1950): 95-100.

Nemiroff, Robert. "Introduction." The Sign in Sidney Brustein's Window. New York: Random House, 1965.

New York Times, 11 October 1964, sec. 2, pp. 1, 3.

"People Are Talking About..." Vogue 133 (June 1959): 78-79.

Ploski and Kaiser. The Negro Almanac, pp. 685-686.

Robertson, Nan. "Dramatist Against Odds." New York Times, 8 March 1959, sec. 2, p. 3.

Toppin. Biographical History of Blacks in America Since 1528, pp. 312-313.

Trewin, J. C. "Promise and Performance." Illustrated London News 235 (12 September 1959): 246.

Turner, Darwin. "The Black Playwrights in the Professional Theatre of the United States of America 1858-1959." In Bigsby, The Black American Writer, vol. 2, pp. 126-128.

Tynan, Kenneth. Curtains: Selections from the Drama Criticism and Related Writings. New York: Atheneum, 1961, pp. 306-309.

Variety, 27 May 1959, p. 16.

The Village Voice, 6 June 1963. (Interview.)

Weales, Gerald. "Thoughts on 'a Raisin in the Sun.'" Commentary 28 (1959): 527-530.

White, E. B. "Talk of the Town." New Yorker, 9 May 1959, p. 335.

Whitlow. Black American Literature, pp. 141-145.

REVIEWS

The Sign in Sidney Brustein's Window:

Carten, John. "Hansberry's Potpourri." New Yorker, 24 October 1964, p. 93.

Ness, D. E. Freedomways 11 (1971): 359-366.

Redding, Saunders. Crisis 73 (March 1966): 175-176.

[1]Current Biography 1959, p. 166.

[2]Gordon, Carolyn, "Lorraine Hansberry," CAAS Bibliographies (Atlanta, Ga.: Center for African and African-American Studies, n.d.), (mimeographed).

[3]Harold Cruse. The Crisis of the Negro Intellectual (New York: Morrow, 1967), pp. 193-238 passim.

HARDEMAN, Beaureguard, Jr. (B. Rap). Born 17 November 1944 in Macon, Georgia. Education: B.S., Morehouse College. Currently living in San Francisco, California. Career: Mathematician, poet, publisher, teacher. Presently employed in the Information Science and Engineering Division of Stanford Research Institute. His "cultural crossword puzzles" have been published in Essence.

POETRY

Metamorphosis of Supernigger: Ten Poems. San Francisco: By the Author, 1973.

Revolution Is. San Francisco: By the Author, P.O. Box 40158, n.d.

INTERJECTIONS

"There is a split in life right down the middle between the two poles of feeling and reason, Humanlike things gravitate in the direction of one or both of these to some degree."

HARDING, Vincent. Born 25 July 1931 in New York City. Career: See Shockley and Chandler, Living Black American Authors.

CRITICISM
    "You've Taken My Hat and Gone." In Clarke, William Styron's Nat Turner, pp. 23-33.
NON-FICTION
    (Anthologies): Barbour, The Black Power Revolt, pp. 85-93; Young, Dissent, pp. 319-354.
    (Periodicals): Crisis, February 1963; Ebony, September 1969; February 1970; Negro Digest, November 1966; February, March 1968; March 1969.
POETRY
    To The Gallant Black Men Now Dead. Atlanta: By the Author, 1967; also in Negro Digest, February 1968.

HARDNETT, Linda G.
    POETRY
    (Anthology): Shuman, A Galaxy of Black Writing.
    SHORT STORY
    (Anthology): Shuman, A Galaxy of Black Writing.

HARE, Nathan. Born 9 April 1934 in Slick, Oklahoma. Education: A.B., Langston University, 1954; M.A., University of Chicago, 1957; Ph.D., University of Chicago, 1962. Career: Instructor, Virginia State College, 1957-58; Assistant Professor, Howard University, 1961-67; Chairman, Department of Black Studies, San Francisco State College, 1968-. (Was the first co-ordinator of a Black Studies Program in the U.S.) Publisher of the Black Scholar.
EDITOR
    With Robert Chrisman. Contemporary Black Thought: The Best from The Black Scholar. Indianapolis: Bobbs-Merrill, 1973*†.
EDITORIALS
    See Black Scholar, 1969-.
NON-FICTION
    Black Anglo-Saxons. New York: Macmillan, 1970†.
    (Anthology): Jones and Neal, Black Fire; In The Death of White Sociology, Edited by J. A. Ladner (New York: Random, 1973); in New Perspectives in Black Studies. Edited by J. W. Blassingame (Urbana: University of Illinois Press.)
    (Periodicals): Published regularly in The Black Scholar and Negro Digest/Black World.
INTERJECTIONS
    "Art must be related to the daily lives of the people and express their needs and aspirations. Black art must, therefore, be art for social change."

HARGRAY, Lorrence.
    POETRY (Periodical): Journal of Black Poetry, Spring 1969.

HARKKON, Omar.
    POETRY (Periodical): Journal of Black Poetry, 1969.

Nathan Hare

HARLESTON, Edward Nathaniel.
POETRY The Toiler's Life: Poems. Introduction by L. S.
  Crandall. Philadelphia: Jenson Press, 1907; facsimile
  ed., Freeport, N.Y.: Books for Libraries*.

HARPER, Frances Ellen Watkins.[1] Born 1825 of free parents in
Baltimore. Died 22 February 1911. Education: She attended
a school for free Negroes conducted by her uncle, William Watkins. At the ages of 13 her education was interrupted and she
was forced to earn her own living as a nursemaid.[2] Later,
she continued her education in Pennsylvania and Ohio.[3] Career:
In 1850, taught domestic science at Union Seminary in Columbus, Ohio; three years later she taught in Little York, Pennsylvania.[4] It was in Little York where she saw her first fleeing
fugitive slave; she was also moved by the true story of the
death of a free Negro who unwittingly had violated Maryland's
laws that forbade free Negroes from entering the State, upon
pain of imprisonment and sale into slavery.[5] The free Negro
who had been caught was sold into slavery into Georgia and had
escaped; before he could reach the North, he was discovered,
remanded to slavery and later died. It was upon his grave
where Frances vowed and pledged herself to the Anti-Slavery
Cause.[6] Later, she wrote, "It may be that God Himself has
written upon my heart and brain a commission to use time, talent and energy in the cause of Freedom." Taking up her cause
in earnest, she volunteered her services to the Anti-Slavery Society as a lecturer. Travelling, she visited Philadelphia, New
Bedford, and Boston. She became so popular as a lecturer
that on 28 September 1854, she was engaged by the Anti-Slavery
Society of Maine as a permanent lecturer.[7] She also travelled
from the North to the South, often speaking under trying conditions.
     After the war, she devoted her time as lecturer and writer
as a representative of the Women's Christian Temperance Union
until her death in 1911. In November 1922, at the World's
W.C.T.U. held in Philadelphia, she was accorded a special
honor when her name was placed on the Red Letter Calendar.[8]
     Her literary career began in 1854 with the publication of her
volume of poems: Poems on Miscellaneous Subjects which sold
10,000 copies in its first five years.[9] Among her writings are
her letters which appear in William Stills, The Underground
Railroad.[10]
NON-FICTION
  Bartram, John. Diary of a Journey Through the Carolina,
    Georgia, and Florida: July 1, 1775-April 10, 1776. (An-
    notated by Frances Harper) Philadelphia: The Philosophical
    Society, 1942.
  "Is Money the Answer?" The Anglo-African, May 1859.
    Reprinted in In Their Own Words: A History of the Amer-
    ican Negro 1619-1865. Edited by Milton Meltzer. New
    York: T. Y. Crowell, 1964, pp. 133-134.
  "Sketches" in Men of Maryland. George F. Bragg. Balti-
    more: Church Advocate Press, 1914.

Women Against Slavery.   New York: Masses and Mainstream, 1955.

(Periodicals): Anglo-African Magazine, Vol. I, 1859, pp. 283-287; Crisis 1 (April 1911): 20.

NOVEL

Iola Leroy: Or Shadows Uplifted.   Philadelphia: Garrigues Bros., 1893; New York: Panther House, 1968*†; New York: AMS Press*; Washington, D.C.: McGrath, 1969*.

POETRY

Atlanta Offering.   Philadelphia: Geo. S. Ferguson, 1895; Freeport, N.Y.: Books for Libraries*.

Effie Afton.   Eventide (Poems & Tales).   Boston: Ferridge, 1854.

Forest Leaves.   Baltimore: Author, 1855.

Idylls of the Bible.   Philadelphia: By the Author, 1901; New York: AMS Press*.

Moses; A Story of the Nile.   2nd ed. Philadelphia: By the Author, 1889; Philadelphia: Menihew and Sons, 1869.

Poems.   Philadelphia: Menihew and Sons, 1871.

Poems.   Philadelphia: Geo. S. Ferguson, 1895; facsimile ed., Freeport, N.Y.: Books for Libraries*.

Poems.   Philadelphia, 1900.

Poems on Miscellaneous Subjects.   Philadelphia: J. B. Yerrinton & Son, 1854.   2nd Series. Philadelphia: Menihew & Son, 1864.

Sketches of Southern Life.   Philadelphia: Menihew, 1872; Philadelphia: Ferguson, 1888.

The Sparrow's Fall and Other Poems, n.p., n.d.

(Anthologies): Adams, Conn and Slepian, Afro-American Literature: Poetry; Atlanta Offerings: Poems, 1895 (Miami: Mnemosyne, 1969); Barksdale and Kinnamon, Black Writers of America; Brawley, Early Negro American Writers; Brown, Davis and Lee, Negro Caravan; Calverton, An Anthology of American Negro Literature; Chambers and Moon, Right On!; Davis and Redding, Cavalcade; Eleazer, Singers in the Dawn; Hayden, Kaleidoscope; Hughes and Bontemps, Poetry of the Negro: 1746-1970; Kendricks and Levitt, Afro-American Voices; Kerlin, Negro Posts and Their Poems; Lomax and Abdul, 3000 Years of Black Poetry; Long and Collier, Afro-American Writing; Majors, Noted Negro Women, pp. 361-363.   Patterson, An Introduction to Black Literature in America; Patterson, A Rock Against the Wind; Randall, The Black Poets; Robinson, Early Black American Poets; Walrond and Pool, Black and Unknown Bards.

(Periodicals): Anglo-African Magazine, Volume I, 1859, pp. 123, 160, 253.

BIOGRAPHY AND CRITICISM ON HARPER

Adams.   Great Negroes Past and Present, p. 147.

Barksdale and Kinnamon.   Black Writers of America, pp. 224-225.

Bardolph.   The Negro Vanguard, p. 80.

Baskin and Runes.   Dictionary of Black Culture, pp. 201-202.

Brawley. Early Negro Writers, pp. 290-292.
_____. Negro Builders and Heroes, p. 234.
_____. The Negro Genius, pp. 116-120.
_____. The Negro in Art and Literature, pp. 44-45, 138.
Bontemps. The Harlem Renaissance Remembered, pp. 63-
   64, 74, 80.
Dannett. Profiles of Negro Womanhood, pp. 102-109.
Davis. The American Negro Reference Book, pp. 35, 854-
   856.
Davis and Redding. Cavalcade, pp. 53, 101.
Du Bois, W. E. B. The Gift of Black Folk, pp. 300-304.
Gayle, Black Expression, pp. 73, 207.
Gloster. Negro Voices in American Literature, pp. 30-31,
   33, 34, 56, 99.
Goldstein, Rhoda L. Black Life and Culture in the United
   States. New York: T. Y. Crowell, 1971, p. 186.
Hughes, Carl M. The Negro Novelist, p. 37.
Jahn. Neo-African Literature, pp. 131, 138, 140.
Jet 23 February 1961, p. 9; 24 February 1966, p. 11.
Kerlin. Negro Poets and Their Poems, pp. 26-32.
Loggins. The Negro Author in America, pp. 211, 245-249,
   324-326.
Majors. Noted Negro Women, pp. 23-27.
Mays. The Negro's God, pp. 118, 120.
Negro History Bulletin (January 1942): 83, 96.
"Negro Novelists Blazing the Way in Fiction." Negro History
   Bulletin 2 (December 1938): 17.
O'Connor, Lillian. Pioneer Women Orators. New York:
   Columbia University Press, 1954.
Oxley, Thomas L. G. "Survey of Negro Literature, 1760-
   1926." The Messenger 9 (February 1927): 37-39.
Ploski and Kaiser. The Negro Almanac, pp. 678-679.
Redding. They Came in Chains, pp. 103, 210.
Riggins, Linda A. "The Works of Frances E. W. Harper."
   Black World 22 (December 1972): 30-36.
Robinson. Historical Negro Biographies, p. 88.
Rollins. Famous American Negro Poets, pp. 22-27.
_____. They Showed the Way, pp. 80-82.
Sillen, Samuel. Women Against Slavery. New York: Masses
   & Mainstream, 1955.
Tischler. Black Masks, p. 150.
Williams. They Also Spoke, pp. 120-136, 143, 217, 223,
   243, 269.
Woodson, Carter G. and Charles H. Wesley. The Negro in
   Our History. Washington: Associated, 1922, p. 469.

MULTI-MEDIA MATERIALS
"Negroes of Achievement: 1865-1915." Chicago: Afro-
   American, 1968. (Study Prints.)
"The Negro Woman." Paramus, N.J.: American Library
   and Educational Service Co., 1966. (LP 2 sides, 33-1/3
   rpm monaural.)

INTERJECTIONS
"Make me a grave where'er you will,

In a lowly plain, or a lofty hill,
Make it among earth's humblest graves,
But not in a land where men are slaves."[11]

[1]The reader may also wish to confer Watkins as well
as Harper when researching further information about
Frances Ellen.

[2]Harry Ploski and Ernest Kaiser, eds., The Negro Almanac (New York: Bellwether, 1971), p. 679.

[3]Richard Barksdale and Keneth Kinnamon, Black
Writers in America (New York: Macmillan, 1972), p. 224.

[4]Benjamin Brawley, Early Negro American Writers
(Freeport, N.Y.: Books for Libraries, 1968), p. 290.

[5]William H. Robinson, Jr., ed., Early Black American Poets (Dubuque, Iowa, Wm. C. Brown, 1969): p. 26.

[6]Brawley, p. 290.

[7]Hallie Q. Brown, Homespun Heroines (Freeport, N.Y.:
Books for Libraries, 1971), p. 99.

[8]Ibid., p. 103.

[9]Ploski, p. 679.

[10]Barksdale and Kinnamon, p. 225.

[11]Brown, p. 101.

HARPER, Michael S. Born 18 March 1938 in Brooklyn. Education: B.A., Los Angeles State College, 1961; M.A., University of Iowa, 1963; M.A., Los Angeles State College, 1963;
post-doctoral fellow, University of Illinois, 1970-71. Currently
living in Providence, Rhode Island. Career: Taught for five
years in the San Francisco Bay Area; was poet-in-residence at
Lewis and Clark College and Visiting Professor in Literature,
Reed College; served as English Professor at California State
College at Hayward; joined the faculty at Brown University in
1970 where he is a director of the writing program. Member:
African Continuum. Awards, Honors: 1971 National Book
Award Nominee; recipient of an Award in Literature from the
National Institute of Arts and Letters, 1971; honored at the
Third Annual Awards Banquet of the Black Academy of Arts and
Letters, Inc., 1972, for his second published book of poetry,
History Is Your Own Heartbeat.

EDITOR
  Heartblow: Black Veils. Urbana: University of Illinois
    Press forthcoming.

POETRY
  Dear John, Dear Coltrane. Pittsburgh: University of Pitts-
    burgh Press, 1970†.
  Debridement. new ed., Garden City, N.Y.: Doubleday,
  History Is Your Own Heartbeat: Poems. Urbana: Univer-
    sity of Illinois Press, 1971*†.
  Nightmare Begins Responsibility. Urbana: University of Illi-
    nois Press, forthcoming.
  Photographs: Negatives: History as Apple Tree. San Fran-
    cisco: Scarab Press, 1973*†.
  Song: I Want a Witness. Pittsburgh: University of Pitts-
    burgh Press, 1972*†.

(Anthologies): Adoff, The Poetry of Black America; Brown,
Lee and Ward, To Gwen with Love; Colley and Moore,
Starting with Poetry; Henderson, Understanding the New
Black Poetry; Randall, The Black Poets; Wilentz and
Weatherly, Natural Process.
(Periodicals): Black Scholar, March 1970; Black World,
September 1973; Chicago Review, Spring 1971; Negro
American Literature Forum, Spring 1972; Negro Digest,
September-October 1968; September 1969; Poetry, Febru-
ary 1968; also published in Poetry Northwest; Quarterly
Review of Literature; Southern Review; december.

WORK IN PROGRESS
Completing a narrative poem on W. E. B. Du Bois.

BIOGRAPHY AND CRITICISM ON HARPER
Contemporary Authors, 33/36.
Kent. "Struggle for the Image," p. 312.
O'Brien. Interviews with Black Writers, pp. 95-107.

REVIEW: Song: I Want a Witness
Palmer, R. Roderick. CLA Journal 16 (June 1973): 529-
531.

INTERJECTIONS
"The function of black art will be the revitalization of the
community. Artists are gifted priests whose duty it is to trans-
late tradition into modal forms. ART IS TESTAMENTAL."

HARRELD, Claudia White.
POETRY Remembered Encounters. Atlanta: Logan Press,
1951.

HARRELL, Dennis. Born 1949.
POETRY (Anthology): Shuman, A Galaxy of Black Writing.

HARRIS, Bill.
DRAMA No Use Crying, 1969.

HARRIS, Helen C.
POETRY
With Lucia Mae Pitts and Tomi Carolyn Tinsley. Triad:
Poems. Washington, D.C.: Plymouth Press, 1945.
(Anthology): Murphy, Ebony Rhythm.

HARRIS, Herman K., II. Born 8 April 1940 in Heath Springs,
South Carolina. Education: A.A., Friendship Junior College,
1960; B.S., Morris College, 1964. Currently living in Rock
Hill, South Carolina. Career: Athletic coordinator; instructor
of physical education; basketball coach; instructor of modern
and contemporary poetry; Minister of Poetry at Friendship Junior College.
POETRY
Hillside Review, 1969; Joy publications, 1971; Longview Journal, 1970; Modern Poetry of America, 1972; New Dawn
publications, 1973; New Writings in South Carolina, 1969;
Night publications, 1969, 1971, 1972; North American

      <u>Mentor</u>, 1970, 1971, 1972, 1973; <u>Painted Poetry Appreci-
ation,</u> 1971.
<u>INTERJECTIONS</u>
  "Live free and leave a print in history."

HARRIS, James Leon. <u>Born</u> 20 May 1934 in New York City.
<u>Education:</u> A graduate of the High School of Art and Design,
and of the Mayer School of Fashion. <u>Currently living in</u> New
York City. <u>Career:</u> Presently working in the advertising field
as a commercial artist on the staff of Mays Department Store.
He composes religious music and directs the True Heart Gospel Singers. He has danced professionally with the Curtis
James Dancers.
<u>NOVEL</u>
  <u>Endurance.</u> New York: Vantage, 1973.
<u>WORK IN PROGRESS</u>
  Screenplay of his novel, <u>Endurance.</u>

HARRIS, Leon R. <u>Born</u> 1886 in Cambridge, Ohio. <u>Education:</u>
Worked for his education at Berea College and at Tuskegee Institute. <u>Career:</u> Taught school in North Carolina. Also
worked in the steel mills in Ohio. Edited the Richmond (Indiana) <u>Blade.</u> [1]
<u>EDITOR</u>
  <u>I'm a Railroad Man.</u> n.p., 1948. (Original railroad songs,
    including the first version of "John Henry.")
<u>NOVEL</u>
  <u>Run Zebra, Run! A Story of American Race Conflict.</u> New
    York: Exposition, 1959.
<u>POETRY</u>
  <u>Locomotive Puffs from the Back Shop.</u> Boston: B. Humph-
    ries, 1946.
  <u>The Steel Makers and Other War Poems...Number One.</u>
    Portsmouth, O.: T. C. McConnell, Printery, 1918.
<u>VIGNETTE</u>
  (Periodical): <u>Phylon,</u> Fourth Quarter, 1957.
     [1]Robert T. Kerlin, <u>Negro Poets and Their Poems</u>
  (Washington, D.C.: Associated, 1923), pp. 181-182.

HARRIS, Leroy.
<u>POETRY</u> (Anthology): Boyd, <u>Poems by Blacks</u>, vol. 2.

HARRIS, Neil. <u>Born</u> 20 February 1936 in Valhala, New York.
<u>Education:</u> Attended Shaw University, 1958-60. <u>Currently liv-</u>
ing in New Rochelle, New York. <u>Career:</u> Established a creative writers workshop at the Mount Morris Drug Rehabilitation
Center under the New York State Narcotic Commission, 1970;
established other workshops at the Logos Drug Rehabilitation
Center in the Bronx, 1972, and in New Rochelle under a grant
from the Westchester Council of the Arts. A one-act play,
<u>The Portrait,</u> was performed at the New Lafayette Theatre
Workshop in 1969, and was produced under a grant from the
American Film Institute, 1973. Another play, <u>Straight from</u>

James Harris (credit: Arthur Harrison)

the Ghetto, was produced at Lincoln Center. Cop and Blow
and Players Inn were performed at the New York Shakespeare
Festival in 1972. He writes for NBC's Sanford and Son, and
is presently director of Black Osmosis Drama-Writers Work-
shop; he also directs "Shades" Drama Workshop, College of
New Rochelle. Member: Writers Guild West. "Rewards":
Life and good health.
DRAMA
    Blues Changes.
    Cop and Blow, 1972.
    Off the Top.
    Players Inn, 1972.
    The Portrait, 1969.
    Yernom.
POETRY
    Straight from the Ghetto. n.p.: By the Author, n.d.
INTERJECTIONS
    "To write is beautiful. To eat is better!"

HARRIS, Tom.
    DRAMA
        The A Number One Family, 1958.
        Always with Love, 1967.

Neil Harris (credit: James Hardy)

Beverly Hills Olympics, 1964.
City Beneath the Skin, 1961.
Cleaning Day, 1969.
Daddy Hugs and Kisses, 1963.
The Dark Years, 1958.
Death of Daddy Hugs and Kisses, 1963.
Divorce Negro Style, 1968.
Fall of an Iron Horse, 1959.
The Golden Spear, 1969.
Moving Day, 1969.
Pray for Daniel Adams, 1958.
The Relic, 1967.
Shopping Day, 1969.
Woman in the House, 1958.

HARRIS, Wendell W.
    POETRY Echoes and Shadows. Philadelphia: Dorrance, 1968.

HARRIS, William J. Born 12 March 1942 in Yellow Springs, Ohio.
    Education: M.A. in Creative Writing, Stanford University,
    1969; Ph.D., 1973. Currently living in Ithaca, New York. Career: Assistant Professor of English and Creative Writing,
    Cornell University; poetry editor of the little magazine, Epoch.

NON-FICTION
(Anthologies): Haskins, Black Manifesto for Education;
Perry and Perry, The Social Web (San Francisco: Can-
field, 1973).
(Periodicals): The American Scholar, Summer 1972.
POETRY
(Anthologies): Adoff, The Poetry of Black America; Cassill,
Intro #3; Chapman, New Black Voices; Colley and Moore,
Starting with Poetry; Davis and Redding, Cavalcade; Jef-
fer and Rayl, Reach Out (Boston: Little, Brown, 1972);
Reed, The Yardbird Reader; Shuman, A Galaxy of Black
Writing; Shuman, Nine Black Poets.
(Periodicals): Antioch Review, Fall 1968; Beloit Poetry Jour-
nal, Winter 1968-69; also in Lillabulero; The Mad River
Review; Pennypaper; Plume and Sword; Southern Poetry Re-
view.
INTERJECTIONS
"I write to understand (to order) the world, to communicate
my feelings to and about it and to change it. As a humanist
intellectual I am still trying to prove that the pen is mightier
than the sword. But whether or not I can change the condition
of man (which doesn't seem very likely) I hope to entertain him
in our dark and cruel time with my poems."

HARRISON, DeLeon. Born 1941 in Little Rock, Arkansas.
POETRY
(Anthologies): Adoff, The Poetry of Black America; Miller,
Dices and Black Bones.
(Periodicals): Black Dialogue; Journal of Black Poetry;
Axolotl.

HARRISON, Eunice B.
POETRY Here Is My Heart. New York: Carlton, 1962.

HARRISON, James Minnis. Born 1873.
POETRY Southern Sunbeams: A Book of Poems. Richmond,
Va.: Saint Luke Press, 1926.

HARRISON, Paul Carter. Born 1936 in New York City.
CRITICISM BY HARRISON
The Drama of Nommo. New York: Grove, 1972*†.
"Black Theater and the African Continuum." Black World
21 (August 1972): 42-48.
EDITOR
Kuntu Drama. New York: Grove, 1974*.
DRAMA
Brer Soul, 1970.
The Great MacDaddy, 1972.
Pavane for a Dead-pan Minstrel. In Podium 20 (November
1965).
Pawns.
Tabernacle. In Couch, New Black Playwrights, pp. 93-180.
Tophat.

REVIEWS: The Great MacDaddy
    Gottfried, Martin. Women's Wear Daily, 14 February 1974.
    Watts, Richard. New York Post, 13 February 1974.

HART, Estelle Pugsley.
    POETRY Thoughts in Poetry. New York: Tobias, 1911.

HASKETT, Edythe R. Career: See Shockley and Chandler, Living
    Black American Authors.
    CHILDREN AND YOUNG ADULTS
        Some Gold, A Little Ivory. New York: John Day, 1971*.
    EDITOR
        Grains of Pepper: Folk Tales from Liberia. New York:
            John Day, 1967*.

HAWKINS, Darnell. Born 24 November 1946 in Sherrill, Arkansas.
    POETRY (Anthology): Boyer, Broadside Annual 1973.

HAWKINS, Jeffery.
    POETRY (Periodicals): Journal of Black Poetry, Fall-Winter
        1971; Negro Digest, September 1969.

HAWKINS, Odie. Born 6 July 1937 in Chicago. Education: Seven-
    teen grammar schools; one high school; the streets of Chicago,
    Los Angeles, New York, Copenhagen, Mexico, Augusta (Geor-
    gia), Stockholm, Philadelphia, Amsterdam, Brussels, London,
    Memphis, and Dumbgum (Mississippi). Currently living in Los
    Angeles. Career: Has three screenplays (MGM, Universal,
    and Warner Brothers) waiting to be filmed; wrote a screenplay
    for Sanford and Son; has given poetry readings at numerous col-
    leges and universities, including New York University, Temple
    University, Howard University, U.C.L.A., San Raphael College,
    Pomona College, Parsons College, and Berkeley.
    NOVEL
        Ghetto Sketches. Los Angeles: Holloway, 1972†.
    POETRY
        Me and Them. Los Angeles: By the Author, 1969.
        (Periodical): Freedomways, Second Quarter 1973.
    UNPUBLISHED WORK
        Four plays.

HAWKINS, Walter Everette. Born 1886 in Warrenton, North Caro-
    lina. Education: Attended the village school of Warrenton and
    the African Methodist school.[1] Career: Was employed by the
    post office in Washington before moving to Brooklyn.[2]
    POETRY
        Chords and Discords. Washington, D.C.: Murray Brothers
            Press, 1909; Boston: R. G. Badger, 1920.
        Petals from the Poppies. New York: Fortuny's, 1936.
        (Anthologies): Byars, Black and White: An Anthology of
            Washington Verse; Kerlin, Negro Poets and Their Poems.
        (Periodicals): Crisis 14 (1917): 130; 27 (1924): 258; 35
            (1928): 232.

[1]Robert T. Kerlin, Negro Poets and Their Poems
(Washington, D.C.: Associated, 1923), p. 121.
[2]Benjamin Brawley, The Negro Genius (New York:
Dodd, Mead, 1937), p. 239.

HAYDEN, Robert.   Born 4 August 1913 in Detroit.   Career: See
Ploski, Lindenmeyer and Kaiser, Reference Library of Black
America.
EDITOR
    Kaleidoscope: Poems by American Negro Poets.   New York:
        Harcourt Brace Jovanovich, 1968.
    With David Burrows and Frederick Paides.   Afro-American
        Literature: An Introduction.   New York: Harcourt Brace
        Jovanovich, 1971†.
POETRY
    A Ballad of Remembrance.   London: Breman, 1962.   Dis-
        tributed in the U.S. by Broadside Press.
    Figure of Time.   Nashville, Tenn.: Hemphill Press, 1955.
    Heart-Shape in the Dust.   Detroit: Falcon, 1940.
    With Myron O'Higgins.   The Lion and the Archer.   Nash-
        ville, Tenn.: Hemphill Press, 1949.
    The Night-Blooming Cereus.   Detroit: Broadside, 1972†.
    Selected Poems, 2nd ed.   New York: October House, 1966.
    Words in the Mourning Time: Poems.   New York: October
        House, 1970.
    (Anthologies): Abdul, The Magic of Black Poetry; Bontemps,
        American Negro Poetry; Brooks, A Broadside Treasury;
        Brown. American Stuff; Brown, Davis and Lee, Negro
        Caravan; Chapman, Black Voices; Chapman, New Black
        Voices; Davis and Redding, Cavalcade; Eastman, The Nor-
        ton Anthology of Poetry; Ellman and O'Claire, The Norton
        Anthology of Modern Poetry; Emanuel and Gross, Dark
        Symphony; Hughes and Bontemps, The Poetry of the Ne-
        gro, 1746-1970; Jordan, Soulscript; Lowenfels, Poets of
        Today; Randall, The Black Poets; Walrond and Pool,
        Black and Unknown Bards; Williams, Contemporary
        Poetry in America.
    (Periodicals): Journal of Black Poetry, Fall-Winter 1971;
        Midwest Journal, Summer 1954; Negro Digest, September
        1965; June 1966; Phylon, Third Quarter 1945; Fourth
        Quarter 1950; Second Quarter 1951; Third Quarter 1958;
        Opportunity, October 1939; April, August, October 1940.
PREFACE
    "Preface to the Atheneum Edition."   The New Negro.
        Edited by Alain Locke.   New York: Atheneum, 1970, pp.
        ix-xiv.
BIOGRAPHY AND CRITICISM ON HAYDEN
    "Black Writer's Views on Literary Lions and Values."   Ne-
        gro Digest 17 (January 1968): 33.
    Davis, Charles T.   "Robert Hayden's Use of History."   In
        Gibson, Modern Black Poets, pp. 43-56.
    Fetrow, Fred M.   "Robert Hayden's 'Frederick Douglass':
        Form and Meaning in a Modern Sonnet."   CLA Journal

17 (September 1973): 79-84.

Malkoff. Crowell's Handbook of Contemporary American Poetry, pp. 136-138.

O'Sullivan, Maurice J., Jr. "The Mask of Allusion in Robert Hayden's 'The Diver.'" CLA Journal 17 (September 1973): 85-92.

Pool, Rosey E. "Robert Hayden: Poet Laureate." Negro
Digest 15 (June 1966): 39-43.

Negro History Bulletin 21 (October 1957): 15.

O'Brien. Interviews with Black Writers, pp. 109-123.

Whitlow. Black American Literature, pp. 133-136.

Young. Black Writers of the Thirties, pp. 166-167, 188,
193-198, 202, 240.

HAYES, Donald Jeffrey. Born 16 November 1904 in Raleigh, North
Carolina.
POETRY
    (Anthologies): Bontemps, American Negro Poetry; Cullen,
    Caroling Dusk; Hughes and Bontemps, The Poetry of the
    Negro, 1746-1970; Johnson, Ebony and Topaz.
    (Periodicals): Good Housekeeping, October 1938; Opportunity,
    July 1927; March 1929. Also published in Harper's Ba-
    zaar and This Week.
BIOGRAPHY ON HAYES
    "Poets." Ebony 4 (February 1949): 41.

HAYNES, Albert.
POETRY (Anthologies): Jones and Neal, Black Fire; The New
    Black Poetry.

HEARD, Josephine Henderson. Born 11 October 1861 in Salisbury,
North Carolina. Education: Scotia Seminary at Concord, North
Carolina; Bethany Institute, New York. Career: Taught in
North Carolina, South Carolina, and Tennessee.[1]
POETRY
    Morning Glories. Philadelphia: n.p., 1890; Atlanta: Frank-
    lin Printing Co., 1901. Poems reprinted in Majors,
    Noted Negro Women, and in Robinson, Early Black Amer-
    ican Poets.
BIOGRAPHY AND CRITICISM ON HEARD
    Majors. Noted Negro Women, pp. 261-268.
    Robinson. Early Black American Poets, 261-263.
        [1]Monroe A. Majors, Noted Negro Women (Freeport,
    N.Y.: Books for Libraries, 1971), p. 261.

HEARD, Nathan C. Born 17 November 1936 in Newark, New Jer-
sey.
NOVELS
    Howard Street. New York: Dial, 1972. Excerpt in Robin-
    son, Nommo.
    To Reach a Dream. New York: Dial, 1972.
SHORT STORY
    (Anthology): Sanchez, We Be Word Sorcerers.

REVIEWS
Howard Street:
    Giovanni, Nikki.   Negro Digest 18 (February 1969): 71-73.
To Reach a Dream
    Watkins, M.   New York Times, 14 July 1972, p. 32.

HENDERSON, David.   Born 1942 in Harlem.   Career: See Con-
    temporary Authors 25/28.
    CRITICISM BY HENDERSON
    "The Man Who Cried I Am: A Critique."   In Gayle, Black
        Expression, pp. 365-372.
    NON-FICTION
    (Anthology): Reed, 19 Necromancers from Now.
    POETRY
    De Mayor of Harlem.   New York: Dutton, 1970†.
    Felix of the Silent Forest.   Introduction by LeRoi Jones.
        New York: Poets Press, 1967.
    (Anthologies): Adoff, Black Out Loud; Adoff, The Poetry of
        Black America; Afro-Arts Anthology; Colley and Moore,
        Starting with Poetry; Gross, A Nation of Nations; Hughes,
        New Negro Poets: USA; King, Blackspirits; Jones and
        Neal, Black Fire; Jordan, Soulscript; Miller, Dices and
        Black Bones; Randall and Burroughs, For Malcolm; Reed,
        Yardbird Reader I; Wilentz and Weatherly, Natural Proc-
        ess.
    (Periodicals): Published in Black World; Essence; Freedom-
        ways; Journal of Black Poetry; Negro Digest; Nickel Re-
        view; Paris Review; New American Review; Evergreen Re-
        view; New York Times; East Village Other; National
        Guardian.
    BIOGRAPHY AND CRITICISM ON HENDERSON
    Lee.   Dynamite Voices, pp. 65-68.
    Middlebrook, Diane.   "David Henderson's Holy Mission."
        Saturday Review 55 (September 1972): 38-40.

HENDERSON, George Wylie.   Born 1904.
    NOVELS
    Jule.   New York: Creative Age, 1946.
    Ollie Miss.   New York: Stokes, 1935.
    CRITICISM ON HENDERSON
    Bone.   The Negro Novel in America, pp. 123-126, 133.
    Gloster.   Negro Voices in American Fiction, pp. 208-209,
        234-235, 237-238.
    Turner, Darwin T.   "The Negro Novelist and the South."
        Southern Humanities Review 1 (1967): 21-29.

HENDERSON, Stephen.
    CRITICISM
    "A Strong Man Called Sterling Brown."   Black World 19
        (September 1970): 5-12.
    Understanding the New Black Poetry: Black Speech and
        Black Music as Poetic References.   New York: Morrow,
        1973†*.

NON-FICTION
    With Mercer Cook.   The Militant Black Writer in Africa and
    the United States.   Madison: University of Wisconsin
    Press, 1969†.
    (Periodicals):   Published in Black Books Bulletin; Black
    World; Ebony; Negro Digest.
SHORT STORY
    (Periodical):   Negro Digest, June 1969.

HENRY, Carol.   Born 8 July 1928 in Newark, New Jersey; grew
up in Staten Island, New York.   Education: B.S. (Piano) Juil-
liard School of Music, 1951; certified music therapist, Essex
County Overbrook Hospital, 1963; M.A. (Performing Arts),
Sarah Lawrence College, 1969; studied dance at New Dance
Group Studio and Merce Cunningham Studio, New York City
1963-70.   Currently living in New York City.   Career: Painter,
pianist, composer, dancer, choreographer, poet.   Her compositions and lyrics have been recorded by various artists.   She
has taught at Southern University, 1953; Florida A & M University, 1953-54; Arkansas AN&M College, 1955-59; SEEK Program, Queens College, 1970-71; Valdosta State College, 1971;
Bennington College, 1971-72; Visiting Lecturer, New York University, 1971-72.   She is founder and director of the inter-
media company, The Innermost Society.   Awards, Honors: Fellowship, Sarah Lawrence College.
POETRY
    (Periodical):   Uptown Beat, 1969-71.
INTERJECTIONS
    "Am dedicated to intermedia as a theater art and as a teach-
    ing tool.   Love teaching children (they are the best teachers)
    but also enjoy teaching and working with adults and exploring
    all the possibilities when working with all age groups and then
    translating all the experiences into my own expression.   Am
    amazed at how I continue to grow."

HENRY, William S.
    FICTION
        Out of Wedlock.   Boston: R. G. Badger, 1931.

HERCULES, Frank.   Born 12 February 1917 in Port-of-Spain, Trinidad, West Indies.   Career: See Contemporary Authors, 2.
    CRITICISM
        "An Aspect of the Negro Renaissance."   Opportunity (Oc-
            tober 1942):   305-306, 317-319.
    NON-FICTION
        American Society and Black Revolution.   New York: Harcourt
            Brace Jovanovich, 1972*.
    NOVELS
        I Want a Black Doll.   New York: Simon & Schuster, 1967*.
        Where the Hummingbird Flies.   New York: Harcourt, 1961.
    REVIEW: Where the Hummingbird Flies:
        Crisis 68 (October 1961):   523.

Carol Henry (credit: Harry Preston)

HERNTON, Calvin. Born 28 April 1932 in Chattanooga, Tennessee.
Education: B.A., Talladega College, 1954; M.A., Fisk University 1956; also attended Columbia University, 1961. Currently
living in Oberlin, Ohio. Career: Social Science Instructor at
various colleges, 1957-61; in social welfare work for the State
of New York, 1956-57, 1961-62; presently an Associate Professor of African and Afro-American Literature, Oberlin College.
CRITICISM BY HERNTON
    "The Umbra Poets." Mainstream 16 (July 1963): 7-13.
NON-FICTION
    Sex and Racism in America. New York: Grove, 1965†.
    White Papers for White Americans. Garden City, N.Y.:
      Doubleday, 1967.
    (Anthologies): Jones and Neal, Black Fire; Simmons and
      Hutchinson, Black Culture; Watkins and David, To Be a
      Black Woman.
    (Periodicals): Negro Digest, October 1963; December 1964.
NOVEL
    Scarecrow. Garden City, N.Y.: Doubleday, 1974*. Ex-
      cerpt in Reed, 19 Necromancers from Now.
POETRY
    The Coming of Chronos to the House of Nightsong: An Epi-
      cal Narrative of the South. New York: Interim, 1964.
    (Anthologies): Adoff, The Poetry of Black America; Hayden,

Kaleidoscope; Hughes, New Negro Poets: USA; Hughes
and Bontemps, The Poetry of the Negro, 1746-1970; Jor-
dan, Soulscript; Lomax and Abdul, 3000 Years of Black
Poetry; Major, The New Black Poetry; Miller, Dices and
Black Bones; Pool, Beyond the Blues; Reed, Yardbird
Reader I.
(Periodicals): Negro Digest, September 1964; Essence,
June 1973; Phylon, First Quarter 1954; Fourth Quarter
1955.
SHORT STORY
(Periodical): Freedomways, Spring 1963.

HERRING, Mel.
POETRY Black Coffee. New York: Umbra Press, n.d.

HERRINGTON, Richard.
POETRY Where I'm Coming From. Houston, Texas: Black Student Union, University of Texas, n.d.

HERSHAW, Fay McKeene.
POETRY Verse Along the Way. New York: Exposition, 1954.

HERVE, Julia Wright.
NON-FICTION
(Periodical): Black Scholar, December 1971.
SHORT STORY
(Periodical): Black World, May 1973.

HIGGS, Oliver.
POETRY Into the Realm. Waterbury, Conn.: Poet's Press,
1954.

HIGHTOWER, Charles.
DRAMA Children's Games, 1969.

HILL, Abram.
DRAMA
Hell's Half Acre, 1938.
With John Silvera. Liberty Deferred, 1936.
Miss Mabel, 1951.
On Striver's Row: A Comedy about Sophisticated Harlem,
1945.
Power of Darkness, 1948.
So Shall You Reap, 1938.
Split Down the Middle. New York: Simon & Schuster, 1970.
Stealing Lightning, 1937.
Walk Hard, 1944.
BIOGRAPHY AND CRITICISM ON HILL
Abramson. The Negro Playwright in the American Theatre,
pp. 96-102.
Crisis 51 (October 1944): 321.
Harrison. The Drama of Nommo, p. 166.
Mitchell. Black Drama, pp. 107, 110, 113, 122-123, 126,
135, 136.

HILL, Anne K.
　　POETRY　Aurora: Poems.　New York: By the Author, 1948.

HILL, Edna White.
　　POETRY　(Anthology): Murphy, Negro Voices.

HILL, Elton (Abu Ishak).　Born 21 January 1950 in Detroit, Michigan.
　　POETRY
　　　　(Anthologies): Alhamisi and Wangara, Black Arts; Major,
　　　　　　The New Black Poetry.
　　　　(Periodicals): Negro Digest, August 1968; other poems in
　　　　　　Black Conscience, Conversations, Michigan Chronicle,
　　　　　　Negro History Bulletin.

HILL, Errol.　Born 5 August 1921 in Trinidad, West Indies.　Education: Diploma, Royal Academy of Dramatic Art (England),
　　1951; Diploma (Dramatic Art), University of London; B.A., and
　　M.F.A., Yale University, 1962; D.F.A., Yale University, 1966.
　　Currently living in Hanover, New Hampshire.　Career: Drama
　　tutor in creative arts, 1962-65, University of West Indies; Associate Professor of Drama, Richmond College, 1967-68; presently Professor of Drama, Dartmouth College, and editor, Bulletin of Black Theatre.　Awards, Honors: British Council Scholarship, 1949-51; Rockefeller Foundation Fellowship, 1958-60;
　　1965-67; Theatre Guild of America Playwrighting Fellowship,
　　1961-62.
　　DRAMA
　　　　Dance Bongo, 1965.　In Caribbean Literature: An Anthology.
　　　　　　Edited by G.R. Coulthard.　London: University of London Press, 1966.
　　　　Dilemma, 1966.
　　　　Man Better Man (folk musical).　In Three Plays from the
　　　　　　Yale School of Drama.　Edited by John Gassner.　New
　　　　　　York: Dutton, 1964.
　　　　The Ping-pong, 1958.
　　　　Oily Portraits, 1966.
　　　　Strictly Matrimony, 1966.　In King and Milner, Black Drama Anthology.
　　　　Wey-Wey, 1966.
　　EDITOR
　　　　Caribbean Plays, vols. 1 and 2.　Trinidad: Extramural Department, University of the West Indies, 1958, 1965.
　　　　The Artist in West Indian Society: A Symposium.　Trinidad:
　　　　　　Extramural Department, University of the West Indies,
　　　　　　1964.
　　NON-FICTION
　　　　The Trinidad Carnival: Mandate for a National Theatre.
　　　　　　Austin, Texas: University of Texas Press, 1972*.
　　　　With Peter Greer.　Why Pretend?　New York: Chandler,
　　　　　　1973.
　　　　(Periodicals):
　　　　"The West Indian Artist."　West Indian Review (Jamaica), 9

Hill, E. (cont.)   378

August 1952.
"The Case for a National Theatre." <u>Public Opinion</u> (Jamaica),
20 September, 4 October, 1952.
"Cultural Values and the Theatre Arts in the English-Speak-
ing Caribbean." <u>Resource Development in the Caribbean</u>
(McGill University), October 1972.
"The Emergence of a National Drama in the West Indies."
<u>Caribbean Quarterly</u> 18 (December 1972).
"West Indian Drama." <u>Trinidad Guardian Federation Supple-
ment</u>, 20 April 1958.
"The West Indian Theatre." <u>Public Opinion</u>, 31 May, 7 June,
21 June, 1958.
"Calypso Drama." <u>Theatre Survey</u> 9 (November 1968).
INTERJECTIONS
"For me, life and art are inseparable. Life is meaningless
without art. Art makes the impossible possible and puts us in
touch with immortality."

HILL, John Calhoun.
POETRY <u>Piccolo,</u> vol. 1. Meridian, Miss.: T. Farmer,
printer, n.d.

HILL, Julious C.
POETRY
A Sooner Song. New York: Empire Books, 1935.
A Song of Magnolia. Boston: Meador, 1937.

HILL, Leslie Pinkney. <u>Born</u> 14 May 1880 in Lynchburg, Virginia.
<u>Died</u> 16 February 1960. <u>Education:</u> Attended the local public
schools in Lynchburg; graduated from East Orange High School,
New Jersey, 1898; received A.B. from Harvard, 1903; M.A.
from Harvard, 1904;[1] Litt.D., Lincoln University, 1929. <u>Ca-
reer:</u> Taught at Tuskegee Institute from 1904-07; became Principal of Manassas Industrial School, Virginia, 1907-13; Principal
of Cheyney Training School for Teachers, 1913-33.[2] Under his
direction, the Cheyney school changed from a private institut-
tion into a standard Normal School of Pennsylvania.[3] He was
also the Founder and President of Chester Community Center;
Founder and Past President of the Pennsylvania State Negro
Council; and served as member of the Delaware County Board
of Assistance;[4] President of American Inter-Racial Peace Committee; Secretary Pennsylvania Association of Teachers of Colored Children; member, Board of Managers, the Armstrong Association, Philadelphia; Trustee of Manassas Industrial School;
Vice-Chairman, Committee on Total Disarmament; American
Academy of Political and Social Science. <u>Member:</u> Phi Beta
Kappa; Kappa Alpha Psi; Pi Gamma Mu; Harvard Club of Phila-
delphia.[5]
DRAMA
Toussaint L'Ouverture, Boston: Christopher, 1928.
POETRY
The Wings of Oppression and Other Poems, 1921; facsimile
ed., Freeport, N.Y.: Books for Libraries*.

(Anthologies): Adams, Conn, and Slepian, Afro-American Literature; Adoff, I Am the Darker Brother; Adoff, The Poetry of Black America; Brown, Davis and Lee, The Negro Caravan; Eleazer, Singers in the Dawn; Hughes and Bontemps, Poetry of the Negro, 1746-1970; Johnson, The Book of American Negro Poetry; Kerlin, Negro Poets and Their Poems; White and Jackson, An Anthology of Verse by American Negroes.
(Periodicals): Crisis 1 (January 1911): 23; 3 (1912): 122; 7 (1914): 181; 10 (1915): 82; 18 (1919): 289; 24 (1922): 16; 34 (1927): 13; 36 (1929): 268; Opportunity 1 (April 1923): 23; 2 (November 1924): 331; 17 (January 1939): 3; Phylon (First Quarter 1941).

BIOGRAPHY AND CRITICISM ON HILL
Bardolph. The Negro Vanguard, p. 160.
Baskin and Runes. Dictionary of Black Culture, p. 212.
Brawley. The Negro Genius, pp. 214-215.
_____. The Negro in Literature and Art, pp. 110-111.
Bond. The Negro and the Drama, p. 189.
Cromwell, Turner and Dykes. Readings from Negro Authors, p. 35.
Dreer. American Literature by Negro Authors, pp. 48-50.
James, Milton M. "Biography." Negro History Bulletin 24 (March 1961): 135-138.
Journal of Negro History (April 1960): 139. (Obituary.)
Kerlin. Negro Poets and Their Poems, pp. 131-138.
Mays. The Negro's God, pp. 179-182.
Meier. Negro Thought in America 1880-1915, p. 258.
New York Times, 16 February 1960, p. 40, sec. 1. (Obituary.)
White and Jackson. An Anthology of Verse by American Negroes, p. 222.
Williams. They Also Spoke, p. 76.
Woodson, Carter G. and Charles H. Wesley. The Negro in Our History. Washington: Associated, 1966, pp. 472, 614.
Yenser, Thomas. Who's Who in Colored America, 5th ed., Brooklyn, Yenser, 1940, p. 256.
    [1]Newman Ivey White and Walter C. Jackson, An Anthology of Verse by American Negroes (Durham, N.C.: Moore 1924), p. 194.
    [2]Thomas Yenser, ed., Who's Who in Colored America (Brooklyn: Yenser, 1940), p. 255.
    [3]White, p. 194.
    [4]Obituary, New York Times, 16 February 1960, p. 40, sec. 1.
    [5]Yenser, p. 255.

HILL, Leubrie. Born 1873. Died 1916. Career: Arranger and writer of popular songs, instrumental rags, and musical comedies.[1]
DRAMA
With Alex Rogers. Dark Town Follies.
With William LeBaron. Hello Paris, 1911.

[1]Eileen Southern, The Music of Black Americans (New York: Norton, 1971), p. 252.

HILL, Mars. Born 18 November 1927 in Pine Bluff, Arkansas. Education: B.S., University of Illinois, 1954; additional studies at University of Washington, Russell Sage College, Afro-American Studio; course work completed for Masters in Afro-American Studies, State University of New York at Albany. Currently living in Albany, New York. Career: Founder and Director of the Black Experience Ensemble in Albany. Presently involved in playwrighting, directing, acting and analysis on the theatre and the cultural development of the Black movement. Member: Congress of African People, North East Regional Committee for the Black Arts Festival in Lagos. Awards, Honors: Community Achievement Award, Neighborhood House (Albany), 1972.
DRAMA
    The Buzzards.
    The Cage.
    First in War.
    To Have and To Have Not.
    House and Field.
    Huzzy.
    The Man in the Family.
    Occupation.
    Peck.
    The Street Walkers.
    Two Ten.
    A Very Special Occasion.
    The Visitors.
    You Ain't Got No Place to Put Yo Snow.

HILL, Mildred Martin.
    POETRY A Traipsin' Heart. New York: Malliet, 1942.

HILL, Quentin. Born 1950 in South Bronx, New York City.
    POETRY
        (Anthology): Major, The New Black Poetry.
        (Periodical): Journal of Black Poetry, Summer 1972.

HILL, Roy L. Born 1925.
    POETRY
        Corrie J. Carroll and Other Poems. Philadelphia: Dorrance, 1962.
        49 Poems. Manhattan, Kansas: Ag Press, 1968.
    SHORT STORIES
        Two Ways and Other Stories. State College, Pa.: Commercial Printing, 1959; New York: Fort Orange Press, 1964.
    REVIEW: Corrie J. Carroll and Other Poems
        Pichette, Kathryn B. CLA Journal 8 (September 1964): 96-97.

HIMES, Chester. Born 29 July 1909 in Jefferson City, Missouri. Education: Attended grammar school in Augusta, Georgia;

Pine Bluff, Arkansas; St. Louis, Missouri; graduated from high
school in Cleveland, Ohio; attended Ohio State University, 1926-
1929. Career: See Barksdale and Kinnamon, Black Writers of
America, pp. 618-621; Contemporary Authors 25/28.

AUTOBIOGRAPHY

The Quality of Hurt: The Autobiography of Chester Himes.
Garden City, N.Y.: Doubleday, 1972*.

CRITICISM BY HIMES

"Dilemma of the Negro Novelist in the U.S." In Williams,
Beyond the Angry Black; also in Miller, Backgrounds to
Blackamerican Literature.

"Introduction." Reed, Yardbird Reader I.

NOVELS

All Shot Up. New York: Berkley, 1960; Chatham, N.J.:
Chatham Booksellers*.

The Big Gold Dream. New York: Avon, 1960; New York:
Berkley, 1966.

Blind Man with a Pistol. New York: Morrow, 1969. (Also
published as Hot Day, Hot Night. New York: Dell, 1970.)

Cast the First Stone. New York: Coward-McCann, 1952;
Chatham, N.J.: Chatham Booksellers*; New York: New
American Library, 1972†.

Cotton Comes to Harlem. New York: Putnam, 1965; New
York: Dell, 1966.

The Crazy Kill. New York: Avon, 1959; New York: Berkley,
1959; Chatham, N.J.: Chatham Booksellers, 1959*.

For Love of Imabelle. Greenwich, Conn.: Fawcett, 1957;
New York: Avon, 1965; Chatham, N.J.: Chatham Booksellers, 1959*. (Originally published as A Rage in Harlem.)

The Heat's On. New York: Putnam, 1966; also published as
Come Back, Charleston Blue. New York: Dell, 1967; New
York: Berkley, 1972†.

If He Hollers Let Him Go. New York: Doubleday, Doran,
1945; Chatham, N.J.: Chatham Booksellers*; New York:
New American Library, 1971†. Excerpt in Negro Digest,
January 1946.

Lonely Crusade. New York: Knopf, 1947; Chatham, N.J.:
Chatham Booksellers*. Excerpt in Hill, Soon One Morning.

Pinktoes. New York: Dell, 1965†. Excerpt in Miller, Blackamerican Literature; Girodais, The Olympia Reader;
Kearns, The Black Experience.

The Primitive. New York: New American Library, 1955†.
Excerpt in Margolies, A Native Sons Reader.

The Real Cool Killers. New York: Avon, 1959; New York:
Berkley, 1959; Chatham, N.J.: Chatham Booksellers,
1960*.

Run Man, Run. New York: Putnam's, 1966; New York: Dell,
1969†.

The Third Generation. Cleveland: World, 1954; Chatham,
N.J.: Chatham Booksellers, 1954*; New York: New American Library, 1956†. Excerpt in Davis and Redding, Cavalcade.

SHORT STORIES

Black on Black: Baby Sister and Selected Writings. Garden City, N.Y.: Doubleday, 1973.

(Anthologies): Barksdale and Kinnamon, Black Writers of America; Brown, Davis and Lee, Negro Caravan; Chambers and Moon, Right On!; Clarke, American Negro Short Stories; Clarke, Harlem; Hughes, The Best Short Stories by Negro Writers.

(Periodicals): Abbott's Monthly, 1932; Atlanta Daily World, 1933; The Bronzeman, 1933; Coronet, February 1941; Crisis, October 1942; January 1943; March 1943; October 1943; November 1943; June 1944; April 1945; July 1948; November 1949; November 1970; Esquire, August 1934; October 1934; September 1936; January 1937; May 1937; March 1940; April 1944; January 1946; October 1959; Negro Story, July-August 1944; December-January 1944-45; May-June 1945; April-May 1946; August-September 1945; Opportunity, March 1939; May 1941; November 1942; Pittsburgh Courier, 1933; also published in Bachelor; Abbott's Illustrated Weekly; Crossroad; The Chicago Defender.

BIBLIOGRAPHIES ON HIMES

Fabre, Michel. "A Selected Bibliography of Chester Himes' Work." Black World 21 (March 1972): 76-78.

Peabody, Ina. "Chester Himes." CAAS Bibliography No. 3. Atlanta: Atlanta University, n.d. (Mimeographed.)

BIOGRAPHY AND CRITICISM ON HIMES

Baldwin, James. "History as Nightmare." The New Leader, 25 October 1947, pp. 11, 15.

Bardolph. The Negro Vanguard, pp. 373, 378, 381, 383, 384.

Bennett, Stephen B. and William W. Nichols. "Violence in Afro-American Fiction: An Hypothesis." Modern Fiction Studies 17 (1971): 221-228.

Bone. The Negro Novel in America, pp. 173-176.

Bryant, Jerry H. "Politics and the Black Novel." Nation, 20 December 1971, p. 21.

Fabre, Michel. "A Case of Rape." Black World 21 (March 1972): 39-48.

Fuller, Hoyt W. "Traveler on the Long, Rough, Lonely Old Road: An Interview with Chester Himes." Black World 21 (March 1972): 4-23.

Gaines, Richard H. Saturday Review, 15 April 1972, pp. 69-70.

Hughes. The Negro Novelist, pp. 206-212.

Kent. "Struggle for the Image," p. 306.

Margolies, Edward. "Experiences of the Black Expatriate Writer: Chester Himes." CLA Journal 15 (June 1972).

_____. "Race and Sex: The Novels of Chester Himes." Native Sons: A Critical Study of Twentieth-Century American Authors. New York: Lippincott, 1969.

_____. "The Thrillers of Chester Himes." Studies in Black Literature 1 (Summer 1970): 1-11.

Mok, M. "Chester Himes." Publishers Weekly, 3 April
     1972, pp. 20-21.
Nelson, Raymond. "Domestic Harlem: The Detective Fic-
     tion of Chester Himes." Virginia Quarterly Review 48
     (Spring 1972): 260-276.
Reed, Ishmael. "Chester Himes: Writer." Black World
     21 (March 1972): 24-38, 83-86.
The Times (London), 28 June 1969, p. 22.
Williams, John A. "My Man Himes: An Interview with
     Chester Himes." In Williams and Harris, Amistad 1,
     pp. 25-94.

HINES, Carl W., Jr. Born 1 September 1940 in Wilson, North
     Carolina. Education: B.S., Tennessee A and I University,
     1962; M.S., University of Tennessee, 1966. Currently living in
     Indianapolis, Indiana. Career: Teaches mathematics in the pub-
     lic schools of Indianapolis; works for the Indianapolis Plan for
     Equal Employment (a program designed to aid in the placement
     of minorities in the Trade Unions); plays in a jazz group on
     weekends; and "writes poetry when inspired."
     POETRY
          (Anthologies): Bontemps, American Negro Poetry; Chambers
          and Moon, Right On!; Hayden, Kaleidoscope; Lowenfels,
          Poets of Today.

HINTON, Henry.
     POETRY (Anthology): Black Poets Write On!

HOAGLAND, Everett. Born 18 December 1942 in Philadelphia.
     Education: A.B., Lincoln University, 1964; M.A., Brown Uni-
     versity, 1973. Currently living in Philadelphia. Career:
     Teacher, secondary-level English, Philadelphia, 1964-67;
     teacher's aide, Operation Headstart, Philadelphia, Summer 1965;
     English teacher, adult evening school, Philadelphia, 1965-66;
     Assistant Director of Admissions, Lincoln University, 1967-69;
     Assistant to the Director of the Black Studies Center, Clare-
     mont College, California, 1969-70; also Instructor in African-
     American Poetry, 1969-71, and Poet-in-Residence, 1970-71; Co-
     ordinator of and teacher in Afro-Culture and Society, Chino In-
     stitute for Men, 1970; Instructor of American and Black Litera-
     ture, Mt. San Antonio College, 1970-71; Instructor of English,
     Upward Bound Program, Claremont College, Summer 1971; Uni-
     versity Fellow in Creative Writing, Brown University, 1971-73;
     Instructor of Humanities, Pre-enrollment Program, Swarthmore
     College, Summer 1972; Assistant Professor of English, South-
     eastern Massachusetts University, 1973 to present. He has al-
     so given poetry readings and presentations in the U.S., France,
     Spain and Mexico. Awards, Honors: Silvera Award for Crea-
     tive Writing, Lincoln University, 1964; listed in "Outstanding
     Young Men of America," 1968-69; recipient, University Fellow-
     ship for Creative Writing, 1971-73.
     POETRY
          Black Velvet. Detroit: Broadside, 1970†.

Ten Poems: A Collection. Lincoln University, Pa.: Amer-
ican Studies Institute, 1968.
(Anthologies): Brooks, A Broadside Treasury; Chapman,
New Black Voices; Major, The New Black Poetry; Randall,
The Black Poets; Welburn, Dues.
(Periodicals): Journal of Black Poetry, Fall-Winter 1971;
Negro Digest, September 1969; also published in Essence,
Evergreen Review and Nickel Review.
UNPUBLISHED WORK
"Niggers and Flies."
WORK IN PROGRESS
"King Dust."
BIOGRAPHY AND CRITICISM ON HOAGLAND
Contemporary Authors 33/36.
INTERJECTIONS
"I am a Baha'i and/but a Black American.....and that says
it all."

HODGES, Frenchy Jolene. Born 18 October 1940 in Dublin, Geor-
gia. Education: B.S. in English, Fort Valley State College,
1964; M.A. in Afro-American Studies with a concentration in
Literature, Atlanta University, 1973. Currently living in De-
troit. Career: Has taught school in Quitman, Georgia, and
Detroit, Michigan. Played the starring roles at Concept East
Theatre in Detroit (God's Trombones, A Hand Is on the Gate,
Baptism, Who's Got His Own), and at the Detroit Repertory
Theater in Larry Blame's Little Old Ladies. Founded the
"frenchy j hodges original" greeting card line in February 1973.
Awards, Honors: Afro-American Studies Fellowship, Atlanta
University, 1972-73; Harold E. Jackmon Memorial Award from
Trevor Arnette Library, Atlanta University.
NON-FICTION
"Dudley Randall and the Broadside Press." Master's Thesis,
Atlanta University, 1973.
POETRY
Black Wisdom. Detroit: Broadside, 1971†.
(Periodical): Phylon, Summer 1972.
CRITICISM ON HODGES
Kent. "Struggle for the Image," p. 315.
INTERJECTIONS
"Life is a legend happening in an eternal minute, and art is
the sapping of substance from reality cased in illusion, helping
man continue through this eternal minute. I fluctuate between
believing that life is a liability and life is an asset. Here late-
ly, more the former; yet, I believe art is very important in
helping man adjust to the latter. City closeness kills percep-
tion and en masse, man loses a lot of his original and natural
grip."

HODGES, George Washington.
WRITINGS
My Souvenirs: Poems and Stories. New York: n.p., 1951.
Swamp Angel. New York: New Voices, 1958.

Frenchy Jolene Hodges

HOLDER, Geoffrey Lamont. Born 1931 in Trinidad, West Indies.
Career: See Current Biography, 1957.
TALES
With Tom Harshman. Black Gods, Green Islands. New
York: Doubleday, 1959; reprint ed., New York: Negro Uni-
versities Press*.
BIOGRAPHY ON HOLDER
Ebony 15 (July 1960): 38-39.
Sepia 8 (July 1960): 14-18.

HOLDER, J. N.
POETRY
Novel Afmerland: Verse to Remember. New York: n.p.,
1953.

HOLDER, James Elliott.
POETRY
The Colored Man's Appeal to White Americans. Atlantic
City, N.J.: By the Author, 1906.
The Negro's Prayer. The Negro's Psalm of Life. Atlantic
City, N.J.: By the Author, 1907.
NON-FICTION
The Problem of America's Destiny. Raleigh, N.C.: n.p.,
1919.

HOLDER, Lawrence.
DRAMA
Closed, 1972.
Grey Boy, 1973.
The Jackass, 1972.
The Journey, 1972.
The Mob, 1972.
Open, 1969.
The Prophylactic, 1970..
The Shadows, 1970.
Street Corners, 1972.

HOLIFIELD, Harold.
DRAMA
Cow in the Apartment, 194?.
J. Toth, 1951.
BIOGRAPHY AND CRITICISM ON HOLIFIELD
Mitchell. Black Drama, pp. 136, 145.

HOLLAND, Mignon.
SHORT STORIES
(Periodicals): Black Creation, Summer 1973; Freedomways,
Second Quarter, 1971.
VIGNETTE
"In the Face of Fire, I Will Not Turn Back." Negro Digest
17 (August 1968): 20-23.
BIOGRAPHY AND CRITICISM ON HOLLAND
"Black Writer's Views on Literary Lions and Values." Ne-
gro Digest 17 (January 1968): 43.

HOLLOWAY, John Wesley. Born 28 July 1865 near Flat Shoals, Merriweather County, Georgia. Education: Studied at Clark University between the ages of 14 and 16; completed a literary course at Fisk University, then returned at a later date to complete the Seminary course. Was a member of the Fisk Jubilee Singers during 1889. Career: Became Assistant Principal in a school in Oklahoma in 1900, serving for four years. Was ordained as a minister of the Congregational Church in 1900; served as pastor in churches in New Jersey, Georgia, and Alabama. Was well-known as a platform lecturer and as Associate Editor of the Georgia Congregationalist.[1]
POETRY
   From the Desert. New York: Neale, 1919.
   (Anthologies): Hughes and Bontemps, The Poetry of the Negro, 1746-1970; Johnson, The Book of American Negro Poetry.
BIOGRAPHY AND CRITICISM ON HOLLOWAY
   White and Newman. An Anthology of Verse by American Negroes, pp. 183-184, 222.
   Who's Who in Colored America, 1932; 1940.
      [1]Newman Ivey White and Walter Clinton Jackson, An Anthology of Verse by American Negroes (Durham, N.C.: Moore, 1924), pp. 183-184.

HOLLOWAY, Lucy Ariel Williams. Born 1905 in Mobile, Alabama.
POETRY
   Shape Them Into Dreams: Poems. New York: Exposition, 1955.
   (Anthologies): Hughes and Bontemps, The Poetry of the Negro, 1746-1970; Johnson, The Book of American Negro Poetry; Walrond and Pool, Black and Unknown Bards.
   (Periodicals): Opportunity, June 1926; September 1929; September 1935.
BIOGRAPHY AND CRITICISM ON HOLLOWAY
   Opportunity 4 (June 1926): 188.

HOLMAN, M. Carl. Born 1919 in Minter City, Mississippi. Education: A.B. (Magna cum laude), Lincoln University, 1944; M.A., University of Chicago; M.F.A., Yale University. Currently living in Washington, D.C. Career: Professor of English and the Humanities, Clark College, 1949-62; editor, The Atlanta Inquirer, 1960-63; served with the U.S. Commission on Civil Rights, 1962-68; joined the National Urban Coalition as co-chairman, and subsequently was elected to the presidency. Member: D.C. Board of Higher Education; Executive Committee, National Committee for the Support of Public Schools; Southwest Community House, Washington, D.C.; Atlanta Committee for Cooperative Action; Greater Atlanta Council on Human Relations; Negotiations Committee, Atlanta Student-Adult Liaison Committee; Atlanta Branch, NAACP; Omega Psi Phi Fraternity; served as member of the board for Field Foundation; Citizen's Conference of State Legislatures; Non-Profit Housing Center; National Institutes of Justice; Council on Foundations,

M. Carl Holman

Inc.; National Committee on Household Employment. Awards,
Honors: John Fiske Poetry Prize, University of Chicago; Blev-
ins Davis Playwrighting Prize, Yale University; Award for Po-
litical Affairs Reporting, American Academy of Political Sci-
ence, 1962; Merit Award, Council on Discrimination, Lockheed
(Georgia) Employees, 1961; Rosenwald Fellowship; John Hay
Whitney Fellowship. The Baptizing, as performed by Tulsa
Little Theatre won first place in the 1971 National Community
Theatre Festival of the American Community Theatre Associa-
tion.

DRAMA
  The Baptizing.
POETRY
  (Anthologies): Adams, Conn and Slepian, Afro-American
    Literature; Adoff, The Poetry of Black America; Bon-
    temps, American Negro Poetry; Hill, Soon One Morning;
    Hughes and Bontemps, The Poetry of the Negro, 1746-
    1970; Jordan, Soulscript.
  (Periodicals): Midwest Journal, Winter 1948, Summer 1949;
    Phylon, 1945; 1948; 1950; 1951; 1952.
BIOGRAPHY ON HOLMAN
  "Poets." Ebony 4 (February 1949): 41.

HOLMES, R. Ernest. <u>Born</u> 24 July 1943 in Harlem. <u>Education</u>:
B.A., New York University, 1966; J.D., New York University
Law School, 1969; post-graduate study at the University of
Southern California's Entertainment Law Institute. <u>Currently</u>
<u>living in</u> Hollywood. <u>Career</u>: Member, New York State Bar;
Associate with Paul, Weiss, Goldberg, Bifkind, Wharton, &
Garrison, August 1969 to present; Senior Counsel, Motown Rec-
ord Corporation. Taught Black American culture at the New
York University School of Continuing Education, 1969-70; lec-
tured on "The Black Man in American Literature," English Department, Washington Square College of Arts and Sciences,
New York University, 1969-71; recruited minority group students for New York University School of Law, October 1969;
worked with Volunteer Lawyers for the Arts, New York City;
co-authored exams in Afro-American history for U.S. Armed
Forces Institute and the University of the State of New York.
<u>Awards, Honors</u>: While in undergraduate school received New
York University scholarships; Leopold Schepp Foundation scholarships; New York State Scholar Incentive Awards; debate and
public speaking awards, including the 41st Annual Griffith
Hughes Memorial Public Speaking Contest, New York University;
Military History Award, Temple University, 1963. While in
law school received the Samuel Rubin Scholarship; Carnegie
Foundation Grant; Dougherty Travel Grant to Universidad de
Concepcion (Chile) and South America, Summer 1967. Was co-
founder and member of the board of directors of the Black
American Law Students' Association.
    POETRY
        (Anthology): Coombs, <u>We Speak as Liberators</u>; Kelly, <u>Points</u>
            <u>of Departure</u>; Patterson, <u>A Rock Against the Wind</u>.
        (Periodicals): <u>Commentator</u>; <u>Liberator</u>; <u>Law Students Civil</u>
            <u>Rights Research Council Bulletin</u>; <u>The Advocate</u>.
    SHORT STORIES
        (Anthology): Coombs, <u>What We Must See</u>.

HOOKS, Nathaniel. <u>Born</u> 1926.
    NOVEL <u>Town on Trial: A Novel of Racial Violence in a South-</u>
        <u>ern Town</u>. New York: Exposition, 1959.

HOPKINS, Pauline Elizabeth. <u>Born</u> 1859 in Portland, Maine. <u>Died</u>
    13 August 1930 in Cambridge, Massachusetts. <u>Education:</u> Was
    graduated from the Girls High School in Boston. <u>Career</u>: Pre-
    sented recitals, concerts and dramatic performances as a mem-
    ber of the Hopkins Colored Troubadours. Became a stenogra-
    pher in 1892, and was employed in turn by two influential Re-
    publicans, by the Bureau of Statistics, and by the Massachusetts
    Institute of Technology. In 1900 she began working and writing
    for the periodical, the <u>Colored American</u>, becoming Literary
    Editor in November 1903, and a founder of the Colored Ameri-
    can League in Boston, which sponsored the <u>Colored American</u>.
    Her stories, biographical sketches and novel serializations were
    published in the magazine. <u>Awards, Honors</u>: At the age of 15
    she was awarded ten dollars for the best essay in a competi-

tion sponsored by William Wells Brown and the Congregational
Publishing Society of Boston.[1]

COLLECTION

Pauline E. Hopkins Papers, Fisk University Library, Nashville, Tennessee.

DRAMA

One Scene from the Drama of Early Days.
Slaves' Escape: or the Underground Railroad, 1879; later
revised and entitled Peculiar Sam, or the Underground
Railroad. (Musical drama.)

NON-FICTION

A Primer of Facts Pertaining to the Greatness of Africa.
Cambridge, n. p., 1905.
(Periodicals): Published regularly in The Colored Magazine;
also in Voice of the Negro, December 1904, February,
March, May, June, July 1905.

NOVEL

Contending Forces: A Romance Illustrative of Negro Life
North and South. Boston: Colored Co-operative, 1900.
Of One Blood, or The Hidden Self. Serialized in The Col-
ored Magazine.
Winona: A Tale of Negro Life in the South and Southwest.
Serialized in The Colored Magazine.

BIOGRAPHY AND CRITICISM ON HOPKINS

Bone. The Negro Novel in America, pp. 14, 19, 26.
Gloster. Negro Voices in American Fiction, pp. 33-34, 56.
Loggins. The Negro Author in America, pp. 326, 405, 453.

REVIEWS: Contending Forces

Colored American 1 (September 1900): 1.
Smith, Alberta Moore. "Comment." Colored American 3
(October 1901): 479.

INTERJECTIONS

"Fiction is of great value to any people as a preserver of
manners and customs--religious, political and social. It is a
record of growth and development from generation to generation. No one will do this for us; we must ourselves develop
the men and women who will faithfully portray the inmost
thoughts and feelings of the Negro with all the fire and romance
which lie dormant in our history, and, as yet, unrecognized by
writers of the Anglo-Saxon race."[2]

[1]Ann Allen Shockley, "Pauline Elizabeth Hopkins: A
Biographical Excursion into Obscurity," Phylon 33 (Spring
1972): 22-26.
[2]Hugh M. Gloster, Negro Voices in American Fiction
(Chapel Hill: The University of North Carolina Press,
1948), p. 33.

HORNE, Frank M. Born 18 August 1899 in New York City. Education: B. S., City College of New York; M. A., University of
Southern California; D. Ophth., North Illinois College of Ophthalmology and Otology. Currently living in New York City. Career:
Practiced ophthalmology in Chicago and New York. Served as Acting Race Relations Advisor of the U. S. Housing Authority. Taught

at the Fort Valley High and Industrial School in Georgia. Awards,
Honors: Won varsity letters for track at City College of New York;
received the 1925 poetry prize from Crisis magazine and the Hoey
Award.

AUTOBIOGRAPHICAL SKETCH
    "I Am Initiated Into the Negro Race." Opportunity 6 (May
        1928): 136-137.
CRITICISM
    "Black Verse." Opportunity 2 (November 1924): 330-332.
POETRY
    Haverstraw. London: Breman, 1963.
    (Anthologies): Abdul, The Magic of Black Poetry; Adoff, The
        Poetry of Black America; Bontemps, American Negro Po-
        etry; Bontemps, Golden Slippers; Braithwaite, Anthology
        of Magazine Verse for 1926; Brown, Davis and Lee, The
        Negro Caravan; Chapman, Black Voices; Hayden, Kaleido-
        scope; Hughes and Bontemps, The Poetry of the Negro,
        1746-1970; Johnson, The Book of American Negro Poetry;
        Johnson, Ebony and Topaz; Kerlin, Negro Poets and Their
        Poems; Lomax and Abdul, 3000 Years of Black Poetry;
        Lowenfels, Poets of Today; Patterson, An Introduction to
        Black Literature in America; Pool, Beyond the Blues;
        Randall, The Black Poets; Rollins, Christmas Gif'; Sim-
        mons and Hutchinson, Black Culture; Walrond and Pool,
        Black and Unknown Bards.
    (Periodicals): Crisis, 1925, 1926, 1927, 1928, 1929, 1965,
        1966, 1967, 1970, 1971; Opportunity, December 1925, July
        1926, July 1929, July 1941; Phylon, Fourth Quarter 1941;
        First Quarter, Fourth Quarter 1943; also published in
        Carolina magazine.
NON-FICTION
    Published in Crisis, Interracial Review, Journal of Inter-
        group Relations, Opportunity, Phylon.
SHORT STORY
    (Periodicals): Crisis 35 (1928): 225; Opportunity (March 1934).
BIOGRAPHY AND CRITICISM ON HORNE
    Johnson. The Book of American Negro Poetry, p. 268.
    Kerlin. Negro Poets and Their Poems, pp. 206-208, 340.
    Opportunity 5 (July 1927): 205, 213.
    "Poets." Ebony 4 (February 1949): 41.
    Primeau, Ronald. "Frank Horne and the Second Echelon Po-
        ets of the Harlem Renaissance." In Bontemps, The Har-
        lem Renaissance Remembered, pp. 247-267.
    Wagner. Black Poets of the United States, pp. 185-186.
    Who's Who in Colored America, 3rd ed. (1930-1931-1932).

HORSMAN, Gallan.
    NOVEL The Noose and the Spear: A Tale of Passion, Adven-
        ture and Violence. New York: Vantage, 1965.

HORTON, George Moses. Born 1797 in Northhampton County, North
    Carolina, the property of William Horton. At the death of his
    master in 1815 he passed to James Horton, a son, and 17 years

later to Hall Horton, son of James. James knew that George
wanted to learn and encouraged him to do so.[1] Education: He
taught himself to read and write by studying the alphabet from
scraps of paper and by reading Methodist hymnbooks.[2] Career:
When Hall Horton realized that George was not the best of field
hands, he permitted him to travel to Chapel Hill to hire his
time. For 30 years, he worked as a janitor at the University
of North Carolina[3] where the college president became his master. He also earned a living writing love poems for the male
students. He charged from 25¢ to 50¢ a lyric, depending upon
the warmth desired. His first book of poems, published in
1829, was to raise funds for manumission. Unfortunately, the
book was a financial failure.[4] He was helped by Mrs. Caro-
line Lee Hentz, herself a poet and novelist, and wife of a new
professor at Chapel Hill. It was she who had his poem, "Liberty and Slavery" published in the Lancaster Gazette where it
was noticed and reprinted as "Slavery" in William Lloyd Garrison's Liberator, 29 March 1934.[5] Later, Mrs. Horace Greeley, having heard of Horton while she was teaching in Warrenton, spoke of him to the editor of the New York Tribune. His
poem, "The Poet's Petition" later appeared in the Tribune. In
1865 Horton went to Philadelphia with a United States Cavalry
Officer, Captain Will H. S. Banks of the 9th Michigan Cavalry
Volunteers.[6]

For most of his life, Horton begged in person, in letters,
and in verse for his freedom. His wish was not fulfilled until
he was an old man, freed by a mandate of occupying Union
forces. He died in Philadelphia in 1883.[7]

POETRY
> Hope of Liberty. Raleigh, N.C.: J. Gales & Son, 1829;
> later printed as
> Poems By a Slave. Philadelphia, 1837; and under this title
> was again bound with the 1838 editions of the poems of
> Phillis Wheatley. Copies of other editions are exceeding-
> ly rare, if indeed they are in existence at all. Harvard
> University houses a copy of Poetical Works (Hillsborough,
> N.C., 1845). There is one copy of Naked Genius at the
> Athenaeum in Boston.
> Rumor has that an autobiography and a collection of his
> works issued in Boston, 1852, 1850, and 1854 are in ex-
> istence.[8]
> Naked Genius. Raleigh, N.C.: 1865.
> Poetical Works of George M. Horton, the Colored Bard of
> North Carolina. Hillsborough, N.C., 1845.
> (Anthologies): Barksdale and Kinnamon, Black Writers in
> America; Breman, You Better Believe It; Brown, Davis
> and Lee, Negro Caravan; Davis and Redding, Cavalcade;
> Du Bois, The Gift of Black Folk; Hayden, Kaleidoscope;
> Hughes and Bontemps, The Poetry of the Negro, 1746-
> 1970; Kerlin, Negro Poets and Their Poems; Long and
> Collier, Afro-American Writing; Patterson, Introduction
> to Black Literature in America; Robinson, Early Black
> American Poets; Turner, Black American Literature;

White and Jackson, <u>An Anthology of Verse by American</u>
<u>Negroes</u>;
See also:
"Pains of a Bachelor's Life" in <u>History of the University of</u>
<u>North Carolina,</u> I. Kemp P. Battle, 1907, pp. 604-605.
"Pleasures of a Bachelor's Life." In <u>History of the Univer-</u>
<u>sity of North Carolina,</u> I. Kemp P. Battle, 1907, p. 604.
(Periodical): <u>Liberator,</u> 29 March 1834.

BIOGRAPHY AND CRITICISM ON HORTON

Bardolph. <u>The Negro Vanguard</u>, p. 80.
Barksdale and Kinnamon. <u>Black Writers in America</u>, pp.
219-220.
Baskin and Runes. <u>Dictionary of Black Culture</u>, pp. 217-218.
Battle, Henry P. "George Horton, Slave Poet." <u>North</u>
<u>Carolina University Magazine</u> 7 (May 1888): 229.
Bergman. <u>The Chronological History of the Negro in Amer-</u>
<u>ica,</u> pp. 79, 163, 248.
Brawley. <u>Early Negro American Writers</u>, pp. 110-122.
_____. <u>Negro Builders and Heroes</u>, p. 233.
_____. <u>Negro Genius</u>, pp. 71-74.
Breman. <u>You Better Believe It</u>, pp. 23-24.
Butcher. <u>The Negro in American Culture</u>, p. 97.
Cobb, Collier. "An American Man of Letters: George
Moses Horton, the Negro Poet." <u>North Carolina Review</u>
(October 3, 1909) and in <u>The University of North Carolina</u>
<u>Magazine</u> (October 1909) and several times reprinted as a
pamphlet, "George Moses Horton: Slave Poet," by Stephen
B. Weeks in <u>The Southern Workman</u> 43 (October 1914):
571; and <u>The Negro Author</u> by Vernon Loggins, New York,
1931, pp. 107-117.[9]
Du Bois. <u>The Gift of Black Folk</u>, p. 304.
Farrison, W. E. "George Moses Horton: Poet for Free-
dom." <u>CLA Journal</u> 14 (March 1971): 227-241.
Gayle, Addison, Jr. <u>Black Expression</u>, pp. 65-70, 73, 109-
110, 205-206.
Jahn. <u>Neo-African Literature</u>, pp. 128, 137, 141.
Jarrett, Calvin. "Illiterate Genius." <u>Negro Digest</u> 13 (July
1964): 62-69.
Joint Commission of the North Carolina English Teachers
Association and the North Carolina Library Association.
<u>North Carolina Authors,</u> 1952, pp. 64-65. (Bibliography.)
Lakum, M. T. T. "George Moses Horton." Master's thesis,
North Carolina College, 1951.
<u>Liberator,</u> 29 March 1834.
Loggins. <u>The Negro Author in America</u>, pp. 104-105, 107-
117, 232, 332, 360, 382-383, 419.
<u>Negro History Bulletin</u> 6 (February 1942): 103.
Porter. <u>Early Negro Writers, 1760-1837</u>, p. 578.
Redding. <u>They Came in Chains</u>, pp. 103, 145.
Robinson. <u>Early Black American Poetry</u>, pp. 18-19.
Toppin. <u>A Biographical History of Blacks in America Since</u>
<u>1528</u>, p. 103.
Weeks, Stephen B. "George Moses Horton: Slave Poet."

Southern Workman 43 (October 1914): 571-577.
White and Jackson. An Anthology of Verse by American Ne-
groes, pp. 6-7, 33-37, 217, 222-224, 235.
INTERJECTIONS
"Born a slave, he gave poignant expression to the predica-
ment of the Black man in what was called a democratic society;
'How long have I in bondage lain, / And languished to be free! /
Alas! and must I still complain, / Deprived of liberty?' "[10]

[1]Benjamin Brawley, Negro Genius (New York: Dodd,
Mead, 1937), p. 71.
[2]Richard Barksdale and Keneth Kinnamon, Black Writers
in America (New York: Macmillan, 1972), p. 219.
[3]Brawley, p. 71.
[4]Peter M. Bergman, The Chronological History of the
Negro in America (New York: Harper & Row, 1969), p.
79.
[5]William H. Robinson, Early Black American Poets
(Dubuque, Iowa: William C. Brown, 1969), pp. 18-19.
[6]Benjamin Brawley, Early Negro Writers (New York:
Dover, 1970), p. 111.
[7]Robinson, p. 19.
[8]Brawley, Early Negro Writers, p. 111.
[9]Ibid., p. 112.
[10]Wade Baskin and Richard Runes, Dictionary of Black
Culture (New York: Philosophical Library, 1973), p. 218.

HORTON, Mary-Louise.
POETRY (Anthology): Black Poets Write On!

HOUGH, Florenz H.
Black Paradise. Philadelphia: Dorrance, 1953.

HOWARD, Alice Henrietta.
POETRY Onion to Orchard: Poems. New York: William Frederick, 1945.

HOWARD, Beatrice Thomas.
POETRY Poems and Quotations. New York: By the Author,
1956.

HOWARD, James H. W.
WRITINGS Bond and Free: A True Tale of Slave Times.
Harrisburg: Edwin K. Meyers, Printer & Binder, 1886;
reprint ed., Miami: Mnemosyne*; College Park, Md.:
McGrath*; New York: AMS Press*.

HOWARD, Sallie.
DRAMA The Jackal, 195?.

HOWARD, Vanessa. Born 1955 in Brooklyn.
POETRY
(Anthologies): Jordan, Soulscript; Jordan and Bush, The
Voice of the Children.

SHORT STORY
   (Anthology): Bambara, Tales and Stories.

HOWARD, Wilbert R.
   POETRY The Rhyme of the Devil-Germs. New York: Pageant,
      1963.

HUFF, William Henry.
   POETRY
      From Deep Within: Poems. Chicago: Dierkes Press, 1951.
      Sowing and Reaping, and Other Poems. Avon, Ill.: Hamlet
         Press, 1950.
      (Anthology): Weisman and Wright, Black Poetry for All
         Americans.
      (Periodical): Crisis, 1937; 1940.

HUGHES, Langston James. Born 1 February 1902 in Joplin, Missouri. Died 22 May 1967. Education: Graduated from Central
   High School in Cleveland, Ohio, 1920; spent one year, 1921-22,
   at Columbia University; graduated from Lincoln University (Pa.),
   1929;[1] received an honorary Litt.D. from Lincoln University,
   1943.[2] Career: In his teens he worked at odd jobs after
   school, and went to see all the road shows he could. Although
   he had not at that time written a poem, he was elected class
   poet of his grammar school. According to Hughes, this was how
   he began to write poetry. When in attendance at Central High
   School, Cleveland, Ohio, he wrote poems and in his senior year
   edited the Yearbook. After spending a summer in Mexico with
   his father, whom he grew to dislike intensely, Hughes returned
   to Cleveland. He wrote "The Negro Speaks of Rivers" which
   was published in Crisis and first won him attention. Leaving
   Columbia University, he settled in Harlem. When he was 20 he
   decided to see the world and signed up on a ship going to Africa.[3] He wandered abroad in Europe, returned to the states
   and attended Lincoln University. Although Hughes had travelled
   to Italy, Paris, and Russia, his home base was Harlem.[4] His
   part-time jobs were various: he was an assistant cook at the
   Grand Duc Cafe, Paris; beachcomber in Spain and Italy; launder-
   er, Washington, D.C.; busboy in New York.
      In 1920, after meeting Vachel Lindsay who introduced him to
   the literary world, he wrote The Weary Blues and won first
   prize in a poetry contest held by Opportunity magazine. He continued to write for both adults and children.[5] He went on cross-
   country tours reading his poetry; became poet-in-residence at
   the University of Chicago Laboratory School in 1949; was a lyri-
   cist, radio writer, and lecturer.[6] He even taught English in
   Mexico;[2] and in 1937 was a Madrid correspondent for the Baltimore Afro-American. In 1933 he assisted in the preparation of
   a scenario for a motion picture to be made in Moscow, Russia.
   Since 1921, when he published his first poem in Crisis, he had
   written many articles, poems, stories, short fiction, and drama.
   Many of these works have been translated into German, French,
   Spanish, Russian, Chinese, Japanese and Dutch. In particular,

his work, <u>Not Without Laughter,</u> not only was published in book form in England, Russia, and France, but was also serialized in <u>Wen Yi,</u> a Chinese literary magazine.[7] <u>Member:</u> National Institute of the Arts and Letters; A.S.C.A.P.;[8] Omega Psi Phi.[9] <u>Awards, Honors:</u> Honorary Litt.D., 1943, from Lincoln University;[10] <u>Opportunity</u> Poetry Prize, 1925; <u>Palms</u> Intercollegiate Poetry Award, 1927; Harmon Award for Literature, 1931; selected by Dr. Charles Austin Beard as one of America's 25 interesting personages with a socially conscious attitude, 1934; Guggenheim Fellowship, 1935.[11]

BIBLIOGRAPHIES ON HUGHES' WORK

Dickinson, Donald C. <u>A Bio-Bibliography of Langston Hughes, 1902-1967.</u> n.p.: Archon Books, 1967.

Emanuel, James. <u>Langston Hughes.</u> New York: Twayne, 1967.

Jahn, Janheinz. <u>A Bibliography of Neo-African Literature from Africa, America and the Caribbean.</u> New York: Praeger, 1965, pp. 274-275.

Libman, Valentina A., comp., Robert V. Allen, trans., Clarence Gohdes, ed. <u>Russian Studies of American Literature.</u> Chapel Hill: University of North Carolina Press, 1969, pp. 106-107.

O'Daniel, Therman B. "Langston Hughes: A Selected Classified Bibliography." <u>CLA Journal</u> 11 (1967): 349-366.

_____, ed. <u>Langston Hughes: Black Genius, A Critical Evaluation.</u> New York: Morrow, 1971.

CRITICISM

"The Negro Artist and the Racial Mountain." <u>Nation</u> 122 (1926): 692-694; also in Gayle, <u>The Black Aesthetic.</u>

"To Negro Writers." <u>American Writers Congress.</u> Edited by H. Hart. New York: International, 1935, pp. 139-141.

"The Twenties: Harlem and Its Negritude." <u>African Forum</u> 1 (1966): 11-20.

"Writers: Black and White." In <u>The American Negro Writer and His Roots,</u> pp. 41-45.

DRAMA

(Full-length Plays)

<u>Emperor of Haiti,</u> 1936. In Turner, <u>Black Drama in America.</u>

<u>Front Porch</u> (three-act comedy-drama, with happy or tragic ending), 1937.

<u>Joy to My Soul</u> (three-act comedy), 1937.

<u>Little Ham</u> (three-act comedy), 1935. In <u>Five Plays by Langston Hughes.</u>

<u>Mulatto</u> (three-act tragedy), 1935. In <u>Five Plays by Langston Hughes;</u> Brasmer and Consolo, <u>Black Drama;</u> excerpt in Watkins and David, <u>To Be a Black Woman.</u>

<u>Simply Heavenly,</u> 1957. New York: Dramatists Play Service, 1959; also in <u>Five Plays by Langston Hughes;</u> <u>The Langston Hughes Reader;</u> Patterson, <u>Black Theater.</u>

<u>The Sun Do Move</u> (music drama), 1942.

<u>Tambourines to Glory</u> (two-act gospel singing play), 1963. In <u>Five Plays by Langston Hughes.</u>

With William Grant Still.   Troubled Island (three-act tragedy), 1936.

With Arna Bontemps.   When the Jack Hollers (three-act comedy), 1936.

(One-act plays)

Angelo Herndon Jones.   (Manuscript in the Yale University Library.)

Don't You Want to Be Free.   In One Act Play Magazine 2 (October 1938): 359-393.

The Em-Fuehrer Jones, 1938.

Mother and Child.   In King and Milner, Black Drama Anthology.

The Organizer, 1938-39.   (Manuscript in Yale University Library.)

Soul Gone Home (one-act fantasy).   In One Act Play Magazine 1 (July 1937); also in Five Plays by Langston Hughes.

Trouble with the Angels.

(Gospel song-plays)

Black Nativity (A Christmas Song-Play in Two Acts), 1961.

Gospel Glory, 1962.

Jericho-Jim Crow, 1963.

The Prodigal Son, 1965.   In Players Magazine 43 (October-November 1967).

(Other plays)

With Jan Meyerowitz.   The Barrier, 1950.

For This We Fight, 1943.

Limitations of Life, 1938.

Little Eva's End, 1938.

Outshines the Sun.

Simple Takes a Wife, 1954.

With Bob Teague.   Soul Yesterday and Today, 1969.

EDITOR

An African Treasury: Articles, Essays, Stories, Poems by Black Africans.   New York: Crown, 1960*; New York: Pyramid†.

The Best Short Stories by Negro Writers: An Anthology from 1899 to the Present.   Boston: Little, Brown, 1967.

With Arna Bontemps.   The Book of Negro Folklore.   New York: Dodd, Mead, 1959*†.

The Best of Simple.   New York: Hill & Wang, 1961*†.

Five Plays by Langston Hughes.   Edited by Webster Smalley. Bloomington: Indiana University Press, 1963†.

The Langston Hughes Reader. New York: Geo. Braziller, 1968*.

Selected Poems of Langston Hughes.   New York: Knopf, 1959.

Good Morning Revolution: The Uncollected Social Protest Writing of Langston Hughes.   Edited by Faith Berry. Westport, Conn.: Lawrence Hill, 1973*†.

AUTOBIOGRAPHY

The Big Sea: An Autobiography.   New York: Knopf, 1940*.

I Wonder as I Wander: An Autobiographical Journey.   New York: Rinehart, 1956; New York: Hill & Wang†; excerpt in Davis and Redding, Cavalcade.

"My Most Humiliating Jim Crow Experience."   Negro Digest

3 (May 1945): 33-34.

CHILDREN AND YOUNG ADULTS

The First Book of Africa, 1960; rev. ed. , New York: Franklin Watts, 1965*.

The First Book of Jazz. New York: Franklin Watts, 1955*.

The First Book of Negroes. New York: Franklin Watts, 1952.

The First Book of Rhythms. New York: Franklin Watts, 1954*.

The First Book of the West Indies. New York: Franklin Watts, 1956.

With Arna Bontemps. Popo and Fifina: Children of Haiti. New York: Macmillan, 1932.

EDITOR

The Book of Negro Humor. New York: Dodd, Mead, 1966*†.

Famous American Negroes. New York: Dodd, Mead, 1954*†.

Famous Negro Music Makers. New York: Dodd, Mead, 1955*.

Four Lincoln University Poets. Lincoln University, 1930.

Lincoln University Poets. New York: Fine Editions, 1954.

New Negro Poets: U.S.A. Bloomington: Indiana University Press, 1964*†.

With Arna Bontemps. The Poetry of the Negro, 1946-1949; rev. ed. , The Poetry of the Negro, 1746-1970; Garden City, N.Y.: Doubleday, 1970, 1973*.

Poems from Black Africa. Bloomington: Indiana University Press, 1963*.

La Poésie Negro-Américaine. Paris: Seghers, 1966.

NON-FICTION

With Milton Meltzer. Black Magic: A Pictorial History of the Negro in American Entertainment. Englewood Cliffs, N.J.: Prentice-Hall, 1967*.

Black Misery. New York: Paul S. Erickson, 1969†. (Photo essay.)

Fight for Freedom: The Story of the NAACP. New York: Norton, 1962*.

With Milton Meltzer. A Pictorial History of the Negro in America, 1956; 3rd rev. ed. , New York: Crown, 1968*†.

With Roy DeCarava. The Sweet Flypaper of Life. New York: Simon & Schuster, 1955*. (Photo essay.)

NOVELS

Not Without Laughter. New York: Knopf, 1930*; New York: Macmillan, 1969†.

Simple Speaks His Mind. New York: Simon & Schuster, 1950.

Simple Stakes a Claim. New York: Rinehart, 1957.

Simple Takes a Wife. New York: Simon & Schuster, 1953.

Simple's Uncle Sam. New York: Hill & Wang, 1965*.

Tambourines to Glory. New York: John Day, 1958; New York: Hill & Wang, 1970*†.

POETRY

Ask Your Mama: 12 Moods for Jazz. New York: Knopf,

Dear Lovely Death. New York: Troutbeck Press, 1931.

Don't You Turn Back. Edited by Lee B. Hopkins. New
York: Knopf, 1969. (Original title: I Bring You My Songs:
Poems of Langston Hughes.)

The Dream Keeper and Other Poems. New York: Knopf,
1932*.

Fields of Wonder. New York: Knopf, 1947.

Fine Clothes to the Jew. New York: Knopf, 1927.

Freedom's Plow. New York: Musette, 1943.

Jim Crow's Last Stand. n. p. : Negro Publication Society of
America, 1943.

Lament for Dark Peoples and Other Poems. Holland: n. p. ,
1944.

Montage of a Dream Deferred. New York: Holt, 1951.

The Negro Mother. New York: Golden Stair Press, 1931;
Freeport, N. Y. : Books for Libraries*.

One-Way Ticket. New York: Knopf, 1949.

The Panther and the Lash: Poems of Our Times. New
York: Knopf, 1967†.

Scottsboro Limited: Four Poems and a Play. New York:
Golden Stair, 1932.

Selected Poems of Langston Hughes. New York: Knopf,
1959*.

With Robert Glenn. Shakespeare in Harlem. New York:
Knopf, 1942.

The Weary Blues. New York: Knopf, 1926.

(Anthologies): Adams, Conn and Slepian, Afro-American
Literature: Poetry; Adoff, Black Out Loud; Barksdale and
Kinnamon, Black Writers of America; Bell, Afro-Ameri-
can Poetry; Bontemps, American Negro Poetry; Cuney,
et al, Lincoln University Poets; Eastman, The Norton
Anthology of Poetry; Ellman and O'Claire, The Norton
Anthology of Modern Poetry; Emanuel and Gross, Dark
Symphony; Ford, Black Insights; Hayden, Kaleidoscope;
Henderson, Understanding the New Black Poetry; Hollo,
Negro Verse; Jordan, Soulscript; Long and Collier,
Afro-American Writing; Patterson, A Rock Against the
Wind; Pool, Beyond the Blues; Randall, The Black Po-
ets; Walrond and Pool, Black and Unknown Bards.

(Periodicals): Black World 2 (April 1971): 27; Crisis 73 (December 1966): 525; 74 (April 1967): 131; (June 1967): 250-
251; 75 (February 1968): 50; 75 (June-July 1968): 194; 77
(November 1970): 367; Freedomways 8 (Spring 1968): 182-
184; Harlem Quarterly (Winter 1949-50); The Negro Quarterly (Spring 1942); (Fall 1942); Negro Digest 13 (September 1964): 54-55; 13 (October 1964): 53; 14 (September
1966); 64; 16 (November 1966): 48; Phylon, (Second Quarter 1941); (First Quarter 1952); (Third Quarter 1957).

SCREENPLAY

With Clarence Muse. Way Down South, 1942.

SHORT STORIES
<u>Laughing to Keep from Crying</u>. New York: Holt, 1952.
<u>Something in Common and Other Stories</u>. New York: Hill &
Wang, 1963*.
<u>The Ways of White Folks</u>. New York: Knopf, 1934*†.
(Anthologies): Bambara, <u>Tales and Stories</u>; Brown, Davis
and Lee, <u>Negro Caravan</u>; Clarke, <u>American Negro Short
Stories</u>; Davis and Redding, <u>Cavalcade</u>; King, <u>Black Short
Story Anthology</u>; Watkins, <u>Anthology of American Negro
Literature</u>.
(Periodicals): <u>Challenge</u>, March 1934; June 1936; <u>Negro
Digest</u>, July 1962; <u>Negro Quarterly</u>, Summer 1942; <u>Negro
Story</u>, October-November 1944; December-January 1944-
45; August-September 1945.

BIOGRAPHY AND CRITICISM ON HUGHES
(See "Bibliographies" listed above for additional citations.)
Abramson. <u>Negro Playwrights in the American Theatre</u>, pp.
67-88.
Anon. "Farewell to Langston Hughes." <u>Crisis</u> 74 (June
1967): 252-254.
Anon. "Langston Hughes and the Example of 'Simple.' "
<u>Black World</u> 19 (June 1970): 35-38.
Anon. "Langston Hughes--45th Spingarn Medalist." <u>Crisis</u>
67 (August-September 1960): 422-423.
Barisonzi, Judith A. "Black Identity in the Poetry of Lang-
ston Hughes." <u>Dissertation Abstracts International</u>, 32:
3291A (Wisconsin.)
Bond. <u>The Negro and the Drama</u>, pp. 114-117.
Bontemps, Arna. <u>Ebony</u> (October 1946): 19-23.
_____. <u>The Harlem Renaissance Remembered</u>, pp. 1-277
passim.
Brawley. <u>The Negro Genius</u>, pp. 246-250.
Brooks, Gwendolyn, et al. "Langston Hughes/Poems and
Tributes Dedicated to the Memory of Langston Hughes."
<u>Negro Digest</u> 16 (September 1967): 31-48.
Bruning, Eberhard. " 'The Black Liberation Movement' und
das amerikanische Drama." <u>Zeitschrift für Anglistic un
Amerikanistik</u> 20 (1972): 46-58.
Carey, Julian C. "Jesse B. Semple Revisited and Revised."
<u>Phylon</u> 32 (1971): 158-163.
Chametzky and Kaplan. <u>Black and White in American Cul-
ture</u>, pp. 187-188, 346, 360-361, 364, 380-384, 386-389.
<u>Current Biography</u>, 1940.
Farrison, W. Edward. "Langston Hughes: Poet of the Ne-
gro Renaissance." <u>CLA Journal</u> 15 (June 1972): 401-410.
Garber, E. D. "Form as a Complement to Content in Three
of Langston Hughes' Poems." <u>Negro American Literature
Forum</u> 5 (Winter 1971): 137-139.
Harrison. <u>The Drama of Nommo</u>, pp. 24, 113, 165.
Hudson, Theodore R. "Technical Aspects of the Poetry of
Langston Hughes." <u>Black World</u> 22 (September 1973): 24-
45.
Joans, Ted. "The Langston I Knew." <u>Black World</u> 21 (Sep-

tember 1972): 14-19.

Johnson, Lemuel A. The Devil, The Gargoyle and The Buffoon, pp. 107-109, 125-131.

Meltzer, Milton. Langston Hughes: A Biography. New York: Apollo, 1972.

Mitchell, Loften. "That Other Man." Crisis 76 (February 1969): 75-77.

_____. Black Drama, pp. 1, 29, 79, 84, 97, 103, 128, 186, 200, 204-205, 145-147, 197-198.

Myers, Elizabeth P. Langston Hughes: Poet of His People. Scarsdale, N.Y.: Garrard, 1970.

O'Daniel, Therman B., ed. Langston Hughes: Black Genius, A Critical Evaluation. New York: Morrow, 1971.

Prowle, Allen D. "Langston Hughes." In Bigsby, The Black American Writer, vol. 2, pp. 77-87.

Taylor, Patricia E. "Langston Hughes and the Harlem Renaissance, 1921-1931." In Bontemps, The Harlem Renaissance Remembered, pp. 90-101.

Wagner. Black Poets of the United States, pp. 385-474.

Waldon, Edward E. "The Blues Poetry of Langston Hughes." Negro American Literature Forum 5 (Winter 1971): 140-149.

Watkins, C. A. "Simple, Alter Ego of Langston Hughes." Black Scholar 2 (June 1971): 18-26.

Whitlow. Black American Literature, pp. 2, 11, 86-92, 96, 134, 141, 185.

Wilkins, R. "Langston Hughes: A Tribute." Crisis 74 (June 1967): 246.

Young. Black Writers of the Thirties, pp. 172-179, 216-219.

    [1]Thomas Yenser, ed., Who's Who in Colored America, 5th ed. (Brooklyn, N.Y.: Yenser, 1940), p. 267.

    [2]A. N. Marquis, ed., Who Was Who in America, vol. 4 (Chicago: Marquis, 1968), p. 472.

    [3]Maxine Block, ed., Current Biography (New York: Wilson, 1940), p. 411.

    [4]Arthur P. Davis and Saunders Redding, eds., Cavalcade (Boston: Houghton-Mifflin, 1971), p. 302.

    [5]Block, pp. 411-412.

    [6]Marquis, p. 472.

    [7]Yenser, p. 268.

    [8]Marquis, p. 472.

    [9]Yenser, p. 268.

    [10]Marquis, p. 472.

    [11]Yenser, p. 268.

HUGHLY, Young.
  DRAMA Place for the Manchild, 1972.

HULT, Ruby.
  DRAMA The Saga of George W. Bush, 1962.

HUMPHREY, Lillie Muse.
NOVEL Aggie. New York: Vantage, 1955.

HUMPHREY, Myrtle "Moss." Born 13 January 1934 in West Point,
Mississippi. Education: B.A. (Sociology), Southern University, 1954; M.S.L.S., University of Southern California, Los
Angeles, 1967; M.L.A. (Certification Medical Librarian 1), University of Southern California, Los Angeles. Currently living
in Los Angeles. Career: Library Assistant, Los Angeles
County Museum of Art; Los Angeles Museum of History and Art,
1960-1964; Librarian Trainee, Los Angeles Public Library,
1965-1966; Reference Librarian, San Fernando Valley State College, 1969; Librarian, Charles R. Drew Postgraduate Medical
School; Senior Medical Librarian, Martin Luther King, Jr. General Hospital, Los Angeles County, 1971 to present. Also holds
poetry readings and one-woman shows. Member: Medical Library Association; Medical Library Group of Southern California.
POETRY
   Be a Man Boy and Other Poems. Los Angeles: Capricorn
      House West, 1973.
   As Much as I Am. Los Angeles: Capricorn House West,
      1973.
NON-FICTION
   Beyond the Walls: Innovations in Library Service. Chicago:
      American Hospital Association, forthcoming.

HUNKINS, Leecynth (Lee Hunkins). Born 8 January 1930 in New
York City. Education: Attended New York University. Currently living in New York City. Career: Has been a claims representative for twenty-five years with the Social Security Administration. Her plays have been produced by community theatres and the CBS Playhouse (now defunct). A two-act play was
presented in the summer festival of the Negro Ensemble Company. Member: Writers Guild of America, East; New York
Chapter of the National Academy of Television Arts and Sciences.
DRAMA
   With Steve Chambers. The Dolls, 1971.
INTERJECTIONS
   "I do not write angry plays, because I believe that if one is
not satisfied with the plight of the Black man, there is more
than one method of getting this message across. I write about
people and problems--not just ghetto life, poverty, drug addic-
tion. True, these are important issues, but our problems are
not limited to just these things. We love, we need, we desire
and we dream--we are Black, but first we are human beings."

HUNT, Evelyn Tooley.
POETRY
   Toad Song: A Collection of Haiku and Other Small Poems.
      New York: Apple, 1966.

Myrtle "Moss" Humphrey

(Periodical): <u>Negro Digest</u>, February 1964; May 1964; September 1964; September 1965; September 1966.

HUNT, Ted.
    <u>POETRY</u> (Anthology): Henderson, <u>Understanding the New Black Poetry</u>.

HUNTER, Eddie.
    <u>DRAMA</u>
        <u>The Battle of Who Run</u>.
        <u>Going to the Races</u>.
        <u>How Come</u>, 1923.
        <u>The Lady</u>, 1944.
        With Alex Rogers. <u>My Magnolia</u>, 1926.
    <u>BIOGRAPHY AND CRITICISM ON HUNTER</u>
        Mitchell. <u>Black Drama</u>, 65-67, 68, 70, 82, 92.

HUNTER, Eleanor.
    <u>POETRY</u>
        (Anthology): Murphy, <u>Negro Voices</u>.
        (Periodical): <u>Harlem Digest</u>.

HUNTER, Kristin (Mrs. John I. Lattany). <u>Born</u> 12 September 1931 in Philadelphia. <u>Education</u>: B.S., University of Pennsylvania,

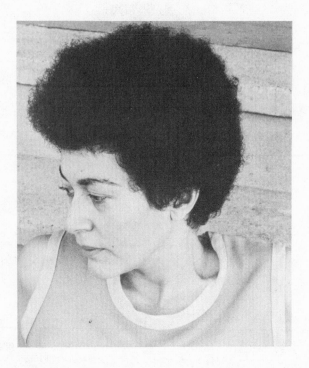

Kristin Hunter (credit: Margery Smith)

1951. <u>Currently living in</u> Philadelphia. <u>Career:</u> Specializes in writing fiction (and sometimes journalism) "about people who happen to be black; in other words, stories that emphasize the rich humanity of black people." Presently writing a novel and a book of light verse while refurbishing an old house and teaching short story writing at the University of Pennsylvania.

<u>Awards, Honors</u>: Received the Lewis Carroll Shelf Award, the National Conference of Christians and Jews Mass Media Award; the Council on Interracial Books for Children Award for <u>The Soul Brothers and Sister Lou</u>; Sigma Delta Chi Best Magazine Reporting of the Year Award, 1968, for the article, "Pray for Barbara's Baby"; <u>Chicago Tribune Book World</u> Award, Best Book for Older Children, 1973, for <u>Guests in the Promised Land</u>.

CHILDREN AND YOUNG ADULTS

<u>Boss Cat</u>. New York: Scribner's, 1971*.

<u>Guests in the Promised Land</u>. New York: Scribner's 1973*.

<u>The Soul Brothers and Sister Lou</u>. New York: Scribner's, 1968*; New York: Avon, 1970†.

NOVELS
  God Bless the Child. New York: Bantam, 1970†.
  The Landlord. New York: Scribner's, 1966; New York: Avon,
    1970†.
SHORT STORIES
  (Anthologies): Hughes, The Best Short Stories by Negro
    Writers; Turner, Black American Literature: Fiction.
  (Periodicals): Black World, June 1972; Essence, April 1971;
    Negro Digest, June 1968.
BIOGRAPHY AND CRITICISM ON HUNTER
  "Black Writer's Views on Literary Lions and Values." Ne-
    gro Digest 17 (January 1968): 40.
  Contemporary Authors, 13/14.
  Whitlow. Black American Literature, pp. 151-154.
INTERJECTIONS
  "Practicing art in America would be no more difficult than
  practicing dentistry (if less remunerative), if people only would
  not weave such an elaborate mystique about it. All that is re-
  quired is that one remain never quite fully grown, so as to
  keep the inner child--the imagination--alive. An artist should
  also have a capacity, even a liking, for hard and lonely drudg-
  ery in the service of that imagination. Pontificating about one's
  'philosophy' is a temptation offered all too often by people who
  imagine that artists are profound and all-knowing; it is one
  which I, however, steadfastly resist, because I know better."

HUNTLEY, Elizabeth Maddox.
  DRAMA What Ye Sow. New York: Court, 1955.

HURST, Janet.
  POETRY (Periodical): Negro History Bulletin, March 1971.

HURSTON, Zora Neale. Born 7 January 1903 in Eatonville, Florida. Died 28 January 1960. Education: Attended the Negro
  Public Schools in Eatonville; high school in Jacksonville, Florida;[1] Morgan Academy in Baltimore; after Morgan, she enrolled
  in Howard University. A scholarship assisted her to transfer
  to Barnard College, where she earned her B.A. in 1928.[2]
  Awarded a private grant from Mrs. R. Osgood Mason, and a
  fellowship from the Rosenwald Foundation, she was able to study
  anthropology and folklore at Columbia University from 1928-32
  under Dr. Franz Boas; and to travel, live and study folklore in
  Haiti and British West Indies on a Guggenheim Fellow from
  1936-38.[3] Career: She worked as a maid and a manicurist in
  order to support herself and attend school. After receiving her
  degree from Barnard College, she became Fannie Hurst's secretary. She began her writing career while in high school and
  wrote her first short story for Stylus, the college literary magazine. Later, she submitted stories to various current magazines. In the winter of 1932 she produced a program of Negro
  spirituals and work songs at the John Golden Theatre in New
  York. In May 1934, she took her troupe to the National Folklore Festival in St. Louis. She also wrote for Paramount Stu-

dios[4] and for Warner Brothers while in Hollywood. She held a
position as librarian at the Library of Congress in Washington,
D.C.;[5] and was formerly head of the drama department of the
North Carolina College for Negroes. Member: The American
Folklore Society; the American Anthropological Society; the
American Ethnological Society; and Zeta Phi Beta.[6] Awards,
Honors: Her first award was for her short story "Spunk"[7] in
the 1925 Opportunity literary contest; in 1939, Morgan College
awarded her the Litt.D. degree. In 1943 she received the An-
nisfield Award, $1000 for Dust Tracks on the Road; Howard Uni-
versity in 1943 bestowed upon her its Alumni Award for distinguished post-graduate work in literature.[8] Although a prolific
writer, Miss Hurston re-appeared in Florida, worked as a maid
in Riva Alto. She died penniless in a hospital in Fort Pierce.
Her funeral expenses were paid by collection and contribution.[9]
However, before she suffered from a stroke she was busy writing a last novel--The Life of Herod the Great.[10]

DRAMA
> With Clinton Fletcher and Tim Moore. Fast and Furious,
> 1931 (Musical). In Burns Mantle and Garrison Sherwood,
> Best Plays of 1931-1932.
> The First One (one act). In Johnson, Ebony and Topaz.
> Great Day, 1927.
> With Langston Hughes. Mule Bone: A Comedy of Negro Life
> in Three Acts, 1931.
> With Dorothy Waring. Polk County, 1944.

NON-FICTION
(Autobiography)
> Dust Tracks on the Road. Philadelphia: Lippincott, 1942*†;
> New York: Arno, 1970*.

(Folk-lore)
> Mules and Men. Philadelphia: Lippincott, 1935; New York:
> Harper & Row, 1970†; New York: Negro Universities
> Press*.
> Tell My Horse. Philadelphia: Lippincott, 1938; English edi-
> tion published 1939, under the title, Voodoo Gods. London:
> J. M. Dent & Sons, Ltd., 1939.
> (Anthologies): Brown, Davis and Lee, Negro Caravan; Cun-
> ard, Negro Anthology; Davis and Redding, Cavalcade.
> (Periodicals): American Legion Magazine (November 1950):
> 12-13, 54-57, 59-60; American Mercury 57 (1943): 450-
> 458, reprinted and condensed in Negro Digest, June 1943;
> Journal of American Folklore 43 (January-March 1930):
> 294-312; 44 (October-December 1931): 317-417; 60 (Oc-
> tober-December 1947): 436-438; Negro Digest 2 (May 1944);
> 2 (June 1944): 25-26; 5 (April 1947): 85-89; Saturday Eve-
> ning Post, 5 September 1942; 8 December 1951; Journal of
> Negro History 12 (October 1927): 664.

NOVELS
> Jonah's Gourd Vine. Philadelphia: Lippincott, 1934*; La Cale-
> bosse de Jonas; traduit par Marcel Duhamel. (In L'arba-
> tete; revue de litterature, Lyon, 1944).
> Moses, Man of the Mountain. Philadelphia: Lippincott, 1939.

Seraph on the Suwanee. New York: Scribner's, 1948.
Their Eyes Were Watching God. Philadelphia: Lippincott,
    1937; New York: Fawcett, 1969*; New York: Negro Univer-
    sities Press*; I loro occhi guardavano Dio, versione itali-
    ana di Ada Prospero, Turino, Frassinelli, 1938.
(Novel excerpts in anthologies): Brown, Davis and Lee, The
    Negro Caravan; Hughes, The Negro Novelist; Hughes, The
    Book of Negro Humor.

SHORT STORIES
    (Anthologies): Barksdale and Kinnamon, Black Writers in
        America; Burnett, E. W. and Martha Foley, Story in
        America (New York: Vanguard, 1934); Clarke, American
        Negro Short Stories; David, Black Joy; Davis and Redding,
        Cavalcade; Locke, The New Negro; Hughes, The Best Short
        Stories by Negro Writers; James, From the Roots; Patter-
        son, An Introduction to Black Literature in America; Wat-
        kins, Anthology of American Negro Literature.
    (Periodicals): Fire 1 (December 1926); Opportunity 2 (De-
        cember 1924): 371-374; 3 (May 1925): 171-173; 4 (January
        1926): 16-21; 4 (August 1926): 246-250, 267.
UNPUBLISHED WORKS
    "Book of Harlem."
    "The Chick with One Hen."
    "The Emperor Effaces Himself in Harlem Language."
    "Polk County, A Comedy of Negro Life in a Sawmill Camp."
BIOGRAPHY AND CRITICISM ON HURSTON
    Adams. Great Negroes Past and Present, p. 147.
    Bardolph. The Negro Vanguard, pp. 202, 206-209, 373.
    Barksdale and Kinnamon, Black Writers in America, pp. 611-
        613.
    Barton. Witnesses for Freedom, pp. 101-114.
    Baskin and Runes. Dictionary of Black Culture, p. 221.
    Bergman. The Chronological History of the Negro in Amer-
        ica, pp. 428.
    Blake, Emma L. "Zora Neale Hurston: Author and Folklor-
        ist." Negro History Bulletin 29 (April 1966): 149-150, 164.
    Bone. The Negro Novel in America, pp. 117, 123, 126-133,
        217.
    Bontemps. The Harlem Renaissance Remembered, pp. 20-21,
        46, 64, 81, 100, 150, 190-214, 229, 233-234, 268, 275.
    Brawley. The Negro Genius, pp. 257-259.
    Butcher. The Negro in American Culture, pp. 45, 48, 94,
        140, 144, 197.
    Byrd, James W. "Zora Neale Hurston: A Novel Folklorist."
        Tennessee Folklore Society Bulletin 21 (1955): 37-41.
    Cherry, et al. Portraits in Color, pp. 25-26.
    Cromwell, Turner and Dykes. Readings from Negro Authors,
        pp. 112-120.
    Dreer. American Literature by Negro Authors, pp. 132-138.
    Gayle. Black Expression, pp. 3, 5, 8, 11, 12, 36, 242,
        254-258, 278.
    Giles, James. "The Significance of Time in Zora Neale

Hurston's Their Eyes Were Watching God." Negro American Literature Forum 6 (Spring 1972): 52.

Gloster, Hugh. "Zora Neale Hurston, Novelist and Folklorist." Phylon 3 (Second Quarter 1943): 153-156.

Helmick, Evelyn Thomas. "Zora Neale Hurston." The Carrell (Journal of the Friends of the University of Miami, Florida, Library) 2 (1970): 1-19.

Hemenway. The Black Novelist, pp. 55-61.

Huggins. Harlem Renaissance, pp. 74-75, 129-133.

Hughes. The Big Sea. New York: Knopf, 1940.

Hughes. The Negro Novelist, pp. 38, 148, 172-178, 238-240, 274, 276, 277.

Hurst, Fannie. "Zora Hurston: A Personality Sketch." Yale University Library Gazette 35 (1961): 18.

Kent. Blackness and the Adventure of Western Culture, p. 32.

Killens. "Another Time When Black Was Beautiful," pp. 20-36.

Kilson, Marion. "The Transformation of Eatonville as Ethnographer." Phylon 33 (Summer 1972): 112-119.

Neal, Larry. "Eatonville's Zora Neale Hurston: A Profile." Watkins, Black Review #2.

Obituaries. Britannica Book of the Year, 1961, p. 515; Current Biography 21 (April 1960): 26; Current Biography Yearbook 1960, 1961, p. 195; New York Times, 5 February 1960, p. 27; Newsweek, 15 February 1960, p. 68; Publishers Weekly, 15 February 1960, p. 144; Time, 15 February 1960, p. 108; Wilson Library Bulletin 34 (April 1960): 552.

Ottley and Weatherby. The Negro in New York, p. 257.

Pratt, T. "Hurston, Zora Neale: A Memoir." Negro Digest 11 (February 1962): 52-56.

Redding. They Came in Chains, pp. 264-266.

Robinson. Historical Negro Biographies, pp. 208-209.

Sato, Hiroko. "Zora Neale Hurston Shiron." Oberon (Tokyo) 34:30-37.

Taylor, Clyde. "Black Folk Spirit and the Shape of Black Literature." Black World 21 (August 1972): 31-40.

Tischler. Black Masks, pp. 143, 158-159.

Turner, Darwin T. In a Minor Chord: Three Afro-American Writers and Their Search for Identity. Carbondale & Edwardsville: Southern Illinois University Press, 1971, pp. 89-120.

_____. "The Negro Novelist and the South." Southern Humanities Review 1 (1967): 21-29.

Warfel, Harry Redcay. American Novelists of Today, p. 233.

Washington, Mary Helen. "Zora Neale Hurston: The Black Woman's Search for Identity." Black World 21 (August 1972): 68-75.

Williams. They Also Spoke, pp. 257-258.

Young. Black Writers of the Thirties, pp. 204, 219-223, 241.

INTERJECTIONS
    Hurston's motto: "Let the people sing." John Chamberlain quite possibly wrote the most perceptive evaluation of her works. He said her story was as earthy as a convivial fishfry, at once "saucy and defiant...vivid as a poinsettia...beautiful as jasmine."[12] Following her death, the editor of the Florida Chronicle summarized: "Zora Neale Hurston went about and didn't care too much about how she looked, or what she said. But Zora Neale, every time she went about had something to offer. She didn't come to you empty."[13]

[1]Sylvia Dannett, ed., Profiles in Negro Womanhood, vol. 2 (Yonkers, N.Y.: Educational Heritage, 1964), p. 240.

[2]Obituary, New York Times, 5 February 1960, p. 27.

[3]Marquis, ed., Who Was Who in America, vol. 3 (Chicago: A.N. Marquis Co., 1963), p. 432.

[4]Maxine Block, ed., Current Biography (New York: H. W. Wilson, 1942), pp. 402-403.

[5]Obituary, p. 27.

[6]Block, p. 403.

[7]Benjamin Brawley, Negro Genius, (New York: Dodd, Mead, 1940), p. 257.

[8]Marquis, p. 433.

[9]Darwin Turner, In a Minor Chord (Carbondale: Southern Illinois University Press, 1971), p. 90.

[10]Obituary. Wilson Library Journal 34 (April 1960): 552.

[11]Dannett, vol. 2, p. 242.

[12]Ibid., p. 243.

[13]Emma L. Blake, "Zora Neale Hurston: Author and Folklorist," Negro History Bulletin 29 (April 1966): 164.

HUTCHINSON, Sylvester.
    POETRY Bride of Whiteness and Other Poems. New York: Vantage, 1967.

HYMAN, Mark.
    SHORT STORY (Anthology): Ford and Faggett, Best Short Stories by Afro-American Writers.

-I-

ICEBERG SLIM see BECK, Robert

IFETAYO, Femi Fumni. (Regina Micou).
    POETRY
    We the Black Woman. Detroit: Broadside, 1970†.
    (Anthology): Patterson, A Rock Against the Wind.

IMAN, Kasisi Yusef.
    DRAMA
    Blowing Temptation Away, 1972.
    The Cause the Cure, 1971.

The Joke On You, 1970.
Libra, 1971.
Mr. Bad, 1972.
Nigger House, 1969.
Praise the Lord, But Pass the Ammunition. Newark: Jihad, 1967.
The Price of Revolution, 1971.
Resurrection, 1970.
Santa's Last Ride, 1970.
Sociology (700 Clean Up Time), 1970.
The Verdict Is Yours, 1970.

POETRY
Poetry for Beautiful Black Women. Newark, N.J.: Jihad, 1969.
Something Black. Newark, N.J.: Jihad, 1967?
(Anthologies): Dee, Glow Child; Jones and Neal, Black Fire; Lomax and Abdul, 3000 Years of Black Poetry; Randall, The Black Poets.

IMBERT, Dennis I.
NON-FICTION
The Negro After the War. New Orleans, Williams Printing Service, 1943.
The Stranger Within Our Gates: A South American's Impression of America's Social Problem. New Orleans: Watson, 1945.

NOVEL
The Colored Gentlemen. New Orleans: Williams Printing Service, 1931.

ISHAK, Abu see HILL, Elton